THE MEDIEVAL ALEXANDER

'Some talk of Alexander...'

THE BRITISH GRENADIERS

I ALEXANDER'S CELESTIAL JOURNEY

THE MEDIEVAL
ALEXANDER

BY

GEORGE CARY

Fellow of Trinity College, Cambridge

EDITED BY

D. J. A. ROSS

*Reader in French in
the University of London*

CAMBRIDGE
AT THE UNIVERSITY PRESS
1956

REPRINTED
1967

Published by the Syndics of the Cambridge University Press
Bentley House, 200 Euston Road, London, N.W. 1
American Branch: 32 East 57th Street, New York, N.Y. 10022

PUBLISHER'S NOTE

Cambridge University Press Library Editions are reissues of out-of-print standard works from the Cambridge catalogue. The texts are unrevised and, apart from minor corrections, reproduce the latest published edition.

First published 1956
Reprinted 1967

First printed in Great Britain at the University Printing House, Cambridge
Reprinted in the United States of America
Library of Congress Catalogue Card Number: 56-59097

FOREWORD

George Cary was born on 12 August 1928, and educated at Eton, whence he passed as an entrance scholar in Classics to Trinity College, Cambridge, in 1945. Two years later he was placed in the First Class in Part I of the Classical Tripos, and next year he repeated his success in Part II of the Modern and Medieval Languages Tripos, specializing in Italian. There can be little doubt that if he had kept to the beaten track he could have found a place, had he so wished, on the University teaching staff, but ordinary academic life did not attract him. His instincts urged him to widen his experience and to explore unfamiliar paths, and with the help of the Jebb Studentship, which he held for two successive years, he started research on the posthumous reputation of Alexander the Great, an enormous theme which had already fascinated him as a schoolboy.

In 1950 the first results of this research won him a Fellowship of his College, and the dissertation which he then submitted is the basis of the present book. What the College looks for in such work is chiefly evidence of originality and intellectual power. The writing is done against time, with scant opportunity for polish or revision, and few dissertations, at all events on literary or historical themes, reach the Electors in a form suitable for immediate publication. Cary's dissertation, though less imperfect than many, was no exception, and in the years immediately following his election he made no attempt to bring it into shape. He certainly hoped to expand it, at some later date, into a comprehensive survey of Alexander's enduring fame in the East as well as in the West. For the moment he was fascinated by those Oriental developments, especially in Persia, which he had barely touched in his dissertation, and he set himself to a serious study of Persian literature and art, partly in the hope of visiting the East and recording photographically as many as possible of the undescribed manuscripts hidden in Persian and Indian libraries. By the width of his interests and his rare qualities of mind he was admirably fitted to advance knowledge in these adventurous ways, and a fascinating field of work lay at his feet, but, before his plans could mature, his health failed and on 9 January 1953, after less than four years of a supremely happy marriage, he died, to his friends' bitter grief, leaving a young widow and an infant son.

Some months after his death Mrs Cary asked me if I saw any possibility of getting his dissertation published. The subject of his research was outside my competence, but it happened that in 1950, in default of anyone better qualified, I had been the Fellow responsible for obtaining expert referees and for presenting his case to the other Fellowship Electors. I now reread the dissertation with care, and one of the referees, Dr F. J. E. Raby, kindly consented to do the same. Dr Raby confirmed my own impression, that the work ought, if possible, to be published, but that this could not be done till it had been thoroughly revised by a specialist. We were fortunate enough to find in Dr David Ross, Reader in French in the University of London, a scholar not only admirably qualified but also unselfishly willing to devote himself to this exacting task, the nature of which he explains in his Editor's Note. The expenses of publication have been met by generous grants from the Syndics of the Cambridge University Press and from the Council of Trinity College.

D. S. ROBERTSON

TRINITY COLLEGE
CAMBRIDGE

EDITOR'S NOTE

Many books were written in the Middle Ages about Alexander the Great and still more books have been written about those books during the past century. It seemed then hardly likely that a thesis entitled 'The Medieval Alexander', upon which I was asked to give an opinion some months ago, would have much new to offer. I was, however, to receive an agreeable surprise. George Cary had approached the problem from an angle completely new, using material which none of his predecessors had exploited. He had asked himself the simple question: What did people really think about Alexander in the Middle Ages? and had sought his answer in unexplored byways. Other writers, in so far as they ever asked themselves this question at all, had confined their inquiries to the most obvious sources, the numerous legendary biographies in prose and verse, in Latin and the vernaculars of Europe, based ultimately for the most part on the Greek Alexander Romance. Cary indeed did not neglect this material and the reader will find that he has studied it with care and originality. But he was not content with the answer to the question: What did the writers of romances think of Alexander? Other, and more serious-minded, sections of educated society in the Middle Ages had shown an interest in the Macedonian conqueror. What did the moralists think of him? and the theologians? and the preachers and authors of books of *exempla* and moral tales? Did all medieval society see him only as a great conqueror, a supreme general, as the historians might be supposed to have viewed him? Or was his well-known secular reputation for open-handed generosity generally accepted? The answers turn out to be various and unexpected, changing from age to age and from group to group.

I felt most strongly that it would be a serious loss to medieval scholarship if so much new material and original study, through the untimely death of the writer, should lie forgotten on the shelves of a college library, and gladly undertook the revision of the text for publication. My acquaintance with George Cary was of short duration, but was sufficient to impress me with his fine personal qualities and the great promise of his scholarship.

The book here presented to the reader is essentially George Cary's thesis as he wrote it in 1950. I have in the main confined my activity to the usual editorial business of abbreviation, correction of details, the addition of some footnotes and stylistic remodelling. The sections on the *Old French Prose Alexander* (pp. 46–8) and the *Parua Recapitulatio* (p. 70) have, however, been entirely rewritten; that on the *Roman de toute chevalerie* (pp. 35–6) has been partially rewritten; and that on the *Histoire ancienne jusqu'à César* (p. 37) is an addition. A few additional notes for which I am responsible are signed with my initials and I have added a brief account (Appendix I) of recent research on the origins of the Greek Alexander Romance. I am also responsible for the selection of most of the plates and for the descriptive notes on them. The general plan of the book and the ideas expressed remain unaltered. I should like to thank Professor R. Weiss and Mr R. Wisbey for valuable corrections and suggestions.

D. J. A. ROSS

BIRKBECK COLLEGE
LONDON

1954

CONTENTS

PART B

The Medieval Conception of Alexander the Great

CONTENTS

ILLUSTRATIONS

PLATES

xii

FIGURES

AUTHOR'S ACKNOWLEDGEMENTS

I must gratefully acknowledge the kindness of many who have helped me in various ways. I would like especially to express my thanks and indebtedness to the following: Professor F. P. Magoun, Jr., of Harvard University, who has presented me with much bibliographical material, and with his copies of many of the scarcer Alexander items; Dr F. J. E. Raby, my Supervisor, for his invaluable suggestions, criticism, and advice; Professor Julio Berzunza, of the University of New Hampshire, for giving me a copy of his Alexander bibliography; Drs Bing and Buchthal of the Warburg Institute for assistance with iconography; Professor Roberto Weiss of the University of London, for advice upon the bibliography of Petrarch; Dr David Ross of Birkbeck College, London, M. Manzalaoui, of the English Faculty, Farouk I University, Alexandria, and Dr G. V. Smithers, of Oxford University, for information upon their particular subjects of research; the library staff of the University Library, and Corpus Christi College, Cambridge, the Warburg Institute, the British Museum, and the London Library, for courteous assistance; and my wife, for much valuable assistance, criticism and encouragement.

G. C.

ABBREVIATIONS

I have used the following abbreviations for the titles of books and series
to which frequent reference has been made:

Ausfeld, *Griechischer Alexanderroman*	A. Ausfeld, *Der Griechische Alexanderroman* (Leipzig, 1907).
B.L.V.	*Bibliothek des literarischen Vereins in Stuttgart.*
E.E.T.S.	Early English Text Society.
O.S.	Original Series.
E.S.	Extra Series.
Grammel	E. Grammel, *Studien über den Wandel des Alexanderbildes in der deutschen Dichtung des 12. u. 13. Jahrhunderts*, Frankfurt diss. (Limburg, 1931).
Hilka, *Altfranzösischer Prosa-Alexanderroman*	A. Hilka, *Der altfranzösische Prosa-Alexanderroman nach der Berliner Bilderhandschrift nebst dem lateinischen Original der Historia de Preliis (Rez. I²) (Festschrift für Karl Appel*, Halle, 1920).
Magoun	F. P. Magoun, *The Gests of King Alexander of Macedon* (Cambridge, Mass. 1929).
Meyer, *A. le G.*	P. Meyer, *Alexandre le Grand dans la littérature française du Moyen Age*, 2 vols. (Paris, 1886).
M.F.R.d'A. I–V	*The Medieval French 'Roman d'Alexandre'* by E. C. Armstrong and others. Vols. I–V (Princeton Univ. Press: *Elliott Monographs*, 36–40, 1937–49).
Migne, *P.L.*	J.-P. Migne, *Patrologia Latina*.
M.G.H.	*Monumenta Germaniae Historica.*
Pfister, *Alexanderroman*	F. Pfister, *Der Alexanderroman des Archipresbyters Leo (Sammlung mittellat. Texte*, VI. Heidelberg, 1912).
R.I.S.	Rerum Italicarum Scriptores.
S.A.T.F.	Société des anciens textes français.

Storost   J. Storost, *Studien zur Alexandersage in der älteren italienischen Literatur: Untersuchungen und Texte* (Romanistische Arbeiten XXIII, Halle, 1935).

Zacher, *Pseudo-callisthenes*   J. Zacher, *Pseudocallisthenes. Forschungen zur Kritik und Geschichte der ältesten Aufzeichnung der Alexandersage* (Halle, 1867).

GENERAL INTRODUCTION

THE legends of Alexander the Great have surely received as much attention from scholars as any other legendary tradition, attention to which they are entitled by their wide dissemination and their great interest, popularity and variety. In particular the European legendary tradition has been carefully studied over the past hundred years; and these enquiries have established the principal features of that tradition beyond reasonable dispute. The labours of Zacher, Zingerle, Meyer, Ausfeld, Kroll, Pfister, Hilka, Magoun, Hamilton and others have made clear the interrelation of the principal texts, which it has been left to others, linguistic specialists, to study in more detail.

But besides the legendary works derived from Pseudo-Callisthenes, there are many other medieval histories of Alexander which depend upon the historical tradition of Quintus Curtius, Justin and Orosius, and finally a third group derives from a combination of both traditions. Though the historical and semi-historical writings upon Alexander have not been altogether neglected, they have not yet been made the object of such intensive study as have the legends. For example, though the *Alexandreis* of Gautier de Châtillon and its descendants have been much studied (but not, it may be noticed, by students of the legend), the accounts of Alexander in such works as the *St Albans Compilation*, in medieval world chronicles, and in commentaries upon the text of Maccabees, have been neglected; and hardly any notice has been taken of the independent references to Alexander in medieval literature as a whole.

This is not surprising, as the interest of scholars in the medieval legend of Alexander has been determined mainly by the fact that the legendary texts are among the earliest writings in the vernacular of their respective countries, and therefore possess great philological interest. Furthermore, the narrative of the Alexander-Romances, recounted with the art of the medieval story-teller, is more attractive than the barren factual accounts of Alexander to be found in chronicles and similar texts. And at the same time the complicated pattern of the interrelations of the various legendary works and their numerous recensions, interpolations, epitomes, translations and adaptations have together formed a tangled web, whose unravelling has successfully attracted and held the attention of scholars.

The first part of this work is necessarily to a great extent derivative. Its purpose is to show how this pattern has been unravelled, how its various strands are connected, and what problems still remain to be solved. In this survey there are included not only the legendary texts, but also those works which are derived principally from the Latin historians of Alexander, and the European descendants of Eastern Alexander tradition. Thus in this first section I have attempted to give a brief conspectus of the history of the medieval Alexander tradition in its principal texts, which may serve both as an introduction to the principal subject of the book, and as an introductory summary for those concerned with other problems in the field.

Such a sketch has been given before by Professor Magoun in the introduction to his *Gests of King Alexander of Macedon*.[1] My survey differs from his in including, not only the derivatives of the Pseudo-Callisthenes tradition, to which he restricted himself, but also the biographies of Alexander based on historical sources, and some of the more important accounts found in general chronicles and world-histories. I have also tried to include the more important Alexander studies which have appeared since 1929, and have treated several of the texts in greater detail. I have omitted or abridged a considerable part of Professor Magoun's survey of Eastern and East-European Alexander material with which the present study is not concerned.

After this preliminary examination of the textual tradition my aim in the rest of the book is to establish the general underlying conceptions of Alexander the Great that were current in the Middle Ages, to discuss their formation and the effect upon them of the various influences to which they were subject, and to show how they reflect the social history of the period.

Most of the critical studies of individual legendary or historical texts or groups of texts contain some remarks upon the conception of Alexander implicit in them; and there have also been studies which discuss the development of the conception of Alexander in national literatures. These have, however, been limited by their preoccupation

[1] F. P. Magoun, *The Gests of King Alexander of Macedon* (Cambridge, Mass., 1929), pp. 22–62.

with legendary texts, and usually also by their subordination to philological interests. Thus Paul Meyer's work[1] contains a few remarks upon the conception of Alexander in French literature; and more recently a monograph has been written by Elisabeth Grammel upon the conception of Alexander in Germany during the twelfth and thirteenth centuries.[2] There is also an excellent but too brief summary of the German conception of Alexander by Hübner.[3]

Storost's work upon the Italian legends is a curious one;[4] while his philological studies, his source criticism and his explanation of the conception of Alexander in each individual author are generally sound, his discussion of larger issues, and especially his attempt to determine the relationship of the medieval writer to his source material, are less satisfactory and rather unoriginal.[5]

Although these and other scholars have dealt to some extent with the conception of the personality of Alexander in the various romances and romantic references which they have studied, there has been no attempt to co-ordinate and correlate the different conceptions of Alexander implicit in the romances of the various European literatures, and to trace in full the growth of the romantic portrait of Alexander, and the influence upon it of changing medieval ideals. Still less has there been any attempt to give the courtly conception of Alexander its proper place, by comparing it with the other views of him current in the Middle Ages. This is because those literary and historical sources of the life of Alexander that are not directly connected with the legend, together with their derivatives and their influence, have, except in the case of the *Alexandreis* and its descendants, been dealt with only in a summary manner, mostly when material from these sources has been incorporated into works essentially of the character of a romance. This study is an attempt to trace, not only the development of that conception of Alexander as the

---

[1] P. Meyer, *Alexandre le Grand dans la littérature française du Moyen Age*, 2 vols. (Paris, 1886).

[2] E. Grammel, *Studien über den Wandel des Alexanderbildes in der deutschen Dichtung des 12. u. 13. Jahrhunderts* (Frankfurt dissertation, Limburg, 1931).

[3] A. Hübner, 'Alexander der Grosse in der deutschen Dichtung des Mittelalters', *Die Antike*, IX (1933), pp. 32–48.

[4] J. Storost, *Studien zur Alexandersage in der älteren italienischen Literatur: Untersuchungen und Texte* (Romanistische Arbeiten, XXIII, Halle, 1935).

[5] Storost, p. 325; for Pfister's comments, see his review in *Zeitschr. f. franz. Spr. u. Lit.* LXI (1937), pp. 235–6.

ideal courtly prince, which has been stressed so often that it has become the accepted version of the medieval Alexander portrait, but also to put that conception in its proper place by showing that it was one among many, and that the assumption often made, that the legendary Alexander was the Alexander best known in the Middle Ages, is founded upon the emphasis that has been laid by most scholars upon that side of medieval Alexander tradition, and their general neglect of references to Alexander outside the field of romance and popular vernacular literature. My object is to summarize, not one but all the general and popular conceptions of Alexander the Great current in the Middle Ages.

Criteria sufficient to justify our regarding an opinion of an historical character as universal, and to establish it as part of the outlook of one class or of one age, may only be found when, as was the case in the Middle Ages, an interest in personality is very restricted, and when knowledge of the famous men of antiquity is drawn, not from original documents, but from opinionated history or anecdote. The existence of universally received standards, whether spiritual or secular, by which a personality is to be assessed, the dependence of medieval writers upon one another, the absence of many historical data from which individual opinions may be formed, and the untrustworthiness of the accessible material, together deprived medieval writers of any opportunity of arriving at a just or even a reasonable opinion of Alexander, and the resultant problems offer to the modern researcher an admirable occasion for a study of conventional medieval opinion. We shall see how the medieval Alexander material, through its retransmission in the hands of patristic, scholastic and mystical writers, of chroniclers and of the writers of popular literature, became, by its gradual accumulation through the centuries, an increasing body of evidence, mainly unreliable, on which a history of Alexander might be based. We shall also note how, as its heterogeneous nature became more and more obvious as the Middle Ages progressed in knowledge, it became a stimulus to historical criticism which could not have existed when no other argument than flat contradiction by an author of greater weight could absolutely destroy the credit of a written, antique and Latin source.

To evoke the dead feelings even of an individual is hard enough; but to catch the echo of a crowd, to hear renewed, not the clear accents of one, but the confused voice of hundreds, cannot be achieved with absolute certainty. We may record only what we seem to hear repeated by the majority. It is in the nature of such a study that it is easily assailable, since, by the attempted conflation of opinions disparate in their authors, if not in their tone, the individual opinion is absorbed in the general, and I may perhaps be accused of deforming individual judgements in fitting them into the framework of a theory intended to embrace them. I have, however, neither attempted to establish a preconceived hypothesis, nor suppressed any material, but have rather tried to follow the lead of contemporary witnesses and to see Alexander through their eyes.

PART A

A BRIEF SURVEY OF THE SOURCES FOR MEDIEVAL KNOWLEDGE OF ALEXANDER THE GREAT, AND OF THEIR PRINCIPAL MEDIEVAL DERIVATIVES

I

THE PRIMARY SOURCES OF MEDIEVAL
KNOWLEDGE OF ALEXANDER
THE GREAT

I. 1. PSEUDO-CALLISTHENES AND
THE INDIAN TRACTATES

I. 1. a

PSEUDO-CALLISTHENES

THE Greek Alexander-Romance[1] owes its name to the fact that a manuscript seen by Casaubon bore an ascription to Callisthenes, an ascription
which he immediately saw to be false. A great deal has been written upon
the sources and evolution of Pseudo-Callisthenes, and unanimity is still far
from being attained. This is, however, no place to enter into the various
theories which have been put forward about the original composition of
the book, which may be studied in the bibliography given, as we are concerned not with the evolution of the primitive work but with the earliest
form of it that is still extant, and its numerous translations and adaptations.

It is generally agreed that the book was originally composed by a native
of Alexandria, at some date after 200 B.C., and possibly much later. His
sources were partly literary and partly the oral legends which were even
then widely told of Alexander. No extant version of Pseudo-Callisthenes
approximates to this original state of the composition, for it was subse-
quently elaborated and enlarged by the addition of much material, especially
of letters supposed to have been written by Alexander and others, and of
Cynic propaganda, in which expanded form alone it survives.

Four recensions of Pseudo-Callisthenes are traceable, of which three are
represented by manuscripts, and the fourth is deduced from the peculiarities common to a group of texts. These recensions are called α, β, γ and

(δ) Pseudo-Callisthenes; and are, in their turn, dependent upon the earliest of them, the α-recension, which is thus the earliest extant source of the immense body of legendary Alexander literature.

The nature and the history of these four recensions is briefly as follows: The α-recension is represented by Paris, Bib. Nat. MS. Fonds Grec 1711 (s. xi);[2] and the various translations from lost manuscripts of the α-tradition are of great value for establishing further the characteristics of the recension. The most important of these translations are:

(i) The Armenian translation,[3] made in the fifth century, which has long been recognized as of considerable use in the attempt to reconstitute the original α-tradition.

(ii) The translation by Julius Valerius, *Res Gestae Alexandri Macedonis*,[4] made *c.* A.D. 320, widely popular in medieval Europe, and the source of many vernacular versions (see pp. 24 ff.).

Also derived from the α-tradition are, in all probability, the account of Alexander in the *Dicts and Sayings of the Philosophers*[5] and the *Metz Epitome*.[6]

The β-recension is a revision of the α-recension, and the majority of the surviving Greek manuscripts of Pseudo-Callisthenes are of this recension.[7] It is probably the work of an Hellenistic writer, and is an attempt to bring the legend closer to historical truth. Its principal derivatives are:

(i) A Bulgarian life of Alexander, written in or before the twelfth century, which was translated and incorporated into the Russian chronographs.[8]

(ii) The fourteenth-century Byzantine Greek poem, ὁ βίος Ἀλεξάνδρου. A similar manuscript was probably used in the Syriac chronicle formerly attributed to Dionysius Telmaharensis.[9]

The γ-recension, represented by Müller's MS. C (Paris, Bib. Nat. MS. Suppl. Grec. 113) and some others, is expanded from a β-type manuscript by a Jew or by one familiar with Jewish sources.[10] Its principal derivatives are:

(i) A Hebrew romance which emphasizes the marvellous element in Alexander's life, and which draws upon several unknown accessory sources.[11]

(ii) The Serbian Alexander, derived from a γ-type manuscript enlarged with some interpolations, and dating from about the fourteenth century.[12] The Serbian Alexander was the source of a Georgian prose translation (fourteenth-century?), later versified.[13]

(iii) The Modern Greek chapbook Alexander, first printed at Venice, 1699.[14]

Closely related to the Serbian Alexander and the Modern Greek chap-book Alexander is the Rumanian prose Alexander.[15]

The (δ)-recension is not represented by any surviving Greek MS., but it survives indirectly in the ultimate (lost) source of a Syriac and an Ethiopic version, and the (lost) Greek manuscript translated into Latin by Archpriest Leo of Naples in the tenth century. This recension was probably based on a good α-type manuscript.[16] Further details of its derivatives are as follows:

The Syriac prose Alexander was probably translated, in or before the sixth century, from a (now lost) Pehlevi translation of a (δ)-type Greek manuscript.[17] In the sixth century Bishop Jacob of Serug made a homily in verse from part of this version.[18]

In the ninth century the Syriac version was translated into Arabic. The Arabic redaction has not survived; but, with interpolations from an α-type manuscript, it was used by the author of an extant Ethiopian version, made between the fourteenth and the sixteenth century.[19]

In the tenth century, about 950, Archpriest Leo of Naples undertook a mission to Constantinople for his master Duke John III of Campania, and found there a (δ)-type Greek manuscript of Pseudo-Callisthenes. He made and brought back with him to Naples a transcript of this manuscript, and was ordered by the Duke to translate it into Latin for his library. This translation, which probably bore the title *Natiuitas et Victoria Alexandri Magni*, but to which, and to its various derivatives, the name *Historia de Preliis*, from its title in the incunable editions, is generally applied, was one of the most important sources for medieval knowledge of Alexander.[20]

Thus, of the various recensions of Pseudo-Callisthenes, only α and (δ) are of importance for the study of medieval knowledge of Alexander in Europe; and the discussion of the numerous texts derived from them through the intermediacy of Julius Valerius and the *Historia de Preliis* forms the second section of this part (pp. 24 ff.).[21]

General Note. Throughout this general sketch of medieval and late antique Alexander-Romances and other Alexander material only the most important bibliographical references are given in full. For further bibliography reference should be made to the passage indicated in Magoun.

[1] EDITIONS. C. Müller, in *Arriani Anabasis et Indica* (Paris, Didot, 1846). Based on a β-type MS., with variants from α and γ.

H. Meusel, 'Pseudo-Callisthenes, nach der Leidener Handschrift hrsg.', in *Jahrbücher f. classische Phil.*, Neue Folge, Supplementband v (Leipzig, 1871), pp. 700–816.

W. Kroll, *Historia Alexandri Magni (Pseudo-Callisthenes)*, vol. I: *Recensio Vetusta* (Berlin, 1926). Alpha text; no more published. Reviewed by A. R. Anderson, *Amer. Journal of Philology*, XLVII (1927), pp. 195–7.

STUDIES. (Only the fundamental studies have here been included). J. Zacher, *Pseudo-callisthenes, Forschungen zur Kritik und Geschichte der ältesten Aufzeichnung der Alexandersage* (Halle, 1867).

A. Ausfeld, *Der Griechische Alexanderroman*, ed. W. Kroll (Leipzig, 1907).

W. Deimann, *Abfassungszeit und Verfasser des griech. Alexanderromans* (Münster diss. 1914, published 1917).

W. Kroll, in Pauly-Wissowa, xx (1919), cols. 1707–23.

Magoun, pp. 22–5 and 35–41 and notes.

[2] Magoun, p. 24 and n. 1.

[3] Magoun, pp. 24–5 and p. 24, n. 2, p. 25, n. 1.

[4] Magoun, p. 25 and n. 2.

[5] Magoun, p. 35 and nn. 1, 2. Below, pp. 22–3.

[6] Below, p. 59.   [7] Magoun, pp. 35–6 and p. 35, nn. 4–5.

[8] Magoun, p. 36 and n. 1.   [9] Magoun, p. 36 and nn. 2–3

[10] Magoun, p. 37 and n. 1.   [11] Magoun, p. 37 and n. 2.

[12] Magoun, pp. 37–8 and p. 37, nn. 3–6, p. 38, n. 1.

[13] Magoun, p. 38 and n. 2.   [14] Magoun, p. 38 and n. 3.

[15] Magoun, p. 38 and n. 4.   [16] Magoun, p. 38 and n. 5.

[17] Magoun, p. 39 and n. 2.   [18] Magoun, p. 39 and n. 1.

[19] Magoun, p. 39 and nn. 3–4. Dr D. S. Rice has recently found an Arabic Pseudo-Callisthenes in Constantinople which may prove to be the lost intermediary. This manuscript is MS. Aya Sofya 3003 and 3004 dated A.H. 871 = A.D. 1466. I thank Dr Rice for this information [D.J.A.R.].

[20] Magoun, pp. 40–1 and p. 41, nn. 1–2. Below pp. 38–58.

[21] For a brief summary of the most recent views on Pseudo-Callisthenes see Appendix I, p. 355–7.

I. 1. b

THE INDIAN TRACTATES

I. 1. b. i

'COMMONITORIUM PALLADII'[1]

This work, an essay upon the Indians, and especially upon the Brahmans, supposed to have been addressed to Alexander, exists in four forms, two Greek and two Latin:

(i) It appears first as an interpolation in Pseudo-Callisthenes (III, 7–16, ed. Müller); cc. 7–10 of this interpolation were probably written by Palladius, bishop of Helenopolis (*c.* 363–*c.* 430).[2]

(ii) The same text as that in Pseudo-Callisthenes III, 7–10 is found independently in various manuscripts, occasionally epitomized and entitled: Παλλαδίου περὶ τῶν τῆς Ἰνδίας Ἐθνῶν καὶ τῶν Βραχμάνων.[3]

(iii) A Latin translation of the work is included in the Bamberg manuscript of the *Historia de Preliis* (see p. 41).[4]

(iv) There also exists an independent Latin version traditionally ascribed to St Ambrose, and known as *De Moribus Brachmanorum*.[5]

[1] BIBLIOGRAPHY. Magoun, p. 44 and nn. 3–5, p. 45 and nn. 1–4.

[2] EDITION. In Müller's edition of Pseudo-Callisthenes (Didot, 1846), pp. 102–20.
INFORMATION. W. Kroll, in Pauly-Wissowa, XX (1919), cols. 1720–1.

[3] EDITION. Sir Edward Bysshe, *Palladius de Gentibus Indiae* (London, 1665; reprinted 1668).
STUDY. P. R. Coleman-Norton, 'The Authorship of the *Epistola de Indicis Gentibus et de Bragmanibus*', *Classical Philol.* XXI (1926), pp. 154–60.

[4] EDITION. F. Pfister, *Kleine Texte zum Alexanderroman* (*Sammlung Vulgärlat. Texte*, IV, Heidelberg, 1910), pp. 1–5.

[5] EDITION. Bysshe. Second text.
INFORMATION. H. Becker, *Die Brahmanen in der Alexandersage* (progr. Königsberg, 1889), pp. 11–23.

I. 1. b. ii

DINDIMUS ON THE BRAHMANS[1]

This tractate corresponds to Pseudo-Callisthenes III, 11–12 (Müller), sometimes falsely attributed to Palladius.[2] It compares the Macedonians unfavourably with the Indians, and echoes the Cynic attack on Alexander. There is a text in the Bamberg manuscript of the *Historia de Preliis*, and a second Latin version, *Anonymus de Brachmanibus*.[3]

[1] BIBLIOGRAPHY. Magoun, p. 45 and nn. 5–8.

[2] EDITION. F. Pfister, *Kleine Texte zum Alexanderroman* (*Sammlung Vulgärlat. Texte*, IV, Heidelberg, 1910), pp. 6–9.

[3] EDITION. Sir Edward Bysshe, *Palladius de Gentibus Indiae* (London, 1665; reprinted 1668); third text.

I. 1. b. iii

'COLLATIO ALEXANDRI CUM DINDIMO PER LITTERAS FACTA'[1]

This work, after the *Epistola ad Aristotelem* the most important of the Indian Tractates, consists of an imaginary correspondence between Alexander and Dindimus, king of the Brahmans. The latter, in answer to Alexander's inquiries about the life of the Brahmans, praises their ascetic life and attacks the Macedonians for their sensuality and idolatry. Alexander, however, replies in a spirited manner, and is allowed to have the last word in the fifth letter of the series, where he ridicules Dindimus' asceticism. This work, in its original form, was supposed to have been directed against Alexander by his Cynic opponents; but Liénard reached a conclusion which will be accepted by most readers of the *Collatio*, that the author's sympathies were with Alexander, and that the work was intended as an attack, either upon the ascetic philosophy preached by the Cynics or, possibly, upon the early Christian accusers of Alexander. By degrees, however, Dindimus came to be accepted as an admirable ascetic, and the work was used against Alexander, whose replies were often mutilated so as to give Dindimus the best of the argument. The work exists in three Latin forms:

Collatio I, the oldest surviving form, is printed by Kübler in his edition of Julius Valerius, and is frequently found subjoined to the text of the Julius Valerius Epitome and the *Epistola ad Aristotelem* in MSS. The date of its composition is probably the fourth century.[2]

Collatio II is the form of the work found in the Bamberg manuscript of the *Natiuitas et Victoria Alexandri Magni* (see p. 41); it is a revision of *Collatio* I, involving alterations in style and the suppression of some pagan elements. It was probably made, like the *Natiuitas et Victoria*, in the tenth century in Naples.[3]

Collatio III is the form in which the correspondence is found in the I[1] recension of the *Historia de Preliis* (see p. 43) and its derivatives. It is an expanded and altered form of *Collatio* II.[4]

The work was widely known in the Middle Ages, and had considerable influence upon the medieval conception of Alexander. The earliest reference to it is in an epigram by Alcuin, who writes to Charlemagne that he is sending him copies of the correspondence between St Paul and Seneca and between Alexander and Dindimus.[5]

[1] BIBLIOGRAPHY. Magoun, pp. 46–7 and nn.

[2] EDITION. B. Kübler, *Julii Valerii...Res Gestae Alexandri Macedonis* (Leipzig, Teubner, 1888), pp. 169–89.

STUDY. E. Liénard, 'Collatio Alexandri et Dindimi', *Revue Belge de Philologie et d'Histoire*, XV, ii (1936), pp. 819–38 (*q.v.* for further bibliographical information).

[3] EDITIONS. B. Kübler, in *Roman. Forschungen*, VI (1888–91), pp. 216ff.

F. Pfister, *Kleine Texte zum Alexanderroman* (*Sammlung Vulgärlat. Texte*, IV, Heidelberg, 1910), pp. 10–20.

[4] EDITIONS. In the various texts in the interpolated recensions of the *Historia de Preliis*: e.g. O. Zingerle, *Die Quellen zum Alexander des Rudolf von Ems* (*Germanistische Abhandlungen*, IV, Breslau, 1885), pp. 220–36 (I[1] recension).

A. Hilka, *Altfranzösischer Prosa-Alexanderroman* (Halle, 1920), pp. 187–200 (I[2] recension).

[5] For various vernacular texts descended from the *Collatio*, see below, pp. 43, 69.

I. 1. b. iv

'EPISTOLA ALEXANDRI AD ARISTOTELEM'[1]

In the Greek Pseudo-Callisthenes III, 17[2] there may be found an epitomized version of a fictitious letter supposed to have been written by Alexander to his master Aristotle, describing the wonders of India. The unabbreviated text of Julius Valerius contains a translation of this which is rather more complete than the surviving Greek text. This seems to have enjoyed a limited independent circulation in South Germany in the thirteenth century.[3] A fuller version of this letter, however, survives in a Latin text, which enjoyed universal popularity in the Middle Ages, and whose usual title is: *Epistola Alexandri Macedonis ad Aristotelem magistrum suum de itinere suo et de situ Indiae*. This text, called by Magoun *Epistola* I,[4] is frequently found in conjunction with the *Zacher Epitome* of Julius Valerius and with *Collatio* I in the manuscripts, but also often occurs by itself. It was translated into Old English as early as A.D. 1000;[5] into Middle Irish;[6] into Icelandic[7] in the fourteenth century; into French in the thirteenth and again probably in the fifteenth century;[8] into Middle English in the fifteenth century;[9] and into German early in the seventeenth century.[10] It was also used in the Letter of Prester John.

In association with the *Zacher Epitome*, *Epistola* I was frequently used by chroniclers and writers of Alexander-books. A revised and abbreviated version of it, *Epistola* II,[11] is found only in the Bamberg manuscript of the *Natiuitas et Victoria* (q.v., p. 41). The *Epistola ad Aristotelem* was finally incorporated, in an abridged form, in the interpolated recensions of the *Historia de Preliis*, and passed thence to many Alexander-books.

By itself it was much used as a standard text-book by writers upon the wonders of the East and upon natural history; Jacques de Vitry, Walter of Metz, Marco Polo, Fulcher of Chartres and Albertus Magnus were among those who referred to it as a work worthy of belief and respect.

[1] BIBLIOGRAPHY. Magoun, pp. 47–9 and nn.

[2] EDITIONS. *Pseudo-Callisthenes*, ed. Müller, pp. 120–5.

INFORMATION. A. Ausfeld, *Der Griechische Alexanderroman* (Leipzig, 1907), pp. 89–96, 179 ff.

[3] See D. J. A. Ross, 'Letters of Alexander', *Classica et Mediaevalia*, XIII (1952), pp. 38–58.

[4] EDITIONS. In *Julius Valerius*, ed. B. Kübler (Leipzig, Teubner, 1888), pp. 190–221.

F. Pfister, *Kleine Texte zum Alexanderroman* (*Sammlung Vulgärlatein. Texte*, IV, Heidelberg, 1910), pp. 21–37.

Stanley Rypins, *Three Old English Prose Texts* (E.E.T.S., E.S. CLXI, 1924), pp. 79–100.

W. W. Boer, *Epistola Alexandri ad Aristotelem ad codicum fidem edita et commentario critico instructa* (The Hague, 1953). Critical text based on twenty-eight MSS. Supersedes Kübler's edition.

[5] EDITION. Rypins, op. cit. pp. 1–50. See for a discussion of this F. Pfister, in *German.-Roman. Monatschr.* XVI (1928), pp. 82 ff.

[6] EDITION. K. Meyer, in W. Stokes and E. Windisch, *Irische Texte* (Leipzig, 1887), II, ii, pp. 43–69 and 100–7.

[7] EDITION. Published by C. R. Unger, in his edition of *Alexanders Saga* (Christiania, 1848), pp. 164–75.

[8] INFORMATION. Meyer, *Alexandre le Grand*, II, pp. 301–5 and 396.

[9] Unpublished. In Worcester Cathedral Library MS. 172, fos. 138–146 verso. Dated 1447.

[10] EDITIONS. First edition of this version by Gabriel Rollenhagen (Magdeburg, 1603); for other editions, see K. T. Gaedertz, *Gabriel Rollenhagen: sein Leben u. seine Werke* (Leipzig, 1881), pp. 103 ff.

¹¹ EDITION. F. Pfister, *Kleine Texte zum Alexanderroman* (*Sammlung Vulgärlat. Texte*, IV, Heidelberg, 1910), pp. 38–41; also edited, in its context in the Bamberg *Historia*, in his *Der Alexanderroman des Archipresbyters Leo* (*Sammlung Mittellat. Texte*, VI, Heidelberg, 1913), pp. 107 ff.

NOTE

The *Epistola ad Aristotelem* must not be confused with the so-called *Epistola de mirabilibus Indiae*,[1] supposed to have been written by Pharasmanes II of Iberia to the Emperor Hadrian, which contains very similar material, is probably connected with the *Epistola ad Aristotelem*, and was likewise early translated into English. A French version was made in the thirteenth century. This text was drawn on by the redactor of *Historia de Preliis*, version I¹.

[1] E. Faral, 'Une source latine de l'*Histoire d'Alexandre*: La Lettre sur les merveilles de l'Inde', in *Romania*, XLII (1914), pp. 199–215, 332–370.

M. R. James. *Marvels of the East* (Roxburghe Club, 1929).

Magoun, p. 49 and nn. 4–6.

I. 2. THE HISTORICAL SOURCES

I. 2. a

Q. CURTIUS RUFUS, 'GESTA ALEXANDRI MAGNI'

THE life of Alexander by Quintus Curtius,[1] written probably in the reign of Augustus, was a work much studied and imitated in the Middle Ages, as is proved, not only by the number of manuscripts which have survived, but by the numerous adaptations and translations made from it during that period. In the so-called *Interpolated Quintus Curtius* the lacunae in the text were supplied by hybrid supplements drawn partly from Quintus Curtius himself, partly from Justin and from the legendary work of Julius Valerius. This adaptation was used by Alberic, the earliest vernacular writer on Alexander, and was translated into French prose by Vasco de Lucena in the fifteenth century.

Of books based upon Quintus Curtius, the two most important were the *Alexandreis* of Gautier de Châtillon and the *Alexander* of Rudolf von Ems. The former, the most popular of medieval Latin epics, was composed between 1184 and 1187, and retells the story of Alexander in the heroic spirit, on the model of the *Aeneid*. The poem of Rudolf von Ems, written about 1230, was a courageous attempt to present a historical portrait of Alexander when that portrait had been completely obscured by the preference of vernacular writers for legendary sources. Another work founded upon Quintus Curtius was the *Triompho Magno* of the Renaissance writer Domenico Falugio.

¹ INFORMATION. The best study of medieval knowledge of Quintus Curtius is in S. Dosson, *Etude sur Quinte-Curce* (Paris, 1887), pp. 360 ff.

I. 2. b
JUSTIN AND OROSIUS

The accounts of Alexander in Justin's Epitome of Trogus Pompeius[1] and the *Historia adversus paganos* of Orosius[2] are very similar; both are violent attacks on Alexander, and reproduce, so far as they represent any philosophic tradition, the Stoic accusations against him. Both authors were widely read in the Middle Ages; and Orosius was the source for the life of Alexander most frequently used by medieval world-chroniclers, who found their material ready prepared in his history. In accounts written exclusively about Alexander, Justin was only used occasionally as a minor source; but Orosius' account was the basis of the *Middle Irish Alexander*, part of the *Parua Recapitulatio* and the *St Albans Compilation* with its derivatives, and thence of the prologue of the *Old French Prose Romance*. It was used largely by the second interpolator of the legendary *Historia de Preliis*, and by the author of the Middle English alliterative *Alexander* Fragment A, and frequently as a minor source. It is also a major source for the history of Macedon in the *Histoire Ancienne jusqu'à César*.

¹ INFORMATION. F. Rühl, *Die Verbreitung des Justinus im Mittelalter* (Leipzig, Teubner), 1871.

Medieval manuscripts listed in M. Manitius, *Hss. antiker Autoren in mitt. Bibliothekskatalogen* (67. *Beih. zum Zentralblatt für Bibliothekswesen*, Leipzig, 1935), pp. 76–8, as follows:

Germany	11	(4 s. ix)
France	8	(1 s. ix, 5 s. xii, 1 s. xiv)
Italy	14	(11 s. xv, only one before 1337)
England	7	
Spain	3	
Total	43	

² INFORMATION. Manitius gives the following entries from medieval catalogues (op. cit. pp. 243–7):

Germany	42	(evenly divided)
France	30	(evenly divided)
Italy	18	(10 s. xv)
England	11	(evenly divided)
Spain	6	(evenly divided)
Total	107	

See also D. J. A. Ross, 'Illustrated MSS of Orosius', *Scriptorium*, IX (1955), pp. 35–56.

I. 3. THE JEWISH GROUP OF TEXTS

I. 3. a

JEWISH SOURCES

THE Jewish sources that contributed to medieval knowledge of Alexander consist of a number of isolated episodes and passages, most of which possess considerable importance in the history of the medieval conception of Alexander. They are:

(i) The *Iter ad Paradisum*,[1] the Latin prose account of Alexander's journey to the Earthly Paradise, very popular in medieval Europe, was derived from a Jewish original, and connected with a version of the story in a part of the Babylonian Talmud which may be dated before A.D. 500.

(ii) Josephus' account of Alexander's negotiations with Sanaballetes ('Saraballa'), and of his entry into Jerusalem,[2] was known in the Middle Ages principally through the intermediacy of the *Historia Scholastica* of Peter Comestor, and through the Latin version of Josephus ascribed to Rufinus.

(iii) The story of how Alexander enclosed the wild tribes of Gog and Magog with a wall at the Caspian Gates,[3] which developed in Jewish tradition, was widely known in the Middle Ages from the version in the *Reuelationes* ascribed falsely to Methodius, bishop of Patara.

(iv) The episode of the Ten Jewish Tribes, enclosed by Alexander with the assistance of God, and the episode of the bones of Jeremiah, used as a foundation deposit in the building of Alexandria to protect the city against serpents,[4] were known in the Middle Ages through the *Vitae Prophetarum* ascribed to Epiphanius, and thence through the *Historia Scholastica* of Peter Comestor.

(v) The prophecies in the book of Daniel relating to Alexander, and the historical sketch of his career in the opening verses of Maccabees.[5]

(vi) The miracle by which God opened the waters of the Pamphylian Sea so that Alexander's army might pass through in pursuit of the Persians;[6] this story was recorded in Josephus, and passed from him to various medieval writers.

---

[1] See below, pp. 19–21.   [2] See below, pp. 127–30.
[3] See below, pp. 130–1.   [4] See below, p. 132.
[5] See below, pp. 119–25.   [6] See below, pp. 126–7.

I. 3. b

'ITER AD PARADISUM'[1]

The strange story of Alexander's journey to the earthly paradise exists in many different forms; the earliest is the account in the Babylonian Talmud, an account which may be dated before A.D. 500. This version has certain evident affinities with the Latin text popular in Europe, the *Iter ad Paradisum*. This Latin prose version of Alexander's journey may be dated after 1100 on linguistic grounds, and before 1175 because it was then incorporated into the *Strassburg Alexander*. It was evidently intended to be added at the end of a life of Alexander, as it carries the story up to his death; and it is, in fact, often found incorporated in manuscripts that contain one or other of the principal legendary accounts. The author of the Latin version, it can be said from internal evidence, was almost certainly a Jew; and five of the fourteen manuscripts are ascribed to 'Salomon didascalus Judaeorum'.

Since this text and the other accounts of Alexander's journey derived from it or similar to it are of great importance for the consideration of the medieval attitude to Alexander, a very brief outline of the plot must be given.

Alexander journeys up the Ganges, with some chosen companions, in search of the Earthly Paradise. At length they come to a smooth city wall extending beside the river, but there is no break or entrance in it. After three more days' journeying upstream, however, they reach a small window set in the wall. Alexander sends some of his companions to knock at the window. When an old man appears in answer to their summons, they demand that the city pay tribute to Alexander, as the king of kings. The old man replies that the city is the abode of the blessed upon earth, and that it will be dangerous for them if they remain longer, as the force of the stream could easily submerge their boat. He gives them a stone to present to Alexander, a stone which conveys a mystic meaning.

Alexander and his men then return home to Babylon with the stone, and puzzle for a long time over its hidden qualities. Sages shrug their shoulders in despair, until an aged Jew, Papas, carried into the presence of Alexander on a litter, at last solves the mystery. He shows that the stone will outweigh any amount of gold that is put in the balance against it; but that if a little dust is scattered upon it the lightest feather will outweigh it. His interpretation is as follows: God favours Alexander in all his designs, but he wishes him to restrain his cupidity; the stone (in some versions of the story it is cut in the shape of a human eye) signifies the ambitious Alexander, powerful and insatiable while he is alive, but deprived of all his might by dusty death—the lightest feather may then outweigh his worth. Alexander rewards the old man for his interpretation, obeys the lesson of this *memento mori*, and ends his days in virtuous peace. In later versions the moral of the stone was of a simpler and more generally edifying nature; it betokened merely the evanescence of all human qualities in the face of death, all power and all glory passing away, and had no longer any specific reference to Alexander's personal cupidity.

The details of this story differ so much in individual versions that it evidently enjoyed great popularity either in lost literary or in oral forms. The two most important literary versions, however, are that which has been summarized from the *Iter ad Paradisum*, which was first translated into German as part of the *Strassburg Alexander*[2] and in a French version, the *Voyage au Paradis Terrestre*, was incorporated into the *Roman d'Alex-andre*;[3] and the version in the *Faits des Romains*, differing in many respects from that described above, which passed into the *Fatti di Cesare*, the *Manchester Epitome*,[4] and other works. The other versions of the story, universally popular in medieval Europe, will be discussed in their place.

[1] EDITIONS. Julius Zacher (Königsberg, 1859).
   M. Esposito, in *Hermathena*, xv (1909), pp. 368–82.
   A. Hilka, in L. P. G. Peckham and Milan S. La Du, *The Prise de Defur and the Voyage au Paradis Terrestre* (Princeton University Press, 1935: *Elliott Monographs*, 35), pp. xli–xlviii.
   STUDIES. I. Levi, 'La légende d'Alexandre dans le Talmud', *Revue des Etudes Juives*, II (1881), pp. 293–300.

PLATE II (*opposite*). This miniature comes from a costly MS. of Jehan Wauquelin's *Histoire du bon roy Alixandre*, written and illustrated for Philip the Good, duke of Burgundy, about 1465. Wauquelin's version of the Wonderstone story differs from those discussed in the text. In it Alexander sails up a great river, so large that it resembles a sea, and comes to a city to which he sends a knight in a small boat to demand tribute and submission. An old man opens a window in the wall, listens to Alexander's message, and, after consultation with the inhabitants of the city, returns, makes the required submission, and as tribute casts a small pebble into the boat. The knight returns with difficulty through a rising storm and delivers the stone to Alexander. Its meaning is explained by an aged Jew who is not named, and the weighing of the stone follows the usual lines. There is no suggestion that the city is the Earthly Paradise.

This version differs considerably from that in the *Roman d'Alexandre*, Wauquelin's usual source, and also, though less markedly, from the Latin *Iter ad Paradisum*. Its exact source is uncertain.

The picture, like all those in the MS., is based directly on the text and no earlier model was used. Alexander is shown in camp on the left and on the right we see the knight in the boat in conversation with the old man at the window.

mer. Si li aduint que enuiron
.viii. iours aprez il arriua deuat
vne cite sa quelle estoit bien p
fout cest a dire bien auat situee
en mer. z pour aler a cesse cite
nauoit voie nusse par ou on v

de tours z de bretesques. mais
il sambloit que pour san chien
netet dicesse esse suist toute en
chartre ainsi come de mousset
Alixandre veant cesse cite com
manda a vnt sien cheualier af

II ALEXANDER AND THE WONDERSTONE

W. Hertz, *Gesammelte Abhandlungen* (Stuttgart and Berlin, 1905), pp. 73–130.

M. Gaster, *Studies and Texts*, II (1925–8), pp. 879 ff. (an attempt to find in the *Iter* the source of the Quest for the Grail; see J. D. Bruce, *The Evolution of Arthurian Romance* (Göttingen, 1923), vol. I, pp. 354 f.

R. Hartmann, 'Alexander und der Rätselstein aus dem Paradies', *Oriental Studies presented to E. G. Browne* (Cambridge, 1922), pp. 179–85.

See also Magoun, pp. 29–30, p. 29, n. 6 and p. 30, nn. 1 and 2.

[2] See below, p. 28.   [3] See below, pp. 31–2.   [4] See below, pp. 373–4.

I. 4. THE ARABIC GROUP OF TEXTS

I. 4. a

THE 'SECRETUM SECRETORUM'[1]

SINCE the *Secretum Secretorum*, the book of counsel supposed to have been written by Aristotle for Alexander, had little effect upon the medieval conception of Alexander, in spite of its great influence upon medieval treatises on political science, its complex history need not be more than briefly recapitulated. It is supposed to have been compiled originally in Syriac during the eighth century. Naturally it claimed to have a Greek origin, and Roger Bacon believed he had seen a manuscript of the Greek version, but no such version has been discovered. From Syriac it was translated into Arabic by the Syrian Christian Yuhanna ibn el-Batrik (Johannes filius Patricii), who died in 815, and was a well-known translator of Aristotelian and pseudo-Aristotelian works. No manuscript survives of his Arabic version, which was in eight books. At some later date three supplementary books were added to the treatise; and finally, the eight books (now divided into ten) and the three supplementary books were considerably enlarged, about 1220, to make a long version of which two manuscripts survive. Steele entitles the original book of Yuhanna ibn el-Batrik the Western version, and the later, or expanded edition, the Eastern version.

The Western version was translated in part into Latin by John of Spain for a Queen of Spain (Theophina or Tarasia) about 1125, a translation which had some vogue. The Eastern version was translated a century later by Philip of Tripoli for a certain Archbishop Guido, a member of the De Vere family of Lincolnshire, the details of whose life date the translation to shortly after 1227. Philip's translation is not extant in its original form; it underwent a revision, in which the most important alteration was the transposition of the section on physiognomy, and survives in the revised version in numerous manuscripts.

Finally, Roger Bacon edited the Latin text of the *Secret of Secrets* about 1257, modelling his edition upon the revised version of Philip of Tripoli, and redividing the text into four books.

The immense popularity of this work is demonstrated by the numerous extant translations into the European vernaculars. The best known of these are the French prose version of Jofroi de Waterford and Servais Copale, the Anglo-Norman verse translation of Pierre d'Abernun, and the translations into English by James Yonge and Lydgate and Burgh. There were other translations into these languages, and also into Italian, Spanish, Dutch, German, and Catalan; while the section on physiognomy circulated widely as an independent treatise.

¹ INFORMATION. For a brief sketch of the history of the *Secret of Secrets*, with a select bibliography of the large literature on the subject, see R. Steele's edition of Roger Bacon's version, *Rogeri Baconi opera hactenus inedita*, fasc. v (Oxford, 1920). Also *Le Secré de Secrez* by Pierre d'Abernun of Fetcham (O. A. Beckerlegge, Oxford, Anglo-Norman Text Soc. v, 1944), Introduction, pp. xviii–xxvi.

For the *Secret of Secrets* in its bearing upon the medieval conception of Alexander, see below, pp. 105–10.

I. 4. b

THE 'DICTS AND SAYINGS OF THE PHILOSOPHERS'¹

This work consists of a number of short lives of ancient philosophers, including Alexander and Aristotle; with each life adorned with the wise sayings attributed to the philosopher concerned. It was written in Arabic about the middle of the eleventh century by Abul Wafar Mubasschir ibn Fâtik, who drew his material about Alexander and Aristotle from an Arabic version of the α-recension of Pseudo-Callisthenes, and from the *Secret of Secrets*.

It was translated into Spanish as the *Bocados de Oro* in the thirteenth century, and from Spanish into Latin, but it was almost unknown in Europe until the fifteenth century. In 1402 Guillaume de Tignonville, provost of Paris under Charles VI, translated it into French prose, and this translation had a great vogue. *Les ditz et faitz des philosophes* was copied in numerous manuscripts, and was many times printed.

This translation was in its turn translated into English prose by Stephen Scrope in 1450; Scrope's translation was examined and re-edited by William of Worcester in 1472. Finally, Lord Rivers retranslated the book from the French, a translation famous as one of the earliest and rarest productions of Caxton's press.

The late popularity of the book was undoubtedly due to its edifying nature. The portrait of Alexander contained in it belongs to the Oriental tradition; he appears as a philosopher king, bent on the suppression of idolatry.

[1] INFORMATION. B. Meissner in *Zeit. d. Deutschen Morgenl. Gesell.* XLIX (1896), pp. 583–627.

H. Knust in his edition of the Spanish version (*Bocados de Oro*), *B.L.V.* vol. CXLI (Tübingen, 1879).

M. Schofield, *The Dicts and Sayings of the Philosophers: a Middle English version by Stephen Scrope* (University of Pennsylvania dissertation, Philadelphia, 1936).

For further information see below, pp. 60, 250–1.

Magoun, p. 35 and nn. 1 and 2.

I. 4. c

'LOS BUENOS PROVERBIOS'[1]

The book of proverbs made by the Nestorian Christian Honein ibn Ishaq in the ninth century was translated into Hebrew by al Harizi in the first half of the thirteenth century, and thence into Spanish as *Los buenos proverbios* in the second half of the same century. It contains many wise sayings attributed to Alexander, most of which are also found in the *Dicts and Sayings*. It did not attain the popularity of the other Arabic works, and was not further translated.

[1] EDITION AND INFORMATION. H. Knust, *Mittheilungen aus dem Eskurial, B.L.V.* vol. CXLI (Tübingen, 1879), pp. 1–65 (text), 519 ff. (discussion).

I. 5. MINOR SOURCES

THE wonderful element in the legendary accounts was supplemented by material drawn from Pliny the Elder, Solinus, Isidore, the source of the *Liber monstrorum*, and others; while Lucan and Aulus Gellius were used very occasionally for the Alexander material that they contained. John of Salisbury also made use of the anecdotes of Alexander in Vegetius and Frontinus.

Much more important than these sources, however, and of far-reaching effect upon the medieval conception of Alexander, is a group of anecdotes in Cicero, Seneca, Valerius Maximus, and the Fathers of the Church, notably St Augustine and St Jerome. The anecdotes told by these authors normally reflect the various ancient philosophic attitudes to Alexander, and were widely known throughout the Middle Ages. Their extensive medieval influence is fully discussed below, pp. 83 ff.

II

THE PRINCIPAL MEDIEVAL
DERIVATIVES OF
PSEUDO-CALLISTHENES

II. 1. JULIUS VALERIUS AND
HIS DERIVATIVES

II. 1. a

JULIUS VALERIUS, 'RES GESTAE ALEXANDRI MACEDONIS'

THE earliest Latin translation of Pseudo-Callisthenes is the prose *Res Gestae Alexandri Macedonis*[1] ascribed in the manuscripts to a certain Julius Valerius Alexander Polemius. This work, divided, like its original, into three books, is a translation from an α-type manuscript of the Greek text, and may be dated from internal evidence c. A.D. 320–30. Various conjectures have been made about the author but nothing is known for certain of him, though it seems probable that he was an African and a freedman.

The work was known to medieval writers, and was used by Alberic and possibly by others of the various authors of the *Roman d'Alexandre*; but it was much more popular in the abridged version known as the *Zacher Epitome*,[2] which was made not later than the ninth century. But from the twelfth century onwards Julius Valerius and the *Epitome* were partially superseded in public favour by the *Historia de Preliis* in its various recensions.

---

[1] EDITIONS. A. Mai (Rome, 1817, and several reprints; from the Ambrosian MS.).
B. Kübler (Leipzig, Teubner, 1888).
STUDIES. J. Zacher, in *Pseudocallisthenes, Forschungen zur Kritik und Geschichte der ältesten Aufzeichnung der Alexandersage* (Halle, 1867), pp. 32–42.
P. Meyer, *A. le. G.* II, pp. 8–18.
A. Ausfeld, *Der Griechische Alexanderroman* (Leipzig, 1907), pp. 10–12.
Magoun, p. 25 and n. 2.
[2] See, J. Zacher, *Iulii Valerii Epitome* (Halle, 1867), and Magoun, p. 33 and nn. 2 and 3. Below, pp. 25–6.

II. 1. b

'ITINERARIUM ALEXANDRI'[1]

This work lies outside the scope of our present study. It was composed in either A.D. 346 or 359, and contains an account of Alexander's peregrinations based on Julius Valerius and Arrian. It survives in one manuscript, and exercised no influence. Its chief interest is as a *terminus ante quem* for dating Julius Valerius.

[1] EDITION. A. Mai (Milan, 1817; reprinted Leipzig, 1818 and Rome, 1835).
INFORMATION. J. Zacher, *Pseudocallisthenes* (Halle, 1867), pp. 42–3.
Magoun, p. 25 and n. 3.

II. 1. c

EPITOMES OF JULIUS VALERIUS

II. 1. c. i

THE 'ZACHER EPITOME'

The so-called *Zacher Epitome*[1] is the only abbreviated version of Julius Valerius to have been widely known and used. Edited by Julius Zacher from a ninth-century manuscript, which fixes the latest possible date of composition, the epitome is a drastic abridgement of Julius Valerius. Speeches and other rhetorical matter have been everywhere omitted; and more has been expunged from book II than from book I, and book III is reduced to a mere fragment. It seems likely that this epitome was made to accompany the text of *Epistola* I which so frequently appears with it in surviving MSS., as the very extensive omissions in book III are largely supplied by the *Epistola*.[2]

The epitome is extant in numerous manuscripts; and together with *Epistola* I supplied the principal source for Thomas of Kent, and for the accounts of Alexander in Vincent de Beauvais, the *Histoire ancienne jusqu'à César* and other chroniclers. It was also a supplementary source of the *Oxford-Montpellier Epitome*, and other legendary texts.

A MS. of the usual composite type, containing the *Epitome* and *Epistola* I, was translated into French prose in the fifteenth century.[3]

[1] EDITION. *Julii Valerii Epitome*, ed. J. Zacher (Halle, 1867).
STUDY, Zacher, ed. cit. introduction.
P. Meyer, *A. le G.* II, pp. 18–26.
Magoun, p. 33 and nn. 2 and 3.

[2] The distribution of the texts of *Zacher Epitome*, *Epistola* I and *Collatio* I in 134 MSS. so far traced is instructive on this point. All three texts occur in twenty MSS., *Epitome* and *Epistola* in twenty-nine, *Epitome* alone in seventeen, *Epistola* alone in thirty-five, *Collatio* alone in twenty-four. The combination *Epistola* + *Collatio* is found eight times and *Epitome* + *Collatio* only once. This would seem to point to an original edition of *Epitome* + *Epistola* with

which *Collatio* I may have been combined, if it was not added later in the textual tradition. The frequent occurrence of *Epistola* and *Collatio* alone is accounted for by the popularity of the former with natural historians and geographers, in whose composite MSS. it is often found, and of the latter with moralists and theologians. We note the relative rarity of *Epitome* occurring alone, seventeen times against forty-nine times in combination. [D.J.A.R.]

³ STUDY. P. Meyer, *A. le G.* II, pp. 301–5.

II. 1. c. ii

THE 'OXFORD-MONTPELLIER EPITOME'

The *Oxford Epitome*, in Corpus Christi College MS. 82, is much fuller than the *Zacher Epitome*, and is closer to its original, Julius Valerius. It was at first supposed, by P. Meyer,[1] that this *Epitome* represented an intermediate stage between Julius Valerius and the *Zacher Epitome*; but G. Cillié[2] showed that it is the result of an expansion of the *Zacher Epitome* with the aid of borrowings from the complete unabbreviated text of Julius Valerius. A second manuscript of this *Epitome* was discovered and published by A. Hilka from Montpellier Fac. de Médecine MS. H. 31,[3] which in its text differs from the *Oxford Epitome* only in minor details.

[1] P. Meyer, *A. le G.* II, pp. 20–6.
[2] G. G. Cillié, *De Julii Valerii Epitoma Oxoniensi* (Strassburg diss., 1905).
[3] A. Hilka, *Romanische Forschungen*, XXIV (1911), pp. 31 ff.
   Magoun, p. 33, n. 3.

II. 1. c. iii

THE 'LIEGNITZ HISTORIA ALEXANDRI MAGNI'

Together with the *Montpellier Epitome*, Alfons Hilka edited,[1] from MS. 31 of the Church of St Peter and St Paul at Liegnitz, an account of Alexander which is generally called the *Liegnitz Historia*. This Latin account of Alexander, 'historia allexandri magni compendiose', was written in prose in the fifteenth century. It is derived from Julius Valerius but it in no way resembles any other edition or epitome of that work. From the nature of various interpolations, and from comparison with the lives of Alexander in Ekkehart of Aura, Godfrey of Viterbo and other chronicles, Hilka suggested that the account was probably intended to be incorporated into a chronicle or history-bible, between the books of Esther and Maccabees, a point at which the life of Alexander is inserted into many vernacular chronicles.

The chief individual characteristic of the work is its use of Peter Comestor's description of Alexander's dealings with Saraballa and his visit to Jerusalem, and there are also some interpolations from the I[3] *Historia de Preliis*. More important is the evidence of some connexion between the *Liegnitz*

Historia, the *Seelentrost* group of Alexander texts, and the Polish chronicler Vincentius Kadlubek. Hilka has shown that these texts frequently agree with one another in individual readings, and suspects some distant common source.

[1] EDITION AND DISCUSSION. A. Hilka, in *Romanische Forschungen*, XXIX (1911), pp. 1–30.
Magoun, p. 33, n. 3.

II. 1. d

ALBERIC AND LAMPRECHT

II. 1. d. i

ALBERIC

There exists only a fragment of the earliest vernacular Alexander-book,[1] written in the first years of the twelfth century by a certain Alberic, possibly a native of Pisançon[2] near Romans in southern Dauphiné. The fragment consists of 105 octosyllabic lines forming fifteen monorhyme tirades or 'laisses' of varying length, and written in a hybrid Franco-Provençal dialect.[3] It breaks off in the middle of a description of Alexander's education. The rest of Alberic's poem, however, which he may possibly have left unfinished, has survived to us in the German version of Pfaffe Lamprecht, which has also supplied us the name of its author and his place of origin.

Alberic's principal sources were Julius Valerius, the I¹ *Historia de Preliis*, and the interpolated Quintus Curtius. His work, besides being translated by Lamprecht into German, was in part rewritten about 1165 to form the *Decasyllabic Alexander*, a part of which survives in two MSS. prefixed to the rest of the *Roman d'Alexandre* in a later form. It was later again rewritten in Alexandrines to form Branch 1 of the *Roman*.

[1] EDITIONS. W. Förster and E. Koschwitz, *Altfranzösisches Uebungsbuch* (5th ed. Leipzig, 1915), cols. 237–46, 323, 324 (text and extensive bibliography).
A. Foulet, in *M.F.R.d'A.* III, pp. 2–8 (discussion), 37 ff. (text).
STUDIES. Meyer, *A. le G.* II, pp. 70–101.
Magoun, p. 26 and n. 2.
A. Schmidt, *Ueber das Alexanderlied des Alberic v. Besançon und sein Verhältnis zur antiken Ueberlieferung* (diss. Bonn, 1886).
[2] V. Crescini, 'Alberico de Pisançon', *Studi Medievali*, II (1929), pp. 196–7.
[3] H. Flechtner, *Die Sprache des Alexander-Fragments des Alberich von Besançon* (Breslau, 1882).

II. 1. d. ii

PFAFFE LAMPRECHT, 'ALEXANDER'

The *Alexander* of Pfaffe Lamprecht,[1] the earliest German Alexander poem, is extant in three manuscripts, but the texts presented by them differ so widely from one another as to offer many problems. The Vorau manuscript gives much the shortest version of the text, while the Strassburg and Basel manuscripts, although of approximately the same length, differ in many respects. The Vorau version is the earliest, having been written about 1155;[2] the Strassburg manuscript was written in 1187, and the Basel manuscript dates from the fifteenth century.

There has been much controversy upon the relationship of the redactions contained in these manuscripts to one another and to the original poem of Lamprecht; but it is generally believed that the *Vorau Alexander* is closest to the original text of Lamprecht, and that the *Strassburg Alexander* and the *Basel Alexander* are interpolated descendants of it.

The *Vorau Alexander* is a Middle High German poem of 1527 lines, incorporated in a composite MS. of German and Latin texts, several relating to Biblical history. As the writer, the priest Lamprecht, says, it is a translation of Alberic; and from the text of Lamprecht that of Alberic may with tolerable certainty be reconstructed, as he was a reliable translator, and, it would seem, seldom omitted or altered anything that Alberic had written. On the other hand he interpolated certain material. He objected to the laudatory superlatives that Alberic heaped upon Alexander—the title of the greatest king upon earth belonged by right to Solomon—since Alexander was a heathen. He added many Biblical and other quotations. And his attitude to Alexander, whom he reproached for his pride and cruelty, lacked the whole-hearted admiration of Alberic.

The poem ends abruptly when Darius is killed by Alexander. The reason for so sudden a conclusion may possibly be that Alberic's poem was cut short by his death, and that Lamprecht completed the poem by making him kill Darius, thus bringing the book swiftly to an end. But whence did he derive the idea that Alexander himself killed Darius? This is found in neither historical nor legendary sources but is believed to be based on I Maccabees i (a book which Lamprecht mentions), where it is said of Alexander: 'et percussit Darium regem Persarum'—a phrase which Lamprecht will have taken too literally.

The *Strassburg MS.*, written in 1187, was destroyed in the war of 1870, but was published by Karl Kinzel in his edition of Lamprecht. It is derived from a reworking (*y*) of a redaction (*x*), which, after omitting the abrupt ending of the original poem, completed the narrative with a long account of the adventures and campaigns of Alexander derived from Leo's *Natiuitas et Victoria* (uninterpolated) and the *Iter ad Paradisum*.

The *Basel Alexander* is found inserted in a world-chronicle. The text presented by this MS. is derived from a separate reworking, probably Swabian, of the redaction (*x*) described above. It differs from the *Strassburg Alexander* both at the beginning, which has been completely altered by the interpolation of the Nectanebus episode from the I² *Historia de Preliis*, and at the end, where a further description of the wonderful adventures of Alexander has been inserted. Some of this added material has evident affinities with the account of Alexander in Jansen Enikel's *Weltchronik*. This final revision of Lamprecht probably dates from the thirteenth century, but its exact relationship to the *Strassburg* and *Vorau* redactions is still disputed.

¹ EDITIONS. K. Kinzel, *Lamprechts Alexander nach den drei Texten, mit den Fragmenten d. Alberic von Besançon* (German. *Handbibliothek*, VI, Halle, 1884) (all three versions).

H. E. Müller, *Die Werke des Pfaffen Lamprecht* (*Münchener Texte*, Heft XII, Munich, 1923) (*Vorau Alexander*).

STUDIES. Th. Hampe, *Die Quellen der Strassburger Fortsetzung von Lamprechts Alexanderlied* (diss. Bremen, 1890).

G. Ehrismann, *Geschichte d. Deutsch. Lit.* II, i (Munich, 1922), pp. 235–55 (with full bibliography).

J. van Dam, *Zur Vorgeschichte des höfischen Epos: Lamprecht, Eilhart, Veldeke* (*Rheinische Beitr. zur german. Philol.* VIII, 1923).

J. van Dam, 'Der künstlerische Wert des Strassburger Alexander', *Neophilologus*, XII (1927), pp. 104–17.

E. Schröder, 'Die deutschen Alexander-Dichtungen des 12ten Jahrhunderts', *Nachrichten v. d. Gesellschaft der Wissen. zu Göttingen*, Phil.-Hist. Klasse (1928), pp. 45–92.

E. Grammel, *Studien über den Wandel des Alexanderbildes in der deutschen Dichtung des 12. u. 13 Jhdts.* (Frankfurt diss. Limburg, 1931), passim.

Magoun, pp. 26–7, p. 26, nn. 3 and 4 and p. 27, nn. 1 and 2.

² E. Sitte, 'Die Datierung von Lamprechts Alexander', *Hermaea*, XXXV (Halle, 1940).

II. 1. e

THE 'DECASYLLABIC ALEXANDER' AND THE 'ROMAN D'ALEXANDRE', WITH ITS ELABORATIONS AND DERIVATIVES

II. 1. e. i

THE 'DECASYLLABIC ALEXANDER', THE 'ROMAN D'ALEXANDRE' AND ITS ELABORATIONS

The *Decasyllabic Alexander*,¹ written about 1165–75, is a poem of 785 lines based principally upon Julius Valerius and the *Historia de Preliis* (I¹), with frequent recurrence to Alberic, and contains an account of Alexander's adventures as far as the campaign against Nicholas.

It was one of the earliest components of the massive and complicated

Roman d'Alexandre,[2] the most important medieval Alexander poem; and it only survives, in fact, in two manuscripts of the *Roman* which preserve in part a redaction made before the final editor, Alexandre de Paris, had recast the decasyllabic poem in Alexandrines to conform with the rest of the poem.

The *Roman d'Alexandre* is at present being studied and edited by a group of American scholars, whose work is still in progress. Their main conclusions are as follows:[3]

At much the same time as the *Decasyllabic Alexander* two other Alexander poems were written, both now lost in their original independent form. These were the poem of Lambert le Tort which described Alexander's adventures in the East and his death, which is called the *Alixandre en Orient*, and another poem dealing with Alexander's death, which is called the *Mort Alixandre*.

The *Decasyllabic Alexander* was the foundation of the first *Roman d'Alexandre* (*RAlix* is the conventional abbreviation). This primitive edition was then thoroughly rewritten by a redactor (called Lambert–2), who interpolated the poem of Lambert le Tort, substituted for Lambert's account of the capture of Babylon and the close of Alexander's life the version of the *Mort Alixandre*, and left the *Decasyllabic Alexander* unchanged. This form of the *Roman* (*RAlix* Lambert–2) was later enlarged by the addition of further material from the *Alixandre en Orient* (*RAlix* Amalgam).

Three manuscripts of the *Roman d'Alexandre*, A, B, and L,[4] present different and distinct revisions of this Amalgam which differ in many particulars from one another and from the usual text; but the intermediate versions of the *Roman* that they provide are of interest only to the student of the textual development of the poem. An interpolated version of that revision of the *RAlix* Amalgam from which MS. B was descended was the basis of the redaction made by Alexandre de Bernai, also called Alexandre de Paris, after 1177, which constitutes the vulgate text of the *Roman d'Alexandre*. Alexandre de Paris made many alterations in the text; he recast the *Decasyllabic Alexander* into alexandrines, interpolated between this and the prologue of Lambert le Tort's poem a reworking of the *Fuerre de Gadres*, composed transitional material before and after this episode, and made a few alterations in the latter part of the poem.

The *Fuerre de Gadres*[5] was originally an independent poem, an imaginative expansion of an episode during the siege of Tyre that was briefly recorded in the I³ *Historia de Preliis*. The descent of the poem is almost as complicated as that of the *Roman* itself. Written by a certain Eustache, it enjoyed great popularity and existed in many different versions, some independent and some incorporated into various Alexander-books. Two of the more important are the version interpolated into Thomas of Kent, and the Latin translation formerly ascribed to Boccaccio, and preserved in one MS. in Florence.

The redaction of the *Roman d'Alexandre* made by Alexandre de Paris is divided into four 'branches',[6] which approximately correspond to the original independent sections of the text.

(i) The birth and childhood of Alexander, the war against Nicholas, the expedition against Athens, the initial steps in the campaign against Darius, the siege, but not the capture, of Tyre.

(ii) The siege of Tyre and its capture, the *Fuerre de Gadres*, the capture of Araine and of Gaza, Alexander's entry into Jerusalem, and the defeat of Darius at the Prés de Paile.

(iii) The pursuit and death of Darius, the descent to the bottom of the sea, the expedition to India and first defeat of Porus, the marvels of India, the second defeat of Porus, the journey to the Pillars of Hercules, the duel between Alexander and Porus, the episode of Queen Candace and the Duke of Palatine, the ascent into the air, the capture of Babylon, the submission of the Amazons, the treachery of Antipater and Divinuspater.

(iv) The death and testament of Alexander, the laments of the twelve peers and the burial of Alexander.

The conception of Alexander in the *Roman d'Alexandre* is well known; he has become the ideal courtly prince. The poem enjoyed great popularity, and many elaborations, mostly works of pure fiction, were composed at various dates, and interpolated into it. These are as follows:

(i) Epic convention demanded that Alexander's death should be avenged, and two poems were written about the vengeance taken upon his murderers. The first of these, the *Venjance Alixandre* of Jean le Nevelon, was probably written shortly before 1181; the second, the *Vengement Alixandre* of Gui de Cambrai, before 1191. Both poems are works of fiction, and they enjoyed equal popularity. Parma MS. 1206 presents a composite text resulting from the combination of the two poems.[7]

(ii) The *Prise de Defur* (*L'épisode du duc Melcis*), an episode interpolated into the body of the Romance, was composed by a Picard about 1250, and is interesting for the strange version of the Wonderstone story that it contains.[8]

(iii) The *Voyage au Paradis Terrestre*, a considerably altered French version of the *Iter ad Paradisum*, is another thirteenth-century poem that is frequently found interpolated into the *Roman*; it has been edited and discussed in conjunction with the *Prise de Defur*.[9]

(iv) The *Voeux du Paon*[10] or the *Roman de Cassamus*, written by Jacques de Longuyon about 1312, was one of the most popular of all late medieval romances, and especially famous for its introduction of the figures of the Nine Worthies. Though its plot is scarcely more than externally connected to that of the *Roman d'Alexandre*, the poem was frequently interpolated into manuscripts of the *Roman*. It occurs as frequently by itself or in combination with one or both of its continuations. In the late Middle Ages the Peacock cycle was by far the most popular element in Old French Alexander-literature. As an independent work it was translated into Spanish, Middle English and Dutch, and appeared as an episode in the two Scottish Alexander-books, the *Buik of Alexander* and the *Buik of King Alexander* (q.v.). It also provided the setting for the fourteenth-century French prose romance *Perceforest*.

The *Restor du Paon*, a continuation, was written before 1338 by Jean Brisebarre, and was followed by a further continuation, the *Parfait du Paon*, written by Jean de le Mote in 1340. Of these poems, the *Restor* accompanies the *Voeux* in several MSS. but the *Parfait* remained unpopular and only two MSS. of it survive.

[1] EDITIONS. P. Meyer, *A. le G.* I, pp. 25–59.
A. Foulet, *M.F.R.d'A.* III, pp. 61–100.
STUDIES. P. Meyer, *A. le G.* II, pp. 102–32.
A. Foulet, ed. cit. pp. 8–11.
[2] EDITIONS. H. Michelant, *Li Romans d'Alexandre*, *B.L.V.* vol. XIII (Stuttgart, 1846).
The Medieval French 'Roman d'Alexandre'; edition prepared by a group of Princeton medievalists, in progress. The volumes so far issued, in the *Elliott Monographs* series, nos. 36–40, by Princeton University Press, are as follows:
Vol. I, *E.M.* 36: *Text of Arsenal and Venice versions*, prepared by M. S. La Du (1937).
Vol. II, *E.M.* 37: *Version of Alexandre de Paris: text*, ed. by E. C. Armstrong, D. L. Buffum, Bateman Edwards, L. F. H. Lowe (1937).
Vol. III, *E.M.* 38: *Version of Alexandre de Paris: variants and notes to Branch I*, prepared by A. Foulet (1949).
Vol. IV, *E.M.* 39: *Le Roman du Fuerre de Gadres par Eustache: essai d'établissement du texte*, par E. C. Armstrong et Alfred Foulet (1942).
Vol. V, *E.M.* 40: *Version of Alexandre de Paris: variants and notes to Branch II*, prepared with an introduction by Frederick B. Agard (1942).
Further volumes to follow.
STUDIES. This edition contains extensive studies of manuscripts, development, etc. Of earlier studies the best is that in Meyer, *A. le G.* II, pp. 133–253; see *Romania*, XI, pp. 213 ff., for Meyer's classification of the manuscripts.
Further bibliography in Magoun, pp. 26–7 and p. 26, nn. 5 and 6 and p. 27, n. 1.
[3] *M.F.R.d'A.* II, pp. ix–xviii.
[4] Edited with full descriptions in *M.F.R.d'A.* I (Arsenal and Venice MSS. A and B), and *M.F.R.d'A.* III, pp. 101–54.

[5] EDITIONS. *M.F.R.d'A.* IV, see above, n. 2; also in R. L. Graeme Ritchie, *The Buik of Alexander*, vol. II (*Scottish Text Society*, new series, no. 17 (1925).

STUDIES. The Princeton edition cited above has superseded all previous studies of the work. See also:

F. Pfister, 'Zur Entstehung und Geschichte des Fuerre de Gadres', *Zeitschr. f. französ. Spr. u. Lit.* XLI (1913), pp. 102–8.

A. Foulet, 'Balaam, Dux Tyri', *Modern Language Notes* (May 1933), pp. 330–5.

Further bibliography in Magoun, pp. 28–9 and p. 28, nn. 2–7, p. 29, nn. 1–4.

[6] See *M.F.R.d'A.* II, pp. xxii–xxiii.

[7] EDITIONS. O. Schultz-Gora, *Die Vengeance Alexandre von Jean le Nevelon* (Berlin, 1902).

Bateman Edwards, *Gui de Cambrai: Le Vengement Alixandre* (Princeton University Press, 1928: *Elliott Monographs*, 23).

E. B. Ham, *Jehan le Nevelon: La Venjance Alixandre* (Princeton University Press, 1931: *Elliott Monographs*, 27).

E. B. Ham, *Five Versions of the Venjance Alixandre* (Princeton University Press, 1935: *Elliott Monographs*, 34).

E. B. Ham, 'An eighth *Venjance Alixandre*', *Modern Language Notes* (1941), pp. 409–14.

STUDIES. K. Sachow, *Ueber die Vengeance d'Alexandre von Jean le Venelais* (diss. Halle, 1902).

E. Walberg, 'Classification des Manuscrits de la *Vengeance d'Alixandre* de Jean le Nevelon', *Från Filologiska Föreningen i Lund, Språkliger Uppsatser*, III (1906), pp. 5–30.

E. C. Armstrong, *The authorship of the Vengement Alixandre and of the Venjance Alixandre* (Princeton University Press, 1926: *Elliott Monographs*, 19).

Bateman Edwards, *A Classification of the Manuscripts of Gui de Cambrai's Vengement Alixandre* (Princeton University Press, 1926: *Elliott Monographs*, 20).

Further bibliography in Magoun, pp. 31–2, and p. 31, nn. 4–5, p. 32, nn. 1–2.

[8] EDITION. L. P. G. Peckham and Milan S. La Du (Princeton University Press, 1935: *Elliott Monographs*, 35), pp. 1–73; with valuable introduction.

[9] EDITION. L. P. G. Peckham and Milan S. La Du, ed. cit. pp. 73–90; with valuable introduction.

Bibliography in Magoun, pp. 29–30, p. 29, n. 6, p. 30, nn. 1–2.

[10] EDITION. Edition of *Voeux du Paon* in R. L. Graeme Ritchie, *The Buik of Alexander* (*Scottish Text Society*, new series, no. 12 (1921) and no. 21 (1927).

Restor and *Parfait* unpublished.

INFORMATION. Meyer, A. le G. II, pp. 268 ff. (details of all three poems).

Meyer, in *Romania*, XI (1882), pp. 247 ff.

A. Thomas, *Hist. Littéraire de la France*, XXXVI, i (1924), pp. 1–100.

Lost Spanish version of *Voeux du Paon*: A. Morel-Fatio, *El Libro de Alexandre* (*Gesell. f. Roman. Lit.* Bd. x, Dresden, 1906), p. xvi.

Middle English version of *Voeux du Paon*: K. Rosskopf, *Editio Princeps des Mittelengl. Cassamus* (diss. Munich, 1911) (edition and information).

Middle Dutch version of *Voeux du Paon*: E. Verwijs, *Bibl. v. Middelnederl. Letterk.*, Afd. 2 (Groningen, 1869) (edition and information).

Bibliography in Magoun, pp. 30–1, p. 30, nn. 3–6, p. 31, nn. 1–3.

II. 1. e. ii

JEAN WAUQUELIN, 'L'HISTOIRE D'ALEXANDRE'

Jean Wauquelin was from 1445 to 1453, the year of his death, one of the most prolific writers under the patronage of the House of Burgundy. His French prose life of Alexander[1] was written before 1448 for Jean de

Bourgogne, Comte d'Etampes and Seigneur de Dourdan (1415–91). Five manuscripts are known, three with fine illuminations; but it was never printed.

The principal sources are a late manuscript of the *Roman d'Alexandre* incorporating the *Prise de Defur*, the *Voeux du Paon* and the *Venjance Alixandre*, and there is mention of a mysterious author called Guillaume, by whom Meyer understood the author of the *Old French Prose Romance*.[2] Wauquelin's use of these sources has been studied by Paul Meyer; he remains faithful to the *Roman d'Alexandre* until after the *Fuerre de Gadres* episode, when he draws from his sources alternately, with much paraphrase and epitomizing, and some attempts to explain the inevitable contradictions.

The book is written in a rather verbose style and conforms to the courtly tradition in the writer's treatment of Alexander, but Wauquelin has little to add of his own except prologues and occasional interjections.

[1] EDITION. The romance as a whole is unpublished, but the *Venjance* section was critically edited by E. B. Ham, *Five versions of the Venjance Alixandre* (Princeton University Press, 1935: *Elliott Monographs*, 34), pp. 59–75.

INFORMATION. Ibid. pp. 45–59. Meyer, *A. le G.* II, pp. 313–29. Magoun, p. 32 and n. 4.

[2] Comparison of the text with its sources shows that Paul Meyer was right in assuming that the *French Prose Alexander* and not its Latin source was used by Wauquelin, who often reproduces this source word for word. The text used was of the second redaction including the Daniel prophecy of the ram and the he-goat (see *French Studies*, VI (1952), pp. 146–7) which appears in Wauquelin. On the other hand, despite Wauquelin's assertion, he made no use of Vincent de Beauvais' *Speculum Historiale* IV either in the Latin or in the French version of Jean de Vignay. Possibly he was misled by the reference to Vincent inserted by the second redactor of *Fr. Prose Alex.* at the end of his prologue into assuming that Vincent was the author of that work. Guillaume remains a mystery. [D.J.A.R.]

II. 1. e. iii

MS. BESANÇON 836

This manuscript,[1] of the fifteenth century, contains a recasting into French prose of the *Roman d'Alexandre* and certain of its continuations, entitled *Fais et Concquestes du Noble Roy Alexandre*. It has not yet been edited or carefully studied.

[1] INFORMATION. P. Meyer, *A. le G.* II, 328–9.

E. P. Ham, *Five versions of the Venjance Alixandre* (Princeton University Press, 1935: *Elliott Monographs*, 34), pp. 79–82.

Magoun, p. 32 and n. 3.

II. 1. f

THE SCOTTISH ALEXANDER-BOOKS

II. 1. f. i

THE 'BUIK OF ALEXANDER'

This fifteenth-century Scottish poem,[1] known only from an edition that appeared in 1580, contains translations into Scottish of the *Voeux du Paon* and the *Fuerre de Gadres*.

[1] EDITION. R. L. Graeme Ritchie, *The Buik of Alexander* (*Scottish Text Society*, new series, no. 12 (1921), and no. 21 (1927), with parallel texts of the French poems).
  INFORMATION. A. Thomas, *Hist. Litt. de la France*, XXXVI, i (1924), pp. 32–3.
  Magoun, p. 28 and n. 7.

II. 1. f. ii

THE 'BUIK OF KING ALEXANDER'

This Scottish poem,[1] written by Sir Gilbert Hay (*fl. circa* 1456), contains a complete life of Alexander including the *Fuerre de Gadres* and the *Voeux du Paon*; it has as yet been little studied. The author claims to be using a French Alexander-book as source.[2]

[1] STUDY. A. Herrmann, *The Forraye of Gadderis, The Vowis*, extracts from Sir Gilbert Hay's *Buik of King Alexander the Conqueror* in *Wissenschaftliche Beilage zum Jahresbericht der 12. Städtischen Realschule zu Berlin* (Berlin, 1900).
  INFORMATION. J. E. Wells, *A Manual of the Writings in Middle English* (New Haven, Yale U.P., 1916), pp. 105–6, 779.
  Dr A. Macdonald has an edition in preparation for the Scottish Text Society.
[2] A brief analysis of the early part of the book in a letter of Dr Macdonald seems to point to the French Prose Alexander as the most likely source, though the *Fuerre* and the *Voeux* must have come from elsewhere. [D.J.A.R.]

II. 1. g

THE DERIVATIVES OF THE 'ZACHER EPITOME'

II. 1. g. i

THOMAS OF KENT, 'ROMAN DE TOUTE CHEVALERIE'

This[1] is an Anglo-Norman verse romance of Alexander derived from the *Zacher Epitome* of Julius Valerius, with supplementary use of the *Epistola ad Aristotelem*, the *Iter ad Paradisum*, and certain passages, mostly descriptive of monsters, from Solinus, Aethicus Ister and several minor sources. The *Fuerre de Gadres* and the lamentation of the peers for the death of Alexander were interpolated from the *Roman* at a later date. The name of the author of the *Fuerre*, Eustasche, occurs in the MSS. erroneously as the author of this poem, but his correct name, Thomas of Kent, has now been established.

The original poem was composed possibly as early as the second half of the twelfth century. It was independent of the continental *Roman d'Alexandre* but was interpolated from it in the first half of the thirteenth century. In this form it survives and can hardly be later in date than *c.* 1250, the approximate date of the Cambridge MS.[2] In its original form, before the *Fuerre de Gadres* was interpolated, it was the principal source of the Middle English *Kyng Alisaunder*. Gower also made use of the *Roman de Toute Chevalerie* for the Nectanebus episode in the *Confessio Amantis*.

[1] EDITION. None; some extracts were printed by Meyer, *A. le G.* I, pp. 195–235.

STUDIES. H. Schneegans, 'Über die Interpolation des '*Fuerre de Gadres*' im altfranz. Roman des Eustache von Kent', *Die Neueren Sprachen*, Ergänzungsband (Festschrift W. Vietor, 1910), pp. 27–61.

Johanna Weynand, *Der 'Roman de Toute Chevalerie' in seinem Verhältnis zu seinen Quellen* (diss. Bonn, 1911).

R. Wolff, *Der interpolierte Fuerre de Gadres im Alexanderroman des Thomas von Kent* (diss. Bonn, 1914).

C. B. West, *Courtoisie in Anglo-Norman Literature* (Oxford, Blackwell, 1938), pp. 71–9.

B. Foster, 'The *Roman de toute Chevalerie*, its date and author', *French Studies*, IX, 1955, pp. 154–8. Also pp. 348–51 (discussion).

D. Legge, *Anglo-Norman in the cloisters* (Edinburgh, 1950), pp. 35–43.

Magoun, pp. 33–4, p. 34, nn. 1–3.

[2] Trinity College, O. 9. 34.

PLATE III (*opposite*). A page (fo. 54b) from the Paris MS. (*c.* 1300) of the *Roman de Toute Chevalerie* of Thomas of Kent, written and illustrated in England with over three hundred miniatures, many of which are unfinished and show only the preliminary pen-drawing. The pictures correspond exactly to those in the fragmentary Cambridge MS. (Trinity College O.9.34, formerly the property of Thomas Gale) of *c.* 1250, and illustrated with a lively series of tinted pen drawings by an artist of the St Albans school. The archetype of these MSS. and of the Durham MS. (Chapter Library C. 4. 27b) which, though un-illustrated, preserves the picture captions, was probably an illustrated MS. of the St Albans school made in the first half of the thirteenth century. The artist, though he occasionally borrowed iconographic details from elsewhere, was himself responsible for the pictures, in which he followed the text closely, often illustrating details found only in the French and absent from the sources used by Thomas of Kent.

The page illustrated shows part of the night battle between Alexander and various wild animals and monsters which he encountered when, in the course of his pursuit of Porus across the Indian desert, he camped by a fresh-water pool. The source is the *Epistola ad Aristotelem*. The subjects are Alexander's encounters with:

(*a*) (left, above): White lions as large as bulls. (*b*) (left, below): Tigers. Both this and the previous miniature show a marked influence of heraldic representational convention. (*c*) (right, above): Bats as large as pigeons. (*d*) (right, below): The terrifying Odontotyrannus, described as being as large as an elephant, with the black head of a horse, and a triple horn on its forehead.

III   ALEXANDER'S BATTLE WITH THE MONSTERS

II. 1. g. ii

'KYNG ALISAUNDER'

This Middle English metrical Romance[1] may be dated before 1330, and is based upon the *Roman de Toute Chevalerie* of Thomas of Kent. It is, however, no close translation but a skilful adaptation by a writer of originality and power, and the best of the English Alexander-books.

Six printed leaves, dated *c.* 1550, contain fragments of an expanded version of *Kyng Alisaunder* which includes the *Epistola ad Aristotelem*.[2]

[1] EDITION. H. Weber, in *Metrical Romances of the Thirteenth, Fourteenth, and Fifteenth Centuries* (Edinburgh, 1810), vol. I, pp. 1–327.

G. V. Smithers, E.E.T.S., O.S. CCXXVII (1952).

STUDIES. T. Hildenbrand, *Die altfranz. Alexanderdichtung 'Le Roman de Toute Chevalerie' des Thomas von Kent und die mittelengl. Romanze 'Kyng Alisaunder' in ihrem Verhältnis zu einander* (diss. Bonn, 1911).

For date and authorship, see G. L. Hamilton in *Mélanges...offerts à M. Antoine Thomas* (Paris, 1927), p. 196 and n. 5.

Magoun, p. 34 and n. 4.

[2] K. D. Bülbring, *Englische Studien*, XIII (1889), pp. 145 ff.

II. 1. g. iii

THE LIFE OF ALEXANDER IN THE 'HISTOIRE ANCIENNE JUSQU'À CÉSAR'

This extremely popular universal history[1] of Antiquity was written for Roger, châtelain of Lille, some time between 1206 and 1230. The principal sources used are Orosius and, for biblical history, Peter Comestor; but prose versions of the Thebes, Aeneas and Troy romances, and an epitome of Geoffrey of Monmouth or of some vernacular 'Brut', have been incorporated. The much commoner first redaction includes a considerable section devoted to the history of Macedon. The author uses Orosius for his account of Philip II and for the wars of the 'Diadochi', but for the life of Alexander himself his principal source was an *Epitome + Epistola* manuscript supplemented from Orosius and, for some episodes, the *Roman d'Alexandre*. Part of the history of the 'Diadochi' was borrowed as an epilogue by the author of the *Old French Prose Alexander*.

[1] Unpublished. List of MSS. in B. Woledge, *Bibliographie des romans et nouvelles en prose française antérieurs à 1500* (Geneva, Droz, 1954), pp. 55–8.

STUDIES. P. Meyer, 'Les premières compilations françaises d'histoire ancienne', in *Romania*, XIV, pp. 36–76.

P. Meyer, *A. le G.* II, pp. 341–7.

D. J. A. Ross, *French Studies*, VI (1952), pp. 135–47.

II. 2. ARCHPRIEST LEO, THE BAMBERG MANU-SCRIPT AND THE BAVARIAN RECENSION OF THE 'HISTORIA DE PRELIIS'

II. 2. a

ARCHPRIEST LEO, 'NATIVITAS ET VICTORIA ALEXANDRI MAGNI' ('HISTORIA DE PRELIIS')

ABOUT the year 950 Archpriest Leo of Naples was sent by his master, Duke John III of Campania, on a mission to Constantinople. He found there a Greek manuscript of Pseudo-Callisthenes, and transcribed it. When he brought this work home to Naples, Duke John ordered it to be translated into Latin for his library. Leo made this translation, and called it *Natiuitas et Victoria Alexandri Magni*;[1] and from this Latin version of a Greek manuscript of the (δ)-recension of Pseudo-Callisthenes the large and complicated *Historia de Preliis*[2] tradition descends.

Leo's version does not survive in its original form; but the details of his journey to Constantinople, his transcription of the manuscript and its translation for the benefit of his patron, are to be found in the prologue which he wrote for it, and which survives in the Bamberg manuscript of the *Historia de Preliis*. This manuscript is generally agreed to provide a text closer to Leo's original version than any other surviving manuscript, and from it was descended the *Bavarian recension*.[3] A different remanipulation of the original *Natiuitas et Victoria*, which contains many interpolations, is known as the I¹ (Interpolated) *Historia de Preliis*; and from this recension the I² and I³ recensions are independently descended.

Before we consider these offshoots and the vernacular texts that depend upon them, it is necessary to examine a German text which is recognized as a translation of some manuscript closer to the original text of Leo than any we now possess. This is the German life of Alexander in *Seelentrost*, which in its turn was the source of other accounts. In this small vernacular group, therefore, we have the closest known descendants of Leo.

---

[1] EDITION AND INFORMATION. F. Pfister, *Der Alexanderroman des Archipresbyters Leo*, (*Sammlung. mittellat. Texte*, VI, Heidelberg, 1913) (this contains the text of the Bamberg MS. with an invaluable introduction describing and tracing the descent of the various recensions of Leo).
Magoun, pp. 40–1 and nn.
[2] *Historia de Preliis* is the title in the incunable editions of the third interpolated recension (I³) of the *Natiuitas et Victoria*. It is now conveniently used to describe all the derivatives of Leo's work.   [3] Below, pp. 41–3.

II. 2. b

'SEELENTROST' AND ITS DERIVATIVES

In the Middle Low German *Seelentrost*,[1] an edifying story-book of wide popularity composed before 1358, there is a life of Alexander based upon legendary sources. The principal source for this narrative, which is full of moral conclusions to be drawn from the study of Alexander's life, is, as Pfister was the first to show, a redaction of Leo closer to the original *Natiuitas et Victoria* than the Bamberg MS. The *Iter ad Paradisum*, and certain isolated passages from the *Zacher Epitome*, were also used.

From the *Seelentrost* life of Alexander various accounts were derived. The first of these, the *Fabelhafte Geschichte Alexanders des Grossen* published by Bruns, is so similar to the *Seelentrost* version that it is essentially the same account. Another direct derivative was the Swedish fourteenth-century *Själens Trost*, to which is closely related the Swedish *De Alexandro Rege*.[2] A more important use of the *Seelentrost* account of Alexander was made in the fourteenth-century *Middle Dutch History Bible* edited by S. Hoogstra. This is derived from *Seelentrost* but certain material has been interpolated, notably miscellaneous anecdotes of Alexander from the *Gesta Romanorum*; while the exemplar and edifying applications of the narrative are curtailed, as inappropriate to a history-bible narrative.

Since Hoogstra's time it has been observed that MS. F of the *Middle Dutch History Bible* presents many individual readings not found in the other manuscripts. Most of these readings appear also in the text of the *Middle Low German History Bible* account of Alexander edited by Barnouw.[3] This text, to be dated about the middle of the fifteenth century, reproduces the interpolations of the Middle Dutch version and is evidently derived from it; so that the two Middle Low German accounts, the *Seelentrost* and the *History Bible*, are connected only through the intermediacy of the Middle Dutch version.[4]

[1] EDITIONS. P. J. Bruns in *Romantische und andere Gedichte in Altplattdeutscher Sprache* (Berlin and Stettin, 1798), pp. 337–66.

A. J. Barnouw, 'A Middle Low German Alexander Legend', *Germanic Review*, IV (1929), pp. 50–77, 284–304, 373–401 (texts of *Fabelhafte Gesch.* from Bruns, Hoogstra's *Tekst* 1 (Middle Dutch Alexander), and *Middle Low German Alexander*, printed in parallel).

STUDY. H. Fuchs, *Beiträge zur Alexandersage*: I. *Alexander im 'Seelentrost'* (progr. Giessen, 1907).

[2] EDITIONS. G. E. Klemming, *Svensk Fornskr. Sallsk.* (Stockholm, 1871–3), pp. 510–532 (*Själens Trost*).

E. S. Bring, *Historia Caroli Magni Suecana* (Lund, 1847) (*De Alexandro Rege*, part I).

J. E. Rietz, *Fabula Alexandri Magni Suecana* (Lund, 1850) (*De Alexandro Rege*, parts II and III).

de feer en fij die gefelle die in he warenoch
ta was alexand in tiviuelinge of he enich va
drie doe foude en he beeouwede dz hijs nz ghe
viaecht en had. So wie datter he doe foude En
ald? So ghingen fi wt eten maer alexander en
mocht nz eten va droefheyde voor dzter he fij
lude feer bade   Hoe der fone boom alxe
ander die derde viage antwoerde en feyde

g iij

FIG. I.   ALEXANDER CONVERSES WITH THE PRIEST OF THE
TREES OF THE SUN AND MOON

From the Dutch Chapbook Alexander, *Historye van den grooten coninc Alexander*.
In this woodcut the trees are, as in almost all pictures of this subject, identified by sun
and moon discs. Alexander stands on the left, his men behind him, wearing contemporary
armour and a long mantle. The priest is dressed in long robes of a rather academic or
clerical type. In this episode, taken from the *Epistola ad Aristotelem*, the trees prophesy
Alexander's imminent death.

40

[3] EDITIONS. S. Hoogstra, *Proza-Bewerkingen van het Leven van Alexander den Groote* ('s Gravenhage, 1898), *Tekst* I, pp. 1–37 (*Middle Dutch Alexander*).

A. J. Barnouw, 'A Middle Low German Alexander Legend', *Germanic Review*, IV (1929), pp. 50–77, 284–304, 373–401.

[4] The Middle Dutch and Middle Low German history-bible accounts of Alexander, inserted between Esther and Maccabees, are called for convenience the Middle Dutch Alexander and the Middle Low German Alexander.

II. 2. c

THE BAMBERG MS. AND THE BAVARIAN RECENSION

II. 2. c. i

'HISTORIA DE PRELIIS', BAMBERG MS.

The manuscript of the *Natiuitas et Victoria* closest to Leo's original translation is Bamberg manuscript E. iii. 14, which also alone contains the full text of the prologue, in which Leo describes how he found the Greek text in Constantinople, and translated it into Latin for his patron.[1] This manuscript, which contains, besides the *Natiuitas et Victoria*, unique versions of the Indian Tractates which were probably made in Naples at the same time as Leo's translation of Pseudo-Callisthenes, was probably brought out of Italy by the Emperor Henry II in 1022, and reached Bamberg soon afterwards. There it supplied Ekkehart of Aura with the material for his account of Alexander. The Bamberg text was also the source of the *Bavarian Recension*, from which the Munich and Paris MSS. of the *Historia de Preliis*, and the fifteenth-century German Alexander-book of Johann Hartlieb, descend.

[1] EDITION AND STUDY. F. Pfister, *Der Alexanderroman des Archipresbyters Leo* (*Sammlung mittellat. Texte*, VI, Heidelberg, 1913) (Text of the Bamberg version of the *Natiuitas et Victoria*; with an invaluable introduction upon the various recensions of the *Historia de Preliis*).

STUDY. W. Bulst, 'Zum Prologus der *Natiuitas et Victoria Alexandri magni regis*', in *Studien zur lat. Dichtung des Mitt., Ehrengabe f. Karl Strecker zum 1. Sept., 1931*, hrsg. W. Stach u. H. Walther (Dresden, 1931, *Schriftenreihe z. Hist. Vierteljahrschrift*, I), pp. 12–17.

Magoun, p. 41 and n. 4.

II. 2. c. ii

THE BAVARIAN RECENSION OF THE 'HISTORIA DE PRELIIS'

Two manuscripts of *Historia de Preliis* have certain features in common with one another and with the Bamberg manuscript, of which they are a reworking. They are:

(i) *Munich MS.* (Cod. lat. Monac. 23489, s. xii–xiii). This manuscript is a thorough revision of the Bamberg text; the style has been corrected, obscure passages improved and grammatical faults rectified. The Brahman Tractates, which are present in the Bamberg manuscript, are omitted, but the prologue of the Bamberg text is included, and a short epigram of four lines has been added at the end of the work. There are no known texts derived from the Munich manuscript.

(ii) *Paris MS.* (BN Nouv. Acq. Lat. 310, s. xii). While certain parts of the text presented by this manuscript are identical with that of the Munich MS., and the first part of Leo's prologue is included, other sections show a conglomerate of the *Historia de Preliis*, the *Zacher Epitome* of Julius Valerius, the *Epistola ad Aristotelem* and Orosius. Pfister sees the Paris manuscript as a sister to M subjected to much interpolation. The Alexander-book of Hartlieb is derived directly from this Paris MS.

Pfister grouped them together as descendants of a *Bavarian recension*,[1] and deduced that the Munich MS. (M) and the Paris MS. (P) were both derived from the same (lost) manuscript of this recension, of which he gives the following stemma:

Bamberg MS.

Bavarian Recension

(Lost MS.)

M   P

[1] EDITIONS. G. Landgraf, *Die Vita Alexandri Magni des Archipresbyters Leo* (*Historia de Preliis*) (Erlangen, 1885). This edition of the *Historia de Preliis* is founded on the Bamberg and Munich MSS., but is extremely unreliable.

STUDIES. F. Pfister, *Der Alexanderroman des Archipresbyters Leo* (*Sammlung mittellat. Texte*, VI, Heidelberg, 1913), pp. 9–14 (discussion of the *Bavarian Recension*).

F. Pfister, in *Rivista di Filologia Classica*, XLII (1914), pp. 104–13 (description of P & M). Magoun, p. 43 and n. 3.

ADDITIONAL NOTE. I have recently found a new MS. of Leo's *Natiuitas et Victoria*. It is Lambeth Palace Library MS. 342, fos. 212–24b. It was written probably in France about 1300. Losses of several folia have left only about five-eighths of the text, which shows signs of grammatical revision. It is however important as it is independent both of Ba and of I[1]. I have an edition in hand. [D.J.A.R.]

II. 2. c. iii

JOHANN HARTLIEB, 'HISTORI VON DEM GROSSEN ALEXANDER'

This Alexander-book,[1] written about 1444 by Johann Hartlieb, Professor of Natural History at Munich, and dedicated to Duke Albrecht III of Bavaria, was first printed at Augsburg in 1473, and enjoyed wide popularity. Friedrich Pfister showed that the basis of Hartlieb's work was either the Paris MS. or a manuscript of exactly similar type; and since the Paris MS. comes from Tegernsee, a place easily accessible to the Munich Professor, it is probable that it was itself his source. The book, written in German prose, is not of great interest. Hartlieb's own contribution consists mainly in certain learned interpolations, explanations and rationalizations of the wonderful adventures of Alexander. Hartlieb's version of the *Collatio* is also found independently in one MS.[2] His work also supplied most of the material for a tragedy by Hans Sachs,[3] and was translated into Danish prose by Peder Pedersen Galthen in 1584.[4]

[1] EDITIONS. Incunable editions listed in *Gesamtkatalog d. Wiegendrucke*, I (Leipzig, 1925), cols. 445–9.
R. Benz, in the series *Deutsche Volksbücher* (Jena, 1924).
STUDIES. S. Hirsch, 'Das Alexanderbuch Johann Hartliebs', *Palaestra*, LXXXII (1909).
H. Poppen, *Das Alexander-Buch Johann Hartliebs und seine Quellen* (diss. Heidelberg, 1914).
E. Travnik, 'Ueber eine Raaber Hs. des Hartliebschen Alexanderbuches', *Münchener Museum f. Philol. d. Mitt. u. d. Renaissance*, II (1913–14), pp. 211–21.
Magoun, p. 43 and n. 4.
[2] INFORMATION. H. Becker, in *Zeitschr. f. Deutsch. Philol.* XXIII (1890), pp. 424–5.
Magoun, p. 43 and n. 5.
[3] INFORMATION. S. Hirsch, op. cit. pp. 133–4.
Magoun, p. 44 and n. 1.
[4] INFORMATION. O. Walde, *Storhetstidens Litterära Krigsbyten* (Uppsala, 1916), II, p. 431.
Magoun, p. 44 and n. 2.

II. 3. THE INTERPOLATED RECENSIONS OF THE 'HISTORIA DE PRELIIS' AND THEIR DERIVATIVES

II. 3. a

'HISTORIA DE PRELIIS', RECENSION I¹

IN the eleventh century an editor of Leo's work improved the style of the book and added a quantity of material; the new edition of the *Historia de Preliis* thus produced is called the I¹ recension.[1] Its date cannot be exactly determined, though it must be earlier than the poem of Alberic (*c.* 1110), in which the recension was used for the first time.

The changes in style are in good taste, and make the narrative more fluent; the additions are considerable, the most important being the incorporation of the Indian Tractates (the *Commonitorium Palladii*, *Dindimus de Bragmanibus*, the *Collatio* (in the form *Collatio* III) and the *Epistola ad*

Aristotelem), in variously abridged versions into the text of the *Historia de Preliis*.

This recension, besides serving as the source of the later interpolated recensions, was used as a secondary source in Alexander-books; though its popularity is not comparable to that of the later recensions. Hilka and Magoun number thirteen extant manuscripts, against thirty-seven of the I^2 and thirty-nine of the I^3 recensions;[2] and as a source, the recension was used by Alberic, Lamprecht, Jacques de Vitry, and in various minor accounts.

[1] EDITION. O. Zingerle, *Die Quellen zum Alexander des Rudolf von Ems (Germanistische Abhandlungen*, IV, Breslau, 1885) (contains the first study and the only edition of the I^1 recension).

INFORMATION. F. Pfister, *Alexanderroman*, pp. 15 ff. (characteristics and derivatives).

F. P. Magoun and A. Hilka in *Speculum*, IX (1934), p. 84 (list of thirteen manuscripts).

Magoun, pp. 50–1 and p. 50, nn. 1–4.

[2] See also F. P. Magoun, 'Photostats of the *Historia de Preliis Alexandri Magni I^3*', *Harvard Library Bulletin*, vol. I (1947), p. 377, n. 5 for list of five additional MSS. of I^1, and D. J. A. Ross in *Scriptorium*, IX (1955), pp. 149–50.

II. 3. b

'HISTORIA DE PRELIIS', RECENSION I^2

The I^2 recension of the *Historia de Preliis*[1] is a revision ofthe I^1 recension, of uncertain date.[2] The wording of the I^1 recension is usually retained, although the redactor has regrouped certain sections so as to make the narrative more logical. The interpolations consist of excerpts principally from Orosius but Valerius Maximus, Pseudo-Methodius, Josephus, Pseudo-Epiphanius, the letter of Pseudo-Pharasmanes to Hadrian and the Indian tractates are also drawn on.

The recension was widely used from the twelfth to the fifteenth century.

[1] EDITION. A. Hilka, *Der Altfranzösische Prosa-Alexanderroman nebst d. latein. Original d. Historia de Preliis (Rez. I^2)*, (Halle, 1920) (with excellent introduction).

STUDY. A. Ausfeld, 'Die Orosius-Recension der *Historia de Preliis* und Babiloths *Alexanderchronik (Festschrift. d. Bad. Gymnasien* (Karlsruhe, 1886), pp. 99–120.

For list of MSS. see F. P. Magoun and A. Hilka in *Speculum*, IX (1934), pp. 84–5.

Magoun, pp. 56–8 and notes.

[2] For G. L. Hamilton's mistaken attempt to establish an eleventh-century date for the recension, see p. 70.

II. 3. c

EPITOMES OF THE I² 'HISTORIA DE PRELIIS'

II. 3. c. i

THE 'PRAGUE EPITOME'

This epitome[1] is contained in a fourteenth-century manuscript, Prague, Oeffentliche und Universitätsbibliothek MS. VIII. C. 24, a miscellany mainly religious in character. The epitome is entitled *Excerptum Alexandri* and is derived from the I² *Historia de Preliis*.

The chief interest of this work lies in the writer's application of the life of Alexander to an exemplar purpose. The text is full of exemplar memoranda; the writer was determined to draw a moral, and often drew very strange morals, from every incident in the life of Alexander that could be turned to his purpose.

[1] EDITION AND INFORMATION. F. P. Magoun, 'A Prague Epitome of the *Historia de Preliis Alexandri Magni* (Recension I²)', *Harvard Studies and Notes in Philology and Literature,* XVI (Cambridge, Mass., 1934), pp. 119–44.

II. 3. c. ii

THE 'HARVARD EPITOME'

The *Epitome* contained in MS. Harvard Latin 122[1] is really a disconnected collection of selected passages, in which the compiler shows an obvious preference for the wonderful element in his source; he reduces the long account of the campaign against Darius to a single phrase, and omits altogether the war with Porus. There is one interpolation, an account of Alexander's horn, borrowed from the *Secret of Secrets*. The text is not complete, beginning at chapter 26, with the siege of Tyre; the source was without doubt a manuscript of the I² recension, but one that does not correspond closely with any of the manuscripts whose readings are known.

[1] EDITION AND INFORMATION. F. P. Magoun, 'The Harvard Epitome of the *Historia de Preliis* (Recension I²)', *Harvard Studies and Notes in Philology and Literature,* XIV (Cambridge, Mass., 1932), pp. 115–32.

II. 3. c. iii

THE 'MANCHESTER EPITOME'

Chetham Library, Manchester, MS. Mum. A. 4. 102 (A. 5. 118) contains an *Epitome*[1] of the *Historia de Preliis* entitled *Gesta Alexandri Regis*, on ff. 98a to 113a, which was written, probably about 1430, by a very ignorant and careless scribe.

This *Epitome* has some characteristics of the I², and some of the I³ recension, and must therefore have had for a source one of the manuscripts of mixed type such as is the source of some other texts.

[1] EDITION AND INFORMATION. S. H. Thomson, 'An unnoticed abridgment of the *Historia de Preliis* (Redaction I²–I³)', *University of Colorado Studies*, I (1941), pp. 241–59.

II. 3. d

THE 'OLD FRENCH PROSE ALEXANDER ROMANCE'

This text, examined by Paul Meyer and edited, with a parallel Latin text of the I² *Historia de Preliis*, by Hilka,[1] is the most important vernacular prose translation of any Alexander text. Sixteen manuscripts survive and it was printed eleven times[2] between 1506 and 1630. It was written some time between 1206, the earliest possible date of the *Histoire ancienne jusqu'à César*, from which the epilogue was borrowed, and *c.* 1290, the approximate date of the earliest surviving manuscripts. A second redaction was made between 1252, date of the completion of the *Speculum Historiale* of Vincent of Beauvais which is quoted in the prologue added to this redaction, and *c.* 1290, approximate date of the earliest surviving second redaction manuscripts. The earlier manuscripts show north-eastern dialectal characteristics and it is likely that the translation was made in north-eastern France. Nothing is known of its author.

The account of Alexander's campaign in Greece is omitted in this version and a considerable part of the correspondence of Alexander and Dindimus is also lacking.[3] It is possible that the translator was working from a manuscript defective in these passages. The reviser responsible for the second redaction added a short prologue giving a brief account of the early history of Macedon down to the marriage of Philip II and Olympias, which was borrowed from a translation of the *Compilation of St Albans*. This was shown some thirty years ago by Professor Magoun,[4] and a manuscript of the translation, formerly, because of the identity of incipit, believed to be a manuscript of the *French Prose Alexander*, has recently come to light in the Fitzwilliam Museum at Cambridge.[5] The second redactor also added a prophecy from the book of Daniel to the account of Alexander's visit to Jerusalem, cut out from the epilogue a considerable passage which he regarded as redundant and made other minor alterations. The Stockholm manuscript contains several interpolations not found elsewhere, including a long passage borrowed from the *Secret of Secrets*.

46

A third redaction was made in the fifteenth century and survives in a single manuscript, Paris, Bibl. Nat. Fr. 788. This was based on a first redaction text and is marked by several rather arbitrary omissions, a turgid and verbose stylistic remodelling, and a considerable number of additions and expansions which close examination shows to have been the product of the redactor's own feeble imagination. No ascertainable sources were used and no real episode is added to the narrative, only a lot of dreary description of persons and places and some imaginary battles in which nothing significant occurs.

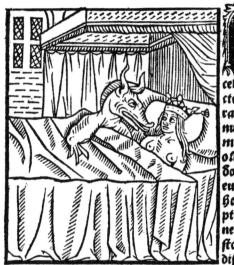

FIG. 2. THE BEGETTING OF ALEXANDER

In Pseudo-Callisthenes and its derivatives the father of the hero is the magician Nectanebus, last independent king of Egypt, who, driven from his throne by a Persian invasion, takes refuge in Macedon where by his magic arts he succeeds in persuading Philip's queen Olympias to receive his advances. He visits her, as in this woodcut, in the form of a dragon. From the *editio princeps* of the French Prose Alexander, *Alixandre le Grant*.

The *French Prose Alexander* is the most successful of the medieval vernacular prose versions of Alexander material. Its author has treated the *Historia de Preliis* as the writers of the romances of antiquity treated their Latin sources—he was certainly familiar with the *Roman d'Alexandre—*

47

and has produced an amusing courtly narrative. The numerous and costly manuscripts bear witness to its success in the later Middle Ages, and the many extremely rare printed editions show that its popularity did not wane in the Renaissance. It was used as a source by Jean Wauquelin.

[1] EDITION. A. Hilka, *Der altfranzösische Prosa-Alexanderroman* (Halle, 1920).
STUDIES. A. Hilka, ed. cit. introduction.
P. Meyer, *A. le G.* II, pp. 305–13.
D. J. A. Ross, 'Some notes on the Old French Alexander Romance in prose', *French Studies*, VI (1952), pp. 136–47.
[2] D. J. A. Ross, *The Library*, ser. 5, vol. VI, pp. 54–7.
[3] Ed. Hilka, pp. 80–94 and 189–99.
[4] F. P. Magoun, *Speculum*, I (1925), pp. 225–32.
[5] D. J. A. Ross, *French Studies*, VI (1952), pp. 353.

II. 3. e

THE ENGLISH FRAGMENTS

II. 3. e. i

'ALEXANDER A'

This is a fragmentary Middle English alliterative poem in Bodleian Library MS. Greaves 60,[1] an Elizabethan MS. of about 1600. The poem begins with the story of Amintas, father of Philip, and after the account of Alexander's conception as the son of Nectanebus, there is a lacuna extending over his birth and early years; the murder of Nectanebus and the taming of Bucephalus are then described, and the fragment breaks off in the middle of a description of the siege of Byzantium by Philip.

The dialect indicates a place of origin in the Gloucestershire area, and a date between 1340 and 1370. The source is a manuscript of the I² *Historia de Preliis* but there are three long historical interpolations describing the antecedents of Alexander, Philip's battles in Greece and the siege of Byzantium, all borrowed from Orosius. The poem's exact relationship with *Alexander B* is uncertain, but it is at least probable that the two fragments are not by the same author.

[1] EDITIONS. W. W. Skeat, *William of Palerne, and a fragment of the Alliterative Romance o Alisaunder*, E.E.T.S., E.S. 1 (1867), pp. 177–218.
F. P. Magoun, jr., *The Gests of King Alexander of Macedon* (Cambridge, Mass., 1929) (first text).

II. 3. e. ii

'ALEXANDER B'

This Middle English alliterative fragment,[1] found only in MS. Bodley 264, is interpolated into a copy of the *Roman d'Alexandre*. In this copy of the *Roman*, an English scribe inserted a note on f. 67 to say that a passage was missing there which he intended to supply; this passage was that contained in *Alexander B*. The fragment is concerned entirely with Alexander's encounter with the Gymnosophists and his correspondence with Dindimus; it breaks off at a description of the pillar set up by Alexander on his departure from the Brahman frontier. The manuscript was written in the second half of the fifteenth century; the date of composition of the original work was between 1340 and 1370, and the place south-west England, possibly Gloucestershire. In spite of the close connexion with *Alexander A* thus suggested, there are differences that make it most unlikely that both fragments are by the same author, though it is possible that *Alexander B* may be part of a continuation of the poem of which *Alexander A* is the beginning. The source, like that of *Alexander A*, was a manuscript of the I² *Historia de Preliis*.

[1] EDITIONS. W. W. Skeat, *Alexander and Dindimus*, E.E.T.S., E.S. xxxi (1878).

F. P. Magoun, jr., *The Gests of King Alexander of Macedon* (Cambridge, Mass., 1929) (second text).

II. 3. f

SEIFRIT AUS OESTERREICH, 'ALEXANDER'

The German verse life of Alexander written about 1352 by Seifrit[1] is founded upon a manuscript of the I² *Historia de Preliis* corresponding in certain peculiarities to the Seitenstett (now Harvard) MS. of that recension used by Zingerle. It contains, however, certain additional material: a version of the *Iter ad Paradisum*, and an anecdote of Alexander ultimately derived from Seneca and widely known in the Middle Ages. Though a close translation of its source in most particulars, Seifrit's book is pleasant reading; and it had some contemporary popularity, as is shown by Gereke's list of eleven manuscripts.

[1] EDITION. P. Gereke, *Deutsche Texte des Mitt.*, Bd. xxxvi (Berlin, 1932).

STUDY. I. Kühnhold, *Seifrits Alexander*, Diss. Berlin (Dresden, 1939).

Magoun, p. 58 and n. 2.

II. 3. g
'KONUNG ALEXANDER'

This Middle Swedish verse translation of a manuscript of the I² recension was written in the late fourteenth century,[1] in octosyllabic couplets. The poet has added little to his source except a prologue, an epilogue and an intermediate moralization. The *Konung Alexander* is not derived from an I² manuscript related to Hilka's text, and without further examination of the I² Latin manuscripts it is impossible to decide its place in the I² tradition.

[1] EDITION. J. A. Ahlstrand, *Konung Alexander: en meteltidens dikt från latinet vänd i svenska rim omkring år 1380 på föranstaltande af riksdrotsen Bo Jonsson Grip, efter den enda kända handskriften* (Stockholm, 1862).

STUDY. F. P. Magoun, 'The Middle-Swedish *Konung Alexander* and the *Historia de Preliis Alexandri Magni* (Recension I²)', *Etudes Germaniques*, III (1948), pp. 167–76 (and see bibliography there cited).

Magoun, p. 60 and n. 2.

II. 3. h
'I NOBILI FATTI D'ALESSANDRO MAGNO'

There are two manuscripts (a third has been lost) and one fragment of this fourteenth-century Italian prose version of an I² text. Of these manuscripts, B is that published by Grion, H is the fragment published by Hilka, and C is that described by Storost and edited by Messner.[1] Although all three texts are evidently derived from the I² *Historia de Preliis*, C contains several passages which are omitted in B and H. Storost, after an examination of the possible explanations for this discrepancy, concluded that C is not connected with B and H at all, but is an independent translation from another I² text.

The book presents no special interest being a close translation of its original, but is noteworthy as a translation from the I² *Historia de Preliis* in a country characterized by its preference for the I³ recension.

[1] EDITIONS. G. Grion, *I Nobili Fatti di Alessandro Magno* (*Coll. di opere inedite o rare*, Bologna, 1872).

C. A. Messner: *Two I² Versions of the Historia de Preliis in Italian Prose, with an Edition of the Nobili Fatti che ffe Alisandro di Macedonio, MS. II. i. 62 of the Biblioteca Nazionale Centrale di Firenze* (unpublished Harvard diss., Cambridge, Mass., 1928).

STUDY. J. Storost, *Studien zur Alexandersage in der älteren italienischen Literatur* (*Romanistische Arbeiten*, XXIII, Halle, 1935), pp. 118–25.

A. Hilka, *Zeitschrift f. rom. Phil.* vol. XLI (1921–2), pp. 234–53.

Magoun, pp. 60–1 and p. 61, n. 1.

II. 3. i

MEISTER BABILOTH, 'ALEXANDERCHRONIK'

This is a fifteenth-century German prose life of Alexander of no especial interest, first printed in 1472.[1] The greater part of the book is a close translation of a manuscript of the I^2 *Historia de Preliis*, but the conclusion is based upon an I^3 text, and contains the characteristic interpolations of that recension.

[1] EDITION. Partial edition only in S. Herzog, *Die Alexanderchronik des Meister Babiloth* (progr., Stuttgart, 1897; and continued, 1903).

STUDY. A. Ausfeld, 'Die Orosius-Rezension der *Historia Alexandri Magni de Preliis* und Babiloths *Alexanderchronik*', *Festschrift d. Bad. Gymnasien* (Karlsruhe, 1886), pp. 97–120 (a study of the I^2 recension).

S. Herzog, ed. cit.

Magoun, p. 55 and n. 4, and p. 58.

II. 3. j

HEBREW DERIVATIVES OF THE I^2 'HISTORIA DE PRELIIS'

I have grouped here three Hebrew translations of the I^2 *Historia de Preliis* which are closely related to one another:[1]

(i) A translation doubtfully attributed to the eleventh- or twelfth-century translator Samuel ben Jehuda ben Tibbon, and called by Magoun *Anon. A.* Excerpts have been published of this translation, which may descend from the *Historia de Preliis* through a lost Arabic version.

(ii) A translation of similar type, called by Magoun *Anon. B*, and probably also made from an Arabic text.

(iii) The account of Alexander in the chronicle of Yosippon (Joseph ben Gorion). This account, as we possess it, consists of two parts: the first, derived direct from the I^2 *Historia de Preliis*, is an interpolation made in the fifteenth century; the second, the original text, is probably derived from *Anon. A* above.

All three of these works were probably written in southern Italy or Sicily, and date from the eleventh and twelfth centuries.

[1] INFORMATION. On these Hebrew translations see:

M. Steinschneider, *Die Hebräischen Uebersetzungen d. Mitt.* (Berlin, 1893), pp. 899 ff.

I. Lévi in *Revue des Etudes Juives*, III (1881), pp. 244 ff.

I. Lévi, *Le Roman d'Alexandre: Texte Hébreu Anonyme...* (Paris, 1887).

L. Wallach, 'Quellenkritische Studien zum Hebräischen Josippon', *Mitteilungen d. Gesells. d. Wissenschaft d. Judentums*, vol. LXXXII (1938), pp. 190–8.

L. Wallach, 'Yosippon and the Alexander Romance', *Jewish Quarterly Review*, new series, XXXVII (1947), pp. 407–22.

Magoun, pp. 58–60, p. 58, n. 6 and p. 59, nn. 1–4.

II. 3. k
'HISTORIA DE PRELIIS', I³ RECENSION

The characteristics of this recension have been listed by Pfister.[1] Derived, independently of I², from the I¹ recension, it shows rhetorical elaborations of style and many interpolations, mainly of a moralizing nature. These interpolations, mostly derived from Oriental sources, include the story of the *Fuerre de Gadres*, the symbolism of the precious stones which compose the steps of Cyrus' throne and the laments of the philosophers at Alexander's tomb. From the character of the interpolations Pfister considered it probable that the redactor was a Jew.

The date of the I³ *Historia de Preliis* is probably before 1150, when it appears to have undergone a revision in England. This second edition has been called the I³ᵃ recension, and is the source of the *Wars of Alexander* and the *Thornton Alexander*; its date may be established by its use in the *Gesta Herewardi* of about 1150.[2]

The earliest work based on the I³ *Historia de Preliis* was the *Alexandreis* of Quilichinus of Spoleto (1236). The recension was as popular as the I² *Historia* and it was widely used, especially in Italy, as the principal source of many Alexander-books.

Several incunable editions of the I³ recension were printed at Strassburg, and it is in them that the title 'Historia de Preliis Alexandri Magni' was first attached to Leo's work.

---

[1] EDITIONS. Incunabula listed in *Gesamtkatalog d. Wiegendrucke*, I (Leipzig, 1925), cols. 440–3, nos. 876–7, 879.

Text of Strassburg incunable of 1494 reprinted in *Prace Filologiczne*, IX (Warsaw, 1920), pp. 23–548.

There is as yet no critical edition of the I³ text.

For list of MSS. see F. P. Magoun and A. Hilka in *Speculum*, IX (1934), p. 85.

STUDIES. F. Pfister, 'Die Historia de Preliis und das Alexanderepos des Quilichinus', *Münchener Museum f. Philol. d. Mitt. u. d. Renaissance*, I (1912), pp. 249–301.

Magoun, p. 51, and nn. 2–3.

[2] G. L. Hamilton, 'A New Redaction (I³ᵃ) of the *Historia de Preliis* and the Date of Redaction I³', *Speculum*, II (1927), pp. 113–46.

Magoun, pp. 55–6, p. 55, nn. 5–6 and p. 56, nn. 1–2.

II. 3. 1

THE 'ALEXANDREIS' OF QUILICHINUS OF SPOLETO AND ITS DERIVATIVES

II. 3. 1. i

QUILICHINUS OF SPOLETO, 'ALEXANDREIS'

This hexameter version of the I³ *Historia de Preliis* was completed in 1236; the author is also known for a short poem, *Preconia Friderici II*, and worked as a judge under Hohenstaufen rule.[1] The *Alexandreis* is of little literary value, and closely follows its original, from which, however, it differs by being divided into three books, of which the first ends with Alexander's coronation as king of Macedonia and the second with his coronation as king of Persia. The poem enjoyed some popularity and was the source of the Italian poem of Domenico Scolari, of the German *Wernigerode Alexander* and of the verse interpolations in the *Darmstadt Alexander*.

[1] EDITION. None; some extracts are published by Pfister in the article cited below, and some by Storost in his chapter on Scolari (*q.v.*).

STUDIES. F. Pfister, 'Die Historia de Preliis und das Alexanderepos des Quilichinus', *Münchener Museum*, I (1912), pp. 249–301. (The basic study and the first to enumerate the characteristics of the I³ *Historia*; reviewed by A. Hilka, *Berlin. Philol. Wochenschrift*, xxxvi (1916), cols. 77–81.)

S. Ferri, 'Per l'edizione dell'Alessandreide di Wilichino da Spoleto', *Bollettino della R. Deputazione di Storia Patria per l'Umbria*, xxi (1915), pp. 211–19.

P. Lehmann, 'Quilichinus von Spoleto', *Berlin. Philol. Wochenschrift*, xxxviii (1918), cols. 812–15.

T. Ferri, 'Appunti su Quilichino da Spoleto e le sue opere', *Studi Medievali*, n.s. ix (1936), pp. 239–50.

Magoun, p. 52 and nn. 1–3.

II. 3. 1. ii

DOMENICO SCOLARI, 'ISTORIA ALEXANDRI REGIS'

The author of this Italian poem in ottava rima[1] was probably a member of a White Florentine family in exile, and a student at Perugia in the early fourteenth century. His poem was written in Umbria, perhaps at Arezzo, and the only known manuscript is dated 1355, and was written at Treviglio, in north Italy. The poem is a fairly close translation of Quilichinus of Spoleto with certain minor interpolations, almost all concerned with wonders, and many corresponding to the interpolations of a similar nature in the I² *Historia de Preliis* which may have been used as a supplementary source. Beside these additions there are various naïve deviations, misreadings, anachronisms and other evidence of no great learning, which have been studied in detail by Storost.

[1] STUDY. Storost, pp. 4ff.

II. 3. l. iii

THE 'WERNIGERODE ALEXANDER'

This work, preserved only in a Wernigerode MS.,[1] is a late fourteenth-century German verse translation of the *Alexandreis* of Quilichinus of Spoleto. The translation keeps fairly close to its source, but the German writer has added some original comments which give the book some value and reveal his own attitude to Alexander.

[1] EDITION. G. Guth, *Der Grosse Alexander aus der Wernigeroder Handschrift* (*Deutsche Texte des Mitt.* XIII, Berlin, 1908).
STUDY. E. Neuling, 'Die deutsche Bearbeitung der *Alexandreis* des Quilichinus von Spoleto', *Beiträge z. Geschichte d. deutschen Sprache u. Literatur*, X (1884), pp. 318–83.
Magoun, p. 52 and n. 3.

II. 3. l. iv

THE 'DARMSTADT ALEXANDER'

A manuscript of the I³ *Historia de Preliis* at Darmstadt, MS. 231,[1] contains some passages in hexameter verse borrowed from Quilichinus. Otherwise the manuscript presents no peculiarities.

[1] INFORMATION. F. Pfister, in *Münchener Museum f. Philologie d. Mittelalters u. d. Renaissance*, I (1912), pp. 253–4.
Magoun, p. 52 and n. 4.

II. 3. m

ITALIAN TRANSLATIONS OF THE I³ 'HISTORIA DE PRELIIS'

II. 3. m. i

COD. RICCARDI, 1922 (Q. II. 12)

This is an Italian prose epitome of the I³ *Historia de Preliis*, preserved in a fifteenth-century manuscript of Tuscan, possibly Florentine, origin.[1] The chief interest of the epitome, which may be founded upon either a Latin or an Italian text of the *Historia de Preliis*, consists in the writer's preoccupation with the wonderful element. The descriptions of battles, sieges, etc., are suppressed, and preference is given to Alexander's marvellous adventures.

The author was a Tuscan, and the work has been attributed to Antonio

Pucci; in which case the epitome would date from the second half of the fourteenth century.

[1] STUDIES. A. Graf, 'Il Zibaldone attribuito a Antonio Pucci', *Giorn. storico della lett. italiana*, I (1883), pp. 285–6.
    Storost, pp. 126–32.

II. 3. m. ii

'ALESSANDREIDA IN RIMA'

This Italian poem in ottava rima, divided into twelve cantos, is a translation of the I³ *Historia de Preliis* with some additions and abridgements, the accounts of battles being noticeably expanded.[1] The poem, cast in the typical form of the Italian *cantare*, has been studied in detail by Storost. It was formerly ascribed to a certain Giacopo di Carlo on the evidence of the early printed editions, but Storost has shown that di Carlo was more likely to have been one of the first printers of the book. The author was probably a native of Gubbio, and wrote about 1430; the book enjoyed great success in the Cinquecento, was first printed in 1512, and went through many subsequent editions.

[1] STUDY. Storost, pp. 180–230.

II. 3. m. iii

THE 'HISTORY OF ALEXANDER' IN FLORENCE, BIBLIOTECA NAZIONALE II. i. 363

This Italian prose history of Alexander is contained in a fifteenth-century MS. completed on 28 June 1473.[1] This is not the date of the work, since Storost has shown that the MS. is only a copy of the original, which, however, was also written in the fifteenth century.

The work is a translation of the I³ *Historia de Preliis*, but contains some interpolations characteristic of I¹ and I², especially in the second half of the text. The conclusion is supplied entirely from I¹ and I². The interpolations are probably due to the use of a manuscript of mixed type, belonging mainly to the I³ tradition, but with interpolations from the other recensions of the *Historia de Preliis*. The work is of no special interest.

[1] STUDY. Storost, pp. 145–67.

II. 3. m. iv

'LIBER ALEXANDRI MAGNI IN VOLGARE'

This work, preserved in a unique manuscript in the library of St Mark's, Venice (It. Cl. VI, 66, Sign. 6033), is a fifteenth-century Italian prose translation of the I³ *Historia de Preliis*.[1] The dialect is North Italian, perhaps

Venetian; the translation is fairly free, and attempts have been made to make the text fluent and readable. But the work is of no especial interest, and presents no new or original conception of Alexander. It is characteristic of late medieval treatment of the Alexander story in its rationalization of the wonderful element and in its adherence to one source. It belongs, not to the Renaissance, but to the medieval group of Italian Alexander-books.

[1] STUDY. Storost, pp. 133–44.

II. 3. m. v

'LIBRO DEL NASCIMENTO'

This is the short title of an Italian prose translation of the I³ *Historia de Preliis* which achieved, for no apparent reason, a greater popularity than any other Alexander-book in Italy, and was many times printed.[1] The first edition was printed at Treviso in 1474, the second at Venice in 1477, the third at Naples in the same year, and Storost has described many other early editions.[2] The translation, made in the fifteenth century, is based entirely upon the I³ *Historia de Preliis*, using a manuscript probably related to the Darmstadt MS.

There is no clue to the identity of the translator or to the place of translation; no manuscripts survive, and dialectal peculiarities have been obliterated in the printed texts. There is nothing of interest to remark in the translation, which keeps, like most Italian Alexander-books, very close to its original.

[1] STUDY. Storost, pp. 168–79.
[2] Incunable editions in *Gesamtkatalog d. Wiegendrucke*, I (Leipzig, 1925), col. 443, nos. 880–3.

II. 3. n

DERIVATIVES OF THE I³ᵃ 'HISTORIA DE PRELIIS'

II. 3. n. i

THE 'THORNTON ALEXANDER'

This text, edited by J. Westlake without critical apparatus for the Early English Text Society,[1] is a slightly abridged English prose translation of the I³ᵃ *Historia de Preliis*.[2] The translation and the unique manuscript are North English, and date from the first half of the fifteenth century. The version has been little studied in relation to its sources, but it is close to its original, and there is little indication of imagination or originality on the part of the translator.

[1] EDITION. J. S. Westlake, E.E.T.S., O.S. CXLIII, 1913.
INFORMATION. J. E. Wells, *A Manual of the Writings in Middle English* (New Haven, Yale U.P., 1916), pp. 105, 779.
Magoun, p. 56 and n. 4.
[2] G. L. Hamilton, in *Speculum*, II (1927), pp. 113–31 (upon the I³ᵃ *Historia de Preliis* and its characteristics).

II. 3. n. ii

THE 'WARS OF ALEXANDER'

This is the title given to a Middle English alliterative poem of considerable merit.[1] It is a translation of an I³ᵃ type manuscript of the *Historia de Preliis*; the additions made by the English writer consist of an introduction, an abridged version of the *Fuerre de Gadres*, and connecting passages at the beginning or the end of the several *Passus* into which he has divided the work for easier reading or listening.

The poem was written probably in pure Northumbrian dialect in the first half of the fifteenth century. It is extant in two manuscripts, Bodleian MS. Ashmole 44, and Trinity College, Dublin, MS. D. 4. 12, both of which are imperfect, and though they normally supplement one another, the conclusion of the poem is missing.

[1] EDITIONS. R. Stevenson (Roxburghe Club, 1849) (extremely unreliable).
W. W. Skeat, *The Wars of Alexander*, E.E.T.S., E.S. XLVII (1886).
STUDIES. J. B. Henneman, *Untersuchungen über das mitteleng. Gedicht 'Wars of Alexander'* (Berlin diss. 1889).
M. Steffens, *Versbau und Sprache des mittelengl. stabreimenden Gedichtes 'The Wars of Alexander'* (*Bonner Beiträge z. Anglistik*, IX, Bonn, 1901).
Magoun, p. 56 and n. 3.

II. 3. o

THE 'HEBREW HISTORY OF ALEXANDER'[1]

In the mid-fourteenth century the *Historia de Preliis* was translated into Hebrew, perhaps from an I³ text, by the Jewish astronomer Immanuel (Bonfils) ben Jacob de Tarascon.

[1] INFORMATION. M. Steinschneider, *Die Hebräischen Uebersetzungen des Mittelalters* (Berlin, 1893), p. 904.
I. Lévi, in *Revue des Etudes Juives*, III (1881), pp. 251–8.
Magoun, p. 62 and nn. 2–3.

II. 3. p

CZECH TRANSLATIONS OF THE I³ 'HISTORIA DE PRELIIS'

In 1433 the I³ *Historia de Preliis* was translated into Czech prose as *Kronika o Alexandru Velikèm.*[1] An unstudied Czech Epitome of the *Historia de Preliis*, Prague University Library MS. XI. D. 2, dated 1469,[2] appears also to be derived from the I³ recension, and may be closely connected to the *Kronika o Alexandru Velikèm*.

A Czech compilation by Matauš Walkenberger, published at Olmütz about 1610,[3] may also be a translation of the *Historia de Preliis*.

[1] F. P. Magoun, and S. H. Thomson, '*Kronika o Alexandru Velikèm*: a Czech prose translation of the *Historia de Preliis*, recension I³', *Speculum*, III (1928), pp. 204–17.
  Magoun, p. 53 and nn. 4–6.
[2] F. P. Magoun, and S. H. Thomson, in *Speculum*, III (1928), p. 217.
[3] Magoun, p. 62 and n. 4.

II. 3. q

POLISH, RUSSIAN AND MAGYAR VERSIONS OF I³ 'HISTORIA DE PRELIIS'

A translation of a Strasbourg I³ incunable made about 1510 entitled *Hystorja Aleksandra Wielkiego Króla Makedońskiego, o Walkach* is found in MS. 79 of the Zamojskii library in Warsaw.[1]

Another translation, probably of an I³ incunable, was published in 1550 with the title *Historya o Zywoćie i Známienitich Spráwach Aleksandra, Króla Makedońskiego*, and eight times reprinted.[2]

Moscow, Lenin Library MS. 2405 contains a Russian version of a Polish translation of I³ *Historia de Preliis*.[3]

A Magyar translation of an I³ incunable forms the first part of John Haller's *Hármas Istoria* published at Kolozsvár in 1696 and several times reprinted.[4]

[1] Magoun, p. 54 and n. 1.
[3] Magoun, p. 55 and nn. 1–3.
[2] Magoun, p. 54 and nn. 1–2.
[4] Magoun, p. 54 and nn. 3–4.

II. 4. MISCELLANEOUS MEDIEVAL DERIVATIVES OF PSEUDO-CALLISTHENES

II. 4. a

THE 'METZ EPITOME'

STILL of uncertain classification is the Epitome preserved at Metz.[1] This work is apparently a Latin abridgement of α Pseudo-Callisthenes independent of Julius Valerius, and is of considerable value for establishing a critical α-text. It contains in particular an independent text of the account of Alexander's death, testament and burial, deriving directly from the source used by Pseudo-Callisthenes, a political pamphlet written immediately after Alexander's death in support of the claims of Perdiccas against those of Antipater to the succession. A fragment of the original survives in Vienna (Papyrus 31954).[2]

[1] EDITION. O. Wagner, *Incerti auctoris Epitome rerum gestarum Alexandri Magni* (Leipzig, 1900).

INFORMATION. E. Wölfflin, 'Die Neue Epitoma Alexandri', *Archiv f. Latein. Lexicographie*, XII (1901), pp. 187–96.

W. Kroll, *Historia Alexandri Magni* I: *recensio uetusta* (Berlin, 1926), pp. xff.

See also Appendix A, pp. 355–7.

[2] See R. Merkelbach, 'Die Quellen des Griechischen Alexanderromans', *Zetemata*, IX (Munich, 1954), pp. 118–51 and (texts) 220–51. Cf. also Appendix A, p. 355.

II. 4. b

THE ABECEDARIAN POEM

Of uncertain origin is the mid ninth-century Latin abecedarian poem telling of Alexander's adventures,[1] of which a fragment is preserved in a Verona MS.[2] Though this date would suggest Julius Valerius as a source, the poem contains some details for which no known source has been found, and a version of the Celestial Journey which resembles that in the *Historia de Preliis*, written a century later. The story was omitted altogether in Julius Valerius. It is possible, therefore, that the poem is derived from a (δ)-type text similar to that from which the *Historia de Preliis* was translated.

[1] EDITIONS AND INFORMATION. F. Zarncke, 'Ueber das fragment eines lateinischen Alexanderliedes in Verona', *Sitzungsber. d. sächs. Akad. d. Wiss.* (1877), pp. 57–69.

P. Meyer, *A. le G.* II, pp. 44–6.

[2] Vatican Codex Reginensis Lat. 195, fo. 50b has a second copy of the first stanza in a hand of the ninth or tenth century. See A. Wilmart, *Codices Reginenses Latini* (Vatican City, 1937), vol. I, p. 468.

II. 4. c

THE 'ERFURT ALEXANDER'

This text, discovered and published by Hilka, has not as yet been thoroughly studied.[1] It is a Latin account of the birth of Alexander as the son of Nectanebus, and of his early youth, composed as a prologue to supplement the *Alexandreis* of Gautier de Châtillon which opens, not with Alexander's birth, but with his youth.

[1] EDITION. A. Hilka, 'Der Zauberer Neptanabus nach einem bisher unbekannten Erfurter Text', *Festschrift z. Jahrhundertfeier d. Univ. zu Breslau* (= *Mittheilungen d. Schlesisch. Gesell. f. Volkskunde*, XIV (1914), pp. 80–9).
    Note by F. Pfister, *Berlin. Philol. Wochenschrift*, XXXVI (1916), cols. 447, 448.
    Magoun, pp. 61–2 and p. 62, n. 1.

II. 4. d

'DICTA ALEXANDRI'

In his *Collectio Salernitana*, S. de Renzi published a work attributed to Giovanni da Procida entitled: *Placita philosophorum moralium antiquorum, ex Graeco in Latinum translata a Magistro Joanne de Procida*.[1] This work contains the life and proverbial sayings of Alexander under the subheading 'Dicta Alexandri', and is evidently a direct translation of some edition (probably Spanish, certainly not Greek) of the *Dicts and Sayings of the Philosophers*, but the text has not been properly examined.

[1] EDITION. S. de Renzi, *Collectio Salernitana*, III (Naples, 1854), pp. 69–150 (full text), 118–30 ('Dicta Alexandri'). The attribution to Giovanni da Procida is now rejected.

II. 4. e

THE DUBLIN FRAGMENT

This fragment of a Middle English prose life of Alexander,[1] incorporated in the Dublin MS. of the *Wars of Alexander*, was printed by Skeat in his edition of the latter poem, and has not yet been studied or assigned to any textual tradition. It is evident, however, from a comparison of the text with that of the '*Dicts and Sayings of the Philosophers*' account of Alexander, that the Dublin fragment is an abridged English version of this work, which was very popular in England in the fifteenth century.

[1] EDITION. W. W. Skeat, *Wars of Alexander*, E.E.T.S., E.S. XLVII (1886), pp. 279–83 (description of the MS., Skeat, p. xviii).
    Magoun, p. 62 and n. 5.

II. 4. f

SPANISH ARABIC AND ALJAMIADO VERSIONS

There must also be noticed two works produced in Spain but belonging to the Oriental Pseudo-Callisthenes tradition: the *Arabic Life of Alexander*[1] edited with a translation by Gómez, and the *Aljamiado Alexander*[2] discussed and edited by Nykl. These two Spanish Arabic works were neither influenced by, nor had any influence on, Western textual tradition.

[1] E. García Gómez, *Un Texto Arabe Occidental de la Leyenda de Alejandro*... (*Istituto de Valencia de Don Juan*, Madrid, 1929).

[2] A. R. Nykl in *Revue Hispanique*, LXXVII (1929).
A. R. Nykl, in *A Compendium of Aljamiado Literature* (New York, 1929).

III

THE PRINCIPAL MEDIEVAL TEXTS
DERIVED FROM HISTORICAL
SOURCES

III 1. DERIVATIVES OF QUINTUS CURTIUS

III. 1. a

THE INTERPOLATED QUINTUS CURTIUS AND
VASCO DE LUCENA

III. 1. a. i

THE INTERPOLATED QUINTUS CURTIUS

In three manuscripts of Quintus Curtius, Vat. Lat. 1869, Vat. Ottob. 2053 and Corpus Christi (Oxford) MS. 82, the lacunae in the text of Quintus Curtius have been filled up with material from various sources: Quintus Curtius himself, Justin, Julius Valerius, Solinus and others.[1] These supplements differ in the various manuscripts, and Vat. Lat. 1869 has three supplements, against two in the other two manuscripts.

The influence of this supplemented text of Curtius is seen in the works of Alberic and Vasco de Lucena. Alberic's indebtedness to an interpolated text of Curtius was first remarked by Foulet in 1935,[2] when he showed that the details of the battle of the Granicus in Alberic-Lamprecht are to be found elsewhere only in the interpolated Quintus Curtius.

The date of the interpolations is necessarily before the date of composition of Alberic's poem, that is to say before the early twelfth century.

[1] STUDIES. S. Dosson, *Etude sur Quinte-Curce* (Paris, 1887), Appendix I, pp. 315–56.

A. Thomas, 'Notice sur un manuscrit de Quinte-Curce', *Revue Critique d'Histoire et de Littérature, XIVe année, 2me semestre* (1880), pp. 75–8.

P. Meyer, *A. le G.* II, Appendix I, pp. 381–6.

[2] A. Foulet, 'La bataille du Granique chez Alberic', *Romania*, LX (1935), pp. 237–41.

III. 1. a. ii

VASCO DE LUCENA

In 1468, Vasco de Lucena, a Portuguese at the Burgundian court, translated the *Interpolated Quintus Curtius* into French prose.[1] His book, dedicated to Charles the Bold, was extremely successful and at least twenty-four manuscripts and six editions survive. In general popularity it largely superseded the Prose Romance of Jean Wauquelin written in the same court twenty years before. Its chief interest is in the prologue and the epilogue, where the translator shows that the wonders told of Alexander are impossible, and condemns the romances as full of lies.

[1] INFORMATION. S. Dosson, *Etude sur Quinte-Curce* (Paris, 1887), pp. 275–7.
P. Meyer, *A. le G.* II, pp. 378–80.
C. Samaran, *Vasco de Lucena à la cour de Bourgogne* (*Documents inédits*) (Lisbon, 1938).
R. Bossuat, 'Vasque de Lucène, traducteur de Quinte-Curce', *Bibliothèque d'Humanisme et Renaissance*, vol. VIII (1946), pp. 197–245.

III. 1. b

THE 'ALEXANDREIS' OF GAUTIER DE CHÂTILLON AND ITS DERIVATIVES

III. 1. b. i

GAUTIER DE CHÂTILLON, 'ALEXANDREIS'

The *Alexandreis* of Gautier de Châtillon,[1] known also as Gautier de Lille, was the most popular of all medieval Latin epics, and its author is acknowledged to have been the most distinguished poet of his time.

This hexameter poem in ten books was written between 1178 and 1182, and dedicated to Gautier's patron William, archbishop of Rheims. The principal source was Quintus Curtius, but use was also made of Justin, Josephus, Julius Valerius, and some minor sources discussed by Christensen. The book describes the life of Alexander in heroic vein, and is full of the inevitable rhetorical digressions and mythological interventions of Latin epic. It is, nevertheless, written skilfully enough to justify medieval opinion of its high merit. There are numerous manuscripts, most of them copiously annotated with explanatory glosses[2] which bear witness to the popularity of the work in the schools. Henry of Settimello borrowed from it, Alanus de Insulis referred to it, and many others testify to its great popularity. But for our purpose the most important evidence of the influence of *Alexandreis* is supplied by the Alexander-books that were founded upon it: the Spanish *Libro de Alexandre*, *Alexanders Geesten* of Jakob van Maerlant, the *Alexander* of Ulrich von Eschenbach, the *Alexanders Saga* of Brand Jónsson, and the Old Czech *Alexandreis*.

[1] EDITIONS. F. A. W. Müldener (Leipzig, 1863). J.-P. Migne, *Patrologia Latina*, vol. CCIX, cols. 459–574.

STUDIES. H. Christensen, *Das Alexanderlied Walters von Châtillon* (Halle, 1905).

C. Giordano, *Alexandreis, poema di Gautier da Châtillon* (Naples, 1917).

M. Bacheler, 'Gualterus' *Alexandreis* in ihrem Verhältnis zum Curtius-Text', *Berliner Philol. Wochenschrift* (1917), cols. 663 ff., 698 ff., 730 ff.

Magoun, p. 22, n. 1.

[2] See R. de Cesare, *Glosse latine e anticofrancesi all' 'Alexandreis' di Gautier de Châtillon* (Milan, 1951).

III. 1. b. ii

JAKOB VAN MAERLANT, 'ALEXANDERS GEESTEN'

This Middle Dutch poem in twelve books is a very close translation of the *Alexandreis* of Gautier de Châtillon, with additional use of the *Iter ad Paradisum* and of one or both of the Vengeance poems; a further alteration is the suppression of the Jerusalem episode, which occurs at the end of Book 1 of the *Alexandreis*.[1] The poem was probably written by Maerlant, one of the best known of Middle Dutch writers, between 1256 and 1260; it is in rhymed couplets.

Alexanders Geesten was later recast into Middle Dutch prose as *Die Historie...des alre Grootsten ende Machtichsten Coninc Alexanders*.[2]

[1] EDITION. J. Franck, *Bibliotheek van Middelnederlandsche Letterkunde* (Groningen, 1882).

INFORMATION. Ibid. Introduction pp. (i–xcvi).

[2] EDITION. S. S. Hoogstra, *Prozabewerkingen van het Leven van Alexander den Groote* ('s Gravenhage, 1898), pp. 38–174 and Introduction, pp. lxxii–cxv.

III. 1. b. iii

'LIBRO DE ALEXANDRE'

The *Libro de Alexandre*[1] is a mid-thirteenth century Spanish poem written in four-line rhyming stanzas, and using as its principal source the *Alexandreis* of Gautier de Châtillon, supplemented by material from the *Historia de Preliis* and the *Roman d'Alexandre*. The poem is extant in two manuscripts, O, the Osuna-Madrid manuscript, of the fourteenth century, and P, the fifteenth-century Paris manuscript; in addition there is a fragment of one leaf preserved in the archives of the Duke of Medinaceli. The texts presented by the two manuscripts differ to such an extent that the latest editor of the poem has thought it best to present parallel editions of the two manuscripts rather than to attempt to make a single critical text; their discrepancies, however, consist rather in linguistic peculiarities and in certain minor divergencies in the narrative, than in any fundamental difference. The Osuna manuscript is unique in containing two letters allegedly written by Alexander to his mother, which were inserted by a copyist from a Spanish translation of the *Dicts and Sayings of the Philosophers*.

The poem was written by an author of considerable skill and Willis has shown how he has contrived to change the atmosphere of the *Alexandreis*, and to make it into a medieval romance by his skilful introduction of episodes from the *Historia de Preliis* and the *Roman d'Alexandre* to supplement the narrative, and by his refusal to admit the heroic and mythological passages of the original into his Spanish rendering.

In spite of the rarity of surviving manuscripts, the *Libro de Alexandre* was well known in Spain; it was used by Alfonso el Sabio in his *Historia General*, imitated by the poet of the *Fernán González*, excerpted in the *Vitorial* of Gutierre Diez de Games, and referred to by the Marqués de Santillana, so that it was evidently not without influence in medieval Spain. The name of the author was at one time presumed to have been Lorenzo Segura; but this name, more correctly Lorenzo d'Astorga, found in the final stanza, is now considered to be merely that of a copyist.

[1] EDITIONS. A. Morel-Fatio, *El libro de Alexandre...* (*Gesell. f. roman. Lit.* x, Dresden, 1906) (Paris MS.).

R. S. Willis, jr., *El libro de Alexandre* (Princeton University Press, 1934: *Elliott Monographs*, 32) (texts of both MSS.).

STUDIES. A. Morel-Fatio, 'Recherches sur le texte et les sources du *Libro de Alexandre*', *Romania*, IV (1875), pp. 7–90.

L. Pistolesi, 'Del posto che spetta al *Libro de Alexandre* nella storia della letteratura spagnuola', *Revue des Langues Romanes*, XLVI (1903), pp. 255–81.

A. G. Solalinde, 'El Juicio de Paris en el '*Alexandre*' y en la 'General Estoria', *Rivista de filologia española*, XV (1928), pp. 1–51.

R. S. Willis, jr., *The Relationship of the Spanish Libro de Alexandre to the Alexandreis of Gautier de Châtillon* (Princeton University Press, 1934: *Elliott Monographs*, 31).

R. S. Willis, jr., *The Debt of the Spanish Libro de Alexandre to the French Roman d'Alexandre* (Princeton University Press, 1935: *Elliott Monographs*, 33).

III. 1. b. iv

ULRICH VON ESCHENBACH, 'ALEXANDER'

The *Alexander* of Ulrich von Eschenbach[1] is the longest medieval Alexander poem, 28,000 lines written in Middle High German rhyming couplets. The poem is divided into ten books, following Gautier, from whom Ulrich derived most of his material. He added, however, a great deal from various other sources; in the first book the account of the birth of Alexander is supplied from the *Historia de Preliis*, while in Book x Ulrich abandons the narrative of Gautier and enters upon a description of the wonders seen by Alexander in the East which is derived from many different sources, including the *Iter ad Paradisum*. The book is a hotch-potch of all available matter relating to Alexander, thrown together with no skill and much repetition and misunderstanding. It concludes with an interminable epilogue, which Toischer considers to have been made so long in order that the book might end at precisely line 28,000.

After the original work had been completed (1270–87) Ulrich added an eleventh book of the same poor quality, an allegory in which Alexander attacks the city of Trintonia, which he is unable to conquer without the help of Aristotle—Valour aided by Wisdom.

In spite of the poverty of the work, it was received with some favour, and several manuscripts exist. It was not, however, used as a source by any later Alexander-book.

[1] EDITION. W. Toischer, *Alexander v. Ulrich von Eschenbach*, B.L.V. vol. CLXXXIII (Tübingen, 1888).

STUDY. W. Toischer, 'Ueber die *Alexandreis* Ulrichs von Eschenbach', *Sitzungsber. d. kaiserl. Akad. d. Wissensch. in Wien. Phil.-Hist. Klasse*, Bd. XCVII (1881), pp. 311–408.

III. 1. b. v

ICELANDIC AND CZECH VERSIONS OF THE 'ALEXANDREIS'

The *Alexandreis* of Gautier de Châtillon was also translated into Icelandic prose by Brand Jónsson (c. 1260),[1] and into Czech verse probably about 1265.[2]

[1] EDITION. C. R. Unger, *Alexanders Saga* (Christiania, 1848).

[2] EDITION. R. Trautmann, *Die alttschechische Alexandreis* (Heidelberg, 1916). Additional notes in *Archiv. f. slav. Philol.* XXXVI (1916), pp. 431–5.

STUDY. H. H. Bielfeldt, *Die Quellen der alttschechischen Alexandreis*. Deutsche Akademie der Wissenschaften. *Veröffentlichungen des Forschungsinstitus für Slawistik*, no. 1 (Berlin, 1951).

III. 1. c

RUDOLF VON EMS, 'ALEXANDER'

The *Alexander* of Rudolf von Ems, written between 1230 and 1250, is extant in two MSS. and one fragment.[1] A poem of 21,643 lines, it is based principally upon Quintus Curtius, but Rudolf used such further material as seemed to him necessary to make the history of Alexander as complete as possible. The most important of these secondary sources was an I² manuscript of the *Historia de Preliis* presenting a text close to that in the Seitenstett MS. used by Zingerle. The Bible, the *Historia Scholastica* of Peter Comestor, Julius Valerius, Epitome, Pseudo-Methodius, the *Alexandreis* of Gautier de Châtillon and other works were also laid under contribution to furnish a complete picture of the historical Alexander. Thanks partly to his skilful combination of different sources, partly to his determination to present only the truth about Alexander, Rudolf's poem is a skilful and artistic unity, the best of the German Alexander-books.

¹ EDITION. V. Junk, *Rudolfs von Ems Alexander, B.L.V.* vols. CCLXXII, CCLXXIV (Leipzig, 1928–9).

STUDIES. A. Ausfeld, *Ueber die Quellen zu Rudolfs von Ems Alexander* (progr. Donaueschingen, 1883).

O. Zingerle, *Die Quellen zum Alexander des Rudolf von Ems* (*Germanistische Abhandlungen*, IV, Breslau, 1885).

R. A. Wisbey, 'Die Aristotelesrede bei Walther von Châtillon und Rudolf von Ems', *Zeits-f-deutsches Altertum*, LXXXV (1954–5), pp. 304ff.

III. 1. d
THE RENAISSANCE ITALIAN ALEXANDER-BOOKS
III. 1. d. i
DOMENICO FALUGIO, 'TRIOMPHO MAGNO'

This Italian poem in twenty-seven cantos in ottava rima was first printed in Rome in 1521,¹ and won for its author the poet's crown from Leo X. Of Falugio himself we know only that he was a native of Incisa–Val d'Arno, and that he published at Rome in 1514 another poem called *Stella d'Amore*. His long Alexander-romance has been studied by Storost. It is founded on Curtius but Falugio has used his source with much freedom, and has treated the life of Alexander in a spirit of Renaissance burlesque.

¹ EDITION. Rome, Marcellus Silber, 1521.

STUDY. Storost, pp. 231–82.

III. 1. d. ii
THE ALEXANDER-ROMANCE IN ROME, BIBLIOTECA
NAZIONALE MS. 1751 (MO. M 10)

This sixteenth-century manuscript contains a fragment of a fine Italian Alexander-romance written in ottava rima and breaking off in the middle of the sixth canto.¹ This is a work of almost pure fiction, though such historical foundation as it possesses is derived from Curtius. In the true style of Renaissance romantic epic, it describes Alexander's life as full of amorous adventure. The writing is fluent and imaginative, the invention unfailing; it is unfortunate that only a fragment of this romantic life of Alexander has survived.

¹ STUDY. Storost, pp. 283–304.

III. 2. DERIVATIVES OF OROSIUS

III. 2. a

THE ST ALBANS AND THE DOUCE COMPILATIONS

III. 2. a. i

THE 'ST ALBANS COMPILATION'

THE so-called *St Albans Compilation*[1] is a Latin prose biography of Alexander found in two manuscripts: Cambridge, Corpus Christi College, MS. 219 (early thirteenth century) and Caius College MS. 54 (later thirteenth century). The first manuscript also contains the *Collatio* I; the second the first two letters of the *Collatio* I and two other letters of Alexander extracted from Julius Valerius.

The book is an uninteresting historical farrago made up of elements from all the various available historical authors but principally from Orosius. It contains no legendary material, and has no originality save that of selection. About half of the work is concerned with the fortunes of the *Diadochi*.

The authorship was variously ascribed by early bibliographers to Radulphus, abbot of St Albans 1146–51, and to Galfridus de Hemlington, monk of St Albans at the same period. Paul Meyer, who was the first to examine it, decided in favour of the ascription to Galfridus but the book itself provides no clue to its author. Meyer also declared that the *St Albans Compilation* had no influence outside England, but Professor Magoun has shown that the Orosian prologue of the second redaction of the *Old French Prose Romance* is based, not directly on Orosius but on the *St Albans Compilation*. The immediate source used by the redactor was a translation of the *Compilation* into Anglo-Norman prose of which one manuscript (MS. CFM 20) survives in the Fitzwilliam Museum, Cambridge[2]. It was also used in the *Douce Compilation*.

[1] EDITION. No complete edition, but selected passages are printed in Magoun, Appendix II, pp. 245–54.
  STUDIES. P. Meyer, *A. le G.* II, pp. 52–63.
  F. P. Magoun, 'The Compilation of St Albans and the Old French Prose Alexander Romance', *Speculum*, I (1926), pp. 225–32.
[2] See D. J. A. Ross, *French Studies*, 1952, VI, p. 353.

III. 2. a. ii

THE 'DOUCE COMPILATION'

This work, written in an English hand at the end of the fourteenth or the beginning of the fifteenth century, is extant in Bodleian Library MS. Douce 299;[1] the compiler was a clerk, and, since he quotes Higden's *Polychronicon*, the compilation probably dates from the last quarter of the fourteenth century. This work is an inept combination of the *St Albans Compilation* and the *Zacher Epitome* of Julius Valerius; its chief interest lies in the preface by the compiler, who there cites the sources from which his book is eventually derived and explains the edifying uses to which the story may be put. This prologue, cited by Meyer, may be compared with the prologue to Leo's *Natiuitas et Victoria*, where the edifying possibilities of the story are similarly expounded.

[1] STUDY. P. Meyer, *A. le G.* II, pp. 63–70.

III. 2. b

SLOANE MS.

The sources of an Alexander compilation in British Museum Sloane MS. 289,[1] which is possibly derived from the *St Albans Compilation*, and certainly from an historical source, are still unidentified.

[1] INFORMATION. E. J. L. Scott, *Index to the Sloane MSS. in the British Museum* (1903), p. 10.

F. P. Magoun, *Speculum*, I (1926), p. 225 n. 4.

III. 2. c

MIDDLE IRISH ALEXANDER

This is an Irish prose life of Alexander based principally on historical sources.[1] It is preserved in the *Book of Ballymote* (*c.* 1400), while a considerable fragment is contained in the *Leabhar breac* (the Speckled Book), written in the first quarter of the fifteenth century. The principal source was Orosius and use was also made of the account of the Jerusalem episode in Josephus, the *Epistola ad Aristotelem*, the *Collatio* and the *Periegesis* of Priscian. The date of the original composition of the work is unknown; a note in the Speckled Book ascribes it to Berchan of the Prophecy (*fl. c.* 690?), who lived at Clonsast. The text given by the Speckled Book, which differs considerably from that in the Book of Ballymote, may date from the eleventh century.

[1] EDITION. K. Meyer, in W. Stokes and E. Windisch, *Irische Texte*, Zweite Serie, Heft II (Leipzig, 1887).
STUDY. R. T. Meyer, 'The Sources of the Middle Irish Alexander', *Modern Philology*, XLVII, i (August 1949), pp. 1–7.

III. 2. d

'PARVA RECAPITULATIO'[1]

The short Latin prose work entitled *Parua recapitulatio de eodem Alexandro et de suis* is found at the end of five English manuscripts containing substantially the same collection of Alexander texts. Despite its title, it is not a brief epitomized life of Alexander but a supplementary tractate. In the manuscripts, of which the oldest (British Museum Royal 13. A. I) dates from the end of the eleventh century, it regularly occurs with the *Zacher Epitome* of Julius Valerius, *Epistola* I, *Collatio* I and various verse epitaphs of Alexander. The *Parua Recapitulatio* was clearly composed as a supplement to these works. The first of the three sections of which it is composed is a correction of Julius Valerius, discrediting the Nectanebus story and suggesting, from no known source, that it was the result of malicious chatter based on Olympias' too great familiarity with the astrologer. Alexander's murderous attack on Nectanebus is similarly rationalized by the suggestion that the cause was resentment on Alexander's part against the harsh discipline to which he was subjected by his tutor. The second section is a full account of Alexander's visit to Jerusalem, recast from Josephus, and the third a brief account of the struggles of the *Diadochi* taken textually from Orosius. The purpose of these two latter sections is clearly supplementary as neither occurs in the *Zacher Epitome*. Presumably the *Parua Recapitulatio* was written in England at the time when this collection of Alexander texts was made, at some date before 1100.

[1] INFORMATION. G. L. Hamilton, *Mélanges...offerts à M. Antoine Thomas* (Paris, 1927), pp. 199–202. (Mostly incorrect as the author had no opportunity of examining the text, on which the above remarks are based. I hope shortly to publish this text.) [D.J.A.R.]

IV

THE PRINCIPAL LATIN CHRONICLE
ACCOUNTS OF ALEXANDER

IV. 1. EKKEHART OF AURA

THE first chronicler to introduce legendary material into his account of
Alexander was Ekkehart, abbot of Aura. The life of Alexander in his
Chronicon Uniuersale[1] begins with an abridged version of the Orosius
account of Alexander, with the addition of the episode of Alexander's
visit to Jerusalem. This historical narrative forms, however, only a small
part of Ekkehart's account. When he has described the life of Alexander
according to historical tradition, he continues: 'Sed quia idem Alexander
multa mire peregisse legitur, quae scire multi delectantur, licet de uita eius
aliqua summatim decerpere, quibus delectationi querentium utcumque
ualeam satisfacere.'

There follows what is called 'Excerptum de uita Alexandri Magni'.[2]
It is, in fact, an abridgement of the Bamberg *Historia de Preliis*, and it is
reasonably supposed that Ekkehart actually used the Bamberg manuscript
as his source. At intervals, where the legendary account of an incident
contradicts the historical account, the latter is placed beside the legend for
purposes of comparison, and the reader asked to form his own opinion
upon which is right. Thus, in the *Historia de Preliis* Porus is killed in single
combat with Alexander; in the historians he is saved, pardoned and restored to his kingdom. Ekkehart is content to juxtapose the two versions,
remarking: 'De hac pugna alii aliter sentiunt, sic scribentes....' This
episode, however, calls Ekkehart's attention to a contradiction in the body
of the legend itself: 'Haec autem diuersitas etiam in epistolis quae ipsius
Alexandri dicuntur ad magistrum suum Aristotilem reperitur, quae si
ipsius sunt, diuersa sibi sentiunt.'

He then compares the account in the *Historia de Preliis* of how Carator,
the son of Candace, is determined to avenge the death of his father-in-law

71

Porus, with the version of the Porus story in the *Epistola ad Aristotelem*, which tells of Alexander's visit to Porus disguised as a simple soldier, of the battle, and of the capture and good treatment of the wounded Porus: 'Haec de dissonantia non solum hystoriographorum, sed ipsius quoque Alexandri, ut dicunt, litterarum idcirco posui, ne quis me de prima huius pugnae descriptione arguat mendacii; ceterum prudens lector eligat, quid sibi de hiis maxime placeat.' This textual crux was often to prove a difficulty to medieval writers.

Ekkehart next proceeds to transcribe the *Epistola ad Aristotelem*, first inserting a preface, in which, as throughout his life of Alexander, he avoids committing himself upon the question of its authenticity. It is here, however, that the veracity of the Letter is first considered to be a matter for serious doubt: '*De mirabilibus rebus quas Alexander uidisse dicitur*: In his ergo itineribus quae et quanta pertulerit et quam miranda conspexerit, ipse, ut fertur, ad matrem suam Olympiadem et magistrum suum Aristotilem scribit, de quibus aliqua ob delectationem noticiae rerum mirabilium breuiando perstringimus, ceterum ueritatem ipsarum rerum iudicio legentium relinquimus.' The abridged version of the Letter practically closes Ekkehart's account, and there is no further point that deserves remark in his life of Alexander.

As a source, Ekkehart supplied material for the accounts of Alexander in Otto of Freising, the *Sächsische Weltchronik*, and Jakob Twinger von Koenigshofen. The account of Alexander in the world-chronicle of Frutolf of Michelsberg, examined by Manitius, drew upon the same sources.

[1] EDITION. In *M.G.H. Scriptt.* vi (ed. D. G. Waitz, 1844), pp. 61–75.
[2] Often found as an independent work in manuscripts.

IV. 2. PETER COMESTOR, 'HISTORIA SCHOLASTICA'

IN the section of his *Historia Scholastica*[1] which is concerned with the book of Esther, Peter Comestor devotes a long passage to an account of Alexander; and as his primary concern is with the Jews, it is from the Jewish point of view that Alexander is here regarded. The account opens with a reference to the Nectanebus legend: 'Cui (Philippo) successit Alexander filius eius adoptiuus, quia legitur Notanabi filius....' Alexander's military career is briefly described, but the main interest centres in Sara-

balla and his intrigues with Alexander, and in Alexander's visit to Jerusalem with all its attendant circumstances. This material is excerpted at
length from Josephus through a Latin translation; and upon the conclusion
of the Jerusalem episode the author abruptly closes his account: 'Porro nos
sub silentio pertransimus qualiter Alexander Darium uicit et Porum, et
quomodo consuluit arbores solis et lunae, et caetera admiratione digna,
quae praeceptori suo Aristoteli per epistolam indicauit, ad ea quae circa
populum Dei gesta sunt festinantes.'

This concludes the biography of Alexander but two short appendices
are added. The first of these is a note on the Temple at Jerusalem; in the
second there is an account of the trees of the sun and moon, which inform
Alexander, in the legend, of his approaching death by poison: '. . . et ita
factum est a sorore.' This strange statement passed from the *Historia
Scholastica* into other accounts, but it is impossible to guess its original
source.

Finally, as an epilogue, we have the story of the Ten Jewish Tribes shut
up by God, at Alexander's prayer, behind two mountains, which God
moves together to form an impenetrable barrier.

Thus Comestor's life of Alexander centres in his relations with the Jews.
The intrusion of the Jewish material thus presented into medieval European
literature, and its influence upon the medieval conception of Alexander, is
of great importance. Peter is content to repeat it, without comment, and
with the addition only of isolated historical and legendary facts. The great
popularity of the *Historia Scholastica* made it an effective vehicle for the
transmission of the Jewish Alexander material, which is told more completely here than in any other medieval historical work of comparable
popularity.

[1] EDITION. *Historia Scholastica*, lib. Esther IV–V: de Alexandro, in Migne, *P.L.* vol.
CXCVIII, cols. 1496A–1498C.

IV. 3. VINCENT DE BEAUVAIS

THE longest of all medieval chronicle accounts of Alexander is that in the
Speculum Historiale[1] of Vincent de Beauvais, where the history of Alexander occupies the whole of the fourth book in the Douai edition. Vincent's
method is that of uncritical collector; he has used most of the accessible
historical and legendary sources and arranged them in rough chronological order, so that his narrative is an incoherent series of contradictory

statements borrowed from conflicting authors, each excerpt preceded by an acknowledgement of its origin.

Justin is the principal historical source, and the *Zacher Epitome*, with the *Epistola ad Aristotelem* and the *Collatio*, the chief legendary authority; but Vincent has also used Quintus Curtius, Valerius Maximus, Seneca, Orosius, Aulus Gellius, St Augustine, St Jerome, St Isidore, Martianus Capella and Peter Comestor—a list which sufficiently shows how he has made his account an anthology of medieval Alexander material. He was the first chronicler to introduce most of the usual, and some of the unusual, anecdotal material into his story. The importance of this will later be made clear.

Vincent's own contribution is confined to occasional comments. In such textual discrepancies as occur, he juxtaposes the various available accounts with the simple comment: 'historia uero Alexandri dicit...', or: 'haec historia Alexandri; Justinus autem dixit...'. 'Historia Alexandri' is his name for the *Zacher Epitome* of Julius Valerius (which, it may be noticed, was never ascribed during the Middle Ages to its author); but although he uses almost the whole of the *Epitome* account of Alexander, and much of its subsidiary material (the *Epistola ad Aristotelem* and the *Collatio*), he does not always regard it as a basic text but sometimes merely uses it for comparison with the historical account of Alexander in Justin. It cannot be said of the life of Alexander in the *Speculum Historiale* that it is derived from one principal source; it is merely a careless anthology of all the Alexander material that came into Vincent's hands.

Besides various unimportant borrowings, one account of Alexander was largely founded on Vincent. It is the life of Alexander in Ranulph Higden's *Polychronicon*, which is modelled upon Vincent's narrative with the addition of some further material.

---

[1] EDITION. *Speculum Historiale* IV (ed. Douai, 1624, pp. 117–37).

PART B

THE
MEDIEVAL CONCEPTION OF
ALEXANDER THE GREAT

NOTE

Superior figures in square brackets refer the reader
to the notes beginning on p. 275.

INTRODUCTION

THE nature of medieval Alexander texts, and the pattern observable in their descent and dissemination, has been now briefly discussed; and we have seen how great a quantity of material dealing with the life of Alexander was readily available in the Middle Ages.

It remains to trace the medieval conception of Alexander as it may be deduced from contemporary testimony. Some individual opinions of medieval writers upon Alexander have already been mentioned in the course of the textual discussion; yet this is to be no attempt at an exact study of the conception of Alexander in the work of individual writers, upon which much has already been written. It is something less precise, more fluid and subtle in its definition. It is not to catch the different influences upon one writer, to show how he used his sources and how he was affected by them—it is rather to be carried along upon the main stream, examining its current, its eddies, and the effect upon its course of confluent tributary waters.

And for this purpose there is no reliance to be placed upon individuals. Although the environmental influence of time and of country upon even the greatest of literary figures may be readily ascertained, yet their approach to the fundamental problems, merely because they have sufficient individuality to separate their work from the general run of literature, cannot be taken as a guide to the direction of contemporary opinion. They may serve only as confirmation of it when it is fully established by other evidence, or as witnesses of the conclusions that general opinion, under their influence or under the influence of ideas they were the first to formulate, is eventually to reach. The safest guide to the establishment of a general conception is a preponderant testimony of mediocre men who have never thought very hard about the matter, and have no reason to be extravagant in their opinions. When we have established a series of points we have to supply the intervening background, to see what remains evidence of an original approach, and what merges into the surrounding context of opinion. I have avoided establishing conceptions by carefully reckoned percentages, or by a slight preponderance of the evidence considered, but have preferred to rely only upon the authority of an uncontestable weight of opinion. I have therefore gathered together as much evidence as may readily be brought to the consideration of the medieval view of Alexander.

Judgements of Alexander in the Middle Ages might be supposed to rest wholly upon the texts, chiefly romances, generally studied hitherto, but this is far from being the truth. The opinion of most medieval writers rests upon that small body of textual material which has not previously been considered, the anecdotal evidence. This anecdotal evidence has its own tradition, its own pattern, and its own great importance. It refuses to be absorbed in the main historical and legendary streams but pursues its own independent line of development.

The biographical material that we have discussed was of primary interest only to those who made it their business to write romance, or epic, or history. To the general reader or hearer, in the Middle Ages as today, history was only remembered in fragments, and the rest, if it was ever learnt, was soon forgotten. An anecdote, a point in the history of a man or of a nation separated from its context and treated by itself, has a more immediate imaginative appeal than the inter- woven chain of influences that has made up the course of that history; and if the history is observed as a whole it is reduced to the anecdotal level, it is looked at through the wrong end of the telescope— 'Alexander, the conqueror of all the world, was conquered by wine' —the reduction of a complicated life to a bald, sententious statement. And if the dogmatic statement is well enough expressed, it becomes an apophthegm—the epigrammatic expression of an incident.

And besides this general human inclination to forget, or to con- centrate upon one summary fact rather than upon a series of real or imaginary facts, there is this in surviving medieval literature, that the greater part of it is not concerned with anecdote for its own sake, for the cleverness or the skill of the narrator, but for the moral that it contains. That alone would assess its value to the spiritual writer; and while the secular writer seeks a different sort of moral, his anecdotes stand in the same illustrative relationship to the rest of his text. An anecdote, to the Middle Ages, was largely a simile to elucidate some point in theology, or morals, or science; in it psychological interest or simple entertainment are the values least considered.

Whence would such anecdotal material concerning Alexander reach medieval writers? There is one evident answer; from those previous collections where anecdotes had already been selected for their moral purpose, from the anecdotes of Valerius Maximus, Cicero, Seneca, and other classical writers, many of which had passed into the writings of the Fathers of the Church. Once such an anecdote is established, it may not be shaken; it is handed on from writer to writer, made better known by its use in a popular work, the *Policraticus* or the *Speculum Historiale*, adapted, altered, confused, but not forgotten. It will be seen how the fund of accessible anecdote was slowly but perceptibly increased by additions from the available material, and we shall discuss in each case the reason why an incident should have received recognition as an anecdote. Throughout the Middle Ages the anecdotal material steadily accumulates—it is used to supplement the regular Alexander material, and to supply stories for the books of *exempla*, until it is known to all classes of society, and is fully and finally enshrined in the didactic poets of the last medieval centuries.

There are four classes of writer with which we are concerned. The first are the philosophers, those who write to instruct in morals, in metaphysics and in the art of government. The second are the theologians and the mystics, who are concerned with the relation of historical truth to religious truth, and with the apposite symbolism to stress that relationship. The third class are the writers of books of *exempla*, the preachers and others in whom an exemplar use of material is evident—those who write for edification. The fourth are the secular writers, which includes not only the writers of romance, of lyrics, and of other vernacular pieces, but all those who intended to amuse rather than to instruct—though the instructive element is never wholly absent.

In each section I have discussed the treatment of inherited material and inherited judgements about Alexander, and the clear emergence of an individual conception. In the fourteenth and fifteenth centuries, however, changing conditions and the consequent change in values had so important an effect upon these separate conceptions of Alexander that it has seemed best to consider the result in a separate section, and finally to trace the transition from the medieval to the Renaissance treatment of Alexander in Italian references of the same period.

I

THE CONCEPTION OF ALEXANDER IN MORALISTS TO THE FOURTEENTH CENTURY WITH A PROSPECT OF THE OPINIONS OF LATER WRITERS

1. INTRODUCTION

THE historical accounts of Alexander presented medieval Europe with established philosophic judgements of his character which preserved, though they were confused in the derivative histories of Curtius, Justin and Orosius, the characteristics of the Peripatetic and Stoic attacks upon him. Alexander was either fundamentally weak or fundamentally bad, and his continued prosperity, ascribed not to his own ability but to Fortune, encouraged his inherent weakness to yield to vicious influences, or his inherent wickedness to worsen as his power increased.

Ethical teaching is more stable and constant than metaphysical speculation. Based upon an abstract idea of good, and not necessarily dependent on the postulation of a God, ethical norms transcend the civilization that gives them birth, and survive the decay of those religious or philosophic ideals upon which they were originally established. Though the coming of Christianity, and the transformation of pagan morality into a rule of Christian conduct through which a man might attain to heaven, affected the orientation of speculative and didactic morality, it did not deprive medieval moralists of sympathy, often of complete agreement, with principles first laid down by pagan writers. They substituted Christian motives and the workings of God for philosophic motives and the working of Fortune, of Natura, or other impersonal forces; but the basic teaching of morality remained much the same.

And Christian morality was especially in sympathy with those philosophers who were most intimately connected with Alexander in the minds of Christian readers. Aristotle, 'maestro di color che sanno', and Seneca, 'maximus ille paupertatis et continentiae sectator, et summus inter uniuersos philosophos morum aedificator', were the most venerated of pagan philosophers; while of those with whom Alexander came into recorded personal contact, Diogenes and the Brahmans were considered admirable examples for the Christian ascetic, and Callisthenes was honoured as the pupil of Aristotle. The philosophers with whom the name of Alexander was connected, in a fashion normally unfavourable to his reputation, were readily understood and appreciated. Thus it was in the denunciations of Alexander by Diogenes, Dindimus and Dionides, supported by Seneca's Stoic attacks, by the summary judgements of the accessible historians, and by the comments of the Fathers of the Church upon the antique material that they transmitted, that medieval moralists found it easiest to establish a judgement upon Alexander; since these were men they could understand, and who presented a judgement of Alexander which, even if it was confused upon particular issues, was at least decisive in condemnation, and ready-made to an exemplar end.

It is, therefore, from the broken survivals of antique tradition that the conception of Alexander in the writings of medieval moralists is principally derived. We shall discuss the perseverance of this tradition in judgements both upon the whole career of Alexander, and upon particular aspects of his character, and show the effect of the impact of other traditions upon this philosophic material, which is merely the continuance of a Greek tradition transmitted through Rome to Christendom. First, however, it is necessary to note the chief problem which faced Christian moralists; a problem for which no solution was ever put forward and which is inherent in every serious medieval judgement of Alexander. The substitution of Christian for pagan ideas necessarily involved the replacement of Fortune, that controlling force in the development of Alexander's character, by Divine Providence. But in the parallel Jewish tradition, in the testimony of the Bible and of Josephus, Alexander is God's instrument of wrath against the Persians, and his career is watched over by God. In Josephus Alexander is, in addition, conscious of the power of God, who accomplishes miracles on his behalf. The same idea is echoed in the Oriental Alexander tradition, and thence in the *Historia de Preliis*; but it is difficult to reconcile with the idolatrous, vicious Alexander of classical tradition, whose vices are ascribed in great part to that very influence of Fortune, and therefore, in the Christian tradition, of God. The questions raised by the conflict between these two traditions will be discussed fully in the second section in dealing with the theological approach to Alexander.

The anecdotal information about Alexander from which almost all knowledge of him in the moralists of this period was derived was supplied principally by Seneca, Valerius Maximus, and Cicero. Of these authors, Seneca naturally reflects the Stoic opinion of Alexander in his anecdotes, Cicero the Peripatetic approach, while Valerius Maximus, as an anthologist like many of the medieval writers themselves, is subject to both philosophic currents. Thus, although there are a certain number of anecdotes which have no connexion with any particular view of Alexander current in antiquity, most of the material known to medieval moralists was derived either from Stoic or Peripatetic sources; and, as we have seen, these anecdotes were necessarily those best adapted for moral use, and of the greatest influence upon medieval opinion of Alexander.

As a very general rule the following principles of anecdotal transmission may be noticed: that the anecdotes derived primarily from Seneca and from Cicero, and retransmitted by the Fathers of the Church, were those best known in the Middle Ages; while those told by Valerius Maximus were widely used only by John of Salisbury among moralists, and passed through his or other intermediacy into the books of *exempla*.

Upon these premises I have adopted the following arrangement in considering the conception of Alexander in the earlier medieval moralists. I have first discussed the history of the anecdotes most popular in the Middle Ages, and the significance of the morals attached to them; I have then dealt with the scattered anecdotal material that appears in the moralists; and finally, I discuss certain special issues and individual judgements. This arrangement has been made necessary by the entire dependence of this class of writers upon scattered references, which makes the assessment of the picture of Alexander presented in any one moralist so fragmentary, so contradictory and so elusive as not to deserve consideration; whereas the discussion of the history of each anecdote shows how its moral became changed, the effect of its popularity upon the general opinion of Alexander, and the fate of individual points of ancient propaganda; so that these parallel vertical traditions, each possessing its particular interest, will by their combination show the trend of the conception of Alexander among medieval moralists down to the fourteenth century, and look forward to the deeper influence of morality upon poetry in the later Middle Ages.

2. THE MOST POPULAR MORAL ANECDOTES OF ALEXANDER, AND THEIR MEDIEVAL HISTORY AND USAGE

In this section the following anecdotes and anecdotal groups have been placed: Alexander's interview with Diogenes; the group of anecdotes in Cicero and Seneca that concern his liberality; his interview with Dindimus; and his encounter with Dionides the Pirate. The reasons for the popularity of these philosophical interviews in the Middle Ages have already been discussed; and it remains now to show how medieval moralists reacted to this material, and how deeply it affected their consideration of Alexander.

(a) ALEXANDER AND DIOGENES

Ancient philosophers worked upon the reputation of the Cynic Diogenes until they had made him the hero of many legendary episodes;[1] and the legend was caught up and enlarged by medieval writers. The fact that Diogenes did not regard his asceticism as a means to a Christian end was not appreciated by medieval observers, who accepted the Senecan and patristic portrait of Diogenes, and were accustomed to see in all asceticism something of Christian saintliness. For it was the ascetic side of him that they took for their example and admiration; the old man sitting in meditation upon a philosophy presumed to be as Christian in its intimations of immortality as it was in its denial of human comfort.

The story of Diogenes in his tub and Alexander interfering with

---

[1] For the ancient legends of Diogenes, see K. von Fritz, *Quellenuntersuchungen zu Leben und Philosophie des Diogenes von Sinope* (Philol., *Suppl.-Band* xxviii), 1926.

his sun is too well known to need retelling here. Its popularity in learned medieval circles was assured by its appearance in authors well established in medieval favour: Cicero, and Valerius Maximus.[1] Valerius Maximus added a proverbial comment: 'Alexander Diogenem gradu suo diuitiis pellere temptat, celerius Darium armis.'[2] And Seneca, in reference to the story, which he does not repeat, also made use of epigrammatic abuse of Alexander: 'multo potentior, multo locupletior fuit [Diogenes] omnia tunc possidente Alexandro: plus enim erat, quod hic nollet accipere quam quod ille posset dare.'[3] And in another place: 'Alexander Macedonum rex gloriari solebat a nullo se beneficiis uictum.'[4]

These comments were often reproduced in the Middle Ages, sometimes with the anecdote and sometimes independently.[1] They point to a moral best expressed by Seneca, and typical of the Stoic treatment of Alexander's character. The world-conqueror, accustomed to boast that nobody could surpass him in liberality, was surpassed by Diogenes, who, by his refusal to accept anything from him except what he could not give, proved himself richer in true riches, and a better man. The emphasis is therefore upon Alexander's making liberality a part of vanity, and on the rebuff that he receives from Diogenes, who asks him to give him back what he cannot give—the sunshine. There is a close parallel in the story of the Gymnosophists later to be discussed, who ask Alexander to give them immortality;[5] and a similar implication—all good gifts come from God.

This moral conclusion was fully maintained where the story was used by learned medieval writers who do no more than repeat the story and the original comments; but it was lost when the story was applied to the purposes of the books of *exempla*. There it took on a wider moral as eminently suited to an edifying purpose as Seneca's judgement was to moral disquisition. This new interpretation was reached by the addition to the anecdote of new material from an Oriental source, which completely changed its character by altering the focus, placing the incident of the sun in the background, and making the episode a lecture on incontinence of a general and conventional type. In this version, which reached Europe through the

---

[1] Cicero, *Tusc. Disp.* v, 32; Valerius Maximus, IV, iii, ext. 4.
[2] Valerius Maximus, loc. cit.   [3] Seneca, *De Ben.* v, iv, 4.
[4] Seneca, *De Ben.* v, vi, 1.   [5] See p. 148.

Disciplina Clericalis, the main part of the narrative is occupied by Diogenes' explanation of his statement that Alexander is 'the servant of his servant'.[2] He explains that his own will is subject to his reason, while Alexander's reason is subject to his will, and therefore Alexander is 'the servant of his servant'. This remark, expounded at considerable length, is preceded by the story of Diogenes' sunshine. This, however, is here not even told of Diogenes and Alexander, but of Diogenes and the servants of Alexander who find him seated in his tub, and to whom he first delivers himself of his epigram on their master. This exemplar anecdote will be examined later; for the moment it is sufficient to note how the incident of the sunshine here became a brief, insignificant, and scarcely noticed introduction to the real theme of the story—Alexander's inability to subject his will to reason.

In its simple form, however, as a comment upon false liberality, and with the comments of Seneca and Valerius Maximus either attached or understood, the application of this story was consistently learned rather than popular, as will be seen from the examples given of its use; it was only when it became attached to the wide moral of the Oriental material that it became known outside learned literature. This restricted application must be considered in conjunction with other Stoic and Peripatetic material relating to Alexander's liberality that was known in medieval times; since, as we shall see, the question of Alexander's liberality was one of great importance in the medieval period, and frequently discussed.

(b) ALEXANDER'S LIBERALITY IN THE MORALISTS

The moral of the Diogenes story is closely connected with that of other Senecan passages; it is also to be related to an anecdote derived from Cicero, and to episodes in the historians known to the Middle Ages. All this material, by its medieval use, illustrates the view of Alexander's liberality held by moralists of this period; and it is of especial importance to establish the evolution of their attitude, because the secular reputation of Alexander for liberality was so pronounced and so remarkable as to suggest some traditional evidence in support of its proverbial fame.[1]

[1] This question is fully discussed in Appendix II, pp. 358–68.

We will first discuss the texts relating to Alexander's liberality best known to medieval writers, and then proceed, from a philosophic definition of liberality, to examine the medieval treatment of these texts, and to consider how far Alexander's liberality was thought true liberality, and how far the effect of mistaken policy or of arrogant vanity.

That this last is the view of Seneca, who represents the Stoic attitude towards Alexander, may be seen not only from his comment upon the Diogenes story, but from two anecdotes which he tells of Alexander's liberality. The first concerns the envoys of an Asiatic city, who advance to offer half their city to the invading Alexander. Alexander replies: 'It is no question of your giving me your city, but of your keeping what I choose to give you back'.[1] The second is the story of the poor veteran who comes to Alexander to beg his release from the army, since he has served his time;[2] he asks for a small gift. Alexander is in the humour to give the man a city. The veteran exclaims in astonishment: 'I am not worthy of so great a gift.' Alexander replies: 'The question is not what it is fitting for you to receive, but what it is fitting that I should give.' This story is compared with that of Antigonus and the Cynic who asks for an obol; when Antigonus suggests that this is no fit gift for a king to give, the Cynic asks for a talent, whereupon Antigonus avoids giving him anything by saying that a talent is no fit gift for a Cynic to receive. Seneca attacks both impartially; Antigonus for his higgling, evasive parsimony, and Alexander for his refusal to consider the feelings of other people, his making liberality a part of vanity, and thence his neglect of all those precepts which should govern the act of giving, the consideration not only of what may reasonably or fittingly be given, but of the ultimate benefit of the recipient: 'Tumidissimum animal! si illum accipere hoc non decet, nec te dare: habetur personarum ac dignitatum portio et, cum sit ubique uirtutis modus, aeque peccat quod excedit quam quod deficit.'[3] The history of this second anecdote, which was widely known in the Middle Ages, belongs not only to the moral, but also to the exemplar and secular attitudes to this question; and there will therefore be frequent reference to it.[4]

[1] *Ep. ad Luc.* LIII, 10.   [2] *De Ben.* II, xvi; the Antigonus story is in *De Ben.* II, xvii.
[3] *De Ben.* II, xvi, 2.   [4] See below, pp. 146–8, 348, 351, 361–2.

An echo of this Stoic approach to Alexander is the passage in Justin where he tells how Alexander gave a kingdom to a peasant, that the gift might be seen to be wholly dependent upon the king's liberality, and not in part upon the rank or true worth of the recipient;[3] while in his preface Justin contrasts the extravagance of Alexander with the parsimony of Philip: 'Frugalitati pater, luxuriae filius magis deditus erat.'[4]

Seneca therefore represents Alexander's liberality as the direct effect of his ὕβρις; and the vigour with which he attacks Alexander for his supposed virtue, and concentrates most of his references to Alexander upon that attack,[1] shows that Alexander had already by this time an established reputation for liberality. And, apart from those references to it which are here unimportant because of their independence of medieval tradition, this reputation is indicated in a passage of Cicero, where he quotes, in a discussion of the true nature of liberality, a famous letter of Philip to the young Alexander.[2] Philip reproaches him for his prodigality, aimed at the acquisition of faithful followers, and points out that he is succeeding only in corrupting the recipients of his prodigality and in diminishing the royal dignity: 'Praeclare in epistula quadam Alexandrum filium Philippus accusat, quod largitione beneuolentiam Macedonum consectetur: "Quae te, malum!" inquit "ratio in istam spem induxit, ut eos tibi fideles putares fore, quos pecunia corrupisses? An tu id agis, ut Macedones non te regem suum, sed ministrum et praebitorem sperent fore?"'

This letter therefore attacks Alexander's liberality on different grounds; it is not derived from vanity, but from mistaken political motives—it is the indiscretion of youth, not the innate conceit of a man. There may be compared with this the correspondence between Zeuxis, Philip, Alexander, and Aristotle in Pseudo-Callisthenes α and Julius Valerius, where the two former reproach the young Alexander for his prodigality;[5] and Alexander and Aristotle reply that it is no prodigality, no careless extravagance of youth, but a careful policy of judicious liberality based on the teaching of Aristotle. It is thus evident that opinion was as divided upon Alexander's liberality

---

[1] Namely De Ben. II, xvi; v, iv, 4; v, vi, 1; Ep. ad Luc. LIII, 10.
[2] Cicero, De Off. II, xv, 53 ff.; the letter is also given in Val. Max. VII, ii, ext. 10. Compare the letter of Olympias in Plutarch, Vita Alex. XXXIX, 5.

in the sources immediately available to the writers of the Middle Ages as in those writers themselves.

The moral of the Ciceronian anecdote, that mistaken liberality does not make friends but prepares enemies, is echoed in Curtius;[6] although in his concluding summary Curtius praises Alexander's liberality whole-heartedly and without reserve.[7]

It was these passages from Cicero and Seneca, transmitted in part through Valerius Maximus and the Fathers of the Church, that provided learned medieval writers with the most accessible material for forming a judgement upon Alexander's liberality. The references to his liberality in legendary texts were unknown or unnoticed by serious writers; the references in the historians, though they have been here adduced as supporting evidence for the principal trends of ancient opinion, similarly went unnoticed outside their contexts, because they are comments on incidents, and were not cast into that anecdotal form so necessary for the wide dissemination of textual material in the Middle Ages.

Before considering the use made of these anecdotes by learned medieval writers it is essential that the fundamental beliefs which determined the medieval attitude to liberality should be examined. William of Conches defined liberality, following Cicero, as: '...uirtus animi beneficiorum erogatrix, quam eandem pro affectu benignitatem, pro effectu beneficentiam appellamus. Haec uirtus tota in distribuendo consistit.'[1] This definition, and especially this division of liberality into two necessary parts, *affectus*, the natural benevolence of the giver, and *effectus*, the objective act of giving, must be taken as the starting-point for any consideration of the medieval attitude to Alexander's liberality; since opinion upon it was to be divided as to the relative importance to be accorded to *affectus* and to *effectus*.

To a philosopher, the emphasis must naturally be upon the *affectus*, the state of mind in the giver; if this is corrupt in any way, if it is not true benignity, but a desire for self-glorification, the groping towards a political end, or careless pleasure in giving, then the *effectus* must lose the name of true liberality. And this *effectus*, be it

---

[1] William of Conches, *Liber Moralium Dogmatis Philosophorum* (under the name of Hildebert of Lavardin) in Migne, *P.L.* CLXXI, col. 1015. For Cicero's definition of liberality, cf. *De Officiis* I, xiv, 42 ff.

noticed, comprises in its original definition all the beneficent results of benevolence; not only material benefits, gifts of money or rank or possessions, but any act of kindness. It includes all those things that benefit the recipient.

To Seneca this definition of liberality was further conditioned by the considerations which attend the act of giving; benevolence does not suffice to make liberality, if the benevolence results in a liberality foolish either because the recipient does not deserve it or because the donor cannot afford it. For Seneca liberality is a careful, philosophic process; and his condemnation of Alexander is especially bitter because he breaks all the rules—his giving does not spring from true benevolence; it considers neither the good of the recipient, nor how much the donor can afford or ought to give.

In contrast to this, Cicero's story of Philip's letter to Alexander is a political comment upon the mistaken use of prodigality for political advantage. The act of liberality is hardly here considered at all; the motives upon which it is based, though they are not benignant, would be excusable as politically expedient. But a measure of political expedience has to be judged by its results, and in this case the results are prophesied to be fatal. This is the view neither of the philosopher, observing the state of mind of the giver, nor of the preacher or the secular writer, who is especially concerned with the amount of the gift; it is that of the counsellor, who examines the action not so much in connexion with liberality as with its expediency as a political act. The medieval use of the story is therefore restricted, and we find it where we should expect to find it—in the *Policraticus*[1] of John of Salisbury, and in encyclopaedists like Vincent de Beauvais and Brunetto Latini.[2] In these citations the original moral is naturally retained.

We return, therefore, to the anecdotes of Diogenes and of the man to whom Alexander gave a city (the anecdote of the Asiatic city appears only in *exempla*[3]), both of which were adorned with savage

---

[1] John of Salisbury, *Policraticus* VIII, ii (ed. Webb, II, p. 235): 'Valerius Maximus, sed et Cicero....'

[2] Vincent de Beauvais, *Speculum Historiale* IV, 19 (ed. Douai, 1624, p. 123).
Brunetto Latini, *Li Livres dou Tresor* II, ii, 80 (ed. Chabaille, p. 418).
Higden, *Polychronicon* III, 27 (ed. Lumby, vol. III, p. 406).
Upon the possible connexion of a passage in Philippe de Novare with this letter, see Meyer, *A. le G.* II, pp. 361–3, and below, p. 362.

[3] See p. 155.

Senecan comments. The history of the Diogenes anecdote and its attendant comments has already been traced, and it has been seen how the emphasis was laid not only upon the character of Alexander, but as much, or more, upon that of Diogenes. It was not the act of giving, but the act of refusing, which was the more significant. This point is well illustrated by the fact that the anecdote is hardly ever introduced into a discussion of the character of Alexander, but often forms part of a panegyric on Diogenes.

The history of the other anecdote is very different, and if we may say that the moral of the Diogenes anecdote is maintained at the same philosophic level, that of the second anecdote declines; it becomes altered for exemplar and secular uses, and ends by bearing a moral the opposite of that intended by Seneca. Seneca's bitter comment upon Alexander's so-called liberality is reproduced, so far as I am aware, only in Petrus Cantor, where the story is still joined to that of Antigonus.[1] The stories are similarly connected, in William of Conches, Giraldus Cambrensis, and others;[8] but the edge has been taken off the anecdote by the omission of Seneca's comment, and the use of a simple transitional phrase, 'melius Alexander', inserted between the story of Antigonus and that of Alexander. This is the intermediate stage in the gradual transformation of the moral attached to the anecdote, which finally emerged, separated now from the Antigonus anecdote, in exemplar and secular writers in a form directly favourable to Alexander.[9]

In its passing through learned into unlearned literature the point of this anecdote was lost; while the moral of the anecdotes of Diogenes was maintained at two different levels, one for learned, and the other for exemplar transmission and interpretation, the anecdote of the man to whom Alexander gave a city was altered for exemplar uses and given an interpretation in keeping with the needs of the parish priest seeking alms for his poor, or the dependent begging money from his patron—transformed into an example of that unphilosophic liberality that we shall later consider more fully. So sharp and subtle a criticism as Seneca's was not to be maintained for long by even the most earnest of medieval moralists, who would consider the Christian uses of extravagance; and to the general observer, Alexander would

---

[1] Petrus Cantor, *Verbum Abbreviatum* XLVII; 'contra eos qui dant non indigentibus', in Migne, *P.L.* vol. CCV, col. 150.

always seem more pardonable than Antigonus, whatever Seneca might have to say upon the question.

Thus Alexander's prodigality was partly admitted; but a more charitable view was taken of it than would be expected from a survey of the surviving material. For medieval views upon prodigality, conditioned by the needs of Christian society, were more fluid and less strict than those of the authors from whom this material was derived; and even the most learned of moralists had, from the ancient viewpoint, a relatively unphilosophic approach to liberality.

(c) ALEXANDER AND DINDIMUS

That the attack of the Brahman Dindimus on Alexander should have so much in common with Greek philosophic attacks on him should cause no surprise; for it was the pleasure of timid and ingenious philosophers among the Cynics to put their abuse of Alexander in the mouth of one of those whom Alexander met in his wanderings, and especially the Brahmans. In their rejection of intellectual life, and their attempt to divest the person of all personal attributes, the Brahmans had certain affinities with the Cynics, and offered an admirable mouthpiece because they were a nation of philosophers.[10]

Dindimus' attack is more valuable than the anecdotal material which we have discussed, for it presents an analysis of the whole character of Alexander, instead of isolated aspects of that character—and the fact that it also contains an account of the ideal ascetic life, with its strange similarity to that preached by Christianity, makes it the more effective as propaganda, in that it demonstrates not only the wickedness of Alexander's life, but also the goodness of the life that should be led.

The *Collatio*,[11] the most influential of the Brahman tracts, also differs from the anecdotes in its literary form, as a comparison between the lives of two men; while in the anecdotes the condemnation of Alexander had been summary and unanswered, the correspondence with Dindimus takes rather the form of a trial in which both sides are heard. If, as we may well believe not only from the tone of the narrative itself, but from the textual researches of M. Liénard, the original author of the *Collatio* aimed at discrediting Alexander's pagan or Christian accusers, personified in Dindimus, his subtle intention was lost to Christian readers, who might well not sympathize with Alexander's vivacious retorts, and who were soon not permitted the opportunity of disapproving, because, in abridged or anecdotal usage, either Alexander's contemptuous remarks upon Dindimus and ascetics in general were suppressed, or Dindimus was allowed to have the last word.

The *Collatio*, like the other Brahman pamphlets which are Cynic accusation in earnest, belongs to the philosophic tradition represented by all the anecdotes in this section; but it was most closely related textually to the legendary tradition, into which it was incorporated in the interpolated *Historia de Preliis*. It enjoyed, however, an independent circulation both before and after that incorporation, and though it is usually linked in the manuscripts to one or other of the main legendary texts, its separate popularity is early shown by the fact that Alcuin sent a copy of the correspondence to Charlemagne.[12]

Before the material which afforded a direct comparison between the Brahmans and Alexander was widely known, the Brahmans had been often proposed by Christian writers as a fit subject for admiration. Tertullian refers to them, St Jerome praises them for their ascetic virtues, while Origen had known of the encounter between Alexander and Dindimus;[1] and in the *De moribus Bragmanorum*, ascribed popularly to St Ambrose,[2] one of the lesser Brahman tractates was connected with one of the greatest of the Fathers.

Thus, when the correspondence between Dindimus and Alexander first began to be known, Christians naturally interpreted it, not as the author had intended, but from the Brahman (or Cynic) point of view. The subtle mockery was lost to that edified mind which saw in the *Collatio* another proof of the admirable asceticism of the Brahmans. From the standpoint of this established reputation, and with a sympathetic prejudice in favour of the ascetic Brahman philosophy, Christian moralists looked upon Alexander's controversy with Dindimus as yet another text that demonstrated the wickedness of Alexander when compared with the Brahmans.

The influence of the correspondence upon the secular conception

---

[1] Tertullian, *Apologeticus* XLII, i (Migne, *P.L.* vol. I, cols. 490–1).

St Jerome, *Contra Iouinianum* II (Migne, *P.L.* vol. XXIII, col. 304).

Origen, *Contra Haereses* I, xliv–xlvii (Migne, *P.G.* vol. XVI, part 3, cols. 3051–2).

[2] On the *De moribus Bragmanorum* ascribed to St Ambrose, see above, p. 12. The text is in Migne, *P.L.* vol. XVII, cols. 1131–46.

of Alexander will be separately considered. Its appearance in those moralists who are our immediate study is infrequent, not for any reason inherent in the character of the text, which was suitable for moral purposes, but because it was neither cast, nor capable of being cast, into a short anecdotal form, and also because it did not follow the usual route of transmission through a well-known classical or patristic writer.

In the twelfth century Dindimus was highly regarded. Abaelard makes his admiration clear; in a discussion of prophecies of the Messiah, he brings forward four pre-Christian kings who foresaw Christ's coming. Two of these are Jewish, two Gentile; David and Solomon, Nebuchadnezzar and Dindimus: 'Iuuat autem et Didimi regis Bragmanorum inferre testimonium, ut in quatuor regum auctoritate nostrae assertio fidei praemineat. Duorum quidem Iudaeorum, et duorum gentilium, David scilicet et Salomonis, Nabuchodonosor et Didimi....Ait itaque Didimus in prima ad Alexandrum epistola...', and he gives Dindimus' declaration of the god that he worships, saying in conclusion: 'Quibus quidem epistolis, si fides exhibenda sit, nulla hominum uita quantumcumque religiosorum innocentiae atque abstinentiae Brachmanorum aequiparanda uidetur.'[1] And he then quotes St Jerome's praise of the Brahmans. Abaelard's deep respect for the nation of ascetics is shown not only by the repetition of this passage in another place, but by a reference to '...illud Brachmanorum sacrificium, hoc est orationes et lacrymae...'.[2]

John of Salisbury, discussing the necessity of justice in a king, cites the correspondence, and says that Alexander left the Brahmans in peace—'...nullam ratus uictoriam, si eorum pacem perpetuam turbaret....'.[13]

Christian admiration for Dindimus showed itself not only by the usual suppression of Alexander's forceful conclusion of the correspondence, but also by such alterations in the text as made Dindimus and his Brahmans into true Christian philosophers. The most interesting of such remanipulations is in the *Pantheon* of Godfrey of Viterbo, who has completely changed the character of the *Collatio*;[3]

---

[1] Abaelard, *Introductio ad Theologiam* I, xxii–xxiii (Migne, *P.L.* vol. CLXXVIII, cols. 1032–3).

[2] Abaelard, *Theologia Christiana* III (Migne, *P.L.* vol. CLXXVIII, col. 1225).

[3] See L. Meyer, *Les Légendes des Matières de Rome, de France, et de Bretagne dans le 'Panthéon' de Godefroi de Viterbe* (Paris, 1933), pp. 82–97, where this original version of the *Collatio* is discussed in full.

not only is Dindimus made the mouthpiece of Christian thought, but Alexander's answers are altered into the arrogant trumpet-blasts of the man who calls himself the son of Jupiter, and Dindimus is allowed the last word by increasing the number of letters to six. A similar Christian treatment appears notably in Jacques de Vitry, Martinus Polonus (von Troppau), and the *Contrefait de Renart*.[141] In these authors varying proportions are given to the several letters of the *Collatio*, but Dindimus is always made singularly Christian, and Alexander is always deprived of his effective retort.

This suppression of Alexander's answers shows the adaptation of a rhetorical controversy to a moral use; the answers of Alexander are too disturbing, too convincing, and too pagan to be allowed a place. The *Collatio* left its impression upon late medieval didactic writers but it did not pass into exemplar literature.

The slight independent popularity of the treatise *De moribus Bragmanorum* is shown by its use in the *Eulogium Historiarum*,[1] a universal chronicle written by a monk of Malmesbury, and in the *Speculum morale*;[2] but the *Collatio* was by far the most influential of the tractates, and the only one whose effect upon the medieval conception of Alexander merits consideration.

The subtlety of Dindimus in the *Collatio* was accepted by Christian moralists; they cut the element of controversy out of the episode, and brought him forward as the conventional ascetic. Alexander appears as the man who received his reproofs; he is reduced almost to the unimportance of the lay-figure that he becomes when this material is re-used in books of *exempla*. Dindimus' reputation was independent of any special connexion with Alexander, but was largely supported by the *Collatio*. Thus the story of Alexander and Dindimus is not so forceful nor therefore so important, even if we neglect the rarity of its appearance in the works of the moralists, as the anecdotal material borrowed from classical and patristic sources, which is closely and personally connected with the character of Alexander. It falls into the category of material of edifying type, the string of moral precepts and pronouncements directed at Alexander, but intending no especial or individual dispraise of him, that we shall meet so often in exemplar literature. The character of the piece caused it to be referred to in

---

[1] *Eulogium Historiarum*, cap. cxxvi (ed. Haydon, vol. I, pp. 432–4).
[2] See below, pp. 297–8.

works of didactic or encyclopaedic intention, while its lack of true anecdotal quality, as well as its textual history, deprived it of lasting popularity among moralists.

(d) ALEXANDER AND DIONIDES THE PIRATE

St Augustine, in the *De Ciuitate Dei*, speaks of the necessity of just government to the establishment of a true kingdom. In illustration he tells a story from the *De Republica* of Cicero, about Alexander and a certain pirate:

Quam similia sunt latrociniis regna absque iustitia

Remota itaque iustitia, quid sunt regna, nisi magna latrocinia? Manus et ipsa hominum est, imperio principis regitur, pacto societatis astringitur, placiti lege praeda diuiditur. Hoc malum si in tantum perditorum hominum accessibus crescit, ut et loca teneat, sedes constituat, ciuitates occupet, populos subiuget, euidentius regni nomen adsumit, quod ei iam in manifesto confert non adempta cupiditas, sed addita impunitas. Eleganter enim et ueraciter Alexandro illi Magno quidam comprehensus pirata respondit. Nam cum idem rex hominem interrogasset, quid ei uideretur, ut mare haberet infestum: ille libera contumacia, Quod tibi, inquit, ut orbem terrarum: sed quia id ego exiguo nauigio facio, latro uocor, quia tu magna classe, imperator.[15]

St Augustine accepts the validity of the pirate's argument; dominion without justice does not make a kingdom, but a *latrocinium*, a robber-kingdom. But a personal application of this moral to Alexander was not easily to be established in the Middle Ages, nor was the question of Alexander's injustice, and of the legitimacy of his empire, to be decided upon the evidence of this anecdote alone, but upon such variable evidence, and with such a variety of resultant opinion, that the discussion of it must be reserved; and comment will here be restricted to the history of the anecdote itself, and to showing that the attached moral, like those of the Senecan anecdotes, veered away from an interpretation unfavourable to Alexander.

St Augustine borrowed the anecdote from Cicero, where it occurs in one of the lost sections of the *De Republica*.[1] But it seems possible

---

[1] The context in the *De Republica* suggests that Cicero used the story much as St Augustine used it; and that in spite of its favourable ending in his version, he did not give it the moral suggested in the *Policraticus*.

that the citation of the anecdote in John of Salisbury, its next use and one which had far-reaching effect, is from the text of Cicero; since the wording differs so substantially from that of St Augustine as to preclude any possibility that John borrowed the anecdote from the *De Ciuitate Dei*.

In the *Policraticus* the speech of the pirate, who is here called Dionides while St Augustine had not named him, is given in more detail.[1] He develops the argument against Alexander at greater length, and inveighs against his ambition and pride: 'Me fortunae iniquitas et rei familiaris angustia, te fastus intolerabilis et inexplebilis auaritia furem facit...tu quo fortunatior, nequior eris.' On hearing the man's arguments, Alexander pardons him, and gives him a place among his own men. This is significant; but even more significant is the position of the anecdote in the *Policraticus*. For it comes after the story of Antigonus, Alexander's tutor, reproving him for playing a lyre:[2] 'Quod et ille (Alexander) patientissime tulit, licet plerumque impatientissimus fuerit, et patrem sicut uirtute ita uitiis superaret.' And the two anecdotes are grouped together under the heading of *patientia*; so that the moral in John's mind becomes evident. He is not here occupied with the question of justice in a king (he shows elsewhere that he thought Alexander unjust[3]), but with the question of self-control; and the two anecdotes are intended to show that Alexander was capable of great self-restraint. The pirate's remarks are not the less true—he speaks 'eleganter et uere', in John as in St Augustine—but their importance here is that they offer, as Antigonus' reproof offered, such an affront to the king as would not have been pardoned by a man less controlled than Alexander. It was a new emphasis; and with this citation of the story in the *Policraticus* the history of the anecdote divides into two streams. In the first tradition the emphasis is, as in St Augustine, upon the pirate's epigram, not necessarily treated as an individual attack upon Alexander, or leading to the conclusion reached by St Augustine upon the illegality of Alexander's empire. In the second the emphasis is concentrated upon the forbearance and kindness shown by Alexander in offering to change the man's fortune for him, and enrolling him among his own

---

[1] John of Salisbury, *Policraticus* III, xiv (ed. Webb, vol. I, p. 225).
[2] *Policraticus* III, xiv (ed. Webb, vol. I, pp. 224–5).
[3] See below, p. 104.

men—this when he has been subjected to an eloquent attack. The second tradition, since it is almost confined to exemplar and secular writers, is of less immediate importance to us.

In the first tradition, Tolomeo da Lucca, Vincent de Beauvais, and Guibert de Tournai reproduce the text of the story given by St Augustine;[16] the first adds the comment that it was for this reason that God transferred world empire from the Greeks to the Romans, and thus he attaches to the story the individual application to Alexander given it by St Augustine. All other citations, however, derive from John of Salisbury. Though this almost universal dependence upon the *Policraticus* version was common to both traditions, and necessary to the second, the pirate's speech, as it is given by John, is most stressed in the first tradition, while in the second it is the conclusion of the *Policraticus* narrative, the mercy shown by Alexander to Dionides, which receives the most attention.

Within the first tradition we may also place the insertion of the anecdote, in its *Policraticus* form, in various Alexander-books, where it is accepted merely as an unstressed passage of narrative;[17] and it was used, with emphasis upon St Augustine's moral, by Chaucer and Gower.[1] In Gower, as would be expected, the didactic element in the story is expanded into a lengthy passage; but in Chaucer it has lost all force of personal criticism, and is a witty remark made to Alexander without any personal application to him being intended:[1]

> To Alisaundre told was this sentence;
> That, for the tyrant is of gretter might,...
> Lo! therfor is he cleped a capitain;
> And, for the outlawe hath but smal meynee,...
> Men clepen him an outlawe or a theef.

The second form of the anecdote had its origins in the innovations of the *Policraticus* version, and seems to have had an especial vogue in Italy, where it occurred most frequently. I have included under this second tradition all those uses of the anecdote where there is a manifest emphasis upon the forbearance shown by Alexander.[18] Two such uses of the anecdote are of especial interest: that by Boccaccio, cited

---

[1] Chaucer, *The Manciple's Tale*, ll. 226–34 (ed. W. W. Skeat, *Works*, vol. IV, p. 562). Gower, *Confessio Amantis* III, ll. 2363 ff. (*English Works*, ed. Macaulay, vol. I, pp. 290 ff.).

in the notes, and that by François Villon in his *Testament*. The story is
here told at length:[1]

> L'empereur si l'araisonna:
> 'Pour quoy es tu larron de mer?'
> L'autre responce luy donna:
> 'Pour quoy larron me faiz nommer?
> Pour ce qu'on me voit escumer
> En une petiote fuste?
> Se comme toy me peusse armer,
> Comme toi empereur je fusse.

But Fortune is against him; so Alexander, when he has heard the
story, changes the pirate's fortune for him. And Villon comments:

> Se Dieu m'eust donné rencontrer
> Ung autre piteux Alixandre....

There can be no more striking example of the way in which the
morals of the Alexander anecdotes were constantly being altered during
the medieval period, generally, except in Germany, in a manner
favourable to Alexander, than in the story of Alexander and the pirate:
which in contrast to its first use by St Augustine to condemn the
injustice and thence the illegality of Alexander's empire, became a
signal instance of his mercy shown in his treatment of a malefactor.

3. MISCELLANEOUS REFERENCES TO ALEXANDER
IN MORALISTS TO THE FOURTEENTH CENTURY

Most of the material here gathered together is unimportant in its
effect upon the medieval moral conception of Alexander, which was,
in fact, established by the anecdotes which we have discussed. But it
is necessary at 'least to note the existence of references to other
material, both favourable and unfavourable to Alexander, in the
works of the earlier moralists.

(a) MISCELLANEOUS MATERIAL UNFAVOURABLE TO
ALEXANDER

(i) '*Victor uictus*', a rhetorical accusation

'The conqueror of all the world was conquered.' Comments based
upon this simple rhetorical pattern were eagerly manufactured by

---

[1] François Villon, *Le Testament* (*Œuvres*, ed. L. Thuasne (Paris, 1923), vol. I, pp. 181–2).

every scribbler who aspired to taste; they were made by the turn of a word or two to apply to whatever vice the writer had especially in mind, or to incidents in Alexander's life—the trickery of Candace, or the poison that killed him.[19] A similar turn of phrase—'he pressed upon the earth with his armies, now he is pressed upon by the earth' —was introduced into Europe in the scene of the philosophers gathered about Alexander's tomb; and was taken up by the author of the school-epigram found among the I³ interpolations of the *Historia de Preliis*.[20] These epigrams, dependent upon the simplest possible verbal play, will be seen from the references given to touch on many aspects of Alexander's life, character and death. How far they reflect the real opinion of their writers, and how far they show merely the desire to make a rhetorical play on words, is not clear.

(ii) *Alexander, women, and wine*

As Dr Tarn has pointed out,[1] one of the most unfair attacks upon Alexander in ancient historians was that upon his chastity; every sort of lie was invented to prove his lecherous incontinence, and these lies appear at their worst in the historical writers accessible to the Middle Ages, but they received no acknowledgement in the anecdotal tradition. The chroniclers of the Middle Ages naturally maintained the libels of Curtius, Justin and Orosius, but without comment; nor did their accounts of Alexander's amorous adventures come to be related outside their historical context. Thus it was that there was no deliberate medieval moral attack upon this aspect of Alexander's reputation before the time of Petrarch;[2] on the other hand, there was in John of Salisbury an overt recognition of Alexander's continence and political wisdom in sending back, untouched, a captive virgin betrothed to a barbarian prince.[3]

As has been seen, there are some rhetorical references to women's conquest of Alexander; but on the whole his reputation did not suffer until the attack of Petrarch, and until the courtly embroideries of the love passage between Alexander and Candace fell into the hands of

[1] See W. W. Tarn, *Alexander the Great*, II (Cambridge, 1948), App. 18, pp. 319–26.
[2] On Petrarch's attack see G. Cary, 'Petrarch and Alexander the Great', *Italian Studies*, v (1950), pp. 43–55.
[3] John of Salisbury, *Policraticus* v, vii (ed. Webb, I, pp. 309–10); the anecdote also occurs in the *Dialogus Creaturarum*, dial. 121: 'De homine et muliere' (ed. Grässe, *B.L.V.* vol. CXLVIII, p. 277).

moral poets.[1] In the late medieval period the anecdote of Campaspe who rode on Aristotle's back, blamed both Alexander and Aristotle impartially for their weakness in dealing with women; while the story of the poison-girl sent to Alexander showed him, if capable of lust, also capable of restraint, and added nothing decisive to the issue.

There were two especial instances of Alexander's addiction to wine which received attention from medieval moralists. The first was the fact that his love of wine was indirectly responsible for his murder, since the poison was introduced into his cup during a drunken orgy; this received due attention from rhetoricians and writers of epitaphs.[2] More important was the anecdote telling how Alexander sentenced a man one night in a drunken rage, and, when the man appealed next morning 'from Alexander drunk to Alexander sober', pardoned him. This incident was used by Giraldus Cambrensis[3] to show how Alexander was at bottom a just man, but was ruined by his vices, and thus to illustrate the Peripatetic viewpoint that is clearly to be perceived in the medieval picture of Alexander's attitude to women and to wine. There is something of pity in such comments, pity for the weak man who gave way to the strongest of all temptations. Wine and women were easily to be pardoned in the Middle Ages; only Petrarch could have no sympathy, and, in his abuse of Alexander for the burning of Persepolis, remarked that it was unpardonable '...tanta de re, Baccho et meretriculae paruisse'.[4]

But the earlier medieval moralists were content with but slight dispraise in their introduction of such rhetorical condemnations of Alexander.

(iii) *Miscellaneous unfavourable evidence*

In addition to those anecdotes already discussed, and those general topics treated below, there are various individual criticisms of Alexander, based upon rare anecdotes or upon the rarer expression of personal opinion, that need, in the interests of completeness, to be

---

[1] For the courtly and late medieval treatment of this question, see pp. 218–20, 231–3.

[2] See below, pp. 282–4, n. 19.

[3] Giraldus Cambrensis, *De Principis Instructione* I, xvii (*Opera*, vol. VIII, ed. Warner, pp. 58–9). Cf. Ranulph Higden, *Polychronicon* III, xxviii (ed. Lumby, vol. III, pp. 440–2). The story was of course originally told of Alexander's father Philip (see Valerius Maximus, VI, 2, ext. 1).

[4] Petrarch, *De Viris Illustribus*, ed. Razzolini, *Collezzione di Opere Inedite o Rare*, vol. I (Bologna, 1874), p. 122.

here catalogued. They refer to the characteristic vices of which Alexander was accused; his pride, ambition, envy and injustice.

The *Policraticus* of John of Salisbury well illustrates the point made at the beginning of this section, that it is impossible accurately to define the attitude of any given medieval moralist to Alexander before the time of Petrarch; we can only observe their importance as transmitters of material, and detect certain tendencies in the medieval interpretation of classical anecdotes. The *Policraticus* contained both favourable and unfavourable comment upon Alexander; but whereas the favourable material is scattered throughout the book, John's unfavourable criticism is almost wholly concentrated in one passage, where, after quoting stories illustrative of the sense of justice in Alexander and Pythagoras, and deciding in favour of the latter as the greater man: 'michi quidem semper (ut tamen pace eorum loquar, qui temeritatem uirtuti praeferunt) ditissimo Alexandro pauper Pitagoras maior erit',[21] he goes on to quote the well-known comparison made by Justin between Alexander and Philip, to which he subjoins a comment apparently his own:[1] the comment begins at 'Ast in uno...'

Quibus artibus orbis imperii fundamenta pater iecit, operis tanti gloriam filius consummauit. Ast in uno non modo patris sed omnium ingenuorum transcendit uitia, quod incontinentissimae fuit inuidiae, adeo ut etiam paterni triumphi ei lacrimas extorquerent ac si ei uirtus paterna omnium gerendorum praeriperet gloriam. Eos etiam aut propriis manibus interficiebat aut rapi praecipiebat ad penam, qui paternae uirtutis praeconia praedicabant.

John quotes elsewhere the well-known story (not so well known in the Middle Ages) of Alexander and Anaxarchus, and his bitter disappointment in learning that there were so many worlds to conquer, when he had not yet conquered one.

The same accusation of ambitious envy was taken up by Alexander Neckham, who showed, however, his profound admiration for Alexander in most respects, and considered it his only great vice. He said that Death took Alexander to show men that he was not a God,[2] a reference not to the Ammon episode, but to Alexander's superhuman endeavours.

---

[1] *Policraticus* v, xii (ed. Webb, vol. I, p. 336). Further on Justin's comparison between Philip and Alexander, see above, p. 87.

[2] Alexander Neckham, *De Naturis Rerum*, ed. by Thomas Wright (Rolls Series, 1863), p. 338.

A reproof supposed to have been administered to the boasting Alexander is cited by Giraldus Cambrensis:[1]

'Quid fui, quid sum, quid ero?' 'Vile sperma, uas stercorum, esca uermium.' Dicitur enim Alexandro Macedoni, gradatim ad dignitates ascendenti et inde iactanti ac glorianti, a Dionysio philosopho sic responsum fuisse.

The emphasis in this anecdote upon Alexander's decline into vice is but rarely paralleled in the early Middle Ages. We have shown that the individual characteristics of the Peripatetic portrait of Alexander were well known; but the Peripatetic account of his vicious deterioration after the conquest of Persia was not normally quoted except in texts immediately derived from Curtius. The reason for this, as has been previously stated, is the preference for a fixed anecdote, with an individual moral application, to an unanecdotal historical evolution, of interest only to the student of the development of personality. Although the group of 'uictor uictus' phrases contain the kernel of the Peripatetic attack, they are judgements upon the final effects of Alexander's decline, and not upon the history of it. The few places outside historical contexts where there is reference to this decline before the late Middle Ages are cited in the notes.[22]

A few further unfavourable comments may be added to this list,[23] but no detailed unfavourable criticism of Alexander appeared before the late Middle Ages; and from the scarcity and individual nature of these comments it is apparent that early unfavourable criticism was principally founded upon those popular anecdotes and anecdotal groups which have already been discussed, and which, by their greater weight and dissemination, are of far greater importance than the isolated condemnations here collected.

(b) MISCELLANEOUS MATERIAL FAVOURABLE TO ALEXANDER

The material under this head is so sparse and individual, that it cannot be arranged in any satisfactory grouping, nor can it be regarded as evidence of any weight in assessing the moral attitude to Alexander. It is almost entirely confined to the small group of humanistic writers represented by John of Salisbury and Giraldus Cambrensis; and is

---

[1] Giraldus Cambrensis, *De Principis Instructione*, praefatio prima (*Opera*, vol. VIII, ed. Warner, p. 5).

derived principally from Valerius Maximus, whose anecdotes are generally favourable to Alexander.

These anecdotes illustrate various aspects of Alexander's continence: his feeling for justice, his chastity, his humility, his trust in his friends, and other amiable qualities.[24] But such material was directly contradicted, and easily overborne in popularity, by the material derived from sources antagonistic to Alexander which we have discussed, and which could be used to point a series of completely contrasting conclusions about Alexander's character. Outside the authors mentioned the influence of this favourable material was negligible, and hardly extended beyond the *Dialogus Creaturarum* which borrowed much of its material from the *Policraticus*. In the later Middle Ages, when the anecdotes derived from Cicero, Seneca and Oriental sources were widely known, this material remained unextracted from the *Policraticus*, and though we may see no deliberate intention in this neglect of evidence favourable to Alexander, it is obvious that the anecdotes of Valerius Maximus were not so popular as those derived from other sources, since their only easy transmission to unlearned medieval authors lay through the *Policraticus*, whereas the anecdotes of Cicero and Seneca, and other unfavourable material, were made known not only through the popularity of the classical authors in which they appear, but also through their quotation in the works of the Fathers, their rapid circulation through books of *exempla*, and their incorporation into legendary texts.

The list of all instances found in which this favourable material is used before the fourteenth century shows clearly that such use is restricted to a few anthologists.

4. ALEXANDER'S PREMATURE DEATH, AND THE QUESTION OF MONARCHY AND EMPIRE

Alexander's early death, at a time when it seemed that nothing could stop him achieving his heart's desire, has always been a subject for earnest reflexion, coloured for Christian moralists by the consideration of its cause and its effect, for writers of *exempla* by a musing upon the futility of all human effort in the face of death, and for the secular writer by regret at the death of so noble a warrior.[1]

[1] For reflexions upon Alexander's death in exemplar and secular writers, see pp. 151–2, 189–95.

Certainly so premature and unforeseen a death argued, to medieval moralists, some direct intervention of God, an intervention that was easily enough explained by Alexander's intolerable vices. But there was a reason more urgent because it was dogmatic to assume such intervention. This was the coincidence in time of the foundation of the Empire by Augustus and of the Church by Jesus, which established the opinion that God ordained it should be so. It followed that, before the Roman Empire, there could have been no Empire and no true Monarchy, a belief which necessarily involved the depreciation of Alexander's achievements.

To medieval thinkers, therefore, beyond the personal moral causes of Alexander's premature death to be found in his evident imperfections, there was frequently a clear connexion of that death with the wide doctrinal reason, that God prevented him from achieving world empire because the time was not yet come. Four causes were directly adduced by medieval moralists for Alexander's death, and in certain cases some comment is added upon God's purpose in depriving him of Empire in favour of the Romans. The four reasons given were:

(i) His injustice, as it was illustrated by the story of the Pirate,[1] to which Tolomeo da Lucca added the comment: 'Ista ergo ratione Romanis a Deo collatum fuit dominium.'[2] This view was also in the mind of John of Salisbury, when he wrote that God deprived an unjust king of heirs to his dominion, and cited the example of Alexander.[3]

(ii) His ambition and his consequent envy of others was suggested by Alexander Neckham as the reason for his death;[4] death took him to show the world that he was not immortal, nor a God. This may be compared with the view that his fate was due to his presumptuous arrogance in allowing himself to be worshipped as the son of Ammon; a view which was especially prevalent in the later Middle Ages.[5]

(iii) The rational reason of treachery assisted by drunkenness was generally brought forward by writers upon kingship, concerned with

---

[1] For St Augustine's use of this anecdote, see pp. 95–6.
[2] Thomas Aquinas (Ptolemaeus Lucensis), *De Regimine Principum* III, v (ed. Mathis, p. 48).
[3] John of Salisbury, *Policraticus* IV, xii (ed. Webb, vol. I, p. 276): 'Quis Alexandro maior in Grecia? Et tamen non suus legitur successisse sed filius saltatricis.'
[4] Alexander Neckham, *De Naturis Rerum* (ed. Wright, p. 338).
[5] See below, pp. 115–16.

the threat of treachery, the need for continence in all things, and the troubles that surround a king.[1]

(iv) Dante, satisfied with the glorious fact of the simultaneous establishment of Church and Empire by God's forethought, does not linger over any explanation of why God deprived Alexander of monarchy; he merely accepts the happy truth as evidence of God's intention to make perfect the coincidence of the spiritual and the temporal monarchy.[25]

The nature of these explanations of Alexander's untimely end is important if they are contrasted with the secular theories upon the subject. It will be seen that moralists, seeking a reason for God's intervention, found it in Alexander's faults, while secular writers were to find a cause for his death in the variability of Fortune, in God's determination to remove Alexander to a greater glory, or in the conspiracy of traitors against him.

But in spite of the reasons given for the cutting-off of Alexander before he had achieved monarchy, he was occasionally described as a monarch in medieval writers;[26] and considering the size of his empire, and the supposed weakness of those peoples who remained unconquered, it is not surprising that many should have chosen to think of him as a monarch even if he did not achieve the solitary dominion of the Romans.

5. ALEXANDER AND ARISTOTLE

The writing of philosophic treatises upon government for the benefit of contemporary rulers, the secluded dictation of cloistered monks to their royal patrons upon the administration of affairs, was a popular occupation in the Middle Ages, and sometimes not un-connected with the prospect of consequent advancement; so that there may be contained among the moral precepts a judicious portion of flattery, aimed at the exaltation of the writer by the exaltation of his patron.

It is with the view of Alexander expressed in works of this type that we are now concerned. The *Secret of Secrets* is evidently the most

---

[1] Medieval comments upon the treachery that brought Alexander to his death are grouped below, pp. 315–17. For comments upon his drunkenness, and the part it played in bringing him to his death, see pp. 282–3.

important document that might have influenced this conception, since it is itself a work supposedly written by the greatest of philosophers for the greatest of princes, and since for Aristotelian writers it became the model of works upon government.[27] And the attitude towards Alexander which we are here to consider is that which is reflected in the circumstances under which the *Secret of Secrets* was supposed to have been composed; it is the attitude of the philosopher, or the learned writer anxious to achieve recognition, towards a king who listened to the counsels of the greatest philosopher so willingly that he ordered all his dominions by the advice of Aristotle, and asked the latter to write him a book on true government. It is Alexander's reverence for letters and for learning that is most considered in these authors, who hope to impress their patron by their own words of wisdom, or to receive some tangible reward for their celebration of his greatness.

There are here three motifs which, while they are founded on such immediate considerations, belong to every writer who considers his dignity as a writer, and every philosopher who wishes to advise a king. The first is the importance of a tutor to a king as demonstrated by the example of Alexander and Aristotle; the second is the necessity, if a prince is to preserve his fame, that he shall surround himself with a circle of learned writers; and the third is the praise of Alexander as a learned prince, and one who encouraged learning in other men.

The first of these points is not only evident in the *Secret of Secrets* (and explicitly in the episodes there recorded of the treatment of conquered Persia,[1] and the girl sent to Alexander by the Queen of the North[2]), but also in other legendary material; the story of the basilisk,[3] and the interpretation of the Wonderstone,[4] besides numerous

---

[1] This incident was used by Guibert de Tournai, *Eruditio regum et principum* (ed. A. de Poorter (*Les Philosophes Belges*, IX, Louvain, 1914)), p. 68; further references to separate articles of advice given by Aristotle to Alexander in the *Secret of Secrets* occur in the *Disciplina Clericalis* (ed. A. Hilka and W. Soederhjelm (*Sammlung mittellat. Texte*, I, Heidelberg, 1911), pp. 10, 37), in the *Gesta Romanorum* (see p. 302).

[2] On the history of the story of the poison-girl see W. Hertz, 'Die Sage vom Giftmädchen', *Gesammelte Abhandlungen* (Stuttgart and Berlin, 1905), pp. 156–277. See also below, p. 231.

[3] For the basilisk episode, which was used in the I³ *Historia de Preliis* and in the *Gesta Romanorum*, see W. Hertz, loc. cit. pp. 192 ff., and F. Pfister, in *Münchener Museum*, I (1912), p. 265.

[4] The best survey of the history of the Wonderstone story is by Hertz, *Ges. Abh.*, pp. 73–130. See also below, pp. 149–51, 347.

inverted adjurations and counsels of Aristotle that are scattered throughout the various Alexander-books.[28] Yet most of this material is Oriental in ultimate origin, and it is noticeable that it is in the antique and the Oriental traditions that the importance of Aristotle's tutorship is most stressed. He is revered in the Western legends, but he is something of a philosophic figurehead, without real effect upon the career of Alexander; and in the *Lai d'Aristote* he becomes a burlesque figurehead.[1] The separation of learned from secular tradition upon this point has been well demonstrated by Hertz's researches into the number of tutors who are supposed to have supervised Alexander's education.[2] Among the Alexander-books it is only in the *Alexandreis* and similar works drawing on older or on moral tradition that Aristotle becomes the only, or even the chief, tutor. In the works of writers upon government, however, as would be expected, Aristotle stands as the philosopher who controlled Alexander's destinies, and the relationship between the king and the philosopher is frequently referred to in learned admonition, more frequently as the Middle Ages became more familiar with the *Secret of Secrets*.[29]

Beside the emphasis upon the importance of having a tutor, we may place the use of the story of the murder of Callisthenes which takes on in works of this type the moral that one should not murder tutors.[30] The emphasis in the Callisthenes episode is here individual and professional. Not here, as in Petrarch and his followers, popular moralists with a foot in the pulpit, is it the aim to demonstrate Alexander's horrible folly, the excess of vanity that led him to so great a crime, but rather to show that sudden anger, and especially anger against a tutor, is undesirable; and that outspokenness in tutors may also be undesired. The Oriental tradition of Aristotle, the tutor whom Alexander obeyed and who always counselled Alexander, and the Peripatetic tradition of Callisthenes, the philosopher sent by Aristotle to teach Alexander and murdered because his counsel was unwelcome, are scarcely compatible, but neither tradition was challenged.

Nor should a prince only have a philosopher to advise and educate him; he should also have philosophical writers of history to com-

---

[1] For the well-known story of Alexander, Aristotle, and Campaspe or Phyllis, see below pp. 231–2.
[2] See W. Hertz, *Ges. Abh.*, pp. 1–33.

memorate him. The prologue to the *Policraticus* of John of Salisbury:[1] 'Quis enim Alexandros sciret aut Caesares, quis Stoicos aut Peripateticos miraretur, nisi eos insignirent monimenta scriptorum?' is typical of an attitude which was especially illustrated by Alexander's famous remarks at the tomb of Achilles, his envy of Achilles that he found so great a poet to celebrate his deeds. The most famous medieval echo of this is in a sonnet of Petrarch's to Laura:

> Giunto Alessandro alla famosa tomba
> Del fero Achille, sospirando disse:
> O fortunato, che sì chiara tromba
> Trovasti, e chi di te sì alto scrisse.[2]

Generally such a statement or such an anecdote appears as an apology for the efforts of the writer, who commends himself by saying that he is conferring literary immortality upon his patron.[31] A pleasing contrast to this self-satisfied attitude is provided by the author of a life of St Martin: 'Postremo Alexandrum, Xersen, Augustum asseclasque eorum comparatione sui (S. Martinus) facit inglorios, dum illi a solis scholasticis recitantur, nec tamen laudantur, istius uero uirtutes ab uniuersa ecclesia memorantur, benedicuntur, et praedicantur.'[3]

But it is best of all that a king, besides surrounding himself with learned men, listening to their counsels and assuring himself of immortality in their panegyrics and histories, should himself be learned; and on this count also mention is made of Alexander, as an example of a learned prince. Giraldus Cambrensis, in his treatise *De Principis Instructione*, uses him as an example of a literary prince, and shows how learning profits a ruler;[4] Alexander Neckham admires his diligence in examining natural phenomena;[5] and many other instances may be cited.[32] The theme appears also in vernacular romance; in every medieval period Alexander's education was represented as including all those subjects which the imagination of the writer considered essential to the perfect prince; and in every case he learnt them well.

[1] John of Salisbury, *Policraticus*, Prologue (ed. Webb, I, p. 12, l. 17).

[2] Petrarch, *Sonetti in vita di Laura* CXXXV, vv. 1–4.

[3] Radbodus, *Libellus de miraculo S. Martini*, in *M.G.H. Scriptt.* xv, ii (1888), p. 1242, ll. 3–4.

[4] Giraldus Cambrensis, *De Principis Instructione* I (*Opera*, vol. VIII, ed. Warner, 1891, p. 7).

[5] Alexander Neckham, *De Naturis Rerum* (ed. Thomas Wright, pp. 141–2; cf. p. 403).

These, therefore, are certain additional elements which colour the conception of Alexander in writers upon government and in other humanistic writers. Like the troubadours, they hope for, if they are not dependent on, the liberality of princes, and therefore seek to impress upon them the value of learning, and the importance of its encouragement. But it would be vulgar and untrue to ascribe their attitude merely to ulterior motives—they are really interested in the importance of the message that they have to give to rulers, and uplifted by the thought that their writings may confer immortality.

Apart from this emphasis upon Alexander's relationship with learned men, and his attitude to learning, is it possible to reach any general conclusion upon the conception of Alexander formed by writers on kingship? For as they are in some sort specialists upon kings, their judgement might reasonably be expected to be at once more elaborate and more just than that of other classes of writers.

It is unfortunate that many of the works written upon kingship in the Middle Ages are as far removed from contact with the actual problems of government as possible, and are composed of quotations from the works of the Fathers and the Scriptures, dreamy theorizing on the ideal state, and platitudinous praise of Christian virtue. In the more considered and more worthy treatises the *Secret of Secrets*, and the definition of an ideal prince contained in it, had a great and lasting influence which began to be felt in the middle of the thirteenth century. But this work had more influence upon general moral judgements than upon any especial consideration of Alexander, who occupies almost as negligible a position in it as the prince to whom any medieval treatise on government was dedicated; and thus these writers' conception of Alexander was inevitably derived—apart from the separate issue of Alexander's regard for learning—from the usual learned sources. And even in that separate issue the *Secret of Secrets* supplied only the fact and the supposed reason for Aristotle's instruction; the tradition of Alexander's interest in learning was chiefly derived from Pliny the Elder, and from the legendary text of Alexander's *Letter to Aristotle*, which gave evidence of such interest in natural history.

These were men of the same learning and the same approach to moral questions as those we have already discussed; it is only that here we are concerned with questions affecting Alexander not as a man, but as a king; and the authors' object is the determination of the nature of true kingship. Where such writers have indulged in usual moral consideration of Alexander they conform to the general tone of learned opinion. They are independent only in so far as they have access to the *Secret of Secrets*, and its portrait of Alexander listening to Aristotle, the perfect relationship of the king and his tutor.

6. ALEXANDER, THE ORACLE OF AMMON, AND CALLISTHENES

We have now to consider the attitude of medieval writers to those incidents on which Stoics and Peripatetics alike based their hatred of Alexander: the interview with the oracle of Ammon, the murder of Cleitus, and the murder of Callisthenes for resisting Alexander's wish to be treated as a god.[33]

This is not an anecdote, but a passage in the life of Alexander; and thus it is impossible to attack the question of its transmission according to previous methods, and to trace its reception as we may trace the moral accorded to a single anecdote. In the form in which it reached the Middle Ages, this train of incidents was linked together in the following order: Alexander goes to the oracle of Ammon, and hears the priest (Justin: after having bribed the oracle) permit his companions (Justin: order his companions) to worship him as a god, the son of Ammon. This deification accentuates Alexander's arrogance; and from it there results indirectly the murder of Cleitus, for comparing Alexander disparagingly with Philip, and the murder of Callisthenes, for advising Alexander against exacting the worship accorded to an Oriental monarch; a murder which is made worse by the fact that Callisthenes had prevented Alexander from committing suicide over the death of Cleitus. He is subjected to lingering tortures, from which he is finally delivered by Lysimachus who gives him the means of committing suicide.[34]

The visit to the oracle of Ammon was to ancient philosophers a turning-point in Alexander's career, an episode of far greater importance than those isolated anecdotal interviews that were quoted by medieval moralists. But before the fourteenth and fifteenth centuries, the story of Alexander's visit to the oracle, the prologue to the story of Cleitus and Callisthenes, was not quoted outside its historical context in the chronicles. The reasons for this silence of the learned are to be found in the nature of the material, and are twofold.

First, why should the story of the visit to the oracle have been cited? Its importance in the deterioration of Alexander's character and its place as the ultimate cause of the murder of Callisthenes are an insufficient answer to the question. We have seen how rarely material from the historians themselves was excerpted for medieval use; anecdotal material was taken, not from the accessible narratives, but from previous excerpts, from Seneca and Cicero through the medium of patristic writers, and from Valerius Maximus. Both these authors and medieval writers chose their anecdotes upon a reasonable principle, that they should bear a general application, and that they should have some sort of intrinsic interest. This episode has, considered by itself, neither of these qualities. What does it say? that Alexander bribed the priests of Ammon to salute him as a god. What does that imply? that Alexander bribed the priests of Ammon to recognize him as a god. What is its moral? that one should not bribe priests to recognize one as a god—this is the only direct moral. This *reductio ad absurdum* shows that the episode is properly only an incident in an historical progression; as Lessing says of the Laocoön, it is the turning-point that teaches us nothing. The indirect consequence, Alexander's punishment for setting himself up as a god, has a moral, and is remembered; but the mere fact of the recognition of his divinity has only the individual and momentary application that is of no service to the moralist. It was therefore rejected by Cicero, Seneca (who ought to have relished it), and Valerius Maximus, and after them by the medieval moralists.

Secondly the preachers, the compilers of books of *exempla*, and such lesser thinkers were further discouraged from reproducing the passage by the stories known to them which represented Alexander as refusing divine honours. One such anecdote, quoted by Seneca from Quintus Curtius, in which Alexander, when he has been wounded, says that the pain of his wound proves him to be no god, was known to the writers of *exempla*.[1] Another is his well-known reply to the Persians who offered him divine honours, which would

[1] See below, pp. 152-3.

III

be known to any reader of the legend;[1] a third is his reply to the Gymnosophists;[2] and a fourth is the reverent attitude of Alexander to God in Josephus,[3] and to a different God in the *Dicts and Sayings*.

These two reasons together account for the uselessness of the Ammon episode as a moral or exemplar anecdote. But there were more possibilities in the murder of Callisthenes, which did, in fact, have a limited independent existence as an anecdote. And this is as easily explained for the merely textual reason that Valerius Maximus used it,[35] and John of Salisbury borrowed it,[4] and for the subjective reason that it shows the contrast between the philosopher and the tyrant—and the philosopher happened to be a protégé of Aristotle, and after his death of the Peripatetic propagandists.

The fullest account of the murder of Callisthenes available to the Middle Ages was in Quintus Curtius.[5] As the incident stands in Justin, we are merely told that Callisthenes was put to death with certain Macedonian nobles for refusing to adore Alexander as a god,[6] although, at a later stage of his narrative, when no longer dealing with the life of Alexander, Justin returned to the death of Callisthenes and described the gruesome tortures to which he was subjected.[7] In Orosius the episode appeared as in the first account of Justin.[8]

This episode, circulated by Peripatetic pamphleteers, did Alexander more harm than any other. From his own time it alienated from him the sympathy of philosophers who felt that a philosophical preceptor, if anyone, should be free from the anger of a tyrant. While no one could rebuke Alexander for his treatment of Diogenes, Dindimus or Dionides, here was a glaring example of his blind vanity, of his refusal to listen to reason and of his cruelty.

The early medieval chronicles, all founded upon Justin and Orosius, reproduce the narrative in which the murder of Callisthenes is dismissed in a sentence. Thus Ekkehart of Aura wrote, following

---

[1] J. Valerius II, 39 (ed. Kuebler, p. 110).

Historia de Preliis II, 22 (ed. Pfister, *Alexanderroman*, p. 100, ll. 23–5): 'Nolo, ut exhibeatis mihi honorem sicut diis, quia corruptibilis et mortalis ego sum. Dubito enim sociare me diis.'

[2] See below, p. 148.   [3] See below, pp. 125–30.

[4] John of Salisbury, *Policraticus* VIII, 14 (ed. Webb, vol. II, p. 333).

[5] The story of the alleged conspiracy, and the subsequent death of Callisthenes, is in Quintus Curtius VIII, v, 5–viii, 23.

[6] Justin XII, vii, 2.   [7] Justin XV, iii, 3–6.

[8] Orosius III, xviii, 11.

Orosius, but omitting the reason given by Orosius for Callisthenes' murder:

Alexander...sanguinem siciens. Unde non solum de extraneis, sed de suis quoque multos occidit, inter quos Amintam consobrinum, Clytum quoque annis grauem et amicicia sibi coniunctum, Callistenen etiam phylosophum sibique apud Aristotilem condiscipulum, cum plurimis regni principibus.[36]

Here the murder of Callisthenes is made to appear, without any reason given, as an example of Alexander's bloodthirsty cruelty. It will be noticed that the name of Cleitus is already closely connected with that of Callisthenes; later this connexion is insisted upon, the events are brought into sequence, and the Cleitus episode made to blacken still further Alexander's murder of Callisthenes.

The story of Callisthenes did not follow the commonest anecdotal route because it appeared only in Valerius Maximus, among classical moralists and anthologists known to medieval writers. It appears in the Middle Ages as an anecdote for the first time in the *Policraticus*, and in an interesting context. The episode does not illustrate vanity or cruelty, but the 'praeceps nobilitas' and 'concitatum ingenium' of noble youths, which should be kept in check by a tactful tutor. John says of Callisthenes that he was sent to Alexander by Aristotle with instructions that he should be cautious and discreet with Alexander: 'At ille, dum Alexandrum Persica salutatione exultantem obiurgat et mores eius studet componere, uita priuatus est.'[1]

This is therefore a moral of quite a different type; it demonstrates the care that tutors should take in their dealings with kings. John of Salisbury introduces the anecdote as a piece of political advice; and from him its history in political writings may be traced through Guibert de Tournai,[2] who used it in the same way in his book on the education of princes, to Aeneas Syluius, who used it as a warning to learned men to keep away from courts, where there are always such lurking dangers.[37]

So far the Ammon episode has not been brought in, nor is the murder of Callisthenes seen in relation to Alexander's visit to the oracle. In the Orosian tradition the episode is an example of Alexander's vanity and cruelty; in the anecdotal field it appears as a warning

---

[1] John of Salisbury, loc. cit.
[2] Guibert de Tournai, *Eruditio Regum et Principum* (ed. de Poorter, p. 22).

to tutors not to try their kings too high. The question of προσκύνησις is given as the immediate reason for the murder of Callisthenes, but it is not linked to the story of the oracle of Ammon, nor is the emphasis upon Alexander's vanity in wishing to be so worshipped, but upon the folly of Callisthenes in being so indiscreet.

Gautier de Châtillon, true to his admiration for Alexander, keeps very quiet about the episode, dismisses it in a few lines, and adds to it a moral similar to that in Aeneas Syluius—the favour of princes does not last.[38] The first movement towards a stronger condemnation of Alexander for the murder of Callisthenes was in Vincent de Beauvais.[1] The reason given is Alexander's demand 'non salutari, sed adorari', and Vincent, with a good knowledge of Justin, mentions the tortures of Callisthenes for the first time in the Middle Ages, adds the story of Lysimachus thrown to the lions for his part in easing Callisthenes' torment, and connects with the murder of Callisthenes the previous murder of Cleitus, when Callisthenes had dissuaded Alexander from committing suicide in his subsequent gloomy repentance.

The change of phrase from 'Persica salutatio' to 'non salutari, sed adorari' is significant; προσκύνησις is beginning to be understood, not as an act of extreme obeisance to a monarch with divine honours, but as an act of worship to a man who wishes to be worshipped as a god, and specifically (though unhistorically) as the son of Ammon. In the long historical narrative of Vincent de Beauvais some chain of supposed historical causation naturally appeared; and the episodes of Ammon, Cleitus, and Lysimachus were combined to place the murder of Callisthenes in a fictitious historical setting, as an act of extreme cruelty inspired by an insane vanity caused by Alexander's visit to the oracle of Ammon. It was the gradual evolution of the murder of Callisthenes from an isolated anecdote of special applica-tion to a link in an historical chain that blackened the case against Alexander by revealing, more clearly than appeared in such authors as John of Salisbury and Guibert de Tournai, the misunderstood cir-cumstances of that murder. Vincent de Beauvais heralded a period in which the Ammon incident first began to be known outside historical texts, and in which the character of Alexander was to suffer from the

---

[1] Vincent de Beauvais, *Speculum Historiale* IV, 33 (Ammon), 45 (Clitus), 46 (Callisthenes) (ed. Douai, 1624, pp. 126 and 129). Cf. Higden, *Polychronicon* III, 27, 28 (ed. Lumby, vol. III, pp. 420 and 446–8).

use of historical narrative in unhistorical writers. The age of anecdote had made way for the age of lengthy historical digression.

Petrarch is the first who, as an ardent follower of the Peripatetic portrait of Alexander, told the Callisthenes story in its full horror.[1] Alexander bribed the priests of Ammon in his insane pride; in the same wild fancy to be thought a god he condemned Callisthenes to a death delayed by lingering tortures—a sentence which was the more revolting and cruel because Callisthenes was his benefactor, not as his tutor alone but as the man who had dissuaded him from committing suicide after he had murdered Cleitus. This incident is cunningly brought in as an obituary comment upon Callisthenes, so that it may linger in the mind of the reader.

The historical scheme has now been accepted. Alexander's murder of Callisthenes is inspired by his mad vanity, which has made him desire to be worshipped as a god. The full lie now became widely known, and was told in detail by Walter Burley[2] and by Boccaccio,[3] from whom it passed through Laurent de Premierfait to Lydgate's *Fall of Princes*.[4] In Petrarch and in Lydgate we have a summary of the feelings aroused in the writer by this supposed truth, this combination of the Stoic accusation of arrogance consequent upon the visit to the oracle with the Peripatetic concentration upon the fate of Callisthenes: Alexander was a prey to all desires, and the worst of those desires was to be thought, or at least to be treated as if he were thought, a god. The policy in arrogating to oneself divine honours could never have been understood by men who regarded kingship as temporal and a king as a deputy holding the reins under God. And if political reasons were set aside, the vain blasphemy and the added horror of the martyrdom of so philosophic a tutor, were clear enough and damning enough.

Thus the combination of the various historical sources, and their introduction into unhistorical literature realized in the fourteenth and fifteenth centuries, caused the Stoic view to triumph over the original

---

[1] Petrarch, *De Viris Illustribus*, de Alexandro Macedone (ed. G. Razzolini, *Collezione di Opere Inedite o Rare* (Bologna, 1874), I, pp. 126 ff.). Cf. G. Cary, 'Petrarch and Alexander the Great', *Italian Studies*, V (1950), pp. 43 ff.

[2] W. Burley, *De Vita ac Moribus Philosophorum* LXVI (ed. H. Knust, *B.L.V.* vol. CLXXVII (Tübingen, 1886), pp. 278–80).

[3] G. Boccaccio, *De Casibus Virorum Illustrium* IV (Paris, Jean Gourmont and Jean Petit, n.d.), f. xxxvii^v to f. xxxviii^v.

[4] John Lydgate, *Fall of Princes* IV, vv. 1109–1421. See on this passage below, p. 257.

Jewish view of Alexander's relationship with God. Alexander was no longer quoted as an example of the reverence in which all, even pagan, kings approached the Jewish God, but as an example of a hideous blasphemer who wished himself to be worshipped as a god. Alexander's blasphemous pride was consequently argued by late medieval moralists as the cause of his death, and in the later editions of the French translation of the *Dicts and Sayings*, we find a contemporary tag attached to that portrait of a reverent and venerable Alexander: 'Plusieurs bons enseignemens et doctrines donna Alexandre, mais enfin il fut deceu par haine et mondaine gloire, car il se souffri adorer comme Dieu et filz de Jupiter Hammon.'[39] The focus had changed; it was no longer the drunkenness, or the injustice, of Alexander that brought him to his death, but his shocking blasphemy —a Stoic accusation become Christian.

Thus the Callisthenes episode comes gradually to be attached to its supposed historical concatenation, to the bribing of the priests of Ammon, the murder of Cleitus, and the savage punishment of Lysimachus, and evolves from an unconnected act of cruelty into the climax of a cruel blasphemy. In the second, minor chain of development it becomes an admonitory anecdote in the hands of writers upon government, 'Keep out of the hands of princes', or (to the princes), 'Don't torture tutors.' Finally it becomes a piece of advice to men aspiring to become courtiers—like Mr Punch's advice to those about to marry—Don't!

7. SUMMARY

In this section it has been seen how the material upon which the ancient moral attack on Alexander was based survived into the medieval period not so much in historical narrative excerpts as in the anecdotes borrowed from Seneca, Valerius Maximus and others. But this persistence of the fundamental material was not, at least before the fourteenth century, paralleled by a similar persistence in the morals attached. The Callisthenes episode was lightly treated, the criticism of Seneca lost all its force, and while the morals of the Diogenes and Dindimus episodes were textually retained, it is evident that the ancient philosophic attack on Alexander lost much of its fervour in the twelfth and thirteenth centuries.

But it must be remembered that the writers concerned formed only a very limited section of medieval society, and that the men most likely to use anecdotal material on a large scale in this period (and especially that material which did not reach them through the intermediacy of the Fathers of the Church, but was borrowed direct from classical authors) were precisely those who could be expected to take a moderately enlightened view of Alexander: the humanistic writers of the twelfth and thirteenth centuries who took some interest in personality, John of Salisbury, Giraldus Cambrensis, and others to whom the study of pagan antiquity made the same appeal. In this small literary group the morals attached to the anecdotes of Alexander were somewhat discounted, but they made this material known to other writers of a less humanistic approach, and their role, considered against the whole medieval background, was that of transmitting most of the material upon which the unfavourable late medieval view of Alexander was founded.

Considered from the standpoint of its regional distribution, use of this moral anecdotal material during the twelfth and thirteenth centuries was almost confined to England and France. The earliest Italian moralist to use it was Brunetto Latini, and when the anecdotes reached Germany in the later Middle Ages, they reached it not through the direct intermediacy of moralists, but through those books of *exempla* and vernacular story-books which had received, adapted and retransmitted that material.

II

THE CONCEPTION OF ALEXANDER
IN THEOLOGIANS AND MYSTICS

1. INTRODUCTION

WE have already considèred the reaction to Alexander of those theological writers who cite moral anecdotes; we have now to discuss those writers who comment upon the passages in the Bible and in Josephus relating to Alexander, and the reflexion of their attitude in other theological literature. These are two different kinds of writer. While the theologians who use anecdotal sources reveal some smattering of humanistic learning, and therefore of humanistic interest, those who interpret the Scriptures are for the most part absorbed in mystical contemplation. They also differ from one another in the sources used, as has been shown. And finally they differ in their view of the sins of a man. For the moralists examine the question of sin with understanding, if not with sympathy; they attempt to find the reason for it and the cure for it. But in the allegorical disquisitions of Biblical interpreters men become types, and thus, if the mind of the commentator first seizes upon a man as sinful he becomes a sinful type; and his sins are not discussed but are taken for granted, as the part of the symbol that makes the symbol. Thus preconceived ideas of Alexander's character become the most important factor in the emergence of the theological approach and the tendency is not, as in the moralists, towards the alteration and alleviation, but rather towards the typification and aggravation, of accepted moral strictures.

The key to this approach to Alexander lies in the view of him as a figure in world history, as the originator of an epoch and the creator of an empire which was eventually to give Antiochus his dominion over the Jews. Such a view involved, not the consideration of isolated philosophic encounters of Alexander, but the portrait of the all-conquering tyrant whose career was foreseen by Daniel, and summarized in Maccabees. Therefore the theologians went back to the historical texts for the amplification of their portrait of the historical Alexander; and especially to Orosius, who had himself presented such a portrait of Alexander in the succession of world history, and whose work was an invaluable and almost inevitable source for all later chronicle writers. Thus those theological accounts of Alexander which we have now to describe were founded upon Orosius' condemnation of Alexander in the supposed light of Scriptural allegorical interpretation.

Orosius did not spare Alexander, rather he carried the Stoic abuse of him to its last extreme for the benefit of his Christian readers. For him Alexander was a ruthless, blood-thirsty conqueror fired by his insane love of glory in battle. At much the same period we find the same view in Fulgentius, who combined Orosius with Julius Valerius in a vituperative attack on Alexander which was the first to be based on a combination of history and legend, and which has, apparently, been neglected by Alexander scholars. These two authors considered Alexander as the ruthless destroyer of Persia; but the later commentaries upon his life in the Orosian tradition were so bound up with the course of Jewish history and with the Scriptural references to Alexander, that they must be examined in close conjunction with the latter group of important texts and the deductions that were made from them.

2. MEDIEVAL COMMENTARY UPON THE PROPHECY OF DANIEL

The two important references to Alexander in the Bible occur in Daniel and Maccabees. The first was interpreted as a prophecy of his coming and of his destruction of the Persian Empire; the other gives a brief narrative of his career of conquest as a prelude to the deeds of his disreputable successor Antiochus.[40] These two passages were connected in the minds of Scriptural commentators and in the minds of their readers by the similarity in both texts of the aspect of Alexander's career considered. In both it is his conquests that interest the writer, and in both the account of Alexander serves only to introduce that of Antiochus, whose acts were of greater significance in Jewish history. The commentaries upon these passages, however, cannot be studied together, since the references to Alexander in Daniel are couched in prophetic and mystical language, and therefore demanded from the first a factual interpretation; while the narrative in Maccabees is historical fact, and was therefore interpreted allegorically by the twelfth-century mystics.

Alexander appears in two allegories in the book of Daniel, in the first as the third of the Four Beasts, a leopard with four wings and four heads, and in the second as a he-goat who attacks the ram with two horns and overcomes him, breaking his horns. The first writer of importance upon these passages was St Jerome, who offered an interpretation which was almost invariably upheld by later commentators, since it is a simple matter of the interpretation of prophecy, and not, as in Maccabees, a question of finding an apposite symbolism.[41]

When Alexander appears as the leopard, his four wings are interpreted as symbolic of the swiftness of his career of conquest, while the four heads are his four successors; as the goat, he attacks Darius, the Ram whose two horns represent his two empires of Media and Persia, and destroys his might. These two prophetic passages, in conjunction with a later reference to the king of Greece who shall come to destroy Persia, are of very great importance in the theological conception of Alexander, for they might only be interpreted as St Jerome interpreted them: Alexander's conquests were due not to his own power but to the will of God.

That the interpretation of these passages in St Jerome has always represented the orthodox view of Scriptural commentators is shown by an interesting passage in the editorial commentary on Dexter Chronologus, who wished to substitute for the usual interpretation of the Four Beasts an astonishing theory of his own which made them represent four invaders of Spain, the Alans, the Vandals, the Suevians and the Goths. The editor gives the following list of commentators who had supported the orthodox view:

> Strauerunt uiam caeteris uetustiores Patres, quos in prologo Danielis cum Eusebio Caesariensi refert sanctus Hieronymus, Theodoretus, Beda, Rupertus: secutique sunt eorum uestigia Albertus Magnus, Hugo Carensis, Lyranus, et recentiores omnes, Hector Pintus, Pereira, Cornelius de Lapide, et alii.[1]

[1] Flauius Lucius Dexter Chronologus, *In Prophetiam Danielis de quatuor animalibus* (Migne, P.L. vol. XXXI, col. 577.

Of later commentators, Peter the Archdeacon reproduces in an abridged form the interpretation of St Jerome,[1] and the *Glossa Ordinaria* formerly attributed to Walahfrid Strabo borrows it.[2] Rupert of Deutz interprets the leopard as representing not Alexander himself, but the kingdom of Macedonia.[42]

References to the use of the prophecies of Daniel in learned and secular works alike could be easily multiplied,[43] but it is noticeable that they were more quoted in Germany than elsewhere, a fact in keeping with that German preoccupation with Alexander's Biblical position which will become increasingly apparent.

3. MEDIEVAL INTERPRETATION OF THE OPENING VERSES OF I MACCABEES

The medieval commentaries upon the opening verses of the first book of Maccabees have been completely neglected by Alexander scholars, although they are of great interest, not only for the light that they throw upon the theological attitude to Alexander, but for the study in medieval symbolism that they provide. I Maccabees opens with a very brief description of Alexander's military career, telling how all nations stood in fear of him, how his Empire was divided after his death, and how the Jews eventually passed under the jurisdiction of the Seleucid Antiochus, the enemy and persecutor of the Maccabees and their followers.[3] In this narrative Alexander is mentioned merely because he is the most important historical predecessor of Antiochus.

Antiochus, as the persecutor of the Jews, became from the early days of Scriptural allegory separated from his chronological setting, and appeared as the conventional type of Antichrist,[4] as did the Maccabees as types of the faithful Christian. Thus he is of the lineage of the Devil: 'Isti (septem pueri) Deum Patrem colunt, ille diabolum: isti uenerantur legem patriam, ille contra Deum rebellans, filium se fatetur esse diaboli.'[5] This quotation from St Gaudentius is a reasonable

---

[1] Petrus Archidiaconus, *Quaestiones in Danielem Prophetam* (Migne, *P.L.* vol. XCVI, col. 1353, the leopard; col. 1355, the goat.

[2] Walahfrid Strabo, *Glossa Ordinaria*; see the note in Migne, *P.L.* vol. CXIV, cols. 63–4.

[3] I Maccabees i, 1 ff.

[4] For references to Antiochus as Antichrist, see Migne, *P.L.* vol. XXV, col. 568; vol. LXXVI, col. 651; vol. CLXIX, col. 1069.

[5] St Gaudentius Brixiensis, *Sermo* XV (Migne, *P.L.* vol. XX, col. 949 B).

exposition of the theme of Maccabees; Alexander is here only the remote historical predecessor of Antiochus and plays no part in the development of the allegory.

A longer account of Alexander in connexion with Maccabees was given by Sulpicius Severus;[1] but it was a strictly historical account, an expansion of the facts briefly stated in the Maccabees passage. This historical tradition in commentary was also followed by Rhabanus Maurus;[2] he was one of those who gave symbolic significance to everything that could bear, and much that could not bear, such an interpretation, but he did not allegorize Alexander. Instead he found in the mention of Alexander an opportunity for a display of learning, and so gave a longer description of Alexander's life than any previous commentator, an historical account based on Orosius and passages of Justin. He follows his authorities fairly closely, the military career of Alexander is his main preoccupation, and stress is laid upon the blood-thirsty nature of his campaigns in true Orosian style. The prophecy of Daniel is placed at the head of the account, and a significant comment is added, that the will of God protected Alexander from death on the field.

In that last scene of the dying Alexander's final interview with his soldiers, Rhabanus allows something of admiration to appear in his account:[3]

> Cumque lacrymarentur omnes, ipse non sine lacrymis tantum, uerum sine ullo tristioris mentis argumento fuit, ut quosdam impatientius dolentes consolatus sit, quibus mandata ad parentes eorum dedit, adeo sicut in hoste, ita et in morte inuictus ei animus fuit.

Rhabanus stresses the fact that Alexander did not leave his dominions divided among several successors, but that the division followed his death, and he concludes with an apology for the digression:[4]

> Haec autem quia in historia Machabaeorum regni Alexandri mentio facta est, ideo ex libris gentilium interposui, ut lector agnosceret non frustra uirtutem Alexandri enarrari, sed magnanimitate atque actione ipsum esse principium [sic. ?praecipuum].

Thus Rhabanus attempts no allegorical interpretation, and it is evident that he found much to admire in the history of Alexander,

---

[1] Sulpicius Seuerus, *Historia Sacra* II, 17 (Migne, *P.L.* vol. XX, col. 139).

[2] Rhabanus Maurus, *Commentaria in libros Machabaeorum* I, i (Migne, *P.L.* vol. CIX, cols. 1127–32).   [3] Migne, *P.L.* vol. CIX, col. 1131.   [4] Ibid.

and took much interest in the telling of the story. He admires his
'magnitudo animi';[1] and from the quotation from Daniel placed at
the head of his account, and his statement that Alexander was preserved in his wars by the will of God, it is apparent that he considers
Alexander in accordance with the official interpretation of Daniel, and
sees him as the Divine instrument of wrath against Darius, as the
robust fulfiller of a prophecy.

In setting the historical career of Alexander against a Biblical background, Rhabanus may be called the first representative of the
German school of learned writers upon Alexander, which was characterized by this attitude.[2]

Walahfrid Strabo reproduces the commentary of Rhabanus; and
there is no further substantial reference to the Maccabees text before
the commentary of Hildebert of Lavardin.[3] Hildebert, true to his
classical instincts, turned the story of the Maccabees into hexameters,
and treated the life of Alexander in the heroic style without committing himself to any opinion upon his character. After describing
the military exploits of Alexander, he cannot resist the temptation of
putting into his mouth a fine death-bed speech to his comrades, in an
heroic style full of classical reminiscence and directly recalling the
last speech in the *Alexandreis*:[4]

> Scio quod me uita relinquit;
> astra uolunt superi nostra uirtute tueri:
> me super astra ferunt, quia pro Ioue ponere quaerunt.
> Forsan ad incursus et tela Typhaea recursus
> Iuppiter expauit, qui me super astra uocauit.
> Si uos, o proceres! quoniam meus inclytus haeres
> aetatis tenerae non posset regna tenere,
> uos, uirtus quorum me collocat arce polorum,
> testor in haeredes.

---

[1] Ibid.   [2] See below, p. 141.
[3] Hildebertus Cenomannensis, *De Machabaeis Carmen* (Migne, *P.L.* vol. CLXXI, col. 1293 A).
[4] Ibid.: cf. *Alexandreis* X (Migne, *P.L.* vol. CCIX, col. 571):

> Summum deinceps recturus Olympum,
> Ad maiora uocor; et me uocat arduus aether,
> Ut solium regni, et sedem sortitus in astris
> Cum Ioue disponam rerum secreta, breuesque
> Euentus hominum, superumque negotia tractem.
> Rursus in aethereas arces, superumque cohortem,
> Forsitan Aetnaeos armat praesumptio fratres;
> Et dura Encelado laxauit membra Pelorus.

And, in contrast to the account given by Rhabanus, Alexander divides his kingdom among several successors. There is here no suggestion of Christian sentiment, only admiration for Alexander as an heroic figure, if not as a desirable character, and the love of school rhetoric.

With the twelfth century, however, there comes an abrupt departure from the earlier practice of giving a simple historical commentary upon these verses of Maccabees in the interpretation given by Hugh of St Victor. In his *Allegoriae in Vetus Testamentum* (if the passage in question is indeed by him) he introduced an original and important symbolic interpretation of the Alexander of Maccabees:

> Machabaeorum fratrum felicia bella silentio non sunt relinquenda. Ipsorum namque certamina gloriosa sanctorum designant agones contra spirituales hostes eorum. Quis enim per Alexandrum Magnum, qui totum pene mundum subiugauit imperio suo, cum tanta erat donata dominandi libido, ut nulli in quantum potuit parceret regno; quis inquam, per illum significatur, nisi diabolus, qui dixit: 'In coelo conscendam; super astra Dei exaltabo solium meum, sedebo in monte testamenti in lateribus aquilonis, ascendam super altitudinem nubium, ero similis Altissimo'? Hic quippe per suam superbiam, et calliditatem, et multitudinem angelorum secum superbientium, et progeniem humani generis in primo parente sibi subiecit. Alexander moriens imperium suum satellitibus suis dimisit, et diabolus in aduentu Mediatoris Dei et hominum, hominis Christi Jesu, suum dominium minui uidens, impiis principibus praesentis saeculi suam malignitatem ad persequendum credentes inspirauit. Ex quibus exibit radix peccati rex Antiochus, filius perditionis Antichristus: qui quanto erit potentior, tanto erit ad persequendum perniciosior.[1]

Antiochus was always the descendant of the Devil, in his role of Antichrist; now the allegory is carried further, and Alexander, as the historical predecessor of Antiochus and the originator of that division of the empire which made him king of Syria, is become the Devil. Hugh holds to the tradition that Alexander left his kingdom divided among several successors and is the first to introduce, not only the interpretation of Alexander as the Devil, but the quotation from Isaiah in illustration of the passage.[2]

In Hugh the working out of a derogatory conception of Alexander in close connexion with the interpretation of Maccabees reaches its climax, though two contemporary accounts, those of Godfrey of

---

[1] Hugo de Sancto Victore, *Allegoriae in Vetus Testamentum* XI (Migne, *P.L.* vol. CLXXV, cols. 749–50 (among 'Exegetica Dubia')).
[2] Isaiah xiv, 13, 14.

Admont and Rupert of Deutz, represent the same opinion of Alexander disguised in allegory of such obscure interest as to require separate discussion.[1]

Peter of Riga in his *Aurora* gives merely an historical summary of Alexander's life;[2] but his unknown interpolator, Aegidius Diaconus, added an irrational interpretation—irrational when it is compared with the conventional interpretation of Antiochus—which he himself introduces later in the commentary; for he makes Alexander the type of Antichrist,[44] which is apparently the only place where such an interpretation occurs.

The trend first shown in the early dependence of commentators upon the Orosius tradition and its attitude to Alexander, reaches its climax in the twelfth century. It is evident that God's use of Alexander as his instrument, which admitted some form of purpose in Alexander's conquest of the world, was, though accepted by Rhabanus Maurus, not recognized by Hugh of St Victor and others of the extreme allegorical school; and that the commentators upon Maccabees, by their reliance upon the historical text of Orosius for the explanation of the historical text of Maccabees, treated Alexander as Orosius treated him, adding that symbolic typification which was usual in their age.

But though the prophecy of Daniel was here neglected, that prophecy is the centre-piece of the passages in Josephus which we have now to discuss, and therefore inevitably plays a large part in those adaptations of Josephus that were to bring his references to Alexander into line with the theologians' customary condemnation of him.

4. MEDIEVAL REACTION TO THE REFERENCES TO ALEXANDER IN JOSEPHUS

Daniel's picture of Alexander as an unwitting instrument of God's purpose to destroy the Persians accorded sufficiently well with the wicked tyrant sketched in Maccabees and described in the historical texts, and God's impersonal use of Alexander for His designs was perfectly to be reconciled with the accepted view of Alexander's

---

[1] See below, pp. 136–40.

[2] See M. Manitius, *Geschichte d. latein. Litt. im Mitt.* III (1931), p. 822; Peter's description of Alexander's life (cited p. 825) is a versification of the opening lines of Maccabees in six distichs.

character, though it provided some apology for his career of conquest, an apology distantly echoed in Alexander's own reply to the Gymnosophists. But Josephus introduced something of discord by his account of the working-out of the prophecy of Daniel in the career of Alexander as seen from a Jewish point of view; for he made God promise to Alexander, in a dream, the conquest of Persia, and work a miracle for him at the Pamphylian sea; and he made Alexander reverence God in His High Priest, and sacrifice in the Temple among the acclamations of the Jewish priesthood and people.

The reaction of medieval theologians to this Josephan material was downright and consisted in the attempt to confine Alexander as there portrayed within the limits of the unwitting instrument of Daniel's prophecies, to discredit or disguise the meaning of Josephus, and thus to reconcile the Jewish with the established theological and historical conception of Alexander. Thus the history of medieval comment upon the Josephan material consists in the explaining away of inconvenient evidence.

Before considering the principal passage in Josephus relating to Alexander which describes his visit to Jerusalem, we will discuss that in which he relates the miracle worked for Alexander at the Pamphylian sea, since this is of minor importance, and was easily brought into line with the usual conception of Alexander.

(a) ALEXANDER AND THE CROSSING OF THE PAMPHYLIAN SEA

Josephus tells how God parted the waters of the Pamphylian sea so that Alexander's troops might pass in pursuit of the Persians.[1] The only significant appearance of this episode in the Middle Ages is in the *Pantheon* of Godfrey of Viterbo, who comments upon it: 'quod miraculum aut ideo fuit, quia Alexander erat magnus Dei cultor, aut quia per eum Deus superbiam Persarum fuerat puniturus.'[45] The first explanation, which would have been unacceptable to any theological writer, is Godfrey's own suggestion, for Josephus expressly states that God let Alexander's army through the sea that they might destroy the empire of the Persians.

And in fact there is no need here of any explaining away to make

---

[1] Josephus, 'Αρχαιολογία II, 348.

the incident concur with the derogatory conception of Alexander. In letting him pass through the Pamphylian sea, God is fulfilling His own desire, which coincides with Alexander's only because God has put into his heart the wish to destroy the Persians. That Alexander plays here, in the opinion of Josephus, the role of the conscious protégé of God is sufficiently evident from the episode of the dream which establishes the Josephan relationship between God and Alexander. A reverent Alexander, however, is not necessary to the explanation of this incident which might as well be a step towards the fulfilment of the Daniel prophecy by an unwitting Alexander.

But Christian thinkers worried over the miracles worked by God for Alexander, over the prodigious signs at his birth, the crossing of the Pamphylian sea and the enclosing of the Ten Tribes. To a muddled thinker it was apparently not evident that God worked these miracles for himself; as we shall see in the case of the Ten Tribes as well as in that of the Pamphylian sea, Richard of St Victor offers an explanation of them typical of the confused but determined efforts to discredit the favourable evidence that were so universal a feature of the theological treatment of Alexander.[46]

(b) THE JERUSALEM EPISODE

This is the most important, and therefore the most frequently attacked of Josephus' references to Alexander. Alexander, descending upon Jerusalem in wrath because a levy has been refused him, does obeisance to the High Priest who comes out with the assembled priesthood and people, in pursuance of a Divine injunction, to greet him. He does so because he reverences in the priest the earthly symbol of that God who had appeared to him in a dream, and told him that he would be assisted in his conquest of Persia and might rest assured of success. He is conducted into Jerusalem by the rejoicing Jews, is shown the prophecy of Daniel relating to him, and makes sacrifice in the Temple. On his departure he makes various concessions to Jerusalem and to the Jews in his empire.[1]

It is upon the basis of this clarification of Alexander's relationship with God that Alexander's role in the episode of the Pamphylian sea

---

[1] Josephus, 'Αρχαιολογία XI, 314 ff. Alexander's dream in XI, 334. For the Eastern versions of this episode, in Pseudo-Callisthenes γ and elsewhere, see F. Pfister, in *Sitzungsber. d. Heidelb. Akad. d. Wissensch.*, Phil.-Hist. Klasse, Bd. v (1914), Abh. 11, pp. 22–30.

and in that of the Ten Tribes should have been interpreted. If Josephus' account had been accepted by theologians Alexander would have been recognized as a reverent worshipper of God, and God as his personal protector, not merely as the Power, unseen of Alexander, that stood behind him in the destruction of the Persian Empire.

Such a view was of course impossible to theologians; but the wide diffusion of the episode, through its incorporation in the *Historia Scholastica* of Peter Comestor and the I² *Historia de Preliis*, made it known, and welcome, to those who took a more charitable view of Alexander.[47] In Antiquity the episode had been accepted by the Jews, who saw in Alexander a hero of their own. From them, through the agency of Josephus, it became known and approved by those who felt a similar admiration for Alexander; but it also reached the theologians, who based their view of Alexander upon different grounds, and consequently approached this material in a determined spirit of depreciation.

St Augustine threw the first stone: 'Hostias sane Alexander immolauit in Dei templo, non ad eius cultum uera pietate conuersus, sed impia uanitate cum diis eum falsis colendum putans.'[1] Alexander's action is here accounted for in a way consonant with the usual theological attacks on him. Alexander adds Jehovah as another god to his collection, not from any supposed political object in conciliating the Jews, still less from any true reverence for God, but in the spirit of a vain collector, a man who worships gods as he finds them. In this connexion there may be cited the passage quoted by St Augustine, St Cyprian, and Minucius Felix in support of the euhemeristic theory of the origin of pagan gods—Alexander's letter to his mother, in which he describes how the priests of Ammon told him how ancestor worship developed into idolatry.[48] But if he disbelieved in the powers of the pagan gods, he yet worshipped them; if then he worshipped Jehovah, who was to say that he believed in his power? Such a line of argument would connect the two passages.

---

[1] St Augustine, *De Ciu. Dei* XVIII, xlv, 2 (Migne, *P.L.* vol. XLI, col. 606).

PLATE IV (*opposite*). This colour-washed drawing shows Alexander kneeling in adoration before the Jewish high-priest Jadus who stands dressed as a bishop with a tonsured cleric behind him and holding the Mosaic tablets of the decalogue. This is the usual iconography of this scene, which occurs with minor variants of detail in most illustrated medieval Alexander-books.

gros namen gottes angeschriben stund
Do saß er von dem pherd vnd gieng al
lain zu dem priester vnd schriat sire des
gottes namen vnd pat in an vnd er auch
den priester des verbunderten sich dy

siglich dy mit im furen vnd wonttn man
het in zaubert do was ainer vnter in der
fragt warumb er der iuden priester an pat
do antburt er im ich hab den priester nicht
angebett Mar har ich angebeten an das

IV   ALEXANDER AT JERUSALEM

This explanation was repeated only in the derivative excerpt of Vincent de Beauvais,[1] and was superseded by an argument based on the fact of Alexander's reverence to Jehovah's High Priest and in his Temple. Unable to ascribe that reverence to any true sense of reverence in the heart of Alexander, theologians were obliged to assume that God compelled Alexander to do him reverence, and that the whole episode of his entry into Jerusalem was a signal manifestation of God's power. God worked upon Alexander to spare the Jews; his mercy shown towards Jerusalem was no act of devout reverence, but was due to a demonstration of God's power which compelled even him to obedience and recognition. The emphasis is on God's omnipotence over Alexander as over all tyrants, Alexander's dream is conveniently forgotten, and he appears as the instrument of God as in the Daniel prophecy—but an instrument which turned awry. It was God's will that Alexander should destroy the Persians—hence the incident at the Pamphylian sea; it was God's will that the Ten Tribes should be shut up—hence the closing together of the mountains; but it was not God's will that Alexander should approach Jerusalem with wrath and vengeance in his heart, and he is deterred from his wicked purpose only by the especial prevision of God on behalf of the Jewish people, which made him appear to the High Priest, and tell him how he should act. In his attack upon Jerusalem Alexander is contravening the purpose of God, his destined task is not accomplished, the invasion of Persia not begun. But Jerusalem is hedged about with a divinity that impresses itself even upon *his* pagan heart, and he is forced into reverence. The development of this opinion is illustrated by the passages cited in the notes;[49] it is the final attempt to discredit the unfortunate evidence of Josephus, and to force it into agreement with a preconceived view of Alexander.

The great popularity of the story of Alexander's entry into Jerusalem ensured its incorporation in many Alexander-books. Except in Germany, however, neither this nor the Daniel prophecy had any apparent effect upon the secular conception of Alexander. If it received any secular interpretation, it was the natural interpretation—that Alexander paid a due reverence to God, and thus showed himself humble.

We have here seen how the theologians built upon the basis of Orosius and the Bible an attack upon Alexander which went far

---

[1] Vincent de Beauvais, *Speculum historiale* IV, xxxii (ed. Douai, 1624, p. 126 (at top)).

enough to interpret all possible material against him. We shall later see how this attack was taken up in Germany, and how the same method of pejorative interpretation was there applied to legendary material. For the moment, there are certain minor episodes to be discussed for their bearing upon the theological attitude to Alexander, and certain writers who deserve individual examination.

5. MEDIEVAL TREATMENT OF MINOR THEOLOGICAL MATERIAL

(a) ALEXANDER AND GOG AND MAGOG

The story of Alexander's building a wall to prevent the tribes of Gog and Magog from invading the civilized world, enormously popular in the Middle Ages, has been much discussed,[50] and had so little effect upon the medieval conception of Alexander as to deserve but brief notice here. This story originated in the Gog and Magog of Ezekiel and the Apocalypse, kings, and later tribes, who were hostile to Israel.[1] Josephus, in two independent passages, mentions that Alexander enclosed the Scythians within an iron barrier, and identifies the Scythians with Gog and Magog.[2] Thus grew the legend, typical of the Jewish attitude favourable to Alexander, that he built a wall against Gog and Magog who would break through it and descend upon the stricken world at the coming of Antichrist. This story was universally known in the Middle Ages,[51] principally through the *Reuelationes* of Pseudo-Methodius,[3] and Gog and Magog were always identified with the peoples who presented the worst contemporary menace; but no deductions were drawn from the episode that reflected upon the character of Alexander. As was natural, the episode was easily confused in medieval minds with the story of the enclosing of the Ten Tribes.[4] It may be noticed that Alexander did not need God's help to shut out Gog and Magog, as he needed it to shut in

---

[1] Ezekiel xxxviii, 1–6 (the kings hostile to Israel). Revelations xx, 1–7.

[2] Ἀρχαιολογία I, 123.

[3] The best edition of the Pseudo-Methodius text is by E. Sackur, *Sibyllinische Texte u. Forschungen* (Halle, 1898), pp. 1–96.

[4] Confusion between the story of Gog and Magog and that of the Ten Tribes occurs in Quilichinus of Spoleto, Rudolf von Ems, and the *Libro de Alexandre*. For text of the passage in Quilichinus and bibliographical notices of the other two passages see Pfister, *Münchener Museum*, I (1912), pp. 294–6.

the Ten Tribes; it was a simple question of building a wall, not the difficult problem of moving two mountains together. The story of the later confusion of the two episodes has been fully discussed by A. R. Anderson in an erudite monograph.

¶ Quomodo Gog et Magog'exeūtes de caſpys mōtibus obtinent terrā Jſrahel

¶ In nouiſſimis vero temporibus ſecunduz Ezechie/ lis prophetiam que dicit. Jn nouiſſimo die conſuma/ tiōis mundi exiet Gog et Magog in terram Jſracl: q̃ ſunt gentes et reges quos recluſit Alexander magnus in finibus aquilonis et in finibus ſeptentrionis Gog et Magog Moſach et Thubal et Anog et Ageg et

FIG. 3. GOG AND MAGOG BREAK THROUGH ALEXANDER'S GATE IN THE LAST DAYS AND OVERRUN THE WORLD

Woodcut from Pseudo-Methodius, *Reuelationes*, ed. Michael Furter.

(b) ALEXANDER AND THE TEN TRIBES

This story, known to the Middle Ages from the version in the *Vitae Prophetarum* of Pseudo-Epiphanius, passed into the *Historia Scholastica* and the I² *Historia de Preliis*, and was thence assured of wide popularity.[52] Of Jewish origin, it tells how the ten exiled Jewish tribes, shut up in shunned seclusion beside the Caspian Sea, beseech Alexander to release them from their natural prison. Alexander, however, informed of God's anger against them, invokes his help to enclose them yet more securely by moving two mountains together. In the circumstances the accompanying remark, 'if God did so much for a heathen, what would he not do for his faithful?' is unjust, with its implication that God is here assisting Alexander to some private end. Alexander is executing the will of God in enclosing the Ten Tribes, and his prayer to God must be granted if God is to fulfil his own intentions. No one could pretend that the enclosing of the Tribes bore no relation to God's especial purposes, so that the interpretation of the episode could only be favourable to Alexander.

The apocalyptic connexions of this story, and its similarity to and confusion with the story of Gog and Magog, assured it a place in numerous chronicles and Alexander-books; but if there is comment upon it in these works, that comment is restricted to the repetition of the accompanying remark. Moralists and theologians, wisely enough, made no attempt to turn this story to the disparagement of Alexander, but deliberately omitted it from their interpretations of his character.

(c) THE BONES OF JEREMIAH

The story of how Alexander brought the bones of Jeremiah to Alexandria, recorded by Pseudo-Epiphanius and repeated in the *Historia Scholastica* of Peter Comestor and some other medieval authors, has been studied in detail by Pfister,[1] but had no effect upon the medieval conception of Alexander. It is merely another aspect of the favourable Jewish attitude to Alexander.

---

[1] See F. Pfister, 'Eine jüdische Gründungsgeschichte Alexandrias, mit einem Anhang über Alexanders Besuch in Jerusalem', *Sitzungsber. d. Heidelberger Akad. d. Wissensch.*, Phil.-Hist. Klasse, Bd. v (1914), Abh. 11, pp. 20-2.

(d) ALEXANDER'S APOCALYPTIC ROLES

Professor Pfister has laid great emphasis on Alexander's apocalyptic role and holds that the episodes of Gog and Magog and the Ten Tribes were of great importance in establishing the medieval conception of him. Even if we assume that Alexander's name was frequently connected with these stories in popular remembrance (and nothing is more likely in view of their prominence in the early annals, where almost nothing else is told of Alexander, and their frequent incorporation into late Alexander-books), it is difficult to see how they can have affected the medieval conception of Alexander. Nobody praised these two actions of Alexander, as they praised other actions of his, and nobody could well dispraise them. The two episodes are connexions in which Alexander's name was popularly mentioned, but they were objective connexions, undeserving of the attention paid them by Professor Pfister.

It is tempting to classify the various ways in which Alexander's name was connected with apocalyptic tradition; but his connexion with Revelations, with the coming of Antichrist and the Second coming of the Messiah, must be reduced in the end to those for which there is ample evidence, and this evidence is confusing mainly because it points in different directions. Alexander is connected with Antichrist in several ways, which cannot be satisfactorily connected together. These apocalyptic roles of Alexander are:

(i) In the story of Gog and Magog, where Alexander appears as the encloser of the tribes that shall break forth over the earth at the coming of Antichrist, and who shall be opposed by Elias and Enoch.

(ii) The story of the Ten Tribes is an episode very similar to the last, similar enough to be confusing to medieval writers. But there is this important difference: that in enclosing the Ten Tribes Alexander is fulfilling the express desire of God, and God helps him in that fulfilment.

(iii) In medieval interpretation of the opening verses of I Maccabees Alexander was interpreted as the Devil from the typification of Antiochus, his eventual successor, as Antichrist; but in one instance, as we have seen, Alexander himself appears as a type of Antichrist.

(iv) Alexander's reign was also connected with the final scene of the Apocalypse, as was that of Nero, by the circumstance of his having ruled twelve years. He was thus regarded as the counterpart of the last king of earth.

It will be apparent, therefore, that Alexander was never firmly established in one apocalyptic role, but that he appeared in various roles, irreconcilable with one another, and of almost equal popularity, except for the last which is rare and of doubtful occurrence.

(e) ALEXANDER'S CELESTIAL JOURNEY

It is well known that many European churches contain representations of Alexander carried up into the sky in a chariot drawn by two or more gryphons, who are enticed upwards by bait spitted on the ends

Ɖât al ɗʒe ſi eu confit l amßʒia et ſee geɪ eut ſa cttepʒinſeɑſ aßatue: iſſe part tiſſe a tout ſon oſt aſſa ſur la rouge ɪ ɑ iſſec ſe fogerento y auoit Ɓng moi ßault et ſi grant l ſemßloit quiſ ſurɪ taſt ſee nues. ɗonʃ panɗʒe monta ſuʃ mont. Aɗonc iſ pʌ enſonʃueur quiſſʌ faire Ɓng engɪͻ p quoy lee oyſe auſɪ

mez grifʒ ſe poʒteroient iuſquee au cieſ: Pource quiſ Ɓouloit noir et Ɓeoit queſſee ʃ ßoſee auoit au cieſ amͻt, ɑ ɗe queſſe foɪ eſtoit ſa terre. Loʒe ɗeſʃenɗut ɗe ſa montaigne et commai

FIG. 4. ALEXANDER'S CELESTIAL JOURNEY

Alexander is shown seated in an iron cage to which four griffins are attached. The bait is a leg of mutton on a spear and the other two objects are sponges soaked in cold water 'por rafrescir lor alaines' as the text says. Below is the earth, shrunk to the size of a small island and surrounded by the stream of Ocean. Ed. Michel le Noir, Paris, 1506.

This is one of the cuts made for this edition but the majority of its illustrations are from a standard set frequently used by this publisher in romances both before and after this date. See also frontispiece and Plate IX, opp. p. 258.

of two lances.[1] This episode, borrowed in most cases probably from the *Historia de Preliis*, and frequently found on façades and misericords, has been long acknowledged to possess some symbolic significance. The exact nature of the symbolic interpretation intended has not yet been established, although many different theories have been produced, ranging from the interpretation of Alexander as Antichrist to the suggestion that the episode is symbolic of the Resurrection.[53]

It seems necessary, however, to remark here that the literary treatment of the story of the Celestial Journey in Germany must automatically suggest that an unfavourable interpretation was attached to the representations of it in German churches, an interpretation which probably concurred with the theological condemnation of Alexander's pride. Thus, in the account of the Celestial Journey in *History-Bible* I and Enikel's *Weltchronik*, an account common to these works but unparalleled elsewhere, Alexander is represented as deterred from ascending further when he has reached a certain height, by a voice which warns him that no man may ascend to heaven who has not deserved to do so by good works.[2] Similarly in the sermons of Berthold von Regensburg the Celestial Journey is introduced as an example of Alexander's 'hohvart'.

This literary evidence suggests that the Celestial Journey was early adapted in Germany to agree with the theological attacks on Alexander, and was the first legendary material to be so treated.

6. ALEXANDER IN THREE INDIVIDUAL THEOLOGIANS

(a) FULGENTIUS

The earliest writer to develop the Orosian tradition was Fulgentius, whose life of Alexander is of especial interest because he was the first writer, except the anonymous author of the *Itinerarium Alexandri*, to use Julius Valerius. Since this account of Alexander has been previously unknown to Alexander scholars, and since it has its own nervous and amusing style, it has been transcribed at length in the

---

[1] The best study on the Celestial Journey that has so far appeared is that by G. Millet, 'L'Ascension d'Alexandre', *Syria*, IV (1923), pp. 85–133. A second article was promised but never published.

[2] See below, p. 258.

Texts (pp. 369–70). The following remarks should be read in the light of the text there given.

In placing Alexander in relation to Jewish history and chronology, and stressing the Orosian attack upon his vices, Fulgentius is typical of the orthodox Christian approach to Alexander which we have seen so consistently maintained; and in his adaptation of legendary material to the purpose of condemnation, he anticipated the later development of the German accusation of Alexander, which was finally to rely largely upon a basis of legend—the Celestial Journey, the *Iter ad Paradisum*, and other episodes.

His remark that Alexander would have ascended into heaven had he been granted wings is interesting in view of the fact that the story of the Celestial Journey was almost certainly unknown in the West at this period—the early sixth century.[1]

(b) GODFREY OF ADMONT

Godfrey of Admont's account of Alexander is contained in a homily upon the first book of Maccabees. After giving the relevant text, he continues:[2]

> Per hoc nomen Alexandri, quod leuans angustiam interpretatur, non incongrue draco ille, serpens antiquus, qui uocatur diabolus et Satanas, accipitur, qui, ex quo primum hominem in paradiso per inobedientiam seduxit, tam inextricabiles angustias et labores initiauit ac leuauit, ut omni posteritati Adae nunquam quotidianae angustiae et labores deessent aut desint, quamdiu homo uiuit super terram. Qui et Philippi Macedo nominatur. Philippus enim os lampadis, Macedo orientalis interpretatur....

This passage sufficiently shows the type of interpretation at which we are now arrived, the misplaced, over-reaching cleverness of a stupid man. Godfrey now continues with a description of Alexander's, or the Devil's, career, related by the dim light of exotic fancy to the text of Maccabees:

> *Hic primus regnauit in Graecia.* Graecia interpretatur sapientia uel eloquentia, in qua idem Lucifer regnauit, quia ob hoc conditus erat, ut in

---

[1] It is, however, interesting to note that among the remarkable third-century mosaics recently discovered at Piazza Armerina in Sicily is one showing a large griffin apparently supporting a cage containing a man. It seems at least possible that Alexander's Celestial Journey is the subject intended. See *Illustrated London News*, 22 Dec. 1951, pp. 1032–3. [D.J.A.R.]

[2] All the quotations are taken from Godfrey of Admont's *Homily on Maccabees* (Migne, *P.L.* vol. CLXXIV, cols. 1130f.).

aeterna sapientia regnaret, et mirifica diuinitatis dulcedine delectaretur, nihilque aliud loqueretur aut ageret, nisi quod ad laudem Creatoris sui pertineret. *Qui egressus est de terra Cethim.* Cethim formido dicitur. Egressus est, proh dolor! de Cethim, quando, formidine Dei contempta, in tantam elatus est mentis superbiam, ut magis sub proprio quam sub Domini dominio esse eligeret, dicens in corde suo: 'Ponam sedem meam ad aquilonem, similis ero Altissimo.' Inde egressus interfecit *Darium regem Persarum atque Medorum.* Darius interpretatur generatio consilii, quo nomine primus parens noster Adam exprimitur,...

Alexander's life is an epitome of the Devil's campaign against the world before the coming of Christ. At the moment of his death— 'post haec decidit in lectum'—the 'lectum', the Cross, delivers men from his thraldom. Antiochus therefore slips naturally into his time-honoured position of Antichrist: '...qui uero radix peccati dicitur, quia eleuatur et extollitur supra omne quod dicitur Deus, aut quod colitur, in quem diabolus pleniter introibit, quem cum uniuersis uitiis et peccatis non solum inuisibiliter, sed et uisibiliter possidebit.'

Thus Godfrey's narrative is a working out of the idea more briefly expressed by Hugh of St Victor, that Antiochus stands in the same relation to Alexander as does Antichrist to the Devil. Godfrey occupies himself with identifying the course of world history from the fall of Adam to the coming of Antichrist with its prefiguration in the Biblical description of the life of Alexander and his successor Antiochus. Such a task of identification explains the tortuous obscurity of interpretation which is here found shrouding the simple sketch of Alexander in Maccabees.

(c) RUPERT OF DEUTZ

Rupert of Deutz,[1] in his *De Victoria Verbi Dei*, an allegorical Scriptural history, begins his account of Alexander by quoting the prophecy of Daniel concerning the Goat and the Ram, and describing the defeat of Darius in a chapter headed by the words: 'Superato per Verbum Dei Persarum et Medorum regno, Macedonum quod in Daniele per hircum caprarum significatur successisse.' The lesson of the defeat of Darius is expounded in characteristically pompous rhetoric, and

---

[1] On Rupert of Deutz see Manitius, *Geschichte d. latein. Litt. im Mitt.* III (1931), pp. 127–35. The quotations are all taken from Rupert of Deutz, *De Victoria Verbi Dei* VIII, xxviii–IX, xiv (Migne, *P.L.* vol. CLXIX, cols. 1397–410).

Rupert proceeds to discuss why the kingdom of Macedon should have been described in the first prophecy of Daniel as a leopard, and in the second as a goat.

Futurum quippe erat ut regnum Macedonum et ferinam pardi ferocitatem, et effeminatam hirci habens libidinem, sua uibraret cornua contra Altissimum, suam obfirmaret saeuitiam contra uerum et uere firmum saepe dictae promissionis uerbum. Ex sacris recitandum est historiis, et postmodum recitabitur, quam ferum et quam fuerit libidinosum, ferocitate crudeli, et crudelitate feroci, sanctos Altissimi conterendo, libidine insana, insania libidinosa populum, et templum Dei contaminando, ferocissimum atque crudelissimum secundum pardi saeuitiam, libidinosum et effeminatum secundum hirci semper in libidinem proni petulantiam, astutum atque uersutum secundum pardi uarietatem, fluxum atque incontinens secundum immoderatum sanguinis hircini calorem.

This is a fair sample of Rupert's style. In his view, therefore, the leopard and the goat do not specifically refer to Alexander, but to the kingdom that he set up, and to Antiochus as the representative of it.

Later he returns to give an unconventional explanation of the goat with its one horn, and the ram with two: 'Bene igitur hirci quidem unum, arietis autem duo cornua uisa sunt, quia uidelicet rex unus regnum Macedonum, duo autem reges [i.e. Cyrus and Darius] Persarum et Medorum roborauerunt imperium.' There follows a digression upon the nature of the princes of the Persians and of the Greeks, who are compared to the wicked angels, and who, in their capacity for stirring up war and bringing suffering, 'potius creaturae quam Creatori seruiebant'. After a brief reminiscence of the passage in Daniel concerning the prince of the Greeks who shall be heard by God, Rupert finally introduces the life of Alexander:

Post annos imperii Persici plus minus ducentos uiginti, Alexander Macedo decedente Philippo in regnum successit, eodem, ut putabatur, Philippo genitus, uirtute et diuitiis [sic] patre maior. Porro, si uerum memorant, qui de illo scripserunt, ueraciter illum adduxit in regnum, et cum peruenit iam dictus ille malus princeps Graecorum, permittente Deo, cuius permissio semper iusta est, licet malignorum principum uoluntas siue intentio semper sit iniusta. Ferunt namque gestorum eius scriptores, Nectanebum quemdam maleficum per maleficia transfiguratum in cornuti Iouis daemonium, quem dicunt Hammonem, Olympiadis uxoris Philippi inisse concubitum, atque exinde Alexandrum hunc fuisse generatum. Ferunt et hoc alii, quia qua nocte eum mater Olympias concepit, uisa est per quietem cum ingenti serpente uolutari.

Apart from the odd misreading 'uirtute et diuitiis' for 'uirtute et uitiis', this passage seems to be very confused. The key sentence, from 'Porro...' onwards, is impossible to construe, but seems to refer to the coming of Alexander as the prince of the Greeks, whose coming will be permitted by God, whose permission is always just. Therefore Alexander is justly allowed to come against Persia, although his private intentions are unjust. The meaning of this passage must be further considered in the light of Rupert's later statements, a dim light at best.

From a suggestion that evil spirits had a hand in his conception Rupert goes on to discuss Alexander's early years and his visit to the oracle of Ammon in a chapter with the explanatory heading:

> *Regem Alexandrum se Hammonis filium uideri uoluisse, idque per hircum caprarum, qui terram non tangebat, Danieli significatum fuisse.*
> Propter felicitatem praedae suae, qua praedatus est mundum, et propter inuictam fortitudinem celeritatemque uictoriarum praesignatus est per cornu insigne quod habebat, inquit Daniel, hircus inter oculos suos. Puer namque acerrimus litterarum studiis eruditus fuisse dicitur, et deinde per quinquennium creuisse sub Aristotele omnium philosophorum nobilissimo doctore, adeptus imperium, regem se terrarum omnium ac mundi appellari iussit....

The interpretation of the goat's single horn has now been changed; and by the introduction of a *quinquennium* of tutorship, Alexander and Aristotle have been brought into a possibly unintentional comparison with Nero and Seneca. Rupert describes how Alexander determined to make the suspicious circumstances of his conception into a reason for pride rather than for shame, bribing the priests of the temple of Jupiter Ammon to recognize him as the son of the God, and wishing to be thought of divine origin. It was for this reason, according to Rupert, that Daniel said of the goat: 'ueniebat ab occidente super faciem totius terrae, et non tangebat terram.' For Alexander was so proud that he lifted himself above the earth, the common level of humanity, in his arrogance.

Rupert now turns to Josephus' account of the entry of Alexander into Jerusalem. His explanation of the reasons that impelled Alexander, the instrument of God, against God's chosen city is typical of the obscure turgidity of his thought:

> Necdum causam commemorat, ut hircus ille, scilicet regnum Graecorum, Judam et Hierusalem, templumque nuper de ruina et igne Chaldaeorum

resuscitatum deuastaret, neque cornu illud insigne ad hoc fuerat deputatum, ut faceret quod faciendum erat per aliud cornu eiusdem hirci, iuxta uisionis supra memoratae mysterium. Sciendum quippe, quia non nisi ob causas manifestas, non nisi ob scelera grandia contigit, ut uel Nabuchodonosor locum illum prius, uel Antiochus desertum redderet posterius. Causas precedentis, id est Babylonicae tempestatis suo loco diximus, causas sequentis postmodum dicemus. Igitur intendebat quidem diabolus contra Deum, contra promissionis Dei uerbum uibrare illud hirci cornu magnum, sed permissus non est, immo manifesta Dei uirtute locus ille defensus est.

Alexander is a passive instrument of God, but the Devil enters into this instrument and turns it against Jerusalem. The goat has acquired another horn, and by analogy should have one for each of the kings between Alexander and Antiochus. Rupert writes nonsense, but fascinating nonsense, the nonsense of a man who is trying very hard to understand. He now recounts the Jerusalem episode without comment, and concludes the passage as follows:

Praeclara uictoriae pars, uictoriae nominis uel uerbi Dei taliter ob implendam ueritatem promissionis, illam gentem reseruantis atque defendentis, ut regnorum capita sibi humiliaret, dum et Babylonis caput Nabuchodonosor prophetam eius procidens adorat, et Macedonum diadema magnus Alexander in sacerdotis ornatu nomen Dei nihilominus adorat, et eorum medius tempore potentissimus Persarum Medorumque rex mysterium uictoriosae passionis eius, sicut suo loco dictum est, appenso Aman in patibulo, licet ignorans, concelebrat.

The next chapter deals with Alexander's death. Rupert tells how he returned to Babylon and was poisoned, and concludes with a long summary of his career which need not be quoted since it is on comparatively conventional lines. He says how small and unimportant Alexander was when compared with God, and how ludicrous it was that he thought himself great. He compared him to a locust who makes a giant leap and thinks himself thereby a giant. And Rupert ends on the customary theme of the evanescence of human glory.

Thus the account of Alexander in Rupert of Deutz is a carrying to absurd lengths of the theological treatment of his life in conjunction with the interpretation of the Bible and of Josephus, an intricate and laboured fantasy.

7. CONCLUSIONS

(a) SUMMARY

The genesis of the theological approach to Alexander may be briefly stated. The prophecies of Daniel and the historical sketch of Maccabees were the foundation on which the theological writers built. By them Alexander was seen as the foreordained destroyer of Persia, and as the predecessor of Antiochus, the accepted type of Antichrist. In order to expand this Alexander portrait for purposes of Biblical commentary theologians turned to the life of Alexander in Orosius, the storehouse of ancient history for those who were neither humanists nor professional historians. And Orosius confirmed the conception of Alexander that was foreshadowed in his bare Biblical role as an instrument of wrath and as the ultimate cause of the reign of the anathematized Antiochus. He was a man of abominable pride, a pride so great that he might admirably symbolize the Devil. This conception of Alexander was first in the field. Already developed in Fulgentius and in St Jerome, it established a prejudice that bore down all evidence favourable to Alexander and brought about his general condemnation.

Although this condemnation of Alexander was the work equally of French and German mystics, its effect in France was nullified for two centuries by the great force and pervasiveness of the courtly tradition, which made most French writers admirers of Alexander. But in Germany the courtly tradition was less influential; and it is significant that throughout the whole of German Alexander literature, from Rhabanus Maurus to the *Middle Low German Alexander*, the tendency was to consider the life of Alexander not as a separate biography but as a chapter in Biblical history, as an extended commentary upon the opening verses of Maccabees, or as the history of the founder of Daniel's third world-kingdom.

This historical tendency to place Alexander against his Biblical background is accompanied by a steady persistence of the theological condemnation of Alexander in Germany during the medieval period. That condemnation was sometimes faintly echoed elsewhere, in France and in England, during the later Middle Ages; but Germany remained always the staunchest upholder of this unfavourable Orosian attitude to Alexander, which made its way into even the most courtly and the most favourable of her Alexander poems.

(b) THE MORAL AND THEOLOGICAL CONCEPTIONS OF ALEXANDER COMPARED

The general conclusions that may be drawn from a comparison of the moral and theological conceptions of Alexander are these:

(i) The twelfth century, with the writings of John of Salisbury and Giraldus Cambrensis, of Hugh of St Victor, Rupert of Deutz, and Godfrey of Admont, saw all the available material presented to medieval readers, and the climax of the development of these two approaches to Alexander.

(ii) The moral conception of Alexander was restricted, during the early period, to England and France; while the theological conception was best represented in Germany.

(iii) These approaches are dependent, the moral upon the anecdotal material presented by classical writers and the Fathers of the Church, and the theological upon the writings of Orosius and other historians, applied to the interpretation of various passages in the Bible and in Josephus.

(iv) The moralists held to, while they modified, the Peripatetic conception of Alexander; the Stoic material known to them lost most of its force in the mild interpretations which they placed upon it.

(v) The theologians, on the other hand, constructed their portrait of Alexander upon the Stoic basis of the account in Orosius; and when they had thus formed their opinion, they modified the Biblical and Josephan material to suit this interpretation of Alexander's character.

(vi) Thus the moralists tended to interpret the material presented to them in favour of Alexander, and the theologians against Alexander.

(vii) From the thirteenth century onwards there appeared a tendency which became much more marked in the fourteenth and fifteenth centuries which resulted in the confusion and submergence of these two conceptions of Alexander in popular didactic writing.

III

THE CONCEPTION OF ALEXANDER
IN THE BOOKS OF 'EXEMPLA'
AND IN PREACHERS

1. INTRODUCTION

UNDER this head we shall consider a group of unliterary and un-reflective writings: the collections of stories made for their edifying nature, and compiled for the assistance of preachers and the devotional needs of the laity. In view of the quantity of anecdotal material upon Alexander in these works, we might think them worthy of elaborate consideration, but their value in assessing a positive medieval conception of Alexander is unreliable for the following reasons.

In the philosophic writers we have a personal application of morality; the incidents related serve not only as a commentary upon the ways of the world, but also as a judgement upon Alexander himself, whose especial vices are examined for the purpose of drawing a general conclusion. But with the transference of anecdotal material to books of *exempla* and related collections of stories intended for edification through amusement the character of the individuals becomes of secondary importance, since such edifying writers are concerned not with the actors but with the universal moral conveyed by the story. There is here no question of a John of Salisbury or a Giraldus Cambrensis, of men who give the morals they draw an individual and direct application to the subjects of their anecdotes, who are concerned with imperfections of character, and who wish to reach a judgement, not upon points of ethics universally admitted by Christian moralists, but upon individual moral situations. This judgement is all the more individual in the case of Alexander, since his life was so well documented, and since such moralists wrote with knowledge of how the cultured men of their own acquaintance were led by the legendary accounts to see in Alexander the paragon of all virtue. The preachers and the compilers of the books of *exempla* might be sure that their literate readers or illiterate hearers knew very little, even though they themselves knew something, of the principal historical and legendary accounts of Alexander; their aim was only to impress upon their public the importance of certain very general precepts in the practice of a Christian life.

The subsistent and universal moral is here the only purpose in telling the tale; characters become unimportant, since the point of the story is no longer even remotely connected with the personality of the actors or the interlocutors, but only with what they have to do or say. Diogenes, Dindimus, Socrates, and the rest have no importance for these writers and their readers as separate people with individual lives and characters; and they tend to become obliterated under the vague description of 'philosophus quidam', confused with one another, or brought together under the most familiar philosophic names. And in most of the exemplar anecdotes Alexander is of even less importance; he is merely the hearer of the precept expressed, the essential cypher without whom the moral point could not have been made.

Thus Diogenes could be *A*, and Alexander *B*; their characters are no longer of the substance of the story which is now the moral truth contained in it. And this disregard for character becomes yet more apparent in the *Gesta Romanorum*, where the anecdotes are no longer illustrations but allegories, and where the interpretation of Alexander as God in one story, and in another as the Devil is in no way incompatible, since each story is meant to be considered alone with its own symbolic significance, and consistency of character is not to be looked for where men are symbols to be interpreted as the various powers of good and evil.

The source material of the *exempla* collections and the preachers is partly those classical anecdotes which have already been discussed, and partly a farrago of material derived mainly from Oriental legend and passed through the lowest written tradition, or through oral tradition, into the books of the compilers. Since both classes of anecdote are used to point the same general morals, they will be discussed together, and the Oriental stories will receive further discussion each in its place.

It would be unwise to see in the varying degree of popularity of different anecdotes any discrimination or purposeful selection among the compilers. In common with those writers who introduced stories of Alexander for more learned purposes, most of them did not use a distant source, but preferred their immediate predecessors, and thus conscious selection cannot be said to have had much hand in the matter. Their elaborate textual relationships are both unprofitable in discussion and incapable of exact definition. It is sufficient to notice that an anecdote, once it had been accepted into two or three of the best known exemplar anthologies, was sure to become very widely known.

It is difficult to offer any positive conjecture upon the opinion of Alexander held by these writers. They received both currents of Alexander tradition, and delivered them to their public with those modifications that best adapted the material for their own purposes. There is, nevertheless, a certain tendency towards approval of Alexander in these modifications, and the material so adapted reached through these writers a large public which was certainly ignorant of that literary Alexander material which affected the view of the more learned medieval authors; so that the influence of their use of the written tradition, even if it cannot be exactly evaluated, was undeniably great and deserving of attention. It may also be added that their public was of course familiar with the popular vernacular Alexander literature which gave a picture of him almost invariably favourable, and no doubt the general tendency towards approval in the *exempla* would have been partly in deference to popular taste.

What follows then is a study of the changes undergone by both historical and legendary material in the hands of simple people. It shows the submergence of any detailed conception of Alexander as a man, and the emergence of general moral views. It is a study, not in the formation of a medieval conception, but in the suppression of two medieval conceptions, and their subordination to the more immediate needs of an illiterate populace in the works of its spiritual teachers. Such an approach stands midway between the approach to Alexander as a subject for philosophical or theological speculation of which we have treated, and the approach to Alexander as a man which we are to discuss.

2. THE EXEMPLAR ANECDOTES OF DIOGENES, THE GYMNOSOPHISTS, THE SCYTHIANS, THE WONDER-STONE, AND THE PHILOSOPHERS AT THE TOMB

The descent of the exemplar form of the Diogenes episode has already been noted but may be restated here. The exemplar anecdote rests upon the combination of the episode of Diogenes and his sun-shine, as it appears in the moralists, with other edifying material derived from an Oriental source; and the result is that the former episode, recounted merely as an incident at the beginning of a sententious lecture by Diogenes, fails of its moral effect. The moral form of the anecdote, however, with the comment of Seneca attached, persisted in one book of *exempla*, the *Dialogus Creaturarum*, which relied mainly upon classical literary sources, and in the *Gesta Romanorum*, where, however, the Oriental form of the narrative appears, attached to the names of Socrates and Alexander, in a different story and a different connexion.[54]

The kernel of the exemplar plot appears in the *Bocados de Oro* under the name of Diogenes,[55] but undoubtedly the most influential early appearance of the anecdote in Europe was in the *Disciplina Clericalis*.[1] Here the story is told 'De Socrate et rege' the king remaining un-specified. A group of the royal retinue come upon a philosopher immersed in cogitation; they stand round him open-mouthed, get in his sun, and are reproached in the traditional fashion for taking away from him that which they have no power to give. They tell him that they are the servants of the king. He says that he is lord of their king who is but the servant of his servant. On hearing this the men (who are thus the servants of the servant of his servant) are annoyed, and threaten to take the life of the old man. At this point the king appears, has the situation explained to him, and asks the philosopher what he meant. He explains that the king is a slave to his will, but that he, as a philosopher, holds his will subject to reason. The king is thus the servant of his servant. He warns the king of the inconstancy of fortune and the vanity of all things in the face of death. The king, always ready to appreciate virtue, commands his servants not to harm the philosopher and departs. In the version of

---

[1] *Disciplina Clericalis*, exemplum XXVIII: de Socrate et rege (ed. A. Hilka and W. Soederhjelm, *Sammlung mittellat. Texte*, I, Heidelberg, 1911, pp. 43–4). Quoted below, p. 278, n. 2.

the *Gesta Romanorum*,[56] the philosopher urges him to govern his kingdom by reason and not by will and the king follows his advice.

In the *Disciplina Clericalis* and the *Gesta Romanorum* this story is told respectively of Socrates and an unnamed king and of Socrates and Alexander; in the *Speculum morale*[57] and in all other versions the persons are Diogenes and Alexander. These discrepancies are, as we have said, characteristic of the exemplar treatment of popular material.

The story arrived in Europe, as appears from the *Disciplina Clericalis*, in a ready-made exemplar form with a philosopher lecturing a king. What philosopher, and what king, was immaterial to the moral; names were added to increase verisimilitude. In the original version the philosopher's part had happened to be ascribed to Socrates. But what more suitable king than Alexander, who was an outstanding example of a king who was ruled by will rather than by reason? And then what better philosopher than Diogenes, the lonely ascetic with whom Alexander was known to have conversed, and who had long been connected with the sunshine part of the anecdote? It was natural at the period to give the best philosophers the best things to say, just as Goldschmidt has shown how the best authors became saddled with every work that they might have written or should have written. In the medieval Alexander tradition there were three philosophers among whom the best things were normally divided: Aristotle, Diogenes, and Dindimus.

Let us now consider the moral and the view of Alexander reflected in it. He is a man ruled by his will; but he has evidently reason enough to see the reasoning of the philosopher, and even to act upon his advice. He is kind to the good man and prevents his retinue from harming him. He shows humility in asking the reason for the philosopher's insulting remark. He is ruled by his will—that is all the positive evil which can be told of him from this anecdote, and it is not very much. The true exemplar theme of man's futility in the face of death plays as important a part in the moral purpose of the story.

Such then is the compiler's conception of Alexander. Subjectively, he is telling a story about a king and a philosopher that teaches men to subdue their will to their reason; he borrows it out of some previous text and is not particularly interested in the character of the king himself, or in the aspect of his character that the story illustrates. None the less the weight of exemplar evidence in favour of a mild view of Alexander accumulates so rapidly that it is difficult to regard this as entirely fortuitous.

There are two further anecdotes which may be closely connected with the Diogenes episode; both, like it, concerned with philosophers, or rather with philosophic peoples, who dissuade Alexander from attacking them by philosophic arguments. The first of these groups is the Gymnosophists. Their dialogue with Alexander was reduced in the *Historia de Preliis* to the final request of the Gymnosophists:[1] 'Give us immortality.' 'I cannot; I am mortal.' 'If you are mortal, why torment us and all the world?' 'Because I am fated by God to do so.' In the *Historia de Preliis* account Alexander really comes off best and the philosophers seem to have found no answer to his uncompromising fatalism. But of course this moral would not do for the writers of *exempla*; they are on the side of the Gymnosophists who express admirably what they themselves want to say: 'We have all to die, so what is the use of aggression?' Alexander's answer is most undesirable in a sermon; it raises the question of free-will and provides a perfect excuse for the man who steals his neighbour's pig: 'We are as the waves of the sea under the wind; what God wills, we must do.' So, very properly, Alexander's answer is cut out, and if the Gymnosophists' question is made to have any effect upon him at all, it is to leave him confused.[58] Thus the episode appears at first sight to have been made much more derogatory to Alexander in adapting it for exemplar purposes. Such, however, is not really the case, because Alexander's confession that he is mortal, and therefore cannot confer immortality, is retained. In other words Alexander goes about to conquer the world, not necessarily because he is proud, but because he is stupid, and does not think, as the Gymnosophists do, and as all good men should, of the approach of death.

The *Collatio* was not used by exemplar writers; and in fact, as we have seen, it lay also outside the moral anecdotal tradition. There was therefore no reason, except its general edifying nature, why it should have provided material for *exempla*.[2]

---

[1] Pseudo-Callisthenes α, III, 5–6, ed. Müller, pp. 99–101 (J. Valerius, ed. Kuebler, p. 120–3): see A. Ausfeld, *Griechischer Alexanderroman*, pp. 88–9.

[2] For the history of the *Collatio* in moralists and in secular writers, see pp. 91–5, 167–84. In the *Prague Epitome* (ed. F. P. Magoun, *Harvard Studies and Notes in Philology and Literature*, XVI (1934), p. 140), the author adds: 'Applica: Totum sicut placet', to the end of the *Collatio*.

To this group of anecdotes must be added a third of the same Cynic type, ultimately derived from Quintus Curtius.[59] This time it is the Scythians who are about to be attacked and send envoys to remind Alexander that the greatest trees can fall in a moment's storm, of the inconstancy of fortune, the futility of desire and similar matters. In the original account, which is of considerable length, Alexander made a suitable and slightly caustic reply; in the exemplar version this is omitted as it is contrary to exemplar convention, and Alexander appears merely to hear a dull little homily based on the comparison of a man with a great tree, perhaps a faint echo of Babrius. Yet a fourth such encounter, when the Amazons dissuade Alexander from invading their land with mundane arguments based upon the peculiarity of the situation,[1] gives rise to no *exemplum* because of the evident rarity of such a situation in everyday life; though the author of the *Prague Epitome* felt that there might be an *exemplum* to be made out of it.[2]

The last three anecdotes have a clear family likeness. In all of them the exemplar form of the narrative favours Alexander. No one tells him that it is *wrong* to go about conquering the world; all they ask is 'What use is it?' The question is not of moral standards but of the uncertain tenure of human life and of the futility of human ambition.

The textual descent of these anecdotes, except for that of Diogenes, is reasonably clear. They pass by the same route as the other anecdotes current in learned circles and are then picked out of the *Policraticus* or some other well-known book by an exemplar compiler whose successors will borrow the story from him. But by the side of this literary descent there were also *exempla* derived from semi-oral material current among the people, and usually of ultimately Oriental origin. In the double narrative of Diogenes both types are to be seen: the usual literary anecdote from Seneca in the *Dialogus Creaturarum*, and the Oriental story of the philosopher and the king in books which draw more immediately upon popular tradition. A more interesting and significant division occurs in the use of the story of the Wonderstone. Here the contrast is not between the historical and the popular tradition, but between the popular tradition and the literary legend form.

---

[1] The Amazons episode is in the *Historia de Preliis*, cc. 82–4 (ed. O. Zingerle, *Die Quellen zum Alexander des Rudolf von Ems* (*Germanistische Abhandlungen*, IV, Breslau, 1885), pp. 206–8).

[2] *Prague Epitome*, ed. Magoun, p. 136: 'Applica quod mulieres etc.' What lies behind the 'etc.'?

W. Hertz, writing of the Wonderstone, remarked that the preachers and the exemplar books made hardly any use of the story.[60] He was surprised at this, and suggested that the compilers were more interested in stronger deterrents from sin when they wrote of Death. This is incorrect as the theme of the Wonderstone is extremely common in the books of *exempla*;[61] and for the simple reason that Alexander stands here for all men, who seek to gain in this world what they must inevitably lose when they die. Hertz can hardly be right in regarding this as but a weak inducement to virtue. Surely it is the most urgent reason why men should turn to goodness, if not to God. No man who is not a mystic can easily imagine the pains of Hell, any more than he can picture the rewards of Heaven. He may talk of them, but will hardly be frightened by them into the active practice of virtue; but put before him the image of death, and he is at once in contact with what he has seen and can understand. The moment of death is the most powerful argument that may be used. It rests on a known fact requiring no exercise of the imagination and it is thus, for the preacher, the strongest of arguments.

The accusation brought against Alexander for his insatiability has naturally no place in the interpretation of the Wonderstone in the books of *exempla*; the stone teaches merely that death takes everything from us. The exemplar form of the narrative, however, is significant. There is no mention here of the journey to the Terrestrial Paradise; the story simply tells of the presentation of the stone, sometimes by a philosopher, sometimes by the citizens of an unspecified city, and of the interpretation of its mysterious powers. Welter saw some connexion with the story of the precious stone which Evax is supposed to have given to Nero, but his view is not convincing.[1] A nearer parallel is to be found in an episode of Ulrich von Eschenbach's *Alexander* where, independent of the story of the visit to the Terrestrial Paradise, which appears elsewhere in that poem, Alexander meets two old philosophers and attempts to exact tribute from them. They reply that they are Elias and Enoch, and present him with a stone which carries the same interpretation as the stone brought from Paradise.[2]

The possible connexion of Elias with Chidr, Alexander's guide to

---

[1] Marbod of Rennes, *Liber de Gemmis* (Migne, *P.L.* vol. CLXXI, col. 1737).

[2] The Elias and Enoch version of the Wonderstone story is in Ulrich von Eschenbach, *Alexander*, vv. 24,444–648; the normal version is vv. 25,265–440.

the Water of Life in Oriental tradition, is a tempting but unsure hypothesis.[1] The main point is that we have here a truly popular tradition: the story of Elias and Enoch, the porters at the gate of the Terrestrial Paradise who shall reappear upon the earth to preach the Faith against Antichrist, which is more familiar in Christian tradition than the Journey of Alexander to the Terrestrial Paradise. How the story of the Wonderstone came to be connected with that of Elias and Enoch, in some confusion of popular legends, of stones and prophets and those who stand at the gates of the Terrestrial Paradise, is not clear; but the stories are so connected not only in the episode of Ulrich von Eschenbach but in the account of the Journey to the Terrestrial Paradise found in the *Faits des Romains* and its derivatives, and also in that in the *Manchester Epitome*,[2] where the lock-keepers who guard the boom across the river and deny entrance to Alexander's lieutenants are evidently Elias and Enoch. It is plain that the exemplar version of the story, in its several forms, is another descendant of the same *popular* version of the Wonderstone story, a version which was originally dissociated[3] from the story of the Journey to the Terrestrial Paradise.

Like the story of the Wonderstone the episode of the Philosophers at the Tomb is derived from Oriental, and immediately from Jewish, tradition. We are told that when Alexander was dead and buried in his golden sarcophagus, a number of philosophers collected round the tomb, and produced each in turn sententious comments upon the futility of man in the face of death. Wherever this episode appears it is a copy or an abridgement of the Oriental version and its earliest appearance in Europe is in the *Bocados de Oro*, the *Disciplina Clericalis*, and the I[3] *Historia de Preliis* interpolations.[4] From the *Disciplina*

---

[1] On this question see I. Friedländer, *Die Chadhirlegende und der Alexanderroman* (Leipzig, Teubner, 1913).

[2] For the version in the *Faits des Romains* see the edition by L.-F. Flutre and K. Sneyders de Vogel, I (Paris, 1937), pp. 397–401; and note in vol. II (1938), pp. 161–2.

One of the most important differences between this and the *Iter* version of the story is that here only Alexander's lieutenants, and not Alexander himself, go up the river. See for a similar version the excerpt from the *Manchester Epitome* given on pp. 373–4.

[3] See I. Levi, 'La légende d'Alexandre dans le Talmud', *Revue des Etudes juives*, II (1881), pp. 293–300.

[4] For these versions of the Tomb story see:

H. Knust, *Mittheilungen aus dem Eskurial, B.L.V.* vol. CXLI (Tübingen, 1879), pp. 46–52.

Disciplina Clericalis, ex. xxxii: de aurea Alexandri sepultura (ed. Hilka and Soederhjelm, pp. 48–9).

F. Pfister, in *Münchener Museum*, I (1912), pp. 271, 278.

Clericalis, this episode passed into books of *exempla*, just as it passed from the I³ interpolations into some of the Alexander-books; and with its, to our ideas, sickening play upon words, proved itself very attractive.[62] The later books of *exempla* tended to abbreviate these comments upon the inevitability of death, perhaps because the compilers and the preachers knew them too well to need to be reminded of them all in their memoranda.

It is the theme of this large group of anecdotes, the futility of man in the face of death, that dominates exemplar morals drawn from the career of Alexander. By their mild, generalized interpretations the compilers of the books of *exempla* softened here the accusations found in the Peripatetic and in the Stoic attacks on Alexander. Such accusations were maintained by individuals, but we have seen how the general exemplar attitude was not ill-disposed towards him.

3. ALEXANDER'S DEIFICATION IN THE BOOKS OF *EXEMPLA* AND THE PREACHERS

The books of *exempla* do not tell the story of Alexander's visit to the oracle of Ammon and the subsequent murder of Callisthenes; its textual descent probably deprived the compilers of any knowledge of this material. On the other hand they used an anecdote of Alexander, told in Quintus Curtius and Seneca,[63] that had passed conveniently unnoticed in philosophic circles, and which threw a very different light upon Alexander's attitude to deification.

Seneca tells how Alexander jumped down into a city and attacked the besieged single-handed. This part of the anecdote was well known, probably through Quintus Curtius and the romances, to medieval authors. But the sequel was omitted when the story was quoted. Alexander received a wound in the course of the engagement and suffered great pain in consequence, whereupon he remarked to those that stood about him: 'All men call me the son of Jupiter, but this wound proves that I am but a man.' Seneca borrowed the story from Quintus Curtius and used it justly enough; remarking that we should learn humility by this example. It is, in fact, the one occasion where Seneca is favourable to Alexander, even though he does not directly praise him for thus disavowing divinity. Yet the passage was conveniently forgotten by all medieval moralists and was first used by Vincent de Beauvais, who included it in his account of Alexander in the *Speculum Historiale*:[1] 'Huius uulneris dolore dum angustiaretur, dicebat: omnes me iurant Iouis esse filium; hoc uulnus hominem esse clamat.'[1]

This quotation must have been known to the numerous learned writers who read Vincent, and yet it appears nowhere else in learned literature. On the other hand the anecdote passed (probably through Vincent) into books of *exempla* and into sermons. The *Tabula Exemplorum* tells the story thus: 'Item Alexander rediens de bello dixit: "Omnes homines dicunt me esse filium Iouis, sed hoc demonstrat uulnus me esse hominem." Sic homo considerans suam miseriam discit humiliari.'[2] The *exemplum* reappears in two other compilations; and twice over in a book of Middle English sermons.[3] In one of these appearances of the anecdote there is an interesting variant. Here the story is told, not of Alexander, but of 'Sares, the son of Alexander'. He comes to a city wounded after a battle and the people acclaim him as the son of Jupiter because of his wondrous beauty. He replies: 'hoc uulnus manifestat oppositum.'

Sares is interpreted as the type of the Hypocrite; his marvellous beauty had made him thought the son of God, but his fair exterior covered a soul that was human and therefore vile; like a hypocrite he was fair without and foul within. This allegorization of the story dissociates the moral assigned to it from any implied reflexion upon 'Sares'. The method of the *Gesta Romanorum* is used here, and the anecdote is not merely an illustration but an allegorical illustration. Why Sares, the son of Alexander? The source of this version is unknown. It may be that 'son of Alexander' is a dittographic misreading, a phrase formed on the analogy of 'son of Jupiter', but the name 'Sares' is unidentifiable. In the other sermon in this collection the story is told correctly of Alexander, and the moral drawn is that suggested in the *Tabula Exemplorum*. It is noticeable that knowledge of this anecdote was practically restricted to English compilers.

The conception of Alexander implied in this episode is evidently favourable, since it shows Alexander capable of humility, which is

---

[1] Vincent de Beauvais, *Speculum Historiale* IV, 51 (ed. Douai, 1624, p. 131).

[2] *Tabula exemplorum*, ed. Welter, exemplum 285, p. 76.

[3] *Middle English Sermons*, ed. W. O. Ross, E.E.T.S., O.S. CCIX (1940), p. 307 (the 'Sares' episode), 323 (normal version).

compatible, not with the proud blasphemer of the theologians, but with the hero of the Romance who refused to allow the Persians to pay him divine honours, and denied to the Gymnosophists that he had anything of immortality about him.

4. ALEXANDER'S LIBERALITY IN THE BOOKS OF *EXEMPLA*

It has been seen how the pungency of Seneca's comments upon Alexander's liberality was weakened by learned medieval writers; though Alexander's liberality still met with disapproval.[1] In the books of *exempla*, however, the Senecan anecdotes were finally made to bear a sense directly favourable to Alexander. As we have seen, the historical Diogenes anecdote makes only a very rare appearance here, and its place has been taken by a story with a more general exemplar moral. But the anecdote of the man to whom Alexander gave a city reached the compilers in its learned form. Seneca's comments are invariably omitted, and the story is often told without comment under the significant heading of *Liberalitas*, but where a moral is given it shows how the compilers regarded Alexander in the light of this story.[64]

In the *Dialogus Creaturarum* the anecdote illustrates a remark of St Isidore, that God often grants to men more than they have asked for in their prayers:

> Verum enim est quod dicit Ysidorus: multi orantes non exaudiuntur petendo, quia illis meliora quam petunt Deus confert. Refert enim Seneca libro de beneficiis, quod Alexander cuidam petenti denarium dedit urbem, et cum ille diceret tantum donum sibi non conuenire, respondit: non quaero quid te deceat accipere, sed quid me dare. Sic enim agit Deus, quia saepe petita non concedit, ut meliora et ampliora donet.[2]

Again, in the *Tabula Exemplorum*, the intended moral is suggested by the heading under which the anecdote is placed:

Misericordia

Item nota quod cum Alexander dedisset uni pauperi preciosum donum, admirans pauper dixit: 'Quare mihi indigno dedisti tantum donum?' Alexander dixit: 'Non quia sis dignus recipere, sed quia me decet tantum dare.'[3]

---

[1] See above, pp. 89–90.

[2] *Dialogus Creaturarum*, dial. 4: de Hespero et Lucifero. (ed. Grässe, p. 142). See also below, p. 325, n. 116.

[3] *Tabula Exemplorum*, ex. 176 (ed. Welter, p. 48).

To the priest seeking alms for the Church and for the support of the poor, the question of the worth of the recipient does not enter into the matter, nor do the means of the giver, since almsgiving does not imply such extravagance as Seneca had in mind. The restriction of liberality in its exemplar application to almsgiving deprives Seneca's judgement of its force because such a judgement is neither desirable nor necessary for Christian preaching and practice in the giving of alms; there should be no measure in giving to the poor, as St Jerome wrote in his letters. Alexander's poor man is no longer a veteran soldier; he is the poor Christian for whom the preacher asks alms, and Alexander is the good and charitable man.

But there is yet another exemplar passage in which a rare anecdote of Seneca's, which in its original wording could by no means be made to bear an interpretation favourable to Alexander, has been made, by deliberate or unconscious alteration, to take on a most favourable meaning. The *exemplum* is quoted by Welter who did not, however, notice the corruption of Seneca's text in the *exemplum*.[1]

Alexander marching into Asia is met by the envoys of a city who offer him half their city; he replies:

Idem de liberalitate Alexandri, ait Seneca (lib. ii° *de Beneficiis*): ueni in Assiriam non ut acciperem id quod dedissetis, sed ut haberetis id.	[*Compare* Seneca, *Ep. ad Luc.* 53, 10: Eo proposito in Asiam ueni, ut non id acciperem, quod dedissetis, sed ut id haberetis, quod reliquissem.]

The anecdote is immediately followed in the exemplar collection by the explicit of the manuscript. The suppression or unintentional omission of the last two words has effectively reversed the meaning of Seneca's anecdote, which was in his text yet another example of Alexander's false liberality; the misreading *Assiriam* for *Asiam*, and the other alterations in the text, argue the use of an imperfect MS. of Seneca or of a derivative of Seneca, and possibly the author either misread or did not notice a lacuna in the original. But whether the alteration was conscious or unconscious, it gave preachers another example of the Christian charity and liberality of Alexander.

[1] See J. Th. Welter, *L'Exemplum dans la litt. religieuse et didactique du Moyen Age* (Paris, 1927), p. 380, n. 1. The manuscript is B.M. MS. Add. 27336, a collection of *exempla* made by a Franciscan in the late fourteenth or early fifteenth century.

5. THE *GESTA ROMANORUM*

The allegorical treatment of stories in the *Gesta Romanorum* led, as has been noticed, to a more complete dissociation from any study of character than is observable in the books of *exempla*. In some of the stories concerning Alexander he is interpreted as God or as Jesus Christ, in others as the Devil; the arbitrary and far-fetched interpretation does not aim at consistent allegory beyond the limits of each one story. But while the *Gesta Romanorum* can therefore convey no conception of Alexander, its popularity was so great that an enumeration of the Alexander anecdotes contained in it is of value and has been given in the notes.[65]

As in most story-books of wide popularity the number of stories in the collection differs from manuscript to manuscript; and the frequency of occurrence of the various stories has been tabulated. From this it appears that the commonest Alexander anecdotes in the *Gesta Romanorum* do not correspond to those commonest in normal exemplar collections, with the exception of the episode of the Philosophers at the Tomb. Of the common stories, most are derived from Oriental sources. An interesting exception, apart from the anecdote of Diogenes and the sun, is the story of Alexander's visit in disguise to the court of Porus.[1] The predominantly Oriental nature of the Alexander material is to be expected in a book where most of the stories are of such provenance; one such story, the story of the man who would not accept mass from a wicked priest, has been traced back to an origin in the Indian version found in the Tripitaka.[2] As a guide to the late medieval popularity of certain anecdotes the *Gesta Romanorum* is untrustworthy. Of the stories commonest in its various manuscripts that of the basilisk, and that of the visit to Porus in disguise, were little known elsewhere; while the story of the pirate, which occurs in only one manuscript of the great number examined by Oesterly, was one of the best known of all the anecdotes of Alexander.

Although no consistent conception of Alexander can be extracted from them, some of the allegorical interpretations have been appended

---

[1] See for discussion of this episode below, p. 365.

[2] See Alexander Haggerty Krappe, 'The Indian Provenance of a Medieval *Exemplum*', *Traditio*, II (1944), pp. 499–502.

for their curious interest. As a source the *Gesta Romanorum* supplied anecdotal material in many scattered cases, and especially to the *Middle Dutch Alexander* and its *Middle Low German* derivative.

6. MISCELLANEOUS *EXEMPLA*

(*a*) UNFAVOURABLE TO ALEXANDER

No stronger evidence for the predominant approval of Alexander in books of *exempla* can be found than the scarcity in them of unfavourable evidence. With the exception of the rare use of the literary Diogenes episode, and of that typical non-committal treatment of unfavourable material which has already been discussed, I have been able to find no more than two unfavourable references to Alexander in books of *exempla*. These references both concern that principal Stoic, and consequently theological, accusation of arrogant pride; and both are evidently a direct reflexion of the theological tradition.

The first is in a book which does not conform to the normal exemplar pattern, the *Speculum Sapientiae*. Here the name of Alexander is coupled with that of Nero, with whom he was uncertainly connected in the Antichrist legend: 'Si autem potentia niteris transcendere et si eius prelatione leuaberis, cum Nerone impiissimo aut cum Alexandro nequissimo praedo eris.' This admonition, in a chapter 'contra appetitum dominationis', sounds very like a reminiscence of the pirate's accusation, taken up by St Augustine, that Alexander was merely a powerful and successful robber.

The second reference to Alexander's pride is in the *Alphabet of Tales*, where his dividing his empire among twelve successors is interpreted as due to the desire that no man should equal him in greatness.[66] The incident, borrowed from the *Historia Scholastica*, is intended to illustrate the tag 'superbus nec in uita nec in morte parem uult habere'.

We may finally mention the most famous of all medieval preachers, Berthold von Regensburg, who keeps to the theological tradition which was so strong in Germany and is entirely out of sympathy with

---

[1] *Speculum Sapientiae* II, 10 (ed. Grässe, p. 46); for the connexion of Alexander with Nero, see pp. 133, 139.

the Alexander portrayed in the *exempla*. All his abuse of Alexander (and he has nothing to say in his favour) is directed at this same vice of 'hohvart', which Berthold sees especially in the episode of the Celestial Journey.[1] Although Berthold, as a preacher, should properly be considered within the exemplar tradition, he stands definitely apart from it both in the material which he uses and in his attitude to Alexander.

It will become apparent from the references given that unfavourable criticism of Alexander is foreign to exemplar literature, and that the few instances of it to be found are derived directly and recognizably from the theological attack upon his pride.

(*b*) FAVOURABLE TO ALEXANDER

But apart from such occasional unfavourable comment as we have discussed, there is to be found in the books of *exempla* a convincing number of miscellaneous anecdotes and incidents that illustrate a favourable attitude to Alexander. The first group is concerned with continence, abstinence, and self-restraint, as exemplified in the life of Alexander; and there are also certain anecdotes that admit of no clear categorical classification.

The exemplar use of the story of the Pirate has already been treated.[2] In the original version, it will be remembered, the moral of the episode had rested upon the pirate's accusation of Alexander as an unjust aggressor, as a robber-chief on an imperial scale. Exemplar and secular writers, however, by their own adaptation of the version of the story in the *Policraticus*, where Alexander, hearing the pirate complain of his bad fortune, changed that fortune and enrolled him among his men, altered the moral emphasis of the story. This was now placed upon Alexander's forbearance in hearing without resentment the pirate's harsh speech, and upon his kindness in changing his bad fortune. This form of the anecdote appears in the *Gesta Romanorum* and the *Dialogus Creaturarum*; but it seems to have been an especial favourite in books of *exempla* and secular writers in Italy.[3]

---

[1] For Berthold von Regensburg's remarks upon the pride exemplified by Alexander in the episode of the Celestial Journey, see *Predigten* xxv (ed. F. Pfeiffer (Wien, 1862), pp. 399 ff.); and for further criticism of Alexander, in conjunction with the Maccabees text, see *Predigten* xxxiii (ed. Pfeiffer, pp. 522, 530, 534).

[2] For the story of the Pirate, see above, pp. 95–8.

[3] For the enumeration of uses of the anecdote in its exemplar form, see pp. 281–2.

There are four anecdotes told only in the *Dialogus Creaturarum* among exemplar books. Most of the material in that collection was derived from literary sources, and especially from the *Policraticus*; the first anecdote, however, does not come from that source. It may possibly be related to the story of the man who appealed from Alexander's anger to his justice, or from Alexander drunk to Alexander sober, but I know of no immediate source. The anecdote is as follows:

Sicut legitur in historiis Alexandri, quod, cum quidam eum grauiter offendisset, nolebat ei dimittere, Aristoteles autem hoc cognoscens perrexit ad eum et ait: 'uolo, domine, quod hodie sis uictoriosus ultra quod fuisti'. Quo respondente ait 'bene uolo'. Cui ille: 'tu, rex, superasti omnia regna mundi, sed hodie tu superatus es, quia, si te permittis superari, uictus es; si tu quoque uincis temetipsum, uictoriosus eris, quia, qui semetipsum uincit, contra omnia fortis est, ut dicit philosophus. Ad haec uerba uindictam remisit Alexander et placatus est.[1]

There is an obvious parallel between this and the exemplar form of the Diogenes anecdote; and its lesson, that Alexander was capable of self-restraint and continence, is borne out by three further anecdotes in the same book. The first is the abusive speech of his tutor Antigonus to Alexander; he tells Alexander that he allows himself to be dominated by pleasure: '...Quasi dicat: indignus es regno ratione aetatis et uoluptatis. Et tamen patientissime (Alexander) tulit.'[2] Here, as in the story of the pirate, the emphasis is upon Alexander's forbearance, and not upon the accusation. It was remarkable to medieval people that a king should so restrain his anger. This anecdote, with its moral, was borrowed from the *Policraticus*, where it occurs in close conjunction with the pirate story.

The second story was also borrowed from the *Policraticus*; it is the well-known tale of the girl engaged to a barbarian prince who fell into Alexander's hands but was sent back to him unharmed;[3] a remarkable instance of continence by medieval standards, when political motives would hardly be suspected except by so discerning a writer as John of Salisbury. The story may be compared with Alexander's treatment of the female entourage of Darius, and with the story in the *Secret of Secrets* of the poison girl and the accompanying lecture by

[1] *Dialogus Creaturarum*, dial. 9: De igne et aqua (ed. Grässe, p. 148).
[2] *Dial. Creat.*, dial. 115: De onagro et apro (p. 269).
[3] *Dial. Creat.*, dial. 121: De homine et muliere (p. 277).

Aristotle on the dangers of incontinence. Both these last passages were cited for exemplar purposes by Malachi in his *Venenum Malachie.*[671] Alexander's chastity was never seriously called in question except by occasional moralists and by Petrarch whose pro-Roman partisanship led him to abuse the Greek hero in the most scurrilous way.

Finally, there is in the *Dialogus Creaturarum* a further incident, borrowed from the *Policraticus*, which tells of Alexander's humble and simple tastes when on the march: '...de Alexandro dicitur, quod in itinere ambulans cum antiquis accepto pane uesci solitus erat.'[1] This may be compared with a story told in the *Fior di Virtù*.[2] Alexander and his men are starving in a desert. One of them finds and brings him some oranges, but he throws the fruit into the river, saying, 'I will not live or die except with my soldiers.' Many jump into the river after the fruit and are drowned; but after a little time they come to a city where they find food. This sounds like a re-manipulation of the story from the *Epistola ad Aristotelem* of the soldier Zephyrus who offered Alexander a drink of water which he had found when all were tortured by thirst in the desert. The compiler says that he found the anecdote 'nelle storie romane', but I have not been able to trace any story exactly corresponding. The sources of the stories in the *Fior di Virtù* are mixed and in great part unliterary.

A well-known example of Alexander's forethought for his soldiers was the story, from Valerius Maximus, of his giving up his seat near the fire to a frozen soldier. This story is told in the *Dialogus Creatura-rum* and the *Gesta Romanorum*.[3] Another anecdote borrowed from Valerius Maximus was the episode of Philip the doctor, which appears in the *Dialogus Creaturarum* as an example of the trust that one should place in one's friends; while Malachi in telling the same tale emphasizes the evil of envy as displayed by Parmenio in attempting to poison Alexander's mind against his friend by saying that Philip wished to poison him.[4]

---

[1] *Dial. Creat.*, dial. 83: De auibus terrenis et aquosis (p. 230). Compare Frontinus, *Strateg.* IV, iii, 10, and John of Salisbury, *Policraticus* V, vii (ed. Webb, I, p. 313).

[2] *Fior di Virtù*, c. XXXIII (ed. B. Fabbricatore, 3rd ed., Napoli, 1870, pp. 105–6): 'Del-l'astinenza si legge nelle storie romane....'

[3] *Dial. Creat.*, dial. 94: De rinocerone, qui despiciebat senem (p. 244). Borrowed from the *Policraticus*.

[4] *Dial. Creat.*, dial. 108: De urso et lupo (p. 259). Malachi, *Venenum Malachie* (Paris, Henri Estienne, 1518), f. 7ᵛ, 19ᵛ.

There is also a small group of stories referring to Alexander's political and strategic wisdom. The *Dialogus Creaturarum* and the *Alphabet of Tales* quote the passage of Justin where it is told how Alexander introduced elderly men into his army in the capacity of military advisers;[68] while the *Dialogus Creaturarum* also praises Alexander's action in burning the spoils taken from the Persians, so that his army should not be deterred by their newly acquired wealth from their business of fighting.[1]

Finally we may mention two references to Alexander's veneration of the High Priest at Jerusalem,[69] and the quotation of his supposed proverbial sayings in the *Fior di Virtù*,[70] where he appears as a wise philosopher in a group of Saints and Stoics.

It will be noticed that these miscellaneous anecdotes are found only in a small number of the numerous surviving books of *exempla*, of which the most important is the *Dialogus Creaturarum*. This shows that they were not so popular as the stories previously discussed; but it does not follow that they were not widely known and accepted, for the *Dialogus Creaturarum* was a book of great popularity and influence. I have no doubt that a thorough search among all the books of *exempla* still in manuscript would produce many more anecdotes of this class, and provide further examples of the use of the anecdotes we have noticed.

7. SUMMARY

It seems justifiable to conclude that the attitude of the writers of *exempla* was generally favourable to Alexander. Such writers might have been expected to reproduce the usual theological or moral approach to Alexander; but they appear to have taken the opposite view for the following reasons.

First, their sources were anecdotal sources. Of the classical anecdotes, they were especially acquainted with those which had passed through such writers as John of Salisbury, who, as has been seen, tended to soften the harshness of ancient moral attack. They also used the Arab-Jewish moralizing material, which contained meditations not so much upon Alexander as upon death, and certain isolated edifying episodes from the legendary works and the historians which contain morals of general application.

---

[1] *Dial. Creat.*, dial. 109: De damula et lupo (p. 262).

Secondly, as we have seen, the tendency of these writers was not to accentuate personal qualities, because they were not interested in them. The portrait of Alexander in their books is not one deliberately constructed by the compilers from their source material; but one that we attempt to deduce from their use of anecdotal material which had evidently, in many cases, passed through some intermediate oral or literary tradition which had made it more favourable to Alexander.

Thirdly, it is permissible to suppose that they had no reason to take an unfavourable attitude to Alexander through prejudice. Unlike the theologians, they did not allegorize his character in connexion with the interpretation of the book of Maccabees; unlike the moralists, they were not interested in the examination of individual reasons for individual actions. And in one episode at least, the giving of the city to the poor man, they saw a totally different side of the question from that which was most apparent to an earnest moralist.

Sermons, however, are on a different level from exemplar anthologies; the latter form the source, the former the employment of it. And the influence of the theological tradition made itself felt on individuals. But the exclusion from the exemplar books of many anecdotes unfavourable to Alexander hindered most preachers from general denunciation of him, since the collections would provide only a very limited range of material for criticism, and few preachers would be acquainted with, or would trouble to use, material borrowed from sources outside the exemplar compilations, the anecdotes which had circulated among the people long enough to be easily remembered and readily appreciated as old favourites.

IV

THE CONCEPTION OF ALEXANDER
IN SECULAR WRITERS TO THE
FOURTEENTH CENTURY, WITH A
PROSPECT OF THE OPINION
OF LATER WRITERS

1. INTRODUCTION

THE evidence previously discussed illustrates three clearly defined
attitudes to Alexander: the weakening of antique moral judgement
in the writings of Christian moralists, its intensification in Scriptural
commentary and related texts, and its deadening in the works compiled for the use of the preaching orders. Each attitude is characteristic of a special class of society: the first of the humanistic clergy,
the second of theologians and mystics, the third of preachers.

In the preachers' manuals we penetrated to the basic and most
simplified form of medieval opinion on the character of Alexander;
certain vague general conclusions which are traceable to some extent
in all medieval writings on him from theology to romance. The work
of these writers is a sort of no-man's-land between that of the theologians and moralists who write to instruct and that of the authors of
romances who write principally to amuse, and it is to this last group
of writers that we now turn our attention.

Moral and didactic elements are inevitably present here as in all
medieval literature; some of the Alexander-books, for instance, were
written by priests who desired them (or professed to desire them) to
be used as a remedy against 'accidia', and therefore assigned to them
a moral value in preserving those who read the life of Alexander from
that dangerous mental inertia. The desire to give historical information is usually present too in an age which distinguished imperfectly
between historical fact and the fiction of romance. But the principal

intention of all this literature is to amuse. To such a literature, and to the conception of Alexander discoverable in it, 'secular' is perhaps the best word that may be applied.

The examination of the opinions of writers in this class is necessarily complex, since we have no longer to consider the view held by a single section of medieval society, but that expressed in a group of writings which comprises all classes among its authors and its public, and which is only united by the common intention to amuse. The history of the attitude of these writers to Alexander is the history of their reaction to the influence of written and oral traditions, pre-medieval and medieval. It is affected by a host of different and variable factors: by the intelligence, character, class and contemporary background of each writer.

First, there is the influence of the texts: the historical group, the legendary group, the Jewish and Arab-Jewish groups, and the miscellaneous anecdotal information that is more generally diffused. And secondly there is the influence of ideas: the moral ideas borrowed from classical sources, the mystical ideas developed in the theologians, the fundamental Christian ideas which were isolated for the preachers' benefit, the feudal ideas of the early medieval period, the courtly ideas that appeared in the twelfth century and the Eastern ideas which were brought in by the new contact with the East established by merchants and crusaders.

And of these two it is the idea that is the real influence, that permeates the mind of the writer and determines the spirit in which he shall approach his text. The text is informed by the idea, but the discrepancies in the text are not necessarily brought into agreement with the idea. In the chroniclers we have contradictory passages from the historical and legendary traditions placed side by side by a writer who has no ideas to formulate about Alexander. If we turn to Gautier de Châtillon or to Alexandre de Paris, we come to the opposite extreme, where the idea has moulded the text into conformity with the conception of Alexander that its author has envisaged. And between the two extremes we have the dull, derivative writers who pass on a text almost unmodified, and give us their own ideas about it in a prologue or an epilogue, or in an occasional naïve comment. And when the ideas so expressed are not even original but borrowed, they are none the less received by the readers of the text, retained and perhaps transmitted by them. And the mediocre writer's views are best judged from such incidental comments in which alone he usually expresses a personal opinion. It will become apparent from the study of secular Alexander texts and references to Alexander in secular writers that the conception of him contained in them differs from that of learned writers on Alexander because in the works of the learned, whether theologians, moralists or authors of books of *exempla*, the view of Alexander expressed has resulted from the reading of certain texts, and this view when established has then influenced the interpretation of other texts. Secular writers on the other hand have approached their sources of information on Alexander with certain preconceived ideas derived from contemporary opinion, and have not hesitated to remodel their material to fit these ideas. And as contemporary secular opinion shifts its emphasis so the resulting secular conception of Alexander is more variable and more volatile than the established views of him expressed in the works of theologians, moralists and writers of *exempla*.

The study of this conception is made more difficult by the fact that we are presented with a number of finished portraits of Alexander, each bearing the strong mark of an individual view, and therefore to be distrusted as evidence for general opinions. Such are especially the portraits of Alexander in Lamprecht, Gautier de Châtillon, the *Roman d'Alexandre*, the *Libro de Alexandre* and Rudolf von Ems. As these portraits have been elsewhere studied in detail, I have examined the Alexander-books only so far as to determine their general presentation of Alexander. That is to say, I have taken the main details of their portraits of Alexander to see how far those details agree with the more reliable testimony to contemporary opinion that is provided by independent references; and have ignored the lesser features of their accounts, which are normally derived directly from the textual tradition. My object throughout has been to avoid giving the secular conception of Alexander any undue emphasis, and rather to allow it to take its proper place among the various views of him held by different groups in medieval society.

For convenience I have taken a number of aspects of the secular conception of Alexander and have in most cases subdivided my examination, taking six texts or groups of texts in order. Thus the first section in each part of the discussion is concerned with Alberic and Lamprecht, and with independent references to Alexander in their period; the second with Gautier de Châtillon, the third with the *Roman d'Alexandre* and its derivatives and elaborations, supported or contradicted by the whole range of French and Provençal courtly references; the fourth with the German Alexander-books from the *Strassburg Alexander* to Ulrich von Eschenbach, supported by German references of this period; the fifth with the Spanish *Libro de Alexandre*; and the sixth with Italian and other testimony. In this way I have divided the field of secular references to Alexander before the four-teenth century; and have tried to reduce the status of the Alexander-books themselves to that of important, but possibly unreliable, witnesses to the feeling of the age.

The conception of Alexander in these works and references is no longer to be deduced from a comparatively small group of anecdotes, but from a large quantity of heterogeneous material; and in dis-cussing the influence of the source material, of learned opinion, and of ordinary contemporary secular opinion upon the medieval secular conception of Alexander I have first discussed the influence of other attitudes to Alexander: the effect of the moralists' condemnation of Alexander and of the theological view of his relationship with God. It will be seen from this survey how the influence of these conceptions of Alexander on secular writers was normally restricted to use of their fundamental texts, without the acceptance of the conceptions to be deduced from them. I have next shown how the attitude of different groups of secular writers towards the exemplar theme of Alexander's death separates them in their attitude to his life. I have then turned from the examination of extraneous themes to the earliest emergence of a secular conception of Alexander. This was built upon the simplest fact that might be known of him, that he was a valiant conqueror; the theme of valour was overlaid by a courtly incrustation during the twelfth and thirteenth centuries, but re-emerged as the chief convention of the Alexander portrait in the later Middle Ages. Alexander's secular reputation for liberality has then been considered, and certain details of the courtly portrait of Alexander discussed.

2. THE SURVIVAL OF MORAL CONDEMNATION IN SECULAR LITERATURE

In the direct sources of legendary Alexander history is to be found as firm a basis for disapproval of Alexander as in the indirect judgements formulated by classical and intensified by some Christian writers. But although many episodes in the legendary material (for example the murder of Nectanebus, the ferocious treatment of the Tyrians, and the device by which the murderers of Darius were discovered[711]) might have sufficed to establish an independent and original adverse judgement, such opinions, if formed, were not expressed by the secular authors with the exception of Lamprecht.

(a) THE AVAILABLE SOURCES

(i) *Legendary*

In the original legendary material, condemnatory judgements of Alexander are contained neither in the prologue nor in the epilogue; for they are found, not in the words of the author, but in those of the Gymnosophists and of Dindimus, in two episodes which echo the Cynic attack upon Alexander.

The early history of the Brahman tractates relating to Dindimus has already been discussed. The episode of the Gymnosophists is earlier, and probably formed part of the original Romance. Wilcken has proved the extreme antiquity of the conversation, and Tarn has found a reference to it in Megasthenes.[721] It concludes with a simple *apologia* for Alexander's conquests, which seems to have been the climax intended by the author. It shows the inconclusive clash of two religious systems—simple self-denying asceticism, and an easy-going fatalism. Alexander's answer is not really a retort; it is an excuse which emphasizes the irreconcilable nature of these beliefs.

In the books of *exempla* the Gymnosophists episode was reduced, as we have seen, to the final exchange of questions relating to immortality, and Alexander's final reply to the Gymnosophists was suppressed for the evident reason that it denied the existence of free-will. Among the legendary texts, the episode was suppressed altogether in the *Zacher Epitome* (though reinstated in the *Oxford-Montpellier*

Epitome) and was reduced to the exchange regarding immortality in Leo and in the interpolated versions of the *Historia de Preliis*.

The *Collatio*, by far the most important of the Brahman tracts, was not composed till the fourth century after Christ.[1] Here we have on each side a reasonable and sustained argument, a rhetorical exercise in which one feels that the heart of the author was with Alexander. But it is evident that from early times the *Collatio* was naïvely interpreted as a document thoroughly Christian in sentiment, and therefore unfavourable to Alexander. Such a misinterpretation of the original purpose of the author resulted from an easy confusion between the ideals of Dindimus and those of a Christian ascetic, and from an opinion of Alexander founded exclusively upon the historical tradition at a time when the legend was little known.

The revised form of the *Collatio* (*Collatio II*) was included among the supplements to the Bamberg manuscript and incorporated in all the interpolated MSS. of the *Historia de Preliis* in the form *Collatio III*. To see in the incorporation of the *Collatio* by the editors of Leo a desire to show Alexander defeated by a near-Christian antagonist is to over-estimate both the intelligence of the interpolators and their capacity for original judgement. The constant accumulation of material relating to Alexander throughout medieval legendary tradition is dependent, not on any desire to accentuate a particular conception of Alexander, but merely upon the instinct to include all the supplementary matter that the author or editor has found which relates to Alexander. This filling in of the gaps by interpolating passages from various contrasting works naturally involves the juxtaposition of passages based upon different conceptions of Alexander; but the choice of those passages springs, not from any wish to vary the conception of Alexander expressed, but from the desire to complete the reader's knowledge of Alexander by presenting him with all the available literature in a single volume.

There is nothing further of importance to notice in the Bamberg *Historia de Preliis*, or in the I¹ and I² recensions;[2] but the additions to the *Historia de Preliis* made by the I³ redactor are of some interest. Most of the possible legitimate or relevant additions to the text had already been made; but the I³ redactor, not content with this, injected a stream of moral reflexions, symbolic interpretations and

---

[1] See above, pp. 13–14.   [2] See above, pp. 43–51.

bombastic phrases.[1] Pfister's argument that the redactor was a Jew is very plausible, but does not rest upon sufficient grounds; he has certainly used Jewish material, but so did other interpolators both before and after him. His outlook is not characteristically Jewish but is rooted in contemporary European symbolism and rhetoric.

He was evidently a man of some learning, acquainted with the Oriental symbolism of jewels and with the principles of rhetoric. Apart from tasteless elaborations of style his principal interpolations are: three narrative passages relating to the siege of Tyre;[2] an expansion of the speech of the dying Darius admonishing Alexander by his example to eschew pride;[173] an interpretation of the precious stones of which the steps in the throne of Cyrus are made—they signify the virtues required in a king; certain legendary episodes; and a number of interpolations in the epilogue. These comprise the praises of Alexander spoken by the philosophers about his tomb; a brief statement of the vices that conquered him, drunkenness and lechery—a statement of the 'uictor uictus' type already studied; a letter from Judas Mardocheus to Alexander, attempting to convert him to Judaism; and two verse epitaphs, one bemoaning the inexorability of death, and the other written in the form of a poetic sermon preached by the spirit of Alexander, reproaching himself for his former pride and exhorting those who follow after him to learn humility by his example.

It is evident that we have here a series of rhetorical school-exercises, a quantity of didactic material introduced by the interpolator for its general moralizing tone, a tone always apparent in epilogue material. They are ill-knit, ill-related to the body of the legendary text, and consist of a number of straggling heterogeneous elements assembled by a man with a special interest in morality. And thus neither they, nor the other rhetorical epitaphs which were produced,[3] remain securely attached to the I[3] tradition, but reappear in varying proportions in the Latin manuscripts and the vernacular Alexander-books founded upon the I[3] recension. But the I[3] Historia de Preliis remained pre-eminently the moral version of the legend.

[1] For the interpolations in the I[3] Historia de Preliis, and the character of the interpolator, see Pfister in Münchener Museum, I (1912), pp. 249–85.

[2] Including the original version of the story of the Fuerre de Gadres; see above, pp. 30–1.

[3] For further epitaphs of Alexander similar to those cited by Pfister, loc. cit., see Romanische Forschungen, XXIX (1911), pp. 69–71.

The only further addition of importance to the moral judgements inherent in the legendary material was made by the *Iter ad Paradisum*. It has already been shown by Hertz how the personal moral of Alexander's insatiability was early reduced, in most versions of the story, to a general moral of the vanity of human endeavour in the face of death.[1] The condemnatory interpretation of the Wonderstone, however, recurs occasionally in the Middle Ages, as we shall see.

From this discussion, therefore, it appears that the moral condemnations of Alexander in the legendary sources are derived, except for the independent *Iter ad Paradisum*, from those individual Stoic and Peripatetic condemnations which were part of the original material or became incorporated into it, and were thus transmitted to all those writers who relied upon the legendary material as their main source.

(ii) *Historical and anecdotal*

Except for Gautier de Châtillon and his followers, and Rudolf von Ems, who by their reliance upon Quintus Curtius were well acquainted with the Peripatetic condemnation of Alexander which his work contains, the influence of historical and anecdotal sources upon secular literature of the period to be considered was limited to the occasional use of moral anecdotes, in which the moral has been usually either altered so as to present a meaning favourable to Alexander, or else ignored and forgotten, and the anecdote considered, not as a moral example, but as a narrative incident in the life of Alexander.

(iii) *Theological sources*

The established theological conception of Alexander received little acknowledgement in secular writings of this period except in Germany. There it is especially reflected in the work of the priest Lamprecht, who in his general outlook is hardly a secular writer, although he is bound textually to the secular tradition and must be considered in connexion with it.

---

[1] For the European history of the *Iter ad Paradisum* and its moral, see W. Hertz, *Gesammelte Abhandlungen* (1905), pp. 73–130.

(b) THE RESULTANT SECULAR CONCEPTION

(i) *Alberic, Lamprecht and their period*

Alberic's poem begins on an unpromising didactic note:

> Dit Salomon, al primier pas,
> Quant de son libre mot lo clas:
> 'Est vanitatum vanitas
> Et universa vanitas.'[1]

But there is comfort in the study of antiquity:

> Solaz nos faz' antiquitas
> Que tot non sie vanitas![2]

And the subject of Alexander has this to commend it: that he was the greatest conqueror the world has ever seen. Alberic describes the youth of the king, and his education and military training, and the fragment of the original breaks off in the enumeration of Alexander's masters and the subjects that they taught. Alberic's professed motive is therefore, like that of the author of the Douce Compilation, that men should be preserved from 'accidia' by reading such a story.[3] And this is a secular explanation; it is no other plea than that of entertainment, of recreation in a spiritual disguise. But even less than Leo would Alberic appear to have paid anything but lip-service to a moral excuse for telling such a story; from so much of his work as survives unaltered in the version of Lamprecht we see only his whole-hearted secular admiration of the feudal Alexander.

But Lamprecht was a priest, and in his Alexander poem he reflected the theological approach to Alexander. Necessarily, by accepting the historical tradition forced on him by Alberic (and he was a faithful translator) he accepted Alexander's valour in war; but he accepted also Orosius' view of him as a bloody tyrant and showed himself hostile to Alexander wherever possible. The superlatives that Alberic had heaped upon his hero cannot be accepted by a good Christian; the title of greatest king on earth belongs by right to Solomon, the greatest king of the Jews:

> ...wande Alexander was ein heiden.[74]

---

[1] Alberic I, vv. 1 ff. (ed. A. Foulet, *M.F.R.d'A.*, III, p. 37).
[2] Alberic I, vv. 7–8 (loc. cit. p. 38).
[3] For the prologue to the *Douce Compilation* see p. 69.

But Lamprecht's criticism goes much beyond Alexander's mere heathendom. He shows how his boldness often degenerated into arrogance and insolence, his courage into rashness, and Alexander's worst qualities appear in the account of the siege of Tyre where his pride and cruelty are evident.[75]

Lamprecht was in close touch with the theological tradition; he frequently interpolates Biblical passages into his translation of Alberic, and is supposed to have derived the strange and abrupt ending to his book, where he makes Alexander kill Darius, from a misunderstanding of the text of Maccabees: 'et percussit Darium regem Persarum'. Although he received from Alberic the portrait of Alexander the conqueror, and although Alexander's good qualities are thus inevitably apparent, his individual criticism emerges throughout the book in his comments upon Alexander's vices and he sees him as the fulfiller of the Biblical prophecy, the ruthless destroyer of Persia. So it may be seen how deeply he was affected by the theological approach to Alexander: he built his book upon a Biblical foundation, concentrated his attention upon the duel between Alexander and Darius, and made of the poem almost a commentary on Maccabees; and he reproduced, as far as his source, full of Alberic's praise of Alexander, would allow him, the abuse of contemporary theologians.

Independent references to Alexander in secular writing of this period are concerned with his role in Maccabees and give an objective portrait of the great heathen conqueror, and no condemnation of him appears in them yet. Lamprecht is the first writer to apply theological treatment to the secular material, the forerunner of later German criticism of Alexander, which was, like his poem, to be founded upon the Biblical presentation of Alexander as it was adapted by medieval theologians to accord with the details of the portrait of him given by Orosius.

(ii) *Gautier de Châtillon*

Gautier made his Alexander into a godlike hero whom his restless and unquenchable spirit drove on across the world from battle to battle, from victory to victory. The spell of Alexander's conquests had fallen upon Gautier, and he saw in him the ideal of what a warrior should be. The ambition that was reproved in the moralists became in the *Alexandreis* a necessary adjunct of magnanimity, the incitement to glory that was ever present in Alexander's mind.

And yet Gautier relied upon Curtius for his source; and Curtius followed the Peripatetics so that his narrative was full of reproach of Alexander. Gautier incorporated something of this adverse criticism in his poem; he reproduced the passage where Curtius laments that Alexander's early virtue should have been undermined by the effects of excessive good fortune,[76] and the account of the visit of the Scythians who attempt to dissuade Alexander from roaming the world in search of glory by showing him its transitory nature.[1] And he recognizes the hand of Nemesis in Alexander's death, the fall of a man who has risen too high. But by a mythological device later to be discussed, he ascribed that fall to the intervention not of Heaven, but of Hell, and thus achieved the effect without detriment to Alexander's position as an elect of Heaven.[2]

But Gautier did not follow out the implications of his use of Curtius' narrative. He received some important material into the *Alexandreis* because it reached him in the text of Curtius;[3] but the details of the Peripatetic attack that are given by Curtius he deliberately and regularly suppressed. The murder of Callisthenes, the destruction of Persepolis and other events which blacken Alexander's character in Curtius are here reduced to a few lines or altogether excluded from the text.[77] Thus most of the evidence for the Peripatetic attack was eliminated from the *Alexandreis*, and only the accusation remained, hesitatingly endorsed by Gautier's inclusion of it in his text, and by

---

[1] *Alexandreis* IX, vv. 418–521 (Migne, *P.L.* vol. CCIX, cols. 548–52). As in other medieval versions of the Scythians episode, Alexander's reply is suppressed. For the use of the episode in books of *exempla*, see above, p. 149.

[2] Upon this episode, see below, pp. 191–3.

[3] E.g. *Alexandreis* VIII, vv. 75–334 (Migne, *P.L.* vol. CCIX, cols. 542–7), gives a long account of the trial and death of Philotas, which was suppressed in the *Libro de Alexandre*.

his recognition of the punishment of pride in the death of Alexander. But there is little enough of condemnation here when set beside the poet's unbounded admiration for his hero.

(iii) The 'Roman d'Alexandre', and related texts and references

(References to the text of the Roman d'Alexandre in this and the following sections are to the critical text: The Mediaeval French 'Roman d'Alexandre', vol. II, Version of Alexandre de Paris, ed. E. C. Armstrong, D. L. Buffum, B. Edwards and L. F. H. Lowe (Princeton, Elliott Monographs, 37, 1937). Abbreviated M.F.R.d'A. II, except where other editions are specified. Reference is to branch, laisse and line.)

In the Roman d'Alexandre, which aims at the exaltation of Alexander as a courtly model, moral condemnation has naturally no place; even the exemplar emphasis on the futility of human life is reduced to a secular lament, the regrès of the peers of Alexander at the passing of all prowess and all largesse from the world.[1] Darius' dying speech no longer contains admonitions against pride;[2] it conveys only the request to Alexander to marry Roxana and to avenge his murder. In the Roman all adverse historical tradition was eliminated by the imagination of the writers which created a new Alexander, an Alexander who is set up as a paragon; and of whom, therefore, moral criticism is impossible.

Most of the imitations and elaborations of the Roman keep the same even tone of admiration, though Thomas of Kent reproaches Alexander for his entanglement with Candace.[3] But there are two important criticisms of Alexander in thirteenth-century French works. The Voyage au Paradis Terrestre presents the usual exemplar explanation of the Wonderstone, the inexorability and omnipotence of death,[4] but this return to didactic material becomes embittered in the Prise de Defur, which reintroduces the older interpretation of the Wonderstone as a direct criticism of Alexander.[5] Here we have the primitive form of the story. A human eye is found by Alexander at the side of

[1] The regrès of Roxana and the peers are in Branch IV, laisses 34–59, vv. 605–1366.
[2] Branch III, laisses 11–12, vv. 269–308.
[3] On Thomas of Kent's treatment of the Candace affair, see C. B. West, Courtoisie in Anglo-Norman Literature (Blackwell, 1938), pp. 75–9, and below, p. 220.
[4] For the Voyage au Paradis Terrestre, see L. P. G. Peckham and Milan S. La Du, La Prise de Defur and Le Voyage d'Alexandre au Paradis Terrestre (Princeton University Press (1935), Elliott Monographs, 35). Text on pp. 73–90.
[5] Prise de Defur, laisses 57–8, vv. 1537–97 (ed. cit. pp. 68–70).

the road; Aristotle demonstrates its peculiar properties and interprets it as a warning to Alexander against the sin of cupidity. Earlier Alexander had given a practical demonstration of that cupidity in the episode of an enchanted stream which turned to blood if a covetous man attempted to drink from it. Alexander shows his cupidity over the matter of a lawsuit; and immediately the stream turns to blood. Alexander retains all his good courtly qualities in this poem, but his cupidity gets the better of him. His frank laugh changes to the harsh chuckle of the miser when he hears of men who are not greedy for wealth,[2]

Quant Alixandres l'ot, si en rit durement;...

His whole character is changed and debased in that instant. A similar and no less important introduction of moral condemnation in a work composed at much the same time, and presenting the conventional portrait of the courtly Alexander in all other respects, occurs in the *Old French Prose Romance*. Here the writer, telling of the ambassadors who bring Alexander presents at Babylon, sees evidence of cupidity in his quibbling over the gifts,[3] and the comment there made does not conform to the picture given elsewhere in the book of Alexander's open-handed, courtly liberality.[78]

In these two mid-thirteenth century works, therefore, there is direct contradiction in individual passages of the ideas embodied in the redaction of Alexandre de Paris. It is significant that both were written at a time when the portrait of Alexander as a model of a courtly prince was already losing popularity. But it is still more significant that both texts rely for their condemnatory passages upon sources foreign to the usual tradition. The version of the Wonderstone story in the *Prise de Defur*, with the Wonderstone as an eye, is evidently derived from a primitive form of the tale, and one which therefore carried with it the primitive interpretation of the stone as a condemnation of Alexander's cupidity.[4]

Thus both these condemnations of Alexander, that in the *Prise de*

---

[1] *Prise de Defur*, laisses 53–4, vv. 1435–75 (ed. cit. pp. 63–5). For a discussion of this episode, see Meyer, *A. le G.* II, p. 200.

[2] *Prise de Defur*, laisse 53, v. 1454 (ed. cit. p. 64).

[3] *Old French Prose Romance*, p. 241. For text, see p. 372.

[4] Cf. A. H. Krappe, 'The Indian provenance of a medieval Exemplum', *Traditio*, II (1944), pp. 499–502.

Defur and that in the *Old French Prose Romance*, are probably related, not to contemporary opinion, but to sources embittered by earlier moral condemnation of his cupidity, either in the Wonderstone episode or in the story of the embassies at Babylon.

And this is more clearly demonstrated by the fact that in independent references to Alexander in French and Provençal literature of this period, there is no vestige of criticism, and, like the courtly Alexander-books, they mention only his most prized courtly qualities, his valour and his liberality.[1]

(iv) *German Alexander-books and references from the 'Strassburg Alexander' to Ulrich von Eschenbach*

In the *Strassburg Alexander*, which is a transitional remanipulation of Lamprecht, a more enlightened spirit prevails throughout than in the *Vorau Alexander*. Lamprecht's insistence that the first place among kings belongs to Solomon is retained,[2] but the author either forgets or is tolerant of the paganism of his heroes in the body of the text, and all the protagonists on both sides have become men of chivalry and honour—a significant step towards the final courtly developments. The typical virtues of the period begin to be ascribed to Alexander; beside his courage and his strength the courtly virtue of 'milte' appears now among his chief qualities.

But in spite of so much admiration expressed throughout the text, there is some final criticism of Alexander which is due to the position of the *Iter ad Paradisum* at the end of the work.[3] It is noticeable that the *Iter* was generally realized to be incompatible with the other legendary material and never became truly united with the legendary tradition. It appears in the Alexander-books in such varying forms as indicate the vicissitudes through which it has passed in the course of its transmission.[4]

The poet sees Alexander's attempt to conquer Paradise as an example of gross pride, as a striving against God; but he follows the Latin tradition of the *Iter* closely enough to make Alexander listen humbly to the old man who gives him the stone, reform his method of life, and end his days in peace and goodness. The closing part of the

---

[1] See below, pp. 322–3, 325–7. [2] See above, p. 171, n. 1.
[3] *Strassburg Alexander*, vv. 6597–7278 (ed. Kinzel, pp. 357–84).
[4] See above, pp. 149–51.

Strassburg Alexander is thus an episode unconnected with the main text, founded closely upon the *Iter ad Paradisum*, and accompanied by the author's own comment upon his interpretation of Alexander's action in seeking to subdue the Earthly Paradise; but the condemnation of Alexander's presumption contained in that comment is annulled by Alexander's conversion to righteousness after his acceptance of the stone.[79] The book ends with a return to the well-worn theme; the world is vanity—trust in God and in His promise of everlasting life:

Nû ist diz liet ze ende comen.
alle di iz habet vernomen,
beide man unde wîb,
denket an den êwigen lîb
und an daz êwige leben.[1]

In the *Basel Alexander* the courtly element has receded, and Alexander appears above all as the type of the conqueror eager for glory; but here the approach to Alexander's ambition is a secular one. It is no ground for condemnation, but for praise, that he is for ever seeking new lands to conquer.[80]

Rudolf von Ems, like Gautier de Châtillon, relied upon Quintus Curtius as his main source; and he shared Gautier's great admiration for the subject of his poem. But he did not make Alexander into an heroic figure; he tried to make him into an historical figure, and, by the inevitable intrusion of the ideals and conventions of his period, succeeded in making him into a figure half historical and half medieval. From his own unhistorical imagination he built up upon the historical sources an Alexander who possesses all the necessary courtly virtues. He therefore omits much that he found in Curtius which detracts from that courtly portrait. He did not include the prognostication of Alexander's decline into tyranny, as did Gautier, nor did he copy from Curtius such details as the debauchery at Babylon, the burning of the palace of Xerxes at Persepolis, and the extravagant excesses to which Alexander abandoned himself after the death of Darius.[2] By these judicious omissions Rudolf shows clearly enough his own opinion of Alexander, whom he represents, in all his own additions to the portrait, as a model of virtue and the ideal of his age.

[1] *Strassburg Alexander*, vv. 7279 ff.
[2] See Grammel, p. 86.

Ulrich von Eschenbach told the story of the Wonderstone twice; once in the mysterious encounter of Alexander with Elias and Enoch, and again, towards the end of his book, following the Latin *Iter*.[1] But though he introduces here the original interpretation of the stone, Alexander's insatiability, he does not linger over this moral, nor does he base on the whole episode of Alexander's journey to the Earthly Paradise an accusation that Alexander fought against God, such as appeared in the *Strassburg Alexander*. In general Ulrich, like Rudolf, customarily portrays Alexander as a model of all the virtues, although here the virtues are milder and more courtly than those extolled by Rudolf. There is, however, one strange passage where, in attempting to christianize Gautier's allegory of Nature and Leviathan who conspire to bring Alexander to his death, Ulrich makes it appear that Alexander died because he was grown proud enough to attempt even the conquest of heaven.[2] But this passage, where Leviathan is represented as telling God that Alexander will attack Heaven after he has attacked Hell, is seen to be only Ulrich's device to give God's sanction to the conspiracy of the powers of evil against Alexander; and throughout the rest of the narrative Alexander is befriended by God. Ulrich, wandering through his twenty-eight thousand lines, is not the sort of author to whom one looks for a clear-cut individual conception of Alexander. In a man of so poor a poetic gift, an 'armer Spielmann', it is not surprising that some condemnation of Alexander is to be discovered in the muddle; it is only strange that so little of it appears, and that Alexander is portrayed throughout the poem in a spirit of generally sustained admiration.

In independent secular German references to Alexander there is already to be seen that tendency to reproduce the abuse of the theologians which became so characteristic a feature of the late German approach to Alexander, and whose force was already apparent, not only in Lamprecht and Berthold von Regensburg[3] and in the frequent German representations of the Celestial Journey,[4] but also in the constant connexion of the life of Alexander in German minds with his Biblical role.[81]

---

[1] Ulrich von Eschenbach, *Alexander*, vv. 24,444–648 (Elias and Enoch version); 25,265–440 (normal version).

[2] See below, pp. 191–3.

[3] On Berthold v. Regensburg and his abuse of Alexander's 'hohvart' see pp. 157–8.

[4] See above, p. 135.

The reflexion of this criticism of Alexander was always to be found in German secular references from the late twelfth century onwards,[82] for the courtly spirit was not so all-pervading in Germany as in France, and its influence passed more rapidly away.

(v) 'Libro de Alexandre'

The slight criticism, inherited from Quintus Curtius, which lingered in the pages of the *Alexandreis*, was forgotten in the *Libro de Alexandre*. In conformity with his intention of omitting all subjective material in his source, the writer did not reproduce the passage in which Alexander's decline into tyranny is foreshadowed; and the murder of Callisthenes is not mentioned. The Philotas episode is compressed into a very few stanzas, compared with the great length of the passage in the *Alexandreis*.[1] Furthermore the Spanish writer took care to introduce from the *Historia de Preliis* only such material as completed the story without detriment to Alexander's reputation; and he therefore omitted the story of Candace, the interview with Dindimus and other legendary matter which he considered unsuitable to a favourable portrait of Alexander.[2]

But as a Christian poet he could not tolerate the machinery used by Gautier to explain Alexander's premature death, the conspiracy of Natura and Leviathan who suborn Proditio and her servant Antipater. He was therefore obliged to allow the death of Alexander to be sanctioned by God and not by these pagan forces of evil. With this intention he introduces into the account of the descent into the sea, which he has interpolated from the *Historia de Preliis*, a criticism of Alexander's pride; this leads to God's anger at Alexander's ceaseless, arrogant ambition, and Nature may then find in God's anger an excuse for her conspiracy with Satan.[3] Thus the necessary christiani-

---

[1] For the severe curtailment of the Philotas episode in *Libro de Alexandre*, MS P, stanzas 1879–86 (cf. *Alexandreis* VIII, vv. 75–334), see R. Willis, jr., *The Relationship of the Spanish 'Libro de Alexandre' to the Alexandreis of Gautier de Châtillon* (Princeton University Press, 1934: *Elliott Monographs*, 31), pp. 10–11 (referred to as: Willis, *Relationship*).

[2] Cf. R. Willis, jr., *The Debt of the Spanish 'Libro de Alexandre' to the French Roman d'Alexandre* (Princeton University Press, 1935: *Elliott Monographs*, 33), pp. 55–6 (referred to as: Willis, *Debt*).

[3] *Libro de Alexandre*, stanzas 2324–457, ed. R. Willis, jr., *El libro de Alexandre* (Princeton University Press: *Elliott Monographs*, 32), pp. 402–7 (referred to as ed. Willis). Cf. Gautier de Châtillon, *Alexandreis* x, vv. 6–167 (Migne, *P.L.* vol. CCIX, cols. 563–7). For a further discussion of this episode, see below, pp. 192–3.

zation of the circumstances that brought Alexander to his death involved a condemnation of him at this point, a condemnation which
is shown by his constant praise of Alexander elsewhere to be untypical
of the author's attitude which was one of warm admiration.

(vi) *Italian and miscellaneous evidence*

The tendency to condemn Alexander in the *Pantheon* of Godfrey
of Viterbo, an historical compilation with a strong moral atmosphere,
has already been noted; and we have seen how Godfrey altered the
Collatio to the great detriment of Alexander's reputation, depriving
him of any effective answer to the moral strictures of Dindimus.[1]

In Quilichinus of Spoleto the Biblical role of Alexander is stressed
in the prologue, in which the writer gives as his reason for recounting
the life of Alexander the necessity of expanding the reference to him
in Maccabees, and where his place in the succession of world-kingdoms is established.[2] But this significant alignment with German
tradition was not accompanied by condemnation of Alexander in the
text, which adheres strictly to the I³ *Historia de Preliis* tradition; and
even the I³ interpolations at the end, with their slight condemnation
of Alexander, are softened here into a long verse epilogue on the usual
'vanity of vanities' theme.[3]

Independent Italian and miscellaneous secular references have
nothing to add to this picture of the effect of moral condemnation
upon the secular conception of Alexander.

(vii) *Summary*

It is apparent from this survey that the condemnation of Alexander
which reached secular writers through their sources had little effect

---

[1] See above, pp. 93–4.

[2] For Quilichinus' prologue, see Pfister in *Münchener Museum*, I (1912), pp. 290–1; after
describing the four ages of the world it ends:

> De regno Greco modicum sacra pagina tractat;
> Ipsius idcirco carmine gesta loquor;
> Quod Machabeorum scripturae subticuerunt, . . .

This introduction also appears in Domenico Scolari, whose poem is founded on that of
Quilichinus; see Storost, p. 25.

[3] For Quilichinus' long epilogue, see Pfister, loc. cit. pp. 296–9; part of this epilogue is
found in the *Darmstadt Alexander* (see p. 54) instead of the normal I³ prose ending. The
Heidelberg manuscript of Quilichinus contains 59 additional lines of epilogue; see Pfister,
loc. cit. p. 299.

upon their view of Alexander except in Germany, where it was allied to the theological attitude to Alexander prevalent in that country. Such other rare individual criticisms of Alexander as appear are probably based upon unknown literary sources, which have forced courtly writers to seem to endorse a condemnation of Alexander foreign to their usual attitude of approval; or else they have been the result of the necessity of making the death of Alexander accord with the purposes of a Christian God.

3. ALEXANDER'S RELATIONSHIP WITH GOD IN SECULAR WRITERS

(a) THE AVAILABLE SOURCES

(i) Legendary

The derivatives of Pseudo-Callisthenes naturally represent Alexander as a thorough-going pagan. Leo implies in his prologue that if Alexander and other heathen accomplished so much fighting for the powers of hell, how much more should he accomplish who is fighting for God?[1] This theme recurs in Vasco de Lucena, and in the usual comment upon the story of the enclosing of the Ten Tribes.

The addition of new material in the interpolated versions of the *Historia de Preliis* was not accompanied by any original expression of opinion upon Alexander's relationship with God; but the *Iter ad Paradisum* introduced a new conception: Alexander appeared there as the favoured worshipper of the Jewish God. He was here not the instrument of God, as in the European theological tradition, but the ally of God, as in the Eastern Alexander-books. The effect of this new conception of Alexander's relationship with God is most noticeable in the *Strassburg Alexander*.

(ii) Theological

The unopposed influence of Orosius upon theological writers had the effect we have noticed upon their opinion of Alexander's relationship with God:[2] his assumption of divine honours became a crime

---

[1] For the passage referred to, in the prologue of the *Natiuitas et Victoria*, see Pfister, *Alexanderroman*, p. 44. For the comment upon the episode of the Ten Tribes, see p. 132; for the epilogue of Vasco de Lucena, p. 332.

[2] See p. 141.

against God which was punished by his death; if he worshipped God in Jerusalem he worshipped him either as one of many gods, or else because the power of God forced itself upon his recognition; if God worked miracles through Alexander he worked them only in the furtherance of his own intentions; and God used Alexander as a passive and pagan instrument, not as his conscious and active servant.

The effect of these opinions upon the secular attitude to Alexander in the period here considered will be seen to be inconsiderable; though in the later Middle Ages their influence increased.

(b) THE RESULTANT SECULAR CONCEPTION

(i) *Alberic, Lamprecht, and their period*

In Alberic the question of Alexander's relationship with God does not appear; he treats his hero in so immediate, so personal a fashion that the question of his religion is allowed no place in his description of Alexander's youth, where he concentrates upon the personal qualities of the king. That Alexander was a heathen is evidently taken for granted; but Alberic's admiration for him passes over his paganism in declaring him the greatest of kings.

But it was not so in Lamprecht, who, as we have seen, deprives Alexander of any claim to have been the greatest king in the world on the grounds that he was a heathen. In his poem the question of Alexander's relationship with God does not go beyond the understanding of the Biblical text, the presumption that Alexander's conquest of the Persians was foreordained of God,[83] although the colloquial conventions of Lamprecht's period place references to God in the mouths of the heathen.[84] In both Alberic and Lamprecht the historical approach to Alexander's paganism is preserved; but in the former the attention of the writer is upon Alexander the king, and in the latter upon the Biblical destroyer—and thus with Lamprecht Alexander's heathendom becomes part of his condemnation. In the independent secular references of this period the objective treatment of Alexander is maintained. In Germany it is frequently joined to the prophecy of Daniel or the historical sketch of Maccabees, and his relationship with God is accepted as the impersonal relationship of the Biblical texts: he is the mere instrument of the Divine Will.

(ii) *Gautier de Châtillon*

The conventions of the Latin epic and the author's personal inclinations lead to a misty mythology in the *Alexandreis*. Mars, Bellona, Victoria, Fortuna, Leviathan, Natura and Proditio all appear in the text as personifications of various powers;[1] but above all there is some single Power which stands behind all Alexander's actions, some divine and stable Fate. It is no Christian God, though in the Jerusalem episode God conventionally promises Alexander his support in the destruction of the Persian Empire,[2] it is some such impersonal power as stood behind Greek mythology, not an immediate, approachable God but a controlling One who acts through lesser natural forces. The introduction of the Jerusalem episode, and of Alexander's desire to be called the son of Jove,[3] remains only textual. It corresponds not to Gautier's imaginative intentions, but to the demands of his sources.

Alexander falls a victim, not to the power of God, but to that of Hell.[4] He expects to be received in a strictly mythological heaven where he will have yet greater things to perform.

There is a strange paganism that infuses all this view of Alexander's relationship to his God. The true power that stands behind him is an unnamed, impersonal God; almost it corresponds to ἀνάγκη, to the power that Alexander acknowledged in his reply to the Gymnosophists. The question of Alexander's relationship to the Christian God does not here enter into the matter because it is of no concern to Gautier who is building up a picture, not of the medieval, but of the glorious, inspired Alexander of antiquity.

(iii) *The 'Roman d'Alexandre', and related texts and references*

Alexander was accepted in the *Roman* as a heathen. But among the courtly conventions of epic and romance none was more usual than the equating of a heathen hero with a Christian hero in all physical

---

[1] For the intervention of these various gods in the life of Alexander, see *Alexandreis* II, vv. 186–200; IV, vv. 401–53; V, vv. 205–55; X, vv. 6–167 (Migne, *P.L.* vol. CCIX, cols. 470, 504–5, 513–4 and 563–7).

[2] For the Jerusalem episode see *Alexandreis* I, vv. 511–64 (ibid. cols. 474–6).

[3] *Alexandreis* III, vv. 241–57 (ibid. col. 491).

[4] For the conspiracy of Natura and Leviathan against Alexander, see below, p. 192; for a citation of Alexander's last speech (*Alexandreis* X, vv. 275 ff. (ibid. col. 568)), compared with a passage in Hildebert of Lavardin, see above, p. 123 and note 4.

qualities and honourable conduct; his heathendom, if it was mentioned, was touched on only with regret that so fine a man should not
have acknowledged the Christian God.

The chief cause of this attitude was the Crusades, when active
conflict with them obliged Christians to acknowledge that the soldiers
of Islam had their valour and their honour. Saladin is the best known
example of the non-Christian hero; and if Balaam in the *Fuerre de
Gadres* is correctly identified as a twelfth-century Syrian emir,[1] he is
a proof, closer to the Alexander tradition, of the admiration for their
opponents inspired in men not too biased by religious prejudice. The
heathen of the earlier period, the cowardly heathen gathered like
vultures round Roland's gallant few in Roncesvalles, are made more
human by closer association with them, and in the last development
we find the pagans of the *chansons de geste* made splendid by the combination of Carolingian material with the Arthurian spirit in the
Italian Renaissance.

This new concentration upon the courtly virtues of heathen heroes
overshadowed their heathendom, and thus helped the writers of
courtly Alexander-books to forget, except in regretful epilogues, that
Alexander was not a Christian.

The parallels between the attitude of Gautier and that of the authors
of the *Roman* to this question are easily observed; but the differences
between the approach of the French scholar and the French courtly
writers are equally evident, and depend upon the varying artistic
demands of the two poems. In the *Roman* God heralds with prodigies
Alexander's appearance in the world;[85] he loves him, and Alexander
reverences God at Jerusalem and sometimes prays to him. Yet the
active intervention of God in Alexander's career is nowhere to be
seen. He does not protect Alexander, nor does Alexander turn to him
for aid in his battles or for the accomplishment of difficult adventures.[86] The prophecy of Daniel and its implications are kept well
in the background; Alexander holds the centre of the stage and owes
nothing of his reputation to God.

Thus, though the Christian God is introduced, the *Roman* resembles the *Alexandreis* in this: that no supernatural forces are allowed
to interfere with Alexander's personal qualities. For the interest of
these writers was in personality; not in the intricate development of

[1] See A. Foulet, 'Balaam, Dux Tyri', *Modern Language Notes*, XLVIII (1933), pp. 330–5.

the details of personal individuality, but in the conventional, unvarying, ideal characteristics of a certain class of person. Romance and lyric are both games, in which each piece, the knight or the shepherd girl, the beloved or the watchman, the king or the bishop, makes his prescribed move; names may be changed but the pieces remain the same. To portray Alexander as the ideal king it was essential to throw all possible emphasis upon his conventional courtly qualities, and the intrusion of God became an obscuring and confusing factor. For the authors of the *Roman* the prophecy of Daniel must have reduced Alexander to a gaudy puppet moved by the supreme power of God. In Gautier Alexander is the godlike king, in the *Roman* the perfect prince; in both his relationship with God is purely formal, since a closer connexion would have destroyed the atmosphere of their poems, which were written in accord, the one with the sentiment of classical epic and medieval imitative epic, the other with twelfth-century French courtly and epic convention.

But even Alexandre de Paris returned at the end to that acknowledgement which, however much a writer on Alexander might become engrossed in the atmosphere of his poem, generally reappeared in his last consideration of his hero. Alexander would have been the best of all men—if he had been a Christian.[87] It is a sad awakening, a retrospective recognition of the fact that the great heroes of antiquity, however much they might be adorned with medieval virtues and Christian ideas, remained always pagan and shut out. And it is thus that so many writers earnestly entreated their readers in bidding them farewell to build their trust upon God; for without God nothing is sure, as nothing was sure even for that greatest among heathen conquerors.

The echo of the attitude to this question adopted in the *Roman* appears also in works influenced by and imitated from it. In the *Old French Prose Alexander*, however, the courtly tradition is confused in the strange speech made by Alexander at the approach of death, where he speaks first of God's close surveillance of his life, and then of the relentlessness of that Fortune which has cut it short.[88] The first phrase is evidently inspired by the Daniel theme, the second is a school reminiscence. Thus the passage, with its incoherent attempt at rhetoric, is a good example of the difficulties experienced by any medieval writer who attempted to reconcile conflicting material relating to Alexander without the intellectual power to consider the problem as a whole.

The question of Alexander's relationship with God does not enter into independent French references of this period, which are principally concerned with his courtly virtues of valour and liberality.[89] He was still, as every one knew, beneath Christian anachronisms a heathen; but this was not to be remembered against him.

(iv) *German Alexander-books and references from the 'Strassburg Alexander' to Ulrich von Eschenbach*

Alexander's relationship with God in the *Strassburg Alexander* has been already in part considered. There is no longer here that emphasis upon the Biblical prophecy which marked the original poem of Lamprecht. The poem has become an extended secular history of a life of conquest, and the pagan heroes are equated with Christians in all the necessary personal virtues.[1] But though the *Strassburg Alexander* echoes so far the *Roman d'Alexandre*, and further echoes it in removing the action from the direct supervision of God, Alexander's relationship with God is necessarily considered in the episode of the *Iter ad Paradisum*.[2] The nature of the conclusions reached by the redactor, from the evidence of this episode, upon Alexander's proud rebellion against God and subsequent repentance, have already been noticed; but we may say that God does not take a prominent part in the action until this Jewish episode is attached at the end of an essentially historical book.

This question assumes a different aspect in Rudolf von Ems. Rudolf, in spite of his attempt to return to historical truth by following Curtius, yielded to the influence, not only of foreign courtly tradition, but also of the characteristic national attitude to Alexander. He therefore accepted the implications of the Biblical passages, of Josephus and Pseudo-Epiphanius, and saw Alexander as the instrument of God's wrath against the unjust.[3] At the same time he modified Curtius, with his doctrine of Fortuna controlling the life of Alexander; although, as we have seen, he was not too devoted to his historical source readily to reject anything that Curtius had written.

---

[1] Cf. Grammel, pp. 41–2.
[2] *Strassburg Alexander*, vv. 6597–7278 (ed. Kinzel, pp. 357–84); see above, pp. 176–7.
[3] See Grammel, pp. 86–8.

He therefore made an attempt to reconcile the two traditions, and Fortune itself is, in the case of Alexander, here subject to the purposeful will of God. Dr Grammel's complicated study of Ulrich's confused narrative does not make plain that his whole conception of Alexander is derived from previously existing textual and conceptual material, and therefore that this confusion owes nothing to the author's originality and everything to his unoriginality.

Ulrich von Eschenbach received from Gautier de Châtillon only the idea of the control of Fortune over Alexander's actions, and though he made a great deal of the Daniel prophecy,[1] he did not logically extend its application to Alexander's personality and life. In the closing passage of his poem, however, Ulrich's alteration of the device by which Gautier brought Alexander to his death in order to bring it into conformity with Christian teaching involved, as will be seen, what was almost a rebellion of Alexander against God;[2] and God sanctioned his death at least by refusing to interfere with the conspiracy against him.

The history of independent German references to Alexander at this time has already been dealt with;[3] and it will be seen from the examples given that Alexander's relationship with God seldom extended beyond the acceptance of his Biblical role in Daniel and Maccabees without consideration of its implications.

(v) 'Libro de Alexandre'

The author of the Libro de Alexandre omitted from his account all that mythological apparatus which cumbered the stage of the Alexandreis, except for Natura and Leviathan (changed into Satan), who meekly take their place in the new Christian order of things. He omitted also the passage in which Alexander called himself the son of Jove.[4]

The action, thus cleared of obscuring mythological intruders, is

[1] Ulrich von Eschenbach, Alexander, vv. 27,697–727 (ed. Kinzel, pp. 736–7).

[2] Ulrich von Eschenbach, Alexander, vv. 27,552–28,000 (ed. Kinzel, pp. 732–44); see W. Toischer, in Sitzungsber. d. k. Akad. d. Wiss. in Wien, Bd. xcvii (1881 for 1880), pp. 324–5.

[3] For independent references of this period see pp. 323–4, 328.

[4] On the omission of pagan deities from the story, see Willis, Relationship, pp. 14–16.

If the Spanish author omitted such pagan intrusions in Gautier, he also omitted the Scriptural digressions in his secondary source, the B Roman d'Alexandre; see Willis, Debt, p. 28. He inserted, however, many moralizing passages upon the vanity of the world (e.g. MS P, stanzas 968–9, 1784–1809).

placed under the discreet and distant surveillance of a Christian God. Alexander, in obedience to courtly tradition, is represented as favoured by that God and as making prayer to Him,[90] and dying he looks to being received, not, as in the *Alexandreis*, into a mythological, but into the Christian heaven.

In the closing passages of the poem, however, as we shall see, it seemed necessary to the Spanish writer that God should show His anger against Alexander and sanction the conspiracy of Nature and Satan that brought him to his death;[1] and his heathendom was inevitably remembered in the injunctions in the epilogue to trust in God and in the sure reward of the faithful Christian.[2]

Thus the *Libro de Alexandre* reflects courtly tradition by Christianizing the atmosphere of the poem, but in the attempt to alter Gautier's concluding allegory it is forced, as is Ulrich von Eschenbach, to show God's wrath against Alexander for his ambition.

(vi) *Italian and miscellaneous evidence*

The emphasis on Alexander's paganism in the *Pantheon* of Godfrey of Viterbo has already been noticed—his aggressive, arrogant treatment of Dindimus and of the Romans.[3] There is nothing else of interest in the Italian treatment of Alexander's relationship to God, which does not normally extend beyond the historical approach, until the fourteenth-century poem of Scolari who follows courtly tradition in his adapted translation of Quilichinus to the extent of making his heroes (on both sides) Christian in all but name, putting Christian invocations and prayers into their mouths, and making them move in an atmosphere of Christian convention. This is due less to originality on the part of Scolari than to the natural expression by a careless writer of the conventions of his age, as Storost has pointed out.[4]

(vii) *Summary*

Alexander's relationship with the Jewish and the Christian God was not normally a question seriously considered by secular writers. In the courtly tradition the same conventions were applied to Alex-

---

[1] On the Natura episode see Willis, *Relationship*, pp. 69–70, and below, p. 192.

[2] E.g. in stanzas 2669–75 (composite numbering).

[3] See pp. 93–4, 286.

[4] See Storost, pp. 4ff., for his discussion of Scolari, and esp. pp. 59ff. For the episode of the Ten Tribes in *I Nobili Fatti* (from the I³ recension), see Storost, p. 125.

ander as to all pagans but it was understood that he remained a pagan; the Jerusalem episode was placidly admitted but it had not the slightest effect. The secular convention of Fortune was at once more natural and more desirable than that a close alliance of God with Alexander should be supposed upon the evidence of Josephus; for it did not reduce Alexander's dignity, or place him under the immediate surveillance of a purposeful God.

But to German writers, following unswervingly the theological tradition of the Biblical Alexander, the question was of more importance, because the Biblical and Josephan testimony was accepted. Lamprecht stood firm upon the Biblical prophecy of Daniel, and saw Alexander's destruction of Darius as foreordained by God. The redactor of the *Strassburg Alexander* saw in the *Iter ad Paradisum* evidence for Alexander's rebellion against, and subsequent reconciliation with, the Jewish God. Rudolf von Ems, relying upon the Jerusalem episode and the story of the enclosing of the Ten Tribes, asked his readers to believe the apparently incredible by remembering that God stood behind Alexander, a theme which was later echoed in the *Wernigerode Alexander*. Even Ulrich von Eschenbach, who, faithful to his model, Gautier de Châtillon, again subjected Alexander to the vagaries of Fortune, felt obliged to represent Alexander's death as the consequence of an indirect threat against God.

Thus the German obsession with Alexander's Biblical role intruded into what was at best a serious secularity; and this intrusion was to become increasingly evident as the Middle Ages progressed. In other countries Alexander was either always a pagan unprotected by God, or he was a courtly hero thinly overlaid with the courtly conventions of Christian chivalry.

4. THE EXEMPLAR TRADITION OF RETROSPECTIVE JUDGEMENT IN THE SECULAR CONCEPTION OF ALEXANDER

Some exemplar purpose, some lesson that the story of Alexander may convey, is professed in many of the Alexander-books, and the expression of that intention ranges from the comprehensive prologue of Leo, in which the story of Alexander is recommended as an example to all classes of men, to the prologue of Alexandre de Paris, with its special emphasis upon the virtue of liberality. But I propose here to deal with the persistence in secular literature of that theme which has been shown to pervade all the literature of *exempla*, the futility of man in the face of death, as it appears in secular biographies of Alexander.

The existence of this idea is a fundamental fact in the medieval view of Alexander, because it rests upon the simplest of premises. A philosophic judgement of Alexander, to be subjective, presupposes some knowledge of his actions, or at the least of his evil actions; but this edifying judgement is based on the simplest possible knowledge because it centres in the one pre-eminent fact of Alexander's career, that he was the greatest conqueror ever seen on earth. All anecdotal material about Alexander, directly or indirectly, rests upon this fact, and in starting from this point we start from the simplest possible oral or written tradition. And on this simplest tradition is based the simplest comment that may be made upon it: that Alexander is dead, and with his death his glory has passed away. To the Christian it is an insistent call to humility; to the pagan it is a tragic comment upon the passing of all things, the theme of *La Ginestra*; to the Christian assailed with pagan thoughts and doubts it carries with it both the sadness and the reflexion. It is not surprising that this is a theme that reappears constantly in medieval comment upon Alexander.

'He was a great conqueror; now he is dead' is the usual form of the theme where it occurs at the end of the life of Alexander, and the whole account of that life has supplied the text for the moral. The theme is, however, of limited force in that it is too simple, that it is a general moral attached to the general fact of death. And thus it is found by itself without comment only in works of simple exemplar purpose. Where a more individual judgement on Alexander's death is expressed this simple fact could appear only as a final and summary comment. The difference between original individual judgement and a simple comment of this kind is really the difference between a mere opinion concerning a fact, in this case Alexander's untimely end, and a considered judgement of the causes underlying the fact, the forces that were responsible for his death. The author of a simple moral *exemplum*, or the author of a legendary or historical biography evaluating the life-story he has written, makes as a *final* judgement on Alexander's career his general comment on the futility of earthly power. The more serious and philosophically minded writer combines that general comment with the expression of his personal view of the forces and causes that lay behind the conqueror's end.

The subjective judgements upon the forces that brought Alexander to his death differ with different classes of observer. The moralists concentrated their attention on Alexander's vices and the direct intervention of God; Gautier and his imitators on the conspiracy of Nature, the personification made popular by Lucan and Alanus de Insulis, and Leviathan; the writers of romance on Fortune and her wheel; and writers upon kingship and its dangers on the immediate instrument, Antipater and his poison, adding a general warning against traitors. Thus the different attitudes towards Alexander are partly defined by the different attitudes that were taken towards his death.

The simple form of exemplar comment is most common, as we should expect, in books of a semi-exemplar type, in edifying poetry and other devotional texts.[91] It is only in such brief passing references to Alexander that we find the comment without any further expression of opinion. Beyond the judgements that we are to consider, such remarks often extended, in historians and secular writers, to an exhortation to the reader to put his faith in God, a natural result of musing over the death of a great pagan. But the judgements upon Alexander's death which precede them are of more interest to our study than the subsequent exhortations to trust in God.

We have already examined the nature of such judgements in the moralists and theologians.[1] They may there divide into three classes. In the first case it was a vice in Alexander that brought him to his death, a personal vice of pride or ambition or injustice. In the second his death occurred as the immediate result of his desire to be worshipped as the son of Ammon, a manifestation of his vain pride that was an insult to God. In the third no reason for Alexander's death is given, but it is understood to result from God's purpose that Alexander should not achieve world empire so that the establishment of the Church and the Empire should coincide in Jesus and Augustus.

These views did not directly affect the secular conception of Alexander in the period under discussion although they are to be found reflected in some of the Alexander poems, and this is especially the case in the account of Alexander's death in Gautier de Châtillon and

---

[1] See above, pp. 103-5.

his imitators. Gautier carried over into his poem something of the Peripatetic feeling of Curtius; and Alexander's ambition is there the cause of his death. But it brings about his death only through a strange chain of personified circumstances; Leviathan, alarmed at Alexander's intention to penetrate the realms of Hell, summons Natura to his aid and together they obtain the alliance of Proditio who suborns Antipater to kill Alexander.[1] This is no divine conspiracy, nor is it divinely approved. Alexander, when he realizes that he is to die, looks confidently to his future reception into heaven. The device, as it stands in Gautier, is thoroughly pagan. It supposes the deliberate intervention of some superhuman power in Alexander's death, and that power has no commission and no authority from God; it is the power of evil. Alexander is a servant of God; but the God of the *Alexandreis* is a god of pagan philosophy, almost the impersonal Plotinic Good opposed to the Evil in Nature. This sharp division of heaven and hell gives an unique point to the death of Alexander. He falls as a punishment for his ambition, but by the hand, not of God, but of Satan. Thus Alexander's ὕβρις is punished while he remains the friend of the heavenly power, though Fortune has forsaken him.[2]

Such a piece of pagan machinery could not be accepted with enthusiasm by Gautier's vernacular followers who were too immersed in Christian sentiment to admit such a device.

The author of the *Libro de Alexandre* made the atmosphere of the poem Christian, cut away the mythological dead wood, the interference of pagan gods, and placed the action under the surveillance of a Christian God.[3] The relationship between God and Alexander is necessarily altered; the Natura episode, thoroughly pagan in Gautier, is to some extent christianized, although the skeleton of Gautier's plot is retained. Natura does not conspire against Alexander until God has made plain His anger against the hero for his ceaseless ambition;

---

[1] The episode occurs in *Alexandreis* x, vv. 6–167 (Migne, *P.L.* vol. ccix, cols. 563–6). See H. Christensen, *Das Alexanderlied Walters von Châtillon* (Halle, 1905), pp. 87–9. The role of Natura in this passage is possibly derived from Lucan, *Pharsalia* x, vv. 39–42; see Christensen, loc. cit.

[2] For the role of Fortuna in the *Alexandreis*, cf. Book II, vv. 186–200 (Migne, *P.L.* vol. ccix, col. 479), where she addresses the Macedonians who are reproaching her bitterly when Alexander has fallen ill after his bathe in the Cydnus, and reminds them that it is her nature to be inconstant, and that men should not praise her when she is with them, and blame her when she is against them.

[3] *Libro de Alexandre*, MS. P, stanzas 2302–435 (MS. O, stanzas 2160–293). See Willis, *Relationship*, pp. 15 ff.

nor does she conspire with the Leviathan of Gautier, but with an orthodox Satan dwelling in a conventional Christian Hell. Alexander is still exalted, still gives thanks to God for bringing his death at the pinnacle of his career, still foresees glory in heaven; but Christian influences have transformed the pagan hero of antiquity into a medieval Christian prince.

Ulrich von Eschenbach, faced with the same difficulty, blundered clumsily and characteristically.[1] He too felt that the action of Leviathan and Natura must receive some sanction from God, and so, in spite of the uniformly favourable conception of Alexander and of his relationship with God which had been maintained throughout the book, Leviathan, faced with Alexander's threat to Hell, is represented as appealing to God for help with the words:

> ist daz er betwinget mich,
> er beginnet vil lîhte suochen dich.

God neither intervenes on his behalf nor opposes him, and Leviathan thereupon invokes the help of Natura who aids him willingly, declaring:

> sît daz er wider mîn gebot
> lebt, sô lebt er wider got.

Ulrich, typically, rounds off the account of Alexander's death with a long exemplar excursus which includes the story of the Philosophers at the Tomb.

Thus both Ulrich von Eschenbach and the author of the *Libro de Alexandre* have come, through their attempt to transform Gautier's allegory into a Christian allegory, almost to the theological reason for Alexander's death. The powers of Hell, with the approval of God, bring him to his death for his blasphemous ambition.

Gautier's allegory, therefore, did Alexander harm by its misuse in the hands of his followers, but the idea of Alexander called to take his place in heaven, which appears in the *Alexandreis*, is present in some of the Alexander-books in a half-Christian form; it is Fortune, working under God, that deprives Alexander of life at the height of his fame, and so does him honour by causing his death at so glorious a moment.[92] The themes of variable Fortune or inflexible Providence reappear frequently in secular references of a meditative type,

---

[1] See on the passage in Ulrich von Eschenbach, Grammel, pp. 108–9. The two quotations are vv. 24,959–60, 24,999–25,000.

and introduce the usual exemplar comment;[93] but the reason for the working of Fortune is in her unreasonable caprice, and the reason for the working of Providence is close to the moral theme 'pride comes before a fall,' and thus this argument is especially to be found in works and references of a didactic type. The statement of Boccaccio that 'Fortune would have brought Alexander low had not death anticipated her' is exceptional, and is a singularly illogical and unconvincing remark which is not further explained.[94]

Finally we leave the reasons for Alexander's death which reflect exemplar, moral and rhetorical conventions and return to a purely secular theme—secular because it is based upon the denial or exclusion of all supernatural forces. This is the poisoning of Alexander by Antipater, not as the instrument of God, or of Fortune, or of Nature, or of Satan, but as a mere traitor. The death of Alexander appears thus when acts of treachery, or treachery in general, are considered; and is related, not to his faults or to the working of divine forces, but to a familiar figure in secular medieval life and literature, the treacherous courtier.[95]

Thus Alexander's dying may be regarded as falling into three stages; first, the intention of the agent who brings Alexander to his death, whether it be God, or Fortune, or Nature, or merely Antipater, and the reasons for that intention; second, the administration of the poison, which gives rise to moral reflexions upon so great a man being laid low by so small a drop of poison; and thirdly, Alexander dead, and the moral, when his life is considered in epilogue, of the passing of all things. By the emphasis which they laid upon the various stages of this episode the approach of various groups of writers to Alexander may be tested. It will be seen how an avenging, a provident, or a merciful God are restricted themes; how Nature is

PLATE V (*opposite*). This page, from the Stockholm MS. of the French Prose Alexander, shows the favourite medieval symbol of Fortune, who here holds a covered cup and an open pot, seated at her wheel on the rim of which appear those whose affairs are prospering on the left, Alexander enthroned at the top and the unfortunate on the right. The accompanying text on Fortune and her wheel is an interpolation into this MS. and does not occur elsewhere. Above, Alexander, left, dictates his will to a notary, right.

The MS. was written in the first quarter of the fourteenth century. Its illustrations are unusual and certainly the work of an artist familiar with Islamic civilization. It was in Portuguese ownership in the fifteenth century and may well have been written and illustrated in southern Spain or Portugal.

Qi dit de larue de fortune coment les uns montent et les autres
des cendent. Les Suns soillent et les autres tresbuche. tels est
huy riches que demain sera poures et tels est huy uif que
de main sera mors. Et ce pouez vous ueoir apertement dou
roi alixandre et des autres plusurs Rois et seignors. Alixan
dre qui monta si haut quil fu seignor et rois sur tos les autres
Rois. Et fu coronez en babiloine a estre emperere de tout
le monde. Et quant de rue fortune lauoit fait seignor elle
par lui que elle auoit henore. Vost demostrer a tous ceaus
que apres lui uendront example. Que nul ne se doit fier
en la gloire terriene. Alixandre qui fu sus haut ou sommet on
de la rue de fortune. Or est de soi tresbuchies tout en sut est
il de cest monde come vos leuez cw cw cw cw

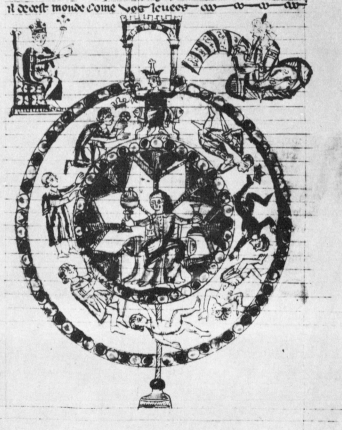

V   ALEXANDER ON THE WHEEL OF FORTUNE

brought forward only in Gautier de Châtillon and his followers; and how the caprice of Fortune is a common and obvious reason for the death of Alexander. The administration of the poison brings from writers of counsel for kings an essay upon traitors, and from the rhetoricians an epigram. The last exemplar moral is universal in all except the late medieval translations of legendary texts, but the moral is overlaid in the courtly romances, where the *regrès* are expressed, not only for his glory, but for his virtues, and especially for his liberality. What is bewailed is not merely the passing of the conqueror but the passing of all courtesy and all 'largesse' from the world.

5. THE BASIS OF THE SECULAR CONCEPTION OF ALEXANDER

Alexander's role as a conqueror always underlay all moral considera-tion of him. The simple portrait of the world-conqueror, first ex-pressed to the medieval world in the Biblical passages and in the annalists, was enlarged and overlaid with a slow accumulation of material but remained always and inevitably the underlying theme of both historical and legendary narrative. The difference between the philosophic, the theological, the exemplar and the secular attitude to this fundamental theme is this. The philosopher discusses the men-tality of the conqueror and his qualities as a ruler; the theologian considers his conquests as ordained by God, and as the explanation of his symbolic role; the exemplar writer records the fact of Alexander's conquests, and adds the second fact, that they availed him nothing at his death. But the secular writer writes of Alexander as a conqueror for comparison with other conquerors of the past or of his own age, or with patrons who would like to be conquerors. Admiration for so great a man inspires his work and provides the basis for the whole secular portrait of Alexander.

It is in this general detachment from philosophic or exemplar issues that the secular attitude to the career of Alexander is first revealed. It is discernible in the early historians and Latin poems, though here the references to Alexander are usually so abrupt that nothing significant may be gleaned. A reference to Alexander the conqueror merely *as* Alexander the conqueror tells us nothing, since it does not reveal the author's opinion of his conquests.[96]

There is by no means one secular attitude invariably maintained towards the conquests of Alexander; since there enters even into such considerations the question of how far God stood behind Alexander, how far he owed his conquests to God. The history of this point has been discussed, and it will have been seen how the tendency was to make God Alexander's friend rather than the active furtherer of his victories.[1] But there emerges early from the fundamental theme of conquest an idea which is purely secular, and dissociated from any tendency to diminish Alexander's prowess by the ascription of his victories to God or to Fortune. This idea is the desire for glory, the belief in his own destiny that drives him on. It is this greatness of mind that is the focal point of his lesser virtues in the secular writers and in some of their sources—of his justice, his courtesy, his liberality, his wisdom, and especially of that valour supported by physical hardiness which enabled him to realize such ambitions.

Personal valour and personal hardiness, no less than greatness of mind, could not only easily be deduced from the Latin sources, but were also necessary to the hero of a *chanson de geste* or of a courtly romance; and the accentuation of these qualities, allied to and inspired by a great desire for glory, is especially secular because it minimizes the controlling influence of God or of a stable Providence, and tends to admit only an inconstant Fortune as the intrusive power from above which can influence Alexander's career. And Fortune, because of its inconstancy, cannot detract from Alexander's personal qualities. It is this view of Alexander as man unaided that lies at the heart of the secular portrait; and the more this aspect of him is stressed, the more may we say that the author or the period concerned is free from the influence of the other conceptions of Alexander already discussed which tend to diminish Alexander's personality and to subject him to a divine directive.

What was the most evident part of true nobility to secular writers was ambition and vanity to moral writers; what was valour to the secular writers was rashness to Seneca and John of Salisbury. As in the discussion of Alexander's reputation for liberality, so here too the changes of meaning in certain words, and the variable value assigned to different virtues at different times and in the several divisions of medieval society must be examined before the outlook of the secular

[1] See above, pp. 181–9.

writer can be seen in clear comparison with the other attitudes to Alexander.

Translating these principal qualities into Latin, we have two pairs of words, *magnanimitas* and *ambitio*, *fortitudo* and *temeritas*; and of these it is *magnanimitas* that is at once the most important quality, and the most subtle and variable in its definition. In the medieval meaning of this word, however, we may see the starting-point of the secular conception of true nobility, and thence of Alexander's nobility seen in the light of that ideal.

Magnanimitas, as a translation of the Aristotelian μεγαλοψυχία, had originally meant a loftiness of spirit, a true nobility of thought and of action dissociated from personal gain.[1] Of such a spirit it is evident that *benignitas*, feeling for others, must form a component quality; but it is a quality subordinate to *magnanimitas*, and thus generosity, itself the practical demonstration of benignity, may be called a grandchild of such a magnanimity.

It was always evident that Alexander displayed generosity in his actions; in his treatment of the female relatives of Darius, of the Persian who sought to murder him, of Philip the doctor, of Dionides and of Diogenes.[97] While it might be alleged, with Cicero or Seneca, that his material liberality did not spring from honest causes but from a mistaken political cunning or from personal vanity, no such attack was made upon his capacity for generous actions; for there was no possible ground for such an attack. But his claim to possess Aristotelian magnanimity as a quality of the character could never have been successfully maintained in learned medieval circles, where his arrogance and his pride, his self-seeking and his general incontinence were the subject of universal reprobation, and the object of informed Christian attack.

In Tertullian, however, Alexander is praised for his *sublimitas*, which stood, like *magnanimitas*, for a translation of the Greek;[98] and it is evident that the meaning of these equivalent terms had already declined from the comprehensive philosophic summary of a character into a nobility which could coexist with or be subordinate to other less praiseworthy qualities. Magnanimity is no longer an exclusive term that sums up the whole man.

---

[1] The classical meaning of *magnanimitas* is defined, after Cicero, *De Officiis* I, 19, by William of Conches in Migne, *P.L.* CLXXI, cols. 1026–7.

The confusion between *anima* and *animus* brought *magnanimitas* into later medieval associations of ideas which *sublimitas* never acquired. Its medieval meaning coincides neither with the ancient nor with the modern meaning, neither with the Aristotelian term nor with the modern application of the epithet 'magnanimous' to a generous man or a generous action. Du Cange gives the medieval meaning of *magnanimus* as 'quick to anger'; but this is a narrowing down of its basic idea which is that of great vital energy. In Alexander, his vast conceptions, the determined and inflexible spirit with which he executed them, his fiery temperament, all those qualities which made him *Magnus*, were understood, in varying proportions, in the application to him of the attribute *magnanimus* by different medieval writers. Fr. Gervase Mathew translates the fourteenth-century *magnanimitas* as 'indomitability';[1] but there was in Alexander's *magnanimitas* more than is suggested by the heavy stubbornness of indomitability, there was a hint also of his *temeritas*, his daring favoured by Fortune.[99] No suggestion of campaigns deliberately planned lay behind such an attribution of magnanimity, nor any Christian association with conquest for the common good; and Alexander is here far from the older Ciceronian definition of *magnanimitas*, based on Aristotelian ideas and reproduced by William of Conches, where 'fortitudo sine audacia' is the foremost quality of a magnanimous man.[100] Thus we shall find in the *magnanimitas* of the medieval historians and writers about Alexander a secular quality dissociated at once from Aristotelian and Christian ideas of true magnanimity, and bearing no relation to those of his actions which we should now call magnanimous, which were qualified in medieval writers, when they were noticed at all, with the epithet *benignus*.[101]

The first Christian text after Tertullian with an important bearing on the subject is Rhabanus Maurus' commentary upon Maccabees, where he remarks of the death of Alexander:[2]

[1] Fr. G. Mathew, 'Ideals of Knighthood in late fourteenth-century England', *Studies of Mediaeval History Presented to F. M. Powicke* (Oxford, 1948), p. 358. 'Magnanimitas' and 'Audacia', the two chief qualities of the fourteenth-century knight, are translated 'indomitability' and 'rashness'.

[2] Rhabanus Maurus, *Commentaria in libros Machabaeorum* I, i (Migne, *P.L.* vol. CIX, col. 1131).

Alexander's invincible spirit in the face of death is quoted, as an independent anecdote borrowed from Justin, in John Bromyard, *Spec. Praed.* Mors (M XI), art. viii, 43 (ed. Nürnberg, 1518, f. ccxix^r, col. 2).

Cumque lacrymarentur omnes, ipse non sine lacrymis tantum, uerum sine ullo tristioris mentis argumento fuit, ut quosdam impatientius dolentes consolatus sit, quibus mandata ad parentes eorum dedit, adeo sicut in hoste, ita et in morte inuictus ei animus fuit.... Tanta illi magnitudo animi fuit, ut cum Herculem filium, cum fratrem Arideum, cum Roxanem uxorem praegnantem relinqueret, oblitus necessitudinem, dignissimum nuncuparit haeredem, prorsus quasi nefas esset uiro forti alium quam uirum fortem succedere, aut tanti regni opes aliis quam probatis relinqui.... Haec autem quia in historia Machabaeorum regni Alexandri mentio facta est, ideo ex libris gentilium interposui, ut lector agnosceret non frustra uirtutem Alexandri enarrari, sed magnanimitate atque actione ipsum esse principium [*sic*; *possibly* praecipuum].

Magnanimity is here suggested to Rhabanus by Alexander's unbroken spirit in his encounter with the weeping soldiers, and by his saying that the man most worthy to succeed him should inherit his empire; the works of gentile historians show that Alexander indeed possessed *uirtus*, and this is defined as 'magnanimitas et (magna) actio'. Magnanimity is therefore here dissociated from any question of physical action; it is a vigorous greatness of mind. That Rhabanus did not associate this magnanimity in Alexander's character with Christian virtues is shown by his account of his life, which, derived from Orosius, shows a blood-thirsty Alexander possessed by the insatiable will to conquer.[1] There is a contradiction in his account between secular admiration of personal qualities and theological doctrine; for Rhabanus, relying upon the prophecy of Daniel and its attendant commentaries, considered that God preserved Alexander in his battles, and thus his *magnanimitas* could properly be attributed to that God who stood behind him. By *uirtus* Rhabanus meant more than courage—he meant the qualities for which Alexander was called Great; and these qualities are divided into greatness of mind and greatness of action, so that there is in the loftiness of spirit associated with Alexander a reminiscence still of earlier definition and usage.

Another magnanimity, a fierce resolution closer to the meaning given by Du Cange, appears in the preface to Ekkehart's account of Alexander, where he says of him:[2] 'Hic paruus statura, ferox natura, uir magni fuit animi, quietis impatiens, semper ad altiora contendens, crudelis et sanguinem sitiens.' The quality, of the will rather than of

[1] See above, pp. 122–4.
[2] Ekkehart of Aura, *Chronicon*, in *M.G.H. Scriptt.* VI (1844), p. 61.

the personality, is again divided off from other aspects of Alexander. To translate it here as 'great-spirited' perhaps comes nearest to Ekkehart's intention. It is a volatile, aggressive will to be great, that takes no account of reasonable warfare or of tactical disadvantage and relies upon itself against all disaster. It was this *magnanimitas* which Seneca called *temeritas*; and it is to such a quality that John of Salisbury referred in a comparison between Alexander and Pythagoras:[1] 'Michi quidem semper (ut tamen pace eorum loquar, qui temeritatem uirtuti praeferunt) ditissimo Alexandro pauper Pitagoras maior erit.' This *uirtus* is very different from that of Rhabanus; while Rhabanus had used the word in a meaning close enough to the narrower classical sense of courage, John of Salisbury intends by it the Christian ideals of virtue, which are opposed to the uncaring fierce foolhardiness of Alexander.

Thus medieval magnanimity, as the term was applied to Alexander, partakes of the nature of many qualities. It means a quality of greatness that may consist in nobility of mind, in the narrower meaning of determined and ambitious bravery, or even in ferocious and foolhardy self-confidence; its exact interpretation must differ in every writer.[102] In common with the interpretation of liberality, its meaning becomes simpler in the later Middle Ages, and magnanimity then comes to be almost synonymous with mere physical courage.

In historians and other writers whose outlook is neither theological nor purely secular, the approach to Alexander's personal valour varies between condemnation of his rashness and admiration of his bravery, between the philosophic and the secular points of view. Secular writers also varied in their definition of the truest valour; as with liberality, valour was not valour in the twelfth and thirteenth centuries if it did not verge upon excess, but in the later centuries it regained a more cautious quality. It is this lack of firm ground for a basis of comparison that must reduce all study of the basic secular approach to Alexander to a summary and partly statistical examination of the evidence contained in that material which alone may give some clue to the prevalence of different attitudes at different places and periods: the original comments of the writers of Alexanderbooks, and the independent references in every form of secular literature.

[1] John of Salisbury, *Policraticus* v, xii (ed. Webb, vol. I, p. 335).

(a) THE AVAILABLE SOURCES

The sources for the basis of the secular conception need no examination; they are the historical and legendary biographies of Alexander which we have already examined, and which contain innumerable references to those predominant qualities which here concern us. It may be noticed that the story of Alexander's rash jump into a besieged city had some independent popularity, and may have served to support the learned condemnation of Alexander's rashness. As a source of secular opinion, however, this condemnation may be entirely ignored, since the rashness attacked by Seneca and John of Salisbury was accepted and admired by writers less philosophic and more ready to admire human prowess.

(b) THE RESULTANT SECULAR CONCEPTION

(i) *Alberic, Lamprecht, and their period*

In Alberic Alexander is the feudal king; in Lamprecht, the Biblical conqueror of Darius. In the former the secular approach to Alexander stands clearly revealed in the poet's pleasure that he is describing the life of the greatest conqueror the world has seen.[103] Alexander's nobility is already a medieval nobility that suffers familiarity with no man of lesser rank, a nobility founded upon feudal discrimination. His youth is devoted to the learning of such necessary arts as shall equip him best for the business of war. Already the medieval development of Alexander's character in the hands of secular writers has begun; although it still extends only to the expression of his foremost qualities in terms of medieval convention, and not to the exaltation of qualities little regarded in the sources.

Lamprecht devoted his whole attention to Alexander's struggle with Darius; the stage was cleared for this scene of Biblical history, this Persian disaster from which arose the third world-kingdom.[104] And he looked on Alexander with a theologian's eye as the proud destroyer. Gautier de Châtillon was also to concentrate upon the portrayal of the clash of Alexander with Darius, conqueror against emperor; but Gautier had a secular purpose in bringing Alexander thus into the unobscured centre of the scene, while Lamprecht was writing a commentary upon Maccabees. And thus the portrait of the hero in the *Vorau Alexander* is no secular portrait in intention, though, being founded upon the text of Alberic, it is materially secular. Lamprecht intended to portray the cruel destroyer who put down Persia from her seat, the man so proud that theologians saw in him the pattern of the Devil.

And the basis of these differing conceptions is reflected in contemporary vernacular references.[105] In France we find the unashamed secular exaltation of Alexander's qualities; in Germany his life is already connected with Biblical exegesis, and is seen as a passage in Jewish history.

(ii) *Gautier de Châtillon*

A god-like fire, an inspired desire for glory drove on the hero of the *Alexandreis*.[106] The supremely personal exaltation of his secular qualities was assured by the removal of the controlling power of Fate to a distant and scarcely noticed eminence, the introduction of Fortune who grants and witholds favours with an impartial hand, and the addition of a group of artificial and unconvincing mythological puppets. Above all these visible superhuman powers moved Alexander, master of himself, the man sent by God, and recalled by God at his death to fight the battles of heaven.

In Gautier's poem Alexander's magnanimity received its secular apotheosis. His desire for glory, his ambition that was attacked by the moralists, is the noblest and the divinest part of the man. In this respect the *Alexandreis* is perhaps the most truly secular of all the Alexander-books.

(iii) *The 'Roman d'Alexandre' and related texts and references*

In the *Decasyllabic Alexander*, as in Alberic, the theme of the prologue is Alexander the conqueror;[107] but references to courtly traits have begun to appear in the text, and Alexander's education now comprises all the requirements of the courtly prince. The preface of Lambert li Tors is concerned almost entirely with the marvellous element in Alexander's life,[108] a preoccupation which corresponds both to the contents of his book (*Alexandre en Orient*) and to the interests of his Crusading period. It may be here noticed that the attention paid by a writer to the wonderful element in Alexander's life does not imply less emphasis upon his military qualities. His high spirit, his valour and his hardiness were not less strikingly displayed in these encounters with unknown terrors than in more ordinary battles. It is in Alexandre de Paris that the courtly themes are most developed, and courtly liberality and courtly love receive most emphasis in his redaction of the life of Alexander. But Alexander's valour is an evident and consistent part of his new character; it is described as *proesce* and *hardemans*, which are two necessary characteristics of a good fighting man. There has been a tendency to suggest that in the *Roman* liberality submerges all other traits in Alexander's character; but valour remains one of his major qualities, and is worked out with characteristic imaginative thoroughness by the courtly revisers. The inspiration of Alexander's valour, his magnanimity, now appears in its true hot-blooded guise; all thought of restraint in his encounter with Nicholas is suppressed,[1] he threatens to destroy Athens with all the uncontrolled anger of a medieval lord,[2] and he has to be restrained by the prudent counsels of Aristotle from extreme rashness.[3] His valour and his strength are emphasized by the conventional stylistic device of the period; a battle is portrayed as a succession of duels in each of which the fortunes of the two combatants are described much as a boxing-match is today described by a running commentator.[4] Like Gautier de Châtillon, who had concentrated attention upon the two principal campaigns of Alexander's career, against Darius and against Porus, omitting the niggling details that confused and weakened the action, the authors of the *Roman* did not want their protagonists crowded; and they achieved their aim by confining attention not only to the great battles, but to the principal episodes of those battles.

[1] The Nicholas episode is in the *Roman d'Alexandre* I, laisses 26–72 (*M.F.R.d'A.* II, pp. 14–36). For a commentary upon this episode in the *Decasyllabic Alexander* and the *Roman* see Meyer, *A. le G.* II, pp. 125–32.

[2] *Roman d'Alexandre* I, laisse 75, vv. 1670 ff. (*M.F.R.d'A.* II, pp. 37–8); cf. Meyer, *A. le G.* II, pp. 146–7. See also Meyer's comments on I, laisses 83–7 (*M.F.R.d'A.* II, pp. 40–2), which describe Alexander's ferocious methods in persuading Philip to divorce Cleopatra (*A. le G.* II, p. 148): 'combien le bouillant héros du poème français diffère du jeune homme calme et subtil à qui le Pseudo-Callisthènes fait dire: "Mon père, lorsque je remarierai ma mère, je vous inviterai aussi aux noces."'

[3] See *Roman d'Alexandre* III, laisses 1–5 (*M.F.R.d'A.* II, pp. 143–5) for Aristotle's reasoning with Alexander; the scene may be compared with that which begins the *Alexandreis* of Gautier de Châtillon.

[4] E.g. in the encounter with Nicholas (above, n. 1), the *Fuerre de Gadres* episode which opens Branch II, and Alexander's battle with Porus, on which see Meyer, *A. le G.* II, p. 170–2.

In the *Roman de Toute Chevalerie* Thomas of Kent emphasizes Alexander's military qualities and his liberality is not so much stressed as in the *Roman d'Alexandre*. The reason for this may lie, not in any conscious originality on the part of the writer, but in the date of the original composition, for the kernel of the poem may date from as early as the middle of the twelfth century. Although it was later enlarged by the addition of much courtly material, this material was not sufficient, since it was interpolated bodily rather than incorporated in the text, to affect the spirit of the poem which remained faithful to the earlier historical approach. The prologue is typical of the feudal rather than of the courtly attitude:[1]

> Ore poet qui voelt oïr un vers merveillus
> D'Alixandre le rei, de Darie l'orguillus,
> Qi Babiloine prist e sis uncles Cyrrus.
> Alixandre conquist itanz isles hidus,
> Ynde & Ethiope, les regnes plentivus,
> Par force de bataille en maint estur dotus,
> Cum l'estorie dirrat, fort fu et vigorous,
> Hardi e conquerant [sages *D*] e enginnus.

But in the more courtly imitations and elaborations of the *Roman d'Alexandre* the same relative importance assigned to Alexander's liberality and Alexander's valour were maintained as in their model; and this parallel interest is supported by references to Alexander in French and Provençal poetry of this period.[109] How far liberality was an obvious and fundamental part of the secular conception of Alexander is considered later; but it is certain that his reputation for those qualities which made him a conqueror flourished even at the height of the courtly period, and there are many references to his prowess, his boldness and his courage. Often his valour and his liberality appear together in comments upon his character, and he is called 'preus et larges', 'larges et hardis'.

His valour is thus regarded, in relation not to historical facts, but to the qualities required of the ideal medieval prince; and thus it is often used as a canon of comparison. It coexists with his reputation for other courtly qualities, his liberality and his love of women; but these themes were evanescent, whereas his reputation for valour,

---

[1] Thomas of Kent, *Roman de Toute Chevalerie*, vv. 26–33, in the partial edition by Meyer, *A. le G.* I, p. 196. Text of MS. *P*.

having a definite historical basis, however much it might be transformed by medieval imaginations, persisted until it became the principal constituent of his popular character.

(iv) *German Alexander-books and references from the 'Strassburg Alexander' to Ulrich von Eschenbach*

In the *Strassburg Alexander* the Vorau picture of Alexander has been enlarged by the addition, not only of much material from the sources, but of courtly details of character, and the antagonistic tone of Lamprecht has been largely eliminated. Alexander is no longer constantly condemned for his pride, nor does his heathendom tell so heavily against him. In the *Vorau Alexander* the dramatic close of the poem, where Darius falls by the hand of Alexander, makes it an account of a single campaign, of the destruction of the Persian Empire prophesied by Daniel. In the *Strassburg Alexander*, however, the narrative is carried on to its end in the *Historia de Preliis*, not to its end in Maccabees. By the lengthy interpolation of legendary elements[1] Alexander's career is deprived of that cataclysmic violence which was its characteristic feature in the earlier poem, and the climax, the clash between Alexander and Darius, is no longer, artistically, the note on which the book ends. It is instead succeeded by a long anticlimax of legendary wanderings. Such a reorganization of the story brings Alexander the destroyer less into the foreground; Alexander's character is more fully, and therefore less sharply defined, and courtly qualities play their part in its formation. But he is still above all a conqueror, and his military qualities, the ambition that inspired him and his valour, are still those most stressed. This emphasis is maintained in the later remanipulation, the *Basel Alexander*,[2] where the courtly tide, which reached its full height in Ulrich von Eschenbach, has already receded, leaving the objective German secular portrayal of Alexander.

In Rudolf von Ems the historical character of the poem gives necessary prominence to the military virtues. Rudolf's general dependence on Curtius, and his determination to produce a book

---

[1] The length of the *Vorau Alexander* is 1533 lines; of the *Strassburg Alexander*, 7302 lines. The material with which the poem has been expanded is derived almost entirely from the I[1] *Historia de Preliis* and the *Iter ad Paradisum*.

[2] On the *Basel Alexander* and the conception of Alexander implied in it, see Grammel, pp. 56–61.

that shall reveal the true Alexander, causes him to stress in him the world-conqueror. Not here, as in more courtly poems, are the sieges and the battles half buried among legendary wonders and picturesque digressions. But Rudolf also thought of Alexander as the weapon of God; God is behind Alexander, and Rudolf asks his readers to believe that anything which shall seem especially wonderful in the book is credible if we consider that Alexander's career was ordained by God.[110] We again encounter the old difficulty; if so much was due to God, how much should Alexander's personal qualities be prized? But we must consider the historical portrait of the valiant conqueror as Rudolf's underlying material; the intrusion of God is a later detail added to the historical text, but without weakening or taking away that character for valour and for noble leadership which was typical of the historical Alexander. God helps Alexander: God uses Alexander: but Alexander is not reduced to the status of the mere instrument of God foretold by Daniel. He remains the magnificent conqueror who occasionally acts in concert with God's desires. Nor do his courtly characteristics shape the poem; they remain a foreign element in an essentially historical account.

There is a different tone in Ulrich von Eschenbach. His poem is founded upon a mass of heterogeneous but closely interwoven textual material, pointing to various morals and to various characteristics in the hero. Yet over all there is some individuality, even if it is the individuality of a tradition and not that of a man. Ulrich built principally upon Gautier; but he took only the text of the *Alexandreis*, and ignored its spirit. He doubled its length,[1] seasoned it with his own ideas and left it unbaked, formless and unpalatable, but distinctly his own.

His seasoning is that of courtly taste; but he emphasized the part of courtly tradition which had received least attention from other writers—the element of love. Ulrich's poem has been called a 'Minneroman': most of the material attributable to his own invention is concerned with the apparatus of courtly love, and this preoccupation with the love element affects his portrait of Alexander the conqueror.[2] Ulrich cannot relish battle scenes because he pictures to

---

[1] In fact there are 5,464 lines in the *Alexandreis* to 28,000 in the *Alexander*. But Ulrich added a great deal of yeast to the mixture; and his lines are shorter.

[2] Further on the love element in Ulrich, see below, pp. 219–20.

himself the sorrow of the ladies at the death of their lovers. While battles and the other encounters of war are necessarily described Ulrich's heart is not in them. Alexander no longer fights for glory and greatness alone, though that theme, derived from Gautier, persists in the German book: he is Candace's chosen knight and fights with her name upon his lips.[1] The older magnanimity is swallowed up in the new exaltation of the knight who does service for his lady.

In independent German references of this period Alexander's valour and strength, and his consequent career of triumphant conquest,[111] were more constantly mentioned than the more exotic courtly qualities. Triumphant valour remained always fundamental in the German view of Alexander, and with the passing of the vogue for French courtly literature it was these fundamental qualities in Alexander which regained their influence on German popular imagination.

(v) The 'Libro de Alexandre'

The author of the Libro de Alexandre, while he naturally followed Gautier in the portrayal of Alexander's character, shifted the emphasis, as did Rudolf, towards the more conventional picture of the medieval king. He surrounds Alexander with the imagery and mise-en-scène of courtly convention, and suppresses Gautier's elaborate mythological machinery. He also, in deference to medieval epic stylistic convention, multiplies lesser combats in the battles, and adds accounts of minor campaigns which Gautier had deliberately omitted in order to concentrate the reader's attention on Alexander's two great struggles, against Darius and against Porus. But, despite these alterations, made in deference to courtly convention, the Libro de Alexandre remains a skilfully constructed and readable poem, which has combined a strongly classicizing source with contemporary courtly elements to produce a successful portrait of a medieval Alexander.[2]

(vi) Italian and miscellaneous evidence

Before the fifteenth century Italian Alexander-books pursued a dreary tradition of close adherence to their Latin sources, in almost every case the I³ Historia de Preliis. Such changes as were made by the

---

[1] Cf. v. 15,236, where Alexander's war-cry is 'süeze Candacis'; and see Grammel, pp. 97–101.

[2] See H. Christensen, Das Alexanderlied Walthers von Châtillon (Halle, 1905), pp. 107–9.

translators in the character of Alexander were made only in the weak, half-unconscious obedience to convention that is typical of their dry and uninspired natures. They appear in the petty anachronisms that extend only to outward description, and not to the transformation of the character of the hero; though he may be thinly overlaid with Christian convention, as in the work of Scolari.[1]

Thus the Italian portrait of Alexander was inevitably the portrait found in the *Historia de Preliis*; and as there is no original approach here, so we find no hot-blooded champion, or courtly, generous prince. In some Italian authors there is, as we shall see, a slight echo of the courtly conception of Alexander;[2] but in independent Italian references as a whole,[3] the same objective, historical approach to Alexander is to be found as appears in the Italian Alexander-books.

(vii) *Summary*

In the chronicle accounts and the references to Alexander in early Latin writers, his conquests were associated with the necessary personal qualities—with greatness of mind, and valour. When these qualities passed into the Alexander poems of the twelfth century, the greatness of mind became a more restless, volatile characteristic, a vigorous force of character that was associated by writers of this period with true nobility; and at the same time valour was naturally made to include accessory hardiness and physical strength displayed in the battles, single combats, sieges and arduous adventures of which such poems are full.

In the late twelfth and thirteenth centuries these qualities in Alexander were placed side by side with, but never obscured by, other conventional qualities of the period: liberality, courtly love and the rest of the chivalric code. In Germany there was added the idea of God's protection of Alexander; but this was never allowed to become so evident as to detract from his personal merit.

By the end of the thirteenth century the two ideas most regularly

---

[1] For the dryness of Italian Alexander-books, and the methods of their authors, see J. Storost, passim.

[2] See below, pp. 217–18.

[3] Most of the Italian independent references to Alexander date from the fourteenth and fifteenth centuries; and the few earlier references have either been dealt with, for convenience, in the late medieval section (see pp. 261–6), or are concerned with Alexander's liberality and have been discussed in the next section.

associated with Alexander in secular literature had come again to be, as in the early period before courtly convention had made its influence felt, his personal valour and the greatness of the empire that he won, but without consideration of the greatness of mind which lay behind that valour and the winning of that empire. The secular attitude to Alexander became more and more obscured with didactic teaching; the living man shrivelled to the embalmed figure of the Nine Worthies, and eventually, out of the decay of the medieval secular tradition, there was evolved the Alexander of Renaissance poetry.

6. ALEXANDER'S SECULAR REPUTATION FOR LIBERALITY

The attribution of magnanimity, of valour, or of physical strength to Alexander is regular and firmly established; the reasons, not only for its original appearance in secular literature, but for its continuance, are immediately evident. But the evolution of Alexander's secular reputation for liberality is less clear, and its origins are disputed and obscure. No theory of its early development has been supported by sufficient evidence to inspire confidence; and the statements which have been made concerning this reputation, which is of great importance for the examination of the secular conception of Alexander, serve only to show the nature of the problems involved.[1]

Paul Meyer's conclusions upon this subject, in his study of the *Roman d'Alexandre*, and its related texts, may be summarized as follows:[2] from the twelfth century until the fourteenth Alexander enjoyed a proverbial reputation for liberality, and the work which contributed most to the establishment of that reputation was the *Roman d'Alexandre*, with its emphasis upon Alexander as a generous giver. This reputation disappeared during the fourteenth and fifteenth centuries when the indiscriminate largesse which supported it fell into disrepute, and was replaced by a reputation for valour such as is emphasized in the *Triomphe des Neuf Preux*. This broad statement has been accepted by all subsequent writers as the fundamental fact of Alexander's secular reputation.

A fresh examination of the available data, and a discussion of Meyer's conclusions, is long overdue. Neither he nor any other

---

[1] See Appendix II, pp. 358–68.   [2] See below, pp. 333–5 for text.

writer has been able satisfactorily to explain the origins of this un-
deniable reputation. Those who have discussed the question have all
been initially handicapped by ignorance of the non-secular conceptions of Alexander studied above. The question cannot be exactly decided, but the previous theories and the discussion of them have been
relegated to an Appendix, where I have also arranged the relevant
evidence, and put forward a new suggestion which is at least based on
some certain facts. The present section is restricted to a brief survey of
the history of Alexander's reputation for liberality before 1350, and
of the evidence that establishes its existence. The discussion of its
eventual decline will be found in the section on the later Middle Ages.

It may be helpful here to restate the difference between the philosophic and the exemplar approach to liberality.[1] The philosopher
examines the state of mind of the giver, the state of his treasury and
the worth of the recipient; these are the three determining factors in
assessing true liberality in the conferment of material benefits. The
preacher considers the giving of alms. To him neither the state of
mind of the giver (which is hoped to be charitable), nor the state of
his treasury (since large gifts are not normally imagined, and charitable
prodigality would be thankfully accepted) nor the worth of the
recipient (being established by the mere fact that he is one of God's
poor) are matters which need serious consideration. The amount of
the gift, that it shall be as large as possible, is the chief factor in the
preachers' definition of liberality, and so for Alexander they have
nothing but praise as a giver of great gifts.

Here, therefore, we have different conceptions of liberality at
different levels of society; and we have now to examine the secular
conception, which we shall see was foreshadowed in the neglect by
the preachers and writers of *exempla* of Seneca's philosophical criteria
and their substitution for them of indiscriminate praise of charitable
prodigality.

(*a*) THE AVAILABLE SOURCES

(i) *Legendary*

The legendary sources are full of references to Alexander's liberality.
The most interesting passage is in the correspondence between
Philip, Zeuxis, Alexander and Aristotle in Julius Valerius, where

---

[1] See above, pp. 85–91, 154–5.

Philip is persuaded by Zeuxis to accuse the young Alexander of stupid prodigality;[1] whereupon Aristotle replies on his behalf that this is no prodigality but a careful policy of judicious liberality founded on his advice. The passage was omitted in the *Zacher Epitome*.

Other relevant passages are the rewarding of the unwelcome envoys of Darius, the visits to the camps of Darius and of Porus in disguise, and the gifts brought to Candace.[2] In the I[3] interpolations there are two passages where Alexander is praised for his liberality.[3]

The *Iter ad Paradisum* contains numerous references to Alexander's liberality,[4] which may have been added by the Latin redactor, since they are not essential to the story and are not found in earlier versions.

(ii) *Historical and anecdotal*

The history of the references to Alexander's liberality in Quintus Curtius and Justin, and of the anecdotes in Valerius Maximus, Cicero and Seneca, as used by medieval moralists, has been discussed.[5] Their intrusion into secular literature will be noticed here and more fully discussed in the Appendix.

(b) THE RESULTANT SECULAR CONCEPTION

(i) *Alberic, Lamprecht, and their period*

In the fragment of Alberic's original text there is no suggestion of Alexander's liberality; it has been deduced, however, from the Vorau text, that Alberic's narrative contained a few references to Alexander's liberality. Grammel[6] remarks of the *Vorau Alexander* upon this question: 'Oft ist seine Freigebigkeit betont, 525, 585, aber nicht fällt der höfische Begriff "Milte".' She has here failed to indicate that

---

[1] The Zeuxis episode is lacking in Pseudo-Callisthenes I, 16 (ed. Müller, pp. 16–17); it occurs in Julius Valerius and the Armenian version. See Ausfeld, *-ischer Griechische Alexanderroman*, pp. 130–1, Zacher, *Pseudo-Callisthenes*, pp. 92–3, and below, pp. 363–4.

[2] For Alexander's visit to the camp of Darius in disguise (*Historia de Preliis* (Bamberg) II, 13, ed. Pfister, *Alexanderroman*, pp. 89–92) and its later transformation into a visit to the camp of Porus, see below, pp. 363–5.

[3] For text of these interpolations, see Pfister in *Münchener Museum*, I (1912), p. 273 (the philosophers praise Alexander's liberality), p. 274 (the Dothomeus epitaph containing praise of his liberality).

[4] See the edition of the *Iter* by A. Hilka, in L. P. G. Peckham and Milan S. La Du, *The Prise de Defur and the Voyage au Paradis Terrestre* (Princeton University Press, 1935: *Elliott Monographs*, 35), p. xlviii.

[5] See pp. 85–91.   [6] Grammel, p. 35.

these two references to Alexander's liberality almost certainly formed part of the text of Alberic, and are in any case of negligible importance as they are merely references to the distribution of plunder such as would come naturally to a medieval writer.[112] In neither Alberic nor Lamprecht is there any important or significant reference to Alexander's liberality.

(ii) *Gautier de Châtillon*

Paul Meyer saw in the opening words of the *Alexandreis*,[1]

> Gesta ducis Macedum, totum digesta per orbem,
> Quam large dispersit opes,...

a possible acknowledgement of Alexander's contemporary secular reputation for liberality. It seems likely, however, that this is a recollection of Alexander's historical reputation for liberality, known to Gautier through Quintus Curtius. In the middle of a passage principally derived from that source in which Aristotle lectures Alexander, Gautier makes him give the following advice on liberality:

> Vulneribus crudis, et corde tumentibus aegro
> Muneris infundas oleam, gazisque reclusis
> Unge animos donis, aurique appone liquorem.
> Haec aegrae menti poterit medicina mederi.
> Sic inopi diues, largusque medetur auaro.[113]

But if money is lacking:

> Non minuatur amor, non desit copia mentis;
> Allice pollicitis, promissaque tempore solue:...

This very un-Aristotelian piece of advice is inserted in a passage probably not founded on the cautious philosophy of the *Secret of Secrets* but which is rather an example of Gautier's own remanipulation of the theory of largesse in the light of contemporary secular ideals.

But liberality plays little part in the *Alexandreis*; Gautier is too occupied with the nobility of Alexander, with his heroic mission, to pay more attention to his liberality than merely to recognize it in passing.

[1] See Meyer, *A. le G.* II, pp. 374-5.

(iii) *The 'Roman d'Alexandre', and related texts and references*

The advance in the influence of courtly convention from Alberic to the *Decasyllabic Alexander* is clearly to be seen in the emphasis upon Alexander's liberality. While in Alberic the youthful Alexander is praised exclusively for his military qualities, in the *Decasyllabic Alexander* there are many courtly elements, and Alexander's liberality is especially praised in two passages whose importance as a possible clue to the origin of Alexander's secular reputation for liberality will be discussed later.[114]

While the prologue of Lambert li Tors reflects the wonderful character of his book, and enumerates the chief events in Alexander's adventurous wanderings in the East, the redaction of Alexandre de Paris returns to the exemplar type of prologue, and asks his hearers to treat the romance as a lesson in the art of living; and the most significant lesson imparted by the life of Alexander is singled out as the art of making friends by liberality. This theme reappears constantly throughout the poem,[115] where it is frequently stressed that it was Alexander's liberality that won him the world by inspiring his followers to deeds of valour. Thus the method of gaining favour condemned by Philip in his letter to Alexander is here thoroughly endorsed; nor does Alexander turn covetous of necessity in the *Roman*, as Philip had predicted; when Porus offers Alexander his treasure Alexander replies with a discourse, interlarded with Christian quotations, upon the evils of cupidity.[1] At his death the two qualities of their king most lamented by the peers are his *largesce* and his *hardemans*;[116] for though liberality is a dominant characteristic of the portrait of Alexander in the *Roman* it is not so dominant that he becomes merely a type of liberality. The character of Alexander is complete, and liberality is only the most notable facet because it is the most original in the poem.

In the *Roman d'Alexandre* and the other texts of this period there is no philosophic approach to liberality. Not only is there that detached admiration for an extravagant spendthrift which appears in a state of society where prodigality is possible in a prince or a private person, but there is also, and naturally so, an intense personal interest in the nature and the extent of his gifts. Most contemporary writers relied

---

[1] See Meyer, *A. le G.* II, p. 171.

upon the liberality of patrons for their existence; with the growth of a new culture in small rival courts only constant liberality could secure and retain the services of a court poet, and the poets responded accordingly. The troubadours and the joglars, like the worse humanists of Renaissance Italy, made their home in that court where they were best rewarded, and combined praise of their liberal lord with as gratifying a disparagement of his close-fisted rivals. The writers of romance similarly hoped for reward as they travelled about the streets and castles, as did also the lesser retailers, remanipulators, botchers and patchers who appropriated their work.

Miss West makes a distinction between the objective type of liberality, the rewarding of followers according to their worth, which she regards as a feudal characteristic, and the subjective rewarding of followers in the attempt to gain popularity, which she considers typical of the courtly period.[1] It may be noticed that the former corresponds closely to the Senecan ideal of liberality and the latter to that political use of liberality condemned by Cicero in his citation of the letter from Philip to Alexander, and upheld in the Zeuxis episode of Julius Valerius and in the rifacimento of the passage from Cicero in Philippe de Novare.[2] Both these aspects of liberality in fact play their part in the courtly conventions. While in his prologue Alexandre de Paris gives the example of the life of Alexander to show how liberality may gain friends, such episodes in the *Roman* as that of the knight to whom Alexander intended to give a city had he not been too base to deserve it,[3] and Aristotle's warning lecture to Alexander upon liberality, show that the worth of the recipient was also appreciated as an ingredient of true liberality, though measure in giving did not come within this unphilosophic definition of liberality, nor was the conception of worth based so much upon true worth of character, as upon worth of conventional character—courage and strength in battle, an air of haughty nobility and high rank. If we observe the personal aspect, that consideration of the question in the mind of the recipient which is naturally evident throughout secular writing, we shall see that the question of the exact *affectus* is of little importance when compared with that of the amount of the *effectus*. It is an inducement to a man to be liberal to tell him that gifts will

---

[1] C. B. West, *Courtoisie in Anglo-Norman Literature* (Oxford, Blackwell, 1938), pp. 73–4.
[2] See below, p. 362 and p. 371 (text).   [3] See below, pp. 360–1.

make him friends, and it is regard for one's own advantage that makes one tell him to be sure to lavish that liberality upon the right people so as to make him good friends. No one subjective aspect of liberality, no one state of mind in the giver, is to be observed here; it is the refusal to stress measure in giving that divides this type of liberality both from the classical definition and from that given to Alexander by Aristotle in the *Secret of Secrets*.

Thus the courtly virtue of *largesce* would bear to the eyes of a philosopher the aspect of prodigality; and it was furthermore the product of a particular and restricted society—a point which greatly influenced the early disappearance of Alexander's reputation for this quality. In connexion with Alexander, courtly *largesce* was first heavily emphasized in the *Roman*; but it had been prefigured, not only in previous courtly poetry, but in the Zeuxis episode in Julius Valerius.

Many of the twelfth- and thirteenth-century vernacular references to Alexander's *largesce* have been collected by Bartsch, Meyer, and Ortiz; to these I have been able to add a number, and the composite list is given in the notes.[1117] It will be seen that Alexander's courtly reputation for liberality, as Meyer was the first to point out, antedates in both romances and lyric poetry the *Roman* as edited by Alexandre de Paris. The question to which this gives rise has been discussed in the Appendix.

It will also be noticed that Alexander's liberality appears more frequently in an unattached proverbial connexion in the troubadours than in romances. This may well be due to the differences between the two poetic forms. The discursive character of a romance allows more space for digressive and comprehensive reminiscence than the compressed and allusive art of the troubadours and trouvères. The rapid forming of convention under these conditions, which necessarily favoured repetitiveness, extended not only to the pattern of the poems, but to the phrases, similes and verbal forms used, so that the catching up of the lines of a previous poet in an allusive reminder to the skilful reader is not uncommon. The constant references to Alexander's liberality throughout the troubadour period show that it was well enough known; but, even though it may be certain that some troubadours knew the *Roman d'Alexandre*, is it not possible that the popularity of theme was in part due to the popularity of some of those who used it, the most famous of whom are Raimbaut de Vaqueyras, Peire Vidal and Aimeric de Pegulhan?

(iv) *German Alexander-books and references from the 'Strassburg Alexander' to Ulrich von Eschenbach*

There is little to remark about Alexander's reputation for liberality in Germany at this period.

His liberality was naturally extolled as one of his chief qualities in the poems that derived directly from the courtly tradition, the *Strassburg Alexander* and Ulrich von Eschenbach.[1118] Even Rudolf von Ems, obedient to the demands of contemporary convention, and supported by the testimony of his source, Curtius, makes frequent reference to it. But that Alexander's character should be so completed in accordance with approved ideals is only to be expected in these long biographical poems. The absolute dependence of Alexander's reputation for this quality upon French models, and the consequent transitory nature of that reputation, are made evident by the independent references to his liberality, which are scarce indeed if they are compared with those which extol his more vigorous and obvious historical qualities, and appear only in writers strongly influenced by French tradition.[1119]

Thus Alexander's reputation for liberality was noticeable in Germany only at the height of the courtly period, and then only in those writers most directly in contact with French literary ideas. It was an exotic addition to the German attitude to Alexander, and one which never became proverbial and soon passed away.

(v) *'Libro de Alexandre'*

In the *Libro de Alexandre* there is no indication of Alexander's courtly reputation for liberality. The Spanish writer was accustomed to omit any subjective material that he found in his sources. He did not transcribe Gautier's opening lines, or Aristotle's advice to Alexander on liberality, or such comments as he found in his principal secondary source, the B *Roman d'Alexandre*. He was a man of an historical bent; he made the epic of Gautier a Christian romance, but he did not follow the courtly tradition so far as to admit its final elaboration of Alexander's liberality and amorous adventures.

In independent Spanish references, however, there is, as might be expected, a dim but observable reflexion of the French tradition.[1]

---

[1] For Spanish references to Alexander's liberality, see Mila y Fontanals, *De los trovadores en España, Obras Completas*, II (Madrid, 1889), p. 528. Cf. also *La vida de Lazarillo de Tormes* (*Clásicos Castellanos*, ed. J. C. y Frauca, Madrid, 1941), p. 110 and n.

(vi) *Italian and miscellaneous evidence*

Storost remarked that the absence of a courtly tradition in Italy prevented Alexander from acquiring a reputation for liberality there, such as he had attained in France and Germany.[1] In the Italian Alexander-books of this period, which follow closely their Latin sources, we find, as we would expect, nothing that suggests a reminiscence of the courtly tradition; but there is scattered evidence which shows that Alexander's reputation for liberality was known in Italy during this period, and it will later be shown that that reputation was accepted by late medieval Italian writers.

Besides the use of the moral anecdotal material relating to Alexander's liberality in Brunetto Latini,[2] there is reference to his secular reputation in two lyrics of the thirteenth century,[120] while Dante notices it in an expression which implies its popular proverbiality: 'E chi non ha ancora nel cuore Alessandro per li suoi reali beneficii?'[121] Boccaccio refers to his prodigality in the distribution of conquered lands,[122] and Petrarch grudgingly admits his liberality, though he will admit little else in his favour.[3] There is thus no reason to suppose that Alexander's reputation for liberality was wholly unknown in Italy; though it is probable that such knowledge of it as existed there was derived, not from any earlier indigenous tradition, but from the French Alexander-books and the troubadour lyrics which were then easily accessible to learned Italians. Latini lived a part of his life in France and wrote his encyclopaedia in French, Boccaccio may have possessed a translation of the *Fuerre de Gadres* into Latin,[4] and was a man of wide reading, while Dante was well versed in Provençal literature, even to the extent of writing Provençal himself, and refers to Alexander in the passage quoted at the same time as he refers to Bertran de Born. Thus there is good reason to see in these references merely a distant echo of Alexander's courtly reputation.

In miscellaneous references of this period there is no perceptible vestige of Alexander's reputation for liberality; and they thus serve

---

[1] Storost, p. 327.

[2] For the use of the moral anecdotal material in Latini, see pp. 349–50.

[3] Petrarch, *De uiris illustribus*, ed. Razzolini, *Collezione di opere inedite o rare* (Bologna, 1872), p. 130. See for Petrarch's opinion of Alexander, G. Cary, 'Petrarch and Alexander the Great', *Italian Studies*, v (1950), pp. 43 ff.

[4] On the Latin version of the *Fuerre de Gadres* and its authorship see *M.F.R.d'A.* IV, pp. 15–21. It is no longer attributed to Boccaccio.

to show that that reputation was a product of the courtly tradition, and extended only as far and as long as the influence of that tradition was felt.

(vii) *Summary*

Certain special questions connected with Alexander's secular reputation for liberality have not yet been considered; these are the questions of its origin, and of its continuance and eventual disappearance in the late Middle Ages.

It may be safely concluded, however, from the evidence already presented that Alexander's secular reputation for liberality was a product of the courtly atmosphere, and was therefore a prominent feature of the Alexander portrait only in France. In other countries where the courtly tradition made itself felt, Germany, Spain and Italy, there was naturally some reference to this reputation and some endorsement of it; but this endorsement is to be found only in works which are either derived or imitated from French models.

7. CONCLUDING STUDIES IN THE DEVELOPMENT OF THE SECULAR CONCEPTION OF ALEXANDER

(a) ALEXANDER AND WOMEN IN COURTLY ROMANCE

The question of Alexander's chastity in the historical sources and in the writings of medieval moralists has already been discussed;[1] and it has been seen how the attacks upon his chastity made by ancient historians were not quoted apart from their contexts, and how his reputation in this respect escaped reproach before the time of Petrarch. The historical material similarly made no impression upon the secular writers, although the story of the poison-girl was widely known in the later Middle Ages.[2]

In the legend chastity was held a necessary requirement before Alexander could approach the trees of the sun and moon; in the *Roman d'Alexandre* and in the *Libro de Alexandre* he was given a shirt which protected its wearer from lechery; and his treatment of Darius' womenfolk provided a remarkable instance of continence to an age not accustomed to such self-control in its conquering princes.[123]

Thus, even if Alexander was not renowned for his chastity, he was not notorious for his unchastity; and the question remained for a time undiscussed. But with the establishment of courtly convention it became essential that he should be amorous, whatever amorousness might imply. In the *Decasyllabic Alexander* women and talk of love have already made their appearance;[1] and in the *Roman* Alexander's amatory instincts are fully developed. In this as in all the other chief courtly romances, the principal object of Alexander's love is Candace who now for the first time becomes an important person in the story of Alexander.

In the legend, it will be remembered, Candace is a queen who has a portrait painted of Alexander, and who, by a series of complicated events, manœuvres him into an embarrassing position, and recognizes him by means of his portrait when recognition may mean death to him from her angry son Carator. No words of love pass between them; on the contrary, Alexander is furious with himself for having let a woman get the better of him.[2]

But in the courtly romances the plot is completely changed. Candace is chosen for Alexander's beloved (or his chief beloved; occasional dalliance, such as that with the maidens of the wood, is pastoral and permissible).[124] He falls in love with her, and she with him. When he comes to her city he stays with her in her palace. In one version of the Celestial Journey the gryphon chariot lands in the grounds of her palace, with an inevitable sequel;[3] and all the skill of the poets is lavished upon her appearance, her clothes and the splendours of her palace.

This treatment of the figure of Candace is to be found in a group of poems; the *Strassburg Alexander*, the *Roman d'Alexandre*, Ulrich von Eschenbach and Seifrit aus Oesterreich;[4] all, except the last, poems of the courtly period. She is accompanied in Ulrich von Eschenbach by a horde of handsome men and beautiful women, and most of the action is subjected to the tyranny of courtly love; the men fight only

---

[1] *Decasyllabic Alexander*, laisse 6, v. 55 (ed. Foulet, *M.F.R.d'A.* III, p. 64):
　　　　Parler ot dames corteisament d'amors,...
[2] For the Candace episode see Julius Valerius III, 28–43 (ed. Kuebler, pp. 135–51); I[2] *Historia de Preliis*, cc. 107–10 (ed. Hilka, pp. 207–21). Upon the contradictions between the various versions of the story, see R. Wilmans in *Zeitschr. f. deutsches Altertum*, XLV, pp. 229–44.
[3] E.g. in Ulrich von Eschenbach, *Alexander*, vv. 24,681–750.
[4] For the love element in the *Strassburg Alexander*, see Grammel, pp. 50–3; in Ulrich von Eschenbach, Grammel, pp. 97–101. For the Candace episode in Seifrit's *Alexander*, see vv. 6897–7586. There is also a return to the courtly treatment of Candace in Hartlieb; see below, pp. 233, 246.

for their beloved, and Ulrich laments the grief that must come to the women through the fall of their lovers in battle and consequently waters down his battles.[125] But though in the *Strassburg Alexander* and the *Roman d'Alexandre* there are a few other amorous episodes, the theme of love is not allowed to exceed episodic limits, and soften the heroic atmosphere of the battles or the marvellous terrors of the journey through the East.

There was also, and in the same courtly period, a revolt against the admission of such a love interest into the life of a conqueror. The Candace episode is omitted by Godfrey of Viterbo, the *Libro de Alexandre* and Rudolf von Ems,[126] while Thomas of Kent and his derivatives, *Kyng Alisaunder* and the version in Gower, introduce a variant which is to Candace's discredit.[127]

Here, though Alexander falls in love with Candace, it is because she is a designing woman, who never rests until she has him within her toils, and this furnishes Thomas with an excuse for a long sermon upon the wiles of women.

Thus the love interest in Alexander's life was entirely an exotic growth, the completion of the courtly portrait in conformity with the approved conventions of the period; and even at the height of that courtly period it was sometimes realized that it was unsuitable to the character of the hero and of his adventures. It had its effect upon occasional independent courtly references to Alexander; but in the later Middle Ages, except in the *Voeux du Paon* and its continuations and adaptations where it remains the source and inspiration of knightly prowess, it disappeared sooner than the rest of the courtly elaborations of Alexander's life and character because it was the uppermost detail added, was most incompatible with his nature, and was entirely unsupported by the Latin sources.

(b) MISCELLANEOUS ASPECTS OF THE SECULAR CONCEPTION OF ALEXANDER FROM THE TWELFTH TO THE FOURTEENTH CENTURY

(i) *The wonderful element*

Little reference has been made to the wonderful element in the Alexander-books and references of this period, though this element has received much attention from scholars. Such apparent neglect has been due to the fact that the accentuation of the wonderful element is a merely textual peculiarity, and that its emphasis and elaboration in the courtly romances did not affect the conception of Alexander except in certain rare instances, such as the Journey to the Terrestrial Paradise, the Celestial Journey, the wood-maidens, the enchanted river and other lesser episodes.[1128] In an age full of the tales of Crusaders and a supposedly scientific lore of marvels much stress was laid upon the wonderful adventures of Alexander in the twelfth and thirteenth centuries, not only by the writers of romance and the lyric poets, but by travellers and natural historians who relied upon the authority of the *Epistola ad Aristotelem*.[1] Such material, however, does not affect the portrayal of Alexander; he is the hero, but interest is centred in the various monsters that he encounters. The decline of the wonderful element in Alexander-books and references is discussed in the next section.[2]

(ii) *Literary iconography*

The Asiatic rhetorical tradition of elaborate description persisted into the Middle Ages. A shield figured with numerous incidents, a bed painted with a universal encyclopaedia, a palace decorated with all the history that the writer could remember afforded an easy method of demonstrating his rhetorical skill, and his learning; while it gave to the careful reader the impression of great richness in the scene described.

In the Alexander legend this rhetorical treatment was especially applied to Alexander's tent, which was decorated, in the *Roman*, with numerous historical scenes, and made of materials of unparalleled splendour.[1129] It was, however, a fairly late addition to the *Roman* and was almost certainly borrowed from the *Roman de Thebes*. Of greater interest are the passages in various poems where the history of Alexander is represented as sculptured, painted, embroidered, woven or in some other visual form, giving the poet an opportunity for a rhetorical digression.

As such it appears first in Ermoldus Nigellus;[3] but Ermoldus was

---

[1] For use of the legend by natural historians see Pfister in *Wochenschr. f. klass. Phil.* XXVII (1910), coll. 675–8; and below, pp. 335–6 for further references.

[2] See pp. 234–6.

[3] Ermoldus Nigellus, *In honorem Hludowici* IV, v. 265 (in *M.G.H. Poet. Lat. Aeu. Carol.* II, p. 65):   Ut quoque Alexander bello sibi uindicat orbem,...

too anxious to show his omnivorous learning to linger long over the representation of the exploits of Alexander, which are dismissed in a line as part of a long series of pictured histories in Charlemagne's palace at Ingelheim.

Alexander then appears, in two of the French *chansons de geste*; among the paintings decorating castles.[1] In both instances these paintings represent various scenes from his legendary history which are briefly described by the poet.

The restriction of these descriptions to the legendary history of Alexander is the natural result of the limited knowledge of Alexander material possessed by these writers, the known predilections of the nobility whose castles were supposed to be described and for whom the poems were written, and the great pictorial possibilities inherent in gryphons and headless men.

The next literary painting of this kind is more detailed; it is that in the famous Italian poem, *L'Intelligenza*, where the life of Alexander is described as it is set out in the frescoes of the palace of Intelligence.[130] Again the emphasis is upon those details of his life which suggest themselves most easily to a pictorial interpretation: the killing of the basilisk, the celestial journey, the submarine descent and other picturesque adventures. There is a similar portrayal in the embroideries of the *Padiglione di Mambrino*,[2] and a brief reference to a pictured life of Alexander in Boccaccio's *Filocolo*.[3]

The last literary account of importance occurs in Boiardo,[4] where the palace of Agramante is decorated with scenes from the life of Alexander, described with the customary rugged swiftness of the Lombard poet. But by his time the use of the life of Alexander in decoration, so long a literary device borrowed from older rhetoric, had become a material fact. In the fourteenth, fifteenth and sixteenth

[1] For the castle of Adamant, where Alexander's deeds are all portrayed, see *Huon de Bordeaux* (Eng. tr. Lord Berners), ed. S. L. Lee, E.E.T.S., E.S. XL, XLI, XLIII, L (1882–7), p. 412. For the similar castle of Noble, see *L'Entree d'Espagne*, vv. 10,430 ff. (ed. A. Thomas, S.A.T.F. (1913), vol. II, p. 89). In this Franco-Italian poem the Italian penchant for literary iconography of Alexander may be said to have its beginning.

[2] See the edition of the *Padiglione di Mambrino* by O. Targlioni Tozzetti (Livorno, 1874).

[3] G. Boccaccio, *Filocolo*, ed. S. Battaglia, *Scrittori d'Italia* (Bari, 1938), p. 103: 'La real sala era di marmoree colonne di diversi colori ornata,...e in quella sala si vedevano ne' rilucenti marmi intagliate l'antiche storie....Nè vi mancava alcuna delle vittorie del grande Alessandro.'

[4] Boiardo, *Orlando Innamorato* II, i, 21 ff.; Agramante is supposed to have been descended from Alexander.

centuries the conservative affection of the nobility for the old romances was accompanied by the appearance of richer furnishings; and many of the tapestries and frescoes of the time represented Alexander, either in the midst of his legendary adventures, or else in his place among the *Neuf Preux*, the group of famous men who had become so popular in the later Middle Ages.[1]

(c) CONCLUSION

The chief developments perceptible in the secular portrait of Alexander to the fourteenth century have now been examined, and the principal constituent qualities of his secular character defined. Besides those virtues that have been discussed, it was natural that Alexander should have been credited, in those poems which portrayed him as a model prince, with the other qualities befitting that model: justice, mercy, honour and other accessories to perfection all receive their due emphasis in such portrayals of Alexander. But these features of his character appear only in Alexander-books; they were details, partly derived from the Latin sources, partly invented in the spirit of the age, to complete the portrait of Alexander presented by the sources; and they had no such hold upon popular imagination as might make them universally remembered as were his valour, his liberality, and his love of women. And thus they do not appear in the general picture drawn here, for they have no place in the broad, general secular conception of Alexander as it may be deduced from independent references.

8. SUMMARY

The basis of the secular reputation of Alexander has always been secular opinion; and upon the shifting ground of contemporary beliefs, institutions and conventions was built the secular portrait of him as it appeared in the twelfth and thirteenth centuries. Moral themes touched it, exemplar themes touched it; but they touched only individuals, or an individual opinion upon an individual point—they

---

[1] The best known example of such material iconography is the pair of Doria Tapestries, discussed below, p. 229. For further references to textiles depicting Alexander, see Francisque Michel, op. cit. (note [129]) vol. I, p. 97, and vol. II, pp. 335, 384. For further iconographic references, see O. Zingerle, *Die Quellen zum Alexander des Rudolf von Ems* (*Germanistische Abhandlugen*, IV, Breslau, 1885), p. 5, n. 4, and below, pp. 343–4. For pageants in which Alexander appeared, see p. 344.

came in loose tags, and did not affect the general attitude of secular writers. It is when literature of the type we have discussed began to decline, when moral and exemplar themes not only influenced secular opinion, but mingled with it in the ideas of new writers, that a new secularity was born, a new piety, or in opposition to it a new lay bitterness; and it is that period that we shall now have to consider. The old Alexander, the conqueror, dwindled into the pageant figure of the Nine Worthies. In the North the moral and didactic writers summed up the medieval conceptions of Alexander and condemned him; while in the South, in Italy, the writers of antiquity were rescued one by one, and their translation and publication provided the ground for a new conception of Alexander, historical rather than legendary.

As we look back upon the development of the secular conception of Alexander, it is evident that it rested upon the historical foundation—upon Alexander as a conqueror with the virtues of a conqueror. This attitude everywhere persisted, and underlay all the developments of the period.

The introduction of the wonderful element, and the increased emphasis laid upon it in the twelfth century, brought no new Alexander to the fore; he became a conqueror not only of known, but of unknown, mysterious antagonists—of strange men and beasts, of the sky and of the deep.

The conventions of French *courtoisie* brought with them the courtly doctrine of liberality: but it was the liberality of a conqueror, that took its place in the portrait of Alexander because it was considered a quality essential to him. It was a new military virtue, a recognition of the need for incentive if a soldier is to give of his best and a significant anticipation of mercenary employment.

The element of love was the most obligatory part of courtly convention; it was foisted upon Alexander, so that he became a conqueror not only of men but of women—or in the disapproval of Thomas of Kent there appeared the rhetorical alternative to this theme, that the conqueror was conquered by women. Much emphasis has been laid by scholars upon this, as upon all the details of the transformation of Alexander into the ideal courtly prince. But that transformation was only a question of the differences effected by a transitory change in values; new virtues came to be highly regarded

VI   ALEXANDER'S FLIGHT AND OTHER SCENES

and were brought into prominence, with such suitable embroidery as adapted them to the requirements of convention—but no permanent change in the picture was brought about by these changes of emphasis. They altered the details of Alexander's character, but his character could only be fitted to his career of conquest, and therefore his basic role as conqueror was to outlive and outgrow the courtly mask that was temporarily fitted upon him.

It is perhaps hardly profitable to read elaborate studies of the portraits of Alexander in the courtly Alexander-books. These writers built upon texts which presented a clear enough picture of Alexander's great virtues, and of the lesser virtues that accompanied them. If they were lazy, or more rarely, if they were determined to give the reader the truth, they did little more than translate. If they were poets in earnest they altered the principal evident virtues to conform with their own courtly ideas. But to read into each little virtue or vice portrayed by the author of an Alexander-book his endorsement of that quality, his testimony that he believed such a quality to exist in Alexander, is as absurd as to maintain that an actor in a play believes what he says to be true. And even if the writer altered the text or added an original comment, there is little enough there, especially in these poems of thousands of lines, to show how far that comment represented his personal view of Alexander. It is only if a theme is recurrent, insistently repeated in the prologue and the epilogue, in interpolations and asides, that we may think it representative of the writer's own approach.

And such themes have been broad, as they must be; it is a question of inclination rather than of invention, of variations upon an unoriginal and invariable theme; and that single theme is the conquests of Alexander, his conquests of men, of countries, of beasts, of the sky and of the sea, and of women, unless they conquered him.

V

THE LATE MEDIEVAL CONCEPTION OF ALEXANDER IN ENGLAND, FRANCE, AND GERMANY

1. INTRODUCTION

In the two last medieval centuries the same bourgeois class that in Italy vacillated between occasional commercial or sexual immorality and frantic repentance, but was best characterized in the money-grubbing, subtle, cautious merchants of Boccaccio, found in the other countries of Europe a different atmosphere. The unsettled political state of Europe, the economic changes, the urge towards religious reform, the disruptive influence of Ockham, the rise of nationalism and the consequent centralization of courts and therefore of most culture—these things contributed to the sobering of ideals, and to the establishment of a new popular literature which owed nothing to the courtly period except some of its material, but derived its cautious secular philosophy and the greater part of its material from the moralists and the preachers. In England Gower and Lydgate, in France Guillaume de Machaut and Eustache Deschamps, are typical representatives of the new literary school.

The disappearance of courtly romance and of the troubadour lyric, save where it was conservatively recopied or destructively remodelled, heralded the disappearance of the courtly conception of Alexander that was there expressed. The various medieval conceptions of Alexander, most clearly discernible from the twelfth to the early fourteenth century, begin to merge together; and secular, exemplar, theological and moral elements are mingled in general decay. But as the circumstances and nature of this deterioration differ in Italy from those prevalent elsewhere, the Italian conception of Alexander during these centuries, when the decay of medieval conceptions co-existed there with the transformation of the Alexander portrait under the influence of new ideas, will be considered separately; and we are here concerned with the late medieval attitude to Alexander in France, England and Germany.

2. THE DECLINE OF THE SECULAR CONCEPTION OF ALEXANDER IN THE LATE MIDDLE AGES

This study is divided into three parts. In the first it is shown how the courtly conception of Alexander dwindled to occasional reminiscences and bookish revivals; in the second, the various forces that contributed to the decline of the secular conception are discussed; and finally, a survey of late medieval Alexander-books and independent references, concluding with those dealing with the *Neuf Preux*, demonstrates how the secular conception of Alexander became in that period purely historical and lacking in interest.

(a) THE DISAPPEARANCE OF THE COURTLY CONCEPTION OF ALEXANDER

Since the secular conception of Alexander rested fundamentally upon the historical and legendary sources of his life, and since some consideration of Alexander as a conqueror, which we have regarded as the basis of the secular conception, was necessary to every mention of him, this basic idea was not to be superseded though it might be obscured by didacticism. But in the light of new ideas and a new criticism Alexander was shorn of his courtly attributes, and became again the valiant conqueror, the man of battles.

The courtly tradition, however, was long in dying, and the memory of the courtly Alexander persists, however feebly, to the end of the Middle Ages. Such conservatism had its especial appeal for the nobility and for the people; it could have little attraction for the middle classes, occupied with their new ideas of morality so opposed to the conventions of the courtly code. And of these two classes the people found no literary expression for their preferences.

Among the nobility, growing centralization of government had greatly reduced the number and the independence of the petty courts whose encouragement and patronage had been the chief support of the authors of courtly lyrics and romances, and with the decline of the patronage on which it relied this literature gradually fell into decay. In France in the fifteenth century a few of the most powerful feudal houses, such as that of Burgundy, Charles d'Orléans at Blois and 'King' René of Provence, continued to keep the old courtly literature half-alive by financing the copying of costly manuscripts for their libraries, and, in the case of Burgundy, supporting a few rather dreary writers of ponderous prose romances, but their activities could not restore life to a culture already moribund. In the end, the courtly conception of Alexander was caught up in Renaissance Italy, where a new aesthetic appreciation of the beauty that was in medieval romance enlivened it and transformed it; and that transformation was effected by the Renaissance poets for the Alexander tradition, as it was for the Carolingian and Arthurian cycles.[1]

Let us return, however, to an examination of the survival of courtly Alexander-romances and courtly feeling about Alexander in late medieval Europe. The fourteenth century produced nothing except the addition of the last elaborations to the *Roman d'Alexandre* in the *Voeux du Paon* and its sequels.[131] In the fifteenth century, however, a revival of courtly interest occurred in the Burgundian court, although most of the literature produced there was not of high quality, and was distinguished more by its bulk than by its beauty.[2] The Dukes of Burgundy were especially fond of the story of Alexander and the ducal library was crowded with copies of the *Roman* and its sequels.[3] Philip the Bold sought to model himself on Alexander, and had a set of tapestries made which illustrated his hero's legendary adventures.[4] A ducal wedding was brightened, among other pageants, by a tableau of the marriage of Alexander to the daughter of the King of Egypt;[5] and two Alexander-books were written for members of the House.

The first of these books was the work of Jean Wauquelin, one of

---

[1] For the portrait of Alexander in Renaissance poetry, see pp. 269–72.

[2] Upon the literature of this court see G. Doutrepont, *La Littérature Française à la cour des Ducs de Bourgogne* (*Bibliothèque du XVe Siècle*, VIII, Paris, 1909).

[3] For the copies of Alexander-books in the ducal library, see Doutrepont, op. cit. p. 113. In the library of Philip the Good there were four copies of the *Voeux du Paon*, one each of the *Restor* and the *Parfait*.

[4] See Doutrepont, op. cit. p. 117; A. Warburg, 'Luftschiff und Tauchboot in der mittel-älterlichen Vorstellungswelt', *Gesammelte Schriften*, vol. 1 (Berlin, 1932), pp. 243–9.

[5] At the wedding of the sister of Edward IV to the Duke of Burgundy at Bruges in 1468, there was a pageant of 'Alexander the great conqueror how he marryed the Doughter of the Kinge of egipt'; see R. Withington, *English Pageantry*, vol. 1 (Cambridge, Mass., 1918), p. 152.

the pensioned writers of the court. His *Histoire du bon roy Alexandre*, dedicated to Jean de Bourgogne, Comte d'Etampes, reflects the spirit of the Doria tapestries, and was evidently based on the Alexander manuscripts in the court library.[1] It is symptomatic, however, of the historical bent of the times, that this rather verbose but not ill-written prose romance is an attempt to combine the *Roman d'Alexandre* with the *French Prose Alexander*, an attempt which leads the author into many morasses of textual contradiction.[2] The spirit of the romance, however, is preserved in it; and the type of public to whom that spirit still appealed is shown by the fact that the work is known only in manuscript, and that three of the five manuscripts are magnificent, copiously illustrated copies made for noble libraries.[3] The Paris fifteenth- and early sixteenth-century press would invest no money in such a rebotch of the old tradition; and it was not able to compete in popularity with the old prose translation of the I[2] *Historia de Preliis* in the chapbook market.

Some twenty years later, in 1468, Vasco de Lucena dedicated the second of these Alexander-books to Charles the Bold. It is nothing more than a French prose translation of the interpolated Quintus Curtius,[4] prefaced by a note in which the author explains how he regards the legendary accounts as all lies, and completed by an epilogue in which he consigns Alexander to his proper place among the damned.[132] Probably because it was a translation of a reputable Latin author this work enjoyed great popularity, not only with the nobility, for whom numerous manuscript copies were made of which at least twenty-four survive, almost all copiously and expensively illustrated, but also with the general public, for whom six editions were published between *c.* 1500 and 1555.[5]

Georges Chastelain, the court poet of Philip the Good, thought as the court thought and won a great contemporary reputation with his

---

[1] For Wauquelin's prose romance, see above, pp. 33–4, and P. Meyer, *A. le G.* II, pp. 313–28. Doutrepont places Wauquelin in his Burgundian literary background (op. cit. pp. 143–5).

[2] See Meyer, *A. le G.* II, pp. 320–1, 324–5.

[3] See Mayer, *A. le G.* II, pp. 313–15. A magnificent manuscript of Wauquelin is described by P. Durrieu, 'L'Histoire du bon roi Alexandre', *Revue de l'Art Ancien et Moderne*, XIII (1903), pp. 49–64, 103–21.

[4] On Vasco de Lucena see above, p. 63.

[5] See R. Bossuat, 'Vasque de Lucène, traducteur de Quinte-Curce (1468)', *Bibliothèque d'Humanisme et Renaissance*, VIII (1946), pp. 197–245. List of twenty-four MSS. and six editions, pp. 204–10.

book 'Les Epitaphes de Hector et Achilles, avec le jugement d'Alexandre le Grand'.[1] One of his poems, addressed to the Duke, might well be placed as an epitaph upon the courtly tradition of Alexander; at the end of each stanza he referred to his patron as:

'Second Hector et dernier Alexandre.'

'Dernier Alexandre'; the old Alexander was passing away with the old society; and such remnants as are to be found of the courtly tradition are dry and uninspired.

Some such survival lingered on also in England in the imitations of the earlier French romances popular at this time when English translators were busy supplying the wants of a new market.[2] In the *Buik of Alexander* Sir Gilbert Hay made a version of the *Fuerre de Gadres* and the *Voeux du Paon* for the benefit of Scotch readers, an experiment which was successful enough to be judged worth the printing as late as 1580, and proved popular enough to be read to pieces, only one copy surviving.[3] But these were only the survivals in a young literature of the second-hand productions of the old and soon disappeared before the competition of more fashionable works.

It has been remarked how apophthegms survive—how men will catch hold of isolated facts or short, summary opinions, when they forget everything else about the figure of whom the fact is told or the opinion expressed. Some details of the courtly Alexander had passed into this sort of popular remembrance of unconnected proverbial features, and although they were reflected but dimly in literature, the reflexion is there.

The chief of these memories is of Alexander's reputation for liberality.[133] An occasional reference to it still appears, almost obliterated by the flat, new attitude to Alexander as conqueror, but sufficient to show that the old idea of a liberal Alexander survived still, despite contemporary opinion and the silence or express denial of the new Alexander-books. If we consider the nature of these references it is evident that we have here no conscious, intentional

[1] Georges Chastelain ('L'Aventureux'), *Le lion rampant*, in *Anthologie des Poètes Français du Xe au XVIe siècle* (ed. A. Dumas, Paris, 1935), pp. 201–2.

[2] Cf. H. S. Bennett, 'The Production and Dissemination of Vernacular Manuscripts in the Fifteenth Century', *The Library*, fifth series, I, iii–iv (1946–7), pp. 167–79.

[3] Edited from Arbuthnot's edition of 1580 by R. L. Graeme Ritchie, *The Buik of Alexander* (*Scottish Text Society*, new series, nos. XVII (1925), XII (1921), XXI (1927) and XXV (1929)).

recalling of an old tradition, but rather the unconsidered transmission of a proverbial saying. The later Middle Ages were full of satires against women—their unchastity, their unfaithfulness, their deceitful ways. The courtly conception of Alexander as a lover of women, and especially of Candace, had received its first shock from the pen of Thomas of Kent, where Candace was represented as a scheming woman who lured Alexander into her toils;[1] and she is so represented also by Thomas of Kent's imitator the author of *Kyng Alisaunder*.[2] In the late Middle Ages, with the decay of poetic invention and the return to the more serious Latin sources, the Candace episode disappeared from most of the Alexander-books; but Seifrit aus Oesterreich surprisingly inserted, in the middle of his strictly derivative text, a Candace episode in the old style.[3] Apart from his work, it is to be found only as a traditional element in the Alexander-books of Jean Wauquelin and Johan Hartlieb.[4] Contrary to the evidence for Alexander's promiscuity, and in additional confirmation of the wickedness of women, the story of the poison-girl from the *Secret of Secrets* rapidly gained in popularity in the late Middle Ages;[5] although the Burgundian pageant to which we have referred, and the love idyll in Boiardo (an idyll of Renaissance type),[6] are evidence for the retention, in a limited circle, of a humanized love interest in the story of Alexander's life.

In the same general connexion we may cite the well-known story of Aristotle and Phyllis or Campaspe. This tells how Aristotle, having seen Alexander in the toils of a beautiful woman, and having lectured his pupil in the approved style upon the dangers of succumbing to

---

[1] See C. B. West, *Courtoisie in Anglo-Norman Literature* (Oxford, 1938), pp. 75–9.

[2] *Kyng Alisaunder*, vv. 7446–785 (ed. G. V. Smithers, E.E.T.S., O.S., ccxxvii (1952), pp. 403–23).

[3] Seifrits *Alexander*, vv. 6897–7586 (ed. Gereke, pp. 113–23).

[4] On the intrusion of courtly love in Hartlieb, see S. Hirsch, *Das Alexanderbuch Johann Hartliebs* (*Palaestra*, LXXXII, Berlin, 1909), pp. 76 ff.; on Alexander's encounter with Candace, pp. 79 ff.

[5] The history of the story of the poison-girl has been exhaustively studied by Wilhelm Hertz, 'Die Sage vom Giftmädchen', *Gesammelte Abhandlungen* (Stuttgart and Berlin, 1905), pp. 156–277, where full details of the medieval references to the story are given. The most important and influential use of the story was in *Gesta Romanorum*, c. 11 (ed. Oesterly, p. 288).

[6] For Boiardo's love idyll, *Orlando Innamorato* II, i, 5 ff., see pp. 270–1. See also above, pp. 99–100, 222, for further Renaissance references to Alexander's love affairs.

the lusts of the flesh, promptly succumbed himself to the same woman and humbled himself so far as to let her ride upon his back, with Alexander sardonically looking down upon the scene from a window.[134] Aristotle, in a way characteristic of late medieval bourgeois literature, turns the incident to his own moral advantage: If she can make such a fool of me, my boy, he says in effect to Alexander, what hope would you have?

This story is typical of its period in its lesson upon the wiles of women, and typical of popular burlesque in its treatment of Aristotle, the

> fronte macer, pallens incompto crine magister

who had lectured Alexander in so many texts from the beginning of the medieval period.[1] There is something refreshing in the attachment of this story to the figure of Aristotle, dignified and immensely sensible in fact and in fiction.

The tale was first told by Henri d'Andeli in his *Lai d'Aristote*; and it was caught up with delight by all Europe. The scene was even carved in wood as a suitable decoration for a church; for it depicted the terrible dangers into which even a wise man falls if he has anything to do with a woman.

Similarly the story of Nectanebus and Olympias was now dwelt upon by misogynists, and also by the haters of sorcery. Gower tells the story at great length[2] and with evident enjoyment; and Guillaume Alexis includes it in his *Contreblason de faulses amours*:

> Pareillement,
> Assemblement
> Fist incongneux
> Magicquement,
> Lubricquement
> Nectabanus,
> Lors que conceups
> Fut et receups
> D'Olympiade anticquement
> Alexandre,...[3]

---

[1] See pp. 105–7.

[2] John Gower, *Confessio Amantis* VI, vv. 1789–2366 (*English Works*, ed. G. C. Macaulay, vol. II, E.E.T.S., E.S. LXXXII (1901), pp. 215–30).

[3] Guillaume Alexis, *Contreblason de faulses amours*, stanza 62 (*Œuvres poétiques*, ed. A. Piaget and E. Picot, S.A.T.F., vol. I (1896), p. 308).

It is surprising that the Italian novellieri did not use a story so appropriate to their usual theme of the wiles of lovers; there is, however, a similar story in Boccaccio, of the friar who persuaded a very stupid woman he was the Archangel Gabriel.[1]

We have here noticed the dwindling survivals of the courtly conception of Alexander. Combined with new material they yielded the Alexander-book of Johan Hartlieb, a book which owes its courtly atmosphere to the fact that it was dedicated to a duke, and that its author was the sort of man to dedicate a book to a duke. But whether it is a concession to aristocratic tradition or the expression of Hartlieb's own feelings, that courtly atmosphere is thin enough, and his book is dusty with the lore of a Professor of Natural History at Munich. The work has much of the new attitude, not only is the strict textual adherence to the Paris manuscript of the *Historia de Preliis* typical of the late medieval approach to sources, as we shall see, but there are many tiresome digressions and learned discussions of the wonders met with by Alexander.[2] The whole, while it breathes a faint odour of the courtly period, is mustily professorial.

So the courtly conception of Alexander was slowly dying during the two last medieval centuries; and we are now to discuss some of the immediate influences that contributed to its decay. In Italy it survived and was regenerated by the Renaissance poets; but the rest of Europe lacked the conditions, material and moral, for such a regeneration. Like a child growing up, a society growing up reaches a point when it is very serious, and thinks that in being as serious as possible consists the art of being grown up. Europe had now reached that stage.

(b) THE NEW APPROACH TO TEXTUAL MATERIAL

This was an age of rationalization and of supposed knowledge, a knowledge that went as far as the desire for historical accuracy and the suppression of poetic invention. The disappearance of the marvellous element except in the close translation of statements in legendary Latin sources used, and the examination of the earlier conceptions of Alexander in the light both of better knowledge of historical texts

---

[1] *Decameron*, fourth day, second story.

[2] For the learned interpolations in Hartlieb, see S. Hirsch, *Das Alexanderbuch Johann Hartliebs*, 1909 (*Palaestra*, LXXXII), pp. 11, 90–9.

and of a desire for accuracy accompanied by lack of imagination, sufficiently explain the dullness of the secular conception of Alexander in this period, and presage the liveliness of moral criticism of him.

Paul Meyer, generalizing upon the medieval conception of Alexander, contradicted himself on this point. In one place he says that the wonderful element in the legend became more and more unpopular from the thirteenth century onwards, as the feeling for historical truth gained force; in another, that the late Middle Ages found greater interest than ever in the marvellous episodes of the legend.[135]

These statements are misleading, and it is doubtful if the wonderful element had ever gained a wide hold over the popular imagination. The romance writers had occupied themselves with it as it was a romantic ingredient in favour at the time of the Crusades, and the natural historians, the encyclopaedists and the travellers, men like Albertus Magnus, Honorius of Autun, Walter of Metz, Brunetto Latini, John de Mandeville and Marco Polo, found matter to interest them in it; but truly popular references to the marvellous element are rare indeed compared with the constant reference to Alexander's liberality and valour.[136] Such few references as are found are concerned with episodes which had evidently some independent popularity; the trees of the sun and moon, the Wonderstone and the maidens of the wood.[137] There can hardly be a question of the disappearance of wide popular favour for the wonderful element, because such favour apparently never existed. Various causes, however, contributed to the late medieval disappearance of the poetic interest of writers of Alexander-books and the learned interest of natural historians, and the emergence of a restricted aesthetic interest in the wonder element which was independent of previous tradition. The first of these was the objective reason, that the supersession of the composite manuscript source consisting of the *Zacher Epitome* of Julius Valerius and the *Epistola ad Aristotelem* by the various interpolated versions of the *Historia de Preliis* as the favourite sources used by writers of late medieval Alexander-books meant that the *Epistola* was now widely known only in an abridged form.[1] A second contributory cause was the new tendency to adhere to one source, to refuse to admit artistic embroidery, and to avoid interpolations.

---

[1] I.e. the shortened version of the *Epistola ad Aristotelem* inserted into the interpolated *Historia de Preliis*.

A third was the deliberate rationalizing examination of the wonderful element, as in Seifrit aus Oesterreich and Vasco de Lucena. But while these factors contributed to the disappearance of such earlier interest as had existed, a new interest in the aesthetic aspect of the wonderful element appeared in Italian literary circles, where it was seen, not from the point of view of scientific worth or of good entertainment, as earlier writers had seen it, but as a beautiful and pictorial element in the story.[1] Such a view of the wonderful element belonged to the literary interests of Renaissance Italy rather than to those of the rest of Europe.

Thus Paul Meyer's statements, though apparently conflicting, do bear some relation to the facts, for interest in the marvellous at once disappeared and increased. The point is that these manifestations of interest are on two different planes, and the difference is that between Albertus Magnus and Boiardo, or, at a lesser interval, between Brunetto Latini,[2] the earnest encyclopaedist, and the pictures of the legend on the wall of the Palace in *L'Intelligenza*.[2] But that interest seems never to have been truly popular and an occasional reference in romance and lyric poetry to some wonderful episode is not sufficient to justify its being called so.

The most interesting contributory factor in the new approach to the textual material was the growth of disbelief in certain details of it. Some such disbelief had been expressed throughout the Middle Ages; but earlier it had affected one or two special points in the story, and was based upon conventional medieval reasoning. The chief passage to arouse such doubts was the story of Alexander's birth as the son of Nectanebus. To historians it was not to be reconciled with the historical account of his birth as the son of Philip; to romance writers of the early period it was inconsistent[138] with the nobility of Alexander that he should have been illegitimate—an argument that did not affect late writers, and least of all those of Renaissance Italy.[3]

But the historians never openly disavowed the Nectanebus story except in the *Parua Recapitulatio*.[4] They put the two versions side by

---

[1] See below, p. 270.

[2] For Latini, see p. 264; for *L'Intelligenza*, see p. 270.

[3] Cf. Alberic, vv. 27–32; *Decasyllabic Alexander*, vv. 58–67 (*M.F.R.d'A*. III, p. 64); Alexandre de Paris I, laisse 4, vv. 182–94 (*M.F.R.d'A*. II, pp. 4–5).

[4] *Parua Recapitulatio*, in British Museum, MS. Royal. 13. A. I. fol. 95: 'Hic alexander secundum ueram hystoriam philippi et olimpiadis fuit filius, aristotelis philosophi et nectanebi phisici discipulus, cuius etiam falso creditus est filius propter familiaritatem nimiam quam filii karissimi gratia habebat olimpias ad ipsum nectanebum.'

side, prefacing the Nectanebus story with a cautious 'fertur', and expressed no preference for either account. And when Alberic wrote:

> Dicunt alquant estrobatour
> Que·l reys fud filz d'encantatour.
> Mentent, fellon losengetour...[1]

he was proceeding, not upon a rational disbelief in magic, but upon a conventional belief in the legitimacy of noblemen. When the Nectanebus episode is first openly disavowed for another reason, by Jean de Courcy, in the middle of our period, his reasoning is still medieval. He rejects it, not because of any inherent improbability, but because it runs counter to the testimony of Aristotle and Maccabees that Alexander was the son of Philip[139]—an argument which, while it appears never to have occurred to any earlier medieval author, relied upon almost the only accepted medieval method of establishing the better of two conflicting opinions: giving preference to the older and more venerable authority.

The *Letter to Aristotle* had also proved hard to swallow for some historians; but here again open incredulity was never shown.[140] Similar wonders were told by adventurous Crusaders or Crusaders with adventurous imaginations, and no one might know for certain. That the wonders were received as truth is shown by their reception into works of natural history, and especially into Albertus Magnus, who relied upon the *Letter to Aristotle* as a textbook of natural history.[2]

But in the fourteenth and fifteenth centuries there arose a new movement towards accuracy, which was accompanied by sufficient education to satisfy some of the desire for it. Such a desire had had an earlier effect on Rudolf von Ems,[3] but he went sadly astray in his choice of sources. Now such spirit as there was was one of calm or passionate scepticism, backed by a greater knowledge of the historical texts; and men examined the sources before them in the light of such knowledge as they had. It was the beginning of true comparative

---

[1] Alberic, vv. 27–9 (ed. A. Foulet, *M.F.R.d'A.* III, p. 38).

[2] See Pfister in *Wochenschr. f. klass. Phil.* XXVII (1910), cols. 675–8, and for similar material in the legend and in Albertus Magnus, *Münchener Museum*, I (1912), pp. 261, 265. See also below, n. 140, pp. 339–40, and pp. 350–1.

[3] Cf. G. Ehrismann, *Gesch. d. deutschen Lit. bis zum Ausgang des Mitt.* (Munich, 1935), vol. II, pp. 23 ff.; Grammel, pp. 65 ff. For the effect of this desire for historical accuracy upon Rudolf's portrait of Alexander, see above, pp. 205–6.

study, of observation and of textual criticism; for the legends it was therefore the beginning of the end.

The first absolute contradiction of an established text occurs in the *Histoire ancienne jusqu'à César*, written between 1206 and 1230, cited by Paul Meyer. The author has read his Orosius, and therefore attacks the courtly conception of Alexander:

> Seignor et dames, li pluisors content e dient que totes bones teches d'onor e de dousor e de largece e de cortesie furent en Alixandre. Mais Orosies dit e tesmoigne, cui on en doit mout bien croire, qu'il n'estoit mie mains crueaus ne mains felons a ses freres ne a ses amis ne a ses parens que il estoit a ses ennemis estranges.[1]

Here we have again the setting aside of one view in favour of that expressed by the authority more revered in the Middle Ages; for Orosius had a high medieval reputation. The same attempt to find a solution of the contradictions in two compared texts, though without any influence on the conception of Alexander, is evident as early as Ekkehart of Aura.[2] The authors of the twelfth and thirteenth centuries, who usually borrowed from many sources, were content to leave the inevitable contradictions as they found them; but the authors of later Alexander-books usually adhered stolidly to a single source and thus avoided all question of direct contradiction, except for the well-known conflict of evidence between Julius Valerius and the *Epistola ad Aristotelem* on the fate of Porus.[141] Contradictions were usually ridden over rough-shod, repaired slip-shod or discussed and let pass; it is only rarely that an author takes up a definite stand upon them.

A more usual method of discrediting textual material was by the rational examination of individual details of the wonderful element. The first sceptical examiner is Seifrit aus Oesterreich, who paints a pathetic picture in dismissing the popular tradition that it was Roxana who tried to drown Alexander in his diving-bell. Some say that she let him down by the chains, and then let go of them, but Seifrit comments:

> 6555 das mag also nit gesein,
> wann die edl chaiserein
> was dannoch zu Persya;

---

[1] *Histoire ancienne jusqu'à César*, quoted by Meyer, *A. le G.* II, pp. 376–7.
[2] See above, pp. 71–2.

der chayser het sy gelassen da.
ob sy dann da gewesen wer,
so wer gewesen doch zu swer
die chetten ir allain zu halden,
der hundert ritter muesten walden.[142]

A good memory, and the imaginative picture of Roxana, already expecting a baby, tugging upon the huge chains, made Seifrit decide to reject this material.

The author of the *Wernigerode Alexander* fell back upon the irrefragable argument first used by Rudolf von Ems, ascribing the most incredible wonders to the intervention of God in the life of Alexander.[143] The prophecy of Daniel, the Jerusalem episode and the story of the Ten Tribes were of great value throughout the medieval period for carrying conviction upon the more dubious points of the narrative. 'God was behind Alexander' was an easy excuse for a writer faced with a wonder which he could not explain. But now God's protection was to cease, as we shall show, and Alexander's long and generally profitable connexion with Christianity was to be liquidated. It was a tax upon the critical imagination too great to be borne.

In the fifteenth century Vasco de Lucena provides a striking example of disbelief arrived at in the light of rational examination. In the preface to his translation of Quintus Curtius, he says scathingly: '...Et pour ce que aucuns pourroient blasmer mon labeur comme superflu, disans que on treuve ces hystoires en françois en rime ou en prose, en six ou sept manieres, je respons qu'il est vray, mais corrompues, changies, fausses et plaines de evidens mensonges.'[1] He then goes on to examine two of these lies: the stories of the ascent into the heavens and the descent into the sea, both of which he shows to have been impossible. It is significant that it was these two episodes that he chose for individual examination, for it seems to show, what might be suspected from their undoubted existence in oral and pictorial tradition, that they were the most popular of the wonders told of Alexander.

It is pleasant to reflect that Vasco's confidence in the authenticity of Curtius had already been shown to be misplaced. In his letter to the Emperor Sigismund, who had asked for a translation of Arrian,

---

[1] Quoted by Meyer, *A. le G.* II, p. 378.

VII ALEXANDER'S SUBMARINE DESCENT

Alexander in his glass diving-bell, accompanied by the three animals whose presence is characteristic of the story. Above, in the boat, the faithless lady has just let drop the chain

Vergerio points out the inaccuracies in the Latin historians of Alexander as sharply as Vasco de Lucena attacked those in the legendary tradition.[1]

The fifteenth-century translator into French of the *Epistola ad Aristotelem* was at least doubtful about the veracity of his text: '...et la seconde partie est son epystre, laquelle il mesmez envoia a son chier maistre prince des philosophes Aristote, de toutes les aventures et mervoillez qu'il eut et vit es derraines parties d'Inde la majour, lesquelles sont moult fortes a croire.'[2]

Favre notes Melanchthon, who refused to write of the marvels told of Alexander because they were too ludicrous;[3] and we may connect with this the Leiden transcript of the *Oxford Epitome*, where the transcriber laid down his pen after the fifth chapter with the comment that the story was grown too absurd to be worth the copying.[4]

Finally we may remark the rude comments of two sixteenth-century readers of Hartlieb scrawled in a copy of the 1472 edition of his book: 'leug nit oder Ich friss dich'; 'leug nit ich friss dich sunst, hat wol mehr gelogen.'[5]

It has already been mentioned that Alexander was no longer in the later Middle Ages portrayed as a Christian or under the protection of the Christian God except in the *Wernigerode Alexander*. This naturally followed from the movement that has been noted towards strict adherence to the source text, a tendency due partly to the determination to get as near as possible to historical truth and consequently to refuse to admit possibly irrelevant material, and partly to the general decline in literary standards, unfavourable to original creation as opposed to mere transcription, that characterized the period. It may be of interest to show how Alexander has again become a heathen in the Alexander-books, and how the sentiment of the Crusading period towards the heathen has worn away with other courtly conventions.

In *Kyng Alisaunder* it is lamented that Alexander did not die a Christian, one instance which may serve to illustrate the new com-

---

[1] For Pier Paolo Vergerio see below, Texts 7, pp. 375-7.

[2] Quoted by Meyer, *A. le G.* II, p. 304.

[3] For Melanchthon's contemptuous comment, see G. Favre, *Mélanges d'Histoire Littéraire*, II (1856), p. 135, n. 1.

[4] The writer, the scholar Perizonius, comments: 'Nolui plura scribere, quoniam nimium fabulosa narrat in sequentibus.' See J. Zacher, *Pseudocallisthenes*, p. 41-2.

[5] Quoted by O. Zingerle, *Die Quellen zum Alexander des Rudolf von Ems* (*Germanistische Abhandlungen*, IV, Breslau, 1885), p. 7, n. 2.

mon-sense approach to his historical relationship with God.[1] In the *Wernigerode Alexander*, the writer sees God working on Alexander's behalf in the episode of the Celestial Journey and elsewhere, but he does not know what to say about this. He stresses the fact that Alexander was a heathen, and, having no explanation to offer of why God should so befriend a heathen, retires behind that usual defence of unhappy controversialists previously used by Rudolf von Ems—the inscrutable ways of God.[2]

Vasco de Lucena is most frank about the whole matter. To him Alexander was a damned heathen, and he suggests that if a heathen accomplished so much, should not a Christian king, armed with the Faith, do much better and conquer the East for Christendom?[3] Gautier de Châtillon had made a different appeal; he had asked for a second Alexander, not a Christian Alexander. Alexander's heathendom is stressed in odd fashion in the *Thornton Alexander*, where Dindimus, Christianized as always in the later Middle Ages, accuses Alexander and the Macedonians of sacrificing their children to 'Mawmetes'.[4]

But outside the Alexander-books, the liveliness of late medieval abuse of Alexander based on the theological approach to him shows the new emphasis upon his heathendom better than the colourless, objective return to historical facts or supposed facts which might be illustrated by numberless references. The attacks on Alexander's idolatry in Lydgate and Gower, the consignment of his soul to the Devil in the *Seelentrost*,[5] the emphasis upon his heathendom in *History-Bible* I,[5] show more positively the new attitude to his relationship with God because they are accusations and condemnations founded upon his heathendom and not merely the record of that fact.

Thus men returned to the bare framework. The inevitable result of the pruning away of medieval accumulations of wonder-material, romantic conventions and Christian interpolations and interpretations, and of the lack of imagination and earnest desire for accuracy which accompanied this pruning, was the return of the secular con-

---

[1] *Kyng Alisaunder*, vv. 8032–3 (ed. Weber, p. 327):

> Alisaunder! me reowith thyn endyng,
> That thou n'adest dyghed in Christenyng!

[2] See below, pp. 341–2, n. 143.
[3] This epilogue is quoted in full below, p. 332, n. 132.
[4] See *Thornton Prose Life*, ed. J. Westlake, E.E.T.S., O.S. CXLIII (1913), p. 83.
[5] On these passages see below, pp. 258–9.

ception of Alexander to that of the world-conqueror, the man of battles whose principal virtue is his magnanimity, his bold valour. For his spirit was now not the fierce, ebullient quality of an earlier age which disappeared with the return to the spirit of the sources; it was a quieter determination that again approached the Aristotelian definition of magnanimity. Thus Alexander, from the fiery chivalrous adventurer, returned to a truer, but a duller role—that of the great, the greatest, conqueror.

(c) THE RETURN TO THE BASIC CONCEPTION OF THE SECULAR ALEXANDER

It now remains to show how Alexander reappeared in the shrivelled, derivative Alexander-books of this period as the world-conqueror, the pattern of military rather than of chivalrous virtues, and how this conception of him is supported by independent secular references. We must remember that such an approach to Alexander was never entirely dormant, but was always sufficiently represented in the duller secular texts and references of the earlier period. Especially in England, in Germany and in Italy, where the influence of courtly ideals was more transitory than in France, Alexander's reputation for his approved historical qualities was always to be seen in independent references; and although the thirteenth-century German Alexander-books reproduced the courtly feeling of the time, independent German references of the same period show a gradual return to the picture of the world-conqueror.[1] In England, except in the imitative work of Thomas of Kent, the courtly conception of Alexander never found a footing; and the vernacular English Alexander-books never ceased to present Alexander first and foremost as a soldier, a presentation supported by independent references.

Remembering the persistence of this attitude to Alexander, let us briefly examine the Middle English Alexander-books of the period from 1300 to 1500. *Kyng Alisaunder*, written about 1330, is a free adaptation of the *Roman de Toute Chevalerie*, with the omission of the interpolated *Fuerre de Gadres*. It is an excellent piece of work, the most individual and imaginative of the English Alexander-books. Like Rudolf von Ems, the writer used his imagination not for the

---

[1] See above, p. 216.

portrayal of the Alexander of courtly fantasy, but to give a clear portrait of Alexander as a mighty conqueror, a man apart. The book breathes, within the trammels of a fairly close adherence to its source, the spirit of Gautier's *Alexandreis* in vernacular feeling and expression; Alexander is the idealized conqueror, but not here, as in the *Alexandreis*, the heroicized conqueror. He is brought into relationship with contemporary convention and belief, and not removed into an atmosphere of the past with a mainly academic appeal. But in the prologue the writer makes a statement which will be recalled later; he says that Alexander was a successful conqueror only because he obeyed the suggestions of his master Aristotle.[1] This is perhaps a result of the growing popularity of the *Secret of Secrets*, which emphasized Alexander's reliance upon the philosopher and proved a valuable tool in the hands of other philosophers faced with would-be Alexanders.

With this poem we may conveniently group the rest of the English Alexander-books, which resemble it in pattern. The fragments *Alexander A* and *Alexander B* are close translations of their sources;[2] and it is typical of the period that *Alexander A* should contain long historical interpolations from Orosius, and that *Alexander B* should have been transcribed into the Bodleian manuscript to supply a supposed gap in the story of the *Roman d'Alexandre* from the scribe's superior knowledge.

Of greater interest is the fifteenth-century *Wars of Alexander*, a spirited translation of the I³ᵃ *Historia de Preliis*. There is no trace of courtly feeling here: in the prologue we are told that some like to hear of knightly adventures, or stories of love, but this is the story of the mightiest emperor that ever existed, the great Alexander,[3] 'as the book tells'. This reference to the book is supported throughout by frequent interjections on the part of the writer to the effect that he has followed his source exactly—a device designed to carry conviction on the knottier points of the narrative by reference to a higher, and

---

[1] *Kyng Alisaunder*, prologue, vv. 29ff. (ed. Weber, p. 4):

> Now pais holdith, and leteth cheste,
> And ye schole here a noble jeste,
> Of Alisaundre, theo riche kyng,
> That dude by his maistres techyng...

and there follows his career of conquest.

[2] For relevant details of *Alexander A* and *B*, see above, pp. 48–9.

[3] *Wars of Alexander*, prologue, vv. 15ff. (ed. W. W. Skeat, E.E.T.S., E.S. XLVII (1888), p. 1).

sometimes a fictitious, authority which was common to many Alexander-books, but was supported in this case by a close adherence to the source text.[144] At much the same time the *Thornton Alexander* was written—an uninteresting prose translation of the I[3a] *Historia de Preliis*, with little to commend it except to a student of fifteenth-century English Prose.[1]

From these English Alexander-books, which present the unadorned portrait of the conqueror, as it is to be found in the legendary sources, we turn to the German and French Alexander-books of the fourteenth and fifteenth centuries. The scope of Seifrit's *Alexander* is sufficiently indicated by the prologue, where, speaking of the book of 'Eusebius' from which he has translated his book (the I[2] *Historia de Preliis*), he says:

> der hab ich mich genomen an
> in deutschew wart zu tichten
> und zu reym richten:
> wie der mylt und der here
> chunig Allexander
> mit seiner mechtigen tat
> alle die welt betwungen hat,
> wie er es an gevie
> und wie es im ze jungist gie,
> als es sag sein hystorie.[2]

But if there is some faint reminiscence there in the epithet 'mylt' of Alexander's courtly qualities, the description of the hero's education shows how the portrayal of his life had returned to the military emphasis of Alberic and his period:

> Der chnab wart gar synn reich:
> czucht und er nam er an sich
> und ander tugent manigvalt.
> do er wart zweliff jar alt,
> do wolt er nicht enpern
> er wolt ritterschaft lern.
> man lernt in justiern,
> stechen und turnyern
> und vechten mit dem swert;
> scirmen man in auch lert,
> unczt er es alles chundt.[3]

---

[1] *Thornton Prose Life*, ed. J. Westlake, E.E.T.S., O.S. CXLIII (1913).
[2] Seifrit's *Alexander*, vv. 12–21 (ed. Gereke, p. 1).
[3] Seifrit's *Alexander*, vv. 605–15 (ibid. p. 11).

Seifrit's account of Alexander is fairly close throughout to his source, the I² *Historia de Preliis*, but he interpolated, beside two passages that have already been discussed (the Candace episode[1] and a comment upon the story of Roxana's attempt to drown Alexander[2]), the Senecan story of the man to whom Alexander gave a city,[3] and a strange version of the *Iter ad Paradisum*.[4] The prevalence in German tradition of versions unknown elsewhere of the *Iter ad Paradisum*, the Celestial Journey and the descent into the sea appears as early as the eleventh century in the *Annolied*, and the reason for the divergence of these stories current in Germany from the usual versions has never been discovered; some scholars ascribe it to some lost intermediate literary text, and others vaguely to oral tradition.[5]

The ruling spirit of Seifrit's poem is that which he found in his source—the portrayal of Alexander as a valiant conqueror. And it may be seen from the independent German references to Alexander at this period that German secular opinion had now returned entirely to this attitude, from which indeed it hardly departed, even at the height of the courtly period.[145]

The author of the *Wernigerode Alexander* translated his text from Quilichinus, but he added certain comments of his own, mainly confined, as has been shown, to curious doubts about the fact that God showed the heathen Alexander such signal favours.[6] Quilichinus' book, in Latin verse of appalling quality, was a direct versification of an I³ *Historia de Preliis* text, with all the interpolations and all the moralizing, but the German writer fortunately substituted some of his own comments for the tiresome reflexions upon the futility of human endeavour in the face of death that pursued Alexander through the Middle Ages. His prologue, however, is a translation of the prologue in Quilichinus which describes Alexander's place in the succession of world-kingdoms and introduces his life as an extended commentary on Maccabees. There was in the later Middle Ages a

---

[1] Seifrit's *Alexander*, vv. 6897–7586 (ibid. pp. 113–23).
[2] Seifrit's *Alexander*, vv. 6545 ff. (ibid. pp. 107–8); see above, pp. 237–8 and below pp. 340–1.
[3] Seifrit's *Alexander*, vv. 8073–94 (ibid. pp. 131–2).
[4] Seifrit's *Alexander*, vv. 6229–374 (ibid. pp. 102–5). In this version the stone is given to Alexander's lieutenants by Michael who breaks a piece off the wall of the city of the blessed and gives it to them. The stone (or the fragment) carries with it the normal interpretation of the vanity of all ambition.
[5] Upon these independent German versions of well-known legendary stories, see pp. 340–1, 346–7. [6] See below, pp. 340–1.

marked tendency to return to the connexion of Alexander's conquests with the text of Maccabees; and Alexander was connected yet further with Judas Maccabeus by the fact that they stood together in the ranks of the *Neuf Preux*.

But if the prologue of the *Wernigerode Alexander* is derivative, the writer sums up at the end of the book his own attitude:

> Ez ist wie Allexander
> Geporn ward und wie er
> Betwang die werlt all gar
> Und wie er für her und dar
> Und waz er wunders hat gesechen.
> Wer ez list, der müss jhehen
> Daz Got wunder mit im wörht,
> Er waz auch selber uner förht,
> Daz waz wol an im schein.[1]

In some mysterious way God chose to assist Alexander; he will go no further towards reconciling the picture of the conqueror with the results of his own observation, the evidences of God's intervention.

Wauquelin's prose romance has already been discussed.[2] The book as a whole, which is full of courtly ideas and feeling, represents a last effort to hold on to the courtly tradition against the influx of historical evidence, as the *Alexander* of Rudolf von Ems was an effort to hold on to historical fact against the influx of courtly ideas. Both were men out of their time, fighting to preserve something foreign to contemporary convention and belief; and both, in a measure, failed.

Vasco de Lucena may be dismissed as an uninspired translator of Quintus Curtius, and the author of a book which supplied after a different fashion, shorn of its wonders and blackened by some smuts, the portrait of Alexander the conqueror, though it was in the spirit of its age and enjoyed considerable success.

So we may pass to the consideration of the two fifteenth-century German authors of Alexander-books, Babiloth and Hartlieb. Of Babiloth[3] there is little to remark. He was a close translator of his source, which appears to have been a manuscript of mixed type,

---

[1] *Wernigerode Alexander*, vv. 6409 ff. (ed. G. Guth, p. 92).
[2] See above, pp. 228–9.
[3] For Babiloth's *Alexanderchronik*, see S. Herzog, *Die Alexanderchronik des Meister Babiloth* (Progr., Stuttgart, 1897, and continued, 1903), which contains a full discussion and a partial edition of the work. See for the I³ ending F. Pfister, in *Münchener Museum*, I (1912), pp. 272, 276.

founded mainly upon the I² *Historia de Preliis*, but containing in its last section all the characteristics of the I³ recension, including the episode of the Philosophers at the Tomb. The book contains the typical rationalizations of the age, but no absolute denial of the courtly spirit—it is what it claims to be, an *Alexanderchronik*, a pseudo-historical sketch of the life of Alexander for the new public that drew so many chronicles of dubious authenticity from the press.

Johann Hartlieb's life of Alexander has already been discussed.[1] His account is little better than a direct translation of the Paris manuscript of the *Historia de Preliis*, with all its interpolations and vagaries. Hartlieb himself claimed to have translated his book from Eusebius, a claim also made by Seifrit aus Oesterreich. Although the *Chronica* of Eusebius naturally contain a brief reference to Alexander, there is nothing that can satisfactorily explain such a statement on the part of translators of the *Historia de Preliis*. This mystery must be set side by side with the ascription of Julius Valerius' translation of Pseudo-Callisthenes in certain manuscripts, which say that it was translated 'ex Aesopo Graeco', a phrase likewise never explained.[2]

Hartlieb added some original material, some courtly reminiscence in his treatment of the love element, and much contemporary scientific lore; but it floated like scum upon the surface—it obscured, but it did not alter the Alexander portrait supplied him by the source text.

Thus we may notice several characteristics common to most Alexander-books of the fourteenth and fifteenth centuries. They are, first, a tendency to return to simple translation from one principal text; secondly, an increasing earnestness in the investigation of truth, an attempt to reconcile opposed authorities and a denial of improbable wonders; and thirdly, a consequent reliance upon the conception of Alexander expressed in the historical and pseudo-historical Latin sources. Alexander is stripped of feasts and frolics and jousts and love-affairs; he is again the warrior and the man of action.

This conception of Alexander is supported by many independent contemporary references; and was also symbolized in his appearance

---

[1] See S. Hirsch, *Das Alexanderbuch Johann Hartliebs* (Palaestra, LXXXII, 1909), and the note by Pfister in *Münchener Museum*, I (1912), p. 282, n. 1.

[2] For transcriptions of the titles and colophons of various manuscripts of Julius Valerius, of which the most important was the Turin palimpsest MS. now destroyed, and a discussion of the various theories put forward about 'Aesop', see Meyer, *A. le G.* II, pp. 13–18.

as one of the Nine Worthies. This group of famous men, occasionally increased to Ten by a writer anxious to please his patron, was first introduced by Jacques de Longuyon in his *Voeux du Paon*, and consisted of three pagan, three Jewish, and three Christian heroes, each characterized by the quality or the action that made him remembered. And Alexander, as one of the three pagans, was here remembered for his conquests and his valour.

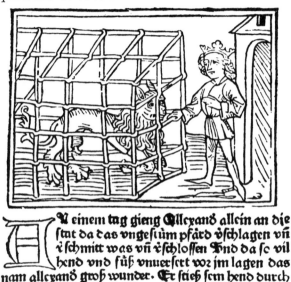

FIG. 5. ALEXANDER TAMES BUCEPHALUS

The fierce man-eating horse kneels in homage before his future master who puts his hand through the bars of the cage to pat him.

From Johann Hartlieb's *Histori von dem Grossen Alexander*. The short cycle of pictures illustrating the incunable editions of Hartlieb's *Alexander* are based on the text, which accounts for the curious half-leonine appearance of Bucephalus here. 'Das pferd het vornen fuss als ein hirss und einen langen hals, einen kopff als ein freysamer leo, und es ass nun menschen fleysch.'

Here, as a symbolic figure in a pageant, his name was woven into a proverbial association with valour, woven in the numerous tapestries that portray the subject; or the yokels, the rabble at Coventry or in Paris would dress up one of their number as Alexander, mumbling such verses as are quoted by Gollancz and Loomis.[146] In this last debasement, whose popularity is symbolized by the *Triomphe des*

Neuf Preux, Alexander is stripped of his character and of his power to move. As in the courtly period, he entered popular imagination in an apophthegm—but that apophthegm did not represent, as did that upon his liberality, one side only of his traditional character; it typified the dull, pseudo-historical, inconsistent dead subject of the contemporary Alexander-books. Thus Alexander's place in the *Neuf Preux* sums up his place in the secular literature of the late Middle Ages, which had returned to supposed historical portraiture suppressing extraneous medieval elaborations.

3. THE LATE MEDIEVAL TREATMENT OF THE EXEMPLAR, THEOLOGICAL, AND MORAL CONCEPTIONS OF ALEXANDER

It is difficult to find any satisfactory way of classifying the remaining evidence. It has seemed best to divide it, except for the section upon the persistence of the exemplar tradition, into sections corresponding with certain movements that reflect, for the first time, strong national differences in the approach to Alexander. As has been shown, the secular attitude to Alexander has now been reduced to a uniform reliance on history or on a bare legendary text, and differences in treatment are rarely important. But the final stage of the moral conception of Alexander which we have now to consider is more complex. This complexity is due in part to the new popularity of the Arabic material, but above all to the general accessibility of ideas and of material which had previously circulated only in one class of society.

In considering the earlier medieval period we proceeded from the moral and theological conceptions of Alexander through the exemplar to the secular attitude. In this study of the late medieval period the order has been reversed, because in that period the secular conception of Alexander quietly died; unless to think of Alexander the Great as the Great Alexander counts for a living view of him. From the discussion of its decay we may return through the persistent and unaltered exemplar tradition, to the living use of the older anecdotal, historical and Oriental material, with its accompanying conceptions of Alexander, in the new and thoughtful vernacular literature and in the works of serious apostles of a new social order.

(*a*) THE PERSISTENCE OF THE EXEMPLAR TRADITION, AND THE LATE MEDIEVAL ASSOCIATIONS OF THE EXEMPLAR THEME OF THE FUTILITY OF MAN IN THE FACE OF DEATH

The collections of *exempla* within this period have already been discussed, since the history of the exemplar treatment of Alexander, with its steady accumulation of a limited store of anecdote, continues unbroken to the end of the Middle Ages, as was indeed natural with anthologies of a derivative and unliterary type. But it is proposed briefly to notice here the later associations, outside the exemplar books themselves, of that theme which has been shown to be the predominant feature of the exemplar approach to Alexander—the futility of man in the face of death.

This theme tended to disappear from the epilogues of Alexander-books, with all other material extraneous to what was considered strict historical narrative; although it persisted, accompanied by abuse of Alexander, in the *Seelentrost* group of texts.[1] But this idea was caught up with delight by didactic writers in the vernacular, who began to conclude with it a new moral treatment of Alexander's death.[2] For his cruelty and his vain blasphemy, taken over from the condemnations of earlier writers, were now more generally given as the causes of his death; or he was punished for his pride, which contrasted so unfavourably with the humility of Diogenes. So that these themes, derived from yet older teaching than the exemplar moral, tended to outweigh in importance that more universal and impersonal moral that might have been drawn from the death of any great man.

But if Alexander's death by itself was now more often considered with the eyes of the didactic philosopher, the simple exemplar theme persisted, attached not only to the name of Alexander, but to that band of illustrious men of whom he was one, the Nine Worthies.[3]

---

[1] For the *Seelentrost* group, see below, p. 258, n. 3; for the text of the epilogue of *Seelentrost*, below, p. 312.

[2] See for examples, pp. 292, 255–7, 315, 346 n. 152.

[3] See above, pp. 246–8.

(b) THE LATE MEDIEVAL CONCEPTION OF ALEXANDER
IN FRENCH MORAL AND DIDACTIC WRITERS

The principal characteristics of the French late medieval approach to Alexander have already been examined. The faint persistence of the courtly tradition and the new popularity of the *Neuf Preux* are the most evident features of the late French attitude, and here more than in any other country Alexander remained reasonably secure from moral attack. But the approach to Alexander was slightly affected by two moral works widely disseminated in the late Middle Ages, the *Secret of Secrets* and the *Dicts and Sayings of the Philosophers*.

The *Secret of Secrets*, although it had been known in Europe from the twelfth century, did not become popular until the fourteenth.[147] The numerous Latin manuscripts and vernacular translations dating from this period are convincing evidence of interest awakened, and this interest was evidently due to the improving morality and useful information contained in the work, cast in a sober, philosophic form that appealed to the new public, and especially to the writers upon political science.

The effect of this popularity upon the reputation of Alexander is hard to gauge. In the *Secret of Secrets* Alexander is merely the recipient of Aristotle's precepts; and the moral counsel that Aristotle conveys, the portrait of the ideal prince that he draws, could not without the use of the imagination be incorporated in the portrait of Alexander himself, though the two anecdotes of Alexander which appear in the book,[1] and its preface in which Alexander asks Aristotle for such a book of counsel,[148] suggest that Alexander's obedience to the precepts of Aristotle was presumed by the author. Such an idea however, was not generally taken up, though Eustache Deschamps used it in his poem of advice for Charles VI;[149] and there it was called for by the necessity of persuading the young king that Alexander owed all his power to a philosopher. But the chief interest of the book for medieval readers lay in its cautious, Aristotelian morality, so popular in the late Middle Ages.

This philosophic tone of the book, this exalted instruction of a prince, is best reflected in French literature in the lyrics of Eustache

---

[1] For these two episodes, the story of how Alexander obeyed Aristotle's advice in his treatment of conquered Persia, and the story of the poison girl, see p. 106, n. 1, and 231, n. 5.

Deschamps. The references to Alexander in his poetry present a fascinating study of the various forces at work in this period of change and decay, and of the coexistence and coalescence of the old conceptions of Alexander.[150] There is in Deschamps a reminiscence of the theological attack, which now first found a faint echo in France;[151] an exemplar musing upon the death of Alexander; a reflexion of the ancient moral approach; occasional survivals of the courtly tradition; but above all a connecting of Alexander with the instruction contained in the *Secret of Secrets* and its portrait of the philosopher king.

The popularity of the *Secret of Secrets* in late medieval France was only equalled by that of the *Dicts and Sayings of the Philosophers*, in the translation of Guillaume de Tignonville.¹ No Alexander-book, however, except for the English *Dublin Epitome*, was ever founded upon this popular work; a fact not so strange if we consider that it owed its popularity, not to its representation of a philosophical Alexander, who occupies a very minor position in it, but to the proverbial philosophy which it contains.

Thus these books had little direct influence upon the late medieval Alexander portrait in spite of their great reputation, for that reputation was due, not to the conception of Alexander contained in them, but to their moral content. It is in their reflexion of late medieval ethical standards that they stand in an indirect connexion with the contemporary Alexander portrait, for they represent the new ideal of the philosophic king by which individual kings were to be judged.

If the approach to Alexander in France in the late Middle Ages can be said to show anything characteristically national it is the continued survival, in an attenuated form, of the old secular portrait of the hero with its courtly elaboration.

¹ On the *Ditz Moraux des Philosophes* see Meyer, *A. le G.* II, pp. 349–50. For its use by Jean de Courcy (who borrowed from it the letter of Olympias to Alexander on pride, and the letter of Alexander to Olympias on his approaching death), see ibid. pp. 351, 354. For editions see Brunet's *Manuel*, s.v. *Dits des philosophes*; for details of the history of the work, of translations into English, etc., see pp. 22–3.

(c) THE LATE MEDIEVAL CONCEPTION OF ALEXANDER
IN ENGLISH MORAL AND DIDACTIC WRITERS

The three most important English writers of this period, Chaucer, Gower, and Lydgate, illustrate admirably the progress of didactic criticism of Alexander, based upon a hotch-potch of all the textual traditions, in late medieval England.

Chaucer's brief reference to the story of Alexander in the *House of Fame*[1] need not detain us. In the *Manciple's Tale* he introduced the story of the pirate.[2] This anecdote was very popular in the later Middle Ages, but in most instances the later version, in which emphasis was laid upon the mercy shown by Alexander to the pirate, was used. It is rare to find, as in Chaucer, an instance of its use where the moral has retained the form which it had taken in St Augustine. Chaucer's version of the story has been quoted elsewhere, and it has been shown that here the pirate's remarks have become an epigram with no personal accusation of Alexander implied.

In the *Monk's Tale*[3] the life of Alexander is told as an illustration of the inconstancy of fortune. This narrative, based on Quintus Curtius, possibly through the intermediacy of Gautier de Châtillon, opens with those famous lines which every writer upon the medieval Alexander feels tempted to put upon his title-page:

> The storie of Alisaundre is so comune,
> That every wight that hath discrecioun
> Hath herd somewhat or al of his fortune.[4]

The life of Alexander is told in a secular spirit of admiration; but it is a significant step that that life should now be fully recounted in narrative poetry to illustrate a moral truth. As we have seen, the transition from the early to the late medieval period, especially in England, is characterized by the appearance of long passages concerning Alexander in moral and didactic prose-writers and poets, instead of the short, abrupt references which were

---

[1] *House of Fame*, v. 915 (ed. W. W. Skeat, *The Works of Geoffrey Chaucer*, Oxford, 1900, vol. III, p. 28).

[2] *The Manciple's Tale*, v. 226–34 (ibid. vol. IV, p. 562); see above, p. 97.

[3] *The Monk's Tale*, vv. 641 ff. (ibid. vol. IV, pp. 264–5).

[4] For a suggestion that Chaucer knew the *Alexandreis*, see H. R. Patch in a review of Magoun's *Gests of King Alexander...*, in *Speculum*, v (1930), p. 118.

the rule in the days of less digressive and more strictly philosophic authors.[1]

Chaucer closes his account with a fine lament upon the death of Alexander:

> Who shal me yeven teres to compleyne
> The deeth of gentillesse and of fraunchyse,
> That al the world welded in his demeyne,
> And yit him thoughte it mighte nat suffyse,
> So ful was his corage of heigh empryse.[2]

The theme of the inconstancy of fortune in connexion with the life of Alexander had also been used by Boccaccio in his *De Casibus Virorum Illustrium*;[3] but he used as his example, not the career of Alexander, but that of Callisthenes. The downfall of Callisthenes consequent upon Alexander's mad vanity, his condemnation, the tortures that he suffered and his death, were described in detail by Boccaccio; and from him the details passed through Laurent de Premierfait to Lydgate, who made great play with them in his *Fall of Princes*. But before we discuss Lydgate's attitude to Alexander, it is necessary to examine that of his predecessor John Gower, and especially the references to Alexander in the *Confessio Amantis* which contains much material concerning him derived from many different sources.[4]

In his prologue Gower refers to Alexander's career of conquest, but the first important passage which he devotes to him is in the third book, where he tells the old story of Alexander and Diogenes in its exemplar form,[5] a point which Pfister appears to have ignored when he considered Gower's source for the story to have been Valerius Maximus, while dismissing, quite correctly, the suggestion that it was taken from the I² *Historia de Preliis*. For Valerius Maximus gives only the incident of the sunshine without that saying of Diogenes, characteristic of the exemplar form and found in Gower, that Alexander is the 'servant of his servant'. Gower must therefore have

---

[1] See above, pp. 110–16, for illustration of this in the history of the medieval treatment of the murder of Callisthenes.

[2] *The Monk's Tale*, vv. 673–7 (ed. cit. vol. IV, p. 265).

[3] G. Boccaccio, *De Casibus Virorum Illustrium* IV (J. Gourmont and J. Petit (Paris, 1525), f. xxxvii^v–xxxviii^v).

[4] On the sources of the references to Alexander in Gower, see G. L. Hamilton in *The Journal of English and Germanic Philology*, XXVI (1927), pp. 491–520, and corrections by Pfister in *Germ.-Rom. Monatschr.* (1928), p. 86.

[5] *Confessio Amantis* III, vv. 1221 ff. (*English Works*, ed. G. C. Macaulay, E.E.T.S., E.S. LXXXI–LXXXII, vol. I, 1900, pp. 259 ff.). See Pfister, loc. cit.

received this anecdote through some source which quoted the exemplar form, possibly from Walter Burley, and he draws from it the exemplar moral of the danger of will uncontrolled by reason.

The second anecdote that Gower tells of Alexander is the story of the pirate.[1] His form of the story belongs to the first, Augustinian tradition, but, as usual in didactic works, the pirate's accusation is excessively swollen. The moral, like that of the Diogenes story, is the necessity of self-control:

> for al the world ne mai suffise
> to will which is noght resonable.

Alexander conquered all the world; he let his will go beyond his reason; but in the end he was poisoned, and what did his unreasonable wars avail him then?

In a later passage the usual theological attack upon Alexander is continued. In a discussion on idolatry, the letter of Dindimus to Alexander is quoted,[2] attacking the Greeks for their numerous gods, and assigning, in a spirit of heavy fantasy, one god to each limb of their bodies. This variant on the euhemeristic theory, coming from the respected pen of Dindimus, is supported by the narration of the legendary story of Alexander and Candeolus, the son of Candace.[3] Gower tells how they came to a cave which, according to Candeolus, was inhabited by the gods. Alexander went in, felt the presence of the gods, and conversed with Serapis.

There is a brief reference, probably borrowed from the *Roman de Toute Chevalerie* which supplied some of Gower's legendary material, to Candace herself and her wily enticement of Alexander with rich gifts.[4] It has already been shown how many episodes in the story of Alexander supplied material for late medieval misogynists.

And indeed the intrigues of Nectanebus are discussed by Gower in the sixth book of the *Confessio Amantis*.[5] He tells at great length and

---

[1] *Confessio Amantis* III, vv. 2363 ff. (ed. cit. vol. I, p. 290 ff.).

[2] Ibid. v, vv. 1453 ff. (ed. cit. vol. I, p. 441 ff.).

[3] Ibid. v, vv. 1571 ff. (ed. cit. vol. I, p. 445).

[4] Ibid. v, vv. 2543 ff. (ed. cit. vol. II, 1901, p. 16).

[5] Ibid. VI, vv. 1790 ff. (ed. cit. vol. II, p. 215). We may notice a reference to Alexander in a poem of Gower's which will serve as a final illustration of his approach: *In Praise of Peace*, vv. 36 ff. (*English Works*, ed. G. C. Macaulay, vol. II, E.E.T.S., E.S. LXXXII (1901), p. 482): 'Alexander chose conquest from God, unlike Solomon who chose wisdom. He gained wha he sought; but he gained it in a miserable pagan world:

(v. 49) Al was vengance and infortune of sinne.'

with evident pleasure the story of the adultery of Nectanebus, and describes Alexander's youth as far as the murder of Nectanebus, with the comment that sorcery did not help him or save him from death. In the part of this account which deals with Alexander's education he is no longer taught fencing and fighting, or the courtly arts of chivalry and love as in earlier days; it is typical of the period that Gower has Callisthenes and Aristotle teach him 'Philosophie, Entenden, and Astronomie'. This leads on to the seventh book which is a long description of Alexander's education. It is based upon the *Secret of Secrets* and contains nothing of interest to our purpose.

Thus Gower used both legendary and moral anecdotal material for his references to Alexander, and his condemnation is principally based upon the Peripatetic contention, that he yielded to himself. Lydgate, however, adopts a different attitude towards Alexander. His main criticism is founded, not upon the anecdotal material used by Gower, but upon the long account of the visit to the oracle of Ammon, the consequent arrogance of Alexander, and the murder of Callisthenes. This he received from Boccaccio; and thus he returns to the theological accusation of pride.

Lydgate's first mention of Alexander, however, in Book 1 of the *Fall of Princes*, introduces the story of Diogenes in its literary form,[1] which he presumably found either in Valerius Maximus or in some intermediary. The moral drawn from this story was that which was usually attached to the exemplar version of it; Alexander's reason was fettered by his wilful sensuality. The fame of such a man shall fade while that of Diogenes shall endure for ever; Alexander was slain by poison but Diogenes continued prosperous, for

> Alisaundre with coveitise was blent;
> The philisophre with litil was content.[2]

This moral was reproduced in two of Lydgate's lyric poems,[152] and it is evident that he considered the story of Alexander and Diogenes a good *exemplum*. It is also expressed, in a form unconnected with the Diogenes story, in the poem 'Mesure is Tresour'[3] where Lydgate tells how Alexander conquered all the world and found the stone of Paradise, but came to misfortune because he did

---

[1] *Fall of Princes* 1, vv. 6233–79 (ed. H. Bergen, Washington, 1923, vol. 1, pp. 176–7).
[2] Loc. cit. vv. 6278–9.
[3] See Lydgate's *Minor Poems*, part II, ed. MacCracken, p. 777.

not know the value of moderation, and let his desires overpower his self-control.

Though there is an evident similarity between this moral and that extracted by Gower from the Diogenes episode, Lydgate has gone a little further in considering the effects of Alexander's lack of control. Gower held to the exemplar form of the story which looks no further than to the general application of Diogenes' rebuke; in Lydgate the contrast is drawn between Diogenes' poverty and Alexander's pride, a reminiscence of the Senecan attack. And it is this pride, sprung from his lack of reasonable control, that brought Alexander to his death; so that Lydgate differed from Gower by his dependence upon a different form of the anecdote, and by the basic theme of his poem, the theme of the *Fall of Princes*, to which Alexander's incontinence is related.

The attack on Alexander's pride foreshadowed here is made more openly in the biographical narrative which Lydgate devotes to Alexander.[1] This account, based upon Quintus Curtius, opens with the conquest of Persia. Lydgate shows how Alexander succumbed

---

[1] See for this long passage *Fall of Princes* IV, vv. 1107ff. (ed. Bergen, vol. II, pp. 504–12, 517–28); the idea, worked out in vv. 1639ff., that Fortune sent Alexander against Darius, is evidently of Peripatetic origin.

PLATE VIII (*opposite*). From a copiously illustrated MS. of the *Historia de Preliis* version I² now in the Stadtbibliothek, Leipzig. This is a vellum MS. written and illustrated in Southern Italy in the second half of the thirteenth century. Small unframed miniatures, often two or more to a page, occur on 171 of its 230 pages making a total of over 200 subjects. These pictures derive directly from a miniature cycle devised originally for the Greek Pseudo-Callisthenes in late Imperial or early Byzantine times and are found also in illustrated MSS. of the γ Pseudo-Callisthenes, the Armenian version, the Serbian Alexander and elsewhere. From the I² *Historia de Preliis* they passed also to its translation the French Prose Alexander where they appear in several MSS. It is probable that the point and date of entry of this cycle into Western Europe was Sicily or South Italy in the first half of the thirteenth century, during the reign of the Emperor Frederick II whose interest in Byzantium was considerable in both the political and the cultural spheres.

The page reproduced (Fol. 8) shows the death of Nectanebus in three scenes:

1. (Above, left) Nectanebus gives Alexander a lesson in astrology.

2. (Above, right) Alexander pushes Nectanebus off the hill when he is not looking, breaking his neck.

3. (Below) Alexander carries the body of Nectanebus, who has declared himself with his dying breath Alexander's father, back to Olympias who awaits him at the door of the palace.

A fourth scene on the following page shows the burial of the astrologer.

ft cognui in fint hoc qa su tebait in euenure
ꝛ ñe dixi tibi qa a filio meo debeo mori. Alex dixit
ergo filius tuus sū ꞇ Nect. ft certe filius ms es.
ꞇ hec dicens expirauit

Alex itaqꝫ pʇna piecate comotus eleuans corꝑ
eius ī humeris suis portauit eu ī palatiū. Cū ergo
vidisset eū olimpiadis dix ti fili Alex quid est hoc
Cui ille ꝶ. corpus nectinabi est. ꞇ illa dix Nec
tanabus pʇ tuus fiut Alex dix Qui admodum
stultitia tua fecit ita est. ꞇ Iussit eu regina sepel
liꞇ

VIII   THE DEATH OF NECTANEBUS

to arrogant pride immediately the conquest was accomplished, and especially describes how Alexander killed first Cleitus and then Callisthenes, whose tortures are enlarged upon, for advising him against accepting divine worship. Lydgate considers that Alexander's bribing of the priests of Ammon to recognize him as a god was the cause of idolatry, a further connexion of Alexander with the euhemeristic theory, and sarcastically remarks, after the account of the murder of Callisthenes, that Alexander was certainly unworthy to be deified.

This biographical passage in the *Fall of Princes* was the most violent attack upon Alexander's whole personality to appear in Northern Europe, as was Petrarch's life of him in Italy. Peripatetic and Stoic features are here combined in a heavy, didactic condemnation, derived from Quintus Curtius, Valerius Maximus and Boccaccio.

But if Lydgate attacked Alexander in his *Fall of Princes*, he also translated the *Secret of Secrets*,[1] with its portrait, by implication, of a philosophic Alexander. But in England, as elsewhere, the undoubted popularity of the *Secret of Secrets* and of the *Dicts and Sayings of the Philosophers* in the fifteenth century had no apparent effect upon the current conception of Alexander. The theological and moral condemnations of him were too firmly established upon the textual evidence, and too obvious to the writer familiar with the most important authorities, to be outweighed by works whose end was professedly moral, and which could not be considered to possess much real importance as reliable histories of Alexander.

We have seen how a little of the courtly spirit lingered in England, and how the Nine Worthies had their own popular reputation in English pageantry. But the most living side of the English late medieval conception of Alexander is represented by the thorough condemnation of him by Gower and Lydgate, who, weary of war and of conquerors, represent the last degradation of the material and the attacks used by the philosophers of antiquity.

---

[1] Lydgate and Burgh's *Secrees of old Philosoffres* has been edited by R. Steele, E.E.T.S., E.S. LXVI, 1894; for the popularity of the *Secret of Secrets* and the *Dicts and Sayings of the Philosophers* in England at this period, see above, pp. 21–3.

(d) THE LATE MEDIEVAL CONCEPTION OF ALEXANDER
IN GERMANY

It has been seen how the attitude of vernacular German literature to Alexander was unfavourable even at the height of the courtly period; and that there developed, from the objective, historical treatment of him in the German world-chronicles, that personal abuse which accompanied the theological interpretation of his Biblical role.[1] Such a tendency was early evident, not only in Lamprecht and in Berthold von Regensburg, but in so many independent references, and even in Alexander-books generally favourable to Alexander, that it is plain that it formed from early times the most native and underivative aspect of the German attitude to Alexander. As the Biblical commentators had interpreted the text of Josephus to fit their attack upon Alexander, so did the German followers of their tradition adapt even the legendary material to the theological condemnation of him; with the result that many legendary themes were used in German writers as an excuse for abuse of Alexander, especially the Celestial Journey and the Journey to Paradise. The unfavourable interpretation of the former[153] in Berthold von Regensburg, the *History-Bible* and Enikel, and of the latter[154] in the *Strassburg Alexander* and Ulrich von Eschenbach, shows how deeply condemnation of Alexander underlay the German approach to this material.

History-Bible I and the group of texts derived from *Seelentrost* are the natural culmination of the German practice of making the life of Alexander an extended commentary upon the Maccabees passage; for here the commentary has swelled so much that it has become an independent book of the Bible, inserted before Maccabees.[2] The accusation of Alexander in the *History-Bible* edited by Merzdorf is concentrated upon the episode of the Celestial Journey, where a voice suddenly bids Alexander return to earth, and warns him that none who has not deserved to do so by good works upon earth shall ascend into heaven. In *Seelentrost* an undisguised condemnation of Alexander runs through the book, and comes to a climax in his eventual consignment to the lowest depths of hell.[3] In both books it is his arrogant, covetous ambition that is singled out for special attack, a

---

[1] See above, pp. 171–2, 176–9.   [2] See below, p. 373.
[3] See below, p. 312. On the importance of this epilogue for deciding the derivation of the

IX ALEXANDER'S CELESTIAL JOURNEY

choice which is typical of the theological attitude to Alexander which saw in him a fit type of Satan.

Independent German references of the late medieval period, where they are not stolidly objective repetitions of the moral anecdotes which were now first widely known in Germany, or mere historical comments, show the same type of attack on Alexander, a fact which emphasizes the aloofness and unrepresentative nature of the writers of late German Alexander-books: Seifrit, Babiloth and Hartlieb.[155]

Middle Dutch Alexander from *Seelentrost*, see A. J. Barnouw, in *Germanic Review*, IV (1929), pp. 54–5 and n. 10.

The *Seelentrost* group comprises the *Fabelhafte Geschichte*, almost identical with *Seelentrost*; two Swedish accounts, *Själens Trost* and *De Alexandro Rege*; and the *Middle Dutch Alexander* and *Middle Low German Alexander* (see pp. 39–41).

Upon the possible connexion between *Seelentrost* and the *Liegnitz Historia*, see above, pp. 26–7.

VI

THE CONCEPTION OF ALEXANDER IN LATE MEDIEVAL AND RENAISSANCE ITALY

1. INTRODUCTION

THIS section cannot claim to be more than a brief survey of a period of transition, when the medieval conceptions of Alexander were being superseded and Renaissance ideas applied to medieval source material or to the Greek historians newly discovered and made known which were replacing them. The effects of the Renaissance upon the Alexander portrait are more far-reaching than may be fully discussed here without occupying too much space in a work devoted to the study of medieval ideas; and the bulk of Renaissance literature is so great that I have been able to make only a very small selection of the most significant and interesting material.

In the discussion of the late medieval period in the rest of Europe it has been shown how the secular conception of Alexander declined, how the exemplar attitude persisted, and how the moral and theological treatment of his character became absorbed and confused in didactic condemnation of him. This movement finds a parallel in the same period in Italy. But there the general decline of the medieval conceptions of Alexander was contemporaneous with the development of a new moral evaluation of him, and the adaptation of the courtly portrait, and of the material upon which it was founded, to Renaissance secular demands. This final section has therefore been divided into two parts; the first is concerned with the disappearance of the medieval approach to Alexander, and the second with the emergence of the Renaissance Alexander portrait.

2. THE DECLINE OF THE MEDIEVAL ALEXANDER CONCEPTIONS IN ITALY DURING THE FOURTEENTH AND FIFTEENTH CENTURIES

(a) THE MEDIEVAL SECULAR CONCEPTION

The discussion of the final stage in the history of the secular conception of Alexander in the rest of Europe began with a description of the disappearance of the courtly tradition. The history of the courtly tradition in Italy during these centuries must be deferred because it is not with its disappearance that we are to be concerned, but with its transformation into the Renaissance portrait of Alexander. The courtly tradition arrived in Italy as a foreign idea, with the introduction of Provençal poetry; it first began to establish itself in native literature in the fourteenth century; and finally passed to the Renaissance language and the Renaissance imagery of quattrocento and cinquecento poets.

But while the courtly tradition of Alexander was thus carried over into the Renaissance, the same movement that was perceptible in the rest of Europe, tending towards the withering of the secular attitude to Alexander, was perceptible also in the late medieval literature of Italy, and it must be remembered that works in the medieval spirit continued to be produced in Italy all through the gradual development of Renaissance literature. The characteristics of this decline that we have noticed in the rest of Europe appear even in the earliest of Italian Alexander-books, in Quilichinus and his imitators, and in the other dreary Italian translations from the I² or I³ *Historia de Preliis*. These texts have been studied in detail by Storost,[1] and are not of sufficient importance or interest to merit a long discussion here. They satisfactorily show only the extreme poverty of the early Italian Alexander tradition, nourished upon no romantic heritage, and sustained by no poetic or imaginative merit. In their unimaginative adhesion to one particular source, in their introduction of numerous

---

[1] For the Alexander-books here referred to, see above, pp. 53–6; and for analysis and discussion, Storost, pp. 14–180. The most important of these works, and one which well demonstrates these characteristics of the medieval Italian Alexander-book, is the *Istoria Alexandri Regis* of Scolari (Storost, pp. 14–117). For survivals of the medieval secular attitude in Italy, in the *Quadriregio* of Federico Frezzi, Giovanni Villani (Gog and Magog), and the *Novelle* of Giovanni Sercambi, see D. Carraroli, *La leggenda di Alessandro Magno* (Mondovì, 1892), pp. 234–83.

anachronisms and other proofs of carelessness or ignorance, in their occasional rationalizations of the wonder element, these translations resemble the worst productions of the late medieval period in the rest of Europe. This treatment of the story of Alexander persisted until well into the Renaissance literary period. From the beginning of the fourteenth century the Renaissance tradition developed parallel to it, but the *Alessandreida*, in the early fifteenth century, was the first Italian Alexander-book to be deeply influenced by Renaissance feeling.

Of the minor elements in the European secular view of Alexander, those which belong to the courtly tradition, the regard for the conqueror's liberality and the introduction of a love interest, in Italy reappeared in the Renaissance approach to Alexander, and will be considered in that connexion. In Italian literature of the pre-Renaissance period the few references to these ideas show unmistakable signs of French influence, and they were never indigenous in Italy.

Of the new elements which contributed to the formation of the late medieval secular approach to Alexander, the Nine Worthies were unknown to Italian writers,[1] while the Oriental material, so popular in France and England, found no acknowledgement except in the translation of the *Dicts and Sayings* formerly attributed to Giovanni da Procida,[2] and the quotations from Honein ibn Ishaq in the *Fior di Virtù*.[3]

Thus the general medieval secular approach to Alexander was represented in Italy in the late Middle Ages only by dry Alexander-books and drier references to his conquests. But the courtly tradition did not disappear, and we shall see how, in the end, it came to inspire the Renaissance secular portrait of Alexander.

[1] Except for the paintings and verses at the castle of La Manta in Piedmont; for details see below, p. 343. It is significant that, of all Italian provinces, Piedmont has always been that most accessible to French influence. The verses in question are in poor Italianized French.

[2] See above, p. 60. The Latin version (*Liber Philosophorum Antiquorum*) is no longer believed to be by Giovanni da Procida. See E. Franceschini, 'Il Liber philosophorum antiquorum', *Atti del Reale Istituto Veneto di scienze, lettere ed arti*, XCI (1931–2), p. 394 and G. Billanovich, 'La tradizione del Liber de dictis philosophorum antiquorum e la cultura di Dante, del Petrarca e del Boccaccio', *Studi Petrarcheschi*, I (1948), pp. 112–13.

[3] For an enumeration of these proverbs see below, p. 349.

(b) THE EXEMPLAR CONCEPTION

The exemplar tradition remained in Italy, as throughout Europe, unalterably based upon the same foundations and the same negative attitude to Alexander, but such a literature was less popular there than in Northern Europe. A new type of devotional literature had grown up in the *Laude*, the *Sacra Rappresentazione* and the books associated with such names as St Francis, St Bernardino da Siena, Girolamo Benivieni, and Savonarola. But besides the book of *exempla* edited by Herzstein, which was composed in Bologna in 1326 and contained the episodes of the pirate and the Wonderstone,[156] and the *Corona de' Monaci* which repeated the anecdote of the pirate[1] (an anecdote which was, in its second form, a favourite in Italy), a certain amount of the traditional exemplar material appeared in the *Fior di Virtù*,[157] one of the most popular of the late medieval Italian books of devotion, where were also retailed some of the proverbial sayings attributed to Alexander in Honein ibn Ishaq.[158]

The chief exemplar theme, that of the futility of man in the face of death, was taken up occasionally by Italian moralists, and notably by Franco Sacchetti who lingers heavily upon it,[2] but it was not a theme to be much appreciated by Renaissance writers, who believed above all in the importance of life, not in the contemplation of death.

(c) THE DISAPPEARANCE OF THE MEDIEVAL MORAL CONCEPTION

Italy had never produced a native theological attitude to Alexander, founded textually upon Orosius and conceptually upon Alexander's place in Daniel and in Maccabees; nor was there an Italian school of allegorical Scriptural commentators, and the nearest any Italian author came to reproducing the theological attacks on Alexander is in the *Pantheon* of Godfrey of Viterbo.[3] Before the Renaissance

---

[1] *Corona de' Monaci*, cap. XLII, es. ii (ed. D. Casimiro Stolfi (Prato, 1862), p. 106): The story of the pirate told at great length as an example of pity and forbearance.

[2] See pp. 311, 316–17.

[3] On the *Pantheon*, and the account of Alexander contained in it, see L. Meyer, *Les Légendes des Matières de Rome, de France, et de Bretagne dans le 'Panthéon' de Godefroi de Viterbe* (Paris, 1933), esp. pp. 55 ff. For individual details of the portrait of Alexander in this work, see above, pp. 93–4 and 188. It is perhaps significant that Godfrey's nationality is in dispute. He may have been a German.

writers of the fourteenth century Italy had not produced humanistic moralists of the type of John of Salisbury and William of Conches; her moralists were the magnificent and the humble moralists of the Church, the Dominicans and the Franciscans, men who relied upon doctrinal explanation or upon the appeal of simple faith, who specialized in preaching and practice, but who were either below or above using the anecdotal material about Alexander to illustrate their teaching.

The first writer to use that material as moralists in the rest of Europe had used it was an encyclopaedist who belonged in spirit to Italian, but in language to French, literary tradition, Brunetto Latini. In his *Livres dou Tresor* he produced a hotch-potch of the usual anecdotal information about Alexander, interspersed with occasional items extracted from the legend.[159] But the moral anecdotes had little appeal in Italy; occasionally during the Renaissance period we find a reference to them,[1] but they seem to have come too late to Italy to be widely popular in a nation which was beginning to study, not the history of moral precepts, but the moral history of individuals.

Dante was thought by his early commentators, earnest students of Orosius, to have immersed Alexander, with Dionysius of Syracuse, up to his neck in boiling blood as a fitting punishment for a bloody tyrant; but it is now generally conceded that he intended by his reference to 'Allessandro fero' not Alexander the Great, but Alexander of Pherae, a more suitable partner for Dionysius.[160] In a later passage of the *Inferno*, when Dante and Virgil cross the arena of burning sand under a fiery hail, reference is made to the similar experience of Alexander's army in India, an evident quotation from the legend, but one which does not correspond to the version of the story in the *Epistola ad Aristotelem*.[161] Benvenuto da Imola, however, proved that it derived from a similar misquotation of the original text which occurs in Albertus Magnus. Thus there is no proof that Dante knew the legend, though the lover of the 'Arthuri regis ambages pulcherrimae'[2] may well have done so.

---

[1] E.g. citations of the Diogenes episode in *Le Novelle Antiche*, XLIX, LXXXII (ed. G. Biagi, *Raccolta di opere inedite o rare*, Florence, 1880, pp. 58, 85); of various anecdotes from Valerius Maximus in Petrarch, *Rerum Memorandarum Libri*, on which see *Italian Studies*, V (1950), p. 54; and citations of the story of Alexander at the tomb of Achilles given above, p. 108.

[2] *De vulgari eloquentia* I, 10.

Dante's reference to Alexander in the *Monarchia*, where he explains how God prevented him from achieving world empire,[1] and his tribute to Alexander's medieval reputation for liberality in the *Convivio*, have already been discussed.[2] The references to Alexander in Dante thus conform closely to the medieval approach. In the intrusion of the divine element, the reference to Alexander's liberality, the citation of the legend as truth—here as in all his writing, Dante sums up medieval opinion.

The didactic element in poetry tended gradually to disappear during the Renaissance but it survived in some poets. Typical of these is the late fourteenth-century writer Franco Sacchetti, the hard-worked Florentine civic official whose novelle, with their mixture of medieval edification and Renaissance ribaldry and obscenity, mark him as a writer of the transition, and his book as a Renaissance form interpreted by a medieval mind. In his lyric poetry the exemplar attitude to Alexander is uppermost, man's futility in the face of death;[3] and the same theme appears in the *Dittamondo* of Fazio degli Uberti, a long didactic poem of the same period.[4] But Sacchetti, in the closing years of the fourteenth century, was the last pillar of medieval morality; his bitter complaints upon the decline of manners in Italy, his feeling that he stood at the end of a period, were justified by the reality.

Another figure in transition, though at an earlier date, was Boccaccio, who combined the Renaissance flavour of the *Decameron* and other works with the medieval must of anthological compilations. One of these latter works, the *De Casibus Virorum Illustrium*,[5] is of special importance because it contains the long historical account of the murder of Callisthenes which passed through Laurent de Premierfait into Lydgate, where, as we have seen, it received the proper degree of horrified emphasis.

But these are isolated writers, or isolated works of writers, in a changing literary atmosphere. Deep in remembrance and tradition

[1] *Mon.* II, 9: see pp. 105, 285–6.   [2] *Convivio* IV, 11: see above, p. 217.

[3] See Franco Sacchetti, *Libro delle Rime* CLXIX, vv. 28–30; CLXXV, vv. 52–6; CCXX, vv. 19 ff. (ed. G. Chiari, *Scrittori d'Italia* (Bari, 1936), pp. 172, 187, 261).

[4] On the passage referring to Alexander in the *Dittamondo* of Fazio degli Uberti, see D. Carraroli, *La leggenda di Alessandro Magno* (Mondovì, 1892), pp. 259–60. For the version of the *Iter ad Paradisum* in this work, see W. Hertz, *Aristoteles in den Alexanderdichtungen des Mitt.* (*Abh. d. k. bayer. Akademie der Wiss.* I Cl., Bd. XIX., Abth. 1, Munich, 1890), pp. 86–7.

[5] G. Boccaccio, *De Casibus Virorum Illustrium* IV (Paris, Jean Gourmont and Jean Petit, 1525, f. xxxvii^v–xxxviii^v). See above, p. 253.

the medieval beliefs about Alexander dimly survived; but we shall see how the Renaissance literary tradition develops ever more clearly a new conception of him to supplant the old.

3. THE EMERGENCE OF THE RENAISSANCE CONCEPTIONS OF ALEXANDER

(a) THE MORAL CONCEPTION—PETRARCH AND CASTIGLIONE

The conception of Alexander in Petrarch has been more fully discussed in a separate study.[1] It is sufficient to note here that Petrarch hated Alexander more than did any other medieval author. He adopted the Peripatetic portrait of Alexander out of Curtius for his biography of him in the *De Viris Illustribus*, suppressed the good in it, and besmirched Alexander by every possible innuendo. This was due in part to the fact that he deduced from Curtius' uneven narrative that Alexander had just such an unbalanced nature as he most despised, for he considered that no man was truly great who did not have a developed and unified personality, and in part to his feeling that the suggestion that Alexander might have conquered Rome, and that he was greater than the greatest Romans, was an insult offered to that city which he loved with a fanatic love. And so he portrayed Alexander as an unbalanced youth protected by Fortune, vain, wild, almost insane; and the resultant picture of him in the *De Viris Illustribus* was unique for the age in its single-minded, deliberate abuse.

In Petrarch's biography we have medieval material worked upon by a Renaissance mind, a step of great importance in the history of moral criticism of Alexander, since with the Renaissance the importance of personality became fully recognized, and references to an individual are no longer regarded only as a means of establishing a general precept.

Petrarch, working upon the frequently used medieval historical source Curtius, inevitably founded his conception of Alexander upon the Peripatetic attack on him. In the succeeding century Curtius was translated into Italian,[2] and his life of Alexander became increasingly

---

[1] See G. Cary, 'Petrarch and Alexander the Great', *Italian Studies*, v (1950), pp. 43 ff.

[2] By Pier Candido Decembrio. For Curtius in the Renaissance, see S. Dosson, *Etude sur Quinte-Curce* (Paris, 1887), pp. 360–80; Storost, p. 317 and nn. 1 and 2, pp. 318–19.

popular throughout the Renaissance. But knowledge of other versions of the life of Alexander had begun with the new humanistic learning, and Vergerio's letter to Sigismund[1] at length established Arrian in his proper place as the most reliable of the Alexander historians. Arrian was translated by Vergerio and by later humanists; and Plutarch also was rediscovered, translated, and his biography of Alexander made readily accessible.[2]

Such an influx of new material was naturally to have its eventual effect upon the moral treatment of Alexander. Most of the history of that change of view lies outside our present field, but we may notice, as a contrast to the violence of Petrarch, the quiet, measured references to Alexander in the *Cortegiano*.[3] Here the principal source is Plutarch; Alexander is a balanced man, a continent and wise ruler. But such a view was not to have wide influence for many centuries. The influence of Curtius maintained its hold over learned historians almost until the present day. It is an attractive moral, and a convenient summary of the man, that he should be seen as perpetually yielding to himself.

But though such familiar medieval ideas persisted, they persisted because they were ancient ideas which the Middle Ages had excerpted and mutilated, but which in later times were used for the assessing, not of isolated aspects of Alexander, but of the development of his personality. Thus the anecdotes used by the medieval moralist lose all their importance; Rabelais points a mocking finger at both Alexander and Diogenes,[4] Machiavelli looks at Alexander's liberality from the point of view of a new political science.[5] Like the legend, the medieval moral material descended in the scale of literary values. As the former was degraded to the chapbooks, so did the latter pass into curious popular tracts.[6] If we are to count such survivals as signs of life the

---

[1] See below, pp. 375-7.

[2] Plutarch's *Lives* were first translated in part into Latin by Guarino da Verona c. 1430, and epitomized by Darius Tibertius in 1501; the *editio princeps* of the Greek text was published by Giunta in 1517.

[3] For the references to Alexander in the *Cortegiano*, see the Index of Names in the edition by Vittorio Cian (Florence, 1929).

[4] Rabelais, *Pantagruel* xxx: Alexander mends old breeches in hell, while Diogenes beats him for not mending his breeches properly.

[5] *Il Principe* xvi: della liberalità: 'E di quello che non è tuo o de' sudditi tuoi, si può essere più largo donatore, come fu Ciro, Cesare e Alessandro, perchè lo spendere quel d'altri non ti toglie riputazione, ma te ne aggiunge; solamente lo spendere il tuo è quello che ti nuoce.'

[6] For example in England the *Collatio* appeared as *The Upright Lives of the Heathen briefly noted: or, Epistles and Discourses between Alexander the Great and Dindimus* (pub. Andrew

medieval moral conception of Alexander was a long time dying; but as a living, distinct tradition it was dead before the fifteenth century.

If this survey of the transition to the Renaissance moral approach to Alexander has been brief, it is because from the beginning of the Renaissance conservative prejudice had less and less effect on the moral attitude to Alexander, and thus it becomes increasingly impossible to study the history of moral opinion about Alexander without frequent reference to individual portraits of him, which would be inappropriate in a study which has rested upon the examination of conventional opinions.

But we may close with one individual estimate—that of one of the great Renaissance moralists, Montaigne. We see in his study the freedom of the man who looks, not to his predecessors in biography, but to the subject of their essays:[1]

> The second of my Three Personages is *Alexander the Great*: For who ever will consider the Age at which he began his Enterprises; the small Means by which he effected so glorious a Design; the Authority he obtained, at so slender an Age, with the greatest and most experienced Captains of the World, by whom he was followed; and the extraordinary Favour wherewith Fortune embraced him, and favoured so many hazardous, I had almost said rash Designs of his!
>
> > ...impellens quicquid sibi summa petenti
> > Obstaret, gaudensque uiam fecisse ruina.
>
> That Grandeur, to have, at the Age of thirty-three Years, passed victorious through the whole habitable Earth, and in half a Life to have attained to the utmost Effort of human Nature; so that you cannot imagine its Duration just, nor the Continuance of his Increase in Virtue and Fortune, even to a due Maturity of Age, but that you must withal imagine something more than Man:...so many excellent Virtues as he was possessed of, Justice, Temperance, Liberality, Truth in his Word, Love towards his own People, and Humanity towards those he overcame; for his Manners, in the general, seem, in truth, incapable of any just Reproach, tho' some particular and extraordinary Action of his may, peradventure, fall under Censure: But it is impossible to carry on so great

Soule, London, 1683). The interview between Alexander and Diogenes appeared as: *A Satirycall Dialogue or a Sharplye-Invective Conference Betweene Allexander the Great and that Truely Woman-Hater Dyogenes* (Dort?, 1615; reprinted, London, 1897, with an introduction by J. S. Farmer).

[1] The extract given is derived from Peter Coste's revision of Cotton's translation of Montaigne (seventh edition, 1759), vol. II, pp. 566-8 (Book II, xxxvi: 'Of Three Most Excellent Men'). The three men are Homer, Alexander and Epaminondas.

Things, as he did, with the strict Rules of Justice; such as he are willing to be judged in gross, by the governing Motive of their Actions...As to his being a little given to Boasting, and a little too impatient of hearing himself ill spoken of; and as to those Mangers, Arms, and Bits he caused to be strewed in the Indies; all those little Vanities, methinks, may very well be allowed to his Youth, and the prodigious Prosperity of his Fortune: And who will consider, withal, his many Military Virtues, his Diligence, Foresight, Patience, Discipline, Subtlety, Magnanimity, Resolution, and good Fortune,...the Excellency of his Knowledge and Capacity, the Duration and Grandeur of his Glory, pure, clear, without Spot or Envy...: Whoever, I say, will seriously consider all these Particulars, will confess, that I had reason to prefer him before Caesar himself, who alone could make me doubtful in my choice:...

In the Middle Ages such admiration of Alexander might be looked for only among the secular writers who, in their own conventional, anachronistic fashion looked at the character of the man rather than at earlier judgements. This attitude of admiration is now gradually transferred to moralists through two concurrent and slow processes: the establishment of the historical truth about Alexander, and the dissipation of all ancient prejudice in the study of that truth.

(b) THE SECULAR CONCEPTION

We have now to trace the aesthetic development of the Renaissance secular portrait of Alexander from the intrusive courtly elements which appeared in Italy in the thirteenth century. In the cultured and imitative literature of that time, we find a clear echo of the French courtly attitude to Alexander. The Franco-Italian *Entree d'Espagne*, the Italian manuscripts of French works, the knowledge of the Romance shown by Brunetto Latini, the Latin translation of the *Fuerre de Gadres* formerly ascribed to Boccaccio, the references to Alexander's liberality in thirteenth-century lyric—all this is evidence that the courtly tradition of Alexander, borrowed and still foreign, was at an early date known to a limited circle of learned Italians.[1]

[1] For reference to Alexander's liberality in *L'Entree d'Espagne*, see below, p. 329. The references to Alexander's valour in the poem, however, far outweigh this: see vv. 3437, 7664, 8113, 8482, 11,805, 12,259, 13,294, 13,850 and 13,938 in the edition by A. Thomas, S.A.T.F., 2 vols. (1913). For knowledge of the Romance in Brunetto Latini, see below, pp. 349–50. For the Latin translation of the *Fuerre de Gadres* see D. Carraroli, *La leggenda di Alessandro Magno* (Mondovì, 1892), p. 278, and M.F.R.d'A. IV, pp. 15–21; text edited by Meyer in *Romania*, XI (1882), pp. 325–32. For the references to Alexander's liberality in thirteenth-century lyric, see below, p. 328.

But these instances are as yet the conscious repetition of foreign ideas, a hot-house culture that influences but does not represent native Italian literary development. It was after the Sicilian and the Tuscan *trovatori* that there arose the first native Italian school of poetry; the poets of the *dolce stil nuovo*. One of the best of them is Dino Compagni, the lively chronicler and the friend of Dante to whom the poem *L'Intelligenza* has been sometimes, though wrongly, ascribed. This poem is full of the philosophic allegory dear to the Middle Ages and the Renaissance alike; it stands between the two ages. But it has a Renaissance sensuality in description which is well shown in the account of the life of Alexander that it contains.[1] His adventures are painted in fresco on the walls of the palace of Intelligence, and just those incidents are portrayed that would strike a Renaissance painter or poet: the adultery of Nectanebus, the descent into the sea, the ascent into the air, the strange beasts encountered—all the most colourful medieval material is here set in a Renaissance frieze.

The poetic treatment of the story of Alexander as an imaginary fresco or carving or embroidery in a palace appears often in the Renaissance; in Boccaccio's *Filocolo*,[2] in the *Padiglione di Mambrino*,[3] and most significantly in the *Orlando Innamorato*[4] of Boiardo. The idea of a coherent, historical conception of Alexander is eliminated in this method of approach; Alexander becomes the fixed centre-piece of each pictorial incident. He is enshrined as in the Doria tapestries, as immutable in each episode of the series as in the pageant of the Nine Worthies.

But whereas the figure of the Nine Worthies is a symbol of valour, a type, the figure of the Renaissance is, in the repeated portrayal of his colourful adventures, intensely individual, the hero of unique experiences. In these poems Alexander retains his character, though necessarily restricted to those aspects of it which can be applied to pictorial uses by a poet. His character as it appears in *L'Intelligenza* and in Boiardo is the courtly portrait reset. The concentration upon

[1] See *L'Intelligenza*, ed. V. Mistruzzi, *Collezione di opere inedite o rare* (Bologna, 1928), stanzas 216–39, pp. 130–51.

[2] G. Boccaccio, *Filocolo*, ed. S. Battaglia, *Scrittori d'Italia* (Bari, 1938), p. 103.

[3] See the edition of the *Padiglione di Mambrino* by O. Targlioni Tozzetti (Livorno, 1874).

[4] Boiardo, *Orlando Innamorato* II, i, 21 ff. Colbert Searles, 'Some notes on Boiardo's version of the Alexandersagas', *Modern Language Notes*, xv (1900), pp. 45–8, is not to be recommended though it is probable, as he suggests from a comparison of certain episodes, that Boiardo's account of Alexander was derived from the *Roman d'Alexandre*.

the wonderful element, here due, not to the usual medieval appetite for marvels, but to aesthetic considerations, and the introduction of the love interest in Boiardo's account,[1] are representative and typical of the whole Renaissance revaluation of medieval poetry. The courtly interest in Alexander's liberality may also be rediscovered in independent Renaissance testimony.[162] If the unknown author of *l'Intelligenza* and Boiardo used, as they almost certainly did, the French Alexander poems,[2] it was a conscious and deliberate choice; for they recognized in the Alexander cycle, as they and other Italian poets recognized in the Carolingian cycle, the medieval material most suitable for their aesthetic purpose.

But for a coherent picture of the development of this new secular Alexander portrait we must turn to the Renaissance Alexander-books. The earliest of these deeply to reflect Renaissance feeling, the *Alessandreida in Rima*,[3] is a typical poem of the *cantare* type, of the period when the French romances first became fully and universally accepted in Italy. It is a poem for the people, full of recapitulations and exhortations addressed to the listening crowd in the square or at the street corner.

The book is in many ways medieval in its repetitions and pedantic accuracies, with frequent reference to the veracity and the authority of the written source (a medieval convention that was accepted also by the Renaissance with the constant references to 'Turpino, che non erra' in Boiardo and Ariosto at the most improbable and absurd points in the story). But, as Storost has noted, the poem is not a close translation of its Latin source. Its author adapts and alters, seeking a more fluent means of expression, and brings it nearer to the form of an historical romance by placing more stress upon the battle scenes than had been allotted to them in the source. This is an intermediate work, a native production which shows the earliest growth of a feeling for historical romance, and a literary disregard for the exact wording of the source accompanied by great pretended respect for it.

---

[1] Boiardo, *Orlando Innamorato* II, i, 29: the story of Alexander and Elidonia.

[2] On the sources of the Alexander episodes in these poems, see D. Carraroli, *La leggenda di Alessandro Magno* (Mondovì, 1892), pp. 247–63.

[3] On the *Alessandreida in Rima*, see Storost, pp. 180–230 (extracts from the text, pp. 214 ff.). The *Alessandreida* continued to be used for popular recitation in Italy until the eighteenth century.

From this poem we pass to the *Triompho Magno* of Falugio[1] and the Alexander-book preserved in the Rome manuscript.[2] If we examine these poems against the background of the contemporary evolution of the romantic epic, we shall see that Falugio, with his love of the satirical burlesque combined with pervasive sentiment, is a writer typical of the Pulci period, of the Florentine bourgeois who took delight in mocking at feudal traditions and everything that had been considered noble. It is typical of Leo X, brought up in the Medici tradition of the *Carmi Carnescialeschi*, that he should have liked such a poem and honoured such a poet.

The author of the poem in the Rome manuscript, on the other hand, has taken that same Renaissance colour that is undeniably present in Falugio, but instead of coarsening it with the crudities of bourgeois Florentine taste, he has enriched it and imbued it with the aristocratic atmosphere of Ferrarese poetry. If there was ever a poem whose spirit was that of Boiardo and Ariosto it is this work. The two poems together illustrate the developments in Renaissance romantic epic poetry that ran from Pulci through Boiardo to Ariosto; when the pictorial element in poetry was raised from vulgarity, and enlarged by its adaptation to classical forms and a classical feeling for words. The vulgar element still appears in the obscenity of Boiardo and Ariosto, but it is not the guttersnipe obscenity of Pulci; rather it is the formal and uninhibited frankness of Renaissance expression.

[1] For discussion and excerpts of the *Triompho Magno* of Falugio, see Storost, pp. 231–82; the poem exists only in one edition printed at Rome, 1521. See above, p. 67.

[2] For discussion and excerpts of this fine poem, unfortunately in a very fragmentary state, see Storost, pp. 283–304. See also above, p. 67.

VII

SUMMARY CONCLUSION

FROM the twelfth century, when the secular conception of Alexander first began clearly to emerge, until the fourteenth the cleavage between the learned and unlearned conceptions of Alexander is most apparent and easily definable. Before the twelfth century, writers on Alexander followed uniformly the historical portrait of him as the conqueror. But the intense literary and intellectual activity of the twelfth century produced two clearly defined learned conceptions of Alexander, the moral and the theological. The first was founded upon the anecdotal material derived from Cicero, Seneca and Valerius Maximus, and reflected the Peripatetic approach to Alexander. The second was based upon the application of the attack directed by Orosius against Alexander's pride to his Biblical role, and culminated in his appearance as a type of the Devil. This development of two independent learned conceptions of Alexander was accompanied by the growth of a secular tradition, which, while it was generally faithful to the legendary sources, was not based on any definite textual foundations but upon universal, though variable, canons of secular morality.

Between the two lay that literature whose intentions were edifying and whose method was exemplar; a literature which verged on one side upon the moral and theological conceptions of Alexander and on the other upon the secular view of him, and whose ideas lay deeply embedded in all medieval literature. Its material, entirely anecdotal in form, was derived from both the philosophical and the legendary traditions, from Eastern and from Western sources. It arrived at a favourable conception of Alexander through the adaptation of the philosophic approach to him to edifying purposes.

The changing economic and social conditions of the last medieval centuries had an inevitable effect upon these various conceptions of Alexander. The new public demanded simple works of instruction and edification, banal revisions and prose versions of the old romances and chapbook histories. In such an atmosphere exemplar literature flourished, while the courtly tradition, the romance and the elaborate allusive lyric, sank into a repetitiveness from which all real life had departed.

The legendary textual tradition is still maintained in unoriginal story-books, but no considered, living judgement of Alexander underlies the picture they give of him. The classical anecdotes are half forgotten, half misused; historical, legendary, Oriental and anecdotal material alike fall into the hands of didactic writers who use all the available Alexander material indiscriminately to set off the truisms of their manuals of popular morality.

But while the medieval conceptions of Alexander crumbled thus into dry confusion the awakening in Italy of an interest in personality, and of a new aesthetic appreciation of literature, assisted the evolution of the Renaissance portrait of Alexander. Petrarch considered the account of Alexander in Quintus Curtius in the light of his Renaissance belief in the necessity for a developed, unified personality, and condemned Alexander by that new standard. Then in the fifteenth and sixteenth centuries the Greek historians of Alexander were rediscovered and translated, and supplied the material for a new moral evaluation of Alexander which, despite long drawn out controversy, has become that generally accepted today.

The special interest of the history of the medieval conceptions of Alexander lies in the sharp cleavage of opinion, in the various contrasting attitudes which the texts imposed on writers, or which writers imposed upon the textual material. I have tried in the preceding pages to present some of the manifold interest of this conflict of prejudice, of sources and of consequent opinion upon the character of Alexander the Great during the Middle Ages.

NOTES

1 In the classification of the great number of citations of the Diogenes story and its attendant comments, some kind of short entry is necessary; and I have therefore indicated in each case whether the story itself is quoted, or only the comments, and what comments are included, by marking each use of the story or the various comments upon it by an ' × ' in the appropriate column below. The following abbreviations have been used:

Story: the literary form of the story (for the exemplar form see p. 278, n. 2).
VMax: the comment of Valerius Maximus.
S1: the first comment of Seneca: multo potentior....
S2: the second comment of Seneca: Alexander Macedonum rex....

Cases where the story was used without direct citation of the Latin texts are separately considered in the latter part of the note.

	Story	*VMax*	*S1*	*S2*
(*a*) St Jerome, *Aduersus Iouinianum* II, in Migne, *P.L.* vol. XXIII, col. 304.	.	.	×	.
(*b*) Peter Abaelard, *Sermo* XXXIII (*De Ioanne Baptista*) in Migne, *P.L.* vol. CLXXVIII, cols. 591–2.	×	.	.	×
(*c*) Idem, *Theologia Christiana* II, in Migne, *P.L.* vol. CLXXVIII, cols. 1189–90.	×	×	×	.
(*d*) John of Salisbury, *Policraticus* V, 17 (ed. C. C. J. Webb (Oxford, 1909), vol. I, p. 359).	.	.	×	.
(*e*) *Dialogus Creaturarum*, dial. 102: de bubalo caligario (ed. J. G. Th. Grässe, *B.L.V.* vol. CXLVIII (Tübingen, 1880), p. 252).	×	×	×	.
(*f*) *Speculum Sapientiae* III, 12 (ed. J. G. Th. Grässe, *B.L.V.* vol. CXLVIII (Tübingen, 1880), pp. 88–9).	.	.	×	.
(*g*) Brunetto Latini, *Li livres dou tresor* II, ii, 100 (ed. P. Chabaille (Paris, 1863), p. 447).	.	.	×	.
(*h*) *Le Novelle Antiche*, c. XLIX (ed. G. Biagi (Florence, 1880), p. 58).	×	.	.	.

275

	Story	VMax	S1	S2
(i) Le Novelle Antiche, c. LXXXII (p. 85).	.	.	×	.
(j) Jacobus de Cessolis, De ludo Scacchorum (ed. F. Vetter, Das Schachzabelbuch Kunrats von Ammenhausen (Frauenfeld, 1892), cols. 171–2).	.	.	×	.
(k) Walter Burley, De uita ac moribus philosophorum L (ed. H. Knust, B.L.V. vol. CLXXVII, Tübingen, 1886, p. 196).	×	×	× (twice)	.
(l) Eulogium Historiarum CXXI (ed. F. S. Haydon, Rolls Series, vol. I (1858), p. 426).	×	×	×	.
(m) Ranulph Higden, Polychronicon III, 20 (ed. J. R. Lumby, Rolls Series, vol. III (1871), pp. 308–10).	×	×	×	.
(n) Gesta Romanorum, c. 183 (ed. H. Oesterly (Berlin, 1872), p. 589).	×	.	.	.
(o) John Bromyard, Spec. Praed., Paupertas (P. III), art. ii, 3 (ed. Nürnberg, 1518, f. cclxxiii^v, col. 2).	×	×	×	.
(p) John Capgrave, Chronicle of England (ed. F. C. Hingeston, Rolls Series (1858), p. 51).	×	.	.	.
(q) Die sogenannte Wolfenbüttler Priamelhandschrift, piece 312 (ed. K. Euling, Deutsche Texte d. Mitt. XIV (Berlin, 1908), pp. 44–5).	×	.	.	.

For other examples of the direct citation of the anecdote and its appended comments, see Oesterly's notes to the Gesta Romanorum, p. 742 (c. 183), and Knust's notes on Walter Burley (c. L, in B.L.V. vol. CLXXVII (Tübingen, 1886), p. 196).

The sun episode was inserted into the I² Historia de Preliis from Valerius Maximus; the latter's comment is omitted, and the hero of the story is not Diogenes, but Anaximenes (ed. A. Hilka, Altfranzösischer Prosa-Alexanderroman (Halle, 1920), pp. 87–8). Thence the episode passed into many derivatives of the I² recension; it was also quoted in this form in independent reference: John Capgrave, Guide of Rome (ed. F. C. Hingeston, Rolls Series, 1858, p. 363): The name of Anaximenes is here rendered as Maximenes, and the connexion with this story is tenuous as we are only told that Anaximenes was sitting in the sun, and, though the source is no doubt the I² *Historia de Preliis*, the point of the story is lost.

Finally we may notice some poetic references to the Diogenes story which deserve separate remark: K. Strecker, *Moralisch-satirische Gedichte Walters von Châtillon*, Heidelberg, 1929, no. XI, pp. 113–15 (Diogenes):

> Quem cum rex muneribus uellet onerare,
> 'Non est nostrum opibus', inquit, 'inhiare,
> sed ne michi subtrahas, quod non potes dare:
> sine solis radios ad me penetrare!'
> Quid, inquam, Diogenes, quid est quod fecisti?
> Rex parabat munera, solem tu petisti!
> O si quisquam diceret hoc sub lege Christi,
> quę Pauli sententia conferretur isti!

Eustache Deschamps, *Balade* CCXIV (*Œuvres*, ed. G. Raynaud and le Queux de St Hilaire, S.A.T.F., vol. II (Paris, 1880), p. 37) (plain speaking no longer in favour):

> Nulz ne veult plus estre Dyogenès
> Qui surmonta l'avarice Alixandre;...

These two examples are doubly interesting because they are to be found in two writers especially favourable to Alexander (see pp. 173–4, 251); they thus demonstrate the pertinacity of the moral condemnation implicit in the Diogenes story, a pertinacity which was not paralleled in the case of any other popular anecdote.

John Lydgate, *Fall of Princes* I, vv. 6224–79 (ed. H. Bergen, vol. I, Washington (Carnegie Institute), 1923, pp. 176–7). An expanded poetic version of the story of the sun, with Lydgate's own, peculiar moral, that Alexander's reason was fettered by sensuality: a moral similar to that of the exemplar Diogenes, vv. 6278–9 (p. 177):

> Alisaundre with couetise was blent;
> The philisophre with litil was content.

The story of Alexander and Diogenes is recalled by Lydgate again in his poem, *Consulo quisquis eris*, vv. 71–88 (*Minor Poems*, II (Secular Poems), ed. H. N. MacCracken, E.E.T.S., O.S., CXCII, 1934, p. 753).

He points the moral 'pride comes before a fall'; Alexander fell while Diogenes prospered:

> He thouht vertu was moor imperrial
> Than his acqueyntaunce, with al his proud language.

It will be noticed from all the examples given of the use of this anecdote that it became most popular in the later Middle Ages; and that in the earlier centuries the story of Diogenes and the sunshine was not so often quoted as was Seneca's comment upon it. These facts are in accordance with two tendencies in the medieval conception of Alexander. The first of these is the increase of moral criticism in the later Middle Ages; the second is the late medieval tendency to give the full text of a story rather than a reference to it; a sign that literature was then intended for a wider and less learned public.

For further comments upon the use of the literary form of the Diogenes story, see above, pp. 255–7.

2   The main cases where this version is used are:

Disciplina Clericalis, exemplum xxviii ('De Socrate et rege') (ed. A. Hilka and W. Soederhjelm, Sammlung mittellat. Texte, I, Heidelberg, 1911, pp. 43–5): Diogenes says to Alexander: 'Voluntas quidem subiecta est et seruit michi, non ego sibi. Tu e conuerso subiectus es uoluntati et sibi seruis, non ipsa tibi. Itaque seruus es eius qui michi seruit.' Alexander, impressed, says to his men: 'Seruus dei est! Videte ne quid molestum ei faciatis aut inhonestum'.

Dialogus Creaturarum, dial. xiv (de smaragdo et annulo) (ed. Grässe, p. 152).

Gesta Romanorum, c. 61 (ed. Oesterly, pp. 368–70). From this is derived the version in the Middle Dutch and Middle Low German Alexander (ed. A. J. Barnouw, Germanic Review, IV (1929), pp. 302–3.

John Gower, Confessio Amantis III, vv. 1221–1311 (English Works, ed. G. C. Macaulay, E.E.T.S., E.S. LXXXI–LXXXII, vol. I (1900), pp. 259 ff.).

For further discussion of the exemplar version of the Diogenes episode, see above, pp. 146 ff.

3   Justin XI, x, 8 ff.; the story of Abdalonimus: 'Cum operam oblocare ad puteos exhauriendos hortosque inrigandos solitus esset, misere uitam exhibentem regem fecerat spretis nobilibus, ne generis id, non dantis beneficium putarent.'

4   Justin IX, viii, 20; the famous comparison between Alexander and Philip of which this forms a part was transcribed by John of Salisbury, Vincent de Beauvais, Ranulph Higden, and others, and was recalled in such phrases as 'uirtute atque uitiis (Alexander) patre maior', which was Justin's summary of his comparison. For an interesting variant on this last phrase, see the study of Rupert of Deutz, above, p. 138.

The phrase here in question was open to misconstruction by medieval writers. The word luxuria, as used by Justin, meant extravagance in all its forms, as contrasted with the frugalitas, or economy, of Philip; for the classical meaning of luxuria included any physical or sumptuary excess. But in the Middle Ages the word came to be used exclusively of sexual excess. This is the meaning given in Du Cange, lussuria in Dante refers to sexual sin, and in the Speculum morale (III, ii, 9) the various forms of luxuria are defined as the various forms of sexual sin.

The inevitable confusion that must have arisen in the reading of this passage in Justin, or in the authors mentioned above, is strikingly confirmed by the two English translations of Higden's Polychronicon, that made by Trevisa and that preserved in British Museum MS. Harley 2261. These two translators render the phrase as follows (in Higden's Polychronicon, ed. J. R. Lumby, Rolls Series, vol. III (1871), pp. 392–3) (spelling modernized):

Trevisa: 'The father gave him to skilful largeness and freeness of gifts, and the son gave him to lechery.'

MS. Harl. 2261: 'The father was given to unliberality, the son to lechery.' Thus in Trevisa *frugalitas* is strangely rendered as 'largeness', and gives to Philip the quality for which Alexander was renowned; and the unequivocal lechery can hardly stand in contrast to that 'largeness'. For the comparison, as it stands in Latin, is an exact balancing of the virtues and vices of father and son, each corresponding with each; and Trevisa has sadly destroyed that balance. On Alexander's attitude to women in the eyes of medieval writers, see above, pp. 99–100.

For other references in Justin to Alexander's liberality, cf. Justin XII, i, 1; XII, xi, 1.

5 *Pseudo-Call.* I, 16 (ed. Müller, p. 16); text only in Julius Valerius, Armenian and Syriac versions. Müller thought the correspondence interpolated because it was not in the Greek text (Meyer, *A. le G.* II, pp. 6–7); Zacher (*Pseudocall.* p. 92) assumed from its presence in the three versions above that it was part of the original text. Ausfeld (*Alexanderroman*, pp. 130–1) rejected it because it was not consistent with the original text: R. Merkelbach, 'Die Quellen des Griechischen Alexanderromans', *Zetemata*, IX (Munich, 1954) shows (p. 49) that these letters formed a rhetorical exercise which was accepted by the author of the Romance but did not form part of the *Epistolary Alexander Romance* which was one of his two principal sources.

6 Curtius VIII, xii, 17 (Alexander's gifts to Omphis, an Indian king): 'Quae liberalitas, sicut barbarum obstrinxerat, ita amicos ipsius uehementer offendit.'

VI, vi, 11 (Alexander's attempts at conciliation): 'Ille, non ignarus et principes amicorum et exercitum grauiter offendi, gratiam liberalitate donisque reparare temptabat. Sed, opinor, liberis pretium seruitutis ingratum est.'

7 Curtius X, v, 28: 'Liberalitas saepe, maiora tribuens quam a dis petuntur....'

For a Christian form of this comment in the *Dialogus Creaturarum*, see above, p. 154, where it is cited and discussed.

8 William of Conches, *Liber Moralium Dogmatis Philosophorum* c. XIII, in Migne, *P.L.* vol. CLXXI, col. 1016: 'Melius Alexander, qui cum daret ciuitatem cuidam dicenti ciuitatem non conuenire humili fortunae suae, respondit: Non quaero quod te oporteat accipere, sed quod me dare.' Similarly in:

Giraldus Cambrensis, *De Principis Instructione* I, viii (*Opera*, Rolls Series, vol. VIII, ed. G. F. Warner, 1891, p. 27).

Brunetto Latini, *Li Livres dou Tresor* II, ii, 79 (ed. Chabaille, p. 412): 'mais Alixandres le fist mieulx....'

9 Fra Salimbene, *Chronica*, s.a. 1248 (*M.G.H. Scriptt.* XXXII, ed. O. Holder-Egger, Hanover and Leipzig, 1905–13, pp. 283–4): 'Erat enim rex, et ideo eum decebat regale munus mittere. Hinc rex Alexander....'

Commendatio Lamentabilis in transitu magni regis Edwardi. (*Chronicles of the Reigns of Edward I and Edward II*, ed W. Stubbs, Rolls Series, vol. II (1883), p. 6):

'Nullus magnificentior in donis, non deliberans cum Antigono quid fortunae postulantis accipere conueniret, sed melius cum Alexandro quantum deceret regalem munificentiam exhibere.'

For exemplar and secular uses of this anecdote, and its further adaptation in the favour of Alexander, see pp. 154–5, 348, 349, 360–1.

10 Cf. E. Liénard, in *Revue Belge de Philologie et d'Histoire*, xv, ii (1936), p. 821. For a general consideration of the connexion of the Brahmans with Alexander, see F. Pfister, 'Die Brahmanen in der Alexandersage', *Berliner Philol. Wochenschrift* (1921), cols. 569 ff. For a description of the basic texts, see pp. 12–14; for the effect of the Brahman texts upon other conceptions of Alexander, see pp. 92–5, 167 ff.

11 For editions and studies of *Collatio I, II, III*, see above, pp. 13–14.

The latest article upon the *Collatio* is that of E. Liénard, 'Collatio Alexandri et Dindimi', *Revue Belge de Philologie et d'Histoire*, xv, ii (1936), pp. 819–38.

M. Liénard reaches the conclusion that it is intended as an attack, not upon Alexander, but upon Dindimus. He supports also the view that it was directed especially against Christian critics of Alexander, by showing that certain passages of Dindimus' letters are directly derived from the *Apologeticus* of Tertullian. While these facts are convincing enough, Pfister's observation of certain un-Christian elements in Dindimus' material must be taken into account; though it is possible either that the author was not acquainted with every detail of Christian doctrine, or that he wished to accuse the Christians of departing from it themselves.

12 For the epigram which Alcuin sent to Charlemagne, in which he intimates that he is sending the correspondence between Paul and Seneca, and that between Alexander and Dindimus, see:

M. Manitius, *Geschichte d. latein. Lit. im Mittel.* I (1911), p. 280.

Cambridge Medieval History, III (1930), p. 516.

G. L. Hamilton, in *Mélanges… offerts à M. Antoine Thomas* (Paris, 1927), p. 197. The text is to be found in Migne, *P.L.* vol. CI, col. 1375.

13 John of Salisbury, *Policraticus* IV, xi (ed. Webb, vol. I, pp. 270–1). As the editor points out, there are some details in this version which do not correspond to the *Collatio*.

There are similar short extracts in:

Jacobus de Cessolis, *De ludo Scacchorum* (ed. F. Vetter, *Das Schachzabelbuch Kunrats von Ammenhausen*, Frauenfeld, 1892, cols. 205–6).

John de Mandeville, *Travels*, ch. XXXIII (ed. P. Hamelius, E.E.T.S., O.S. CLIII (1919), pp. 195–6; ed. M. Letts, Hakluyt Soc. (1953), pp. 204–5, 399–400, 468–9).

14 Jacques de Vitry, *Historia Hierosolymitana* I, ii, in *Gesta Dei per Francos* (Hanover, 1611), pp. 1108–11. Alexander's replies are here completely suppressed.

Martinus Polonus, *Chronicon* II, iv (Antwerp, Plantin, 1574), pp. 67–72. A similar treatment; all we are told of Alexander's reaction to the long letter sent him by Dindimus (all notion of *correspondence* is here obliterated) is the brief comment (p. 72): 'Et recepta epistola Alexander, iratus propter illatam diis suis iniuriam, indignanter illi rescripsit.' But the text of the reply is suppressed.

Contrefait de Renart, see Meyer, *A. le G.* II, pp. 339–40. Here the *Collatio* is made into a medieval attack on idolatry. There is a similar use of it in Gower, *Confessio Amantis* v, vv. 1453 ff. (*English Works*, ed. G. C. Macaulay, vol. I, E.E.T.S., E.S., LXXXI (1900), pp. 441 ff.). Further upon the passage in Gower, see above, p. 254.

Other uses which deserve notice are:
Vincent de Beauvais, *Speculum Historiale* IV, 66–71 (ed. Douai, 1624, pp. 135–7).
Eulogium Historiarum, caps. CXXII–CXXV (ed. F. S. Haydon, Rolls Series, vol. I (1858), pp. 428–32). Here the correspondence runs: Dindimus–Alexander–Dindimus–Alexander–Dindimus. This is immediately followed by the extract from the *De moribus Bragmanorum*.

15 St Augustine, *De Ciu. Dei* IV, iv (Migne, *P.L.* vol. XLI, col. 115) (Cicero, *De Republica* III, xv). Compare Porus' letter to Alexander in *Historia de Preliis* III, ii (ed. Pfister, *Alexanderroman*, p. 103): 'Indorum rex Porus latroni Alexandro, qui latrocinando optinet ciuitates,…'

16 St Thomas Aquinas (Ptolemaeus Lucensis), *De Regimine Principum* III, v (ed. J. Mathis (Rome, 1948), p. 48). The conclusion is added: 'Ista ergo ratione Romanis a Deo collatum fuit dominium.'

Vincent de Beauvais, *Speculum Historiale* IV, li (ed. Douai, 1624, p. 131).

Guibert de Tournai, *Eruditio Regum et Principum* (ed. A. de Poorter, Louvain, 1914 (*Les Philosophes Belges*, IX), p. 49). His source is almost certainly Vincent de Beauvais.

17 These versions are as follows:
Ulrich von Eschenbach, vv. 24,024–172, ed. W. Toischer, *B.L.V.* vol. CLXXXIII (Stuttgart, 1888), pp. 639–43. *Alexander Hystorie*, Tekst II in S. Hoogstra's *Proza-bewerkingen v. h. leven Alex. d. Groot in het middelnederlandsch* (s' Gravenhage, 1898), pp. 112–13. Closely connected with this version is that interpolated into MS. Br. 4 (Breslau Town Lib.) of the I² *Historia de Preliis*, and mentioned by Hilka, *Altfranzösischer Prosa-Alexanderroman*, p. xxxv and n. 5.

The versions in the *Middle Dutch* and *Middle Low German Alexander* are derived from that in the *Gesta Romanorum*, which belongs to the second tradition; but as they place no emphasis upon the forbearance of Alexander, as does the *Gesta Romanorum* version, they should be included here. See A. J. Barnouw, in *Germanic Review*, IV (1929), pp. 375–7.

Other versions of the pirate story belonging to the first tradition, and derived from the *Policraticus*, are here listed for completeness. They are:
Dialogus Creaturarum, dial. 79: 'de perdice fure' (ed. Grässe, *B.L.V.* vol. CXLVIII, p. 224).

Ranulph Higden, *Polychronicon* III, xxvii (ed. Lumby, vol. III, pp. 422–4).

18 The following are citations of the anecdote in which the emphasis is

definitely upon the forbearance of Alexander, and which therefore belong to the second tradition:

Tractatus de diuersis historiis Romanorum, ex. 1 (ed. S. Herzstein, Erlangen, 1893 (*Erlanger Beit. z. Englischen Philol.* xiv), pp. 1–2).

G. Boccaccio, Epist. v (to Niccolò Acciaiuoli, 1341) in *Opere Latine Minori*, ed. A. F. Massera, *Scrittori d'Italia* (Bari, 1928), p. 126: '...come del pirata Antigono [sic] la fortuna rea in buona trasmutò Alessandro, così da voi spero doversi la mia trasmutare.' The form *Antigono* for the name of the pirate is evidently due to a confused reminiscence of the linked episodes in the *Policraticus*, where the story of Dionides succeeds that of Antigonus; see the text.

Gesta Romanorum, c. 146 (ed. Oesterly, p. 504–5): 'De principibus et aliis magnatibus fortiter arguendis pro eorum forefactis.' Alexander rewards the pirate's outspokenness by establishing him among his men: '...de latrone factus est princeps et zelator justicie.' The story is thus interpreted: the pirate is the sinner, Alexander the prince or prelate who must lead him back into the ways of righteousness. But the prelate must first be sure of his own righteousness. For the use of this version in the *Middle Dutch* and *Middle Low German Alexander*, see above, p. 281, n. 17. The anecdote is of very rare occurrence in the MSS. of the *Gesta Romanorum*; see pp. 156, 302.

Heinrich von Beringen, *Schachgedicht*, vv. 726–75 (ed. P. Zimmermann, *B.L.V.* clxvi (Tübingen, 1883); cited by Grammel, *Alexanderbild*, p. 118).

Fior di Virtù, c. ix, *Della virtù della misericordia* (ed. B. Fabbricatore (3rd ed., Napoli, 1870), pp. 42–3). Quoted below, pp. 348–9.

Corona de' Monaci, c. xli, *Dell'amore del prossimo e correzione*, es. 2 (ed. D. Casimiro Stolfi (Prato, 1862), p. 106). See above, p. 263.

François Villon, *Le Testament*, stanzas xvii–xx (*Œuvres*, ed. Louis Thuasne (Paris, 1923), vol. i, pp. 181–2). This is borrowed from the French version by Jean de Vignay of Jacobus de Cessolis, *De ludo Scacchorum*. For further comments upon the history of the second tradition, see pp. 158, 348–9.

19 'Alexander, the conqueror of all the world, was conquered...'

(*a*) *By Diogenes*

In the moral form of the Diogenes episode, with the comments of Seneca and Valerius Maximus; see pp. 83–5.

(*b*) *By wine*

I² *Historia de Preliis*, c. 129 (Hilka, *Altfranzösischer Prosa-Alexanderroman* (Halle, 1920), pp. 259–60): 'Victor omnium uidebatur, sed uino et ira uictus est.' Thence in some derivatives, e.g. in the *Prague Epitome*, ed. Magoun (*Harvard Studies and Notes in Philology and Literature*, xvi, 1934), p. 144: 'Fuit itaque Alexander uictor omnium, set ira et uino uictus.'

Giraldus Cambrensis, *De Principis Instructione* i. xvii (*Opera*, vol. viii, ed. Warner, pp. 58–9). For a discussion of this passage see above, p. 100.

NOTE 19

Epitaph quoted by A. Hilka, *Romanische Forschungen*, XXIX (1911), p. 70 (from MS. Kk. iv. 25, Cambridge University Library (s. xiii), l. 11.

I³ *Historia de Preliis*; see F. Pfister in *Münchener Museum*, I (1912), pp. 272–6.
Brunetto Latini, *Li Livres dou Tresor*, I, i, 27 (ed. Chabaille, p. 37): 'Il estoit victorieus sor toutes gens, mais il estoit vaincuz par vin et par luxure.'
Chaucer, *Monk's Tale*, ed. W. W. Skeat, *Works* (2nd edn. 1900), vol. IV, p. 264, vv. 3834–6:

> Save wyn and wommen, no-thing mighte aswage
> His hye entente in armes and labour;
> So was he ful of leonyn corage.

Benvenuto da Imola (quoted in W. W. Vernon, *Readings on the Inferno of Dante* (Oxford, 1906); vol. I, p. 432, note on *Inf.* XII, 106–8): 'Orbis uictor ab ebrietate uictus est, ut ait Augustinus.'
Old French translation of the *Epitome of Julius Valerius*, quoted by P. Meyer, *A. le G.* II, p. 304: '...par vin et par venin fut vaincus....'

(c) By women, lust, or love

I³ *Historia de Preliis*: see F. Pfister in *Münchener Museum*, I (1912), pp. 272, 276.
Brunetto Latini, *Li Livres dou Tresor* I, i, 27 (quoted under (*b*) above).
Chaucer, *Monk's Tale*, vv. 3834–6 (quoted under (*b*) above).
Boiardo, *Orlando Innamorato* II, i, 29–30:

> Dapoi che vinto egli ha ben ogni cosa,
> Vedesi lui che è vinto d'Amore;...

G. Betussi, *Il Raverta*, in *Trattati d'Amore del Cinquecento*, ed. G. Zonta, *Scrittori d'Italia* (Bari, 1912), p. 139: 'Alessandro Magno, che tutto il mondo vinse, non si lasciò poi vincere ad Efestione, alla quale portò tanto amore?' (This is reminiscent of the *rifacimenti* of Anacreon, and of Michelangelo's sonnets, in which homosexuality was similarly disguised by the alteration of gender throughout.) The same is done deliberately in the interest of morality by Vasco de Lucena in the introduction to his French version of the interpolated Quintus Curtius. See A. Bossuat, *Bibliothèque d'Humanisme et Renaissance*, VIII (1946), pp. 235–6.

(d) By poison

Epitaph quoted by Hilka, *Romanische Forschungen*, XXIX (1911), p. 70, l. 24.
Old French Prose Romance, c. 124 (ed. Hilka (Halle, 1920), p. 260): 'Chi gist Alixandres, rois de Macedone, qui par fer ne pot estre vaincus, mais l'ochist le venim....'
Old French Translation of the *Epitome of Valerius*, quoted by Meyer, *A. le G.* II, p. 304 (quoted under (*b*) above).
For references to the poisoning of Alexander more immediately connected with the theme of treachery, see below, pp. 315–18.

283

(e) By his own will

The exemplar form of the Diogenes anecdote, where Diogenes calls Alexander the servant of his servant, the will; for citations of this story, see pp. 146–9.

(f) By anger

I² *Historia de Preliis*, c. 129 (ed. Hilka, *Altfranzösischer Prosa-Alexanderroman*, pp. 259–60): see under *(b)* above for quotation.

Petrarch, *Sonetti sopra diversi argomenti* XIX:

> Vincitore Alessandro l'ira vinse,
> E fel minore in parte, che Filippo....

(Cf. Val. Max. IX, iii, ext. 1: Alexander's anger, that caused the deaths of Cleitus and Callisthenes, deprived him of heaven.)

20 For the tomb story see H. Knust, *Mittheilungen aus dem Eskurial, B.L.V.* vol. CXLI (Tübingen, 1879), pp. 45–55. F. Pfister in *Münchener Museum* I (1912), pp. 271–8; *Disciplina Clericalis*, ex. xxxii (ed. A. Hilka and W. Soederhjelm, *Sammlung mittellat. Texte*, I (Heidelberg, 1911), pp. 48–9). For further references to this story, and further discussion of it, see pp. 151–2, 300–1.

For the epitaph see Hilka in *Romanische Forschungen*, XXIX, p. 70.

Cf. also the conclusion of the *Libro del Nascimento*, quoted by Storost, p. 179:

> Però ceto si spande
> La fama: il nome: e i fatti di colui
> Che vinse tutto: e morte vinse lui.

21 John of Salisbury, *Policraticus* V, xii (ed. Webb, vol. I, p. 335). The anecdote here told by John of Alexander's justice is that he complimented the judges who decided a case against him, on placing justice before other considerations. This does not agree with his statement elsewhere that Alexander had no heirs because he was an unjust king; see above, p. 104.

22 These passages are as follows:

Giraldus Cambrensis, loc. cit. (p. 282, n. 19).

Thomas Aquinas (Ptolemaeus Lucensis), *De regimine principum* III, viii (ed. J. Mathis, Rome, 1948, p. 47): (when Alexander was no longer a favourite of his soldiers, he was poisoned by his sister (*sic*)); 'et praecipue, quia post uictoriam Darii accepta filia in coniugem, militaria coepit postponere, luxui uitae intendens, et sui immemor factus dolorosa morte uitam finiuit.'

Upon the well-known passage in Gautier de Châtillon, *Alexandreis* III, vv. 241 ff. see above, p. 173.

23 For the Anaxarchus story, see:

Val. Max. VIII, xiv, ext. 2.

Policraticus VIII, v (ed. Webb, II, p. 247).

Dialogus Creaturarum, dial. 82 (ed. Grässe, *B.L.V.*, vol. CXLVIII, pp. 228–9).

Marsilio Ficino, *Theologia Plat.* XVI; see Nesca Robb, *Neoplatonism of the Italian Renaissance* (1935), p. 73; in this example the episode is treated in a

Renaissance spirit, as illustrating the ambition that every man should have to develop his personality to the full.

We may finally cite two references to Alexander's cruelty, in *The English Conquest of Ireland* (ed. F. J. Furnivall, E.E.T.S., O.S. CVII (1896), pp. 34–5), and Brunetto Latini, *Li Livres dou Tresor* II, ii, 72 (ed. Chabaille, p. 399); and a generally abusive passage in Walter Map, *De Nugis Curialium* II, 23 (Eng. tr. F. Tupper and M. B. Ogle (London, 1924), p. 117) (of Llewellyn, king of the Welsh): 'For he was like Alexander of Macedon and all those whom insatiable desire hath set free from all check—prodigal, watchful, active, bold, quick-witted, affable, lickerous, wicked, treacherous, and pitiless.'

24 The following anecdotes favourable to Alexander are told in the *Policraticus* (ed. Webb):

III, xiv (I, pp. 224–5): the stories of Antigonus and Dionides; see above, pp. 95–8.

v, vii (I, pp. 309–10): the story of the cold soldier to whom Alexander gave up his seat at the fire (Frontinus, *Strateg.* IV, 6), and that of the captive virgin whom he sent back untouched (Frontinus, II, 11): 'Fertur et aliud de eodem: quod, cum uirgo eximiae pulchritudinis, finitimae gentis principi desponsata, inter captiuas adesse nuntiaretur, ei abstinentia summa pepercit, ut ne illam quidem aspexerit; qua mox ad sponsum remissa, uniuersae gentis per hoc beneficium sibi mentes reconciliauit. Sic humanitate suorum alienorum animos sibi iustitia deuinxit.'

v, vii (I, p. 313): Emilianus Scipio took simple meals during the marches of his army; so did Alexander (Frontinus, IV, 3).

v, xii (I, p. 335): Alexander praised the judges for condemning him at a trial, and placing justice before consideration of rank. See above, p. 284.

VI, xiv (II, p. 37): discipline in the army; how Alexander trained his small body of troops to perfection.

VII, xxv (II, p. 224): Alexander's reply to Parmenio. The Parmenio episode is derived from Val. Max. VI, iv, ext. 3.

For uses of many of these episodes in books of *exempla*, especially the *Dialogus Creaturarum*, see pp. 158–61.

The episode of the judges also occurs in Guibert de Tournai, *Eruditio Regum et Principum*, ed. A. de Poorter (*Les Philosophes Belges*, IX, Louvain, 1914), p. 79: 'Legimus enim in iudicio causam fuisse damnatam Machedonis Alexandri, unde et iudicibus egit gratiam quia praetulerant iustitiam potestati.'

For the favourable references in Giraldus Cambrensis, which refer to Alexander's learning and encouragement of learning, see pp. 108, 290.

25 Dante, *Monarchia* II, ix (among attempts to achieve world empire previous to the Romans): 'Praeter istos et post, Alexander rex Macedo maxime omnium ad palmam Monarchiae propinquans, dum per legatos ad deditionem Romanos praemoneret, apud Aegyptum, ante Romanorum responsionem, ut Liuius narrat, in medio quasi cursu collapsus est. De cuius etiam sepultura ibidem existente, Lucanus in octauo, inuehens in Ptolemaeum regem Aegypti, testimonium reddit dicens:

> Ultima Lagaeae stirpis perituraque proles
> Degener, incestae sceptris cessure sorori,
> Quum tibi sacrato Macedo seruetur in antro.

"O altitudo diuitiarum sapientiae et scientiae Dei!" quis hic te non obstupere poterit? Nam conantem Alexandrum praepedire in cursu coathletam Romanum, tu, ne sua temeritas prodiret ulterius, de certamine rapuisti.'

This passage raises the question of Alexander's own relations with Rome; of the embassy which the Romans were supposed to have sent to him, and of his intentions towards them. Would he have conquered Rome, had he lived? Many medieval authors thought it probable—especially Gautier de Châtillon, and F. Frezzi in his *Quadriregio*, IV, vii, 49 ff. (ed. E. Filippini, *Scrittori d'Italia* (Bari, 1914), p. 306).

Petrarch, however, a fanatic lover of Rome, supported Livy's contention that Alexander could never have conquered Rome, abused the 'frivolous Gauls' who supposed it possible, and ridiculed Alexander's power. See G. Cary, 'Petrarch and Alexander the Great', *Italian Studies*, V (1950), p. 53.

In the *Pantheon* of Godfrey of Viterbo (Part XI), there is an imaginary hostile correspondence between Alexander and the Romans, started shortly before the former's death. No source for this correspondence is known, and it seems likely that it was Godfrey's own invention. But his reasons for inventing such a correspondence are undiscoverable. For a full discussion of the passage involved, see L. Meyer, *Les Légendes des Matières de Rome, de France, et de Bretagne dans le 'Panthéon' de Godefroi de Viterbe* (Paris, 1933), pp. 108–13.

26 De Quincey, in *The Caesars* (*Works*, vol. IX (Edinburgh, 1880), p. 6), thus gives the narrowest definition of monarchy: 'The Caesar of Western Rome— he alone of all earthly potentates, past or to come, could be said to reign as a *monarch*, that is, as a solitary king. He was not the greatest of princes, simply because there was no other but himself.'

Examples of the medieval use of the terms 'monarch' and 'monarchy' in reference to Alexander are as follows:

Rhabanus Maurus, *Commentaria in Libros Machabaeorum* I, i (Migne, *P.L.* vol. CIX, cols. 1127–9. In explanation of the phrase that Alexander 'primus regnauit in Graecia', Rhabanus says that Alexander's empire was the only one previous to that of the Romans to be called a *monarchia*.

St Thomas Aquinas (Ptolemaeus Lucensis), *De Regimine Principum* (ed. Mathis), III, viii (p. 47): 'Alexander, quamdiu cum reuerentia suos tractauit Macedones,...optime processit in monarchia....' III, xii (p. 53): 'Secunda uero monarchia, uidelicet Medorum et Persarum, durauit usque ad tempora Alexandri.... Sed monarchia Graecorum in Alexandro incipit, et in eodem finitur.'

Rudolf von Ems, *Alexander*, vv. 15,653 ff.:

> 'unz er mit hôher werdekeit
> den namen und den prîs erstreit
> daz er hiez mônarchus.'

'Mônarchus' is then interpreted as meaning 'vürste aller küneg'.

For the succession of empires, and the suggestion of God's purpose in delegating monarchy to the Romans, cf. Folcuinus, *Gesta Abbatum Lobiensium*, in *M.G.H. Scriptt.* IV (ed. G. H. Pertz, 1841), p. 55, ll. 25 ff.: 'Inde ad Macedones, quos multo sanguine sibi acquisiuit Alexander ille, quem Daniel uel aes in statua uel pardum in uisione nominat, magnus utique, magnus ille gurges miseriarum; ad postremum Romanis,...non sine nutu Dei cessit imperium.'

Abaelard notes an advantage of the monarchical system in the preservation of peace, and refers to the troubles that succeeded upon the death of Alexander (in Migne, *P.L.* vol. CLXXVIII, col. 266 c): 'Unde etiam Alexandro mortuo, multiplicatis regibus mala quoque multiplicata sunt.'

Much reference was made in the Middle Ages to the troubles that succeeded his death, and the division of his kingdom. Such references generally had especially in view the plight of the Jews under Antiochus. In the *Alphabet of Tales* this division of the empire among several successors is adduced as an example of pride—Alexander was so proud that he wanted no man to possess as great dominion as himself.

See, for commentary upon Maccabees, pp. 121–5; for the passage in the *Alphabet of Tales*, p. 157.

27 See L. K. Born, 'The Perfect Prince', *Speculum*, III (1928), pp. 470–504.

The principal writers upon government to borrow largely from the *Secret of Secrets* were Thomas Aquinas (Ptolemaeus Lucensis), Innocent III, Guillaume Perrault, Hoccleve, Egidio Colonna (Egidius Romanus), and Ximenes.

On Walter Milemete, see the edition of his work by M. R. James (Roxburghe Club, 1913).

For the *Secret of Secrets* and its influence, see pp. 21–2; for its effect upon the late medieval conception of Alexander, see pp. 250–1.

The best brief sketch of the history and effect of the *Secret of Secrets* is by R. Steele, in his Introduction to Roger Bacon's edition of the work (*Rogeri Baconi opera hactenus inedita*, fasc. V (Oxford, 1920), pp. ix–lxiv) with select bibliography.

28 Passages in the Alexander-books where Aristotle advises Alexander are so numerous that only a few of the most important are given here:

Gautier de Châtillon, *Alexandreis* I, 69 ff. (Migne, *P.L.* vol. CCIX, cols. 465 ff.); reproduced with some alterations in the derivatives of the *Alexandreis*.

In Ulrich von Eschenbach's *Alexander*, the additional book XI is an allegory, with frequent borrowings from the *Secret of Secrets*, in which the city of Trintonia cannot be taken by Alexander until Aristotle gives his advice; see W. Toischer, in *Sitzungsber. d. kaiser. Akad. d. Wissen.*, Phil.-Hist. Kl., Bd. xcvii (1881 for 1880), pp. 325–6.

Derived from the passage in the *Alexandreis* referred to above, which contains a long speech of Aristotle to the young Alexander, is Rutebeuf's *Dit Aristote*; see Meyer, *A. le G.* ii, p. 372.

Roman d'Alexandre iii, laisses 1 ff.; see Meyer, *A. le G.* ii, p. 162.

On the seventh book of Gower's *Confessio Amantis*, which contains an account of Alexander's education entirely derived from the *Secret of Secrets*, see above, p. 255.

29 The following are representative references illustrative of Alexander's relationship with his tutor:

(i) The letter of Philip to Aristotle, desiring him to direct Alexander's education, was quoted by:

John of Salisbury, *Policraticus* iv, vii (ed. Webb, i, p. 256).

Guibert de Tournai, *Eruditio Regum et Principum*, ed. de Poorter, p. 22.

(ii) The advantage to Alexander of such a tutor as Aristotle was emphasized by innumerable accounts and episodes which illustrated the value of Aristotle's counsel. Among detached comments upon the benefit to Alexander of Aristotle's tutorship, we may notice the following:

St Jerome, *Epistola* cvii (ad Laetam de institutione filiae), sec. xiii (Migne, *P.L.* vol. xxii, col. 878): Jerome will nourish and instruct the infant Paula as a Bride of Christ, more glorious than Aristotle, who taught Alexander, the king who was to die by poison in Babylon.

Moses of Bergamo, quoted in Manitius, *Geschichte der lat. Lit. im Mittelalter*, iii (1931), p. 684: Alexander took the advice of Aristotle in the field, Scipio Africanus that of Polybius.

Antonius Astesanus, *Carmen de eius uita et fortunae uarietate* ii, 939, in R.I.S. xiv (1908–12), p. 30: Aristotle was not ashamed to be the tutor of Alexander.

Guillaume Perrault, *De Eruditione Principum* i, 2 (Aquinas, *Opera Omnia* (Parma, 1852–71), vol. xvi (1864), p. 394: A prince should have if possible a philosopher to help him through life, as Alexander Aristotle, and Nero Seneca.

(iii) The danger of bad tutors was illustrated by the story of the tutor Leonidas, who passed on to Alexander a defect in his gait; the story was quoted by St Jerome (Migne, *P.L.* vol. xxii, col. 872), and fairly frequently in the Middle Ages; e.g. by Guillaume Perrault, op. cit. v, 9 (ed. cit. p. 431), and for exemplar citations see p. 304.

(iv) Alexander's reverence for his tutor was also attested not only by his attitude to Aristotle in the various texts, but by a remark of his cited in the *Bocados de Oro* (ed. H. Knust, *Mittheilungen aus dem Eskurial, B.L.V.* vol. cxli (Tübingen, 1879), p. 311): 'E dixeronle: "Porque honrras a tu maestro mas que a tu padre?" E dixo: "Porque por mi padre he la vida finable e por mi maestro la vida fincable".' Further references are given in Knust's note; and there may be added an independent citation in a letter of Olympia Morata, in *Opuscoli e Lettere de' Riformatori Italiani del Cinquecento*, ed. G. Paladino, vol. II (*Scrittori d'Italia*, Bari, 1927), p. 172: 'A patre enim uiuendi, a magistro bene uiuendi initium sumpsisse.'

Examples of reference to Alexander's reverence for Aristotle in German literature are given by Grammel, p. 118, and are as follows:

Heinrich von Beringen, *Schachgedicht*, vv. 2385 ff.

Wälschen Gast, vv. 6414 ff.

Hugo von Trimberg, *Renner*, v. 16,409.

For the importance of the relationship between Alexander and Aristotle in the late medieval period, see pp. 250-1. The best study of the relationship between them in Alexander-books is that by W. Hertz, *Aristoteles in den Alexander-dichtungen des Mittelalters*, in *Ges. Abh.*

30 See above, pp. 112-16, for the full history of this episode; the instances of its use in writers of this type are as follows:

John of Salisbury, *Policraticus* VIII, 14 (ed. Webb, II, p. 333).

Guibert de Tournai, *Eruditio Regum et Principum*, ed. de Poorter, p. 22.

Aeneas Syluius, *De Curialium Miseriis Epistola*, ed. W. P. Mustard (Baltimore and O.U.P., 1928), p. 55.

31 The references under this head have been divided into two groups; the first consists of citations of the Achilles episode, the second of comments similar to that in the Prologue of the *Policraticus*, upon the preservation of Alexander's fame in the historians of his deeds, and his consequent indebtedness to them:

(i) The Achilles episode:

St Jerome, *Vita S. Hilarionis*, prologus (Migne, *P.L.* vol. XXIII, col. 29 A).

Chronicon S. Andreae III, prologus, in *M.G.H. Scriptt.* VII (ed. G. H. Pertz, 1846), p. 539, l. 39.

Petrarch, *Sonetti in vita di Laura*, CXXXV, vv. 1-4.

G. Boccaccio, *Epistola* XIX (to Pietro da Monteforte, 1373), in *Opere Latine Minori*, ed. A. F. Massera, *Scrittori d'Italia* (Bari, 1928), p. 199.

Pietro Aretino, *Secondo Libro delle Lettere* no. CDXCI (to the Marchese di Vasto) (ed. F. Nicolini, *Scrittori d'Italia* (Bari, 1916), II, part 1, p. 212).

(ii) General comments upon the preservation of Alexander's fame:

Giraldus Cambrensis, *Symbolum Electorum*, Ep. XV (to King Richard) (*Opera*, vol. I, ed. Brewer, p. 243).

Walter Map, *De Nugis Curialium* V, Prologue (Eng. translation, F. Tupper and M. B. Ogle (London, 1924), pp. 254-5).

Richard of London, *Itinerarium Peregrinorum*, prologus (*M.G.H. Scriptt.* XXVII (1885), p. 195).

F. Sacchetti, *Rime*, CLXXIII, vv. 122-6 (ed. Chiari, *Scrittori d'Italia* (Bari, 1936), vol. I, p. 182).

PART B. THE MEDIEVAL CONCEPTION OF ALEXANDER

Iacobus de Guisia, *Annales Hanoniae*, prologus iii (ed. E. Sackur, in *M.G.H. Scriptt.* xxx, i (1896), p. 80 at bottom).

Pier Paolo Vergerio, *Epist.* LXXXI (*Epistolario*, ed. L. Smith, *Fonti per la Storia d'Italia* (Rome, 1934), p. 192).

Fra. Johannes Ferrariensis, *Ex annalium libris Marchionum Estensium excerpta*, dedication to Borso d'Este (ed. L. Simeoni, *R.I.S.* xx, ii (Bologna, n.d.), p. 3, ll. 10–11).

32 Ranulph Higden, *Polychronicon*, III xxiv (ed. Lumby, vol. III, p. 366): 'Item Plinius, libro septimo: Alexander Magnus inflammatus cupidine noscendi naturas animalium....'

L'Ymage dou Monde, quoted by Le Roux de Lincy, *Le Livre des Légendes* (Paris, 1836), p. 215:

> Les gens Alexandres ki fu
> Rois et bons clers de grant vertu,...

Eustache Deschamps, *Balade* CCLXXII, v. 15 (*Œuvres*, ed. Raynaud and Le Queux de Saint Hilaire, S.A.T.F., vol. II (1880), p. 117):

> (Alexander, Julius Caesar,
> Charlemagne, Judas Maccabee)
> Furent tous clers et grans fereurs d'espee.

Cf. also *Bal.* XCIX (vol. I, p. 208), CCII (vol. II, p. 22).

John Lydgate, in *Minor Poems*, ed. H. N. MacCracken, vol. I, E.E.T.S., E.S. CVII (1911), p. 72:

> Off Alisaundre clerkys synge and reede,
> Afftir his conquest slayn in Babilon;...

John Capgrave, *Chronicle of England* (ed. Hingeston (Rolls Series, 1858), pp. 53).

33 For the historical facts of the Ammon and Callisthenes episodes, see W. W. Tarn, *Alexander the Great*, I (Cambridge University Press, 1948), pp. 77–82.

For the question of Alexander's deification, and the historical evidence involved, see W. W. Tarn, *Alexander the Great*, II, pp. 347–74; and P. Schnabel, 'Zur Frage der Selbstvergöttung Alexanders', *Klio*, XX (1926), pp. 398–414.

For disapproval of the Ammon episode in sources available to medieval writers, cf. Curtius IV, vii, 29ff., and Aulus Gellius XIII, iv, 1ff., where Olympias writes to Alexander begging him not to cast doubts on her respectability by calling himself the son of Ammon.

34 Relevant passages in the sources are as follows:

Ammon episode: Curtius IV, vii, 5–32.
> Justin XI, xi, 2–12.
> Orosius III, xvi, 12–14.

Cleitus episode: Curtius VIII, i, 19–52.
> Justin XII, vi, 3–18.
> Orosius III, xviii, 8.

Callisthenes episode: Curtius VIII, v, 5–viii, 23.

Justin XII, vii, 1–2; xv, iii, 3–6.

Orosius III, xviii, 11.

For an interesting account of the Ammon episode by a theologian, Rupert of Deutz, see above, p. 139.

35 Val. Max. VII, ii, ext. 11 (details of Aristotle's advice to Callisthenes, that he should be cautious); 'At ille, dum Alexandrum Persica Macedonem salutatione gaudentem obiurgat et ad Macedonicos mores inuitum reuocare beniuole perseuerat, spiritu carere iussus seram neglecti salubris consilii poenitentiam egit.'

Compare also Val. Max. IX, iii, ext. 1 (three deeds of Alexander's committed in anger deprived him of heaven): '...Lysimachus leoni obiectus et Clitus hasta traiectus et Callisthenes mori iussus.'

36 Ekkehart of Aura, *Chronicon*, in *M.G.H. Scriptt.* VI (ed. D. G. Waitz, Hanover, 1844), p. 61, ll. 29–36.

Compare Rhabanus Maurus, in his *Commentaria in Libros Machabaeorum* I, (Migne, *P.L.* vol. CIX, col. 1130).

The episode of Callisthenes does not appear in the early annalistic accounts of Alexander or in Hugh of St Victor, Matthew Paris, or Roger of Wendover.

37 Aeneas Sylvius, *De Curialium Miseriis Epistola*, ed. W. P. Mustard (Baltimore and Oxford University Press, 1928):

p. 32: 'Clitum, suae nutricis filium, quod sibi ausus Philippi patris laudes comparare fuisset, Alexander Macedo sua manu interemit.'

p. 55: (the miseries of court life; the uncertain temperament of kings): 'Nec tu mihi Aristotelem obiicias, summum philosophum, Alexandri Magni castra sequentem; nescis enim qua uoluptate hoc egerit, et an sibi libertas fuerit aliter faciendi. At secuti sunt Alexandrum complures alii, Callisthenes philosophus, Clitus frater collactaneus, Lysimachus miles et philosophus insignis. Callisthenes dum adorari more Persico Alexandrum prohibet, truncatis manibus et pedibus, effossis oculis, naribus et auribus amputatis, miseram uitam in carcere ducere cogebatur; cui cum Lysimachus in remedium aerumnarum uenenum obtulisset, leoni obiectus est. Clitus cum Alexandrum Philippi patris laudibus detrahentem redarguisset, ab eodem, ut supra retuli, in conuiuio est occisus.'

38 Gautier de Châtillon, *Alexandreis* IX, 3 ff:

'...quam (*i.e.* Indiam) dum petit ille deorum,
aemulus in terris, Clytus, Hermolaus, et eius
doctor (Aristoteli praeter quem nemo secundus)
extremum clausere diem, documenta futuris
certa relinquentes, etenim testatur eorum
finis, amicitias regum non esse perennes.'

The murder of Callisthenes is omitted altogether in the *Libro de Alexandre*; though the fate of Clitus and Hermolaus is fully described, with a warning similar to that in Gautier, that one should beware of the favour of kings. See *Libro de Alexandre*, stanzas 1969–72 (composite numbering; ed. Willis, p. 342).

Ulrich von Eschenbach also omits the Callisthenes episode; though he includes that of Clitus (vv. 19,231 ff.).

39 For sixteenth-century editions of the *Dits Moraux*, see Brunet, *Manuel du Libraire*, 5th ed., vol. II, cols. 765–6 under 'Dits des philosophes'. Compare with this phrase:

Haymo of Halberstadt, *Comm. in Isaiam* II, xx (ed. Cologne, 1531), f. 67ᵛ: 'Alexander magnus quum se putaret esse ut deum, ueneno periit....' This was quoted in Fra Salimbene, *Chronica*, s.a. 1250 (*M.G.H. Scriptt.* XXXII, ed. O. Holder-Egger (Leipzig and Hanover, 1905–13), p. 441).

Brunetto Latini, *Li Livres dou Tresor* I, i, 27 (ed. Chabaille, p. 37) (Olympias had spread about that Alexander was the son of a God): 'Et certes il demena si haute vie que on pooit bien croire que il estoit filz d'un dieu....Il estoit victorieus sor toutes gens, mais il estoit vaincuz par vin et par luxure.'

40 I Maccabees i, 1–8.

Daniel, vii, 6; viii, 3–26; xi, 1 ff. These passages are as follows:

vii, 6: (in the succession of Beasts) 'Post haec aspiciebam, et ecce alia quasi pardus, et alas habebat quasi avis, quatuor super se, et quatuor capita erant in bestia, et potestas data est ei.'

viii, 3–26: The allegory of the ram attacked by the goat.

xi, 1 ff: The king of Greece who shall overcome the king of Persia.

41 St Jerome, *Comm. in Danielem* (Migne, *P.L.* vol. xxv, cols. 529 ff. The most important passages in this commentary are these:

cols. 529–30: commentary on vii, 6; the leopard is Alexander; (col. 530) 'Quodque additur: "et potestas data est ei", ostendit, non Alexandri fortitudinis, sed Domini uoluntatis fuisse.'

cols. 536 ff.: commentary on viii, 3 ff.: Darius is the ram, Alexander the goat.

cols. 557–8: commentary on xi, 1 ff.: 'Et ecce princeps Graecorum, id est, Macedonum, ueniebat, et ingressus est in conspectu Dei, ut accusaret Persarum principem atque Medorum: ut in locum eorum regnum Macedonum succederet. Et reuera mira sacramenta Dei....' Alexander destroyed the Persians in vindication of the prophecy.

42 For the strange interpretations of Rupert of Deutz, see above, pp. 137–40.

Another deviation from the usual interpretation appears in Peter Comestor, *Historia Scholastica, lib. Danielis* VII (Migne, *P.L.* vol. CXCVIII, col. 1456A): '"Et ecce hircus ueniebat ab occidente, et non tangebat terram." Hic est Alexander quasi uolans, per inuia quaeque gradiens, ut hircus, ut ab hircis oculorum, quod diuersi coloris habuit.' This reference to the differing colour of Alexander's eyes is an evident reminiscence of the legend with which Peter Comestor was well acquainted; see above, pp. 72–3.

Among miscellaneous Latin references to the prophecy we may cite the following:
St Jerome, *Vita S. Hilarionis*, prologus (Migne, *P.L.* vol. XXIII, col. 29A);
Comm. in Jeremiam I, v, 6 (Migne, *P.L.* vol. XXIV, col. 742B). 'Pardum autem
uocat ob uarietatem, et quia plurimis sibi subditis gentibus contra Medos dimi-
cauit et Persas'; also *Comm. in Isaiam* v, xx (Migne, *P.L.* vol. XXIV, col. 195A–B).
Folcuinus, *Gesta Abbatum Lobiensium* in *M.G.H. Scriptt.* IV (1841), p. 55,
ll. 25 ff. (quoted above, p. 287).
Romuald of Salerno, *Chronicon*, in R.I.S. VII, i (Città di Castello, n.d.), p. 32
(quotation of St Jerome's commentary).
Ranulph Higden, *Polychronicon* (ed. Lumby, vol. III, pp. 128, 136).
The prophecy appeared similarly in many chronicle accounts.

43 Some of the more important references to Daniel in Alexander-books are
as follows:
Vorau Alexander, vv. 471–7 (ed. Kinzel, p. 68).
Ulrich von Eschenbach, *Alexander*, vv. 27,697–727.
A lengthy interpolation in the second redaction of the *Old French Prose
Romance*; see Hilka, *Altfranzösischer Prosa-Alexanderroman*, pp. 68–9, and D. J. A.
Ross in *French Studies*, VI (1952), pp. 144 and 147.

44 Manitius III, p. 823: 'Darauf folgen vier Distichen, in denen Alexander als
der Typus des Antichrist hingestellt wird, dessen Herrschaft auf drei und ein
halbes Jahr bemessen wird.' This is followed by the usual presentation of Antiochus as Antichrist (ibid.).
On a conceivable connexion of Alexander with Antichrist, see W. Bousset,
The Antichrist Legend (English tr., London, 1896), p. 63; Alexander's reign of
twelve years is balanced by that of the last king on earth.
For another description of Alexander and Antiochus in Acardus de Arroasia
(*fl. c.* 1115), *Super Templo Salomonis*, see Manitius III, p. 1001.

45 Godfrey of Viterbo, *Pantheon*, part XI (ed. 1578, p. 163, col. 2): 'De Alexandro narrat Josephus, dicens: Cum Alexander persecutus Persas usque ad
Pamphylicum mare uenisset, ipsum mare ultro apertum est ei: et ipse sicco pede
transiuit, sicut olim per mare rubrum filii Israel transierunt. Quod miraculum
aut ideo fuit, quia Alexander erat magnus Dei cultor, aut quia per eum Deus
superbiam Persarum fuerat puniturus.' See L. Meyer, *Les Légendes des Matières
de Rome, de France, et de Bretagne dans le 'Panthéon' de Godefroi de Viterbe* (Paris,
1933), p. 66, n. 3.

46 Richard of St Victor, *Explicatio in Cantica Cant.* XXI (Migne, *P.L.* vol.
CXCVI, col. 469C): 'Signa uero interdum facta sunt ab infidelibus, siue etiam
reprobis, utpote ab Alexandro Macedone et Juda proditore, et aliis multis, qui
ad damnationem haec faciebant.'
John of Salisbury refers to the eagles sitting upon the roof-tree of the palace,
and the lightning, which accompanied Alexander's birth, without, however,

offering a theological or rational explanation of the phenomena (*Policraticus* I, xiii, ed. Webb, vol. I, p. 57, l. 20, and p. 63, l. 24). The form of Richard's reference, however, suggests that he is thinking more specifically of the enclosing of the Ten Tribes (see above, p. 132) which might be said to have been a miracle accomplished by Alexander himself, and was never satisfactorily turned to his discredit.

47 Peter Comestor, *Historia Scholastica*, lib. Esther, IV (Migne, *P.L.* vol. CXCVIII, cols. 1496–8) and I¹ *Historia de Preliis* (ed. O. Zingerle, *Die Quellen zum Alexander des Rudolf von Ems* (*Germanistische Abhandlungen*, IV, Breslau, 1885)), pp. 149–53.

There were besides many independent quotations of the episode from the Latin translation of Josephus, e.g. in the *Middle Irish Alexander* (see above, p. 69); but Comestor's account was of great influence, as the following list of some of its more important derivatives will show:

(*a*) *Chronica regia S. Pantaleonis*, in G. Eccardus, *Corp. Hist. Med. Aeu.* I (Leipzig, 1723), cols. 711–13.

(*b*) Vincent de Beauvais, *Spec. Hist.* IV, 32 (ed. Douai, 1624, pp. 125–6).

(*c*) Ranulph Higden, *Polychronicon* III, 27 (ed. Lumby, vol. III, pp. 412 and 418–20).

(*d*) *Liegnitz Historia*; see Hilka, in *Roman. Forsch.* XXIX (1911), pp. 23–4.

(*e*) *Historienbibel* I; see Pfister, *Alexanderroman*, p. 29, n. 1.

48 Minucius Felix, *Octavius* XXI, 3 (ed. G. H. Rendall, Loeb Classical Library, 1931, pp. 373–4): 'Alexander ille Magnus Macedo insigni uolumine ad matrem suam scripsit, metu suae potestatis proditum sibi a diis hominibus a sacerdote secretum: illic Vulcanum facit omnium principem, et postea Iouis gentem.' There are similar passages in St Cyprian, *De Idolorum Vanitate* III (Migne, *P.L.* vol. IV, col. 568–9) and St Augustine, *De Ciuitate Dei* VIII, 27, XII, 10 (Migne, *P.L.* vol. XLI, cols. 256 and 358). See further D. Carraroli, *La leggenda di Alessandro Magno* (Mondovì, 1892), p. 143.

For Tertullian's reference to Alexander in a discussion of euhemerism, see *Apologeticus* XI (Migne, *P.L.* vol. I, cols. 336–7), quoted below, p. 318. For a discussion of this passage in a history of the theory, see J. D. Cooke: 'Euhemerism: a medieval interpretation of classical paganism', *Speculum*, II (1927), pp. 396–410.

For Gower's use of Dindimus' criticism of Alexander's gods, in which he assigns one god to every limb of the body, see above, p. 254.

49 The development of this view may be seen in the following quotations: St Jerome, *Comm. in Danielem* III, xlvii (Migne, *P.L.* XXV, col. 504): '"Vere Deus uester Deus deorum est, et Dominus regum, et reuelans mysteria, quoniam potuisti aperire hoc sacramentum." Ergo non tam Danielem, quam in Daniele adorat Deum, qui mysteria reuelauit. Quod et Alexandrum magnum regem Macedonum in Pontifice Joiada fecisse legimus.'

Sedulius Scotus, *Liber de Rectoribus Christianis* xvIII (Migne, *P.L.* vol. cIII, cols. 327–8) (what should not Christian princes do in the service of God?): 'Si rex impius Nabuchodonosor Deum Israel honorat, si Alexander Magnus cum esset paganissimus illius templum adiit, illius maiestati ceruicem subdidit, se genibus prouolutus curuat, ab illo auxilium efflagitat, illi uictimas immolat, atque insuper sancti pontificem templi Jaddum plurimis honoribus sublimat.'
 Vita Heriberti Archiep. Colon., auctore Lantberto, in *M.G.H. Scriptt.* IV (1841), p. 749, ll. 8 ff.: 'Sic Alexander Magnus cum Hierusalem conaretur irrumpere, territus est a simili pontificii ueteris imagine, prohibente, ne quam uim suis inferret ciuibus, nisi gratus sibi esset praesens uitae exitus.'
 Thomas Aquinas (Ptolemaeus Lucensis), *De Regimine Principum* II, xvi (ed. Mathis, p. 36) (God is above all princes): 'Circa quod etiam monitus Alexander, ut historiae tradunt, cum proposito uadens in Iudaeam destruendi regionem, cum appropinquanti Hierusalem ei irato in albis Summus Pontifex occurrisset cum ministris templi mansuefactus, et de equo descendens, ipse eum uice Dei reueritus est, et ingressus templum, maximis honorauit donis, et gentem totam pro diuina reuerentia libertate donauit.'
 The best example of such treatment of the Jerusalem episode, however, is to be found in the *De Victoria Verbi Dei* of Rupert of Deutz, discussed above, pp. 139–40.

50 The most thorough study is that by A. R. Anderson, *Alexander's Gate, Gog and Magog and the Enclosed Nations (Medieval Academy of America Publications, no. xII, Cambridge, Mass., 1932*), which should be consulted for further bibliography.
 Still of importance are:
 A. Graf, *Miti, Leggende, e Superstizioni del Medio Evo*, I (Turin, 1892), pp. 73–126.
 F. Kampers, *Alexander der Grosse und die Idee des Weltimperiums in Prophetie und Sage* (Freiburg-im-Breisgau, 1901).

51 The following are a few representative references to the legend in medieval literature (see also A. R. Anderson, op. cit. and F. Pfister in *Handwörterbuch des deutschen Aberglaubens*, III (s.v. *Gog und Magog*), cols. 914–16):
 St Jerome, *Epistola* LxxVII, 8 (ed. Hilberg, *Corp. Scriptt. Eccl. Lat.* LV (1912), p. 45).
 Alcuin (Migne, *P.L.* vol. cI, col. 1296).
 Honorius of Autun, *De Imagine Mundi* I, xi (Migne, *P.L.* vol. cLxxII, col. 123): 'mons Caspius...inter quem et mare Gog et Magog, ferocissimae gentes, a magno Alexandro inclusae feruntur.'
 Godfrey of Viterbo, *Pantheon*, part xI (see L. Meyer, *Les Legéndes des Matières de Rome, de France et de Bretagne dans le 'Panthéon' de Godefroi de Viterbe* (Paris, 1933), pp. 101–6).
 Ralph de Diceto, *Abbreuiationes Chronicorum (Opera Historica*, ed. W. Stubbs, Rolls Series, vol. I, 1876, p. 48) (from Aethicus Ister, *Cosmographia*).

Redaction C of the Letter of Prester John, in the edition by Fr. Zarncke, *Abh. d. sächs. Gesell.*, Phil.-Hist. Klasse, VII (1879), p. 911.

Interpolated into the *Historia de Preliis* by the I³ redactor; see Pfister, in *Münchener Museum* I (1912), pp. 267–8.

Interpolated into I² *Historia de Preliis*, MS. Br. 4 (Breslau Town Lib.); quoted by Hilka, *Altfranzösischer Prosa-Alexanderroman*, p. xxxi: '. . . et nominauit illum locum Alexander in Bactria et fecit scribere ad portam: Hic inclusit Alexander duas gentes immundas, scilicet Gogh et Machgogh. Quos tamen Antichristus inde reducet et eos habebit comites secum euntes. Contra quos uenientes Elias et Enoch predicabunt de fide Christi. Ipsi uero interficient eos, magnam hic stragem facientes hominum.'

Lucidarius, ed. F. Heidlauf, *Deutsche Texte des Mitt.* XXVIII (Berlin, 1915), p. 11.

52 On the story of the Ten Tribes and its origins, see F. Pfister in *Rhein. Mus.* LXVI (1911), pp. 464 f.; on its confusion with the story of Gog and Magog, A. R. Anderson, *Alexander's Gate, Gog and Magog, and the Enclosed Nations (Medieval Academy of America Publications*, no. XII, Cambridge, Mass., 1932), pp. 70–86.

For typical medieval references cf.:

(a) Peter Comestor, *Historia Scholastica* (Migne, *P.L.* vol. CXCVIII, col. 1498 A).

(b) Giraldus Cambrensis, *Descriptio Kambriae* I, xvi (*Opera*, vol. VI, ed. Dimock, p. 199).

(c) *Das Zeitbuch d. Eike v. Repgow* (ed. H. G. Massmann, *B.L.V.* vol. XLII (Stuttgart, 1857), pp. 68–9).

(d) Godfrey of Viterbo, *Pantheon*, parts X, XI (ed. Pistorius, *Rer. Germ. Scriptores*, II (1613), p. 155, cols. 1–2, p. 165, col. 2).

(e) *Sächsische Weltchronik*, s. XIII, in *M.G.H. Deutsche Chroniken*, II (Hanover, 1877), p. 78.

(f) *Seelentrost* and derivatives, ed. A. J. Barnouw, in *Germanic Review*, IV (1929), pp. 287–8.

(g) Bishop Antoninus of Florence, *Chronica* IV, i, 10 (ed. P. Mauturus (Lyons, 1586), pp. 117–18).

It also appears frequently in chronicles: e.g. in Matthew Paris, Romuald of Salerno, Vincent de Beauvais, Ranulph Higden, Jakob Twinger von Koenigshofen and the *Histoire ancienne jusqu'à César*. These later accounts are derived, almost without exception, from that in the *Historia Scholastica*.

53 The principal attempts at symbolic interpretation of this subject are:

(a) J. Durand, 'La légende d'Alexandre le Grand', *Annales Archéologiques*, XXV (1865), pp. 141 ff.

(b) A. L. Meissner, 'Bildliche Darstellungen der Alexandersage in Kirchen des Mittelalters', *Archiv für das Studium der neueren Sprachen*, LXVIII (1882), pp. 177–90.

(c) R. S. Loomis, 'Alexander the Great's Celestial Journey', *Burlington Magazine*, XXXII (1918), pp. 177 ff.

(d) G. Boffito, 'La Leggenda Aviatoria di Alessandro Magno', *Bibliofilia*, XXII (1920), pp. 316–30 and XXIII (1921–2), pp. 22–32.

(e) E. Jamison, 'Notes on Santa Maria della Strada at Matrice', *Papers of the British School at Rome*, XIV (1938), pp. 67–9.

54 *Dialogus Creaturarum*, dial. 102: De bubalo caligario (ed. Grässe, *B.L.V.* vol. CXLVIII (Tübingen, 1880), p. 252).

Gesta Romanorum, c. 183 (ed. Oesterly, p. 589).

For uses of this version in books of semi-exemplar type, see above, pp. 84–5.

55 *Bocados de Oro*, ed. H. Knust, *Mittheilungen aus dem Eskurial*, *B.L.V.* vol. CXLI (Tübingen, 1879), p. 144.

A similar abbreviated version of the exemplar story appears in:

Dialogus Creaturarum, dial. 14: 'de smaragdo et annulo' (ed. Grässe), p. 152.

W. Burley, *De Vita ac Moribus Philosophorum*, ed. H. Knust, *B.L.V.* vol. CLXXVII (Tübingen, 1886), p. 204. For ancient and Oriental versions of the story see Knust's note on the *Bocados de Oro* version (ibid. p. 144).

56 *Gesta Romanorum*, c. 61 (ed. Oesterly, pp. 368–70).

From this is derived the version in the *Middle Dutch* and *Middle Low German Alexander* (ed. A. J. Barnouw, *Germanic Review*, IV (1929), pp. 302–3).

For the use of the episode in the *Confessio Amantis* of John Gower, see below, pp. 353–4.

57 E. Ph. Goldschmidt, *Mediaeval Texts and their First Appearance in Print* (Bibliographical Society, 1943), pp. 93 ff.; a discussion of the unconscious methods by which a work might become attributed to the wrong author.

There is an interesting group of passages in the *Speculum Morale*, two concerned with the exemplar story of Diogenes, and one with that of Alexander's encounter with Dindimus in the *De Moribus Bragmanorum* attributed to St Ambrose; compared with one another, they well demonstrate the extreme similarity between the two stories and between the legendary characters of Diogenes and Dindimus. These passages are as follows:

I, iii, 97 (ed. Douai, 1624, col. 524): Alexander's messengers find a naked philosopher contemplating the nature of things, seated by a fountain in a wood. He says he is the lord of their lord, and explains his remark. Alexander does not appear, nor is Diogenes called by name.

This is followed by an extract from the *Collatio* where Dindimus calls Alexander a slave to his desires.

I, iii, 104 (ibid. cols. 569–70): The Brahmans and their manner of life and Alexander's interview with the Gymnosophists (Dindimus is represented as asking the questions normally ascribed to the Gymnosophists). This is followed by an extract from the *De Moribus Bragmanorum*. Alexander's men find Dindimus in a wood by a fountain and ask him to come to Alexander; he refuses and says he does not fear any punishment that Alexander may exact. Alexander then comes to Dindimus in person and is rewarded by a lecture on continence.

III, iii, 9 (ibid. col. 1030): Alexander's messengers find a naked philosopher by a fountain in a wood; his only belongings are a cup to drink water, and a tub. When it rained he would turn the tub upside down. When he sees the messengers drink water with their cupped hands he throws the cup at them. They run towards him in his tub and he asks them not to take away what they cannot give him—the sunlight. They ask him why he threw away the cup; he explains that he has now learnt that Nature provides a cup in one's cupped palms. They say they are messengers of the lord Alexander, and he says he is lord of their lord. They bring him to Alexander and he proves his statement. There is no mention of Alexander's subsequent treatment of the philosopher who is again not mentioned by name. The story of the cup is told again expressly of Diogenes (ibid. col. 569).

58 The episode, with Alexander's answer suppressed, is given as follows:

(a) Jacques de Vitry, *Historia Hierosol*. I, ii (in *Gesta Dei per Francos* (Hanover, 1611), p. 1108).

(b) Humbert de Romans, in *Maxima Bibliotheca Veterum Patrum* (Lyons, 1677), xxv, p. 566, col. 1: '*Exemplum de Alexandro*: Ideo Bragmani Alexandro qui mandauerat eis ut peterent ab eo, quid uellent, et ipsis petentibus immortalitatem, quam summe optabant, et Alexandro respondente "Ego mortalis cum sim, quomodo uobis immortalitatem dare possum?" bene responderunt dicentes: "Tu mortalis cum sis, quare tot mala faciendo discurris?" quasi dicere deberent: "Recogitatio mortis te deberet facere cessare a malis".'

(c) *Speculum Laicorum*, c. lii (*De Mortis Memoria*), no. 394 (ed. J. Welter (Paris, 1914), p. 77).

(d) *Alphabet of Tales*, no. DXIV (ed. M. M. Banks, E.E.T.S., O.S., CXXVI–CXXVII (1904–5), p. 348–9).

(e) John Bromyard, *Spec. Praed.*, Mors (M xi), art. xv, 86 (ed. Nürnberg, 1518, f. ccxxiii^v, col. 1).

(f) John Capgrave, *Guide to Rome* (ed. Rev. F. C. Hingeston, Rolls Series (1858), p. 362).

The author of the *Prague Epitome* merely adds a marginal *Nota* (ed. F. P. Magoun, *Harvard Studies and Notes in Philology and Literature*, XVI (1934), p. 137).

For further references see *Speculum Laicorum*, ed. J. Th. Welter (Paris, 1914), p. 141 (note on no. 394).

59 The Scythians episode occurs in Quintus Curtius VII, viii, 8 ff. Alexander there replies to the Scythians (VII, ix, 1): 'Contra rex fortuna sua et consiliis eorum se usurum esse respondet; nam et fortunam, cui confidat, et consilium suadentium, ne quid temere aut audacter faciat, secuturum.'

It is mistakenly ascribed by Jacobus de Cessolis to Valerius Maximus. See S. Dosson, *Etude sur Quinte-Curce* (Paris, 1887), p. 369, and Jacobus de Cessolis, *De Ludo Scacchorum* (ed. F. Vetter, *Das Schachzabelbuch Kunrats von Ammenhausen* (Frauenfeld, 1892), cols. 61–4).

For its use in the *Alexandreis* of Gautier de Châtillon, see above, p. 173. Other examples of its use, in all of which Alexander's answer is suppressed, are:

(*a*) *Dialogus Creaturarum*, dial. 1, De sole et luna; dial. 82, De bubone qui uoluit habere dominium alitum (ed. Grässe, pp. 139, 228–9).

(*b*) *Alphabet of Tales*, no. XLIX, Ambiciosi reprimendi sunt a sapientibus. (ed. Banks, p. 33). The Scythians have here been transformed into 'one of the prophets'.

(*c*) Walter Burley, *De Vita ac Moribus Philosophorum*, ed. Knust, pp. 278–80.

(*d*) Fr. Johannes Ferrariensis, in R.I.S. xx, ii (Bologna, n.d.), p. 45, ll. 35–8.

(*e*) A possible reference of the 'quidam philosophus' type to the episode is in *Speculum Laicorum*, c. VI ('De amore mundi et eius fallaciis'), no. 39, i (ed. Welter, p. 11: 'Refert Quintus Curcius: De quodam philosopho et Alexandro.'

60 W. Hertz, *Gesammelte Abhandlungen* (Stuttgart and Berlin, 1905), p. 115: 'Die Prediger scheinen übrigens von dieser Geschichte wenig Gebrauch gemacht zu haben. Sie war ihnen offenbar zu fein. Wenn sie in den Exempelsammlungen das Stichwort *Mors* aufschlugen, suchten sie stärkere Schreckmittel.' And he quotes only the instance in John Bromyard.

61 References to the Wonderstone story in books of *exempla* are as follows:

(*a*) *Tabula Exemplorum*, ex. 185 (s.v. Mors) (ed. J. Th. Welter (Paris, 1926), p. 51): Alexander comes to a city, and is honourably received; the wise citizens give him a beautiful stone of great powers, worth a magnificent treasure. But if a little dust is placed upon it it loses all its power. Alexander asks the citizens the meaning of this phenomenon; they say that he resembles the stone: 'quia tum [l. cum] uiuebat erat pulcher, potens et ualens, sed quando super se habuerit modicum de terra et post mortem et sepulturam omnia simpliciter amitteret.

Versus: Forma, genus, mores, sapiencia, sensus, honores,
      Morte ruunt subita, sola manent merita.'

(*b*) *Speculum Laicorum*, c. XLI ('de humilitate et eius effectibus'), no. 315 (ed. Welter, p. 65): 'Legitur in gestis Alexandri Magni: De lapide quodam diuersi ponderis Alexandro dato.'

The heading, and the reference to the 'Gesta Alexandri', make it possible that the *Iter ad Paradisum*, incorporated in a manuscript of legendary texts, is here intended, with its moral of humility and self-restraint.

C. LII ('De mortis memoria', no. 390 (ibid. p. 76)): the same. Here the heading makes it probable that the anecdote has reverted to the usual exemplar interpretation.

(*c*) *Tractatus de Diuersis Historiis Romanorum*, c. XLII ('Qui potentes et nobiles se credunt') (ed. S. Herzstein, *Erlanger Beiträge zur engl. Philol.* XIV (Erlangen, 1893), p. 18): 'Cum Allexander nauigaret per quendam fluuium paradisi, ut ueniret ad ortum eius, quidam senex apparens de rupe ei suasit regressum deditque ei lapidem preciosum dicens ei, quod in eius pondere congnosceret ualorem suum. Lapis ergo ille positus in statera omnia preponderabat, quecunque in alia lance ponerentur; coopertus puluere nichil ponderabat, sed ei una festuca preponderabat.

In hoc dabatur intelligi, quod uiuus omnibus aliis preponderabat, mortuus autem nichil.'

(d) *Eulogium historiarum*, c. CXXVI (ed. F. S. Haydon, Rolls Series, I (1858), p. 434; here included because it contains an exemplar version of the Wonderstone story): 'Ferunt historiae nonnullae quod cum satellites Alexandri abdita Indiae loca perlustrassent, affuit quidam ambitionem Alexandri uehementer redarguens, qui lapidem modicum et oculatum illis tradidit, domino suo proferendum: asserens procul dubio dominum eorum Alexandrum illi lapidi per omnia fore simillimum. Relato lapide, haesitatum est diu quorsum congrueret similitudo praetaxata. Tandem illi ponderositatem parui lapidis mirantes in statera positus est; tamdiu omnia sibi applicata pondere suo eleuauit, donec modica argilla obuolutus leui libramine resultaret. Simili modo Alexandro regnante per omnia, par in mundo sibi non coaequatur; ipso mortuo, pauperem habet parem.'

(e) *Alphabet of Tales*, no. DXVI (*Mors*) (ed. Banks, pp. 349–50): 'Mors hominem quantumcumque adnichilat.'

(f) John Bromyard, *Spec. Praed.*, Mors (M xi), art. xviii, 121 (ed. Nürnberg, 1518, f. ccxxviii^r, col. 1): here also the stone is sent to Alexander.

For further references in books of *exempla*, see Welter's notes to the passages cited from the *Tabula Exemplorum* and the *Speculum Laicorum*; these notes are suspect, however, because of Welter's confusion between the story of the Wonderstone and that of the stone sent to Nero by Evax. In fact it was not a stone but a book on the properties of stones that formed the present of Evax to Nero.

For further comments upon the influence of the *Iter ad Paradisum* and the story of the Wonderstone, see p. 347.

62 Other references to this episode, mostly derived from Petrus Alfonsi, are these:

(a) *Dialogus Creaturarum*, dial. 122 (ed. Grässe, p. 279): 'recitat Alfonsus in tractatu suo de prudentia...' (also referred to: Dial. 1, De sole et luna, p. 139).

(b) Johannes Gualensis or Vallensis, *Summa de regimine uitae humanae. Breuiloquium* II, v: De Prouidentia (cited by H. Knust in *B.L.V.* vol. CXLI, pp. 556–7).

(c) *Tabula Exemplorum*, ex. 182 (s.v. Mors) (ed. Welter, p. 50).

(d) *Speculum Laicorum*, cap. lii, De mortis memoria, ex. 391 (ed. Welter, p. 76).

(e) *Alphabet of Tales*, no. DXI (s.v. Mors) (ed. Banks, p. 347–8).

(f) Ulrich von Eschenbach, *Alexander*, vv. 27,233–27,525:

> Uns schrîbet Alphunsus,
> ein werder philosophus....

(g) John Bromyard, *Spec. Praed.*, Mors (M xi), art. xxiv, ex. 149 (ed. Nürnberg, 1518, f. ccxxxi^r, col. 1).

(h) *Gesta Romanorum*, c. 31 (ed. Oesterly, pp. 329–30). From this is directly derived the version in the *Middle Dutch* and *Middle Low German Alexander*, ed. A. J. Barnouw, *Germanic Review*, IV (1929), pp. 395–6.

(i) *Fior di Virtù*, c. VI (ed. B. Fabbricatore, 3rd ed., Napoli (1870), pp. 34–5); on this version, not from Alfonsi, see below, p. 348.

63 Seneca, *Ep. ad Luc.* VI, vii (59), 12 (flattery makes a man think himself perfect): 'Alexander cum iam in India uagaretur et gentes ne finitimis quidem satis notas bello uastaret, in obsidione cuiusdam urbis, dum circumit muros et inbecillissima moenium quaerit, sagitta ictus diu persedere et incepta agere perseuerauit. Deinde cum represso sanguine sicci uulneris dolor cresceret et crus suspensum equo paulatim obtorpuisset, coactus apsistere "Omnes", inquit, "iurant esse me Iouis filium, sed uulnus hoc hominem esse me clamat." Idem nos faciamus. Pro sua quemque portione adulatio infatuat.'

S. Dosson (*Etude sur Quinte-Curce* (Paris, 1887), pp. 31 f.) quotes the versions of the story in Curtius VIII, x, 27 ff., and in Seneca as above, and reaches the conclusion that Seneca borrowed the anecdote from Curtius. Curtius' wording of Alexander's remark is slightly different: '... dixisse fertur se quidem Iouis filium dici, sed corporis aegri uitia sentire.' It is evident from the wording of the medieval citations of the anecdote that they are in all cases derived from Seneca.

64 E.g. *Tractatus de diuersis historiis Romanorum*, c. 6 (ed. S. Herzstein, *Erlanger Beit. z. engl. Philol.* XIV (Erlangen, 1893), pp. 3–4): De liberalitate Allexandri.

Fior di Virtù, cap. XI (ed. B. Fabbricatore, 3rd ed. (Napoli, 1870), p. 50): Della liberalità si legge in Alessandro....

For a discussion of this use of the episode, and of various uses of it in secular literature, see Appendix II, below, pp. 360–1.

65 The following details of the stories are taken from Oesterly's edition. I have indicated in the case of each story how frequently it appears in the 138 manuscripts listed by Oesterly (pp. 9–241); I have also indicated whether it appears in the following works: Sidney J. H. Herrtage, *Gesta Romanorum; early English version*, E.E.T.S., E.S. XXXIII, 1879 (indicated by 'E.E.'); W. Dick, *Die Gesta Romanorum nach der Innsbrucker Handschrift vom Jahre 1342 und vier Münchener Handschriften hrsg. von Wilhelm Dick (Erlanger Beit. z. Engl. Phil.* VII, Erlangen, 1890) (indicated by 'Dick'). The numbers assigned to the stories, and the page numbers, are from Oesterly's edition.

c. 11 (p. 288): Alexander and the poison girl. Aristotle advises against contact with her, and a malefactor is ordered to touch her; when he does so, he dies immediately. Alexander is the Christian firm in his faith so long as he resists the flesh and the devil. The Queen of the North, who sends the poison girl to him, signifies abundance of worldly goods; the girl is lechery and gluttony; Aristotle is conscience; the malefactor is the perverse man who does not obey the will of God.

PART B. THE MEDIEVAL CONCEPTION OF ALEXANDER

SOURCE. *Secret of Secrets*; for further details see above, p. 231, n. 5.

FREQUENCY. In 18 MSS. of Oesterly, Dick (p. 10), E.E. (p. 340).

c. 31 (p. 329–30): The story of the philosophers at Alexander's tomb bemoaning his fate. Alexander is the rich man of this world, the man who is overcovetous and can never be sated; the soul of such a man goes to hell.

SOURCE. Petrus Alfonsi, *Disciplina Clericalis*; see above, pp. 151–2.

FREQUENCY. In 47 MSS. of Oesterly, Dick (p. 44).

c. 34 (pp. 331–4): 'Legitur de rege Alexandro, qui habebat Aristotelem magistrum, de cuius doctrina multum profecit et multas uirtutes ab eo didicit.' The seven rules of conduct given by Aristotle at Alexander's request: 'Rex in istis septem miro modo studebat et sic profecit quamdiu uixit.'

SOURCE. *Secret of Secrets*.

FREQUENCY. In 18 MSS. of Oesterly, Dick (pp. 47–8).

c. 61 (pp. 368–70): Socrates and his wife; she falls ill and Socrates weeps. Alexander, out hunting, meets Socrates who says to him that he is the servant of his servant. The exemplar Diogenes anecdote then follows as usual. 'Ab illa die cepit rex regnum suum racione gubernare et non uoluntate.' Alexander is the man ruled by will rather than reason but who may be set right by holy instruction.

SOURCE. See above, pp. 146–7.

FREQUENCY. In 10 MSS. of Oesterly, Dick (pp. 124f.).

c. 139 (pp. 493–4): Alexander and the basilisk, which he kills, by the advice of a philosopher, by holding a mirror against it. The mirror is the consideration of one's own infirmity.

SOURCE. On the sources of this episode, and its interpolation into the I³ *Historia de Preliis*, see Pfister, *Münchener Museum*, I (1912), pp. 263–5.

FREQUENCY. In 51 MSS. of Oesterly, Dick (p. 20), E.E. (pp. 240–1).

c. 146 (pp. 504–5): Alexander and the pirate; the exemplar version of the story. The pirate is the sinner; Alexander the prince or the prelate who is to lead him back to righteousness. But let the prince or prelate first be sure that he himself is not worse than the man he is trying to correct.

SOURCE. See above, pp. 95–8.

FREQUENCY. In 1 MS. of Oesterly, Dick (p. 69).

c. 183 (p. 589): Alexander and Diogenes; literary version. Diogenes is any mortal; the tub is our life; the sun is Christ; Alexander is the devil who shows us the vanities of the world.

SOURCE. See above, pp. 83–5.

FREQUENCY. In 42 MSS. of Oesterly, Dick (p. 46).

c. 184 (p. 589–90): The story, from Valerius Maximus, of the boy who holds a burning coal in his hand when assisting with Alexander at a sacrifice. Alexander is Christ; the boy is any of us; the burning coal is the fire of the devil's temptation.

SOURCE. Valerius Maximus III, iii, ext. 1; see for a similar allegorical use *Prague Epitome*, ed. Magoun, pp. 129–30.

FREQUENCY. In 3 MSS. of Oesterly.

c. 198 (pp. 610–11): Alexander goes to the palace of Porus disguised as a simple soldier, and takes his gold cups as they are feasting. Alexander is Christ as Man; the palace is the world, Porus is the devil, the gold cups are the saints born before the incarnation of Christ.

SOURCE. For this story, see below, pp. 364–5.

FREQUENCY. In 35 MSS. of Oesterly.

For independent references to these stories, especially of the ancient and post-medieval periods, see Oesterly's notes. For the popularity of the *Gesta Romanorum* in the fifteenth and sixteenth centuries, with a list of early printed editions, see E. P. Goldschmidt, *Mediaeval Texts and their First Appearance in Print*, pp. 9–10.

66 *Alphabet of Tales*, no. DCCXXXVII (ed. Banks, pp. 492–3). This citation is interesting because it contains the singular detail that Alexander was poisoned by his sister. This, first occurring in Peter Comestor, *Historia Scholastica*, lib. Esther, c. IV (Migne, *P.L.* vol. CXCVIII, col. 1498A: 'et ita factum est a sorore'), passed thence into various accounts. Besides the *Alphabet of Tales*, it is to be found in Bishop Antoninus of Florence, *Chronica* IV, i, 15 (ed. P. Mauturus (Lyons, 1586), p. 121: 'Comestor dicit ei uenenum propinatum a sorore sua'), in *History-Bible* I (*Do Got in Siner Magenkraft*, ed. J. F. L. Th. Merzdorf, *B.L.V.* vols. C–CI (Tübingen, 1870), p. 552), and in Ulrich von Eschenbach, *Alexander*, vv. 27,541–8.

On this last passage see W. Toischer in *Sitzungsber. d. kaiserl. Akad. d. Wissen. in Wien*, Bd. XCVII (1881 for 1880), p. 397; Ulrich refers to his source as the 'heilige Mann Josaphat', which Toischer cannot explain; could this be an intended reference to Josephus who is the principal source of Peter Comestor's account?

The source of this strange tradition is unknown.

67 Malachi, *Venenum Malachie* (Paris, Henri Estienne, 1518), f. 23ʳ (*Venenum luxuriae*): 'Et hoc est quod dicit Aristoteles in Epistola ad Alexandrum...' against cohabitation, and 'making men into women'.

F. 24ᵛ (Ibid.): Alexander and the poison girl.

68 *Dialogus Creaturarum*, dial. 40: De quinque dentalibus et piscatore (ed. Grässe, p. 182): 'Et propter hoc Alexander obtinuit uictoriam, qui consilio gubernauit exercitum.'

Alphabet of Tales, no. CIV: Bellantes debent esse cauti et experti (ed. Banks, p. 76).

69 *Speculum Laicorum*, c. XXX, no. 230: De ecclesia (ed. Welter, p. 49): 'Refert magister historiarum: De Alexandro Magno Jerosolymam intrante et summum sacerdotem adorante.'

Welter mentions in his notes a parallel *exemplum* in Etienne de Bourbon.

70 See below, p. 349. For the sake of completeness, it may be added that the anecdote of Alexander's tutor Leonides, who imparted to him a defect in his gait, first told in St Jerome among Christian writers (see above, p. 288), was fairly frequently used in *exempla*: e.g. in the *Speculum Laicorum*, c. XVII, no. 110; c. LXXXI, no. 541 (ed. Welter, pp. 24, 105).

See for further references Welter's note *ad loc.*

71 The murder of Nectanebus in Pseudo-Callisthenes, where Alexander pushes him over a precipice, was originally derived from a humorous story of a star-gazer; see Otto Weinrich, *Der Trug des Nektanebos* (Leipzig and Berlin, 1911), and A. Haggerty Krappe, 'Tiberius and Thrasyllus', *American Journal of Philology*, XLVIII (1927), pp. 359–66.

See below, p. 305, n. 75, for Lamprecht's comments upon Alexander's ferocity at the siege of Tyre.

Alexander's breaking of his word, in the trick used to discover the murderers of Darius, was unnoticed by medieval writers (Julius Valerius II, 36–7, ed. Kuebler, pp. 177–80).

72 For the early versions of the conversation with the Gymnosophists, see U. Wilcken, 'Alexander der Grosse und die indischen Gymnosophisten', *Sitzungsber. d. Preuss. Akad. d. Wissen.*, Phil.-Hist. Klasse (1923), pp. 150–83, and W. W. Tarn, *Alexander the Great*, II (Cambridge, 1948), pp. 363 and 437.

For the version of the conversation in Pseudo-Callisthenes, see Ausfeld, *Griechischer Alexanderroman*, pp. 88–9; thence the conversation passed into the Syriac and Armenian versions, and Julius Valerius III, 10–13 (ed. Kübler, pp. 120–23); and from there into the *Oxford-Montpellier Epitome* (ed. A. Hilka, *Romanische Forschungen*, XXIX (1911), pp. 60–1).

For the version in the *Historia de Preliis*, in which most of the conversation is omitted, see ed. Pfister, *Alexanderroman*, pp. 106–7, and Pfister's note *ad loc.*

For exemplar versions of the story see above, p. 148.

The story is used in the English fragment *Alexander B* to supply a supposed gap in the *Roman d'Alexandre*; see above, p. 49.

73 Such admonitions against pride bear not the slightest relationship to the spirit of the text, where Alexander is shown to be the reverse of proud. For instance, his reply to the second letter of Darius when he says that his god is against the proud, and his reply to the Persian request for his deification, which he refuses—'dubito enim sociare me diis'. Such incompatibility has two contributory causes: first, the tendency which we have noticed for moral judgements to bear little relation to the story; and second, because judgements of Alexander, and especially those expressed in the epilogues, consider, not the question of his personal pride, but the fact of his personal power, and are thus primarily of exemplar intention. For a further discussion of such epilogue judgements, see pp. 189–95.

74 *Vorau Alexander*, vv. 61–70; copied, and slightly expanded, in *Strassburg A*, vv. 65–82, ed. K. Kinzel, *Lamprechts Alexander*, Germanische Handbibliothek, VI (Halle, 1885), pp. 30–1. Vorau text:

Diser rede wil ich mich irvaren.
Salemon der was ûz getân,
der sich ûz allen kunegen nam.
dô diu frowe regina austri zû im kom,
unde si sînen hof gesach,
mit rehter wârheit si sprah,
daz von mannes geburte
nî sô frumer kunic wurte.
man mûste in wol ûz sceiden,
wande Alexander was ein heiden.

75 Alexander's war against Tyre was unjustified (*Vorau*, v. 952); he should not have destroyed so fine a city (vv. 713–26). See further *Vorau*, vv. 1001–8 (ed. Kinzel, pp. 116, 86–8 and 120–2).
For further details of Lamprecht's hostile attitude see Grammel, pp. 27–39. Dr Grammel, however, does not provide a sufficient picture of the nature of the source material used by Lamprecht, and gives no details at all of the fundamental theological attitude to Alexander which she deduced only from the vernacular German works of Lamprecht and Berthold v. Regensburg. The theological texts studied above have hitherto always been ignored.

76 *Alexandreis* III, vv. 241 ff. (Migne, *P.L.* vol. CCIX, col. 491):

Tantus enim uirtutis amor tunc temporis illi
pectore regnabat, si perdurasset in illo
ille tenor, non est quo denigrare ualeret
crimine candentem titulis infamia famam,
uerum ubi regales, Persarum rebus adeptis,
deliciae posuere modum, suasitque licere
illicitum et licitum, genitrix opulentia luxus,
corripuit fortuna physin, cursuque retorto
substitit unda prior, uitiorum cautibus haerens.
Qui prius ergo pius erat hostibus, hostis amicis,
impius in caedes et bella domestica, demum
conuersus, ratus illicitum nil esse tyranno.

77 For the suppression of details in Quintus Curtius unfavourable to Alexander, see H. Christensen, *Das Alexanderlied Walters von Châtillon* (Halle, 1905), pp. 108–9.
Cf. especially Gautier's brief dismissal of the murders of Cleitus, Hermolaus and Callisthenes in *Alexandreis* IX, vv. 3 ff. (Migne, *P.L.* vol. CCIX, col. 551):

...quam (i.e. Indiam) dum petit ille deorum
aemulus in terris, Clitus, Hermolaus, et eius
doctor (Aristoteli praeter quem nemo secundus)

extremum clausere diem, documenta futuris
certa relinquentes; etenim testatur eorum
finis amicitias regum non esse perennes.

For medieval treatment of the murder of Callisthenes, see above, pp. 110–16.

78 The question is discussed by Hilka, *Altfranzösischer Prosa-Alexanderroman*, p. vii. Compare his comment on the passage (p. xii): 'hier die merkwürdige Angabe, dass Alexander auch geizig war, was in Widerspruch zu seinem sonstigen Charakterbild in diesem Roman steht'.

References to Alexander's liberality are as follows:

(p. 46): Philip portrayed as the type of a covetous king, 'um dadurch Alexanders vielgerühmte "largece" in desto helleres Licht zu rücken' (p. ix).

Praise of Alexander's largesse by the messenger of the Queen of the Amazons; see Hilka, p. 159.

(pp. 243–4): Aristotle warns Alexander in a letter to reward every man who has served under him: 'car il n'en est nulle choze qui tant soit contre nature comme services qui n'est guerredonnés et espandement de sanc qui n'est amendés.'

79 In the *Iter ad Paradisum* passage of the *Strassburg Alexander*, Grammel (pp. 53–6) saw a return on the part of the author to what she calls the Cluniac spirit, expressed best in Germany by the attitude to Alexander in the *Vorau Alexander*.

The truth is that the redactor of the *Strassburg Alexander* has done no more than reproduce the story of the Latin *Iter*, the story of a good man, favoured by God, who fails only in one particular, his ambitious cupidity. Although the redactor gives his own comment upon the material thus presented, it is a comment upon the Alexander of this individual episode, and Alexander is later represented as converted to humility and ending his days in virtue. The Jewish Alexander has been attached to the historical Alexander; the redactor lacks the imagination to alter the Alexander portrait in his source material, and accepts both his presumption and his conversion.

80 In the *Basel*, as in the *Strassburg Alexander*, the contradiction of a favourable conception of Alexander by the *Iter* is inevitable; but in the *Basel* version he is not converted by the homily of his adviser to humility and self-restraint, as in the earlier poem; he continues his adventures and explores the skies and the depths of the sea.

Here again it is textual tradition that has changed the atmosphere of the poem. The addition, by the redactor of the *Basel Alexander*, of wonder material subsequent to the *Iter* has made it necessary to dispense with that quiet conversion, that living in peace which occupied the last years of his life in the conclusion of the Latin work. Since he has still to ascend the heavens and descend into the sea he must pursue his old path of adventure undeterred by the warning of the Wonderstone. But the ambition that remains with him to the end of his life has been made secular; it is not a sin but a glory.

See, for a fuller description of the *Basel Alexander* portrait of Alexander, Grammel, pp. 56–61, who again has not indicated that the change in the conception of Alexander rests in great part upon the changed arrangement of the textual material.

81 For the constant connexion of the life of Alexander with his Biblical role in German writers, cf. the following examples:

(*a*) The life of Alexander in Rhabanus Maurus, *Commentaria in libros Machabaeorum*, I, i (Migne, *P.L.* vol. CIX, cols. 1127–32).

(*b*) In the *Annolied* and the *Kaiserchronik* Alexander is first introduced as the founder of Daniel's third world-kingdom; see p. 321.

(*c*) The life of Alexander in Rupert of Deutz, *De Victoria Verbi Dei* VIII, xxviii–IX, xiv (Migne, *P.L.* vol. CLXIX, cols. 1397–1410); see above, pp. 137–40.

(*d*) The position of the *Vorau Alexander* in its manuscript (Grammel, p. 28): 'Der Redaktor hat die Gedichte seiner Handschrift in der Art einer christlichen Weltgeschichte geordnet, und der Alexander steht zwischen den Gedichten alttestamentarischen und neutestamentarischen Inhalts.'

(*e*) The references to Biblical passages in the *Vorau Alexander* and its derivatives, in Rudolf von Ems, and in Ulrich von Eschenbach.

(*f*) The effect of Alexander's Biblical role upon Rudolf von Ems' view of him; see pp. 205–6.

(*g*) The position or intended position of many lives of Alexander in the middle of world-chronicles: Ekkehart of Aura (see pp. 71–2); Otto of Freising (see p. 72); Jakob Twinger v. Königshofen (see pp. 342–3); Martinus Polonus (see p. 342); *Chronica Regia S. Pantaleonis* (ed. J. G. Eccardus, *Corp. Hist. Med. Aeu.* I (Leipzig, 1723), cols. 708 ff.); *Basel Alexander* (see Grammel, pp. 22–3); *Liegnitz Historia* (see Hilka, *Romanische Forschungen*, XXIX (1911), pp. 1–16); Enikel's *Weltchronik* (see below, pp. 346–7).

(*h*) The History-Bible accounts of Alexander: *Middle Low German Alexander* (see p. 346); *History-Bible* I (see p. 347).

(*i*) The *Prague Epitome* (see above, p. 45).

82 See for independent German references of this period derogatory to Alexander, Grammel, pp. 121–2; the most important are:

Heinrich von Beringen, *Schachgedicht*, vv. 308 ff. (a version of the Gymnosophists episode; also in Thomasin von Zirclaria, *Wälschen Gast*, vv. 3577 ff.).

Thomasin von Zirclaria, *Wälschen Gast*, v. 3433; Alexander is portrayed as distrustful.

See also below, pp. 330–1, for comments on the Candace episode.

83 For the connexion of the life of Alexander with the text of Maccabees, so typical of German treatment of Alexander (see above, n. 81), and cf. *Vorau Alexander* (ed. Kinzel, p. 26), vv. 7 ff.:

> Alexander was ein wîse man,
> vil manec rîche er gewan,

er zestôrte vil manec lant.
Philippus was sîn vater genant.
diz mugit ir wol hôren
in libro Machabeorum.

For the conclusion of the *Vorau Alexander*, where Darius falls by the hand of
Alexander, and its possible indebtedness to Maccabees, see Grammel, pp. 28–32,
and Alfred Foulet in *M.F.R.d'A.* III, p. 6, nn. 18–19.

For reference to the prophecy of Daniel, see vv. 473–8 (ed. Kinzel, p. 68);
for other references to the Bible in the *Vorau Alexander*, and the reasons why
they should be ascribed to Lamprecht rather than to Alberic, see A. Foulet,
op. cit. p. 5.

84 For references to a God in the mouth of Alexander and his followers, see
Vorau, v. 590.

Grammel remarks of the *Vorau Alexander* (p. 37): 'Die heidnischen Götter
werden hier noch gar nicht erwähnt. Im Laufe der Betrachtung der Alexander-
dichtungen werden wir gerade in dieser Hinsicht, in Bezug auf die Auffassung
der Heiden und ihrer Götter, eine grosse Wandlung wahrnehmen. Lamprecht
nimmt auch hier, wie es ihm zukommt, die typisch vorhöfische Haltung ein.'
It is extremely doubtful, however, if Lamprecht was responsible for this suppression. Alberic was jealous for Alexander's good reputation; he abused the
liars who had said he was the son of Nectanebus (see p. 236). How much more
likely would he be than the critical Lamprecht to suppress Alexander's heathen
characteristics.

85 *Roman d'Alexandre*, branch I, laisse I, vv. 27–9 (on the prodigies attending
Alexander's birth):

> Ce fu senefiance que Dieus fist esclarcir
> Por moustrer de l'enfant qu'en devoit avenir
> Et com grant seignorie il avroit a baillir.

86 For the elimination of divine influence, see especially the account of the
Celestial Journey where the sources represented Alexander as redirected to earth
by a beneficent Divine power:

(*Roman d'Alexandre*, branch III, laisse 280, vv. 5054–61):

> Li rois s'est porpensés, s'il perdent la volee,
> Il charra a la terre s'iert sa vie finee
> Et sa gent en sera dolente et esgaree,
> Car toutes gens le heent qui terre il a gastee.
> Il rabaisse sa lance, vers terre l'a clinee;
> li oisel famelleus la sieuent la volee,
> Jus s'asieent a terre en mi lieu de la pree;
> Li rois est la dedens, fait ot bone jornee.

For the Jerusalem episode see branch II, laisse III, vv. 2436–55.

87 Cf. *Roman d'Alexandre*, branch iv, laisse 67, vv. 1556–8.

> Se il fust crestïens, ainc tels rois ne fu nés,
> Si cortois ne si larges, si sages, si menbrés,
> Si cremus en bataille, ne d'armes redoutés.

Branch iv, laisse 74, v. 1679:

> Se il fust crestïens, onques ne fu teus ber.

88 Upon the confusion of pagan and Christian elements in the *Old French Prose Romance*, see Hilka, *Altfranzösischer Prosa-Alexanderroman* (Halle, 1920), pp. xii–xiii.

Interpolations by the French writer which have a bearing upon the question are as follows:

(*a*) The insertion of a long account of the prophecy of Daniel into the Jerusalem episode (pp. 68–9). This is, however, an addition of the second redactor. See D. J. A. Ross in *French Studies*, vi (1952), pp. 146–7.

(*b*) When Alexander hears from the speaking trees of his approaching death, he prays to God to have pity upon him (p. 246). Here 'Sire Dieus...' replaces 'Jupiter omnipotens...' in the Latin.

(*c*) Alexander's Will, mentioned in the text; this passage (pp. 252–3) is given on pp. 312–13.

89 For independent French references of this period, see pp. 322–3, 325–6.

It may be noticed here that the Jerusalem episode was interpolated from Peter Comestor into the *Histoire ancienne jusqu'à César* described by Meyer; see *A. le G.* ii, p. 345. The same work also contains the account of the enclosing of the Ten Tribes from the same source, with the usual comment: If God did so much for a pagan, what will he not do for his own if they trust him?

90 On the interjection of Christian prayers, etc., see Willis, *Relationship*, pp. 67–72; for Alexander's final prayers to God, cf. P stanzas 2562–4, 2595:

> Sere del Rey del çielo altamente rresçebido
> quando a mi aya tenersa por guarido
> sere en la su corte honrrado e servido
> todos me laudaran por que non fue vençido.

This forms part of Alexander's last speech (P stanzas 2587–97, corresponding to O stanzas 2458–68), a Christianized version of *Alexandreis* x, vv. 405–17 (Migne, *P.L.* vol. ccix, col. 571).

But in spite of the fact that Alexander is here made so Christian, the lament that Christendom has no such ruler as Alexander, in *Alexandreis* v, vv. 491–520 (Migne, *P.L.* vol. ccix, col. 518) is entirely omitted.

91 The comments on Alexander's death here cited are those which reproduce most simply the exemplar themes of the vanity of human affairs and the inexorability of death. They are divided into three groups; in the first there are included those independent references which conform to the popular formula

'Where is now Alexander?'; in the second, miscellaneous references to the vanity of human existence and the inexorability of death; and in the third I have briefly noticed the Alexander-books which place most emphasis upon the simple exemplar theme in their epilogues.

(i) *Where is now Alexander?*

(*a*) Herimannus Contractus, *Opusculum diuerso metro compositum*, vv. 767–70. (ed. E. Dummler, in *Zeitschrift f. deutsch. Altertum*, XIII (1867), p. 406):

> ubi Ninus, Arbaces, Cirus,
> ubi nunc Alexander ferus?
> Octauianus, Julius,
> clarusque noster Karolus?

(*b*) *La Vie de Saint Auban*, quoted by R. Ortiz in *Giornale Storico della Letteratura Italiana*, LXXXV (1925), p. 78:

> ù est Alexandres li prince alosé?

(*c*) *Les Fortunes et Adversitez de Jean Regnier* (ed. E. Droz, S.A.T.F., Paris, 1923, p. 179, vv. 29–30).

> Ou est Helene, la belle simple et quoye,
> Alexandrë et sa chevalerie,...?

(*d*) Pen try-out in the *Wernigerode MS.*, quoted in the edition by G. Guth, *Deutsche Texte des Mitt.* XIII (1908), p. vi:

> Vbi sampson uir fortissimus
> ubi salomon prudentissimus
> ubi alexander magnanimus
> aut ubi darius?

(*e*) Eustache Deschamps, *Balade* CCCXXX, v. 52; *Balade* CCCLXVIII, v. 3 (*Œuvres*, ed. Raynaud and Le Queux de Saint Hilaire, S.A.T.F., vol. III, Paris, 1882, pp. 35, 113).

(*f*) John Lydgate, *As a Mydsomer Rose* (*Minor Poems* II (Secular), ed. H. N. MacCracken, E.E.T.S., O.S. CXCII (1934), p. 783):

> And wher is Alisaundir that conqueryd al?

(ii) *Miscellaneous reflexions of exemplar type upon the death of Alexander in independent references*

(*a*) Alexander Neckham, *De Vita Monachorum* (*Minor Anglo-Latin Satirists*, ed. T. Wright, Rolls Series, vol. II (1872), p. 193):

> Magnus erat quidem, totoque potentior orbe,
> Nunc quem, sic mundus ceperat, urna capit.
> Sic et Alexander fortissimus ille Macedo,
> Clauditur angusto puluis et ossa loco.

(*b*) Nicholas Bozon, *Contes Moralisés* (ed. L. Toulmin Smith and P. Meyer, S.A.T.F., Paris (1889), p. 44).

(c) *Exemplum*, in J. Klapper, *Exempla aus Hss. des Mitt. (Sammlung mittellat. Texte*, II, Heidelberg, 1911), *exemplum* 2, pp. 7–8: 'De Alexandro Magno.' This *exemplum* consists merely of a short account of Alexander's life, ending with the edifying reflexion which is evidently the reason for the biographical account: 'Sic perit gloria mundi. O quam breui tempore durauit gloria eorum!'

(d) Federico Frezzi, *Quadriregio* II, xix, vv. 145 f. (ed. E. Filippini, *Scrittori d'Italia*, Bari, 1914, p. 192).

(e) Cino da Pistoia, *Rime dubbie* II, vv. 25–7 (*Rimatori del dolce stil nuovo*, ed. G. di Benedetto, *Scrittori d'Italia*, Bari, 1939, p. 221).

(f) Franco Sacchetti, *Libro delle Rime* CLXIX, vv. 28–30; CLXXV, vv. 52–6; CCXX, vv. 19–30 (ed. G. Chiari, *Scrittori d'Italia*, Bari, 1936, vol. II, pp. 172, 187, 261).

(g) John Gower, *In Praise of Peace*, vv. 281–7 (*English Works*, ed. G. C. Macaulay, vol. II, E.E.T.S., E.S. LXXXII, 1901, p. 489): The Nine Worthies have passed away; all is vanity.

(h) John Lydgate, *A Thoroughfare of Woe* (*Minor Poems*, II (Secular Poems), ed. H. N. MacCracken, E.E.T.S., O.S. CXCII (1934), p. 824): The best things pass; be content with your lot:

> What myght the conquest of Alysaundre availe?

(i) *Anglo-Norman Life of S. Modwenna*, stanzas 178–9, vv. 709 ff. (*Anglo-Norman Text Society*, vol. VII, ed. A. T. Baker and A. Bell (Oxford, 1947), p. 26):

> Alisandre le cunquerant
> Ne li autre rei poant
> Pur ren, qu'il usent en lur vivant,
> De mort ne poent aver garant.
> Sanz repeir s'en sunt alé;
> De quanque il orent conquesté,
> Oveoc els n'unt ren porté
> Fors lur bien e lur peché.

(iii) *References in Alexander-books*

It may be said that in every Alexander-book the simple exemplar theme is overlaid by other considerations to be discussed later. Here we will note only the texts and groups of texts in which the exemplar theme is most prominent in the epilogue material:

(a) I³ *Historia de Preliis* and Quilichinus of Spoleto; see Pfister, *Münchener Museum*, I (1912), pp. 271–8, 296–300.

(b) Otto of Freising, *Chronica*, ed. A. Hofmeister (Hanover and Leipzig, 1912), p. 98: 'O mortalium conditio, o mentes miseras et cecas! Nonne iste est Alexander, qui Persarum nobile ac superbum imperium destruxit et ad Macedonas transtulit? Numquid ipse non est, quem totus orbis tremens etiam non uisum expectare non ausus ultro se seruituti dedit? Et tamen tantus talisque unius potus poculo, unius ministri insidiis extinguitur, unius morte totus mundus concutitur. Regni Macedonum monarchia, quae ab ipso cepit, ipso mortuo cum ipso finitur. Nos uero hoc non adtendimus, qui mundum diligimus, qui ipsi tanquam aeternae rei ac permanenti inherere uolumus. Cadimus cum cadente, labimur cum labente, uoluimur cum rotante, postremo perimus cum pereunte.'

But the Church of Christ is founded on a firm rock; we must build our faith in Christ.

(c) *Strassburg Alexander*, vv. 7279–302 (ed. Kinzel, pp. 384–5); see above p. 177.

(d) Gautier de Châtillon, *Alexandreis* (Migne, *P.L.* vol. CCIX, col. 572):

> O felix mortale genus, si semper haberet
> Aeternum prae mente bonum, finemque timeret,
> Qui tam nobilibus, media quam plebe citatis
> Improuisus adest, animae discrimine magno
> Dum quaeruntur opes, dum fallax gloria rerum
> Mortales oculos uanis circumuolat alis....

(e) *Libro de Alexandre*, stanzas 2669–75 (composite numbering), ed. Willis, pp. 460–1: One should not put one's trust in earthly things but in God; the vanity of earthly things.

(f) Ulrich von Eschenbach, *Alexander*, vv. 27,552–642 (ed. Toischer, pp. 732–4); a long moral epilogue in which men are exhorted to put their faith in God; see W. Toischer, in *Sitzungsber. d. kaiserl. Akad. d. Wissen. in Wien*, Phil.-Hist. Klasse, Bd. XCVII (1881), pp. 324–5.

(g) *I Nobili Fatti* (ed. G. Grion, *Collezione di opere inedite o rare* (Bologna, 1872), p. 183): 'E perciò, signori, ogn'uomo si brighi a Dio servire, e acquistare il regno del cielo, che mai non fallerà. Chè bene avete udito, come le signorie di questo mondo sono vane e brieve. Quie finiscie Alessandro, che bene v'ho divisato tutto dal suo nascimento infino alla fine. Amen.'

(h) *Seelentrost* (ed. A. J. Barnouw, *Germanic Review*, IV (1929), p. 396) (Epilogue): 'Also gink ot ome; de wile dat he levede, do was he woldich over alle lude, nu is siner de duvel woldich. Korte wile vor he wol, nu scal he ewichliken ovel varen; hir was he rike ene clene tit, nu scal he arm wesen ane ende. Hir en konde siner nemet vullen mit gude, nu wert he vorvullet mit dem helleschen vure. Hir en wolde he nicht holden de bot unses heren, nu mot he horsam wesen dem duvel. Kint leve, dut lat dy en lere wesen, dat du de gebot goddes gerne willest holden, updat du dar nicht enkomest, sunder dat du komest dar alle godes hilgen sin mit gode. Dat we dar al komen, des helpe uns de vader un de sone unde de hillighe gheyst. Amen.'

On this passage see also above, pp. 258–9.

92 The most singular such instance is in Alexander's unique Will, in the *Old French Prose Romance*, c. 127 (ed. Hilka, pp. 252–3): 'Je Alixandres, fius de deus

Amon et de la roïne Olimpias, rois des rois et sires de la terre, fais savoir a tous ceaus qui sont et qui cest present testament verront et orront que, comme il soit ensi choze ke par la volenté de Dieu le totpoissant avoec l'effors de nos hommes je aie conquise la segnorie dou monde et de celle me fis coroner em Babilone a tel solempnité et a tel noblece com a tel chose apartenoit, Fortune qui jusques celui jour m'avoit assis au souverain siege de sa roe, plus haut et plus noble que n'eüist onques fait houme jusques a celui jour, quant elle de tout m'avoit fet segnor, et celle par moi qui elle avoit honoré volt demoustrer a tous ceaus qui apres moi vendront que nus ne se doit fier en la glore terriene, car de tant comme l'en en quide plus estre au desus, en est l'en au desous. Le jour meïsmement que je me fis coroner et quidoie estre venus a la fin de mon travail et au commencement de repos, par ceaus meïsmes que je avoie norris et alevés tant chierement comme mes enfans, je fui empoisonés de tels poisons dont je sui certains qu'il me couvendra morir. Mais por ce que je ne vorroie mie que Fortune se peüist vanter que elle m'eüist aussi mis au desous, fais savoir que pour entendre la renoumee de mes oevres, laquele Fortune ne me puet tolir, fais je mon testament des terres et des meubles que je ai conquis.'

For the medieval use of the Wheel of Fortune, see H. R. Patch, *The Goddess Fortuna in Mediaeval Literature* (Cambridge, 1927).

[Alexander appears occasionally on the Wheel of Fortune in the illustrations of Alexander-books and chronicles. A clumsy marginal drawing in MS. Brussels, Bibliothèque Royale 12012, f. 31ᵛ, of the *Alexandreis* of Gautier de Châtillon, shows this subject. The Stockholm MS. (V. u. 20) of the *French Prose Alexander* has a similar picture on f. 78 (Plate V, opp. p. 194). A frequently copied frontispiece for book five of *La Bouquechardière* which contains the history of Macedon (see P. Meyer, *A. le G.* II, pp. 347–55) shows, in one of its two compartments, Alexander at the top of the wheel and again seated on the ground sorrowfully contemplating his crown and sceptre, symbols of his fallen greatness. Finally a few MSS. of the *Histoire ancienne jusqu'à César* contain, in the account of the life of Alexander, a picture of Fortune and her Wheel, but the text shows that this does not refer to the conqueror himself. (D.J.A.R.).]

93 There are here arranged two groups of independent references. In the first group the emphasis is upon the role of Fortune at Alexander's death; in the second it is upon the intervention of God's Providence to cut short the career of an ungodly and unjust man. With the latter may be compared the views on the subject expressed by the moralists (see above, pp. 103–5).

(i) *Fortune and Alexander's death*

(a) Alcuin, *De clade Lindisfarnensis monasterii* IX, vv. 35–6 (*M.G.H., Poet. Lat. Aeu. Carol.* I, p. 229):

> Victorem mundi medio sors, ecce, secundis
> Rebus Alexandrum inuida flore tulit.

(b) *Epitaph* at end of *Liegnitz Historia*, cited by Hilka, *Romanische Forschungen*, XXIX (1911), p. 69:

> Magnus Alexander, rex ordine, gente Macedo,
>   Conditur Aegypto nominis urbe sui,
> Graecia quem profert, tremit Aethiops, Indus adorat,
>   Imperii limes clauditur Oceano.
> Amplius huic Fortuna dedit licuisse secunda,
>   Stare diu summo sed malefida negat....

(The other epitaphs quoted by Hilka, loc. cit. pp. 70–1, also contain various references to the theme of the part played by Fortune at Alexander's death.)

(c) *Epitaph* quoted by Pfister in *Münchener Museum*, I (1912), p. 278.

(d) Frate Stoppa de' Bistichi, quoted by Ortiz in *Giornale Storico della Lett. Italiana*, LXXXV (1925), p. 85:

> Il potente Assuero
> signor del mondo fu, quand'altrui piacque,
> e Alessandro altero
> segnoreggiò la terra e l'aria e l'acque;
> e annullossi e tacque,
> po' la fortuna volse
> e la vita gli tolse
> colei che tutte cose mena a tondo.

(e) Franco Sacchetti, *Libro delle Rime* CCXX, vv. 19–30 (ed. G. Chiari, *Scrittori d'Italia* (Bari, 1936), p. 261):

> O quanti re, e qual reo e qual buono,
> secondo l'opre loro fortuna volse,
> infino a Dario con li suo' tesori!
> Fidandosi costui ne'vani errori,
> sconfitto fu da Alessandro Magno,
> il qual di tutto il regno ebe guadagno.
> Quanti re vinse e quanto mondo tenne,
> e 'nfine dove venne
> tanto signor, insuperbendo, a morte!
> Antipater le sorte
> gli diede del velen con falsi fregi;
> po' venne 'l suo sotto diversi regi.

(f) *Morte Arthure*, vv. 3409 ff. (ed. Brock, E.E.T.S., O.S. VIII (1865), p. 100): Arthur dreams of a mysterious chair hanging from the wheel of Fortune; he sees the kings who tried the chair, the first of whom was Alexander.

(g) John Lydgate, *Mumming at London* (*Minor Poems*, II (Secular poems), ed. H. N. MacCracken, E.E.T.S., O.S. CXCII (1934), p. 684): (on Fortune)

> She made Alexaundre wynnen al,
> That noman him with stonde dare,
> And caste him doune, er he was ware.

(*h*) F. Villon, *Poésies diverses*, xii: *Probleme* (on Fortune), vv. 25–7 (*Œuvres*, ed. L. Thuasne (Paris, 1923), i, p. 289):

> Alixandre, qui tant feist de hemee,
> Qui voulut veoir l'estoille pouciniere,
> Sa personne par moi fut envlimee;...

(ii) *God's intervention at Alexander's death*

(*a*) Antonius Astesanus, *Carmen de eius uita et fortunae uarietate* iii, vv. 2031–4, in R.I.S. xiv (1912), p. 66:

> Est et alexander, domitor quasi totius orbis,
> Mortuus, incaute dira uenena bibens.
> Sic deus omnipotens uoluit, iustissimus ille
> Non impunitum passus abire malum.

(*b*) Unknown poet quoted by I. V. Zingerle, 'Ueber die Wiltener Meister-sängerhandschrift', *Sitzungsber. d. kais. Akad. in Wien.*, Phil.-Hist. Klasse, Bd. xxxvii (1861), p. 345: the greatest kings owe their sovereignty to God, who destroyed all the might of Ahasuerus and Alexander at their deaths.

(*c*) *Middle English Sermons*, ed. W. O. Ross, E.E.T.S., O.S. ccix (1940), p. 335: Who was a greater king than Alexander? But yet in his most royalty he was poisoned, nor might any of his heirs rejoice in his lordship.

The moral is that earthly power is useless without the grace of God. This sounds much like a reminiscence of a remark in the *Policraticus*; see above, p. 104.

94 G. Boccaccio, *Amorosa Visione* xxxv, 1 ff. (ed. V. Branci, *Scrittori d'Italia* (Bari, 1939), vol. vi, p. 224): *Della medesima Fortuna, dove pone Alessandro, vinto il mondo, esser poi alla morte e non poter niente.*

> 'Tu puoi', ricominciò la Donna a dire,
> 'veder qui Alessandro, ch'assalio
> il mondo tutto, per velen morire,
> e non esser però il suo disio
> pien, ma più che giammai esser ardente,
> e 'n tale ardor, come vedi, morio:
> lo qual fu quanto alcuno altro possente.
> Né però averia questa lasciato,
> che se fosse vivuto, che vilmente
> lui non avesse in infimo voltato
> della sua rota; ma quel che costei
> non fe', morte adempié nel nominato.

95 For references to Alexander's death by poison, without a concomitant reference to treachery, see the *Victor uictus* group cited above, p. 283.

(i) Comments upon Alexander's death by poison at the hands of a traitor are as follows:

PART B. THE MEDIEVAL CONCEPTION OF ALEXANDER

(a) *Floriant et Florete*, vv. 225–8 (ed. H. F. Williams, *University of Michigan Publications, Language and Literature*, XXIII (1947), p. 46 (reflexion on treason):

> Li rois Daires en fu murtris
> Et Julïus Cesar occis
> Et Alixandre empoisonnez
> Et li rois Pepins enherbez....

(b) *Chanson de Roland, Venice text* (V.7), laisse CLXIV (ed. W. Förster, *Altfranzösische Bibliothek*, VI, Heilbronn, 1883, p. 156) (reflexion on treason):

> Alixandre qui tant fu conquiranz
> Ke fu enposonez par li culuert sodiuanz....

(c) Peire Vidal, *Ben viu a gran dolor* IV, vv. 45–8 (*Poésies*, ed. J. Anglade (Paris, 1913), p. 120) (reflexion on treason):

> Qu'Alexandres moric
> Per sos sers qu'enriquic,
> E·l reis Daire feric
> De mort cel que·l noiric.

(d) *Commendatio lamentabilis militum* (*Chronicles of the Reigns of Edward I and Edward II*, ed. W. Stubbs, Rolls Series, vol. II (1883), p. 15): Alexander's death by treachery is compared to the death of Richard I by a wound.

(e) *Vita Edwardi Secundi auctore Malmesberiensi* (*Chronicles of the Reigns of Edward I and Edward II*, ed. W. Stubbs, Rolls Series, vol. II (1883), p. 234) (on the loss of Berwick by treachery): 'Sic ille magnus Graecorum imperator Alexander, totius orbis domitor, cum cunctas nationes armis subicit, per familiares proditores toxicatus occubuit.'

(f) *Stockholm MS. of the Old French Prose Romance*, unique prologue (ed. A. Hilka, *Altfranzösische Prosa-Alexanderroman* (Halle, 1920), p. iii–iv): After all his exploits Alexander was poisoned by his servant 'Jobal'.

(g) Guillaume Perrault, *De Eruditione Principum* I, I (Aquinas, *Opera Omnia* (Parma, 1852–71), vol. XVI (1864), p. 391): The troubles that beset a king—Alexander was poisoned by traitors.

(h) F. Sacchetti, *Libro delle Rime*, CCXX, vv. 25 ff.: quoted above, p. 314, n. 93.

(i) H. v. d. Türlin, *Krône*, vv. 11,578 ff. (ed. C. H. Fr. Scholl (Stuttgart, 1852); see Grammel, p. 119).

(j) Ferreto de' Ferreti Vicentino, *Historia rerum in Italia gestarum* II (ed. C. Cipolla, *Fonti per la Storia d'Italia*, vol. I (Rome, 1908), p. 175, l. 15): Alexander fell a victim to poison; beware of traitors.

(ii) Besides this final case of treachery, Alexander's life provided medieval writers with certain other morals in connexion with treachery; these are here quoted for completeness:

(a) The proper punishment of traitors shown by Alexander's treatment of the murderers of Darius, in *The Book of Fayttes of Arms and of Chyvalrye*, translated and printed by Caxton from Christine de Pisan (ed. A. T. P. Byles, E.E.T.S., O.S. CLXXXIX (1932), p. 56, l. 9).

(b) Alexander's punishment of the guides who led him wrong, in *L'Art de Chevalerie*, ed. U. Robert, S.A.T.F. (1897), pp. 89–90.

(c) Alexander betrayed by a woman in *Amadas et Ydoine*, vv. 5849 ff. (ed. J. R. Reinhard, *Classiques franç. du moyen âge* (Paris, 1926), p. 220):

> Si refu treciés et traïs
> Li preus, li larges, li hardis
> Alixandres qui tant valut:
> Bien sai sa feme le deçut.

(d) Alexander's fitting punishment of Philotas, who suppressed for three days information about a traitor, in *Vita Edwardi Secundi auctore Malmesberiensi* (*Chronicles of the Reigns of Edward I and Edward II*, ed. W. Stubbs, Rolls Series, vol. II (1883), p. 245).

(e) Darius' fate at the hands of his servants was frequently referred to in the Middle Ages; cf. F. Sacchetti, *Rime*, CXCVII, vv. 124–33 (ed. G. Chiari, *Scrittori d'Italia* (Bari, 1936), pp. 223–4), and the quotation from Peire Vidal on p. 316.

We may finally add here two independent citations of the story of the treacherous attack made on Alexander by a Persian dressed in Macedonian armour:

(f) William of Malmesbury, *Gesta Regum* (ed. W. Stubbs, Rolls Series, vol. II (1889), pp. 364–5).

(g) Michael Scot, *Mensa Philosophica*, De Armigeris; see S. Dosson, *Etude sur Quinte-Curce* (Paris, 1887), p. 369, n. 12.

96 The following independent early references to Alexander in medieval Latin works are concerned with his valour, and are independent of accounts of his life:

(a) Liutprand of Cremona, *Legatio* XXIX (Eng. tr. F. A. Wright, Routledge (London, 1930), p. 252): the Greek soldiers were not valiant heroes cast in the mould of the great Alexander (Migne, *P.L.* vol. CXXXVI, col. 921).

(b) Fredegarius Scholasticus, *Chronicon* II (*M.G.H. Scriptt. Rer. Meroving.* II (1888), p. 46, ll. 1–2).

(c) *Rhythmus in Odonem regem* VIII, 1–4 (*M.G.H. Poet. Lat. Aeu. Carol.* IV, i, ed. P. de Winterfeld (Berlin, 1898), p. 138):

> Ut Alexander Maximus
> pugnator sis aptissimus,
> tibique sit contrarius
> ceu fugiens Pompegius.

(d) Monachus Sangallensis, *Gesta Karoli* II (*M.G.H. Scriptt.* II, ed. G. H. Pertz (1829), p. 758, l. 31): 'Non audistis, quod fecerit paruus Dauid ingenti illi Goliaht, uel breuissimus Alexander procerissimis satellitibus suis?'

(*e*) Rangerius Lucensis, *Vita Metrica S. Anselmi Lucensis*, vv. 4047ff. (*M.G.H. Scriptt.* xxx, ii (Leipzig, 1934), p. 1241):

> Scilicet haec Pirrus faciebat, et ille Philippi
> Fortis Alexander, quem Darius timuit;
> Qui, ne nulla sequi posset uictoria, molles
> Erubuit gladios faemineasque manus.
> Turpe uiro forti mulierem uincere, uinci
> Turpius;...

(*f*) Nicolaus de Braia, *Carmen de Gestis Ludovici VIII Regis*, in *M.G.H. Scriptt.* xxvi (ed. O. Holder-Egger, 1882), p. 487, vv. 1854–5.

(*g*) Canonicus Leodiensis, *Chronicon Rhythmicum*, in *M.G.H. Scriptt.* xii (ed. G. H. Pertz, 1856), p. 420 (vv. 471–4).

97 For medieval references to these magnanimous acts, see pp. 154, 158–60, 282; the following are not recorded elsewhere, and are strictly secular in character:

(*a*) *Alexander's forgiveness of the Persian who tried to murder him.* William of Malmesbury, *Gesta Regum* (ed. W. Stubbs, Rolls Series, vol. ii (1889), pp. 364–5): (William Rufus compared to Alexander): 'A magni quondam Alexandri non degener gloria, qui Persam militem se a tergo ferire conatum, sed pro perfidia ensis spe sua frustratum, incolumem pro admiratione fortitudinis conseruauit.'

(*b*) *The story of the cold soldier to whom Alexander gave his seat at the fire* (see also p. 160). G. Boccaccio, *Epist.* xii (to Francesco Nelli, 1363), in *Opere Latine Minori*, ed. A. F. Massera, *Scrittori d'Italia* (Bari, 1928), p. 160.

(*c*) *The man to whom Alexander gives a cloak.* F. Frezzi, *Quadriregio* iv, iii, vv. 154ff., ed. E. Filippini, *Scrittori d'Italia* (Bari, 1914), p. 289.

98 Tertullian, *Apologeticus* xi (Migne, *P.L.* vol. i, cols. 336–7): 'Quot tamen potiores uiros apud inferos reliquistis? aliquem de sapientia Socratem, de iustitia Aristidem, de militia Themistoclem, de sublimitate Alexandrum....'

For a reference to this passage in connexion with the euhemeristic theory of the origin of idolatry, see above, p. 294.

Facciolati defines *sublimitas* as 'perfectio, excellentia', and cites as an example a passage from Pliny, *Hist. Nat.* x, 36 (67): 'illa fuit uera et incomparabilis animi sublimitas, captis Pompeii scriniis epistolarum, concremasse ea optima fide atque non legisse.'

Petrarch, in a note in his copy of Pliny, compared this action of Caesar's with that of Alexander in opening the letter of Sisines (Curtius iii, vii, 11–15), and abuses the latter; see P. de Nolhac, *Petrarque et l'humanisme*, ii (1907), p. 79.

99 Seneca, *De Ben.* i, xiii, 3 (Alexander's desire to be thought to follow in the steps of Hercules): 'Quid enim ille simile habebat uesanus adulescens, cui pro uirtute erat felix temeritas? Hercules nihil sibi uicit: orbem terrarum transiuit non concupiscendo, sed uindicando. Quid uinceret malorum hostis, bonorum uindex, terrarum marisque pacator? At hic a pueritia latro gentiumque uastator, tam hostium pernicies quam amicorum, qui summum bonum duceret terrori

esse cunctis mortalibus, oblitus non ferocissima tantum, sed ignauissima quoque animalia timeri ob uirus malum.'
On Heracles and Alexander, see A. R. Anderson, 'Heracles and his successors', *Harvard Studies in Classical Philology*, XXXIX (1928), pp. 7–58.
For an extremely important passage defending Alexander's *temeritas*, see Gautier de Châtillon, *Alexandreis* IX (Migne, *P.L.* vol. CCIX, col. 558 (at bottom). Cf. Curtius IX, v, 2.
This follows an account of his jump into the besieged city, the best-known example of his rashness, and one which was borrowed from the *Alexandreis* by Willelmus Britto, *Philipis* IV, vv. 425–8, ed. A. Molinier, A. Pannenborg, and G. Waitz, in *M.G.H. Scriptt.* XXVI (1882), p. 329.
For a further independent reference to the jump, see *Roman de la Rose ou de Guillaume de Dole*, vv. 5306–7 (ed. G. Servois, S.A.T.F. (1893), p. 159).

100 William of Conches, *Liber Moralium Dogmatis Philosophorum* XXVIII, 'De magnanimitate', ascribed to Hildebert of Lavardin following Cicero, *De officiis*, I, 19 (Migne, *P.L.* vol. CLXXI, cols. 1026f.): 'Haec uirtus, cum ad aspera ineunda aliquem promptum faciat, communem utilitatem quam suam potius attendit. Sicut enim scientia, quae est remota a iustitia, potius quam sapientia est appellanda calliditas; sic animus ad pericula paratus, si sua cupiditate non communi utilitate impellitur, temeritatis potius nomen quam fortitudinis habet.'
This Ciceronian definition of magnanimity, expanded over several paragraphs, shows how far the medieval version of magnanimity had departed from the selfless cautious bravery ('Temeritas' is specifically abused) of older writers.

101 E.g. in the Prologue of the *Natiuitas et Victoria Alexandri Magni*, ed. Pfister, *Alexanderroman*, pp. 44–5: 'Licet namque et spirituales homines audire, quae et qualia certamina uel quam benignas operationes propter amorem saeculi in se habebant pagani ab initio usque ad aduentum Christi, ut merendo considerent, quam sapientes et pios uiros tunc possidebat diabolus excecando mentes illorum, ne suum agnoscerent creatorem et seruirent creaturae potius quam creatori. . . .'

102 The association of magnanimity with greatness in the medieval period is especially perceptible in the following passages:
(*a*) St Augustine, *De Ciu. Dei* IV, 7; XVIII, 42 (Migne, *P.L.* vol. XLI, cols. 117, 602): The magnificence combined with the brevity of Alexander's empire.
(*b*) *Chronica regia S. Pantaleonis* (Eccardus, *Corp. hist. medii aeui*, I (Leipzig, 1723), c. 719): 'Decessit Alexander Magnus mensem unum et annos tres et triginta natus, uir supra humanam potentiam magnitudine animi praeditus.'
(*c*) John Lydgate, *Ballade*, to King Henry VI (*Minor Poems*, II, ed. H. N. MacCracken, E.E.T.S., O.S. CXCII (1934), p. 627):

> And that thou mayst beo Goddes Chaumpyoun,
> As that he was, Iudas the Makabe;
> With Alysaundres magnanymyte,...

The association with Judas Maccabee, and thus with the characters of the *Neuf Preux*, makes it certain that 'magnanymyte' is here understood as noble valour, which is Alexander's conventional characteristic among the *Neuf Preux*. See above, pp. 246–8.

103 See Alberic, laisse 2 (ed. Foulet, *M.F.R.d'A.* III, p. 38):

> En pargamen no·l vid escrit
> Ne per parabla non fu dit
> Del temps novel ne del antic
> Nuls hom vidist un rey tan ric
> Chi per batalle et per estric
> Tant rey fesist met ne mendic
> Ne tanta terra conquesist
> Ne tan duc nobli occisist
> Cum Alexander Magnus fist,
> Qui fud de Grecia natiz.

Cf. laisses 8 ff. (ibid. pp. 39–40) for a description of the personal qualities of Alexander, and of his physical appearance.

104 The portrait of Alexander in the *Vorau Alexander* is fully studied by Grammel, pp. 27–39.

For Alexander's Maccabean role in Lamprecht, see above, p. 172.

Grammel remarks of the *Vorau Alexander*, without indicating that the qualities in question are derived from Alberic (p. 33): 'Tapferkeit und Mut sind seine Haupteigenschaften, eine Tapferkeit, die mit Waffenkunst und Kriegslist gepaart ist, ein Mut, der vor nichts zurückschreckt, der oft bis zur Vermessenheit und Tollkühnheit führt.'

105 Independent vernacular references during this period are as follows:

(i) *In France*

(*a*) Etienne de Fougères, *Le livre des manières*, stanzas 28–9 (ed. Talbert, 1877):

> Si donques aveit en mimoire
> D'Alexandre le proz l'estoire,
> Com il ala par le desert,
> Comment l'ocistrent li cuivert,
> Et com il fat peis descovert,
> Idonc savreit tot en apert.

(*b*) Wace, *Roman de Rou*, vv. 41 ff. (ed. H. Andresen (Heilbronn, 1877), vol. I, p. 12):

> Alisandre fu reis puissanz,
> Duze regnes prist en duze ans,...

(*c*) *Aymeri de Narbonne*, vv. 9–10 (ed. L. Demaison, S.A.T.F., vol. II (1887)):

> Et por ice dirai, sanz plus atendre,
> Del plus preudome qui fust puis Alixandre.

These quotations should be taken in conjunction with the Latin references given above, p. 319, n. 102, and with the absence of references to liberality at this period; see above, p. 211.

(ii) *German references*

Two important lives of Alexander occur in independent German works of this period: in the *Annolied* and the *Kaiserchronik*, both printed in *M.G.H. Deutsche Chroniken*, 1 (Hanover, 1895). The *Annolied* account, with which the *Kaiserchronik* substantially agrees, opens with an account of Alexander as the founder of the third world-kingdom, and goes on to describe his life, with especial emphasis upon his wonderful adventures, including the visit to the trees of the sun and moon, the Celestial Journey, and the descent into the sea (in the individual German version, see below, pp. 340–1). Both accounts, as Grammel points out, concentrate upon the presentation of Alexander in the midst of his great deeds and wonderful adventures. This is therefore an objective portrait of Alexander; but the connexion with Biblical testimony is significant.

See further Grammel, p. 113, and cf. *Rolandslied*, vv. 3974–6 (ed. C. Wesle (Bonn, 1928)).

106 The theme of Alexander the conqueror is at once brought forward:

> Gesta ducis Macedum, totum digesta per orbem,
> quam large dispersit opes, quo milite Porum
> uicerit et Darium, quo principe Graecia uictrix
> risit, et a Persis rediere tributa Corinthum,
> Musa refer:...
>
> (Book I, vv. 1–5, Migne, *P.L.* vol. ccix, cols. 463–4).

Alexander is subtly introduced, not at a disadvantage as a new-born baby, but as the youth already chafing with high-flown ambition, who is encouraged by Aristotle (Book I, vv. 92 ff., in Migne, *P.L.* vol. ccix, cols. 466 ff.). Typical of his restless, unceasing ambition is the scene before Arbela, where he is so consumed with restless care that he cannot sleep until the Gods send sleep to him (Book IV, cols. 505 f.). Cf. also Book IX, col. 562 c:

> Thracas Asiamque subegi,
> proximus est mundi mihi finis, et absque deorum
> ut loquar inuidia, nimis est angustus hic orbis
> et terrae tractus, domino non sufficit uni;...

Compare also the famous passage at the end of Book V (col. 518 B–C), where Gautier regrets that France has not so great a king to lead Christendom against the Saracen, and asks that God should grant her another Alexander:

> Si gemitu commota pio, uotisque suorum
> flebilibus, diuina daret clementia talem
> Francorum regem, toto radiaret in orbe,
> haud mora, uera fides, et nostris fracta sub armis
> Parthia baptismo renouari posceret ultro:

quaeque diu iacuit effusis moenibus alta
ad nomen Christi Carthago resurgeret, et quae
sub Carolo meruit Hispania soluere poenas,
erigeret uexilla crucis, gens omnis, et omnis
lingua Deum caneret, et non inuita subiret
sacrum sub sacro Remorum praesule fontem.

Bellona, at the instigation of Mars, attempts to prevent Alexander fighting; but he fights even against the will of the gods (Book v, col. 513, vv. 205 ff.).

Christensen has pointed out how Gautier omitted all minor campaigns and battles, in order to concentrate attention upon the conflict between his two great pairs of protagonists, Alexander and Darius, Alexander and Porus; see H. Christensen, *Das Alexanderlied Walters von Châtillon* (Halle, 1905), pp. 107–9.

107 *Decasyllabic Alexander*, vv. 1 ff. (ed. Foulet, *M.F.R.d'A.* III, p. 61):

Chançon voil faire per rime e per lioine
Del fil Felip lo rei de Macedoine,
C'est d'Alixandre qui conquist Babiloine,
Perse e Afrique e Tirë e Sidoine,
E tot lo mont mist en si grant aigoine
Qui ne le volt servir per son espoine
Nel pot garir ne l'escuz ne la broine,
Morir l'estut, unc ne fu prise essoine.

108 Lambert li Tors, Prologue (*Roman d'Alexandre* III, vv. 6 ff.) (*M.F.R.d'A.* II, p. 143):

...De Gos et de Magos que il enclost et prist,
Que ja mais n'en istront jusqu'au tans Antecrist,
Ainsi com Apellés s'ymage contrefist,
Du duc de Palatine qu'il pendi et deffist,
la roïne Candace qu'en sa chambre le mist
Et de la vois des arbres qui de sa mort li dist,
Ainsi com Aristotes l'entroduist et aprist,
La verté de l'estoire, si com li rois la fist,
Uns clers de Chastiaudun, Lambers li Tors, l'escrist,
Qui du latin le traist et en romans le mist.

109 Not all the references which deal both with Alexander's valour and his liberality have been included here, to avoid unnecessary repetition; they are given on pp. 325–7.

The references are divided into French and Provençal:

(i) *French references to Alexander's valour and military qualities*

(a) Filippe Mousket, *Historia regum Francorum*, vv. 19,266–9, 24,553, in *M.G.H. Scriptt.* XXVI (1882), pp. 736, 769. Vv. 19,266–9:

Et li quens Felipres de Flandres,
Ses parins, ki plus k'Alixandres
Fu larges et preus et hardis,
Ala sor lui jusqu'a Senlis....

(b) *Les Enfances Guillaume*, laisse 1, vv. 1–2, LXIV, v. 2650, ed. Patrice Henry (S.A.T.F., Paris, 1935), pp. 3, 112. Vv. 1 f.:

> Chanson de geste plaroit vos a entandre?
> Teis ne fut faite de lo tans Alixandre;...

(c) *Roman de la Rose*, vv. 18,763–86, ed. E. Langlois (S.A.T.F., vol. IV (1922), pp. 242–3: Alexander's career of ceaseless conquest is briefly described, including a curious reference to an attempted conquest of hell.

(d) *La Branche des Royaus Lingnages*, vv. 15,716 ff. (*Recueil des Hist. des Gaules et de la France*, vol. XXII (1865), p. 245, vv. 15,716–9); the conquests of Alexander (also vv. 12–13, p. 173; vv. 11,241–5, p. 201).

(e) *L'Entrée d'Espagne*, laisse 46, vv. 965–6; laisse 529, v. 12,259, ed. A. Thomas (S.A.T.F., 2 vols., 1913), vol. I, p. 38, and vol. II, p. 155: two references to Alexander's war with Nicholas.

(f) *Amadas et Ydoine*, vv. 5849–52, ed. J. R. Reinhard, *Classiques franç. du moyen âge* (Paris, 1926), p. 220.

(g) *Florimont*, vv. 13,590–604, ed. A. Hilka, *Gesell. f. roman. Lit.*, Bd. XLVIII (Göttingen, 1933), pp. 535–6.

(ii) *Provençal references*

These have been collected by Karl Bartsch in *Germania*, II (1857), pp. 449–64; see for references to Alexander's valour, from Arnaut Daniel, Serveri de Gironne, Gaucelm Faidit, and others, pp. 455 ff. and below, pp. 326–7.

110 The best discussion of Rudolf von Ems' belief in God's surveillance of Alexander is in O. Zingerle, *Die Quellen zum Alexander des Rudolf von Ems* (*Germanistische Abhandlungen*, IV, Breslau, 1885), pp. 13 f. On the passage where Rudolf excuses the fact that one and a half million Persians were killed in battle by ascribing it to the intervention of God, who willed, as Josephus says, that Alexander should destroy the heathen (vv. 12,873 ff.), he comments: 'Ein starker Autoritätsglaube, der Glaube an Alexanders göttliche Mission, nicht etwa hier das einzige Mal ausgesprochen, halfen über das wunderlichste Zeug hinweg. In dieser Beziehung charakterisiren den Dichter auch folgende Verse, die sich der Erzählung von Alexanders Geburt und der Beschreibung seiner Gestalt anschliessen' (vv. 1335 ff.).

See also Grammel, pp. 86–8.

111 For independent German references of this period, see Grammel, pp. 114–24. Some of the more important are as follows:

(a) *Moriz von Craun*, v. 99 (*Zwei altdeutsche Rittermären*, ed. E. Schröder, Berlin, 1913): Alexander's attack upon Greece.

(b) Enikel's *Weltchronik* (*M.G.H. Deutsche Chroniken*, III): for a discussion of this important text, see below, pp. 346–7, where it is examined in conjunction with the similar *Historienbibel* I account. Alexander's wonderful adventures are emphasized throughout the account of his life, and occupy by far the larger part of the narrative.

(c) Heinrich v. d. Türlin, *Krône* vv. 12,280 ff. (ed. G. H. F. Scholl, Stuttgart, 1852):

> Daz Alexander, der küene man,
> Porum dar umbe verkôs,
> Daz er zer tjost sîn ors verlôs,
> Unz ime anderz brâht wart.

(d) Thomasin v. Zirclaria, *Wälschen Gast*, vv. 1049 f. (ed. H. Rückert (Quedlinburg and Leipzig, 1852)):

> lât niht verderben iuwer jugent:
> gedenket an Alexanders tugent.

(e) Der Stricker, *Karl der Grosse*, vv. 4002 ff. (ed. K. Bartsch (Quedlinburg and Leipzig, 1857)).

(f) *Die Heidin*, vv. 1134 ff. (ed. L. Pfannmüller, *Mittelhochdeutsche Novellen*, 1 (Bonn, 1912), p. 32).

(g) Rudolf von Ems, *Weltchronik*, vv. 1473–90 (Gog and Magog), 3588 ff. (ed. G. Ehrismann, *Deutsche Texte des Mitt.*, Bd. xx (1915), pp. 21, 50).

(h) Heinrich von Beringen, *Schachgedicht*, vv. 2124–35 (ed. P. Zimmermann, *B.L.V.* vol. CLXVI (Tübingen, 1883), pp. 71–2): Alexander's conquests.

(i) Albrecht von Kemenaten, *Dietrichs Abenteuer*, stanzas 868, 936 (ed. J. Zupitza, *Deutsches Heldenbuch*, v (Berlin, 1870), pp. 159–71).

All of these references are concerned simply with Alexander's valour and conquests.

112 The two passages in the *Vorau Alexander* are as follows (ed. Kinzel, pp. 72 and 76):

525, Thelemone (Mothona) is captured, and its wealth distributed to the troops; cf. Julius Valerius I, 16–17 (ed. Kuebler, pp. 26–8).

585, Alexander, speaking to the Macedonians, promises to furnish them with all that they will need; cf. Julius Valerius I, 19 (ed. Kuebler, pp. 28–9), *Historia de Preliis*, c. 25 (ed. Pfister, pp. 60–1).

113 *Alexandreis* I, vv. 157 ff. (Migne, *P.L.* vol. CCIX, col. 467 C). For the practical demonstration of this theory on Alexander's part, cf. the Argument to Book v:

> Ad donatiua maniplos
> Conuocat Aeacides, et donis uulnera curat.

And col. 516 D:

> Nec mora, distribuens celebres apud Arbela gazas
> Munificus Macedo, tantis ardenter onusto
> Rebus, et inuenta satiato milite praeda
> Transcurrit Syriam, . . .

114 *Decasyllabic Alexander*, laisse 5, vv. 44–7 (*M.F.R.d'A.* III, p. 63):

> Chivalers aime e honore forment,
> Quant que il a tot lor met em present.
> Tant per es larges ne prisa or ne argent,
> Les chivalers teneit toz a talent.

Laisse 8, vv. 79–82 (ibid. p. 65):

> Ot lui esteit de jovne gent asez,
> De filz de contes e de filz d'amirez
> Qui tuit lo servent volenters e de grez;
> Chivaus lor dona e mulez sojornez.

See below, pp. 360–6, for comment on these references.

115 Most of the important references to Alexander's liberality in the *Roman d'Alexandre* are concentrated at the beginning, except for the story of the jongleur and the city of Trage, and the story of the knight and the city of Araine. See below, pp. 360–1, 364.

For other references to Alexander's liberality, see *Roman d'Alexandre* I, laisse 1, vv. 16–19; I, laisse 2, vv. 43–6; I, laisses 5–6, vv. 195–216; III, laisse 2, vv. 19–27 (*M.F.R.d'A.* II, pp. 1–5 and 143). Most of these quotations, it may be noticed, are concerned with the political value of Alexander's liberality in obtaining friends and encouraging his soldiers to conquer the world. Compare the Zeuxis episode, below, p. 362, and Philippe de Novare, below, p. 371.

116 *Roman d'Alexandre* IV, laisses 34–59, vv. 605–1399 (*M.F.R.d'A.* II, pp. 334–51). Compare also the epilogue in laisses 71–4, and especially v. 1684 (ibid. pp. 356–8):

> Plus donast Alixandres qu'autres n'osast penser.

Is this a reminiscence of Curtius, x, v, 28: '...liberalitas saepe maiora tribuens quam a dis petuntur...'?

117 These references are arranged in two groups, the first French, the second Provençal. Late medieval references are given below, pp. 332–3.

(i) *French references (excluding all Alexander-books)*

(*a*) Chrétien de Troyes, *Erec*, vv. 2259–60 (cited Meyer, *A. le G.* II, p. 374):

> Erec de doner et de despendre
> Fu pareilz le roi Alixandre.

Cf. Hartmann v. d. Aue, *Erec*, vv. 2819–21.

(*b*) *Les Enfances Guillaume*, vv. 2703 ff. (ed. B. Henry, S.A.T.F. (1935), p. 114; vv. 2703–5, in a description of Charlemagne):

> A col li pendent une targe listee,
> Rois Alixandres la donait une fee
> Ke l'aportait d'outre la mer salee.

(*c*) Filippe Mousket, *Historia regum Francorum*, in *M.G.H. Scriptt.* XXVI (1882), p. 736: (vv. 19,266f.). See p. 322, n. 109.

(*d*) *Roman de la Rose*, vv. 1130, 12,667 (ed. E. Langlois, S.A.T.F., vol. II (1920), p. 58; vol. III (1921), p. 251).

(*e*) Henri d'Andeli, *Dit du chancelier Philippe*, v. 77, in *Romania*, I, p. 211: largesse of his hero compared to that of Alexander.

(*f*) Henri d'Andeli, *Lai d'Aristote*, in *Œuvres*, ed. A. Héron, p. 3: after telling of the deeds accomplished by Alexander, he says:

> ...ce li fist larguesce, sa mere.

See Meyer, *A. le G.* II, p. 376.

(*g*) Philippe de Novare, *Les Quatre Ages de L'Homme*: see below, p. 371.

(*h*) *L'Entrée d'Espagne*: for references to Alexander's liberality in this Franco-Italian poem, see below, p. 329, n. 120.

(*i*) *Roman d'Eledus et Serene*, vv. 2841 ff. (ed. J. R. Reinhard, University of Texas, 1923): Alexander's liberality in giving away the lands he conquered.

(*j*) Guillaume Guiart, *Branche des royaux lingnages* (*Rec. des Hist. des Gaules et de la France*, XXII (1865), p. 222) (vv. 4333–4, in praise of Robert d'Artois):

> ...Et le plus large pour despendre
> Qui fust puis le tens Alixandre....

(*k*) Rutebeuf, *La Complainte du Conte de Poitiers*, vv. 80–2 (ed. A. Kressner, Wolfenbüttel, 1885, p. 94):

> L'en nos a parlé d'Alixandre,
> De sa largesce, de son senz,
> Et de ce qu'il fist a son tenz:...

(For the important passage in which Rutebeuf quotes Aristotle's advice to Alexander on liberality, in the *Dit d'Aristote*, see text and discussion in A. Héron, 'La Legende d'Alexandre et d'Aristote', *Précis analytique des travaux de l'Académie des Sciences...de Rouen, pendant l'année* 1890–1 (Rouen, 1892), pp. 332–4).

For later references to Alexander's liberality in French poetry (almost entirely restricted to Eustache Deschamps), see below, pp. 332–3.

(ii) *Provençal references*

(*a*) *Unknown poet* in Paris B.N. MS. supp. fr. 683:

> Alixandris fon lo plus conquerens
> e lo plus larcs de nostres ancessors,
> e Tristans fo de totz los amadors
> lo plus lejals e fes mais d'ardimens,
> e Ectors fon lo melher ses falhensa
> de cavaliers en fatz et en parvensa,
> el plus cortes Galvans totas sazos,
> el plus savis fon lo reis Salamos.

(*b*) Raimbaut de Vaqueyras, on Boniface de Montferrat:

> Aleyxandres vos laisset son donar
> et ardimen Rotlans elh dotze par
> el pros Berartz domney e gent parlar.

(c) Gaucelm Faidit (*Planh* for Richard Coeur de Lion):

> qu'Alixandres lo reis, qui venquet Daire,
> no cre que tan dones ni tan mezes....

(d) Aimeric de Pegulhan (*Planh* on Guillelmo da Malaspina):

> De bos mestiers el mon par no li sai,
> qu'anc no fo tan larcs segon mon parer
> Alexandres de manjar ni d'aver,
> ni ges Gavains d'armas plus no valia
> ni no saup tant Ivans de cortezia,
> nis mes Tristans d'amor en tant assai.

(e) Henry, Duke of Rhodez (in *Tenso* with Guiraut Riquier):

> Guiraut Riquier, a mi ven d'agradatje
> que prendals dos; qu'Alissandris avia
> per sos grans dos mes sotz son senhoratje
> aquest mon mays que per cavalaria
> ni per sabers.

(f) Unknown poet (MS. in Bibl. Chigi):

> Senher Marco, Alexandres per dar....

(g) Peire Vidal (and in ed. by Anglade, Paris, 1923, p. 120):

> Qu' Alixandres moric
> per sos sers qu'enriquic,
> e·l rei Daire feric
> de mort cel q'el noiric.

(h) Chansonnier de Berne, piece 164:

> Et menbre vos d'Alixandre le roi;
> Celi d'Ailiers qui tant fu prous et lairges.

(i) Pier de la Mula:

> Per dar conquis Aleysandres Roays
> E per tener perdet Daire lo Ros
> La batalha....

(j) G. Fabre de Narbonne:

> Onc no vec de pretz ni d'onor
> Alixandres, segon qu'aug dir,
> Per trop tener thesaur en tor
> Mas quar volc ben dar e partir
> Lo sieu de gran coratge.

See also p. 323.

118 For references to Alexander's liberality in the *Strassburg Alexander*, see Grammel, p. 47: 'Vor allem aber wird seine "Milte" gepriesen, wird er doch in der höfischen Epik und Lyrik der Prototyp des milden Ritters.' In Rudolf von Ems, Grammel, pp. 77–8: 'Keine Tugend ist so oft erwähnt und so sehr betont wie Alexanders "Milte".' In Ulrich von Eschenbach, Grammel, p. 96: 'An der Spitze seiner Tugenden steht seine Freigebigkeit...'.

This enthusiasm is perhaps a little rash in its emphasis on Alexander's liberality as it appears in the German Alexander-poems. Alexander's generous liberality is not much to the fore in the *Strassburg Alexander*, while in Rudolf von Ems and Ulrich von Eschenbach it is subsidiary to other qualities.

119 Independent German references collected by Grammel, pp. 115ff., are as follows:

(a) Hartmann v. d. Aue, *Erec*, vv. 2819–21 (ed. A. Leitzmann (Halle, 1939), p. 73) (cf. Chrétien de Troyes above, p. 325):

> sîn milte dûhte si sô groz
> diu gemâzte in niemen ander
> wan dem milten Alexander.

(b) Walther v. d. Vogelweide XVII, vv. 7–10 (ed. K. Lachmann, Berlin, 1907):

> swelch künec der milte geben kan,
> si gît im daz er nie gewan.
> wie Alexander sich versan!
> der gap und gap, und gap sim elliu rîche.

(c) Meister Sigeher (to Ottocar of Bohemia) (Grammel, p. 115):

> ...seht an Alexander, der gab unverspart,
> des vert sin lob in allen richen witen.

(d) Heinrich von Beringen, *Schachgedicht*, vv. 2577ff. (ed. P. Zimmermann, *B.L.V.* vol. CLXVI, Tübingen, 1883): the episode of Alexander's visit in disguise to the camp of Porus; discussed below, p. 365.

(e) *Der Junker und der treue Heinrich*, vv. 922ff. (ed. K. Kinzel, Berlin, 1880, p. 64).

(f) Thomasin von Zirclaria, *Wälschen Gast*, vv. 3767ff.: here Alexander's liberality is condemned because he devoted it to his own ambitious purposes; see Grammel, p. 117, and below, pp. 362–3.

120 The two quotations are given by R. Ortiz in *Giornale Storico della Lett. Ital.* LXXXV (1925), p. 87, who does not study them in relation to other Italian comments on Alexander's liberality, and are as follows:

Guittone d'Arezzo:

> E se valesse a condizion d'amore
> in ciascuna vertù compiutamente,
> quanto Alessandro re valse in donare,
> si ti dispregierebbe il conoscente.

Anonymous poet:

> Se fossi ricco come fu Nerone
> e passass' Alessandro di larghezza
> e 'l buon Hector di Troja di prodezza
> e avess' el saver di Salomone....

We may also notice here the two references to Alexander's liberality in the

Franco-Italian *L'Entrée d'Espagne*, in the edition by Anthoine Thomas, S.A.T.F., 2 vols. (1913):

Laisse 121, v. 2971 (vol. I, p. 110): liberality is a requisite for love:

...Car d'amor n'avra joie qui ne suet Alexandre.

Laisse 452, vv. 10,430 ff. (vol. II, p. 89): the paintings in the Château de Noble depicting the exploits of Alexander are pointed out in a speech beginning:

'Veez qe feit largece....'

121 *Convivio* IV, 11. Dante turns from the discussion of material riches to that of their dispersal in liberal acts. He has shown why material riches are unjustly acquired: '...Per che è manifesto in ciascuno modo quelle ricchezze iniquamente avvenire; e però nostro Signore inique le chiamò, quando disse: 'Fatevi amici della pecunia della iniquità', invitando e confortando gli uomini a liberalità di beneficii, che sono generatori d'amici. E quanto fa bel cambio chi di queste imperfettissime cose dà, per avere e per acquistare cose perfette, siccome li cuori de' valenti uomini! Lo cambio ogni dì si può fare. Certo nuova mercatanzia è questa dell' altre, che credendo comperare un uomo per lo beneficio, mille e mille ne sono comperati. E chi non ha ancora nel cuore Alessandro, per li suoi reali beneficii?'

An interesting problem is suggested by this passage. Is Dante referring to the Senecan anecdotes of Alexander's liberality, which he must have known, not only from Seneca himself but from Brunetto Latini, or to the secular tradition? It seems by no means certain that he knew the legendary history of Alexander (see p. 364), and 'reali' might refer to the point of the Senecan anecdote of the man to whom Alexander gave a city, that the gift 'should befit a *king*'—thereby endorsing Latini's, and denying Seneca's, application of the anecdote (see p. 350). On the other hand Dante is referring to a popular reputation, and shortly afterwards mentions such men as Saladin and Bertran de Born; which would bring us to what is most probably the foundation for his statement, Alexander's reputation for liberality in the troubadours, with which he must certainly have been acquainted.

122 G. Boccaccio, *Epist.* XII (to Francesco Nelli) in *Opere Latine Minori*, ed. A. F. Massera, *Scrittori d'Italia* (Bari, 1928), p. 171: '...Alessandro di Macedonia, il quale ha ardire con poca compagnia d'assalire il mondo, e da poi i sottoposti reami per ragione di guerra immantinente e con lieto viso donare.'

Cf. Alexander's reply to Philip in Philippe de Novare, below, p. 371.

123 For the trees of the sun and moon, see below, p. 337. For the shirt which protects its wearer from lechery or drunkenness, see the *Decasyllabic Alexander*, laisse 26, vv. 264–73 (ed. Foulet, *M.F.R.d'A.* III, p. 75) and the *Libro de Alexandre*, stanzas 99f. in P. ed. Willis, p. 24.

For Alexander and the women of Darius, cf. especially the praise of Gautier de Châtillon, *Alexandreis* III (Migne, P.L. vol. CCIX, col. 491 at top). Alexander's well-known comment that he would not allow himself to be defeated by women (a comment paralleled by his remarks upon the Amazons), appears as a saying in the *Bocados de Oro* (ed. Knust, *Mittheilungen aus dem Eskurial, B.L.V.* vol. CXLI (Tübingen, 1879), p. 311): 'Fea cosa es que nos vençamos los omnes, lidiando ellos connusco, e que nos vençan sus mugeres, seyendo ellas nuestras presas.' Cf. also Erasmus, *Apophthegm.* VIII, 10, and Castiglione, *Cortegiano* III, 39 (ed. V. Cian, Firenze, 1929, p. 355): '...rimettovi alla continenzia solamente di dui grandissimi signori giovani, e su la vittoria, la quale suol far insolenti ancora gli omini bassissimi: e dell'uno è quella d'Alessandro Magno verso le donne bellissime di Dario, nemico e vinto....'

On the original versions of this story, see W. W. Tarn, *Alexander the Great*, II (Cambridge, 1948), pp. 337-8.

124 Upon the maidens in the wood, a story possibly of Oriental origin, see Meyer, *A. le G.* II, pp. 181-2.

See, for an independent reference to these ladies in Ulrich von Gutenburg, Grammel, p. 115-16; and cf. Guillem de la Tor, cited by K. Bartsch in *Germania*, II (1857), p. 458:

Plus que las domnas que aug dir
c'Alixandres trobet el bruoill,
qu'eran totas de tal escuoill,
que non podion, ses morir,
outra l'ombra del bruoill anar,...

125 For Ulrich's treatment of all women as beautiful and virtuous, and for the effect of his introduction of the code of courtly love into the poem, see Grammel, pp. 92-101; p. 94: 'Wir sehen, die Ritter sind zu Frauenrittern geworden, die alle ihre Rittertaten im Dienste ihrer Dame ausüben, und wo der Dichter nur immer Gelegenheit hat, nimmt er sie wahr, auf die Dame des Ritters Bezug zu nehmen.'

126 For the omission of the Candace episode in Godfrey of Viterbo, see L. Meyer, *Les Légendes des Matières de Rome, de France, et de Bretagne, dans le 'Panthéon' de Godefroi de Viterbe* (Paris, 1933), p. 101.

For its omission in the *Libro de Alexandre*, see Willis, *Debt*, p. 56, who points out that the Spanish author omitted everything that could be construed as unfavourable to Alexander.

For its omission in Rudolf von Ems, see Grammel, p. 69; but Rudolf, who gives a substitute in a love scene with Thalestris, queen of the Amazons, may have intended to include it as his unfinished poem does not extend so far.

127 For Thomas of Kent's treatment of the episode, see C. B. West, *Courtoisie in Anglo-Norman Literature* (Oxford, Blackwell, 1938), pp. 72, 75-9.

Cf. the derivative attacks upon Candace in *Kyng Alisaundre*, vv. 7446-7785 (ed. G. V. Smithers, E.E.T.S., O.S. CCXXVII (1952), pp. 403-23), and Gower, *Confessio Amantis* V, vv. 2543-6 (*English Works*, ed. G. C. Macaulay, vol. II, E.E.T.S., E.S. LXXXII (1901), p. 16).

Candace is similarly attacked in Hugo von Trimberg, *Renner*, vv. 21,021 ff., on which see Grammel, p. 121; and possibly (though Roxana may be intended), in *Amadas et Ydoine*, vv. 5849 ff. (ed. J. R. Reinhard, *Classiques franç. du moyen âge* (Paris, 1926), p. 220):

> Si refu treciés et traïs
> Li preus, li larges, li hardis
> Alixandres qui tant valut;
> Bien sai sa feme le deçut.

128 For these episodes see as follows:
(a) The Journey to the Terrestrial Paradise: pp. 151-2.
(b) The Celestial Journey, pp. 134-5.
(c) The Wood-maidens, p. 330, n. 124.
(d) The Enchanted River, p. 175.

The following episodes may also be mentioned for their possible effect upon the conception of Alexander:
(a) The Killing of the Basilisk, p. 302.
(b) The Trees of the Sun and Moon, p. 337.
(c) The Descent into the Sea, pp. 340-1, n. 142.

129 The tent is described in the *Roman d'Alexandre*, branch I, laisses 91-8; see A. Foulet's note in *M.F.R.d'A.* III, p. 329.

For a discussion of the materials described, see Francisque Michel, *Recherches sur le commerce, la fabrication, et l'usage des étoffes de soie, d'or et d'argent, et autres tissus précieux en occident, principalement en France, pendant le Moyen-Age* (Paris, 1872-4), vol. II, pp. 89 ff.

For the description of a wonderful tent which once belonged to Alexander, see Guido of Ivrea, *Versus Eporedienses*, vv. 147-68, ed. E. Dümmler, *Zeitschr. f. deutsch. Altertum*, XIV (1869), pp. 249-50; and cf. Manitius, *Gesch. d. lat. Lit. im Mitt.* III (1931), p. 866.

For a description of the tent in the poem of the first Crusade composed in imitation of Baudri de Bourgueil, see Meyer, *A. le G.* II, pp. 370-1 (text in *Romania*, V, pp. 1-63).

There is a further reference to the tent in *La Conquête de Jerusalem*, vv. 5493-4 (ed. C. Hippeau, Paris, 1868, p. 219).

130 See *L'Intelligenza*, stanzas 216-39 (ed. V. Mistruzzi, *Collezione di opere inedite o rare* (Bologna, 1928), pp. 130-51).

Stanza 216 (p. 130):

> Dall'altra parte del luogo giocondo
> Evi 'ntagliato Alessandro signore,
> Come si mosse ad acquistar lo mondo,
> Al tempo del re Dario, a grand' onore;
> Tutto, come cercò del mare il fondo,

> In un'olla di vetro a chiar colore;
> E come in aria portârlo i griffoni,
> E come vide tutte regioni....

For further commentary upon *L'Intelligenza*, see above, p. 270.

131 The *Voeux du Paon* was written by Jacques de Longuyon, between 1304 and 1312. It was very popular, and was famous for its introduction of the *Neuf Preux* into literature. For the translation of this work into Scots, as the *Buik of Alexander*, see p. 35. The *Voeux du Paon* was followed by a sequel, the *Restor du Paon*, composed by a certain Jean Brisebarre before 1338, and this by the *Parfait du Paon*, composed by Jean de le Mote in 1340, which completed the cycle.

These works are only externally connected by the names of their protagonists with the *Roman d'Alexandre*. For further details of them and of their authors see Meyer, *A. le G.* II, pp. 267–72, 396, and A. Thomas in *Histoire Littéraire de la France*, vol. XXXVI (1927), pp. 1–100.

132 This epilogue by Vasco de Lucena is quoted by Meyer, *A. le G.* II, p. 379: 'Puisque Alexandre conquist tout Orient sans grant nombre de gens d'armes, sans geans, sans enchantemens, sans miracles et sans sommes d'argent moult excessives, comme il appert assez par ce livre, il n'est pas doncques impossible que ung autre prince le puist reconquester. En oultre, s'il n'a point samblé difficile a Alexandre de conquester tout Orient pour saouler le vain appetit de sa gloire, il m'est advis que moins difficille devroit sembler a un bon prince christien icelui conquester pour le reduire a la foy de Jhesu Crist, car ja soit ce que le traveil et la paine d'Alexandre et du christien fust egal, le prouffit et gloire mondaine de tous deux en ce cas presque pareil, touteffois Alexandre y gaigna ou acrut sa dampnacion, et le christien y acquerroit sa gloire perpetuelle. Alexandre tua millions de gens pour regner en Orient sans l'oster de nul erreur, et le bon chrestien y regneroit ostant les presens et advenir de erreurs et de mort perpetuelle.'

133 Instances of late medieval references to Alexander's reputation for liberality are as follows:

Chronique Rimé attribué à Geffroi de Paris, vv. 4613–14 (*Rec. des Hist. des Gaules et de la France*, vol. XXII, 1865, p. 134):

> Alixandre par dons conquist,
> Daire par tenir se forfist....

For earlier references of this pattern, which thus indicate its proverbial nature, see pp. 326–7.

Eustache Deschamps, *Lay* IX (*Le Lay du tresbon Connestable*), vv. 21–4 (*Œuvres*, S.A.T.F., vol. II, ed. Le Queux de Saint-Hilaire (1880), p. 325):

> Car en largesce passoit
> Alixandre et surmontoit
> En sa prouesce Achilles,
> Plus doulz que Paris estoit....

For earlier references of this pattern, see p. 326.

E. Deschamps, *Balade* CCCLIII, vv. 48–9 (S.A.T.F., vol. III, ed. cit. (1882), p. 83):
qualities of a good general include largesse—remember Alexander.
For other references to Alexander's largesse in Deschamps see G. Raynaud,
the joint editor, in vol. XI (1903), pp. 203–4, where, quoting Meyer's views on
the decay of Alexander's reputation for liberality during these centuries, he says
that Deschamps more often respects tradition by referring to Alexander's
liberality. For further remarks on Deschamps, see above, pp. 250–1. It is possible
that his references to Alexander's liberality owed something to the fact that he
was well acquainted with the *Secret of Secrets*, with its counsel of liberality given
to Alexander by Aristotle.

On the references to liberality borrowed from the *Secret of Secrets*, and used
by Gower in Book VII of the *Confessio Amantis*, see A. H. Gilbert in *Speculum*,
III (1928), p. 88.

For late medieval German references to Alexander's liberality, see p. 328;
for a Spanish reference, p. 216, n. 1; and for Italian references, p. 351.

134 The best sketch of the medieval history of this episode is still that by
A. Héron, *La légende d'Alexandre et d'Aristote* (Académie des Sciences, etc., de
Rouen, 1892), pp. 367–84, which deals with the *Lai d'Aristote* and later versions
of the story. See also A. Borgeld, *Aristoteles en Phyllis* (Groningen, 1902).

For the use of the episode as an *exemplum*, see *Die exempla aus den Sermones
feriales et communes des Jakob von Vitry*, hrsg. J. Greven (*Sammlung mittellat. Texte*,
IX, Heidelberg, 1914), no. 15 (pp. 15–16): 'De Aristotele et uxore Alexandri',
and works there cited.

135 The two passages are as follows:
(*a*) *A. le G.* II, pp. 69–70:
'Dans les premiers temps, au xiie siècle, alors qu'apparaissent les premiers
romans (au sens étymologique du mot) d'Alexandre, l'histoire du conquérant
macédonien est, comme celle de Charlemagne, une matière à développements
poétiques, un sujet particulièrement approprié à l'expression des sentiments
chevaleresques. Les poètes se plaisent à orner leur héros de toutes les vertus qui
conviennent à un roi chevalier. Ils ne se contentent de le représenter comme un
grand conquérant, ils lui attribuent encore la qualité la plus prisée au moyen
âge: ils en font le type du souverain à la main libérale. La largesse d'Alexandre
devient, grâce à eux, proverbiale pendant tout le moyen âge. Aussi les versions
de Pseudo-Callisthènes et les textes de l'antiquité latine ne sont-ils pour eux
qu'un recueil de renseignements où ils puisent à volonté, prenant les traits qui
leur plaisent, rejetant ceux qui ne conviennent pas au type idéal qu'ils se sont
formé.

'Plus tard, au xiiie siècle et plus encore au xive, les sentiments chevaleresques
s'affaiblissent, sans que la curiosité des choses merveilleuses se soit émoussée.
Les aventures d'Alexandre plaisent non plus par leur côté épique, mais par les
événements étranges ou surnaturels qui s'y rattachent. Dès lors rien de ce que

contiennent les versions latines du Pseudo-Callisthènes n'est omis: des faits monstrueux qui avaient choqué les premiers romanciers, tels que l'histoire de Nectanebus, sont admis par Thomas de Kent, et vers le même temps apparaît et se reproduit rapidement à un grand nombre d'exemplaires la traduction en prose française de l'*Historia de Preliis*.'

(*b*) *A. le G.* II, pp. 376–7:

(Alexander's reputation for largesse in the early romances): '...Mais, dès le xiiie siècle, ce trait du caractère d'Alexandre s'efface peu à peu. Déjà, dans cette histoire universelle composée avant 1230, dont nous avons traité dans un chapitre précédent, nous rencontrons une sorte de protestation... [quoted, p. 237]. Et un peu plus tard, dans la version de l'*Historia de Preliis*, nous avons vu Alexandre qualifié de "convoitous et eschars" [see p. 372]. Dans le cours du xive siècle, la largesse d'Alexandre cesse d'être proverbiale. La transformation des conditions sociales amène une modification correspondante dans les idées: donner sans compter ni prévoir n'est plus une vertu comme au beau temps des jongleurs. En même temps, le sentiment de la vérité historique gagne du terrain. Les aventures merveilleuses, qui du Pseudo-Callisthènes à Lambert le Tort avaient intéressé tant de générations, ne semblent plus avoir autant d'attrait que par le passé, et Alexandre redevient ce qu'il fut pour l'antiquité: le type du conquérant.'

It will be observed that these two passages contradict one another, and especially on two points; the growth of the feeling for historical truth, and the duration of Alexander's reputation for liberality. The second of these points is discussed elsewhere (pp. 360–8).

Two individual statements of Meyer, however, upon this question need to be considered here; they deal with the St Albans Compilation (see p. 68), and the *Speculum Historiale* of Vincent de Beauvais (see pp. 73–4).

(i) Meyer, *A. le G.* II, p. 63: 'La Compilation de St.-Alban était née du désir de substituer aux fables de Pseudo-Callisthènes un récit authentique. Ce fut là un effort remarquable vers la critique.' (See also ibid. pp. 52–3.)

There is little evidence for this view. In the middle of the twelfth century, the period of the Compilation, most chronicles founded their accounts of Alexander exclusively upon historical material, especially upon Orosius, the main source of the Compilation. There is no such overt protest against the authority of the legend in the Compilation as appears in the *Parua Recapitulatio* (see p. 235, n. 4) or in Vasco de Lucena (see p. 332). The fact that the legendary material is nowhere mentioned may argue ignorance of it rather than the desire to protest against it, which would be normally shown by derogatory reference.

Thus, although the Compilation may have been a tacit protest against the authority of the legend, there is no more reason to suppose it so than to suppose every chronicle account of Alexander founded exclusively upon historical sources to be such a protest.

(ii) Meyer, *A. le G.* II, pp. 333–4: 'Vincent de Beauvais, ou frère Vincent, comme il serait plus sûr de l'appeler, a certainement contribué pour une grande part à maintenir aux fables du Pseudo-Callisthènes une certaine autorité, alors que, selon le progrès naturel de l'instruction et du bon sens, elles tombaient de plus en plus dans le discrédit. A une époque où l'*Alexandreis* de Gautier de Lille, rédigée d'après Quinte-Curce, était en possession de la faveur publique, où l'Angleterre possédait sur Alexandre une compilation purement historique, frère Vincent a eu l'idée d'écrire l'histoire d'Alexandre en combinant de la façon la plus maladroite l'*Epitome* de Valerius, qu'il cite sous le titre d'*Historia Alexandri*, avec Justin, Quinte-Curce, Valère Maxime et autres écrivains de l'antiquité. Nous avons vu plus haut qu'il avait fait également usage des lettres d'Alexandre et de Dindimus. La massive compilation de Vincent ne tarda pas à acquérir de l'autorité, surtout lorsqu'elle eut été mise à la portée des lecteurs laïques par la traduction de Jean du Vignay; et, bien qu'il ne s'y trouvât absolument rien d'original, on ne se fit pas faute de la citer comme une des sources de l'histoire d'Alexandre.'

There are two points here deserving of examination. The first is the statement that at the time of Vincent (the middle of the thirteenth century) the legendary material was falling increasingly into discredit; the second is the suggestion that the *Speculum Historiale* helped to keep it in favour with the general public.

In individual instances disapproval and disavowal of the legend was apparent from an early period, in the question of Alexander's conception as the son of Nectanebus, or the contradiction between the legendary and the historical account of the fate of Porus. If we compare the number of legendary to the number of historical Alexander-books written in each medieval century, we shall find that the proportion remains almost constant; and that, if there was any tendency, it was for Alexander-books to be founded more and more upon the legend. The *Middle Irish* Alexander, the *Parua Recapitulatio*, the *St Albans Compilation*, Gautier de Châtillon's *Alexandreis*, Rudolf von Ems' *Alexander*—these historical books were all the products of the eleventh, twelfth and thirteenth centuries.

Secondly, the direct influence of the *Speculum Historiale* is to be seen only in Ranulph Higden, Guibert de Tournai, and an occasional *exemplum*. In addition it offered a text in which historical and legendary accounts possessed equal importance, and were brought into contrast with one another; one which would therefore stimulate, rather than discourage, a return to historical truth by affording an opportunity for comparison between the contradictory historical and legendary texts.

136   (i) *Borrowings of the wonder material by natural historians, etc.*

(*a*) In Albertus Magnus; see Pfister in *Münchener Museum*, I (1912), pp. 261, 265, and *Germanisch-Romanische Monatschrift*, XVI (1928), p. 83.

PART B. THE MEDIEVAL CONCEPTION OF ALEXANDER

(b) In Jacques de Vitry, *Historia Hierosolymitana* i; see *Gesta Dei per Francos* (Hanover, 1611), pp. 1108 ff.; Pfister, *Alexanderroman*, p. 38.

(c) In Giraldus Cambrensis; see note 137 (b), p. 337.

(d) In Fulcher of Chartres, *Historia Hierosolymitana*; see M. Manitius, *Gesch. d. lat. Lit. im Mitt.* iii (1931), pp. 429–30.

(e) In Peter Comestor, *Historia Scholastica* (Migne, *P.L.* vol. cxcviii, cols. 1075 B, 1497–8).

(f) In Honorius of Autun, *Imago Mundi*; see Pfister, *Germanisch-Romanische Monatschrift*, xvi (1928), p. 84.

(g) In Alexander Neckham; see *De naturis rerum*, ed. T. Wright, pp. 141–2, 403.

(h) In Marco Polo; see D. Carraroli, *La leggenda di Alessandro Magno* (Mondovì, 1892), p. 275.

(i) In Mandeville; see the edition by P. Hamelius, E.E.T.S., O.S. cliii (1919), pp. 194 ff.; also in *Abh. d. sächs. Gesellsch.*, Phil.-Hist. Klasse, viii (1883), p. 143.

(j) In the letter of Prester John; see L. Olschki, 'Der Brief des Presbyter Johannes', *Historische Zeitschrift*, cxliv (1913), pp. 1–13, esp. pp. 5–6.

(k) For the story of the magic mirror in Benjamin of Tudela, the Letter of Prester John, etc., see A. Hilka in *Roman. Forschungen*, xxix (1911), pp. 8–13.

For general comments upon the use of the Alexander material in such writers, see R. Wittkower, 'Marvels of the East', *Journal of the Warburg and Courtauld Institutes*, v (1942), pp. 179–80.

(ii) *The wonder material in romances*

(a) For borrowings in romances, see Meyer, *A. le G.* ii, pp. 369–72; for the marvellous element in romances with remarks upon the influence of the Alexander marvels, see E. Faral, *Recherches sur les sources latines des contes et romans courtois du moyen âge* (Paris, 1913), pp. 307–83.

(b) For borrowings of the account of Alexander's tent, see above, p. 331.

(c) For borrowings of the description of ebony in the *Roman d'Alexandre*, see G. L. Hamilton in *Speculum*, ii (1927), pp. 121–7.

(d) For borrowings of the story of the wood-maidens, see above, p. 330.

(e) For a passage borrowed from the *Roman d'Alexandre*, in *Doon de Nanteuil*, see *Doon de Nanteuil, fragments inédits*, vv. 50 ff. (ed. P. Meyer, in *Romania*, xiii, 1884, p. 16):

Onques par Aristote qui sot d'enchantement,
Qui fit l'omme d'airain parler si hautement
De nonante langaige par ung tuel d'argent,
N'ot si buen Alexandre es desertz d'Abilant
Quant hipopotamus le firent le torment.

For the introduction of wonderful material into Alexander-books, we may cite the following instances:

(a) Thomas of Kent's *Roman de toute chevalerie* is crammed with wonders borrowed chiefly from Solinus and Aethicus Ister. See J. Weynand, Der 'Roman de toute chevalerie' des Thomas von Kent in seinem Verhältnis zu seinen Quellen (Diss. Bonn, 1911), passim.

(b) Basel Alexander, where wonderful material from Enikel's Weltchronik is interpolated; see pp. 346–7.

(c) Ulrich von Eschenbach, who concentrates the wonderful material in the tenth book of his Alexander: see W. Toischer, in Sitzungsber. d. k. Akad. d. Wiss. in Wien., Phil.-Hist. Klasse, Bd. xcvii (1881 for 1880), p. 324.

(d) Domenico Scolari, who inserted many wonders into the text of his Italian translation of Quilichinus; see Storost, pp. 52–3.

For epitomes of the Historia de Preliis in which the wonderful element has been retained in preference to the battles, see:

(a) The Harvard Epitome of the I² Historia de Preliis (ed. F. P. Magoun, Harvard Studies and Notes in Philology and Literature, xiv, 1932, pp. 115–34); see above, p. 45.

(b) Cod. Riccard. 1922, an Italian prose epitome of the I³ Historia de Preliis; see Storost, pp. 126–32; and above, pp. 54–5.

137 For the story of the prophetic trees of the sun and the moon that foretold Alexander's death, see Julius Valerius iii, 24–7 (ed. Kuebler, pp. 131–5); Epistola ad Aristotelem (ed. Kübler, pp. 209–17).

Independent citations as follows:

(a) Peter Comestor, Historia Scholastica, lib. Esther iv (Migne, P.L. vol. cxcviii, col. 1497–8).

(b) Giraldus Cambrensis, Topographia Hibernica ii, iv (Opera, vol. v, ed. Dimock, p. 81, l. 18). Cf. M. Manitius, Gesch. d. lat. Lit. im Mitt. iii (1931), p. 626.

(c) L'Art de Chevalerie, ed. U. Robert (S.A.T.F., 1897), pp. 89–90.

(d) L'Ymage dou Monde, cited in Le Roux de Lincy, Le Livre des Légendes (1836), p. 213 (cf. Caxton's Mirrour of the World, ed. Prior, E.E.T.S., E.S. cx (1913), p. 75).

(e) For the use of the story in Marco Polo, see G. Favre, Mélanges littéraires (1856), ii, p. 119 and H. Yule and H. Cordier, The Book of Ser Marco Polo, vol. i (London, 1926), pp. 127–39.

(f) John de Mandeville. See M. Letts, Mandeville's Travels (London, Hakluyt Society, 1953 for 1950), pp. 37, 208, 491.

(g) John Lydgate, Reson and Sensuallyte, ed. Sieper, E.E.T.S., E.S. lxxxiv (1901), vv. 4367–426, pp. 115–16.

For popular references to the story of the Wonderstone, see pp. 149–52, 347; to the story of the maidens in the wood, see p. 330.

138 References to this most evident of all the contradictions between the various sources are so numerous that only a few of the more interesting may be cited here:

(*a*) Fulgentius; see pp. 369–70 for the text of his account, the first in Latin to mention Nectanebus' paternity.

(*b*) Alfred the Great, in his translation of Orosius, refers to the Nectanebus legend; see G. L. Hamilton, in *Mélanges...offerts à M. Antoine Thomas* (Paris, 1927), p. 197.

(*c*) For references in Alberic, the *Decasyllabic Alexander*, and the *Roman d'Alexandre*, see p. 235, nn. 3, 4.

(*d*) The story is referred to, although it is of course rejected, in Gautier de Châtillon, *Alexandreis* I, vv. 46–7; III, vv. 167–8 (Migne, *P.L.* vol. CCIX, cols. 463, 489). The author of the *Libro de Alexandre* rejected the Nectanebus story, accessible to him in the *Historia de Preliis*, as incompatible with the text of the *Alexandreis*; see Willis, *Debt*, p. 56. Ulrich von Eschenbach, on the other hand, adds the Nectanebus episode to supply the supposed omission at the beginning of the *Alexandreis*; see W. Toischer, in *Sitzungsber. d. kaiser. Akad. d. Wissen. in Wien*, Phil.-Hist. Klasse, Bd. XCVII (1881), p. 322.

(*e*) Ekkehart of Aura, *Chronicon*, in *M.G.H. Scriptt.* VI (ed. D. G. Waitz, 1844), p. 61: 'Alexander Magnus, Philippi, ut putabatur, et Olimpiadis filius....' On p. 62 the Nectanebus episode is told from the Bamberg MS. of Leo.

(*f*) Otto of Freising, in *M.G.H. Scriptt.* XX (1868), p. 154, ll. 20–2 (ed. R. Wilmans): (Alexander) 'De quo traditur, quod non Philippi, sed cuiusdam magi Aegyptiorum regis Nectanabi filius fuerit.'

(*g*) Godfrey of Viterbo, *Pantheon*, part XI; see L. Meyer, *Les Légendes des Matières de Rome, de France, et de Bretagne dans le 'Panthéon' de Godefroi de Viterbe* (Paris, 1933), pp. 59–60.

(*h*) Vincent de Beauvais, *Speculum Historiale* IV, 1 (ed. Douai, 1624, p. 171): 'Alexander Philippi et Olympiadis filius nascitur, quod tamen illi uulgatae Alexandri historiae non uidetur omnino congruere, quae eum narrat a Nectanebo, iam extra regnum facto, generatum fuisse.'

(*i*) *Old French Prose Romance* (ed. Hilka, Halle, 1920), pp. 5–6: 'Apres che Phelippes de Macedone rois engenra en sa feme Olimpias le bon roi Alixandre; mes Vinchens, uns jacobins qui cerka toutes les ystoires du monde, dist en son livre la ou il parolè d'Alixandre, que Nectanebus rois d'Egypte fu ses peres et l'engendra en la roïnne Olimpias et jut a li en forme de dragon.' This is an addition of the second redactor.

(*j*) *Histoire ancienne jusqu'à César*, cited by Meyer, *A. le G.* II, p. 342: '*De Neptanabus le roi d'Egypte, qui fu peres Alixandre, si come pluisor content et dient*: Dit vous ai ariere que li pluisor cuidoient et cuident encore que cis Alixandres estoit fiz au roi Neptanabus d'Egypte, e si vos dirai por quoi il le cuidoient e disoient et dient encore....' He goes on to tell the story of Nectanebus' device.

[It is to be noted that the method of composition of this author is a most unintelligent juxtaposition of sources. As a result of this many episodes are duplicated, and the duel of Alexander and Porus is told three times following the *Zacher Epitome*, the *Epistola*, and the *Roman d'Alexandre* respectively. D.J.A.R.]

(*k*) Nectanebus is substituted for Philip as the father of Alexander in the *Basel Alexander*, vv. 1-534 (ed. K. Kinzel, Halle, 1884), pp. 3-24.

(*l*) *Eulogium Historiarum* (ed. Haydon), vol. I, pp. 60, 310.

(*m*) Reference to the story cited by S. Lattès, 'La plus ancienne Bible en vers italiens (Manuscrit Vatican 4821)', *Ecole française de Rome, Mélanges d'Archéologie et d'Histoire*, année 49 (1932), p. 194.

(*n*) John Lydgate, *Fall of Princes* IV, vv. 711-14 (ed. H. Bergen, Washington, 1923), vol. II, p. 493: 'Men say that Nectanebus begat Alexander.'

(*o*) For the fanciful genealogy of Alexander in the *Florimont* of Aimon de Varennes (1188), which makes Florimont the father of Philip and grandfather of Alexander, and Olympias a Carthaginian princess, see the edition by A. Hilka, *Gesell. f. roman. Lit.* XLVIII (Göttingen, 1932), who discusses the episode at length in his introduction, pp. cvi-cix, and suggests a possible connexion with Oriental tradition. In vv. 3883-93 (p. 152) there is a reference to the Nectanebus story:

> Les gens en dissoient folie
> Qu'Olimpias fut s'amie,
> Alixandres ses fils estoit.
> Mai cil mantoit qui le dissoit;
> Grant mensonge fut c'on le dist;
> Car Alixandres puels l'osist.

For Alexander's genealogy in this work, see vv. 11,386, 11,410, 13,581ff. (pp. 448-9 and 535). Vv. 13,590-603 contain a short description of Alexander's life (pp. 535-6).

139 Jean de Courcy first tells the story of the birth of Alexander as the son of Nectanebus; and, as Meyer says (*A. le. G.* II, p. 350): 'Mais déjà le titre de ce chapitre: "De la conception du roy Alixandre, comme l'en disoit", indique un esprit sceptique.'

The next chapter (*Boucachardière* v, xii) begins as follows (ibid. p. 351):

> '*De ung signe qui apparut en la groisse sa mere, et comme il fut né*
> Combien que cy dessus vous aye compté toute l'opinion d'aucuns hystoriens, et comme ja pieça en escript le mirent, si n'est pas tele la moye opinion; et est l'une des causes qui me meut ad ce dire que la sainte Bible tesmoigne le contraire ou premier livre des Machabeux ou il dist de Alixandre et Phelippe son pere, cellui qui premier en Grece regna.... L'autre cause si est par Aristote qui mon opinion tesmoigne veritablement, qui tout vit celle chose advenir, car il fut conseillier d'icellui roy Phelippe. Repairer nous convenient au vray histoire comme le roy Phelippe revint de sa conqueste pour l'iver temps qui de pres le hastoit....'

140 For doubt thrown upon the authenticity of the *Epistola ad Aristotelem*, see the remarks of Ekkehart of Aura, quoted and discussed above, p. 72; and Otto of Freising, in *M.G.H. Scriptt.* xx (Hanover, 1868, ed. R. Wilmans), p. 155, ll. 27–31: (Porus' palace) '...de cuius domo aurea, uinea quoque argentea et aurea, racemisque ex gemmis preciosis, qui scire uult, legat epistolam Alexandri ad Aristotilem philosophum praeceptorem suum, in qua pericula eius quae passus est, de simulacrisque solis et lunae, quae ei mortem praedixerant, et multa quae tam mirabilia sunt, ut etiam incredibilia uideantur, diligens inquisitor rerum inueniet.'

For an early secular show of doubt about the deeds of Alexander, dissipated by the facts of the career of Frederick II, cf. Aimeric de Peguilhan, *La Metgia* iv, vv. 28–32, in *Poesie Provenzali Storiche* (ed. V. de Bartholomaeis, vol. i (Rome, 1931), *Fonti per la Storia d'Italia*), p. 248:

> Quel sieu perden, venc, meten e donan,
> Sai conquerir l'Emperi Alaman.
> Oimais crei ben, cor qei anes doptan,
> Los faitz c'om ditz d'Alixandre comtan.

141 In the Porus crux, the *Epitome* of Valerius says that Alexander killed Porus in a duel at their first encounter; in the *Epistola ad Aristotelem* Porus is represented as pardoned and guides Alexander through the desert. In the historians Alexander and Porus become allies.

The contradiction was reconciled in Godfrey of Viterbo and the *Roman d'Alexandre* in a similar way; Porus, saved from the battle, guides Alexander across the desert, and then plots treason against him. Alexander thereupon kills him in a duel. See L. Meyer, *Les Légendes des Matières de Rome, de France, et de Bretagne dans le 'Panthéon' de Godefroi de Viterbe* (Paris, 1933), pp. 78–80; Meyer, *A. le G.* ii, pp. 186–7.

For the treatment of the Porus episode in the *Libro de Alexandre*, see Willis, *Relationship*, pp. 16–17. See also Vincent de Beauvais, *Speculum Historiale* iv, 49 (ed. Douai, (1624) p. 130) for a statement of the contradiction; and Meyer, *A. le G.* ii, pp. 324–5.

For a further crux, concerning the siege of Tyre, see Meyer, *A. le G.* ii, pp. 162–3 (*Roman d'Alexandre*), 320–1 (Wauquelin).

142 The full passage, in Seifrit's *Alexander*, vv. 6545–62, begins as follows (ed. P. Gereke, *Deutsche Texte des Mittelalters*, xxxvi (Berlin, 1932), pp. 107–8):

> Das das nit war sey das in sein
> weib in das mer liess.
> 6545 Sumleich ritter sagent ein mer
> das gar vast gelogen wer.
> das daucht mich ungelaublich
> das Allexander der reich
> der edlen frawen sein,
> 6550 Roxanen der chaiserein,

die chetten geb zu halten,
das sy der solt walten.
da lies an der selben stundt
vallen die chetten in des meres grundt.
6555   das mag also nit gesein....

This story is told of Alexander's queen (Roxana is not mentioned by name) in
History-Bible I and Enikel's *Weltchronik*, and obviously descends from the same
undiscovered source as that which is responsible for the unique version of the
Celestial Journey found in these two texts. See upon this version below, pp. 346–7.

The account of the attempt to drown Alexander may be connected with another
detail of the submarine descent unique in German texts, and first appearing in
the *Annolied*. This detail is that Alexander took down with him into the sea a
dog, a cat, and a hen, which assisted him by their peculiar properties. When he
was stranded at the bottom of the sea by the letting down of the chains, Alexander killed the hen; and the sea, unwilling to tolerate blood, cast the contrivance
out upon the beach, and Alexander was saved.

For a Latin literary source of this account, and for a discussion of the questions
involved, see A. Hilka, *Altfranzösischer Prosa-Alexanderroman*, pp. xxxviii–xli,
who quotes a relevant passage from MS. M1 (München, cod. lat. 824) of the
I² *Historia de Preliis*.

[Curiously enough, though nothing of all this appears in the *French Prose
Alexander*, three of the MSS. show by their illustrations that some version of
this kind must have been current in France in the fourteenth century. British
Museum Royal 20. A.V. fol. 71b and 20. B. XX. fol. 77b both show Alexander in the glass barrel with his three animals, and the latter, and Royal 19 D.I.
fol. 37b, show the queen cutting the cable. The aberrant version of the *Roman
d'Alexandre* (MS. L. Bib. Nat. Fr. 789) contains such an account, but no picture
illustrates it. I hope shortly to complete a literary and iconographic study of
Alexander's bathyscaphe. D.J.A.R.]

143   There are two relevant passages in the *Wernigerode Alexander*:
    (i) The author's comment on the divine interference in the Celestial Journey
(vv. 5629–39, ed. Guth, p. 81):
                                    ...alsus
        tet Got mit im wunder vil
        und mer als ich gelauben wil
        er ye getet mit kainem man
        in solhen jorn, als ich hon
        gelesen. Allexander
        yn zehen jarn und mer
        zwayer jar ward er gemain
        aller werlt her allain.
        waz daz nit ain wunder gröss
        daz ez die Gotheit nit verdrozz
        daz er im ie so hoch gedaht?

341

(ii) His final comment upon God's interference (vv. 6284-304, p. 90):

Als ich main besünder,
ist ez ain wunder gröss
daz Allexander beslozz
die zehen gesleht,
als man auch vil rëht
in der heiligen geschrift list,
wie er sie mit list
beslüst, Gög und Magög.
Grosser wunder gesach nÿ aüg,
die ye getet kain haydnisch man.
Het ez sant Peter getan,
ez wer wünders mer dann vil.
Ez kann nymmant an ain zil
sagen waz im Got verhangt
ze tün. Dar umb mich nit belangt
waz die Gothait da mit maint
daz sie im so vil erschaint
wunders auf der erde.
Nymmant sich dor an kere:
ez waiz Got wol wor umb ers tet.
Da von nymmant ze sagen stet.

144 See for examples of this Skeat's introduction to his edition, p. xxi.

Out of the numerous examples in other Alexander-books, we may cite Lambert li Tors' reference to his Latin source (see above, p. 322); Lamprecht's reference to Alberic; Seifrit aus Oesterreich's and Hartlieb's references to the book of 'Eusebius' from which their translation was made; and numerous references in Rudolf von Ems, cited by O. Zingerle, *Die Quellen zum Alexander des Rudolf von Ems* (Breslau, 1885).

See also above, p. 271.

145 For a discussion of the principal late German accounts of Alexander, see below, pp. 258-9.

We may notice here two chronicle lives of Alexander which present no especial interest, except that they indicate the tendency to return to an historical foundation, as is made evident in the omission of the wonder element.

The first of these, the life of Alexander in the Latin chronicle of Martinus Polonus (von Troppau), is derived from the I² *Historia de Preliis*. It contains a long Jerusalem episode and a long Candace episode, but the wonders are much abridged. See Martinus Polonus, *Chronicon* II, iv (ed. Plantin, Antwerp, 1574), pp. 59-77.

The second, in the German chronicle of Jakob Twinger v. Koenigshofen, is founded upon the account of Alexander in Ekkehart of Aura (see above, pp. 71-2): but the historical narrative from Orosius which opens Ekkehart's version is omitted, and the text follows Ekkehart's transcription of the Bamberg *Historia de Preliis.* But the wonderful material (including the *Epistola ad Aristotelem*) is entirely omitted, and the reader who wishes to know of Alexander's adventures is referred to 'the book of Alexander'. See *Chronike* I, xcv–cxvii (ed. J. Schiltern, Strassburg, 1698), pp. 40–9.

146 For a list of texts illustrative of the Nine Worthies, see I. Gollancz, *The Parlement of the Thre Ages* (Roxburghe Club, 1897), Appendix II, pp. 119–45. The list was supplemented with further literary and some iconographic evidence by R. S. Loomis, 'Verses on the Nine Worthies', *Modern Philology*, XV (1917), pp. 211–19.

Of these texts we may cite some of the more interesting in their references to Alexander.

Gollancz:

Nos. III and IV (pp. 121–30). Relevant extracts from the *Voeux du Paon* and the *Buik of Alexander*.

No. VI. *Ane Ballet of the Nine Nobles* (s. xiv exeunte), stanza II, vv. 325 ff.

(p. 132):
> Alexander als nobil a kyng,
> In xij yeris wan throw hard feichtyng,
> Al landis vnder the formament!

No. VII. Early Mumming Play (s. xv); Alexander says (p. 135):
> And in romaunce often am I leyt
> As conqueror gret thow I seyt.

No. IX (pp. 139 f.). Prologue to the *Fabelhafte Geschichte*.

No. X (pp. 140–3). Passages from the two Scottish Alexander-books.

Loomis:

No. II (pp. 211–12). Stanzas of great interest below the fifteenth-century mural paintings (made between 1411 and 1430) of the Nine Worthies in the castle of La Manta in Piedmont.

Alexander is represented as saying:
> Jay coquis por ma force les illes d'outramer;
> D'Orient jusques a Ocident fuge ja sire apeles.
> Jay tue roy Daire, Porus, Nicole larmires;
> La grant Babiloina fige ver moy encliner;
> E fuy sire du monde; puis fui enarbres;
> Ce fut III. C ans devant que Diu fu nee.

No. V (p. 215). Verses made on a series of copper engravings made in 1464 by the Meister mit den Bandrollen; of Alexander it is said:

> *Rex Alexander*
> Secondus fuit alexander uocatus
> qui de macedonis fuit natus
> in paradiso (...) tributum

> sicut continet historia scriptum
> trecentis annis obiit prius
> in babilonia quam nasceretur xps.

No. VII (p. 217). Verses spoken on the reception of Queen Margaret at Coventry in 1455, from the Coventry Leet Book; the verses about Alexander are given thus in *Two Coventry Corpus Christi Plays*, ed. Hardin Craig, E.E.T.S., E.S. LXXXVII (1902), Appendix III, p. 112:

> I, Alexander, that for chyvalry berith the balle,
> Most curagious in conquest, thro the world am y-named.

Loomis gives a comprehensive list of bibliographical references on the iconography of the *Neuf Preux*. On the *Neuf Preux* in pageants, see R. Withington, *English Pageantry*, vol. I (Cambridge, Mass., 1918), pp. 79, 99, 138 and n. 4, 150, 164, 191 and n. 2, 192, 195; also pp. 22, 23, and 94.

For a literary reference unnoticed by the above authors, see Stephen Hawes, *Pastime of Pleasure*, vv. 5551–7 (ed. Mead, E.E.T.S., O.S. CLXXIII, 1928, p. 212).

We may conclude with Gower's reference to the vanity of all things symbolized by the passing away of the *Neuf Preux*: *In Praise of Peace*, vv. 281–6 (*English Works*, ed. G. C. Macaulay, vol. II, E.E.T.S., E.S. LXXXII, 1901, p. 489).

147 For bibliographical details, and other material dealing with the late medieval popularity of the *Secret of Secrets*, see above, pp. 287–8; for a list of works founded on the *Secret of Secrets*, see R. Steele's introduction to his edition of the translation by Lydgate and Burgh (E.E.T.S., E.S. LXVI, 1894), pp. xii–xiii.

For the use of the work by Gower and others, see A. H. Gilbert, 'Notes on the Influence of the *Secretum Secretorum*', *Speculum*, III (1928), pp. 84–98.

For its use in Germany, see W. Toischer, *Die altdeutsche Bearbeitungen des pseudo-aristotelischen Secreta Secretorum* (Prague, 1884), and A. Mussafia, in *Sitzungsber. d. kaiserl. Akad. d. Wissen. in Wien*, Phil.-Hist. Klasse, Bd. CVI, pp. 507 ff.

For its use in the Stockholm manuscript of the *Old French Prose Romance*, see W. Soederhjelm, 'Notice et extraits du MS. fr. 51 de la Bibliothèque Royale de Stockholm', *Neuphilol. Mittheilungen* (Helsingfors, 1917), pp. 307–33.

148 For various prefaces to the *Secret of Secrets*, see R. Steele's edition of Roger Bacon's version of the work (*Rogeri Baconi Opera Hactenus Inedita*, fasc. V, Oxford, 1920), p. 1; also his edition of Lydgate and Burgh's *Secrees of old Philosoffres*, E.E.T.S., E.S. LXVI (1894), pp. 1–2, vv. 50 ff. (p. 2):

> This Alysaundre / the Crowne whan he took,
> Knyghtly dispoosyd / of herte and of Corage.
> In whoos worshepe / compyled was this book
> By Arystotyl / whanne he was falle in Age, . . .

Cf. also Rutebeuf, *Le Dit d'Aristote*, vv. 1–6 (ed. A. Kressner, Wolfenbüttel, 1885, pp. 176–8):

Aristotles a Alixandre
Enseingne et si li fet entendre
En son livre versifié
Enz el premier quaier lié
Coment il doit el siecle vivre,
Et Rustebues l'a tret del livre;...

The 'livre versifié' in question is the *Alexandreis*, from the first book of which Rutebeuf extracted his poem.

149 See Eustache Deschamps, *Balade* XCIX (*Œuvres*, S.A.T.F., vol. I, ed. M. de Queux de S -Hilaire, 1878, pp. 208–10): this consists of various pieces of advice extracted from the *Secret of Secrets*, with the *Envoi* (p. 210):

Princes, ces poins tint cilz Roy et ama,
Qui tout le monde obtint et subjuga
Et d'ensuir les vertus fut vray hoir;...

Cf. *Balade* CCII (vol. II, pp. 22–3): the poem contains advice to the young Charles VI, using the example of Alexander.

150 For a discussion of the references to Alexander in Deschamps, see G. Raynaud in a note in volume XI of his works (S.A.T.F., 1903), p. 203. Only the most important references are given here.

For Alexander's liberality see *Lay* IX, vv. 21–2 (vol. II, p. 325), *Balade* CCCLIII, vv. 48–9 (vol. III, p. 83). For quotation and discussion of these passages see pp. 332–3.

For references to Alexander's learning, see the previous note, and *Balade* CCLXXII, v. 15 (vol. II, p. 117), *Balade* CCCLVI, vv. 25 ff. (vol. III, p. 88).

For Alexander's death at the hands of his servants (with emphasis upon the vanity of human affairs), see *Balade* CCCXXX, v. 51; *Balade* CCCLXVIII, v. 3 (vol. III, pp. 35, 113); for further references see Raynaud, loc. cit.

For criticism of Alexander, see *Balade* CCXIV, vv. 1–2 (vol. II, p. 37) (plain speaking no longer in favour):

Nulz ne veult plus estre Dyogenès
Qui surmonta l'avarice Alixandre;...

For emphasis upon Alexander's late medieval role of conqueror, see *Balade* CCXCIII, vv. 1–2 (vol. II, p. 150): (Deschamps wishes the Duc d'Orléans)

Du sens que Dieu donna a Salemon
Et du pouoir au grant roy Alixandre;...

Compare a similar remark in Gower, cited on p. 254, n. 5; and for the connexion between Alexander and Solomon in the *Vorau Alexander*, see above, pp. 171–2. For a similar treatment of Alexander, cf. *Balade* CCII (vol. II, p. 23), where Alexander is 'hardis et preus', and Raynaud, loc. cit. For three similar references in Guillaume de Machaut to 'li meschiès qu'Alixandres fist Daire', see his *Poésies lyriques* (ed. V. Chichmaref, 1909), vol. I, p. 180; vol. II, pp. 438, 558.

151   E.g. in the epilogue of Vasco de Lucena (p. 332), who, recalling Alexander's heathendom, consigns his soul to hell as does the author of *Seelentrost* (p. 312). It is further observable in the comment attached to many sixteenth-century editions of the *Ditz Moraux*: 'Plusieurs bons enseignemens et doctrines donna Alexandre, mais enfin il fut deceu par haine et mondaine gloire, car il se souffri adorer comme Dieu et filz de Jupiter Hammon.'

Laurent de Premierfait's translation of Boccaccio's *De Casibus Virorum Illustrium* also helped to introduce abuse of Alexander of a theological or Stoic type into France.

152   These two references are as follows:

Benedictus Deus in Donis suis, stanza 5, vv. 35 ff. (*Minor Poems*, part I, ed. H. N. MacCracken, E.E.T.S., E.S. CVII (1911), p. 8):

> [God] Made Alysaundre a myghty conquerour,
> Pore Dyogynes lyst do hym no reuerence,
> Be-twen hem two ther was gret difference,
> The toon in pride, the tother in poverte,
> Texempleffye, breffly in sentence,
> What euer Iesu sent blyssed mot he be.

Consulo quisquis eris (*Minor Poems*, part II, ed. MacCracken, p. 753). Here the story is used to point the moral that 'pride comes before a fall'; Alexander fell while Diogenes prospered:

> He thouht vertu was moor imperrial
> Than his acqueyntaunce, with al his proud language.

153   For Berthold von Regensburg's remarks upon the pride exemplified by Alexander in the Celestial Journey, see *Predigten* XXV (ed. F. Pfeiffer, vol. I (Vienna, 1862), pp. 399–400).

For the account of Alexander in *History-Bible* I ('Do Got in Siner Magenkraft'), see J. F. L. Theodor Merzdorf, *Die Deutschen Historienbibeln des Mittelalters*, *B.L.V.* vols. C–CI (Tübingen, 1870), vol. II, pp. 543–52. For the very similar version of the story in Jansen Enikel's *Weltchronik*, see vv. 19,445–600 in the edition by Ph. Strauch, *M.G.H. Deutsche Chroniken*, III (Hanover, 1900), pp. 371–3.

The accounts of the Celestial Journey and of the descent into the sea (see pp. 340–1) found in these works are descended from a common but unknown source. See the valuable note by Pfister, *Alexanderroman*, p. 29, n. 2.

The date of this mysterious source is established by the fact that the version of the descent into the sea in the *Annolied*, the *Kaiserchronik*, and the *Basel Alexander*, is evidently derived from it, and it must therefore be necessarily prior in date to the *Annolied* account, with which that in the *Kaiserchronik* substantially agrees (see p. 321).

Besides the descent into the sea, the *Basel Alexander* contains versions of the *Iter ad Paradisum* and the Celestial Journey very similar to those in Enikel's *Weltchronik*, and probably derived from that source. For a discussion of the relationship between these interpolations in the *Basel Alexander* and Enikel's *Weltchronik*, see Grammel, pp. 25-6.

154 For a discussion of the role of the *Iter ad Paradisum* in the *Strassburg Alexander*, the *Basel Alexander*, and Ulrich v. Eschenbach, see above, pp. 176-9. For the version of the *Iter* in *History-Bible* I, see Merzdorf, loc. cit. pp. 546-8; in Enikel, see vv. 18,995-19,224, in *M.G.H. Deutsche Chroniken*, III (Hanover, 1900), pp. 362-6. In this version Alexander gets ready 200 ships, with food sufficient to last five years; the stone, cut in the shape of an eye, cannot be outweighed by wood, iron, or lead, until it is covered with earth. Alexander is warned not to go against the will of God. On this version, see W. Hertz, *Aristoteles in den Alexanderdichtungen des Mittelalters* in *Gesammelte Abhandlungen*, (Stuttgart and Berlin, 1905), pp. 119 ff.

For the *Iter* in similar world-chronicle accounts of the 14th and 15th centuries, see Hertz, loc. cit. pp. 119-20.

For the use of the *Iter* as a warning against pride in Frauenlob's tenson with Regenboge on the words 'wîp' and 'vrouwe' (*Heinrichs von Meissen des Frauenlobes Leiche, Sprüche*, etc., ed. L. Ettmüller (Quedlinburg and Leipzig, 1843), Spr. 163-7), see Hertz, loc. cit. pp. 82-3, and Grammel, p. 122.

On a story of Ulrich Boner (*c.* 1350), in his collection of tales (c. 87, ed. F. Pfeiffer, Leipzig, 1844, p. 154), 'Von einem edeln steine eins keisers von angedenkunge des todes', see Hertz, loc. cit. p. 123, Grammel, p. 122. Alexander's name is not mentioned here.

Alexander's connexion with Wonderstones was well known in Germany; Wolfram v. Eschenbach, *Parzival*, v. 77,323 refers to him as 'steinkundiger'. But this may have been in part due to another story of Alexander and a Wonderstone which found its way into Europe, the Oriental tale of the lucky stone which Alexander lost when it was swallowed by a serpent. For this story and its European descendants, see W. Printz, 'Gilgamisch und Alexander', *Zeitsch. d. deutschen morgenl. Gesell.* LXXXV (1931), pp. 196-206. This stone is the mysterious *Claugestiân*, referred to in *König Rother*, v. 4952-65 (ed. H. Rückert, Leipzig, 1872, pp. 244-5).

For the use of the *Iter* in *Seelentrost*, see above, pp. 258-9; in Seifrit, see above, p. 244 and n. 4.

155 The independent German references to Alexander dating from this period have been scattered over many sections of this book: see for a reference to the Pirate Story, p. 282; to the story of Diogenes, p. 276; to God's intervention in the fall of Alexander, p. 315. For references lying between the two secular periods, see pp. 323-4; and for the life of Alexander in Jakob Twinger von Königshofen, p. 342.

347

A number of other references are given here; and it will be seen that they conform to the usual characteristics of the German Alexander tradition: *Sächsische Weltchronik*, ed. L. Weiland, in *M.G.H. Deutsche Chroniken*, II (Hanover, 1877):

pp. 77–8: brief account of Alexander's life, from Ekkehart of Aura and Peter Comestor, including the episode of the Ten Tribes.

p. 83: Alexander marries Roxana...:

> 'De dese wunder al wil weten,
> de lese Alexandrum Magnum
> [i.e. Ekkehart's chronicle]
> unde dat bok Machabeorum.'

p. 383: the Turkish Sultan at the siege of Constantinople; he wishes to emulate Alexander. See on Sultan Muhammad II's admiration for Alexander, Pfister in *Wochenschr. f. klass. Phil.* (1911), cols. 1152–9.

Braunschweigische Reimchronik, vv. 8486–9 in *M.G.H. Deutsche Chroniken*, II (Hanover, 1877), p. 564: Alexander's valour.

Hugo vom Trimberg, *Renner*, vv. 19,085–8 (cited Grammel, p. 119):

> er tet mêr in zwelf jâren
> denne die drîzic jâr kunic wâren,
> Dô er machte zwelf grôze stete
> der ieglich sînen namen hete!

Der Saelden Hort, vv. 5415 ff. (ed. H. Adrian, *Deutsche Texte d. Mitt.* XXVI, 1927, p. 97): Alexander's wonderful adventures.

156 *Tractatus de Diuersis Historiis Romanorum*, ed. S. Herzstein (*Erlanger Beitr. z. Englischen Philologie*, IX, Erlangen, 1893):

No. 1 (pp. 1–2): the pirate story in the *Policraticus* version, though St Augustine's name heads the citation. No moral attached; Alexander will change pirate's fortune: 'Fecitque eum milicie ascribi, ut posset inde facilius legibus militare.'

No. 6 (pp. 3–4): the story of the man to whom Alexander gave a city, quoted without Seneca's comment, as an example of true liberality.

No. 42 (p. 18): the story of the Wonderstone, quoted above, pp. 299–300.

157 *Fior di Virtù*, ed. B. Fabbricatore (third ed., Napoli, 1870). The following anecdotes are told of Alexander:

(*a*) Cap. VI (pp. 34–5), *Del Vizio della Tristizia, e della Morte di Alessandro*. The chapter is occupied with a long description of the episode of the Philosophers at the Tomb (see above, pp. 151–2), told, unusually, as an example of immoderate grief, and concludes with the words: 'E allora cominciò tutta la gente a piangere, e fecero il maggiore corrotto, che mai fosse udito.'

(*b*) Cap. IX (pp. 42–3): *Della virtù della misericordia*: 'Della misericordia è scritto nelle storie romane che, essendo un ladro che rubava per mare, sì fu menato dinanzi Alessandro.' The story is told in the usual exemplar fashion and

348

concludes: 'Sicchè, vedendo il re Alessandro la franchezza di costui, sì gli fè misericordia, veggendo ch'egli non era ladro se non per povertà; e per compassione ch'egli ebbe della sua miseria, sì gli perdonò la morte, e fecelo de' suoi cavalieri; e fu poi de' migliori che il re avesse.' The Italian fondness for the exemplar form of the pirate anecdote has been previously remarked. Of especial interest is the quotation from Boccaccio, which will be requoted here for convenience: G. Boccaccio, *Epist.* v (to Niccolò Acciaiuoli, 1341), in *Opere Latine Minori*, ed. A. F. Massera, *Scrittori di Italia* (Bari, 1928), p. 126: '...come del pirata Antigono la fortuna rea in buona trasmutò Alessandro, così da voi spero doversi la mia trasmutare.' The form 'Antigono' of the pirate's name is evidently derived from a confused remembrance of the linked episodes in the *Policraticus*, where the story of Dionides follows that of Antigonus; see above, p. 96.

(c) Cap. XI (p. 50): *Della virtù della liberalità.* The story of the man to whom Alexander gave a city. On the strange version of the story here given see below, p. 360.

(d) Cap. XVI (p. 65): *Della pazzia.* A madman refuses to move out of Alexander's path; when the soldiers attempt to shift him, Alexander says: 'Let him be; for he is not a man' (i.e. he is no true man). I have been unable to discover the source of this story; could it be a delightful modification of one of Alexander's various interviews with philosophers?

158 The proverbial sayings ascribed to Alexander are in the following pages and chapters of the *Fior di Virtù* (ed. cit.):

(a) Pp. 41–2 (cap. IX, *Della virtù della misericordia*): 'Alessandro dice: La possanza delle persone cresce in due modi; per acquistare amici, e per fare misericordia e perdonare a' nemici; chè vendetta senza danno non puote essere.'

(b) P. 46 (cap. XI, *Della virtù della liberalità*): 'Alessandro dice: Dona ad altrui, se tu vuoi che sia donato a te.' Cf. p. 372 (Wauquelin).

(c) P. 60 (cap. XV, *Della prudenza*): 'Alessandro dice: La notte fu fatta per pensare quello che l'uomo debbe fare il dì.'

(d) P. 79 (cap. XX, *Della falsità*): 'Alessandro dice: In cui ti debbi fidare, non avere mai sospezzion di lui, o non ti fidare; chè la sospezzione dà cagione di fare male.'

(e) P. 100 (cap. XXXI, *Della umiltà*): 'Alessandro dice: Dalla nobiltà di cuore viene a ricordarsi de' servigi, e dimenticare le 'ngiurie.'

(f) P. 114 (cap. XXXVII, *Della moderanza*): 'Dalla cortesia ebbe incominciamento la gentilezza; e, secondo che dice Alessandro, la gentilezza si è belli costumi e virtudiosi, e antica ricchezza, cioè costumi di laudabili virtudi, e ricchezza bene acquistata.'

159 The passages in *Li Livres dou Tresor* concerned with Alexander are referred to by the edition of P. Chabaille (Paris, 1863). In the following passages reference is made to certain of the marvellous adventures of Alexander.

I, iv, 123 (p. 160). The Ichthyophagi.

I, v, 141 (p. 193). The Basilisk.

I, v, 185 (p. 233). An experiment to prove the longevity of deer.

I, v, 189 (p. 243). The elephants of Porus defeated by heated brazen statues.

II, ii, 79 (p. 412). The Senecan story of the man to whom Alexander gave a city, told as it was told by William of Conches, and subjoined to the story of Antigonus with the intermediate comment: 'Mais Alixandres le fist mieulx....' This anecdote was used fairly frequently in late medieval Italy; see pp. 348–9, 351.

II, ii, 100 (p. 447). Comparison of Alexander with Diogenes.

Proverbial sayings of Alexander are cited on pp. 399, 440; and there is a short biography of him in I, i, 27 (pp. 36–7), with reference to the legend, on which see D. Carraroli, *La leggenda di Alessandro Magno* (Mondovì, 1892), pp. 247–50, who also discusses the Alexander material in the *Tesoretto*.

160 *Inferno* XII, vv. 106–8:

> Quivi si piangon li spietati danni:
> Quivi è Alessandro, e Dionisio fero,
> Che fe' Sicilia aver dolorosi anni.

On this passage see U. Bosco, 'Particolari Danteschi', *Annali della Scuola Normale Superiore di Pisa*, II, xi (1942), pp. 133–47. The views of early commentators and of Dante scholars are summarized by W. W. Vernon, *Readings on the Inferno of Dante*, 2nd ed., vol. I (1906), pp. 432 ff. Most of the early commentators asserted that Alexander the Great was meant, the most violent of them being Benvenuto da Imola, whose commentary is quoted by Vernon, and who quotes Orosius on the wickedness of Alexander. Other commentators suggested Alexander Balas and Alexander of Pherae.

Modern scholars have tended to identify the Alexander here mentioned with Alexander of Pherae, and this view is supported in the article mentioned above.

161 Dante, *Inferno* XIV, 28 ff.

> Sopra tutto il sabbion d'un cader lento
> Piovean di foco dilatate falde,
> Come di neve in alpe senza vento.
> Quali Alessandro in quelle parti calde
> D'India vide sopra lo suo stuolo
> Fiamme cadere infino a terra salde;...

For a summary of opinions upon this passage, see W. W. Vernon, *Readings on the Inferno of Dante*, vol. I (1906), pp. 499–500.

The passage in Albertus Magnus, *De Meteoris* I, iv, 8, runs: 'Admirabilem autem impressionem scribit Alexander ad Aristotilem in epistola de mirabilibus Indie dicens quemadmodum niuis nubes ignite de aere cadebant quas ipse militibus calcare praecepit.'

The passage in the *Epistola ad Aristotelem* of which this is a misquotation is:

'...et frigus ingens uespertino tempore accrescebat. Cadere mox in modum uellerum immensae coeperunt niues. Quarum aggregatione metuens ne castra cumularentur, calcare militem niuem iubebam, ut quam primum iniuria pedum tabesceret...' (ed. Kuebler, p. 208, ll. 5–9).

In the latter version it is the snow, in the two former the fire, that is trampled.

162 The following references to Alexander's liberality should be considered in conjunction with the references given above, pp. 328–9, and the exemplar uses of the moral anecdotes relating to Alexander's liberality given on pp. 348–9.

(a) Fra Salimbene, Chronica, s.a. 1248, in M.G.H. Scriptt. xxxii (ed. O. Holder-Egger, Hanover and Leipzig, 1905–13), pp. 283–4 (the gift of Jeroboam): '...erat enim rex, et ideo eum decebat regale munus mittere. Hinc rex Alexander dixit cuidam, qui munus suum recusabat, eo quod humili sue fortune disconueniens erat: "Non considero", ait, "quid te oporteat accipere, sed quid me deceat dare."'

(b) Brunetto Latini, Li livres dou Tresor II, ii, 79 (ed. P. Chabaille, Paris, 1863, p. 412): another version of the Senecan story. These two final Italian references to the story of the man to whom Alexander gave a city must be added to the exemplar uses of the story in Italy (in the Fior di Virtù and the Tractatus de diuersis historiis Romanorum) given above, pp. 348–9; the Fior di Virtù version is discussed below, p. 360. It is thus evident that the story of the man to whom Alexander gave a city, like that of Alexander and the Pirate, was a special favourite in Italy.

(c) For the story of Alexander's liberality in the Novellino, and its derivation from the Roman d'Alexandre, see below, pp. 361 (discussion), 374–5 (text).

In the Renaissance we may cite the following examples:

(d) Annales Foroliuienses, s.a. 1433–5, ed. Giuseppe Mazzatinti, R.I.S. xxii, ii (Città di Castello, 1903), p. 91, l. 44: (of Filippo Maria Visconti) '...et omnes capti ducti sunt ad Philippum Mariam, qui paulo post eos dimisit, libertatem donauit, faciens eos dignos clementie et largitate (sic) ac munificentie sue, ut de Alexandro legitur....'

(e) Giuseppe Betussi, La Leonora, in Trattati d'Amore del Cinquecento, ed. Giuseppe Zonta, Scrittori d'Italia (Bari, 1912), pp. 316–17: 'Capello: Onde, senza chiederla, essendomi da voi donata questa grazia, tanto più sarò obligato a riconoscere la liberalità vostra maggiore di quella d'Alessandro, il quale, se bene donava largamente, non però donava che le cose di fortuna, e voi oggi ci farete dono di tesori più preziosi e più stabili.

Leonora: Ancorchè la cosa sia differente, dirò pure ch'ei dava del suo, ed io sarò largo dell'altrui.'

(f) Niccolò Machiavelli, Il Principe xvi, quoted above, p. 267, n. 5; it is possible that this statement is based upon the classical evidence for Alexander's liberality, and not upon the memory of his medieval reputation.

APPENDICES

I

RECENT STUDIES ON PSEUDO-
CALLISTHENES

PART A, I. i. a, pp. 9–12 above, gives a picture of the views generally held
on the question of the origin and transmission of the Greek Alexander-
Romance at the time when that chapter was written. Recently two important studies on the subject have appeared and some new and significant
material has come to light which considerably alter the picture. It has
therefore been judged desirable to give a brief account of the new material
and of most recent views in this appendix.

The new material consists of four papyrus fragments. The first of these,
Berlin Papyrus 13044, was published thirty years ago by Wilcken in his
study of the episode of Alexander's meeting with the Indian gymnosophists.[1]

The second is Vienna Papyrus 31954 containing a brief extract from
Alexander's political testament, agreeing partly with the version of Pseudo-
Callisthenes, partly with that of the Latin Metz Epitome.[2]

The other two, Hamburg Papyrus 129,[3] and Papyrus of the Società
Italiana 1285,[4] contain parts of a collection of letters by and to Alexander
most of which appear also in Pseudo-Callisthenes. The Hamburg Papyrus
is of the first century B.C. and so helps to date the letter-collection which
it contains.

Of the two recent studies on the sources and origin of Pseudo-Callisthenes the first, by Friedrich Pfister, appeared in 1946.[5] This study contains
(pp. 29–39) a brief account of the history of the problem, of the principal
texts and the most important studies devoted to them, and a short study
on the sources and relationship of the Metz Epitome, which Pfister distin-
guishes from the account of Alexander's death and testament in the same
MS. (*Alexander's last days*), showing that the latter is an independent tract.

[1] U. Wilcken, *Alexander der Grosse und die indischen Gymnosophisten*, Sitzungsberichte
d. preuss. Akad. d. Wissensch. (Berlin, 1923), pp. 160–83.

[2] See M. Segré in *Rivista di Filologia*, XI (1933), pp. 225 ff. and Fuhrmann in *Archiv für
Papyrusforschung*, XI (1935), pp. 107 ff. Also Merkelbach, op. cit. infra, pp. 243–4.

[3] See *Griechische Papyri der Hamburger Staats- und Universitätsbibliothek*, Band II (1954),
pp. 51–74.

[4] See D. Pieraccioni in *Papiri della Società Italiana*, XII, 2 (Florence, 1951).

[5] 'Studien zum Alexanderroman', *Würzburger Jahrbücher* (1946), Heft 1, pp. 29–66.

There follows a stemma of the earlier versions (p. 40). Pfister considers that the archetype of the Romance as it has reached us was a conflation of an original Romance of the nature of a Greco-Egyptian 'Volksbuch', a collection of Alexander-letters and an historical source. On pp. 42–4 twelve different attributions are listed and discussed.

The second section of Pfister's study, pp. 44–50, is a discussion of the hypothetical original (Volksbuch) Romance and the interpolations made by the redactor responsible for the archetype of surviving versions. The last section, pp. 50–66, is an attempt to reconstruct the original Greco-Egyptian 'Volksbuch' and includes a very interesting study of its relationship to Egyptian traditions of the Egyptian world-conqueror Sesonchosis or Sesotris, mentioned several times in the Romance.

A much fuller and more important study of the sources and transmission of Pseudo-Callisthenes is that of Reinhold Merkelbach.[1] The author believes that the Alexander-Romance was the work of a Greco-Egyptian working in Alexandria about A.D. 300 and using two main sources.

The first of these was a romanticized history of Alexander of a highly rhetorical type depending on the Cleitarchus tradition. This was responsible for the historical elements in the Romance. The second was a collection of Letters of which the basis was an *Epistolary Romance of Alexander* written in the first century B.C. which gave the story of Alexander's life and campaigns in a series of imaginary letters in the tradition of the rhetorical schools supposed to have been written by the protagonists. To this were added, first, the two long letters of Alexander to Aristotle and Olympias describing the marvels of India, originally separate tractates, secondly, the account of Alexander's meeting with the India gymnosophists, found also in Plutarch's life of Alexander and elsewhere, and thirdly *Alexander's Last Days*, which Merkelbach shows to have been originally a political pamphlet written in 321 B.C. immediately after Alexander's death supporting the claims of Perdiccas and his party against those of Antipater. This was later interpolated by the Rhodians, probably about 300 B.C.

The author of the Romance used his sources most unintelligently, frequently upsetting the chronological order and sometimes repeating the same episode twice. He also added a good deal of his own invention or from Egyptian popular tradition, notably the whole of the Nectanebus episode at the beginning.

Merkelbach gives (pp. 74–112) a critical analysis of the Romance with numerous valuable textual emendations, and in a series of appendices dis-

---

[1] 'Die Quellen des griechischen Alexanderromans', *Zetemata*, IX (Munich, 1954).

cusses the principal sources in detail. He shows that the I[1] redaction of Archpriest Leo's *Historia de Preliis* is of special importance for the reconstruction of the original of that version of the Romance. In a brief discussion of the later Greek versions he divides the γ-tradition into two, γ and λ. He also shows that Julius Valerius was probably himself the author of the *Itinerarium Alexandri* which has hitherto been regarded as the work of a writer drawing on Julius Valerius. In a supplement he publishes the texts of the *Epistolary Romance* (pp. 195–219) using the Papyrus fragments as well as Pseudo-Callisthenes. This is followed by a parallel text of the Pseudo-Callisthenes and Metz Epitome versions of *Alexander's Last Days* (pp. 220–51).[1]

D.J.A.R.

[1] It is to be noted that Pfister's article, though published in 1946, was hardly accessible in this country in 1950 when the thesis on which this book is based was completed, and that the real significance of the Papyrus fragments, the two most important of which were published after that date, was not realized before the appearance of Merkelbach's book in 1954. It was also not the author's intention to treat the subject of the Greek Alexander Romance in detail as it lay outside the period with which he was concerned. My own object in adding this appendix has been to draw the English reader's attention to the latest work in the field.

II

THE ORIGINS OF ALEXANDER'S SECULAR
REPUTATION FOR LIBERALITY

1. INTRODUCTION

(a) PREVIOUS THEORIES

P. MEYER[1] considered that the classical sources may have contributed to
the growth of Alexander's secular reputation for liberality, but he believed
the portrayal of that liberality in the *Roman d'Alexandre* to be merely a
natural courtly development, and ascribed the popularity of the theme to
the popularity of the *Roman*. The passage in Philippe de Novare[2] which
we are to discuss was in his opinion derived from the letter of Philip to
Alexander in Cicero through the intermediacy of an 'enjolivement roma-
nesque', and he saw in the passage on the embassies to Alexander in the *Old
French Prose Romance*[3] a protest by the author against Alexander's contemporary reputation for liberality.

A little later than Meyer Carraroli[4] contrasted the erotic spirit of the
troubadour lyric with the heroic feeling of French epic and romance, and
suggested, as a probable influence upon the Provençal poets, the Arabic
proverbs relating to Alexander's generosity which passed into Europe
about this time. As an instance of the material thus introduced he quoted
the story of Aristotle and his pupils.[5] Aristotle asks his princeling pupils
how they will reward him when they become kings. Each promises something different, but Alexander says that he cannot promise anything
because the future is too uncertain, and he cannot be sure what it will be
in his power to give, he can say only that it will not be unworthy of his

---

[1] Meyer, *A. le G.* II, pp. 371–7; see for a discussion of part of this passage, above, pp.
[2] Texts, 2, p. 371.
[3] For discussion of this passage, see above, pp. 175–6; and Texts, 3, p. 372.
[4] D. Carraroli, *La Leggenda di Alessandro Magno* (Mondovì, 1892), pp. 224–5.
[5] For this story, see Julius Valerius I, 9 (ed. Kuebler, p. 17, ll. 1–16), and *Bocados de Oro*,
ed. H. Knust in *Mittheilungen aus dem Eskurial, B.L.V.* vol. CXLI (Tübingen, 1879), p. 313:
'...E dixo Aristotiles: De cierto se yo que tu seras grand rrey, que la tu natura lo muestra
e la faccion del tu rrostro.' Cf. for the Pseudo-Callisthenes version, Zacher, *Pseudo-Kallis-
thenes*, pp. 91–2, and Ausfeld, *Griechischer Alexanderroman*, pp. 38–9, 130–1. The story immediately precedes the Zeuxis correspondence.

master. This, in the view of Carraroli, is just the sort of proverbial tale to influence the twelfth-century writers with their emphasis upon boundless liberality; and he quotes in additional support the theory of liberality expounded in the *Enseignemens d'Aristote*,[1] a theory which he believes to have been widely known and widely appreciated in these references to Alexander's liberality.

Dr West's comments upon the possible differences between the feudal and the courtly conceptions of Alexander's liberality have already been discussed.[2] She also saw a possible contributory cause of his reputation in the classical sources, citing Plutarch, but giving no other classical references.

(b) RELEVANT CONCEPTUAL EVIDENCE

It has been shown that the Ciceronian and Senecan anecdotes of Alexander's liberality were widely known among moralists in the Middle Ages. The original morals attached to these anecdotes condemned Alexander's liberality as thoughtless or vain prodigality, but this attitude was altered in other types of medieval literature, and especially in the books of *exempla*, to one of unqualified approval. This development dated from the thirteenth century. In some moralists, however, the critical attitude of Cicero and Seneca to Alexander's liberality was well maintained; and thus we may say that there coexisted, from the twelfth century onwards, two moral views of Alexander's liberality, one condemning, and the other condoning, his reputation for that quality.[3]

(c) RELEVANT TEXTUAL EVIDENCE

In the arrangement of this material I propose to proceed upon a presumption, not because I claim that it solves all difficulties, but rather because some previous hypothesis is necessary to a comprehensible classification of the evidence.

This hypothesis is that the basis of the secular reputation of Alexander for liberality is to be found in the Latin legendary and anecdotal sources, that its continuance was due in part to the influence of this material, in part to the wide popularity of the *Roman d'Alexandre*, which together established it as a proverbial quality; and that the influence of the Oriental material was very slight.

[1] The French translation of the *Secret of Secrets* by Jofroi de Waterford. See below, p. 367.

[2] C. B. West, *Courtoisie in Anglo-Norman Literature* (Oxford, Blackwell, 1938), pp. 73–4; for a discussion of this view, see above, pp. 214–15.

[3] For the approach to Alexander's liberality in moralists and exemplar writers, see above, pp. 85–91, 154–5.

2. THE SECULAR USE OF MORAL ANECDOTAL MATERIAL

(a) THE SENECAN STORY OF THE MAN TO WHOM ALEXANDER GAVE A CITY

The popularity of this story from early times may not be doubted. It occurs not only in numerous moral references which have already been discussed, but in the *Bocados de Oro*, in a form which is evidently the result of confusion with the Antigonus episode with which it is linked in the text of Seneca: 'E entro un omne a el, e dixole: "O rrey, mandame dar dies mill maravedis." E dixole: "Non los mereces." E dixole el: "Si yo non los meresco haver tu los mereces dar."'[1]

This transference of the wit from Alexander to his interlocutor suggests some early confusion with the Antigonus episode. In the *Fior di Virtù*, the anecdote has again been much altered, in a way reminiscent of the alteration of the story about the Asiatic city in the book of *exempla* cited by Welter: (Alexander offers the man a city) 'e il povero disse, che così grande dono non si convenia a lui. Alessandro rispose: "Io non guardo a quello che si convegna ricevere, ma quello che a me si conviene."'[2] The omission of the word 'dare' makes the correct interpretation of the anecdote a matter of some doubt.

This evidence for the early corruption of the anecdote in popular citation, suggesting that it was in fact well known to secular writers, is supported by the variant of the story in the *Roman d'Alexandre*.[3] Alexander offers to a knight who has asked him for a gift the city of Araine; the knight, 'qui mout ot le cuer bas', declines this gift and asks for other things: gold, silver and clothing. Alexander replies:

> Je ne sai qui te tient ne le cuer que tu as,
> Mais itel sunt li don al roi mascedonas.

And instead of the city he has five hundred marks given to the man:

> Ce fu li menres dons au roi macedonas.

This was evidently intended as an improvement upon the Senecan anecdote, an improvement which is based upon the remark of the veteran

---

[1] *Bocados de Oro*, ed. Knust, p. 310. Knust's note gives only the normal Senecan parallel; he has apparently not noticed the variant form of the story.

[2] *Fior di Virtù*, c. XI: 'Della virtù della liberalità appropriata all' aquila' (ed. B. Fabbricatore, 3rd ed., Napoli, 1870, p. 50).

[3] *Roman d'Alexandre*, branch II, laisses 89–90, vv. 2095–135. *M.F.R.d'A.* II, p. 120.

that he did not think himself worthy of so great a gift, and which, by following out the implications of that remark, destroys the original moral of the story. If this alteration was not due to the author of Branch II of the *Roman* it is evidently of courtly origin; for it is typical of the courtly attitude to regard as a man 'qui ot le cuer bas' one who refused a great gift from his lord.

A similar version of the story appears in Seifrit aus Oesterreich, where, however, the incident takes place at Babylon at the end of Alexander's life, and his interlocutor is a poor man.[1] When the man is reluctant to accept the gift of a city Alexander has ten gold marks given him.

A most interesting variant of the story in the *Roman d'Alexandre* occurs in the *Novellino*, and since it seems to have attracted no attention it is given in the Texts.[2] Here the story of a knight who did not want a city is thoroughly confounded with the incident, also found in the *Roman d'Alexandre*,[3] of the jongleur whose native town had been destroyed by Alexander's troops, and was consoled by Alexander by the gift of the lordship of the city of Trage. This episode, ultimately derived from the legendary story of the athlete who secured for the Thebans permission to rebuild their city, and confused with that of the musician Ismenias' attempt to dissuade Alexander from destroying Thebes, is further discussed below, and it is evident that the *Novellino* account is derived from a confusion of the two stories which argues their probable independent popularity.

(b) THE STORY OF ALEXANDER AND DIOGENES

The Senecan anecdote of Alexander and Diogenes was widely known throughout the medieval period, and found its way into popular literature in the later Middle Ages.[4] In the I[2] *Historia de Preliis* and its descendants it was compounded with the story of Anaximenes before the gates of Athens, and his deliverance of that city from the vengeful anger of Alexander; and

---

[1] Seifrit's *Alexander*, vv. 8073-94 (ed. Gereke, pp. 131-2):

> Das ain arm man Allexandrum
> umb ain phennyng patt.

(vv. 8089 ff.)   'ich wais nicht was dir mag zemen
> oder was dir taugt ze nemen.
> ich wais wol was ich geben schol,
> das meinen ern zymet woll.'
> er hies das man im geben solt
> zechen markch von gold.

[2] Texts 6, pp. 374-5.
[3] Branch I, laisses 125-8, vv. 2597-665 (*M.F.R.d'A.* II, pp. 58-60).
[4] For the history of the episode of Alexander and Diogenes, see above, pp. 83-5.

thus the story of the sunshine (though not the attendant comments of Valerius Maximus and Seneca) was known to all users of that tradition.

But the fact that the Diogenes story always retained its original form (a fact true also of the exemplar version of the story) indicates that it did not possess that secular popularity which may be ascribed to the preceding anecdote, and that it was transmitted through literary channels.

(c) PHILIP'S LETTER TO ALEXANDER REBUKING HIS PRODIGALITY

Philippe de Novare includes in his book upon the Four Ages of Man an interesting passage in which he tells of Alexander's war against Nicholas, of his subsequent triumphant campaigns, and his constant liberality. Philip, his father, who is here represented as a proud and parsimonious man, thereupon writes to Alexander reproaching him for his liberality, which he says will make his men regard him not as a king but as a steward. Alexander replies accusing his father of niggardliness and pride, and declaring that he will conquer the world with the help of his judicious use of liberality.

This passage[1] is obviously connected, as Meyer pointed out,[2] with the letter of Philip to Alexander quoted in the De Officiis; Philip's reference to Alexander's making himself seem not a king but a steward is an evident parallel. The latter anecdote, therefore, must have undergone an inter-mediate remanipulation in the hands of some writer favourable to Alex-ander, who recast it on the lines of the Zeuxis episode in Julius Valerius. An interesting point is the similar context of the passages in Cicero and in Philippe de Novare. In both the example of the correspondence is used to instruct contemporary youth on the correct political use of liberality; and as one condemns, and the other approves Alexander's liberality as a model, they stand all the more completely in contrast.

This passage in Philippe de Novare, therefore, is evidence that some secular sympathizer with Alexander, and with his liberal practices, was acquainted with the passage in the De Officiis and altered it to suit his own opinion of Alexander.

(d) PERSISTENCE OF MORAL CONDEMNATION

The persistence of moral criticism of Alexander's liberality in secular works is striking and significant, for there was no secular evidence on which such a criticism could legitimately be built, and writers who

[1] Texts, 2 p. 371.   [2] Meyer, A. le G. II, pp. 361-3.

admired Alexander would not be likely to draw a conclusion unfavourable to him on the basis of non-existent evidence.

It must therefore be presumed that the condemnations of Alexander's liberality found in the *Old French Prose Romance*, Jean Wauquelin and an independent German reference were inherited from moral writers.

The first of these instances has already been discussed, and its probable derivation from a moral source established;[1] while the passage from Wauquelin, given in the Texts side by side with that in the *Old French Prose Romance*,[2] is very similar both in context and in spirit, and is in fact borrowed from it. Wauquelin's criticism of Alexander is especially reminiscent of the moral attitude to his liberality, with its emphasis upon the supposed political advantage that he derived from it, an emphasis paralleled in the letter of Philip to Alexander in the *De Officiis*. The same criticism of Alexander's liberality is to be found in the quotation from the *Wälschen Gast* of Thomasin von Zirclaria cited by Grammel,[3] where Alexander is accused of using liberality to further his personal ambition.

From considering these reflexions of the moral texts and ideas relating to Alexander's liberality, we pass to the observation of the influence of certain important passages in the legendary sources which refer to that quality.

3. THE SECULAR USE OF LEGENDARY ANECDOTAL MATERIAL

(a) THE ZEUXIS CORRESPONDENCE

This correspondence[4] is perhaps the most interesting legendary reference to Alexander's liberality, with its evident tone of an *apologia* in answer to the critics, and perhaps in answer to that very letter of Philip to Alexander which was so widely known, and was so carefully remodelled in the text of Philippe de Novare.

Alberic certainly, and the successive authors and editors of the *Roman d'Alexandre* possibly, were acquainted with the unepitomized text of Julius Valerius, the only legendary text to contain the correspondence.[5] It includes an endorsement, from Aristotle himself, of the ideals of twelfth-century liberality. Why, then, was all mention of the episode omitted by Alberic and his successors?

I would suggest that it was omitted because it is a collection of letters,

---

[1] Pp. 175–6. [2] Texts 3, p. 372.
[3] *Wälschen Gast*, vv. 3767ff.; see Grammel, p. 117.
[4] See pp. 210–11. [5] See M.F.R.d'A. III, p. 5, n. 15.

and therefore of no interest to the type of public who encouraged the writing of romances. The spirit of the letter was transferred to the material acts of liberality of the young Alexander. This is an unsupported conjecture, but it must at least be acknowledged that these writers were probably acquainted with material admirably suited to their purpose and made no apparent use of it, while they made frequent reference to Alexander's youthful acts of liberality, which find no acknowledgement in the Latin sources.

(b) ALEXANDER AND THE JONGLEUR

One of the most signal instances of Alexander's liberality in the *Roman d'Alexandre* takes place at the city of 'Trage' or Tarsus;[1] when a jongleur who entertains him, being asked whence he comes and what reward he desires, explains that his native city has been destroyed. Alexander thereupon gives him the lordship of the city of 'Trage'.

Meyer maintained that this story did not derive from any episode in Pseudo-Callisthenes; but, as Foulet remarks, it is ultimately descended from the story in Julius Valerius and the *Historia de Preliis* of the athlete who restored the city of Thebes after its annihilation at the hands of the wrathful Alexander.[2] Alexander admires his prowess at the games, asks the name of his city, and what reward he desires. The man replies that he is a citizen of no city, since his city is Thebes which Alexander has destroyed; and he asks that the citizens be permitted to rebuild their city. Alexander grants his request. The remanipulation of this episode is evidently the work of a secular writer who was more interested in jongleurs than in athletes.[3]

A most interesting conflation of this story with that of the knight who was offered the city of Araine, found in the *Novellino*, is studied above.

(c) ALEXANDER'S VISIT TO THE CAMP OF
DARIUS OR PORUS

In the *Historia de Preliis* it is told of Alexander how he paid a visit to the camp of Darius in disguise, was invited to dinner, and detected in the act of stealing a gold cup.[4] Asked to justify his action, he explained that his master, Alexander, was accustomed to allow his men to keep their cups for themselves at the conclusion of every meal, such was his liberality.

[1] *Roman d'Alexandre*, branch I, laisses 125–8 (*M.F.R.d'A.* II, pp. 58–60).

[2] See A. Foulet, op. cit. p. 336; cf. *Zacher Epitome* I, 45–7, *Historia de Preliis*, cc. 39–40.

[3] Or perhaps it is more likely that the episode was in part based on the story of the musician Ismenias who tried to dissuade Alexander from destroying Thebes (Pseudo-Callisthenes I, 46, ed. Müller, pp. 51–3; Julius Valerius I, 51–3, ed. Kuebler, pp. 62–4).

[4] Bamberg *Historia*, II, 13 f. (ed. Pfister, *Alexanderroman*, pp. 89 ff.).

Alexander was shortly afterwards recognized by one of Darius' suite and forced to flee. At a later stage in the story he visited the camp of Porus in disguise, and persuaded Porus, who questioned him about his antagonist, that Alexander was a decrepit old man tottering on the brink of the grave. In the *Gesta Romanorum* and an independent German reference, the two episodes have become confused; the story of the cup is related as having happened at the camp of Porus, where Alexander went in disguise.[1] In the independent German account of the incident this evidence of Alexander's liberality is said to have brought many of Porus' knights over to his side. The anecdotal use of this story, and the confused form in which we find it in the fourteenth century, suggests that it had some popularity independent of its context in the *Historia de Preliis*.

4. CONCLUSIONS

Meyer argued that the portrait of a liberal Alexander in the *Roman d'Alexandre* contributed most to the establishment of his proverbial reputation for that quality; although he admitted that Alexander's courtly reputation for liberality preceded the appearance of the *Roman d'Alexandre*, since it found its first acknowledgement in the *Erec* of Chrétien de Troyes. But liberality, although it was certainly a conventional quality of the courtly king, was not normally one of the most important qualities of all; and the emphasis placed upon Alexander's liberality in the *Roman d'Alexandre* is with difficulty to be ascribed only to the desire of the redactor to make his Alexander portrait conform to courtly tradition, for it is a greater emphasis than would be explained by such a desire.

If we concede it to be necessary that the redactor of the *Roman d'Alexandre* based his exaltation of Alexander's liberality upon some Latin source (and, as we have shown, the two most important *individual* liberal acts of Alexander in the *Roman* are derived from Latin anecdotal sources), his enthusiasm becomes clear; he found in the testimony of the sources evidence for just such a quality as he would have wished to find in his hero, and upon the basis of this evidence he extolled Alexander's liberality not merely to that conventional level demanded by courtly tradition, and reached by every other courtly hero, but to a height whence it dominated

---

[1] *Gesta Romanorum*, c. 198 (ed. Oesterly, pp. 610–11); Heinrich von Beringen, *Schachgedicht*, vv. 2469ff., on which see Grammel, pp. 117–18. There is a version of the story similar to that in the *Gesta Romanorum* in Jacobus de Cessolis, *De Ludo Scacchorum*, ed. F. Vetter, *Das Schachzabelbuch Kunrats von Ammenhausen* (Frauenfeld, 1892), cols. 261–9.

the *Roman*, and established itself in the minds of all who read the poem as the chief characteristic of Alexander's personality.

As to the references to Alexander's courtly reputation which may not be explained by reference to the *Roman*, the references in *Erec* and the *Strassburg Alexander*, these must be supposed to rest upon that same foundation of Latin anecdotes which we have shown to be directly recalled in so many passages of secular writers. Alexander's reputation for liberality among moralists and exemplar writers was striking enough to suppose that some connexion must have existed between the moral and the courtly traditions, and that connexion is sufficiently supplied by the anecdotes which were known through every class of medieval society.

It seems most probable, therefore, that Alexander's proverbial reputation for liberality was originally founded upon knowledge of these anecdotes and of the Alexander portrait in the *Roman*, which itself drew inspiration from the anecdotes.

Carraroli's view that Alexander's secular reputation for liberality was founded upon Oriental material is scarcely tenable. His assertion that the majority of references to Alexander in the troubadours are concerned with his liberality is incorrect, and the story of Aristotle and his pupils, which he cites in support of his theory from Julius Valerius and the *Bocados de Oro*, proves little, as it is never referred to elsewhere and was apparently not generally known. It demonstrates the virtue of cautious liberality, in Alexander's reserved statement that he will wait and see how far it will be in his power to reward Aristotle, a statement reminiscent of Aristotle's advice to Alexander in the *Alexandreis*—'If you haven't the money, put them off with promises.' Such a story, typical of the approach to liberality in the *Secret of Secrets* and the proverbial material in the *Dicts and Sayings*, would hardly have commended itself to a twelfth-century secular writer who probably had bitter experience of promises.

But in the late Middle Ages, the *Secret of Secrets*, with its Aristotelian advice to Alexander on liberality, had wide influence. The substance of this advice is thus given in the Anglo-Norman *Secré des Secrés*:

> E si est de largece la sustenance:
> Volentiers parduner sans dotance,
> Ne ne fet des privetez d'autrui
> Ne des secrez enquerre, saciez de fi,
> Ne ne fet pas a remenbrer
> Chose donee ne a rehercer,
> E si est de bunté e vertu
> Renumbrer ceo k'est avenu,

E tort volentiers relesser,
E honurables honurer;
E si deit ausi a simple gent
Aidier debonerement.
As innocens li deit suvenir
A lur defautes peremplir;
Respundre deit benignement
A salutation de la gent,
E sa lange deit refrener,
E tort a tens dissimuler,
E feindre de fol la folie
Ausi c'um ne la sache mie.[1]

As Héron remarks, this definition of largesse includes all acts of benevolence, generosity and charity. It is, in fact, an attitude that returns closely to the Senecan conception of beneficence, of which *liberalitas* is a part. We therefore have two parallel traditions, the classical and the Arabic, which almost agree in their definition of liberality. In both traditions Alexander's liberality is placed in close connexion with this definition; in the classical tradition he is condemned, in the Arabic tradition he is by implication extolled in the *Secret of Secrets*, and certainly extolled in the *Dicts and Sayings*.

It is, however, doubtful if these Arabic works, preaching a standard of liberality easily appreciable by the later medieval writers, and praising Alexander by that standard, had any effect upon the survival of Alexander's secular reputation for liberality into the later Middle Ages.

We have examined the late medieval references concerned, and it may be seen that in spite of the fact that they occur in Deschamps who borrowed largely from the *Secret of Secrets*, they are cast in the old phraseology and exhale the old spirit, musty but undiluted. It is a proverbial reputation that we have considered, and not a petty association of ideas that needs bolstering up. Such a reputation as had been established in the twelfth and thirteenth centuries might not easily be destroyed, when it survived, not as long as those ideas upon which it was founded survived, but as long as any person might remember to catch up from oral or from written tradition the proverbial sayings that were evolved upon the basis of those ideas. For a proverbial reputation should be expressed in general terms independent of any specific anecdotal association—'as liberal as Alexander', not 'as liberal as Alexander when he gave the city to the poor man'.

The reproaches of a few scholars, pedants or misanthropes cannot make

---

[1] Quoted by A. Héron, *La légende d'Alexandre et d'Aristote* (Rouen, 1892), p. 25.

a proverbial saying the less proverbial. It is proverbial so long as its common meaning is generally understood, so long as it is an image which would normally and conventionally be used with respect to some quality or some attribute. Thus Meyer's scattered quotations decrying the liberality of Alexander could never be accepted as signifying the end of Alexander's proverbial reputation for liberality. However rarely we find them, the fact that we find references of *proverbial* type to Alexander's liberality in fifteenth- and sixteenth-century writers in France, Italy, and Spain shows that Alexander's proverbial reputation for liberality existed throughout the whole of the later Middle Ages. It was not specifically rejected; it died slowly and over centuries, as proverbs will, becoming obsolete and archaic, disappearing from popular remembrance and surviving only in the dusty productions of learned writers.

For the dissociation of literature from the court and its retirement into the closet, the emergence of the satirist, the world grown old in its own estimation and writers more reflective, had their effect upon this as upon Alexander's reputation for valour. The new bourgeois class brought their philosophy of cautious liberality with them, and largesse, the unconsidered and unconsidering effusion of wealth, was seen as the destroyer of private and national economy, or, simply, as a waste of money, according as the philosopher or the merchant was uppermost. The courtly view of liberality depended for its existence upon certain conditions of society; if he is a court poet a man will regard extravagance as liberality, but to those who spend their time in philosophic study, in the counting-house, or in the council chamber deciding how much the king ought to spend on his poet, liberality is generosity combined with cautious finance.

III

TEXTS

1.

Fabius Claudius Gordianus Fulgentius, *De aetatibus mundi et hominis* x, xxxvii–xl (ed. R. Helm, Leipzig, Teubner, 1898, pp. 164–7).

Ea igitur tempestate fortuna quodam aestu turbulentiae grauidata in paruo Macedonum regno clarissimum peperit nefas. Namque Alexander dubia sub opinione Philippi Macedonis filius incerti patris crimine maculatus exsurgit. Quidam enim ferunt, Dictanabo uaporante libidinis, clandestino Olimpiada magico conpressisse figmento, alii quod draconis squamifero fermentante complexu uirulentum ediderit grauidata puerulum. Sed quid his opus est: ex quo Philippi in hoc negotio uacillauit auctoritas patris, nulla nominum inuentio opus est ad ornandum adulterium genetricis. Habere enim non dicitur uirum cui suppetunt multa nomina maritorum. Hic ergo quamuis patre tyrannice crudeliterque regnante ampliatum Macedonum regnum susceperit, tamen ultra mundi terminos aestuans insatiabile imperium protelauit; non contentus in id quod pater crudeli tyrannide peruaserat, sed mundum sibi breuiorem aestimans ultra saeculum aliquid exquirebat. Et primum quidem Babilonicum regnum arripuit mille annorum dominatu fulcitum, tot triumphis ac totius orbis uictoriis enthecatum. Illuc etenim et Israhelitica confluxerat gloria et Aegyptiaca olim famosa conmigrarat potentia, illuc Spartana, illuc Athenaica atque insuperabilis uirtus deuoluta cesserat Scytica. De quo regno a uicies milies centum octoginta milia tribus proeliis cesa feruntur nec tamen tantae cladis sensit Babilonia detrimentum. Quis ferat haec, domine Deus meus, totius orbis ineffabilis conditor? Deficit supputatio morientum in numero: aerumnae locus Partiaco non paruit regno. Si inaestimabile est quod una prouincia perdidit, quis tua, orbis, opera sufficiens enarrabit? Igitur Alexandri rapidos regnandi ad cupiditatem animos tantae inmensitatis multitudo non terruit, sed indubitanter pugnam insperatam arripuit, et insperato uictoriam dubitatam inuenit. Vincit in paruo quibus sufficere non poterat numerando; superat effugatum, sequitur fugitiuum, inuenit uulneratum aureo catenarum ligamento constrictum. Praebet inanem misericordiae sepulturam illo; filias etiam quas sorores.... Iuste quidem ille uitam perdidit, regnum amisit, qui maternum uiolans sacramentum suum se maluit esse uitricum, patrem etiam germanarum; nec puduit illuc partem turpissimam libidinans obicere corporis, unde primum prodierat imago nascentis. Post haec regni etiam Persici uictoria non contentus, quo totius mundi confluxerat dominatus, qui posset et uniuersas auaritiae saturare uoragines—et nihil ultra post hunc quaereret qui etiam aliquando saturari non posset—, tamen Indicos fines ante cuiquam inaccessos sollicitat et ignotos nostro saeculo fines ardenti cupiditate penetrat. Et primum quidem feras in aciem belli propositas statuarum aere succenso debilitat et ignitis amplexibus rabidas fugat. Post haec Poro Indico rege captiuo Fasiacas primus inuadit latebras. Illic aurum fastiduit Macedo qui saturari non potuit toto orbe possesso. Dehinc nudos Bragmones, exustos Eoas, Foebeos Passadras, Caucasii montis incolas, Drancas et Uergetas, Hyrcaniae populos, Corasmos et Daas, Ocionitidis quidem Amazonas ut ferus adit, ut inportunus prouocuit, ut praedo peruasit; incognitam quoque saeculis Meroen et ultra Sieneticos uapores Falernis liquoribus ruptuantem inpatiens penetrat; Candacen Aethiopicam, quamuis praeceps, non tamen securus, sollicitat; Atlanteas Niliaci liquoris diffusitrices cataractas intrepidus exspectat. Quid dicam pertemtata Maeotide inertes thirofagos, asperos antropofagos, nudos etiam ictiofagos lacessisse? Solis quoque ac Lunae loquentia nemora regis ipsius interitum praedicantia laboriosus inuestigator accessit. Et quid pluribus: nulla secreta mundi misteria, nulla gens abstrusis terrarum angulis exulata, nulla Oceani semotior insula Atlantei marginis aestu roriflua, quae non Alexandrum aut dominum timuit aut repentinum expauit aut praedonem inuenit. Quisnam est, domine Deus meus, hominum tam inconsideratus appetitus? Lassatur peragrando mundus, non erat iam quod humanis ostenderet oculis, et auaritiae non saturatur affectus. Paruum est uisu quaerenti Alexandro quod fecisse suffecerat Deo; posset et in caelum ascendere, si aut natura pinnarum concessisset aut semita. Et quia mundum peragrando paruum sibi esse credidit, ideo tribus contentus sepulchri cubitis obdormiit. Discat ergo ex hoc humana natura nihil esse de potentia praesumendum, ex quo mors communiter heres est potentum et pauperum. Vidit enim et Aethiopicas uires et Atlanticas moles et Foebeos ignes et Scythicas glacies. Sed quid profuit omnia inuicta uincere et seruili ueneno succumbere? Huius actus huiusque mortem qui semper mente considerat, moriturum se esse non credat; numquam enim mortis malo terretur qui alieno malo considerato corrigitur.

2.

Philippe de Novare, *Les quatre âges de l'homme* II, secc. 67–70 (ed. M. de Fréville, S.A.T.F., 1888, pp. 39–41).

(67) Li vaillant jone qui a bien béent et a conquerre, redoivent volantiers savoir et avoir en remenbrance .i. respons que Alixandres dist a son pere. Il avint que li rois Phelipes, li peres Alixandre, fu mout crueus et orguilleus et eschars, et vost toz jors avoir le servise de ses genz par fierté et par seignorie, sanz bienfait et sanz largesce. Il avoit a voisïn .i. fort roi qui avoit a nom Nicholas; cil avoit si sozmis le roi Phelipe que, chascun an, li randoit mout grant treu. Seur ce, avint que Alixandres fu d'aage, chevaliers preuz et hardiz et larges seur touz homes. Adonques avint que li mesage dou roy Nicholas vindrent querre le treu. Alixandres en ot mout grant desdaig, et dist qu'il meïsmes li porteroit et paieroit, si comme il afferoit.

(68) Et maintenant assambla touz les bachelers et tous les bons chevaliers qu'il pot trover; si ala sor le roi Nicholas, et se conbati a lui et le vainqui, et gaaigna quanqu'il avoit, mueble et eritage. Et dès iqui ala avant conquerant, et tout quanqu'il pooit gaaignier et conquerre anterinement, donoit si largement que riens ne l'an demoroit. Ses peres l'oï dire, si li manda letres don la tenor en fu tele:

(69) 'Biaus filz, il m'est avis que tu ne viaus mie que tes genz te taignent por roi ne por seignor, mais por prevost; car rois et signor doit estre serviz par seignorie et par fierté, et prevos doit avoir servise por doner, et doit porchacier amis por ce qu'il est balliz, se il avient que on le praigne, que li ami li aident a delivrer, et se on le reant, que il li aident a sa raençon.'

(70) Alixandres li respondi a ce: 'Sire, je ain miaus avoir meniere de prevost, de tant come monte a largesce, et par ce conquerre, que avoir meniere de roi ou de seignor cruel et eschars, et par ce estre au desouz de mes anemis, et randant treuage come serf. Et sachiez, sire, que je bée a tout conquerre, se Dieu plest, et tout doner si largement que ja riens n'an demorra a moi que la seignorie et l'onor tant seulement, et en moi ne vueil qu'il ait escharseté que une: ce est de retenir a moi proprement l'onor et l'amor de mes genz et de touz mes serveors; et por ce avrai la seignorie dou monde; et tout quanque je porrai conquerre et avoir, je le donrai a celz par cui je le conquerrai.'

3.

The episode of the Embassies at Babylon in the *Old French Prose Romance* and Jean Wauquelin (see p. 175).

Old French Prose Romance, c. 123 (cited by Meyer, *A. le G.* II, pp. 312–13):

Et quant Alixandre fu entrés en la cité, si trova ileuc messages de toutes les parties dou monde,... dont il avint que les Romains li manderent grant quantité d'or. Dont Alixandre dist que ceaus qui li avoient ce present mandé l'amoient, dont on pooit bien par ce conoistre qu'il estoit covoitous par nature et eschars. Les François li manderent escu, lequel il reçut molt en gré, et dist que tout aussi com il estoient par nature et par usage la plus vigoreusse gent dou monde, et il devoient mander present qui fust convenables a lui qui le devoit resevoir et a çaus qui le tenoient; et ce dissant, qu'il avoient fait, car li escu li estoit convenables por ce qu'il avoit conquis a lui tout le monde a sa conoissance.

Jean Wauquelin, *Histoire d'Alexandre* II, 87 (cited by Meyer, *A. le G.* II, pp. 326–7):

...ceulx de Romme luy envoyerent une tresgrant some d'or par mullés et chevaulx qui le porterent et conduisirent. Pour lequel present il les rechut moult honnourablement et grandement, et leur dist en tel maniere: 'Je voy', dist il, 'clerement que ceulx qui nous ont rechupt et ce present envoiié nous ayment d'une amour cordialle. Et pour ce nous les retenons a noz tresespeciaulx amis.' Par laquelle parole on parchupt clerement et seult on que de sa proppre nature il estoit convoitteux et escars, et combien que toudis on lui ait donné le nom de larguesse. Touteffoix ne l'estoit il point par nature, mais il estoit tellement a chou induis, et ossi il veoit clerement que par ses dons il possesoit de plus grans. Et pour ce c'est ung mot veritable qui se dist: *Date et dabitur uobis*, qui est a dire en franchoix: 'Donnez et on vous donra.' The passage concludes with a longer account of the embassy of the French, which contains much in praise of the gallant French nation.

4.

Historienbibel I ('Do Got in siner Magenkraft')—account of the Celestial Journey, in J. F. L. Th. Merzdorf, *Die Deutschen Historienbibeln, B.L.V.* vols. C–CI (Tübingen, 1870), vol. II, pp. 548–9.

'Nun wisst ich gern wass wunders uff dem himel wär. Daz wil ich versûchen.' Und hiess im jung griffen ussniemen und uss ainem nest bringen und hiess ims schön ziechen und sprach. 'Ich wil zû himel faren und wil minen lib wol bewaren daz mir nútz geschicht.' Und do die griffen ains halben jǎrs alt wurdent do hiess er im ain schönen sessel bringen. Daruff sass er mit siner kron. Und hiess zwo ysni stangen mit ysen an den sessel binden und hiess an ain yegklich an daz ort binden flaisch. Und band die griffen an ain stang und fûrtend inn die griffen über sich gegen dem himelschen tron. Dô kam ain stimm zû im die sprach zornklich zû im: 'Alexander, wa wilt du hin? Du tûst torlichen daz du wider got strebest. Es mag niement zû himel denn der es mit gûten wercken verdienent und dem es sin got gan.' Nun waz dem Alexander also hiess in den hochen wolcken daz er verbrunnen wolt sin und sprach zû der stimm: 'Sag mir wahin sol ich faren syd ich zû den engeln nit komen mag.' Dô sprach die stimm: 'Far uff daz ertrich das ist dir gût.' Dô sprach er: 'Ich sich nútz denn wasser und ainen hût daruff schweben.' Dô sprach die stimm: 'Der hût ist das ertrich.' Zû hand hûb er die stang mit dem flaisch under sich gegen dem ertrich. Dô fûrtend inn die griffen wider uff das ertrich.

Darnǎch tett er die griffen von im und lousst die riemen uff und wär gern by sinem volck gewesen daz hett er by dem mer gelaussen. Dô was er wol anderthalb hundert myl wegs von inen.

5.

Iter ad Paradisum; a version similar to that in the *Faits des Romains* (see p. 151).

Manchester Epitome, after Zingerle, c. 90 (ed. Prof. S. H. Thomson, *University of Colorado Studies*, I (1941), pp. 257–8).

Rursus idem Alexander postquam fuit in Egipto scire uoluit originem Nili fluminis qui spergitur super regnum Egipti. Unde fecit preparare nauem cum hominibus munitis uictualibus et rebus necessariis per unum annum et nauigauerunt per sex menses per dictum flumen et uenerunt ad quoddam palacium album supra Nilum ubi erat quedam cathena que constringebat totum illum flumen ita quod nemo poterat transire ultra dictam cathenam per Nilum. Unde naute clamantes uersus palacium fortiter uoces suas exaltarunt pro consilio habendo qualiter possunt dictam cathenam transire cum naui. Quibus responsum fuit datum a quodam induto ueste alba quod hoc non crederetur ab Alexandro nisi aliquod signum haberet credibile. Quibus datus fuit quidam lapis preciosus ad similitudinem oculi qui in se habuit ista[m] proprietatem quod si ipse poneretur super quoddam pondus, si dictus lapis esset discoopertus quod non ualeret contrapensum ab alio latere poni qui superaret illum lapidem, sed si terra fuerit coopertus levis erit sicut alius lapis tante quantitatis. Itaque factum est et reuersi sunt ad Alexandrum et omnia que ipsis acciderunt narrauerunt ei. Quo audito Alexander fecit probare et experimentum facere de dicto lapide super palacium ciuitatis Babilonie uidentibus suis principibus et baronibus et populis uniuersis experimenti ueritati. His uero factis Alexander dixit ariolo astrologo suo quid talia significabant. Qui respondit quod 'Lapis discoopertus signat personam tuam quoniam contra te nemo poterit preualere nec tibi resistere dum uiuis, sed lapis coopertus qui non plus ponderat quam alius lapis eiusdem quantitatis signat quod mortuus fueris et corpus tuum coopertum non ualebit plus alio corpore mortuo.'

6.

Alexander, the knight, and the jongleur (see p. 361). *Le Novelle Antiche*, no. IV (ed. G. Biagi, *Raccolta di opere inedite o rare*, Firenze, 1880, pp. 9–11).

Stando lo Re Allexandro alla città di Giadre con moltitudine di gente ad asedio, uno nobile cavaliere era fuggito di pregione. Essendo poveramente ad arnese misesi ad andare ad Allexandro che lli donasse, acciò che lo mondo parlava d'Allexandro che donava più che altro sengnore larghissimamente. Andando questo cavaliere per lo camino, trovò uno homo di corte molto nobilemente ad arnese: dimandòlo ov'elli andava. Lo cavaliere rispuose: Io vado ad Allexandro. Perchè vai? disse l'omo di corte. Perchè io ò inteso che largamente dona; ond'io vado perchè largamente mi doni, sì che io possa in mia contrada orrevilemente ritornare. Allora lo giularo parlò et disse: Che vogli che io ti dea? et dàrmi ciò che Allexandro ti darae. Lo cavaliere rispuose: Donami cavallo da cavalcare et somieri et robbe et dispendio condonevile (?convenevile) a rritornare in mia terra. Lo giularo lil donoe et furono in concordia. Cavalcano et giunseno ad Allexandro, lo quale avea conbattuto aspramente la città di Giadres et era partito dalla battaglia et faciasi disarmare sotto uno bello padiglione: et lo cavaliere et lo giularo si trassero davanti. Et lo cavaliere fece sua dimanda. Alexandro humilemente no lli fece motto neente nè non li fece rispondere. Lo cavaliere si partio dallo giularo et misesi in via per ritornare in sua terra. Pocho dilungato lo cavaliere, avenne che lli nobili cavalieri di Giardes recharo le chiavi della cittade ad Allexandro con pien mandato d'ubbidire li suoi comandamenti come al loro singnore. Allora lo Re Allexandro si volse verso li baroni et disse: V'è chi mi dimandava dono? Et allora fue mandato per lo cavaliere che domandasse dono. Lo cavaliere ritornò ad Allexandro. Parlò et disse: Nobile cavaliere, prendi le chiave della nobile città di Giardes che io la ti dono vollontieri. Lo cavaliere rispuose: Messer, non mi donate cittade, ma pregovi che mi doni oro et argento et robe, come ti sia in piacere. Allora Allexandro sorrise et comandò che lli fossero dati ij M marchi d'ariento. Et questo si scrisse per lo minore dono ch'elli facesse unqua. Lo cavaliere prese li marchi et dielli al giulare. Il giularo fu dinanzi Allexandro et dimandòli che facesse ragione, et fece sostenere lo cavaliere et propuose così: Messer, io trovai costui in camino; domandàlo ov'elli andava et perchè. Dissemi che andava ad Allexandro perchè li donasse. Io feci co llui patto di darli quello che detto he, ed egli mi promise di darmi ciò che Allexandro li donasse. Onde egli m'a rotto li patti, chè à rifiutata la nobile città di Giardres et à preso li marchi d'argento. Perchè, io dinanzi dalla vostra singnoria dimando che mi faciate sodisfare tanto quanto più vale la città che i marchi. Allora lo cavaliere parlò; primieramente confessò li patti pienamente, poi disse: Ragione vuole quelli che mi dimanda; si è giulare et in corte di giularo non può discendere singnoria di cittade: lo suo pensiere fu d'argento et d'oro et la intenzione sua fue tale. Io l'ò pienamente fornita. Onde la tua singnoria provegha innella mia diliberanza sechondo che piacerà al tuo savio consiglio. Allexandro colli suoi savi asciolseno lo cavaliere, et lodollo di grande savere.

7.

Pier Paolo Vergerio, *Epistola* cxxxviiii (To the Emperor Sigismund) in *Epistolario*, ed. L. Smith (*Fonti per la Storia d'Italia*, Rome, 1934), pp. 379–84.

Iussisti me, Sigismunde, clementissime imperator, ut Arriani historiam, qui res gestas Alexandri Macedonis greco sermone conscripsit, in latinum uerterem; non quod ueterum Grecorum magnifica olim opera et apud suos tam metro quam soluta oratione sine fine celebrata Latinis sint incognita; illa presertim illustriora, inter que Alexandri bella et uictorie longe maiores quam bella inprimis connumerantur; sed quod Arrianus in eis describendis certiores secutus sit auctores, atque ideo fide dignus uideatur. Nam ex ceteris quidem historie scriptoribus, qui multi fuerunt multumque sibi inuicem dissonantes, aliqui, uulgarem famam secuti, non que gessit Alexander, sed que de eo passim ferebantur, ea tanquam uere gesta conscripserunt. Alii fauore gentis et domestice glorie studio in enarrandis ad laudem eius operibus modum excesserunt. Nonnulli e contra, odio uel inuidia, siue ut aliis morem gererent, qui tanti nominis splendore offendebantur, detrahere rebus gestis conati sunt; quidam insuper, priuatim ambitione querendi nominis et proprie laudis cupiditate, non quid gestum ab eo fuerit, sed quid decore de illo scriptum memorie posterorum mandari posset, hoc solum extimauerunt; nec tam ueritatem rerum quam figmentorum lenocinium amplexi sunt. Atque hec tanta scribentium uarietas perplexitatem legentibus afferre non modicam consueuit, cum essent incerti quibusnam fidem adhiberi pre ceteris conueniret, et fabulasne an historiam ueram legerent. Tu igitur hinc adductus, ea que Arrianus de gestis Alexandri scripsit tanquam ueriora cupis agnoscere, laudandus profecto, siue quia ueritati studes, que rebus omnibus preferenda est, siue quod historie notitia tantopere delectaris ut domesticis non contentus etiam externa requiras. Est autem in historia simul cum iocunditate fructus plurimus, ualetque magnopere rerum gestarum frequens cognitio, tum ad peritiam gerendarum augendam, tum ad satietatem minuendam iugiter concomitantium tediorum. Decet autem omnes homines, sed eos precipue qui magnis administrationibus presunt, ad utrunque conari laborareque summo studio ut sciant se quidem inprimis; deinde, si quibus forte est in alios imperium, etiam subditos optimis rationibus regere, ac per honestas delectationes, quantum fieri potest, sine molestia uitam agere; te uero ante omnes, qui in supremo rerum culmine constitutus es, et qui magna semper animo uoluis, curare conuenit Alexandri Magni opera, que haud dubie magna fuerunt, certius agnoscere, et que ex eis digna sunt laude, ea non tam palpitando sectari uelle quam precurrendo superare. Sed et michi quoque non est uisum alienum, preter causas alias, que me ad hoc uel impulerunt uel coegerunt; nam, te quidem iubente, necesse erat parere; ut in honorem quoque scriptoris, qui Latinus fuit, laborem hunc non inuitus assumerem, et que de rebus Grecorum grece scripsit, in latinum Latinus transferrem, illumque tibi traditum et michi per te commendatum, Latinis uero prorsus incognitum, tandem quasi longo postliminio in patriam reuocarem et suis utcunque darem agnoscendum. Qua in re licere michi sum arbitratus, tibi uero non futurum ingratum certus sum, si plano ac pene uulgari stilo sensus tantum, non uerba transferrem, ut, eo nunc primum e Grecia redeunte et externa narrante, a Latinis quibusque uel indoctioribus rerum gestarum tenor possit agnosci. Ornatum autem orationis et dicendi elegantiam, quibus ille uel in aliena lingua plurimum eminet, si quis forsitan cum rerum notitia pariter desiderat, ea non a me, alieni sermonis interprete, sed ab ipso historie auctore et conditore requirat.

BIBLIOGRAPHY

The principal modern editions of ancient and medieval works are listed under their author, or in the case of anonymous works under the title.

ABAELARD. *Introductio ad Theologiam*, Migne, *P.L.* CLXXVIII. *Theologia Christiana*, ibid.

Abecedarian Poem on Alexander, ed. F. Zarncke, 'Ueber das Fragment eines lateinischen Alexanderliedes in Verona', *Sitzungsberichte der Sächsischen Akademie der Wissenschaften* (1877), pp. 57–69.

AENEAS SYLVIUS (PIUS II). *De Curialium Miseriis Epistola*, ed. W. P. Mustard (Baltimore and O.U.P., 1928).

AHLSTRAND, J. A. *Konung Alexander: en meteltidens dikt från latinet vänd i svenska rim omkring år 1380 på föranstaltande af rikdrotsen Bo Jonsson Grip, efter den enda kända handskriften* (Stockholm, 1862).

Aimeri de Narbonne, ed. L. Demaison, S.A.T.F. (1887).

AIMERIC DE PEGULHAN. *La Metgia* in *Poesie Provenzali Storiche*, ed. V. de Bartholomaeis, *Fonti per la Storia d'Italia* (Rome, 1931).

AIMON DE VARENNES. *Florimont*, ed. A. Hilka, *Gesellschaft für romanische Literatur*, Bd. XLVIII (Göttingen, 1933).

ALBRECHT VON KEMENATEN. *Dietrichs Abenteuer*, ed. J. Zupitza, *Deutsches Heldenbuch*, V (Berlin, 1870).

ALCUIN. *Opera*, Migne, *P.L.* CI.
De Clade Lindisfarnensis Monasterii, in *M.G.H. Poetae Latini Aeui Carolini*, I.

Alexandri Magni Iter ad Paradisum.
    Ed. A. Hilka, in L. P. G. Peckham and M. S. La Du, *The Prise de Defur and the Voyage au Paradis Terrestre*, *Elliott Monographs* 35 (Princeton Univ. Press, 1935), pp. xli–xlviii.
    Ed. M. Esposito, in *Hermathaena*, XV (1909), pp. 368–82.
    Ed. J. Zacher (Koenigsberg, 1859).

Aljamiado Alexander, ed. A. R. Nykl, *Revue Hispanique*, LXXVII (1929).

Alphabet of Tales, ed. M. M. Banks, E.E.T.S., O.S. CXXVI–CXXVII (1904–5).

Amadas et Ydoine, ed. J. R. Reinhard, *Classiques français du moyen âge* (Paris, 1926).

ANDERSON, A. R. *Alexander's Gate, Gog and Magog and the Enclosed Nations*, *Medieval Academy of America Publications*, XII (Cambridge, Mass., 1932).
    'Heracles and his successors', in *Harvard Studies in Classical Philology*, XXXIX (1928), pp. 7–58.

Annales Foroliuienses, ed. G. Mazzatinti, *Rerum Italicarum Scriptores*, XXII, ii (Città di Castello, 1903).

ANTONINUS (Bishop of Florence). *Chronica*, ed. P. Mauturus (Lyons, 1586).

ANTONIUS ASTESANUS. *Carmen de ejus Vita et Fortunae Varietate*, *R.I.S.* XIV (1908–12).

AQUINAS, THOMAS. *Opera Omnia* (Parma, 1852–71).

ARMSTRONG, E. C. *The authorship of the Vengement Alixandre and of the Venjance Alixandre*, *Elliott Monographs* 19 (Princeton Univ. Press, 1926).

BIBLIOGRAPHY

Art de Chevalerie, L', ed. U. Robert, *S.A.T.F.* (Paris, 1897).

AUGUSTINE, ST. *De Ciuitate Dei*, Migne, *P.L.* XLI.

AUSFELD, A. *Der griechische Alexanderroman*, ed. W. Kroll (Leipzig, 1907).

Die Orosius-Recension der Historia de Preliis und Babiloths Alexanderchronik, Festschrift der Badischen Gymnasien (1886), pp. 99–120.

Ueber die Quellen zu Rudolf von Ems Alexander. Programm Donaueschingen (1883).

BABILOTH, MEISTER. *Alexanderchronik*, partial ed. S. Herzog, *Programm* (Stuttgart, 1897 and 1903).

BACHELER, M. 'Gualterus Alexandreis in ihrem Verhältnis zum Curtius-text', in *Berliner Philologische Wochenschrift* (1917), cols. 663 ff., 698 ff., 730 ff.

BARNOW, A. J. 'A Middle Low German Alexander Legend', in *Germanic Review*, IV (1929), pp. 50–77, 284–304, 373–401.

BARTHOLOMAEIS, V. DE. 'Poesie Provenzali Storiche', in *Fonti per la Storia d'Italia* (Rome, 1931).

BARTSCH, K. 'Alberic von Besançon', in *Germania*, II (1857), pp. 449–64.

BECKER, H. 'Die Brahmanen in der Alexandersage', *Programm* (Koenigsberg, 1889). In *Zeitschrift für Deutsche Philologie*, XXIII, pp. 424–5.

BENEDETTO, G. DI. *Rimatori del dolce stil nuovo, Scrittori d'Italia* (Bari, 1939).

BENNETT, H. S. 'The Production and Dissemination of Vernacular Manuscripts in the Fifteenth Century', in *The Library*, fifth series I (1946–7), pp. 167–79.

BERTHOLD VON REGENSBURG. *Predigten*, ed. F. Pfeiffer (Vienna, 1862).

BETUSSI, GIUSEPPE. *Il Raverta*, in *Trattati d'Amore del Cinquecento*, ed. G. Zonta, *Scrittori d'Italia* (Bari, 1912).
La Leonora, ibid.

BIELEFELDT, H. H. *Die Quellen der alttschechischen Alexandreis*, Deutsche Akademie der Wissenschaften, *Veröffentlichungen des Forschungsinstituts für Slawistik*, I.

BILLANOVICH, G. 'La tradizione del Liber de dictis philosophorum antiquorum e la cultura di Dante, del Petrarca e del Boccaccio', in *Studi Petrarcheschi*, I (1948), pp. 112–13.

BOCCACCIO, G. *Amorosa Visione*, ed. V. Branchi, *Scrittori d'Italia* (Bari, 1931).
De Casibus Virorum Illustrium, ed. J. Gourmont and J. Petit (Paris, s.d.).
Filocolo, ed. S. Battaglia, *Scrittori d'Italia* (Bari, 1938).
Opere Latine Minori, ed. A. F. Massera, *Scrittori d'Italia* (Bari, 1931).

BOFFITO, G. 'La Leggenda Aviatoria di Alessandro Magno', in *Bibliofilia*, XXII (1920), pp. 316–30, and XXIII (1921–2), pp. 22–32.

BONER, ULRICH. (Collection of tales by) ed. F. Pfeiffer (Leipzig, 1844).

BORGELD, A. *Aristoteles en Phyllis* (Groningen, 1902).

BORN, L. K. 'The Perfect Prince', in *Speculum*, III (1928), pp. 470–504.

BOSCO, U. 'Particolari Danteschi', in *Annali della Scuola Normale di Pisa*, I (i), pp. 27 ff.

BOSSUAT, R. 'Vasque de Lucène, traducteur de Quinte-Curce', in *Bibliothèque d'Humanisme et Renaissance*, VIII (1946), pp. 197–245.

BOUSSET, W. *The Antichrist Legend* (London, 1896).

BOZON NICHOLAS. *Contes moralisés*, ed. L. Toulmin Smith and P. Meyer, S.A.T.F. (Paris, 1889).

Braunschweigische Reimchronik, ed. *M.G.H. Deutsche Chroniken*, II (Hanover, 1877).

BROMYARD, JOHN. *Speculum Praedicatorum*, ed. (Nürnberg, 1518).

BRUNET, J. C. *Manuel du Libraire*, 5th ed. (Reprinted Berlin, Fraenkel, 1921.)

BRUNETTO LATINI. *Li Livres dou Tresor*, ed. P. Chabaille (Paris, 1863).

BRUNS, P. J. *Fabelhafte Geschichte Alexanders des Grossen*, in *Romantische und andere Gedichte in Altplattdeutscher Sprache*, pp. 337–66.

Buik of Alexander, ed. R. L. G. Ritchie; *The Buik of Alexander*, Scottish Text Society, new series, XII, XVII, XXI, XXV (1921–9).

BULST, W. *Zum Prologus der 'Natiuitas et Victoria Alexandri magni regis'*, in *Studien zur lateinischen Dichtung des Mittelalters*, *Ehrengabe für Karl Strecker zum 1. Sept. 1931*. Schriftenreihe zum Historischen Vierteljahrschrift, I, pp. 12–17.

BURLEY, WALTER. *De uita ac moribus philosophorum*, ed. H. Knust, *B.L.V.* CLXXVII (Stuttgart, 1886).

Cambridge Medieval History (Cambridge, 1911).

CANONICUS LEODIENSIS. *Chronicon Rhythmicum*, ed. G. H. Pertz, *M.G.H. Scriptt.* XII (1856).

CAPGRAVE, JOHN. *Chronicle of England*, ed. F. C. Hingeston, Rolls Series (1858). *Guide to Rome*, ibid.

Carmen de Gestis Ludovici VIII Regis, ed. O. Holder-Egger, *M.G.H. Scriptt.* XXVI (1882).

CARRAROLI, D. *La Leggenda di Alessandro Magno* (Mondovì, 1892).

CARY, G. 'A note on the Mediaeval History of the Collatio Alexandri cum Dindimo', in *Classica et Mediaevalia*, XV (1954), pp. 124–9.

'Petrarch and Alexander the Great', in *Italian Studies*, V (1950), pp. 43–55.

CASTIGLIONE, BALDASSARE. *Il Cortegiano*, ed. V. Cian (Firenze, 1929).

CAXTON, WILLIAM. *Book of the Fayttes of Arms and of Chyvalrye*, ed. A. T. P. Byles, E.E.T.S., O.S. CLXXXIX (1932).

Mirrour of the World, ed. Prior, E.E.T.S., E.S. CX (1913).

CESARE, R. DE. *Glosse latine ed anticofrancesi all' 'Alexandreis' di Gautier de Châtillon* (Milan, 1951).

Chanson de Roland, Venice text (V. 7), ed. W. Förster, *Altfranzösische Bibliothek*, VI (Heilbronn, 1883).

CHASTELAIN, GEORGES. *Le Lion rampant*, in *Anthologie des poètes français du Xe au XVIe siècle*, ed. A. Dumas (Paris, 1935), pp. 201–2.

CHAUCER, GEOFFREY. *Works*, ed. W. W. Skeat (Oxford, 1900).

CHRISTENSEN, H. *Das Alexanderlied Walters von Châtillon* (Halle, 1905).

Chronica Regia S. Pantaleonis, in G. Eccardus, *Corpus Hist. Medii Aevi* (Leipzig, 1723).

Chronicon S. Andreae, in *M.G.H. Scriptt.* VII, ed. G. H. Pertz (1846).

CINO DA PISTOIA. *Rime dubbie*, in *Rimatori del dolce stil nuovo*, ed. G. di Benedetto, Scrittori d'Italia (Bari, 1939).

COLEMAN-NORTON, P. R. 'The Authorship of the Epistola de Indicis Gentibus et de Bragmanibus', in *Classical Philology*, XXI (1926), pp. 154–60.

Collatio Alexandri cum Dindimo per litteras facta.
   Version I, ed. B. Kuebler, in *Julii Valerii Res Gestae Alexandri Macedonis* (Leipzig, Teubner, 1888), pp. 169–89.
   Version II, ed. F. Pfister, in *Kleine Texte zum Alexanderroman*, Sammlung Vulgär-lateinischer Texte, IV (Heidelberg, 1911), pp. 10–20.

Commendatio lamentabilis in transitu magni regis Edwardi, in *Chronicles of the Reigns of Edward I and Edward II*, ed. W. Stubbs, Rolls Series (1883).

Commendatio lamentabilis militum, in *Chronicles of the Reigns of Edward I and Edward II*, ed. W. Stubbs, Rolls Series (1883).

Conquête de Jérusalem, La, ed. C. Hippeau (Paris, 1868).

COOKE, J. D. 'Euhemerism: a medieval interpretation of classical paganism', in *Speculum*, II (1927), pp. 396–410.

Corona de' Monaci, ed. D. C. Stolfi (Prato, 1862).

CRAIG, H. *Two Coventry Corpus Christi Plays*, E.E.T.S., E.S. LXXXVII (1902).

CRESCINI, V. 'Alberico de Pisançon', in *Studi Medievali*, II (1929), pp. 196–7.

CYPRIAN, ST. *De Idolorum Vanitate*, Migne, *P.L.* XLI.

DAM, J. VAN. 'Der künstlerische Wert der Strassburger Alexander', in *Neophilologus*, XII (1927), pp. 104–17.

Zur Vorgeschichte des höfischen Epos: Lamprecht, Eilhart, Veldeke. *Rheinische Beiträge zur germanischen Philologie*, VIII (1923).

De Alexandro Rege (Swedish).

Ed. E. S. Bring, *Historia Caroli Magni Suecana* (Lund, 1847).

Ed. G. E. Klemming, *Svensk Fornskr. Sallsk.* (Stockholm, 1871–3).

Ed. J. E. Rietz, *Fabula Alexandri Magni Suecana* (Lund, 1850).

De Moribus Brachmanorum, ed. Migne, *P.L.* XVII.

DE QUINCEY, T. *The Caesars*, in *Works*, vol. IX (Edinburgh, 1880).

DEIMANN, W. *Abfassungszeit und Verfasser des griechischen Alexanderromans* (Münster, 1917).

DESCHAMPS EUSTACHE. *Œuvres*, ed. G. Raynaud and Le Queux de S. Hilaire, S.A.T.F. (Paris, 1880, etc.), 11 vols.

DEXTER CHRONOLOGUS. *In Prophetiam Danielis de quatuor animalibus*, Migne, *P.L.* XXXI.

Dialogus Creaturarum, ed. J. G. T. Grässe, *B.L.V.* CXLVIII (Tübingen, 1880).

Dicta Alexandri, ed. S. de Renzi, *Collectio Salernitana*, III (Naples, 1854).

Dindimus on the Brahmans, or *Dindimus de Bragmanibus*.

Ed. F. Pfister, *Kleine Texte zum Alexanderroman*, *Sammlung Vulgärlateinischer Texte*, IV (Heidelberg, 1910), pp. 6–9.

Ed. Sir Edward Bysshe, *Palladius de gentibus Indiae* (London, 1665), third text.

DOMENICO FALUGIO. *Triompho Magno* (Rome, Marcellus Silber, 1521).

Doon de Nanteuil, ed. P. Meyer, *Romania*, XIII (1884), p. 16.

DOSSON, S. *Etude sur Quinte-Curce* (Paris, 1887).

DOUTREPONT, G. *La Littérature française à la cour des Ducs de Bourgogne. Bibliothèque du XVe Siècle*, VIII (Paris, 1909).

DUMAS, A. *Anthologie des Poètes Français du Xe au XVIe Siècle* (Paris, 1935).

DURAND, J. 'La Légende d'Alexandre le Grand', in *Annales Archéologiques*, XXV (1865), pp. 141 ff.

DURRIEU, P. 'L'Histoire du bon roi Alexandre', in *Revue de l'Art Ancien et Moderne*, XIII (1903), pp. 49–64, 103–21.

Dutch Chapbook Alexander, *Historye van den grooten coninc Alexander* (Delft, Christian Snellaert, 1488).

EDWARDS, B. *A classification of the Manuscripts of Gui de Cambrai's Vengement Alixandre*, Elliott Monographs 20 (Princeton Univ. Press, 1926).

EHRISMANN, G. *Geschichte der deutschen Litteratur bis zum Ausgang des Mittelalters* (Munich, 1935).

EIKE VON REPGOW. *Zeitbuch*, ed. H. G. Massmann, *B.L.V.* XLII (Stuttgart, 1857).

EKKEHART OF AURA. *Chronicon Universale*, ed. D. G. Waitz, *M.G.H. Scriptt.* VI (Hanover, 1844).

Excerptum de uita Alexandri Magni, ibid.

Enfances Guillaume, Les, ed. P. Henry, S.A.T.F. (1935).

English Conquest of Ireland, The, ed. F. J. Furnivall, E.E.T.S., O.S. CVII (1896).

Entree d'Espagne, L', ed. A. Thomas, S.A.T.F. (Paris, 1913).

Epistola Alexandri ad Aristotelem (Epistola I).

Ed. W. W. Boer, *Epistola Alexandri ad Aristotelem ad codicum fidem edita et commentario critico instructa* (The Hague, 1953).

Ed. B. Kübler, *Julii Valerii...Res Gestae Alexandri Macedonis* (Leipzig, Teubner, 1888), pp. 190–221.

Ed. S. Rypins, *Three Old English Prose Texts*, E.E.T.S., O.S. CLXI (1924), pp. 79–100.

Epistola Alexandri ad Aristotelem. (Epistola II, Bamberg Version), ed. F. Pfister, *Kleine Texte zum Alexanderroman, Sammlung Vulgärlateinischer Texte*, IV (Heidelberg, 1912), pp. 21–37.

Epistola de mirabilibus Indiae.

Ed. E. Faral, 'Une source latine de l'*Histoire d'Alexandre: La Lettre sur les merveilles de l'Inde*', in *Romania*, XLII (1914).

Ed. M. R. James, *Marvels of the East*, Roxburghe Club (1929).

Erfurt Alexander, ed. A. Hilka, 'Der Zauberer Neptanabus nach einem bisher unbekannten Erfurter Text', *Mitteilungen der schlesischen Gesellschaft für Volkskunde*, XIV (1914), pp. 80–9.

ERMOLDUS NIGELLUS. *In Honorem Hludowici*, in *M.H.G. Poetae Latini Aeui Carolini*, II.

ETIENNE DE FOUGÈRES. *Livre des manières*, ed. Talbert (1877).

EULING, K. *Die sogenannte Wolfenbüttler Priamelhandschrift, Deutsche Texte des Mittelalters*, XIV (Berlin, 1908).

Eulogium Historiarum, ed. F. S. Hayden, Rolls Series (1858).

Faits des Romains, ed. L. Flutre and K. Sneyders de Vogel (Paris, 1937–8).

FARAL, E. *Recherches sur les sources latines des contes et romans courtois du moyen âge* (Paris, 1913).

FAVRE, G. *Mélanges d'Histoire Littéraire*, II (Geneva, 1856).

FERRETO DE' FERRETI VICENTINO. *Historia rerum in Italia gestarum*, ed. C. Cipolla, *Fonti per la Storia d'Italia*, I (Rome, 1908).

FERRI, S. 'Per l'edizione dell'Alessandreide di Wilichino da Spoleto', in *Bolletino della Reale Deputazione di Storia Patria per l'Umbria*, XXI (1915), pp. 211–19.

FERRI, T. 'Appunti su Quilichino da Spoleto e le sue opere', in *Studi Medievali*, n.s. IX (1936), pp. 239–50.

Fior di Virtù, ed. B. Fabbricatore, Naples (1870).

FLECHTNER, H. *Die Sprache des Alexanderfragments des Alberich von Besançon* (Breslau, 1882).

Floriant et Florete, ed. H. F. Williams, *University of Michigan Publications, Language and Literature*, XXIII (1947).

FOLCUINUS. *Gesta Abbatum Lobiensium*, ed. G. H. Pertz, *M.G.H. Scriptt.* IV (1841).

FÖRSTER, W. and KOSCHWITZ, E. *Altfranzösisches Uebungsbuch*, 5th ed. (Leipzig, 1915).

Fortunes et Adversitez de Jean Regnier, Les, ed. E. Droz, S.A.T.F. (Paris, 1923).

FOSTER, B. 'The *Roman de toute Chevalerie*, its date and author', in *French Studies*, IX (1955), pp. 154–8. Also pp. 348–51 (discussion).

FOULET, A. 'Balaam, Dux Tyri', in *Modern Language Notes*, XLVIII (1933), pp. 330–5. 'La bataille de Granique chez Alberic', in *Romania*, LX (1935), pp. 237–41.

FRANCESCHINI, E. 'Il Liber philosophorum antiquorum', in *Atti del Reale Istituto Veneto di scienze, lettere ed arti*, XCI (1931–2), p. 394.

FRAUENLOB (HEINRICH VON MEISSEN). *Heinrich von Meissen des Frauenlobes Leiche, Sprüche etc.*, ed. L. Ettmüller (Quedlinburg and Leipzig, 1843).

FREDEGARIUS SCHOLASTICUS. *Chronicon, M.G.H. Scriptores Rerum Merovingicarum*, II (1888).

FREZZI FEDERICO. *Quadriregio*, ed. E. Filippini, *Scrittori d'Italia* (Bari, 1914).

BIBLIOGRAPHY

FRIEDLÄNDER, I. *Die Chadirlegende und der Alexanderroman* (Leipzig, Teubner, 1913).

FRITZ, K. VON. *Quellenuntersuchungen zu Leben und Philosophie des Diogenes von Sinope*. *Philol.*, Supplement-Band XXVIII (1926).

FUCHS, H. *Beiträge zur Alexandersage*, Programm (Giessen 1907).

FUHRMANN, H. in *Archiv für Papyrusforschung*, XI (1935), pp. 107–9.

FULGENTIUS, FABIUS CLAUDIUS GORDIANUS. *De aetatibus mundi et hominis*, ed. R. Helm (Leipzig, Teubner, 1898).

GAEDERTZ, K. T. *Gabriel Rollenhagen: sein Leben und seine Werke* (Leipzig, 1881).

GARCÍA GÓMEZ, E. *Un Texto Arabe Occidental de la Legenda de Alejandro* (Madrid, Istituto de Valencia de Don Juan, 1929).

GASTER, M. *Studies and Texts*, II (1925–8), pp. 879 ff.

GAUDENTIUS BRIXIENSIS, ST. *Sermones*, Migne *P.L.* XX.

GAUTIER DE CHÂTILLON. *Alexandreis*, ed. Migne, *P.L.* CCIX.

Moralisch-Satyrische Gedichte Walters von Châtillon, ed. K. Strecker (Heidelberg, 1929).

GEFFROI DE PARIS. *Chronique Rimé attribué à*, in *Recueil des Historiens des Gaules et de la France*, XXII (1865).

Gesamtkatalog der Wiegendrücke (Leipzig, 1925).

Gesta Romanorum.

Ed. W. Dick, *Die Gesta Romanorum nach der Innsbrucker Handschrift vom Jahre 1342 und vier Münchener Handschriften herausgegeben*. *Erlanger Beiträge zur englischen Philologie*, VII (Erlangen, 1890).

Ed. H. Oesterly (Berlin, 1872).

English version, ed. S. H. J. Herrtage, E.E.T.S., E.S. XXXIII (1879).

GILBERT, A. H. *Notes on the Influence of the Secretum Secretorum*, in *Speculum*, III (1928), pp. 84–98.

GIORDANO, C. *Alexandreis, poema di Gautier da Châtillon* (Naples, 1917).

GIOVANNI DA PROCIDA. *Placita Philosophorum moralium antiquorum*, ed. S. de Renzi, *Collectio Salernitana*, III (Naples, 1854).

GIRALDUS CAMBRENSIS. *Opera*, ed. Brewer, Dimock and Warner, Rolls Series, 7 vols.

GODFREY OF ADMONT. *Homilia super Macchabaeis*, Migne, *P.L.* CLXXIV.

GODFREY OF VITERBO. *Pantheon*, ed. Pistorius, *Rerum Germanicarum Scriptores* (1613).

GOLDSCHMIDT, E. P. *Medieval Texts and their First Appearance in Print*, Bibliographical Society (1943).

GOWER, JOHN. *English Works*, ed. G. C. Macaulay, E.E.T.S., E.S. LXXXI–LXXXII (1901).

GRAF, A. 'Il Zibaldone attribuito a Antonio Pucci', in *Giornale storico della letteratura italiana*, I (1883), pp. 285–6.

Miti, Leggende e Superstizioni del Medio Evo (Turin, 1892).

GRAMMEL, E. *Studien über den Wandel des Alexanderbildes in der deutschen Dichtung des 12. und 13. Jahrhunderts*, Frankfurt diss. (Limburg, 1931).

GREVEN, J. *Die exempla aus den Sermones feriales et communes des Jakob von Vitry, Sammlung Mittellateinischer Texte*, IX (Heidelberg, 1914).

Griechische Papyri der Hamburger Staats- und Universitätsbibliothek, II (1954).

GUI DE CAMBRAI. *Le Vengement Alixandre*, ed. B. Edwards, Elliott Monographs 23 (Princeton Univ. Press, 1928).

GUIART, GUILLAUME. *La Branche des Royaus Lingnages*, in *Recueil des Historiens des Gaules et de la France*, XXII (1865).

GUIBERT DE TOURNAI. *Eruditio regum et principum*, ed. A. de Poorter, *Les philosophes belges*, IX (Louvain, 1914).

383

BIBLIOGRAPHY

Guido of Ivrea. *Versus Eporadienses*, ed. E. Dümmler, *Zeitschrift für deutsches Altertum*, xiv (1869).

Guillaume, Alexis. *Contreblason de faulses amours*, in *Œuvres poétiques*, vol. I, ed. A. Piaget and E. Picot, S.A.T.F. (1896).

Guillaume de Machaut. *Poésies lyriques de Guillaume de Machaut*, ed. V. Chichmaref (Paris, 1909).

Haller, John. *Hármas Istoria* (Kolozsvár, 1696).

Hamilton, G. L. *A New Redaction* (I^{3A}) *of the Historia de Preliis and the Date of Redaction I^3*, in *Speculum*, II (1927), pp. 113–46.

'Quelques notes sur l'histoire de la légende d'Alexandre en Angleterre au moyen âge', in *Mélanges...offerts à M. Antoine Thomas* (Paris, 1927), pp. 195–202.

'Studies in the Sources of Gower', in *Journal of English and Germanic Philology*, xxvi (1927), pp. 491–520.

Hampe, Th. *Die Quellen der Strassburger Fortsetzung von Lamprechts Alexanderlied*, diss. (Bremen, 1890).

Hartlieb, Johann. *Histori von dem grossen Alexander*, ed. H. Benz, *Deutsche Volksbücher* (Jena, 1924).

Hartmann von der Aue. *Erec*, ed. A. Leitzmann (Halle, 1939).

Hartmann, R. 'Alexander und der Rätselstein aus dem Paradies', in *Oriental Studies presented to E. G. Browne* (Cambridge, 1922), pp. 179–85.

Hawes, Stephen. *Pastime of Pleasure*, ed. Mead, E.E.T.S., O.S. clxxiii (1928).

Haymo of Halberstadt. *Commentaria in Isaiam* (Cologne, 1531).

Heidin, Die, ed. L. Pfannmüller, in *Mittelhochdeutsche Novellen*, I (Bonn, 1912).

Heinrich von Beringen. *Schachgedicht*, ed. P. Zimmermann, *B.L.V.* clxvi (Tübingen, 1883).

Heinrich von der Türlin. *Diu Krône*, ed. C. H. F. Scholl (Stuttgart, 1852).

Henneman, J. B. *Untersuchungen über das mittelenglische Gedicht 'Wars of Alexander'*, diss. (Berlin, 1889).

Henri d'Andeli.

Dit du chancelier Philippe, in *Romania*, I, 1872, p. 217.

Lai d'Aristote, in *Œuvres d'Henri d'Andeli*, ed. A. Héron (Rouen, 1881).

Herimannus Contractus. *Opusculum diuerso metro compositum*, ed. E. Dummler, in *Zeitschrift für deutsches Altertum*, xiii (1867).

Héron, A. 'La Légende d'Alexandre et d'Aristote', in *Précis analytique des travaux de l'Académie des Sciences...de Rouen, pendant l'année 1890–1* (Rouen, 1892).

Herrmann, A. *The Forraye of Gadderis, The Vowis, extracts from Sir Gilbert Hay's Buik of King Alexander the Conqueror*, in *Wissenschaftliche Beilage zum Jahresbericht der II. Städtischen Realschule zu Berlin* (Berlin, 1900).

Hertz, W. 'Aristoteles in den Alexanderdichtungen des Mittelalters', in *Abhandlungen der königlichen bayerischen Akademie der Wissenschaften*, I Cl., xix. Bd., I Abt. (Munich, 1890). *Gesammelte Abhandlungen* (Stuttgart and Berlin, 1905).

Hildebert of Lavardin, or Hilderbertus Cenomannensis. *De Machabaeis Carmen*, Migne, *P.L.* clxxi.

Hildenbrand, T. *Die altfranzösische Alexanderdichtung 'Le Roman de Toute Chevalerie' des Thomas von Kent und die mittelenglische Romanze 'Kyng Alexander' in ihrem Verhältnis zu einander*, diss. (Bonn, 1911).

Hilka, A. *Der altfranzösische Prosa-Alexanderroman nebst dem lateinischen Original der Historia de Preliis (Recension I^2)* (Halle, 1920).

'Die Berliner Bruchstücke der ältesten italienischen Historia de preliis', in *Zeitschrift für romanische Philologie*, XLI, pp. 234–53.

(Review of F. Pfister, *Die Historia de preliis und das Alexanderepos des Quilichinus*), *Berliner Philologische Wochenschrift*, XXXVI (1916), cols. 77–81.

HILKA, A. and F. P. MAGOUN. 'A list of manuscripts containing texts of the Historia de preliis Alexandri Magni', in *Speculum*, IX (1934), pp. 84–6.

HIRSCH, S. 'Das Alexanderbuch Johann Hartliebs', in *Palaestra*, LXXXII (1909).

HONORIUS OF AUTUN. *De Imagine Mundi*, Migne, *P.L.* CLXXII.

HOOGSTRA, S. *Proza-Bewerkingen van het Leven van Alexander den Groote in het middelnederlandsch* (The Hague, 1888).

HÜBNER, A. 'Alexander der Grosse in der deutschen Dichtung des Mittelalters', in *Die Antike*, IX (1933), pp. 32–48.

HUGH OF ST VICTOR. *Allegoriae in Vetus Testamentum*, in Migne, *P.L.* CLXXV.

Huon de Bordeaux (Eng. tr. Lord Berners), ed. S. L. Lee, E.E.T.S., E.S. XL, XLI, XLIII (1882–7).

IACOBUS DE GUISIA. *Annales Hanoniae*, ed. E. Sackur, *M.G.H. Scriptt.* XXX, i (1896).

Intelligenza, L', ed. V. Mistruzzi, *Collezione di opere inedite o rare* (Bologna, 1928).

Itinerarium Alexandri, ed. A. Mai (Milan, 1817).

JACOBUS DE CESSOLIS. *De Lude Scacchorum*, ed. F. Vetter, *Das Schachzabelbuch Kunrats von Ammenhausen* (Frauenfeld, 1892).

JACQUES DE LONGUYON. *Voeux du Paon*, ed. R. L. G. Ritchie, *The Buik of Alexander*, Scottish Text Society, new series, XII (1921) and XXI (1927).

JACQUES DE VITRY, *Historia Hierosolymitana*, in *Gesta Dei per Francos* (Hanover, 1611).

JAKOB VAN MAERLANT. *Alexanders Geesten*, ed. J. Frank, *Bibliotheek van Middelnederlandsche Letterkunde* (Groningen, 1882).

JAMISON, E. 'Notes on Santa Maria della Strada at Matrice', in *Papers of the British School at Rome*, XIV (1938), pp. 67–9.

JANSEN ENIKEL. *Weltchronik*, ed. P. Strauch, *M.G.H. Deutsche Chroniken*, III (Hanover, 1900).

JEAN LE NEVELON, or JEAN LE VENELAIS.
La Venjance Alixandre, ed. E. B. Ham, *Elliott Monographs* 27 (Princeton Univ. Press, 1931).
Five Versions of the Venjance Alixandre, ed. E. B. Ham, *Elliott Monographs* 34 (Princeton Univ. Press, 1935).
'An eighth *Venjance Alixandre*', *Modern Language Notes* (1941), pp. 409–14.

JEROME, ST.
Commentaria in Danielem, Migne, *P.L.* XXV.
Commentaria in Isaiam, Migne, *P.L.* XXIV.
Commentaria in Jeremiam, Migne, *P.L.* XXIV.
Contra Iouinianum, Migne, *P.L.* XXIII.
Epistolae, Hilberg, *Corpus Scriptorum Ecclesiasticorum Latinorum*, LV (1912).
Epistolae, Migne, *P.L.* XXII.
Vita S. Hilarionis, Migne, *P.L.* XXIII.

JOHANNES FERRARIENSIS. *Ex annalium libris Marchionum Estensium excerpta*, ed. R. Simeoni, R.I.S. XX, ii (Bologna, n.d.).

JOHANNES GUALENSIS or VALLENSIS. *Summa de regimine uitae humanae*, ed. H. Knust, *B.L.V.* CXLI (Tübingen, 1879), pp. 556–7.

JOHN DE MANDEVILLE. *Travels.*
   Ed. P. Hamelius, E.E.T.S., O.S. CLIII and CLIV (1919–23).
   Ed. M. Letts, Hakluyt Society (1953).
JOHN OF SALISBURY. *Policraticus,* ed. C. C. J. Webb (Oxford, 1909).
JÓNSSON, BRAND. *Alexanders Saga,* ed. C. R. Unger (Christiania, 1848).
JULIUS VALERIUS. *Res Gestae Alexandri Macedonis,* ed. B. Kuebler (Leipzig, Teubner, 1888).
   Oxford-Montpelier Epitome, ed. G. Cillié, *De Julii Valerii Epitoma Oxoniensi* (Strasbourg, 1911); ed. A. Hilka in *Romanische Forschungen,* XXIX (1911).
   Zacher Epitome, ed. J. Zacher, *Julii Valerii Epitome* (Halle, 1867).
Junker und der treue Heinrich, Der, ed. K. Kinzel (Berlin, 1880).
Kaiserchronik, ed. M.G.H. *Deutsche Chroniken,* I (Hanover, 1895).
KAMPERS, F. *Alexander der Grosse und die Idee des Weltimperiums in Prophetie und Sage* (Freiburg-im-Breisgau, 1901).
KLAPPER, J. *Exempla aus Handschriften des Mittelalters. Sammlung Mittellateinischer Texte,* II (Heidelberg, 1911).
KNUST, H. *Mitteilungen aus dem Eskurial, B.L.V.* CXLI (Tübingen, 1879).
König Rother, ed. H. Rückert (Leipzig, 1872).
Konung Alexander, ed. J. A. Ahlstrand (Stockholm, 1862).
KRAPPE, A. H. 'The Indian provenance of a Medieval Exemplum', in *Traditio,* II (1944), pp. 499–502.
   'Tiberius and Thrasyllus', in *American Journal of Philology,* XLVIII (1927), pp. 359–66.
KÜHNHOLD, I. *Seifrits Alexander,* Diss. Berlin (Dresden, 1939).
Kyng Alisaunder.
   Ed. H. Weber, *Metrical Romances of the thirteenth, fourteenth and fifteenth centuries* (Edinburgh, 1810).
   Ed. G. V. Smithers, E.E.T.S., O.S. CXXVII (1952).
   Expanded version, fragment, ed. K. D. Bülbring, *Englische Studien,* XIII (1889).
LAMPRECHT, PFAFFE. *Alexander,* ed. K. Kinzel, *Germanische Handbibliothek,* VI (Halle, 1884).
LANDGRAF, G. *Die Vita Alexandri Magni des Archipresbyters Leo* (*Historia de Preliis*) (Erlangen, 1885).
LANTBERT. *Vita Heriberti Archiepiscopi Coloniensis, M.G.H. Scriptt.* IV (1841).
LATTÈS, S. 'La plus ancienne Bible en vers italiens (Manuscrit Vatican 4821)', in *Ecole française de Rome, Mélanges d'Archéologie et d'Histoire,* année 49 (1932).
Lazarillo de Tormes, La vida de, ed. J. C. y Frauca (Madrid, *Clásicos Castellanos,* 1941).
LE ROUX DE LINCY. *Le Livre des Légendes* (Paris, 1836).
LEGGE, D. *Anglo-Norman in the cloisters* (Edinburgh, 1950).
LEHMANN, P. 'Quilichinus von Spoleto', in *Berliner Philologische Wochenschrift,* XXXVIII (1918), cols. 812–15.
LÉVI, I. 'La legende d'Alexandre dans le Talmud', in *Revue des Etudes Juives,* II (1881), pp. 293–300.
   Le Roman d'Alexandre: Texte Hébreu Anonyme... (Paris, 1887).
   'Les Traductions hébraïques de l'histoire légendaire d'Alexandre', in *Revue des Etudes Juives,* III (1882), pp. 238–65.
Libro de Alexandre, ed. R. S. Willis, *Elliott Monographs* 32 (Princeton Univ. Press, 1934).
Liegnitz Historia Alexandri Magni, ed. A. Hilka, *Romanische Forschungen,* XXIX (1911), pp. 1–30.

BIBLIOGRAPHY

LIÉNARD, E. *Collatio Alexandri et Dindimi*, in *Revue Belge de Philologie et d'Histoire*, xv, ii (1936), pp. 819–38.

LIUTPRAND OF CREMONA. *Works*, English translation, F. A. Wright (London, Routledge, 1930).

LOOMIS, R. S. 'Alexander the Great's Celestial Journey', in *Burlington Magazine*, XXXII (1918), pp. 177 ff.

'Verses on the Nine Worthies', in *Modern Philology*, xv (1917), pp. 211–19.

Lucidarius, ed. F. Heidlauf, *Deutsche Texte des Mittelalters*, XXVIII (Berlin, 1915).

LYDGATE, JOHN. *Fall of Princes*, ed. H. Bergen (Washington, Carnegie Institute, 1923).

Minor Poems, ed. H. N. MacCracken, E.E.T.S., O.S. CXCII (1934).

Reson and Sensuallyte, ed. Sieper, E.E.T.S., E.S. LXXXIV (1904).

LYDGATE, JOHN and BURGH. *Secrees of old Philosoffres*, ed. R. Steele, E.E.T.S., E.S. LXVI (1894).

MAGOUN, F. P. *Gests of King Alexander of Macedon* (Cambridge, Mass. 1929).

'Photostats of the Historia de Preliis Alexandri Magni I³', in *Harvard Library Bulletin*, I (1947), p. 377.

'The Compilation of St Albans and the Old French Prose Alexander Romance', in *Speculum*, I (1925), pp. 225–32.

'The Middle-Swedish Konung Alexander and the Historia de Preliis Alexandri Magni (Recension I²)', in *Etudes Germaniques*, III (1948), pp. 167–76.

'A Prague Epitome of the *Historia de Preliis Alexandri Magni*', *Harvard Studies and Notes in Philology and Literature*, XVI (1934), pp. 119–44.

'The Harvard Epitome of the *Historia de Preliis*', *Harvard Studies and Notes in Philology and Literature*, XIV (1932), pp. 115–32.

MAGOUN, F. P. and THOMSON, S. H. 'Kronika o Alexandru Velikèm, a Czech prose translation of the Historia de Preliis, recension I³', in *Speculum*, III (1928), pp. 204–17.

MALACHI. *Venenum Malachie* (Paris, Henri Estienne, 1518).

MANITIUS, M. *Hss. antiker Autoren in mittelälterlichen Bibliothekskatalogen*, Beiheft 67 of *Zentralblatt für Bibliothekswesen* (Leipzig, 1935).

Geschichte der lateinischen Literatur im Mittelalter (1911–31). 3 vols.

MAP, WALTER. *De nugis curialium*, English translation by F. Tupper and M. B. Ogle (London, 1924).

MARBOD OF RENNES. *Liber de Gemmis* in Migne, *P.L.* CLXXI.

MARCO POLO. Ed. H. Yule and H. Cordier, *The Book of Ser Marco Polo* (London, 1926).

MARTINUS POLONUS (VON TROPPAU). *Chronicon* (Antwerp, Plantin, 1574).

MATHEW, FR. G. 'Ideals of Knighthood in late fourteenth-century England', in *Studies of Mediaeval History presented to F. M. Powicke* (Oxford, 1948).

MEISSNER, A. L. 'Bildliche Darstellungen der Alexandersage in Kirchen des Mittelalters', in *Archiv für das Studium der neueren Sprachen*, LXVIII (1882), pp. 177–90.

MEISSNER, B. 'Mubašširs Aḫbâr el-Iskender', in *Zeitschrift der deutschen morgenländischen Gesellschaft*, XLIX (1895), pp. 583–627.

MERKELBACH, R. *Die Quellen des Griechischen Alexanderromans*, Zetemata, IX (Munich, 1954).

MERZDORF, J. F. L. T. *Die Deutschen Historienbibeln des Mittelalters*, B.L.V. C and CI (Tübingen, 1870).

MESSNER, C. A. *Two I² Versions of the Historia de Preliis in Italian, with an edition of the Nobili Fatti che ffe Alisandro il Macedonio, MS. II. i. 62 of the Biblioteca Nazionale Centrale di Firenze*, Harvard dissertation (1928, unpublished).

387

Metz Epitome, ed. O. Wagner, *Incerti auctoris Epitome rerum gestarum Alexandri Magni* (Leipzig, 1900).

MEYER, L. *Les Légendes des Matières de Rome, de France, et de Bretagne dans le 'Panthéon' de Godefroi de Viterbe* (Paris, 1933).

MEYER, P. *Alexandre le Grand dans la littérature française du moyen âge*, 2 vols (Paris, 1886).
'Les plus anciennes compilations françaises d'histoire ancienne', in *Romania*, XIV, pp. 36–76.

MEYER, R. T. 'The Sources of the Middle Irish Alexander', in *Modern Philology*, XLVII, pp. 1–7.

MICHEL, F. *Recherches sur le commerce, la fabrication, et l'usage des étoffes de soie, d'or et d'argent, et autres tissus précieux en occident, principalement en France, pendant le Moyen-Age* (Paris, 1872–4).

Middle English Sermons, ed. W. O. Ross, E.E.T.S., O.S. CCIX (1940).

Middle Irish Alexander, ed. K. Meyer, in W. Stokes and E. Windisch, *Irische Texte*, II, ii, pp. 43–69, 100–107.

MILA Y FONTANALS. *De los trovadores en España, Obras Completas*, II (Madrid, 1889).

MILEMETE, WALTER. *Works*, ed. M. R. James, Roxburghe Club (1913).

MILLET, G. 'L'Ascension d'Alexandre', in *Syria*, IV (1923), pp. 85–133.

MINUCIUS FELIX, ed. G. H. Rendall, *Loeb Classical Library* (1931).

MONACHUS SANGALLENSIS. *Gesta Karoli*, *M.G.H. Scriptt.* II, ed. G. H. Pertz (1829).

MONTAIGNE. Cotton's translation, revised by P. Coste, 7th ed. (1759).

MOREL-FATIO, A. *El libro de Alexandre, Gesellschaft für romanische Literatur*, X (Dresden, 1906).
'Recherches sur le texte et les sources du Libro de Alexandre', in *Romania*, IV, 1875, pp. 7–90.

Moriz von Craun, in *Zwei altdeutsche Rittermären*, ed. E. Schröder (Berlin, 1913).

Morte Arthure, ed. E. Brock, E.E.T.S., O.S. VIII (1865).

MOUSKET FILIPPE. *Historia regum Francorum*, in *M.G.H. Scriptt.* XXVI (1882).

MÜLLER, H. E. *Die Werke des Pfaffen Lamprecht, Münchener Texte*, XII (Munich, 1923).

MUSSAFIA, A. 'Mittheilungen aus romanischen Handschriften, I. Ein altneapolitanisches Regimen Sanitatis', in *Sitzungsberichte der Kaiserlichen Akademie der Wissenschaften in Wien*, Phil.-Hist. Klasse, CVI (1884), pp. 507–626.

NECKHAM, ALEXANDER. *De Naturis Rerum*, ed. T. Wright, Rolls Series (1863).
De Vita Monachorum, ibid.

NEULING, E. 'Die deutsche Bearbeitung der Alexandreis des Quilichinus von Spoleto', in *Beiträge zur Geschichte der deutschen Sprache und Literatur*, X (1884), pp. 318–83.

NICOLAUS DE BRAIA. *Carmen de Gestis Ludovici VIII Regis*, *M.G.H. Scriptt.* XXVI, ed. O. Holder-Egger (1882).

Nobili fatti d'Alessandro Magno, I, ed. G. Grion, *Collezione di opere inedite o rare* (Bologna, 1872).

NOLHAC, P. DE. *Pétrarque et l'humanisme* (Paris, 1907).

Novelle Antiche, Le, ed. G. Biagi, *Raccolta di opere inedite o rare* (Florence, 1880).

NYKL, A. R. *A Compendium of Aljamiado Literature* (New York, 1929).
'El Rrekontamiento del Rrey Ališandere', in *Revue Hispanique*, LXXVII (1929), pp. 409–611.

OLSCHKI, L. 'Der Brief des Presbyter Johannes', in *Historische Zeitschrift*, CXLIV (1913), pp. 1–13.

ORIGEN. *Contra Haereses*, Migne, *Patrologia Graeca*, XVI.

OROSIUS. *Historia aduersum paganos*, ed. C. Zangemeister (Leipzig, Teubner, 1889).
ORTIZ, R. 'La Vie de Saint Auban', quoted in *Giornale storico della Letteratura Italiana*, LXXXV (1925), p. 78.
OTTO OF FREISING. *Chronica*, ed. A. Hofmeister (Hanover and Leipzig, 1912). Ed. R. Wilmans, *M.G.H. Scriptt.* XX (Hanover, 1868).
Padiglione di Mambrino, ed. O. Targlioni Tozzetti (Livorno, 1874).
PALADINO, G. *Opuscoli e Lettere de' Riformatori Italiani del Cinquecento, Scrittori d'Italia* (Bari, 1927), vol. II.
PALLADIUS, bishop of Helenopolis. Παλλαδίου περὶ τῶν τῆς 'Ινδίας ἐθνῶν καὶ τῶν Βραχμάνων, ed. Sir Edward Bysshe, *Palladius de Gentibus Indiae* (London, 1665). *Palladius de gentibus Indiae*, ed. ibid.
Parlement of the Thre Ages, The, ed. I. Gollancz, Roxburghe Club (1897).
PATCH, H. R. Review of F. P. Magoun, *Gests of King Alexander of Macedon*, in *Speculum*, V (1930), p. 118.
The Goddess Fortuna in Mediaeval Literature (Cambridge, 1927).
PEIRE VIDAL. *Poésies*, ed. J. Anglade (Paris, 1913).
PERRAULT, GUILLAUME. *De eruditione principum*, in Aquinas, *Opera Omnia* (Parma, 1852–71), vol. XVI.
PETER COMESTOR. *Historia Scholastica*, Migne, *P.L.* CXCVIII.
PETRARCH. *De uiris illustribus*, ed. G. Razzolini, *Collezione di opere inedite o rare*, I (Bologna, 1874).
PETRUS ALFONSI. *Disciplina Clericalis*, ed. A. Hilka and W. Söderhjelm, *Sammlung Mittellateinischer Texte*, I (Heidelberg, 1911).
PETRUS ARCHIDIACONUS. *Quaestiones in Danielem Prophetam*, in Migne, *P.L.* XCVI.
PETRUS CANTOR. *Verbum Abbreviatum*, in Migne, *P.L.* CCV.
PFISTER, F. 'Auf den Spuren Alexanders des Grossen in der älteren englischen Literatur', in *Germanisch-Romanische Monatsschrift*, XVI (1928), pp. 81–6.
'De codicibus "Vitae Alexandri Magni" vel "Historiae" quae dicitur "de preliis"', in *Rivista di Filologia Classica*, XLII, pp. 104–13.
'Die Brahmanen in der Alexandersage', in *Berliner Philologische Wochenschrift* (1921), cols. 569 ff.
'Die Historia de Preliis und das Alexanderepos des Quilichinus', in *Münchener Museum für Philologie des Mittelalters und der Renaissance*, I, pp. 249–301.
'Die 'Οδοιπορία ἀπὸ 'Εδὲμ τοῦ παραδείσου und die Legende von Alexanders Zug nach dem Paradies', in *Rheinisches Museum*, LXVI (1911), pp. 458–71.
'Eine jüdische Gründungsgeschichte Alexandrias mit einem Anhang über Alexanders Besuch in Jerusalem', in *Sitzungsberichte der Heidelberger Akademie der Wissenschaften*, Phil.-Hist. Klasse, V (1914), Abh. 11, pp. 22–30.
'Eine sagenhafte Jugendgeschichte Alexanders des Grossen', in *Berliner Philologische Wochenschrift*, XXXVI (1916), cols. 447–8.
'Gog und Magog', in *Handwörterbuch des deutschen Aberglaubens*, III, cols. 914–16.
(Review of A. Hilka, *Zur Alexandersage*, Breslau, St Mathias Gymnasium, 1909), in *Wochenschrift für klassische Philologie*, XXVII (1910), cols. 675–8; ibid. XXVIII (1911), cols. 1152–9; in *Romanische Forschungen*, XXIX (1911), pp. 69–71.
'Studien zum Alexanderroman', in *Würzburger Jahrbücher*, Heft 1 (1946), pp. 29–66.
PHILIPPE DE NOVARE. *Les Quatre Ages de l'homme*, ed. M. de Fréville, S.A.T.F. (Paris, 1888).
PIERRE D'ABERNUN. *Secré des Secrés*, ed. O. A. Beckerlegge, Anglo-Norman Text Society, V (Oxford, 1944).

PIETRO ARETINO. *Secondo Libro delle Lettere*, ed. F. Nicolini, *Scrittori d'Italia* (Bari, 1916).

PISTOLESI, L. 'Del posto che spetta al Libro de Alexandre nella storia della letteratura spagnuola', in *Revue des Langues Romanes*, XLVI (1903), pp. 255–81.

POPPEN, H. *Das Alexanderbuch Johann Hartliebs und seine Quellen*, diss. (Heidelberg, 1914).

PRINTZ, W. 'Gilgamisch und Alexander', in *Zeitschrift der Deutschen Morgenländischen Gesellschaft*, LXXXV (1931), pp. 196–206.

PSEUDO-CALLISTHENES. Ed. H. Meusel, *Pseudo-Callisthenes nach der Leidener Handschrift herausgegeben, Jahrbuch für classische Philologie*, Neue Folge, Supplementband V (Leipzig, 1871).

Ed. C. Müller, *Arriani Anabasis et Indica* (Paris, Didot, 1846).

Ed. W. Kroll, *Historia Alexandri Magni (Pseudo-Callisthenes)*, vol. I, *Recensio Vetusta* (Berlin, 1926).

PSEUDO-METHODIUS. *Revelationes*, in E. Sackur, *Sibyllinische Texte und Forschungen* (Halle, 1898).

RADBODUS. *Libellus de miraculo S. Martini*, in *M.G.H. Scriptt.* XV, ii (1888).

RALPH DE DICETO. *Abbreuiationes Chronicorum*, *Opera Historica*, ed. W. Stubbs, Rolls Series, vol. I (1876).

RANGERIUS LUCENSIS. *Vita Metrica S. Anselmi Lucensis*, *M.G.H. Scriptt.* XXX (Leipzig, 1934).

RANULF HIGDEN. *Polychronicon*, ed. J. R. Lumby, Rolls Series (1871).

RHABANUS MAURUS. *Commentaria in Libros Machabaeorum*, Migne, *P.L.* CIX.

Rhythmus in Odonem regem, ed. P. de Winterfeld, *M.G.H. Poetae Latini Aeui Carolini*, IV (Berlin, 1898).

RICHARD OF LONDON. *Itinerarium Peregrinorum*, in *M.G.H. Scriptt.* XXVII (1885).

RICHARD OF ST VICTOR. *Explicatio in Cantica Canticorum*, Migne, *P.L.* CXCVI.

ROBB, N. *Neoplatonism of the Italian Renaissance* (London, 1935).

Rolandslied, ed. C. Wesle (Bonn, 1928).

Roman d'Alexandre.

Ed. H. Michelant, *Li Romans d'Alexandre*, *B.L.V.* XIII (Stuttgart, 1846).

The Medieval French 'Roman d'Alexandre', Elliott Monographs 36–40 (Princeton Univ. Press, 1937–49). In progress. (Abbreviated *M.F.R.d'A.* I–V.)

Vol. I, *Text of Arsenal and Venice Versions*, ed. M. S. La Du, *E.M.* 36 (1937).

Vol. II, *Version of Alexandre de Paris, text*, ed. E. C. Armstrong, D. L. Buffum, B. Edwards, L. F. H. Lowe, *E.M.* 37 (1937).

Vol. III, *Variants and notes to Branch I*, ed. A. Foulet, *E.M.* 38 (1949).

Vol. IV, *Le roman du Fuerre de Gadres*, ed. E. C. Armstrong and A. Foulet, *E.M.* 39 (1942).

Vol. V, *Variants and notes to Branch II*, ed. F. B. Agard, *E.M.* 40 (1942).

Roman d'Eledus et Serene, ed. J. R. Reinhard (University of Texas, 1923).

Roman de la Rose, La, ed. E. Langlois, S.A.T.F., 5 vols. (1920 ff.).

Roman de la Rose ou de Guillaume de Dole, ed. G. Servois, S.A.T.F. (1893).

ROMUALD OF SALERNO. *Chronicon*, R.I.S. VII, i (Città di Castello, n.d.).

ROSS, D. J. A. 'Letters of Alexander', in *Classica et Mediaevalia*, XIII (1952), pp. 38–58.

'Some notes on the Old French Alexander Romance in prose', in *French Studies*, VI (1952), pp. 136–47 and 353.

'Some unrecorded MSS of the *Historia de Preliis*.' *Scriptorium*, IX, 1955, pp. 149–50.

'The printed editions of the Old French Prose Alexander Romance', in *The Library*, Ser. 5, vol. VI, pp. 54–7.

ROSSKOPF, K. *Editio Princeps des Mittelenglischen Cassamus*, diss. (Munich, 1911).
RUDOLF VON EMS. *Alexander*, ed. V. Junk, *B.L.V.* CCLXXII and CCLXXIV (Leipzig, 1928–9).
Weltchronik, ed. G. Ehrismann, *Deutsche Texte des Mittelalters*, XX (1915).
RÜHL, F. *Die Verbreitung des Justinus im Mittelalter* (Leipzig, Teubner, 1871).
RUPERT OF DEUTZ. *De Victoria Verbi Dei*, in Migne, *P.L.* CLXIX.
RUTEBEUF. *Werke*, ed. A. Kressner (Wolfenbüttel, 1885).
SACCHETTI, FRANCO. *Libro delle Rime*, ed. G. Chiari, *Scrittori d'Italia* (Bari, 1936).
SACHOW, K. *Ueber die Vengeance d'Alexandre von Jean le Venelais*, diss. (Halle, 1902).
Sächsische Weltchronik, ed. L. Weiland, *M.G.H. Deutsche Chroniken*, II (Hanover, 1877).
Saelden Hort, Der, ed. H. Adrian, *Deutsche Texte des Mittelalters*, XXVI (1927).
SALIMBENE, FRA. *Chronica*, *M.G.H. Scriptt.* XXXII, ed. O. Holder-Egger (Hanover and Leipzig, 1905–13).
SAMARAN, C. *Vasco de Lucena à la cour de Bourgogne (Documents inédits)* (Lisbon, 1938).
Satirycall Dialogue or a Sharplye-Invective Conference Betweene Allexander the Great and that Truely Woman-Hater Dyogenes (Dort ?, 1615; reprinted London, 1897, with an introduction by J. S. Farmer).
SCHILTERN, J. *Chronike* (Strassburg, 1698).
SCHMIDT, A. *Ueber das Alexanderlied des Alberic von Besançon und sein Verhältnis zur antiken Ueberlieferung*, diss. (Bonn, 1886).
SCHNABEL, P. 'Zur Frage der Selbstvergöttung Alexanders', *Klio*, XX (1926), pp. 398–414.
SCHNEEGANS, H. 'Ueber die Interpolation des "Fuerre de Gadres" im altfranzösischen Roman des Eustache von Kent', in *Die Neueren Sprachen*, Ergänzungsband (Festschrift W. Vietor, 1910), pp. 27–61.
SCHRÖDER, E. 'Die deutschen Alexander-Dichtungen des 12ten Jahrhunderts', in *Nachrichten von der Gesellschaft der Wissenschaften zu Göttingen*, Phil.-Hist. Klasse (1928), pp. 45–92.
SCOTT, E. J. L. *Index to the Sloane MSS. in the British Museum* (London, 1903).
SCROPE, STEPHEN. *The Dicts and Sayings of the Philosophers*, ed. M. Schofield, University of Pennsylvania Dissertation (Philadelphia, 1936).
SEARLES, C. 'Some notes on Boiardo's version of the Alexandersagas', in *Modern Language Notes*, XV (1900), pp. 45–8.
Secret of Secrets (Secretum Secretorum), ed. R. Steele, *Rogeri Baconi opera hactenus inedita*, fasc. V (Oxford, 1920).
SEDULIUS SCOTUS. *Liber de rectoribus Christianis*, Migne, *P.L.* CIII.
SEGRÉ, M. In *Rivista di Filologia*, XI (1933), pp. 225 ff.
SEIFRIT AUS OESTERREICH. *Seifrits Alexander*, ed. P. Gereke, *Deutsche Texte des Mittelalters*, XXXVI (Berlin, 1932).
SITTE, E. 'Die Datierung von Lamprechts Alexander', *Hermaea*, XXXV (Halle, 1940).
Själens Trost, ed. G. E. Klemming, *Svensk. Fornskr. Sallsk.* (Stockholm, 1871–3), pp. 510–32.
SKEAT, W. W. *Alexander and Dindimus*, E.E.T.S., E.S. XXXI (1878).
William of Palerne and a fragment of the Alliterative Romance of Alexander, E.E.T.S., E.S. 1 (1867).
SÖDERHJELM, W. 'Notice et extraits du MS. fr. 51 de la Bibliothèque Royale de Stockholm', in *Neuphilologische Mitteilungen* (Helsingfors, 1917), pp. 307–33.
SOLALINDE, A. G. 'El Juicio de Paris en el Alexandre y en la General Estoria', in *Revista de Filología española*, XV (1928), pp. 1–51.
Speculum Laicorum, ed. J. Welter (Paris, 1914).
Speculum Sapientiae, ed. J. G. T. Grässe, *B.L.V.* CXLVIII (Tübingen, 1880).

STEFFENS, M. 'Versbau und Sprache des mittelenglischen stabreimenden Gedichtes "The Wars of Alexander"', in *Bonner Beiträge zur Anglistik*, IX (Bonn, 1901).

STEINSCHNEIDER, M. *Die Hebräischen Uebersetzungen des Mittelalters* (Berlin, 1893).

STOROST, J. *Studien zur Alexandersage in der älteren italienischen Literatur, Romanistische Arbeiten*, XXIII (Halle, 1935).

STRICKER, DER. *Karl der Grosse*, ed. K. Bartsch (Quedlinburg and Leipzig, 1857).

SULPICIUS SEVERUS. *Historia Sacra*, in Migne, *P.L.* XX.

Tabula Exemplorum, ed. J. T. Welter (Paris, 1926).

TARN, W. W. *Alexander the Great* (Cambridge University Press, 1948).

TERTULLIAN. *Apologeticus*, in Migne, *P.L.* I.

THOMAS, A. *Histoire Littéraire de la France*, XXXVI, i (1924), pp. 1–100 (on the cycle of the *Voeux du Paon*).

'Notice sur un manuscrit de Quinte-Curce', in *Revue Critique d'Histoire et de Littérature*, 14me année, 2me semestre (1880), pp. 75–8.

THOMASIN VON ZIRCLARIA. *Wälschen Gast*, ed. H. Rückert (Quedlinburg and Leipzig, 1852).

THOMSON, S. H. 'An unnoticed abridgement of the *Historia de Preliis* (Redaction I²-I³)', *University of Colorado Studies*, I (1941), pp. 241–59.

Thornton Alexander, ed. J. S. Westlake, E.E.T.S., O.S. CXLIII (1913).

TOISCHER, W. *Die altdeutschen Bearbeitungen des pseudo-aristotelischen Secreta Secretorum* (Prague, 1884).

'Ueber die Alexandreis Ulrichs von Eschenbach', in *Sitzungsberichte der kaiserlichen Akademie der Wissenschaften in Wien*, Phil.-Hist. Klasse, XCVII (1881), pp. 311–408.

TOLOMEO DA LUCCA (PSEUDO-THOMAS AQUINAS). *De regimine principum*, ed. J. Mathis (Rome, 1948).

Tractatus de diversis historiis Romanorum, ed. S. Herzstein (Erlangen, 1893), *Erlanger Beiträge zur Englischen Philologie*, XIV.

TRAUTMANN, R. *Die alttschechische Alexandreis* (Heidelberg, 1916).

In *Archiv für slawische Philologie*, XXXVI (1916), pp. 431–5.

TRAVNIK, E. 'Ueber eine Raaber Handschrift des Hartliebschen Alexanderbuches', in *Münchener Museum für Philologie des Mittelalters und der Renaissance*, II (1913–14), pp. 211–21.

ULRICH VON ESCHENBACH. *Alexander*, ed. W. Toischer, *B.L.V.* CLXXXIII (Tübingen, 1888).

Upright Lives of the Heathen briefly noted: or, Epistles and Discourses between Alexander the Great and Dindimus, The (pub. Andrew Soule, London, 1683).

VERGERIO, PIER PAOLO. *Epistolario*, ed. L. Smith, *Fonti per la Storia d'Italia* (Rome, 1934).

VERNON, W. W. *Readings on the Inferno of Dante* (Oxford, 1906).

Vie de S. Modwenna, ed. A. T. Baker and A. Bell, Anglo-Norman Text Society, vol. VII (Oxford, 1947).

VILLON, FRANÇOIS. *Œuvres de François Villon*, ed. L. Thuasne (Paris, 1923).

VINCENT DE BEAUVAIS. *Speculum Historiale* (ed. Douai, 1624).

Speculum Morale (ed. Douai, 1624).

Voyage au Paradis Terrestre, ed. L. P. G. Peckham and M. S. La Du, *The Prise de Defur and the Voyage au Paradis Terrestre, Elliott Monographs* 35 (Princeton Univ. Press, 1935).

WACE. *Roman de Rou*, ed. H. Andersen (Heilbronn, 1877).

WALAHFRID STRABO. (attributed falsely to) *Glossa Ordinaria*, in Migne, *P.L.* CXIV.

WALBERG, E. 'Classification des Manuscrits de la Vengeance d'Alixandre de Jean le Nevelon, in *Från Filologiska Föeningen i Lund, Språkliger Uppsatser*, III (1906), pp. 5–30.

WALDE, O. *Storhetstidens Litterära Krigsbyten* (Uppsala, 1916).

WALLACH, L. 'Quellenkritische Studien zum Hebräischen Josippon', in *Mitteilungen der Gesellschaft der Wissenschaft des Judentums*, LXXXII (1938), pp. 190–8.

'Yosippon and the Alexander Romance', in *Jewish Quarterly Review*, new series XXXVII (1947), pp. 407–22.

WALTHER VON DER VOGELWEIDE. Ed. K. Lachmann (Berlin, 1907).

WARBURG, A. *Luftschiff und Tauchboot in der mittelälterlichen Vorstellungswelt*, in *Gesammelte Schriften*, I (Berlin, 1932).

Wars of Alexander, ed. W. W. Skeat, E.E.T.S., E.S. XLVII (1888). Ed. R. Stevenson, Roxburghe Club (1849).

WEINRICH, O. *Der Trug des Nektanebos* (Leipzig and Berlin, 1911).

WELLS, J. E. *A Manual of the Writings in Middle English* (New Haven, Conn. Yale Univ. Press, 1916).

WELTER, J. TH. *L'Exemplum dans la littérature religieuse et didactique du moyen âge* (Paris, 1927).

Wernigerode Alexander, ed. G. Guth, *Der Grosse Alexander aus der Wernigeroder Handschrift*, Deutsche Texte des Mittelalters, XIII (Berlin, 1908).

WEST, C. B. *Courtoisie in Anglo-Norman Literature* (Oxford, 1938).

WEYNAND, J. *Der 'Roman de Toute Chevalerie' in seinem Verhältnis zu seinen Quellen*, Diss. (Bonn, 1911).

WILCKEN, U. 'Alexander der Grosse und die indischen Gymnosophisten', in *Sitzungsberichte der Preussischen Akademie der Wissenschaften*, Phil.-Hist. Klasse (1923), pp.150–83.

WILLIAM OF CONCHES. *Liber Moralium Dogmatis Philosophorum*, in Migne *P.L.* CLXXI.

WILLIAM OF MALMESBURY. *Gesta Regum*, ed. W. Stubbs, Rolls Series (1889).

WILLIS, R. S. *The Debt of the Spanish Libro de Alexandre to the French Roman d'Alexandre*, Elliott Monographs 33 (Princeton Univ. Press, 1935).

The Relationship of the Spanish Libro de Alexandre to the Alexandreis of Gautier de Châtillon, Elliott Monographs 31 (Princeton Univ. Press, 1934).

WILMANS, R. In *Zeitschrift für deutsches Altertum*, XLV, pp. 229–44.

WILMART, A. *Codices Reginenses Latini*, vol. I (Vatican City, 1934).

WISBEY, R. 'Die Aristotelesrede bei Walther von Châtillon und Rudolf von Ems', *Zeits. f. deutsches Altertum*, LXXXV, 1954–5, pp. 304 ff.

WITHINGTON, R. *English Pageantry* (Cambridge, Mass., 1918).

WITTKOWER, R. 'Marvels of the East', in *Journal of the Warburg and Courtauld Institutes*, V (1942), pp. 159–97.

WOLFF, R. *Der interpolierte Fuerre de Gadres im Alexanderroman des Thomas von Kent*, diss. (Bonn, 1914).

WÖLFFLIN, E. 'Die neue Epitoma Alexandri', in *Archiv für lateinische Lexicographie*, XII (1901), pp. 187–96.

ZACHER, J. *Pseudocallisthenes, Forschungen zur Kritik und Geschichte der ältesten Aufzeichnung der Alexandersage* (Halle, 1867).

ZARNKE, F. 'Ueber das Fragment eines lateinischen Alexanderliedes in Verona', in *Sitzungsberichte der sächsischen Akademie der Wissenschaften* (1877), pp. 57–69.

Edition of Prester John Letter in *Abhandlungen der sächsischen Gesellschaft*, Phil.-Hist. Klasse, VII (1879), pp. 827–1030.

ZINGERLE, I. V. 'Ueber die Wiltener Meistersängerhandschrift', in *Sitzungsberichte der kaiserlichen Akademie in Wien*, Phil.-Hist. Klasse, XXXVII (1861).

ZINGERLE, O. *Die Quellen zum Alexander des Rudolf von Ems*, Germanistische Abhandlungen, IV (Breslau, 1885).

INDEX

INDEX

Jesus Christ, 104, 137, 168, 191, 302–3, 312, 319, 346
  Alexander interpreted allegorically as, 156
Jewish Alexander material and tradition, 10, 18, 19, **118–42**, 151, 169, 186, 202
  view of Alexander, 72–3, 81, **125–32**, 306
Jewish High Priest reverenced by Alexander, *see* Jerusalem
Jews, 10, 19, 20, 52, 57, **118–42** *passim*, 169, 171, **292–7**
  Alexander's relations with, 72–3, **118–42**, **292–7**
Jofroi de Waterford and Servais Copale, *Enseignemens d'Aristote*, 22, 359 n.
Johannes Ferrariensis, *Ex annalium libris Marchionum Estensium excerpta*, 290, 299
Johannes filius Patricii (Yuhanna ibn el-Batrik), 21
Johannes Gualensis or Vallensis, *Summa de regimine uitae humanae*, 300
John III, duke of Campania, 11, 38
John de Mandeville, 234, 280, 336, 337
John of Salisbury, *Policraticus*, 23, 79, 82, 89, 93, **96–7**, 99, 101, 102, 103, 104, 108, 112, 113, 114, 117, 142, 143, 149, 158, 159, 160, 161, 196, 200, 201, 264, 275, 278, 280, 282, 284, 285, 288, 289, 293, 294
John of Spain, 21
Joiada, 294, *see* Jadus
jongleur, given the city of Trage by Alexander in the *Roman*, 325, **361**, **364**
Joseph ben Gorion, *Yosippon*, 51
Josephus, 18, 63, 67, 69, 70, 73, 81, 112, 118, **125–30**, 139, 140, 142, 186, 189, 258, 294, 303, 323
'Αρχαιολογία, 127 n., 128 n.; Latin version ascribed to Rufinus, 18, 73, 294
Judas Iscariot, 293
Judas Maccabeus as one of the *Neuf Preux*, 245, 290, 319–20
Judas Mardocheus, letter of, to Alexander, 169
Julius Caesar, 267 n., 269, 310, 316, 318
Julius Valerius, *Res Gestae Alexandri Macedonis*, 10, 14, 15 n., 16, **24**, 25, 26, 29, 59, 62–3, 67, 69, 70, 87, 112 n., 135, 148 n., 210, 211 n., 214, 215, 219 n., 234, 237, 246, 279, 304, 324, 335–6, 337, 351, 357, 358 n., 362, 363, 364, 366
  Oxford-Montpelier Epitome, 25, **26**, 167–8, 239, 304; Leiden transcript, 239
  Turin palimpsest MS., 246 n.
  Zacher Epitome, 14, 24, **25–6**, 35, 37, 39, 42, 69, 70, 167, 211, 234, 335, 339, 340, 364 n.; derivatives of, 35–7; entitled *Historia Alexandri* by Vincent de Beauvais, 74; French version, 25, 283
Junker und der treue Heinrich, Der, 328

Jupiter, 94
  Alexander denies that he is son of, 152–3
Justin, Epitome of the *Historiae Philippicae* of Trogus Pompeius, 1, 16, 62, 74, 80, 87, 99, 101, 110, 112, 114, 161, 198 n., 211, 278, 279, 290, 291, 335
  comparison of characters of Alexander and his father Philip, 87, 101, 278–9

Kaiserchronik, 307, 321, 346
Karolus (i.e. Charlemagne), 310
'King' René of Provence, 228
knight to whom Alexander gives a city, 214
König Rother, 347
Konung Alexander, middle Swedish Alexander poem, 50
Kronika o Alexandru Velikèm, 58
Kyng Alisaunder, 36, 37, 220, 231, 239–40, **241–2**, 330
  expanded version, fragment, 37

La Manta, castle of, Nine Worthies fresco in, 262 n., 343.
Lai d'Aristote, see Henri d'Andeli
Lambert le Tort of Châteaudun, author of *Alexandre en Orient*, 30, 202, 213, 322, 334, 342.
Lamprecht, Pfaffe, **27–9**, 44, 62, 165, 166, 167, 170, **171–2**, 176, 178, 182, 186, 189, **201–2**, 205, 211, 212, 258, 304, 305, 308, 320, 342.
  Alexander, 177 n., 293, 307, 311, 324, 339; Biblical quotations in, 28
  See also *Basel, Strassburg* and *Vorau Alexanders*
Lantbert, *Vita Heriberti Archiepiscopi Coloniensis*, 295
largesce, 213, 215, 306, **366–7**, 371
late medieval moral and didactic writers, opinion of Alexander in, 250–9, 274, 344–7
  in England, 252–7, 346
  in France, 250–1, 344–6
  in Germany, 258–9, 346–7
late medieval opinion of Alexander, 79, 83, 102, 104, 117, 141, 142, 182, 210, 217, 218, 220, **226–59**, **260–6**, 273–4, 277–8, 287, 289, **330–48**, **366–8**
  in France, 250–1, 344–6
  in England, 252–7, 346
  in Germany, 258–9, 342–3, 346–7
  in Italy, 260–6, 348–51
Latin Chronicle Accounts of Alexander, 71–4
Latin epic, conventions of, 63, 183, 185
Laude, 263
Laurent de Premierfait, 253, 265, 345
  French version of *De casibus virorum illustrium* of Boccaccio, 345